R. Gupta's®

Popular Master Guide

BCA

Bachelor of Computer Applications

ENTRANCE EXAMINATION

by

RPH Editorial Board

2026
EDITION

RAMESH PUBLISHING HOUSE, NEW DELHI

Published by
O.P. Gupta *for* Ramesh Publishing House

Admin. Office
12-H, New Daryaganj Road, Opp. Officers' Mess
New Delhi-110002 ✆ 23275224, 23245124

E-mail: info@rameshpublishinghouse.com
For Online Shopping: www.rameshpublishinghouse.com

Showroom
- Balaji Market, Nai Sarak, Delhi-6 ✆ 23282525 📱 9354373464
- 4457, Nai Sarak, Delhi-6, ✆ 23918938

Book Code: R-57

ISBN: 978-81-7812-385-1

Price: ₹ 530

Printed at : Deepak Offset, Delhi

CONTENTS

Previous Years' Paper, 2024 ...... **1–16**

Previous Years' Paper, 2023 ...... **17–35**

Previous Years' Paper, 2022 ...... **36–43**

Previous Years' Paper, 2020 ...... **44–55**

Previous Years' Paper, 2019 ...... **56–71**

Previous Years' Paper, 2018 ...... **72–83**

Previous Years' Paper, 2017 ...... **84–104**

QUANTITATIVE ABILITY **1–116**

Arithmetical Mathematics; Logarithms and Exponents; Linear and Quadratic Equation; Sequences and Series; Binomial Theorem; Permutations and Combinations; Matrices and Determinants; Sets, Relation and Function; Limit and Continuity; Differentiation; Application of Derivatives; Integration and Area Under Curve; Straight Line and Circle; Vector; Trigonometry; Probability; Mensuration; Statistics.

GENERAL INTELLIGENCE & REASONING **1–68**

Letter Series; Wrong Letter Series; Repeat Series; Number Series; Wrong Number Series; Word Analogy; Number Analogy; Odd One Out; Coding and Decoding; Statement Analysis; Place Arrangement; Direction Sense; Blood Relationships; Rows and Ranks; Permutations and Combinations; Symbol Substitution; Missing Numbers; Alphabet Problems; Logical Diagram; Syllogism; Venn Diagrams; Non-Verbal Series; Non-Verbal Analogy; Odd Man Out.

GENERAL ENGLISH **1–80**

Comprehension Passages; Cloze Test; Spot the Error; Sentence Improvement; Reordering Words; Ordering of Sentences; Sentence Completion; Nouns, Numbers & Pronouns, Prepositions; Adjectives, Adverbs & Degree of Comparison;

Determiners & Articles; Conjunctions; Tenses & Verbs; Narration; Active & Passive Voice; Synonyms, Antonyms & Homonyms; One Word Substitution; Idioms, Phrases & Proverbs; Modals & Auxiliaries; Non Finites; Commonly Confusing Words; Spelling Errors; Punctuation.

COMPUTER KNOWLEDGE 1–84

Introduction; Characteristics of Computers; History of Computers; Computer System; Generations of Computers; Various Types of Computer Systems; Input/ Output Devices; Hardware & Software; Computer Memory; Software; Operating System; Programming Languages; Data Processing; Data Processing System; Computer Networks; Internet; Intranet and E-mail; Electronic Commerce; Mobile Computing; Office Automation Systems and Transaction Processing Systems; Glossary; Computer Abbreviations; Multiple Choice Questions.

GENERAL AWARENESS 1–92

Our India; National Symbols; The Universe; United Nations Organisation; Indian Constitution & Polity; Planning in India; General Science; Space Research; Indian History; World Geography; First in India; Cultural Activities; Awards; Sports; Multiple Choice Questions.

Previous Years' Paper

Bachelor of Computer Applications (BCA)

Entrance Exam, 2024

(Exam held on 24-06-2024)

1. What is the symbol of Gold?
1. Ag 2. Au
3. Ca 4. G

2. Who invented the telephone?
1. Marie Curie
2. Mark Marturello
3. Alexander Graham Bell
4. Nikola Tesla

3. What is the national animal of India?
1. Dolphin 2. Parrot
3. Lion 4. Bengal Tiger

4. What is the minimum age for becoming a Lok Sabha candidate?
1. 27 2. 25
3. 26 4. 28

5. Who was the first election commissioner of India?
1. Sukumar Sen 2. Rajiv Kumar
3. Om Birla 4. Dhananjaya

6. What is a "free throw" commonly associated with?
1. Football 2. Badminton
3. Basketball 4. Cricket

7. Which day is celebrated as World Press Freedom Day?
1. 10 April
2. 15 February
3. 18 December
4. 3 May

8. Who is the author of the famous book "We the People"?
1. Kushwant Singh
2. Charles Dickens
3. Emily Bronte
4. Nani Palkhivala

9. Who appoints the Advocate General of each state of India?
1. President
2. Governor of a State
3. Prime Minister
4. Solicitor General

10. Who has been appointed as the new Chief of Research and Analysis Wing (RAW)?
1. Ravi Sinha
2. Tapan Kumar Deka
3. Ravindra Kaushik
4. Ajay Kumar Singh

1. 2	**2.** 3	**3.** 4	**4.** 2	**5.** 1	**6.** 3	**7.** 4	**8.** 4	**9.** 2	**10.** 1

11. If PINK is coded as 1691411, then RED will be coded as:

1. 1963 2. 1853
3. 1854 4. 1954

12. Which of the following is the odd one from the given alternatives?

1. Diving 2. Driving
3. Swimming 4. Sailing

13. Which of the following pairs of words are differently related?

1. Kind : Cruel
2. Stale : Fresh
3. Slow : Sluggish
4. Truth : Lie

14. Drama : Stage : : Tennis : ....

1. Court 2. Net
3. Tournament 4. Racket

15. The day before yesterday was Saturday. What will be the day after tomorrow?

1. Wednesday 2. Monday
3. Friday 4. Thursday

16. Look at the series: 36, 34, 30, 28, 24, ... What number should come next?

1. 26 2. 20
3. 23 4. 22

17. Which word is odd one out?

1. Fondness 2. Liking
3. Hate 4. Attachment

18. Pointing to a photograph of a boy Suresh said, "He is the son of the only son of my mother". How is Suresh related to that boy?

1. Uncle 2. Brother
3. Cousin 4. Father

19. The sum of ages of 4 friends A, B, C and D is 70 years. What would be the total of their ages after 5 years later?

1. 90 2. 85
3. 75 4. 65

20. A man walks 1 km to East and then he turns to South and walks 5 km. Again he turns to East and walks 2 km. After this he turns to North and walks 9 km. Now, in which direction he is from starting point?

1. North 2. South
3. North-East 4. West

21. Which of the following compound is mainly used in hand sanitizer?

1. Alcohol 2. Acetic acid
3. Aldehyde 4. Ketone

22. Which of the following glands is present in the human mouth?

1. Adrenal 2. Pituitary
3. Gonads 4. Salivary

23. What is the basic unit of our neural system?

1. Neutron 2. Neuron
3. Nephron 4. Nucleon

24. Name the part of the body on which corona-virus affects the most?

1. Heart 2. Liver
3. Kidney 4. Lungs

25. About 70% part of the sun is made up of:

1. Hydrogen 2. Oxygen
3. Carbon 4. Helium

26. A Universal donor person have a blood group:

1. A 2. AB
3. O 4. B

11. 3	**12.** 2	**13.** 3	**14.** 1	**15.** 1	**16.** 4	**17.** 3	**18.** 4
19. 1	**20.** 3	**21.** 1	**22.** 4	**23.** 2	**24.** 4	**25.** 1	**26.** 3

27. Name an instrument which is used to measure the Density of milk?

1. Lactometer 2. Hydrometer
3. Barometer 4. Hygrometer

28. Which of the following is/are the symptoms of Black Fungus?

(*a*) Facial Swelling
(*b*) Nasal Congestion
(*c*) Headache

1. Only (*a*) 2. Only (*b*)
3. Both (*b*) and (*c*) 4. (*a*), (*b*) and (*c*)

29. Which of the following is used in pencils?

1. Silicon 2. Graphite
3. Charcoal 4. Phosphorous

30. The gas usually filled in the electric bulb:

1. Hydrogen
2. Oxygen
3. Nitrogen
4. Carbon dioxide

31. The sum of first 20 odd counting numbers is:

1. 20 2. 100
3. 400 4. 313

32. The positive integer which is nearest to 1000 and divisible by 2, 3, 4, 5 and 6 is ....

1. 1020 2. 1040
3. 960 4. 1030

33. How many times is the HCF of 48, 36, 72 and 24 contained in their LCM?

1. 12 2. 10
3. 24 4. 14

34. The LCM of 5, 8, 12, 20 will not be a multiple of ....

1. 3 2. 9
3. 8 4. 5

35. A man sold 250 chairs and had a gain equal to the selling price of 50 chairs. His profit percentage is ....

1. 25% 2. 10%
3. 5% 4. 50%

36. In an election between two candidates, one got 55% of total valid votes. 20% of the votes were invalid. If the total number of votes were 7500, the number of valid votes that the other candidates got were ....

1. 2700 2. 2900
3. 3000 4. 3100

37. A man's basic pay for a 40 h week is ₹ 20. Overtime is paid for at 25% above the basic rate. In a certain week, he worked overtime and his total wage as ₹ 25. He therefore, worked for a total of ....

1. 45 h 2. 47 h
3. 48 h 4. 50 h

38. If the cost price of 36 books is equal to the selling price of 30 books, then the gain percentage is ....

1. 20% 2. 25%
3. 16% 4. 30%

39. A dealers makes a profit of 20% by selling an article. What would be the percentage change in the profit percent if he had paid 20% less for it and the current paid 10% more for it?

1. 225% 2. 125%
3. 200% 4. 160%

40. The average weight of a class of 29 students is 40 kg. If the weight of the teacher be included, the average rises by 500 g. What is the weight of the teacher?

1. 40.5 kg 2. 50.5 kg
3. 45 kg 4. 55 kg

27. 1	**28.** 4	**29.** 2	**30.** 3	**31.** 3	**32.** 1	**33.** 1
34. 2	**35.** 1	**36.** 1	**37.** 3	**38.** 1	**39.** 4	**40.** 4

41. The averages of square of natural numbers from 1 to 35 is ....

1. 436 2. 426
3. 416 4. 446

42. If A takes 4 h to cover a distance and he is 2 times faster than B, then what time will B take to cover the same distance?

1. 6 h 2. 8 h
3. 9 h 4. None of these

43. A motor car does a journey in 9 h, the first half at 12 km/h and second half at 15 km/h. Find the distance.

1. 120 km 2. 100 km
3. 124 km 4. 96 km

44. A man is walking at a speed of 9 km/h. After every km he takes rest for 9 min. How much time will he take to cover a distance of 27 km?

1. 6 h 2. 6 h 45 min
3. 6 h 54 min 4. 6 h 35 min

45. At what rate of interest per annum will a sum becomes 5 times in 20 years at SI?

1. 20% 2. 16%
3. 25% 4. 10%

46. The difference between the compound interest and simple interest on a certain sum at 5% for 2 years is ₹ 1.50. The sum is ....

1. ₹ 600 2. ₹ 500
3. ₹ 400 4. ₹ 300

47. What principal will amount to ₹ 1352 in 2 years at 4% compound interest?

1. ₹ 1520 2. ₹ 1260
3. ₹ 1250 4. ₹ 1220

48. A and B can do a piece of work in 72 days; B and C can do it in 120 days; A and C can do it in 90 days. In what time can A alone do it?

1. 150 days 2. 120 days
3. 100 days 4. 80 days

49. A can do a certain job in 12 days. B is 60% more efficient than A. The number of days, it takes to do the same piece of work, is ....

1. 6 2. 25/4
3. 15/2 4. 8

50. A pipe can fill a tank in 6 h. Due to leak in the bottom it is filled in 8 h. If the tank is full, how much time will the leak take to empty it?

1. 24 h 2. 20 h
3. 18 h 4. 12 h

51. Find the third proportional to the numbers 5 and 10.

1. 20 2. 2.5
3. 25 4. 30

52. Ratio of boys to the girls in a class is 5 : 4. Which of the following cannot be the number of students in the class?

1. 45 2. 72
3. 108 4. 98

53. In an educational institution there are 15 more boys than girls. If the number of boys is increased by 20% and number of girls is increased by 15% there would be 29 more boys than girls. How many girls are there in the institution?

1. 250 2. 255
3. 230 4. 220

54. Two oranges, three bananas and four apples cost ₹ 15. Three oranges, two bananas and one apple cost ₹ 10. I bought 3 oranges, 3 bananas and 3 apples. How much did I pay?

1. ₹ 15
2. ₹ 8
3. ₹ 10
4. Cannot be determined

41. 2	**42.** 2	**43.** 1	**44.** 3	**45.** 1	**46.** 1	**47.** 3
48. 2	**49.** 3	**50.** 1	**51.** 1	**52.** 4	**53.** 4	**54.** 1

55. How many prime factors are there in the expression $(12)^{43} * (34)^{48} * (2)^{57}$?

1. 282 2. 237
3. 142 4. 61

Directions (Q. Nos. 56-60): A survey film watching habits of people living in 5 cities I, II, III, IV and V is summarised below. The column (1) gives percentage of film-watchers in each city who see only film a week. The column (2) gives the total number of film-watchers who see more than one film per week. Read the table and answer the questions.

City	(1)	(2)
I	50	3200
II	30	3500
III	65	7000
IV	25	5400
V	80	2900

56. How many film-watchers in City II see only one film a week?

1. 900 2. 1500
3. 1600 4. 3200

57. Which city has the highest number of film-watchers who see only film a week?

1. I 2. II
3. III 4. IV

58. The city with the lowest number of film-watcher is ....

1. I 2. II
3. IV 4. V

59. The city with the highest number of film-watcher is ....

1. I 2. V
3. IV 4. III

60. The total number of all film watchers in the five cities who see only one film a week is ....

1. 31100 2. 29500
3. 28600 4. 28300

61. High-capacity computers used primarily for research purposes are:

1. Microcomputers
2. Minicomputers
3. Mainframes
4. Supercomputers

62. Which piece of hardware do you need to connect to the internet?

1. An ISP Account
2. A Modem
3. A Browser
4. Internet Explorer

63. Which one of the following is ***not*** a network topology?

1. Star 2. Bus
3. Linear 4. Ring

64. Which of the following device could ***not*** be a part of a wired LAN based on star topology?

1. Switch 2. Repeater
3. Hub 4. Router

65. Which key strokes switch a user between simultaneously running applications in windows?

1. FN + TAB
2. ALT + TAB
3. CTRL + TAB
4. SHIFT + TAB

66. Which of the following operating systems use preemptive scheduling?

1. Mac OS 8 2. Window 3.x
3. Windows 95 4. DOS 6.0

55. 1	**56.** 2	**57.** 3	**58.** 2	**59.** 4	**60.** 1
61. 4	**62.** 2	**63.** 3	**64.** 2	**65.** 2	**66.** 3

67. What does URL stand for?

1. Uniform Resource Locator
2. Universal Resource Locator
3. Uniform Retrieval Locator
4. Universal Retrieval Locator

68. Which of the following is non-volatile memory?

1. RAM 2. Cache
3. CPU Register 4. ROM

69. Which port is typically used to connect a monitor to a computer?

1. USB 2. Ethernet
3. HDMI 4. Audio Jack

70. Which Linux command is used to change file permission?

1. chmod 2. chperm
3. perm 4. chown

71. In Windows, what is the shortcut key to open Task Manager?

1. Ctrl + Alt + Delete
2. Ctrl + Shift + Esc
3. Alt + F4
4. Ctrl + Esc

72. Which part of an email address comes after the '@' symbol?

1. Username
2. Domain name
3. Subject
4. Service Provider Name

73. Which of the following is ***not*** a web browser?

1. Google Chrome
2. Mozilla Firefox
3. Microsoft Edge
4. Ubuntu

74. What is the purpose of "Bcc" (Blind Carbon Copy) field in an email?

1. To send a copy of the email to additional recipients without their address being visible to other recipients
2. To attach files to the email
3. To set the priority of the email
4. To format the email text

75. What does the acronym 'IM' stand for in internet communication?

1. Instant Messaging
2. Internet Messaging
3. International Messaging
4. Internal Messaging

76. Choose the correct antonym (opposite) for the word 'CORDIAL' given from the options below:

1. Unfriendly 2. Sweet
3. Affable 4. Frigid

77. Choose the correct synonym for the word 'STRIFE' given from the options below:

1. Concord
2. Peace
3. Truce
4. Battle

78. Which of the following will be the correct sentence in passive voice?

Active Voice: They sun-dried the fenugreek leaves to make spices.

1. The spices were made by sun-dried fenugreek leaves.
2. The fenugreek leaves were sun-dried to make spices.
3. They made the spices by sun-drying the fenugreek leaves.
4. The sun-dried fenugreek leaves were used for making species.

67. 1	**68.** 4	**69.** 3	**70.** 1	**71.** 2	**72.** 2
73. 4	**74.** 1	**75.** 1	**76.** 1	**77.** 4	**78.** 2

79. Which of the following will be the correct sentence in passive voice?

Active Voice: I saw the thief leaving the house.

1. The thief was seen to be leaving the house.
2. Leaving the house, I saw the thief.
3. The thief had been seen leaving the house
4. The thief was seen leaving the house by me.

80. Spot the error:

Two hours after its (*a*) / take-off, the flight reached (*b*) / Mumbai Airport, when (*c*) / it stopped for a short Interval (*d*).

1. (*a*) 2. (*b*)
3. (*c*) 4. (*d*)

81. Spot the error:

While four of them surrendered, three others (*a*) / escaped under the cover of heavy firing at Handwara (*b*) / in the Kupwara district, about 70 km from state capital Srinagar (*c*).

1. (*a*) 2. No error
3. (*b*) 4. (*c*)

82. Three of four words given in this question are spelt wrong. Select the word that is spelt correctly:

1. irelevant 2. irrelevent
3. irrelevant 4. irrelevant

83. Fill in the blank with an appropriate preposition or conjunction. She is not very talented, ……….. she is highly successful.

1. yet
2. despite
3. however
4. in spite

84. Fill in the blank with an appropriate preposition or conjunction ………… he was an illiterate, he managed to achieve success through hardwork.

1. In spite of
2. Despite
3. As if
4. Although

85. Fill in the blank with an appropriate tense.

Only one of the boys ……… not done the home-work given yesterday.

1. have
2. has
3. can
4. could

86. Select the correct transformation of the following direct speech to indirect.

He said, "I will go to college tomorrow".

1. He said that he would go to college the next day.
2. He says that he would go to college the next day.
3. He says that he would go to college tomorrow.
4. He said that he would go to college tomorrow.

87. Select the correct transformation of the following direct speech to indirect.

He said to me, "Why are you troubling me?"

1. He asked me why am I troubling him.
2. He asked me why have I been troubling him.
3. He asked me why I was troubling him.
4. He asked me why was I troubling him.

79. 4	**80.** 3	**81.** 2	**82.** 3	**83.** 1	**84.** 4	**85.** 2	**86.** 1	**87.** 3

88. Choose the correct spelling:

1. Perceved
2. Perceived
3. Perseived
4. Percieved

89. Out of given alternatives, choose the word which can be substituted for the given word/ sentence.

The action or an instance of making a judgment about something.

1. Assessment
2. Conservation
3. Evolving
4. Chaos

90. Out of given alternatives, choose the word which can be substituted for the given word/ sentence.

The act of using someone or something unfairly for your own advantage.

1. Evolving
2. Severity
3. Exploitation
4. Bolster

91. Out of given alternatives, choose the word which can be substituted for the given word/ sentence.

Satisfactory or acceptable in quality or quantity.

1. Restoration
2. Adequate
3. Recognizing
4. Spanning

92. The question below contains four scattered segments of a sentence. Indicate the sequence which correctly assembles the segments and completes the sentence:

(*a*) his contribution to the
(*b*) completely ignored as soon
(*c*) as he retired from work
(*d*) field of astronomy were

1. (*a*), (*c*), (*b*), (*d*)
2. (*b*), (*a*), (*c*), (*d*)
3. (*a*), (*b*), (*d*), (*c*)
4. (*a*), (*d*), (*b*), (*c*)

93. Rearrange the following jumbled sentences to make a meaningful one:

(P) are inhibiting progress
(Q) they look for creative
(R) rather than the conventional solution of outsourcing
(S) solutions to the problems that

1. SRQP 2. PQRS
3. QSPR 4. QRPS

94. In the given question, a short passage is given with one of the lines in the passage missing and represented by a blank. Select the best out of the four answer choices given, to make the passage complete and coherent.

As people return to life and work post the lockdown, some predictions point to a mad rush to do even more than before. Travel more, buy more, meet more people, eat out more -do more of more. .... Much more is anticipated from the State. Some see it as an opportunity to overtake China.

1. The government too is expected to do more to restore economic growth and livelihoods.
2. One pathway is to shift from a mindset of scarcity to a mindset of abundance.
3. Last but not least, let's unlock our spiritual treasure trove.
4. Neurosciences and behavioural sciences increasingly corroborate this ancient wisdom

88. 2	**89.** 1	**90.** 3	**91.** 2	**92.** 4	**93.** 3	**94.** 1

95. In the given question, a short passage is given with one of the lines in the passage missing and represented by a blank. Select the best out of the four answer choices given, to make the passage complete and coherent.

The fragmentation of the anti-XYZ vote now gives a clear edge to the incumbent party. But beyond the arithmetic, the collapse of the possible alliance in Delhi sends out two messages. It reinforces XYZ's narrative that opposition parties are weak and squabbling, dominated by narrow interests .... And while seven seats may not be a lot, the battle in Delhi has always been symbolic and watched widely across the country. While calling it a bellwether state may be somewhat of an exaggeration, the party which wins Delhi has usually done well nationally.

1. with so much commons.
2. without commons
3. with little in common
4. with ecstasy

Directions (Q. Nos. 96-100): Read the following comprehension and answer the questions based on it.

A balanced diet means getting the right types and amounts of foods and drinks to supply nutrition and energy for maintaining body cells, tissues, and organs, and for supporting normal growth and development. Eating a balanced diet means choosing a wide variety of foods and drinks from all the food groups. It also means eating certain things in moderation, namely saturated fat, trans fat, cholesterol, refined sugar, salt and alcohol. The goal is to take in nutrients you need for health at the recommended levels. Your balanced diet must be planned at your own calorie level, and portion size is key. You want to get the most nutrients for the calories by choosing food with a high-nutrient density. Nutrient-dense foods provide substantial amounts of vitamins and minerals and relatively few calories, such as fresh fruit and vegetables, lean meat and fish, and whole grains and beans. Low-nutrient dense foods have few vitamins but lots of calories, such as candy bars, soda, donuts and onion rings. Nutrition guidelines recommend eating a wide variety of foods. But, there's a school of thought that eating variety of foods leads to overeating. There is the tendency to stay hungry longer and eat more food when flavours are diverse and keep changing because we fill up on fewer calories when flavour variety is controlled. We have seen this principle in action when we come home with a load of groceries and want to sample the wide variety of tasty foods.

96. Which two categories of food mentioned in the passage are opposite to each other in nutritional values?

1. The two food categories are 'Nutrient-dense foods' and 'low-nutrient dense foods'.
2. The two food categories are 'A balanced diet' and 'A unbalanced diet'.
3. The two food categories are 'A high calorie food' and 'A low calorie food'.
4. The two food categories are 'A high sugar food' and 'A sugar-free food'.

97. Which word in the passage means the same as adequate?

1. Over-eating
2. Refined
3. Recommended
4. Substantial

95. 3	**96.** 1	**97.** 4

98. A balanced diet means:

1. a diet consisting of the right kind and quantity of food for carrying out growth, development and body functions.
2. a diet consisting of a particular range of food stuffs which provide energy for body to carry out its functions.
3. a diet consisting of a large amount of calories required to carry out the body functions.
4. a diet consisting of vitamins and minerals which are necessary for the body.

99. How does eating a variety of foods lead to over-eating?

1. People cannot manage the portion size of food items which can result in over-eating.
2. People tend to indulge in tasting more flavors which can result in over-eating.
3. People tend to eat more of calorie laden food which results in over-eating.
4. People tend to eat more food thinking that it would make their diet balanced and this results in over-eating.

100. What does the phrase a school of thought' mean?

1. It means a school which is started by great thinkers and philosophers.
2. It means a school where it is taught how to think and meditate.
3. It means a school where thoughts are put into practice.
4. It means a particular idea or set of ideas held by a specific group.

EXPLANATORY ANSWERS

1. (2): The chemical symbol for Gold is Au, derived from its Latin name 'Aurum'. It is a precious metal known for its lustre and high economic value.

2. (3): He is credited with inventing the telephone in 1876. Bell's invention revolutionized communication and laid the foundation for modern telecommunication.

3. (4): The Royal Bengal Tiger is the national animal of India. It symbolizes strength, power, and grace, and represents the rich wildlife heritage of the country.

4. (2): The minimum age to contest Lok Sabha elections in India is 25 years, as per Article 84(b) of the Indian Constitution.

5. (1): Sukumar Sen was the first Chief Election Commissioner of India, appointed in 1950. He oversaw the country's first general elections in 1951–52.

6. (3): A free throw is a shot taken from the free-throw line in basketball, awarded after certain fouls. It is unopposed and worth one point.

7. (4): World Press Freedom Day is observed every year on 3rd May to raise awareness about the importance of freedom of the press and to remind governments of their duty to uphold the right to freedom of expression.

8. (4): The book "We the People" was authored by Nani Palkhivala, a renowned Indian jurist and constitutional expert, and it contains his reflections on the Indian Constitution and democracy.

9. (2): The Advocate General of a state is appointed by the Governor under Article 165 of the Indian Constitution. The person must be qualified to be a judge of a High Court.

10. (1): Ravi Sinha was appointed as the Chief of the Research and Analysis Wing (RAW), India's external intelligence agency, in June 2023, succeeding Samant Goel.

98. 1	**99.** 2	**100.** 4

11. (3): Given,

P I N K
↓ ↓ ↓ ↓
16 9 14 11 ←Positions in Alphabet

Similarly,

R E D
↓ ↓ ↓
18 5 4 ←Positions in Alphabet

Hence, RED is coded as 1854.

12. (2): All others — Diving, Swimming, and Sailing — are water-related sports/activities. Driving is unrelated to water, so it's the odd one out.

13. (3): All other pairs are antonyms (Kind–Cruel, Stale–Fresh, Truth–Lie), while Slow–Sluggish are synonyms, hence differently related.

14. (1): Drama is performed on a Stage.

Tennis is played on a Court. So, the correct analogy is Court.

15. (1): If day before yesterday was Saturday, then:

- Yesterday = Sunday
- Today = Monday
- Tomorrow = Tuesday
- Day after tomorrow = Wednesday.

16. (4): The pattern is:

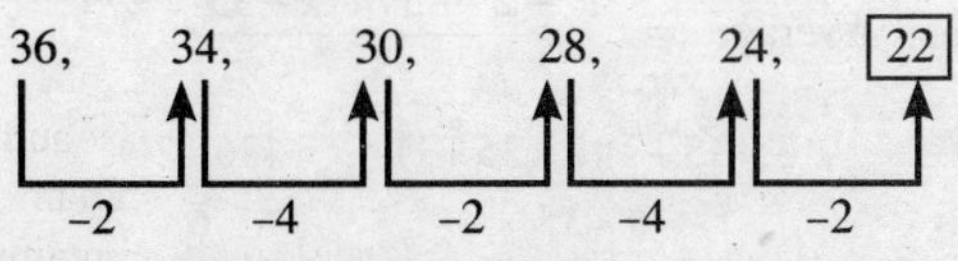

Hence, 22 will come next.

17. (3): All other words (Fondness, Liking, Attachment) are positive emotions, whereas Hate is negative, hence it's the odd one out.

18. (4):

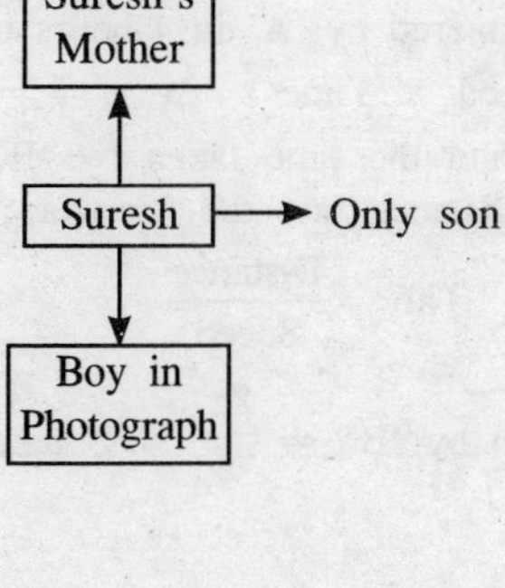

"The only son of my mother" = Suresh himself.

So, "He is the son of Suresh" ⇒ Suresh is the father of the boy.

19. (1): The current total age of A, B, C, and D is 70 years.

After 5 years, each will be 5 years older.

So, total increase in age

$= 5 \times 4 = 20$ years.

Therefore, total age after 5 years

$= 70 + 20 = 90$.

20. (3): Break down the man's movement:

- 1 km East
- 5 km South
- 2 km East (total East = 3 km)
- 9 km North (net North = 9 - 5 = 4 km)

So, final position is 3 km East and 4 km North of start ⇒ Direction = North-East.

21. (1): The main ingredient in most hand sanitizers is alcohol, especially ethanol or isopropyl alcohol, due to its effectiveness in killing bacteria and viruses.

22. (4): The salivary glands are present in the human mouth and secrete saliva, which helps in digestion and keeps the mouth moist.

23. (2): The basic unit of the neural system is the neuron, which is responsible for transmitting nerve impulses throughout the body.

24. (4): The coronavirus (COVID-19) primarily affects the lungs, leading to symptoms like cough, breathlessness and pneumonia.

25. (1): About 70% of the Sun's mass is composed of hydrogen, which fuels the Sun through nuclear fusion reactions.

26. (3): A person with O negative blood group is called a universal donor because their blood can be transfused to people of any other blood group.

27. (1): A lactometer is used to measure the density or purity of milk, which helps determine if water has been added to the milk.

28. (4): Black fungus (Mucormycosis) symptoms include facial swelling, nasal congestion, and headache, especially in immunocompromised individuals.

Hence, correct options are (*a*), (*b*) and (*c*).

29. (2): Graphite is the substance used in pencil leads due to its smoothness and ability to leave a mark on paper without being toxic.

30. (3): Nitrogen gas is usually filled in electric bulbs to prevent the filament from oxidizing and breaking quickly during heating.

31. (3): The sum of the first n odd natural numbers $= n^2$.

Here, $n = 20 \Rightarrow$ Sum $= 20^2 = 400$

32. (1): LCM of 2, 3, 4, 5, and 6 = 60

Now, find the multiple of 60 nearest to 1000:

$60 \times 17 = 1020 \Rightarrow$ Nearest = 1020

33. (1): Numbers: 48, 36, 72, 24

HCF = 12

LCM = 144

Now, $144 \div 12 = 12$

34. (2): LCM of 5, 8, 12, 20 = 120

Check divisibility:

$120 \div 9$ = not exact (remainder $\neq 0$)

So, 120 is not a multiple of 9.

35. (1): Selling Price of 250 chairs = SP

Gain = SP of 50 chairs

So, Profit % = $(50/200) \times 100 = 25\%$

36. (1): Total votes = 7500

Invalid votes = 20% of 7500
= 1500

Valid votes = 7500 − 1500
= 6000

Votes for one candidate = 55% of 6000
= 3300

So, other candidate got = 6000 − 3300
= 2700

37. (3): Basic wage for 40 hours = ₹ 20

Basic rate = ₹ 20 ÷ 40 = ₹ 0.50/hour

Overtime rate = ₹ 0.50 + 25%
= ₹ 0.625/hour

Let overtime hours = x

Then, total wage = $20 + 0.625x$ = ₹ 25

So, $0.625x = 5$

$\Rightarrow \quad x = 8$ hours

Total time worked = 40 + 8 = 48 hours

38. (1): Let cost price (CP) of 1 book = ₹ 1

Then, CP of 36 books = ₹ 36

Given: SP of 30 books = ₹ 36

So, SP of 1 book = ₹ 36 ÷ 30 = ₹ 1.20

Profit on each book = ₹ 1.20 − ₹ 1 = ₹ 0.20

Profit % = $(0.20 / 1) \times 100 = 20\%$

39. (4): Let original cost price = ₹ 100

Original profit = 20%

Selling price = ₹ 120

Now, cost price reduced by 20%

New CP = ₹ 80

Selling price increased by 10%

New SP = ₹ 132

New profit = ₹ 132 − ₹ 80 = ₹ 52

Old profit = ₹ 120 − ₹ 100 = ₹ 20

Increase in profit = ₹ 52 − ₹ 20 = ₹ 32

% increase in profit = $(32 / 20) \times 100 = 160\%$

40. (4): Average weight of 29 students = 40 kg

Total weight = $29 \times 40 = 1160$ kg

Average becomes 40.5 kg for 30 people

New total weight = $30 \times 40.5 = 1215$ kg

Teacher's weight = 1215 − 1160 = 55 kg

41. (2): To find the average of squares of natural numbers from 1 to 35, use the formula:

$$\text{Average} = \frac{1^2 + 2^2 + 3^2 + ... + 35^2}{35}$$

$$= \frac{35(35+1)(2\times35+1)}{6\times35} = \frac{(36)(71)}{6}$$

$$= \frac{2556}{6} = 426.$$

So, the average is 426.

42. (2): Let the speed of 'B' = x.

Then the speed of 'A' = $2x$.

Distance covered by 'A' in 4 hours is Distance

= Speed × Time = $2x \times 4 = 8x$.

Now, to find the time taken by 'B' to cover the same distance, use the formula:

$$\text{Time} = \frac{\text{Distance}}{\text{Speed}}$$

Time taken by 'B' = $\frac{8x}{x}$ = 8 hours.

43. (1): Let total distance = $2x$

First half: x at 12 km/h ⇒ time = $x/12$

Second half: x at 15 km/h ⇒ time = $x/15$

Total time = 9 hours

So,

$$\frac{x}{12}+\frac{x}{15} = 9$$

$$\Rightarrow \quad \frac{5x+4x}{60} = 9$$

$$\Rightarrow \quad \frac{9x}{60} = 9$$

$$\Rightarrow \quad x = 60$$

Total distance = $2x$ = 120 km

44. (3): Distance = 27 km

Walking speed = 9 km/h

⇒ Time walking = 27 ÷ 9 = 3 hours

Rest after every km except the last

⇒ 26 rests of 9 min each

Total rest = 26 × 9 = 234 minutes

= 3 h 54 min

Total time = 3 h + 3 h 54 min

= 6 h 54 min

45. (1): Let principal = ₹ 100

Amount becomes 5 times ₹ A = ₹ 500

Simple Interest = 500 – 100 = ₹ 400

Time = 20 years

Using SI formula:

$$SI = \frac{P \times R \times T}{100}$$

$$\Rightarrow \quad 400 = \frac{100 \times R \times 20}{100}$$

$$\Rightarrow \quad 400 = 20R$$

$$\Rightarrow \quad R = 20\%$$

46. (1): Given: CI – SI = ₹ 1.50, Rate = 5%, Time = 2 years

Use formula for difference between CI and SI for 2 years:

$$\text{Difference} = \frac{P \times R^2}{100^2} = \frac{P \times 25}{10000}$$

$$= \frac{P}{400} = 1.50$$

$$\Rightarrow \quad P = 1.50 \times 400 = ₹\,600$$

47. (3): Let principal = P, rate = 4%, time = 2 years

Amount = ₹ 1352

$$A = P\left(1+\frac{4}{100}\right)^2$$

$$= P \times (1.04)^2$$

$$= P \times 1.0816$$

$$\Rightarrow \quad P = \frac{1352}{1.0816} = ₹\,1250$$

48. (2): Let total work = 360 units

A + B = 360 ÷ 72 = 5 units/day

B + C = 360 ÷ 120 = 3 units/day

A + C = 360 ÷ 90 = 4 units/day

Add: (A + B) + (B + C) + (A + C)

= 5 + 3 + 4 = 12

So, A + B + C = 12 ÷ 2 = 6 units/day

Then A = (A + B + C) – (B + C)

= 6 – 3 = 3 units/day

Time by A alone = 360 ÷ 3 = 120 days

49. (3): A can do job in 12 days

B is 60% more efficient

⇒ Efficiency ratio A : B

= 100 : 160 = 5 : 8

So if A does 5 units/day, B does 8 units/day

Work = 12 × 5 = 60 units

Time by B = 60 ÷ 8 = 15/2 days

50. (1): Filling rate without leak = 1/6

Filling rate with leak = 1/8

Leak's rate = 1/6 – 1/8

= (4 – 3)/24 = 1/24

So leak empties tank in 24 hours

51. (1): To find the third proportional to 5 and 10:

Let the third proportional be x, then:

$$\frac{5}{10} = \frac{10}{x}$$

$$\Rightarrow \quad 5x = 100$$

$$\Rightarrow \quad x = 20$$

52. (4): Ratio of boys to girls = 5:4

$\Rightarrow$ Total parts = 9

So total number of students must be divisible by 9

Check options:

- $45 \div 9 = 5$
- $72 \div 9 = 8$
- $108 \div 9 = 12$
- $98 \div 9 = 10.89$

Since 98 is not divisible by 9, it is not valid.

53. (4): Let the number of girls = x

Then number of boys = $x + 15$

Now, after increase:

- Boys become: $1.2 \times (x + 15)$
- Girls become: $1.15 \times x$

Given:

$1.2(x + 15) - 1.15x = 29$

Expand:

$$1.2x + 18 - 1.15x = 29$$

$$\Rightarrow \quad 0.05x = 11$$

$$\Rightarrow \quad x = \frac{11}{0.05} = 220$$

So, number of girls = 220

54. (1): Let Orange = O, Banana = B, Apple = A

Equation 1: 2O + 3B + 4A = 15

Equation 2: 3O + 2B + 1A = 10

We want: 3O + 3B + 3A = ?

Add equations (1) and (2):

(2O + 3B + 4A) + (3O + 2B + 1A)

= 5O + 5B + 5A = 25

$\Rightarrow$ Divide by 5: O + B + A = 5

So, 3O + 3B + 3A = 3 × 5 = ₹ 15

55. (1): Break each number into primes:

- $12 = 2^2 \times 3$
- $34 = 2 \times 17$
- $2 = 2$

Now count prime factors with powers:

$(12)^{43} = (2^2 \times 3)^{43} = 2^{86} \times 3^{43}$

$(34)^{48} = (2 \times 17)^{48} = 2^{48} \times 17^{48}$

$(2)^{57} = 2^{57}$

Total:

- Power of 2 = 86 + 48 + 57 = 191
- Power of 3 = 43
- Power of 17 = 48

Total prime factors = 191 + 43 + 48 = 282

For Q.No. 56-60:

Let's compute required values step-by-step using the data:

City	% Watching 1 Film/Week	Watchers >1 Film/Week	Let Total Watchers = x
I	50%	3200	Let x = total $\Rightarrow$ 50% of $x = x/2$ = only-1-film $\Rightarrow$ So, $x/2 = x - 3200 \Rightarrow x = 6400$
II	30%	3500	30% of $x = x - 3500 \Rightarrow 0.3x = x - 3500 \Rightarrow 0.7x = 3500 \Rightarrow x = 5000$
III	65%	7000	$0.65x = x - 7000 \Rightarrow 0.35x = 7000 \Rightarrow x = 20000$
IV	25%	5400	$0.25x = x - 5400 \Rightarrow 0.75x = 5400 \Rightarrow x = 7200$
V	80%	2900	$0.8x = x - 2900 \Rightarrow 0.2x = 2900 \Rightarrow x = 14500$

Now compute number of only-one-film watchers for each city:

- City I: 50% of 6400 = 3200
- City II: 30% of 5000 = 1500
- City III: 65% of 20000 = 13000
- City IV: 25% of 7200 = 1800
- City V: 80% of 14500 = 11600

56. (2): City II ⇒ 30% of 5000 = 1500

57. (3): Only-one-film watchers highest in:
- I: 3200
- II: 1500
- III: 13000
- IV: 1800
- V: 11600

So, highest is City III

58. (2): Total watchers per city:
- I: 6400
- II: 5000
- III: 20000
- IV: 7200
- V: 14500

Minimum = City II

59. (4): Maximum total watchers = 20000 in City III

60. (3): Sum of only-one-film watchers: 3200 (I) + 1500 (II) + 13000 (III) + 1800 (IV) + 11600 (V) = 31100

61. (4): Supercomputers are high-capacity machines used primarily for complex computations, scientific research, and weather forecasting due to their extremely fast processing capabilities.

62. (2): To connect to the internet, you need a modem (modulator-demodulator), which converts digital signals into analog and vice versa, enabling internet connectivity via your ISP.

63. (3): Star, Bus, and Ring are standard network topologies. Linear is not recognized as a formal topology; it may informally describe a bus network but is not a standard term.

64. (2): In a wired LAN based on star topology, devices like hub, switch, and sometimes even router can be part of the network structure. However, a repeater is not typically used in a star topology.

Repeaters are used to regenerate signals over long distances in linear or bus networks, not within the centralized structure of a star topology.

65. (2): ALT + TAB is the keyboard shortcut used in Windows to switch between open applications or windows quickly.

66. (3): Windows 95 introduced preemptive multitasking, which allows the operating system to forcibly take control of the CPU from running tasks to ensure fair CPU time distribution. Earlier systems like DOS or Windows 3.x used cooperative multitasking.

67. (1): URL stands for Uniform Resource Locator. It is the address used to access resources on the internet, such as websites (e.g., https://www.example.com).

68. (4): ROM (Read-Only Memory) is non-volatile, meaning it retains its contents even when power is turned off. RAM, cache, and CPU registers are volatile and lose data when power is lost.

69. (3): Monitors are typically connected to computers using an HDMI port (High-Definition Multimedia Interface), which transmits both video and audio signals.

70. (1): In Linux, the command used to change file permissions is chmod (change mode). It allows you to define who can read, write, or execute a file.

71. (2): The direct shortcut to open Task Manager in Windows is Ctrl + Shift + Esc.

(Note: Ctrl + Alt + Delete brings up a menu that includes Task Manager, but doesn't open it directly.)

72. (2): In an email address (like user@example.com), the part after the @ symbol is the domain name (e.g., example.com).

73. (4): Ubuntu is an operating system based on Linux, not a web browser.

Browsers like Google Chrome, Firefox, and Microsoft Edge are used to access the web.

74. (1): To send a copy of the email to additional recipients without their address being visible to other recipients:

The Bcc field hides the addresses from others in the recipient list, providing privacy.

75. (1): IM stands for Instant Messaging, a form of real-time text communication over the internet (e.g., WhatsApp, Messenger).

76. (1): The word 'cordial' means warm, friendly, and polite. The opposite of that is unfriendly.

77. (4): Strife means conflict or struggle, especially violent or bitter disagreement. The correct synonym is Battle.

Other options like Concord, Peace, and Truce are all antonyms.

78. (2): The fenugreek leaves were sun-dried to make spices.

This sentence changes the focus from the doer to the action/object (passive voice) while maintaining the meaning of the original sentence.

Correct passive: The fenugreek leaves were sun-dried to make spices.

79. (4): The thief was seen leaving the house by me.

This sentence correctly converts the active voice to passive, retaining both the subject and the action in the correct order.

Correct passive: The thief was seen leaving the house by me.

80. (3): The error lies in "when". The sentence uses "when" incorrectly in a completed action context. It should be "where" or should be rephrased.
Correct form: "...Mumbai Airport, where it stopped..."
Correct error part: (c)

81. (2): The sentence is grammatically correct and properly structured; no error is present in any part.

82. (3): The correct spelling is irrelevant. The other options are misspelled.

83. (1): Correct sentence: She is not very talented, yet she is highly successful.
"Yet" correctly connects contrasting ideas here.

84. (4): Correct sentence: Although he was an illiterate, he managed to achieve success through hard work.
"Although" is the correct conjunction for this contrast.

85. (2): "Only one of the boys has not done the homework given yesterday."
"One" is singular, so the singular verb "has" is correct.

86. (1): He said that he would go to college the next day.
In indirect speech, "will" changes to "would" and "tomorrow" changes to "the next day."

87. (3): He asked me why I was troubling him.
In reported speech, the question is converted into a statement and the tense changes from present continuous to past continuous.

88. (2): The correct spelling is perceived.

89. (1): The action or instance of making a judgment about something is called an assessment.

90. (3): The act of using someone or something unfairly for your own advantage is exploitation.

91. (2): The word that means satisfactory or acceptable in quality or quantity is adequate.

92. (4): Sequence:
(*a*) his contribution to the
(*d*) field of astronomy were
(*b*) completely ignored as soon
(*c*) as he retired from work

Complete sentence: His contribution to the field of astronomy were completely ignored as soon as he retired from work.

93. (3): Sequence:
(Q) they look for creative
(S) solutions to the problems that
(P) are inhibiting progress
(R) rather than the conventional solution of outsourcing

Complete sentence: They look for creative solutions to the problems that are inhibiting progress rather than the conventional solution of outsourcing.

94. (1): The government too is expected to do more to restore economic growth and livelihoods.

This sentence fits best after the first line, maintaining coherence and flow about expectations post-lockdown.

95. (3): Correct phrase to complete the passage:

It reinforces XYZ's narrative that opposition parties are weak and squabbling, dominated by narrow interests with little in common.

96. (1): The two food categories are 'Nutrient-dense foods' and 'low-nutrient dense foods'.

These two categories are opposite in nutritional values as described in the passage.

97. (4): The word "substantial" in the passage means enough or adequate amounts, matching the meaning of "adequate."

98. (1): a diet consisting of the right kind and quantity of food for carrying out growth, development and body functions.

This is the precise definition of a balanced diet according to the passage.

99. (2): People tend to indulge in tasting more flavors which can result in over-eating.

Eating a variety of flavors leads to eating more because people want to sample different tastes.

100. (4): It means a particular idea or set of ideas held by a specific group.

The phrase "a school of thought" refers to a specific set of ideas or beliefs shared by a group.

Previous Paper (Solved)

CUET-UG

(Common University Entrance Test for UG Programmes)

Bachelor of Computer Applications (BCA), 2023*

ENGLISH LANGUAGE

Directions (Qs. No. 1-5): *Read the following passage to answer the questions:*

The village school was located in a prominent place where apart from the school, there were a few shops, a small temple and a government dispensary. The headmaster of the school was a learned and scholarly man loved by all. The dispensary was looked after by a doctor and a male nurse. The doctor attended the dispensary very punctually and used to retire to his residence after the duty hours and never allowed anyone to visit his residence after the duty hours.

The school was housed in dilapidated building and very often the headmaster used to take the children out to the nearby garden where they could play and take part in various sports and games under the able supervision of the headmaster.

One day a stray dog entered the garden when the children were playing. One of them pelted a stone at the dog and it started barking and all of a sudden became boisterous and bit a child in the leg. The boy was very badly hurt and his leg started bleeding. The children who by this time became panicky rushed to the headmaster who together with a few students, took the child to the nearby dispensary and then to the doctors residence.

The headmaster knocked at the door of the doctor for help. But the doctor refused to open the door and made it clear that he would not attend to anyone howsoever serious he may be, during his leisure hours. However the headmaster continued to knock at the door and finally the doctor opened the door when he saw the headmaster trembling with fear and the student in agony and pain.

The doctor mellowed down now and took the child to the dispensary for bandaging and giving necessary injections and medicines. The doctor was impressed by the dedication and sincerity of the headmaster. He realized his folly and decided to attend to the needy and sick even during his leisure hours.

1. The village school was located near the:

A. Forest B. Market
C. Library D. Pond

2. After the duty hours the government dispensary doctor normally:

A. Slept and dreamt
B. Spent time with his family
C. went to his private clinic
D. Rested at home and never allowed visitors

3. All of a sudden a dog became boisterous and it bit a child in the leg. The dog got angry mainly because:

A. One boy did mischief
B. Dog was feeling hungry
C. Dog saw another dog
D. Boy did not give food to the dog

4. The head master was trembling with fear at the doctor's residence along with the injured boy. The doctor was:

* Exam held on 16-6-2023 conducted by NTA

A. afraid of higher officials
B. afraid of student's parents
C. not opening the door
D. impressed with the dedication of the headmaster

5. Find the synonym from a passage which means "To become less extreme in behaviour".

A. stray B. boisterous
C. mellowed D. folly

Directions (Qs. No. 6-10): *Read the following passage to answer the questions:*

The needs of a nations people are bigger and much more important than any other considerations. The mission of parliament is that it has to be alive and dynamic over issues vital to the existence of our very nationhood. Our freedom did not come as a gift. The whole country struggled for decades to achieve the first vision of independence, so we have to protect it. There were excellent leaders in all walks of life-science, education and industry. To preserve this freedom from intruders and others who would compromise it is our bounden duty and not a matter of choice and convenience. No ideology is above the security and prosperity of our country. No agenda is more important than harmony among the people. Students should get ready to transform India into a developed nation. Ignite your minds and think big.

A teacher once said, 'Give me a five-year-old child. After seven years, no God or Devil will be able to change the child.' Will all teachers be such gurus? The administrators have a great opportunity to link the people and political leaders. They should always take decisions that are good for the people I believe it is only executives like empowered district collectors who can assist transformation. The state-Central integrated fund has to be deployed in mission mode programmes.

6. We have to protect our nations Independence as we got it after:

A. Excellent leader
B. War and Fight
C. Struggle for decades
D. Help from foreign country

7. To transform India into a Developed Nation Dr. A.P.J. Abdul Kalam expects his students to:

A. Ignite the minds B. Fire the mind
C. Use the mind D. Clean the mind

8. The one who can link the people and political leaders even to assist for transformation. They are known as:

A. Leader B. Administrators
C. Manager D. Major

9. The existence of Nationhood is maintained by:

A. Country B. Office
C. Collectorate D. Parliament

10. Find the synonym from the passage which means:

'Trespasser'

Choose the correct option:

A. Leader B. Teacher
C. Intruder D. Collector

Directions (Qs. No. 11-15): *Read the following passage to answer the questions:*

Village Resource Centres (VRCs) were established by the Indian Space Research Organisation (ISRO) as part of its societal mission of bringing space-based services emanating from Satellite Communication (SatCom) and Earth Observation (EO) to rural society. While SatCom provides the method for an effective delivery of information and services across vast regions, EO provides community-centric information regarding geo-referenced land records; natural resources; the environment; sites for exploiting ground water for potable use and recharging: wasteland and reclamation; watershed profile; and cropping patterns. It can also provide customized local area information. These systems are very useful for predicting disaster, giving early warning and vulnerability-related information.

ISRO has undertaken the mission of assisting the VRC programme with a portfolio of services which are being established in collaboration with forty partner agencies across twenty-two states. A total of 473 VRCs have been set up with plans for rapid expansion in the future. Each VRC essentially has digital connectivity; specialty health care providers enabled via the Indian National Satellite System (INSAT); Spatial information on natural resources facilities for primary health care and distance education.

11. Village resource centres were set up by the ______ to bring space based centres to rural society:

A. SatCom
B. Indian Space Research Organisation
C. Earth observation
D. Indian National Satellite system

12. ISRO has undertaken the mission of assisting the village Resource Centres Programme with forty partner agencies across ______ states.

A. Twenty One B. Twenty Two
C. Twenty Three D. Twenty Five

13. Match List-I with List-II:

List-I	List-II
(*a*) SatCom	(*i*) Village Resource Centres
(*b*) VRCs	(*ii*) Indian National Satellite System
(*c*) ISRO	(*iii*) Satellite Communication
(*d*) INSAT	(*iv*) Indian Space Research Organisation

Choose the correct answer from the options given below:

	(*a*)	(*b*)	(*c*)	(*d*)
A.	(*iii*)	(*iv*)	(*i*)	(*ii*)
B.	(*iv*)	(*ii*)	(*iii*)	(*i*)
C.	(*ii*)	(*iv*)	(*i*)	(*iii*)
D.	(*iii*)	(*i*)	(*iv*)	(*ii*)

14. Find a word from the passage that means the same as 'to assume things before it happens'.

A. Communications B. Observations
C. Information D. Prediction

15. Find a word from the passage that is an antonym of the word 'safe/secure'.

A. Exploitation B. Expansion
C. Vulnerable D. Collaboration

16. Fill in the blank with the correct determiner:

The teacher asked him ______ questions.

A. much B. a few
C. any D. every

17. Change the following into direct speech:

He requested me to shut the door.

A. He told, "The door should be shut."
B. He said, "Please shut the door."
C. He said, "Shut the door."
D. He ordered, "Close the door."

18. Fill in the blank with the correct adverb:

I ______ met him at the conference on Sunday but discussed a lot of things.

A. Always B. Never
C. Briefly D. Finally

19. Which of the following sentences does ***not*** use the correct modals.

(*a*) I swim across the river when I was young.
(*b*) It may rain next Friday
(*c*) I expected that I would get a first class
(*d*) One ought to respect the environmental laws
(*e*) This used to be a dense jungle.

Choose the ***correct answer*** from the options given below:

A. (*a*) and (*d*) only B. (*a*) only
C. (*e*) only D. (*c*) and (*d*) only

20. Complete the sentence by choosing the appropriate options:

He gave ______ European ______ one-rupee coin.

A. the, an B. a, a
C. an, an D. the, a

21. Complete the sentence by choosing the appropriate set of prepositions:

He is notoriously mean ______ his treatment ______ his servants.

A. in, of B. with, of
C. of, with D. for, of

22. Synonym of the word "alleviate".

(*a*) worsen (*b*) grow
(*c*) lessen (*d*) increase
(*e*) reduce

Choose the ***correct answer*** from the options given below:

A. (*a*) and (*e*) only B. (*c*) and (*e*) only
C. (*b*) and (*d*) only D. (*a*) only

23. Choose the correct Exclamatory sentence of the given sentence:

The Night is very beautiful.

A. How beautiful is the night!
B. Night is so beautiful!
C. What beautiful night!
D. Night is too beautiful!

24. Choose the option that has been correctly changed from Direct to Indirect speech.

Adesh said, "Please shut the door behind you."

(*a*) Adesh requested me to please shut the door behind me.
(*b*) Adesh said that I request you to shut the door behind you.
(*c*) Adesh said to shut the door behind you.
(*d*) Adesh said to me that I request to shut the door behind you.

Choose the ***correct answer*** from the options given below:

A. (*a*) only B. (*b*) only
C. (*c*) only D. (*d*) only

25. Match the underline phrases with their meanings:

List-I ***(Phrases)***	**List-II** ***(Meanings)***
(*a*) I had so much work to do but the fever got the best of me	(*i*) Peaceful time
(*b*) They spent their halcyon days in a village	(*ii*) Vulnerable/ Weak spot
(*c*) He earned really well but ended up penniless. Gambling was his achilles heel	(*iii*) Competent for a work
(*d*) A doctor worth his salt will advise people for healthy eating	(*iv*) Take advantage of something

Choose the ***correct answer*** from the options given below:

	(*a*)	(*b*)	(*c*)	(*d*)
A.	(*iv*)	(*i*)	(*ii*)	(*iii*)
B.	(*iv*)	(*ii*)	(*i*)	(*iii*)
C.	(*i*)	(*iii*)	(*ii*)	(*iv*)
D.	(*iv*)	(*iii*)	(*ii*)	(*i*)

26. Choose the correct meaning of the underlined word from the following sentence:

The minister entered the hall with his entourage.

A. cars
B. belongings
C. following subordinates
D. police

27. Find out the adverbs from the given sentence and tick the correct option given below:

People often complain about foolish things and easily try to escape from the reality.

A. complain, reality
B. often, easily
C. easily, complain
D. often, escape

28. Choose the option with the same meaning:

Camouflage

(*a*) disguise (*b*) cover
(*c*) demonstrate (*d*) fabric

Choose the ***correct answer*** from the options given below:

A. (*a*) only B. (*b*) only
C. (*c*) only D. (*d*) only

29. Complete the sentence using the correct options:

When I reached the station, the train

A. been leaving
B. had been already leaving

C. had already left
D. has left

30. State the kind of clause for the underlined part of the given sentence:

The Children whom I teach in standard 8 are very disciplined.

A. Adverb clause B. Adjective clause
C. Noun clause D. Adverb clause of time

31. Match List-I with List-II to complete the idioms:

List-I	List-II
(*a*) At one's	(*i*) tongue
(*b*) Hold one's	(*ii*) fingertips
(*c*) Lose one's	(*iii*) head
(*d*) Win	(*iv*) hands down

Choose the ***correct answer*** from the options given below:

	(*a*)	(*b*)	(*c*)	(*d*)
A.	(*ii*)	(*i*)	(*iii*)	(*iv*)
B.	(*i*)	(*ii*)	(*iii*)	(*iv*)
C.	(*iv*)	(*iii*)	(*ii*)	(*i*)
D.	(*ii*)	(*i*)	(*iv*)	(*iii*)

32. Find the correct Antonym of the word 'Terrible':

A. scaring B. soothing
C. horrible D. frightening

33. Match List-I with List-II for suitable antonyms:

List-I (*Word*)	List-II (*Antonym*)
(*a*) Charming	(*i*) Hide
(*b*) Occasional	(*ii*) Miser
(*c*) Generous	(*iii*) Hideous
(*d*) Exhibit	(*iv*) Regular

Choose the correct answer from the options given below:

	(*a*)	(*b*)	(*c*)	(*d*)
A.	(*iii*)	(*iv*)	(*ii*)	(*i*)
B.	(*iv*)	(*ii*)	(*iii*)	(*i*)
C.	(*iii*)	(*ii*)	(*i*)	(*iv*)
D.	(*ii*)	(*i*)	(*iv*)	(*iii*)

34. Arrange the following in the correct sequence:
(*a*) With telling us about
(*b*) Has been mainly occupied
(*c*) The finite world has been analysed
(*d*) The elements into which
(*e*) The language of man

Choose the correct answer from the options given below:

A. (*e*), (*b*), (*a*), (*d*), (*c*)
B. (*a*), (*e*), (*b*), (*d*), (*c*)
C. (*e*), (*a*), (*b*), (*d*), (*c*)
D. (*e*), (*d*), (*a*), (*b*), (*c*)

35. Match the phrases with their meaning:

List-I	List-II
(*a*) Set in	(*i*) to treat with contempt
(*b*) Wind up	(*ii*) extinguished
(*c*) Look down upon	(*iii*) begin
(*d*) Put out	(*iv*) bring to an end

Choose the correct answer from the options given below:

	(*a*)	(*b*)	(*c*)	(*d*)
A.	(*ii*)	(*iii*)	(*iv*)	(*i*)
B.	(*iv*)	(*ii*)	(*iii*)	(*i*)
C.	(*iii*)	(*i*)	(*iv*)	(*ii*)
D.	(*iii*)	(*iv*)	(*i*)	(*ii*)

36. Choose the option that gives the correct meaning of the foreign word:

'animus'

A. good intention B. bad intention
C. mean while D. self love

37. Identify the correct passive voice form of the following sentence:

One should keep one's promises.

A. Promises need to be kept.
B. Promises should be kept.
C. Nobody keeps promises.
D. One has kept one's promises.

38. Complete the sentence with suitable option:

You ______ stood by your friends in their bad times.

A. ought to have B. should
C. must D. can have

39. Choose the correct question tag for the given sentence:

She doesn't really know how to get out of the problem?

A. Isn't she? B. doesn't she
C. does she? D. Is it?

40. Choose the correct option to change the following sentence into passive voice.

Your behaviour astonished me.

A. I was astonished by you with your behaviour.
B. You are astonished by me with behaviour.
C. I was astonished by your behaviour.
D. With your behaviour you were astonished

41. Choose one word which can be substituted for the given sentence:

'One who acts against religion'.

A. Egoist B. Heretic
C. Optimist D. Stoic

42. Fill in the blank with the suitable homonym. Choose the correct one from the following.

Ravi writes in his note book today.

The marriage is performed as per Hindu ______.

A. Rites B. Wrights
C. Rights D. Raight

43. Parts of a sentence are given in a jumbled order. Arrange the parts in the correct sequence to form a meaningful sentence.

(*a*) the resistance (*b*) of
(*c*) depend on (*d*) what does
(*e*) a conductor

Choose the ***correct answer*** from the options given below:

A. (*d*), (*a*), (*e*), (*c*), (*b*)
B. (*d*), (*a*), (*b*), (*e*), (*c*)
C. (*b*), (*a*), (*d*), (*e*), (*c*)
D. (*d*), (*a*), (*c*), (*b*), (*e*)

44. Choose the correct idiomatic expression.

The staff agreed to execute the plans.

A. Carry away B. Lay out
C. Turn down D. Carry out

45. Complete the omitted/grammatically correct sentence:

"Asoka two lives, one as ruthless conqueror and the as a compassionate ruler"

(*a*) Asoka led two lives one as the most ruthless conqueror and the as a compassionate ruler.
(*b*) Asoka led two various lives, one ruthless conqueror and the as a compassionate ruler.
(*c*) Asoka led two live one as ruthless conqueror and the as a famous compassionate ruler.
(*d*) Asoka led two lives one as ruthless conqueror and the other as a compassionate ruler.
(*e*) Asoka led two lives one as ruthless conqueror so and the as a compassionate ruler.

Choose the correct answer from the options given below:

A. (*a*) only B. (*b*) only
C. (*e*) only D. (*d*) only

46. Choose the correct subject for a letter of enquiry for a course in Choreography:

A. Enquiry for choreography
B. Course in choreography
C. Enquiry regarding course in choreography
D. Enquiry in course of choreography

47. Choose the correct Assertive sentence of the given sentence:

Alas that youth should pass away!

A. It is sad that youth has passed away
B. It is sad to think that youth should pass away
C. It is sad that youth shall pass away
D. It is sad that youth passes away

48. Complete the sentence in List I with the correct preposition from List II:

List-I	List-II
(*a*) ____ the street the piper slept	(*i*) in
(*b*) Little Jack Horner sat ____ a corner	(*ii*) into
(*c*) Old mother Hubbard went ____ the cupboard	(*iii*) over
(*d*) The cow jumped ____ the moon	(*iv*) to

Choose the correct answer from the options given below:

	(*a*)	(*b*)	(*c*)	(*d*)
A.	(*ii*)	(*i*)	(*iv*)	(*iii*)
B.	(*i*)	(*ii*)	(*iv*)	(*iii*)
C.	(*iii*)	(*ii*)	(*i*)	(*iv*)
D.	(*ii*)	(*iii*)	(*iv*)	(*i*)

49. Find out which part of the sentence has an error.

The captain along with his team are practicing very hard for the forthcoming matches.

A. The Captain along with his team
B. are practicing very hard
C. for the
D. forthcoming matches

50. Spot the Error

(*a*) Copernicus proved
(*b*) that Earth
(*c*) moves
(*d*) round
(*e*) the sun

Choose the ***correct answer*** from the options given below:

A. (*b*) only B. (*c*) only
C. (*d*) only D. (*e*) only

COMPUTER SCIENCE

51. Which one of the following statement is not true in context of relational data model?

A. Foreign Key can take NULL Value
B. A database schema is the design of a database
C. A tuple is a unique entity whereas attribute values can be duplicate in the table
D. If no single attribute in a relation is able to uniquely distinguish the tuples, then it is not possible to form a Primary Key

52. The statement in SQL which allows to change the definition of a table is ....

A. ALTER B. UPDATE
C. CREATE D. SELECT

53. Which of the following block always execute regardless of exception occurance?

A. try block B. finally block
C. else block D. except block

54. NULL is ....

A. the same as 0 for integer
B. the same as blank for character
C. the same as 0 for integer and blank for character
D. unknown value

55. What will be the output when applying following MySQL command?

SELECT LEFT ("UNIVERSITY", 5);

A. UNIVY B. UNIVE
C. RSITY D. UVYNIV

56. When pickle.load() function is used, it generates exception of EOF (End Of File). In which two ways this exception could be handled?

(*a*) with statement
(*b*) try and except
(*c*) avoid EOF exception
(*d*) assert
(*e*) reload

Choose the correct answer from the options given below:

A. (*a*) and (*c*) only

B. (*c*) and (*e*) only
C. (*a*) and (*b*) only
D. (*d*) and (*e*) only

57. Identify the error/errors in the following code:
(*a*) Line 1 - import pickle
(*b*) Line2 - data=['one', 2, [3, 4, 5]]
(*c*) Line 3 - with open('data2.dat', 'rb') as f
(*d*) Line 4 - pickle.dump(data, f)

Choose the correct answer from the options given below:
A. (*a*), (*b*) and (*c*) only
B. (*a*) and (*b*) only
C. (*c*) and (*d*) only
D. (*a*) and (*c*) only

58. Match List-I with List-II

List-I	List-II
(*a*) char (n)	(*i*) for numbers
(*b*) Int	(*ii*) fixed numbers of characters
(*c*) varchar (n)	(*iii*) variable numbers of characters
(*d*) float	(*iv*) for fractional numbers

Choose the correct answer from the options given below:

	(*a*)	(*b*)	(*c*)	(*d*)
A.	(*ii*)	(*i*)	(*iii*)	(*iv*)
B.	(*i*)	(*ii*)	(*iii*)	(*iv*)
C.	(*i*)	(*iv*)	(*ii*)	(*iii*)
D.	(*iii*)	(*ii*)	(*iv*)	(*i*)

59. Meta-data is also known as:
A. Database Instance
B. Data Constraint
C. Database Schema
D. Data Dictionary

60. Match List-I with List-II

List-I	List-II
(*a*) IP Address	(*i*) 198.20.2.18
(*b*) MAC Address	(*ii*) 12:CD:3E:56:5F:C3
(*c*) Network topology requires central controller or hub	(*iii*) Star
(*d*) Internet an example of this topology	(*iv*) Mesh

Choose the correct answer from the options given below:

	(*a*)	(*b*)	(*c*)	(*d*)
A.	(*i*)	(*ii*)	(*iii*)	(*iv*)
B.	(*iv*)	(*iii*)	(*ii*)	(*i*)
C.	(*i*)	(*iii*)	(*ii*)	(*iv*)
D.	(*iii*)	(*i*)	(*ii*)	(*iv*)

61. Arrange the following steps in sequential order of handling exception:
(*a*) Exception is raised
(*b*) Create an exception object
(*c*) Executes the code
(*d*) Runtime system searches for exception handler
(*e*) Program terminates

Choose the correct answer from the options given below:
A. (*a*), (*b*), (*d*), (*c*), (*e*)
B. (*b*), (*a*), (*d*), (*c*), (*e*)
C. (*a*), (*d*), (*b*), (*c*), (*e*)
D. (*a*), (*b*), (*c*), (*e*), (*d*)

62. Which of the following can be handled by a gateway?
A. Protocol conversion
B. Packet resizing
C. Data encapsulation
D. Regeneration of weakened signals

63. What will be the correct output, When applying ROUND() function in the following MySQL command:

SELECT ROUND(2912.564, 1)

A. 2912.5 B. 2912.56
C. 2912.6 D. 2912

64. Match List-I with List-II

List-I	List-II
(*a*) Repeater	(*i*) Device that receive data, analyse and transmit it to other networks
(*b*) Switch	(*ii*) Serves as the entry/exit point of a network

(*c*) Router (*iii*) Regenerate the signals on the cables to which it is connected

(*d*) Gateway (*iv*) Device used to connect multiple computers

Choose the correct answer from the options given below:

	(*a*)	(*b*)	(*c*)	(*d*)
A.	(*ii*)	(*iv*)	(*iii*)	(*i*)
B.	(*iii*)	(*iv*)	(*i*)	(*ii*)
C.	(*i*)	(*ii*)	(*iii*)	(*iv*)
D.	(*ii*)	(*iv*)	(*i*)	(*iii*)

65. Match List-I with List-II

List-I	List-II
(*a*) IP Address	(*i*) A name against IP address
(*b*) MAC Address	(*ii*) Physical or Hardware address
(*c*) URI	(*iii*) A unique address to uniquely identify each node in a network
(*d*) Domain Name	(*iv*) A unique address for each resource located on the web

Choose the correct answer from the options given below:

	(*a*)	(*b*)	(*c*)	(*d*)
A.	(*i*)	(*ii*)	(*iii*)	(*iv*)
B.	(*iv*)	(*iii*)	(*i*)	(*ii*)
C.	(*iii*)	(*iv*)	(*ii*)	(*i*)
D.	(*iii*)	(*ii*)	(*iv*)	(*i*)

66. A .... allows to insert/delete elements from front as well as rear:

A. Stack B. Deque
C. Queue D. List

67. For the table Emp_Salary, you need to modify a column, choose the correct SQL statement that modify the datatype of column salary from into float:

A. Alter table Emp_Salary add column salary float
B. Alter table Emp_Salary modify column salary float
C. Alter table Emp_Salary change column salary float
D. Alter table Emp_Salary modify salary float

68. Which of the following keys should be unique in Database?

(*a*) Foreign Key
(*b*) Primary Key
(*c*) Candidate Key
(*d*) Composite Primary Key

Choose the correct answer from the options given below:

A. (*a*) and (*c*) only
B. (*a*) and (*b*) only
C. (*b*), (*c*) and (*d*) only
D. (*a*), (*c*) and (*d*) only

69. What is time complexity for n elements in an insertion sort?

A. n B. n^2
C. $\log_2 n$ D. 1

70. How many total number of swaps will be done while sorting the given list using insertion sort list:

9	6	12	1	–7	3

A. 13 B. 5
C. 11 D. 9

71. It is easy to identify and isolate the fault in which of the following topology?

A. Mesh B. Bus
C. Ring D. Hybrid

72. Which of the following elements would cause collision in hashing if we apply the hash function List[i]%10, for the list [2,4,18,24,30,45,54]

(*a*) 2, 4
(*b*) 24, 54
(*c*) 4, 24
(*d*) 24, 30
(*e*) 45, 54

Choose the correct answer from the options given below:

A. (*a*) and (*b*) only
B. (*b*) and (*c*) only

C. (*a*), (*d*) and (*e*) only
D. (*a*), (*b*) and (*c*) only

73. Which elements will remain in the stack after performing following operations
PUSH(4)
POP()
PUSH(6)
PUSH(2)
PUSH(8)
POP()

A.
8
2
6
4

B.
4
8
2
6

C.
2
6

D.
2
4

74. The number of attributes in a relation is called:
A. Cardinality B. Domain
C. Tuple D. Degree

75. What will front and rear of queue contain after execution of following statements, the Queue already had the given elements in FIFO order:

1 ⟶ 8 ⟶ 7 ⟶ 9
↑ F (at 1), ↑ R (at 9)

enqueue (11)
enqueue (3)
enqueue (6)
dequeue ()
dequeue ()
enqueue (9)
enqueue (8)
dequeue ()
A. Front - 1 Rear - 8
B. Front - 8 Rear - 1
C. Front - 9 Rear - 8
D. Front - 8 Rear - 9

76. Which of the following is not an SQL Data Definition Language (DDL) statement?
A. CREATE TABLE
B. ALTER TABLE
C. DROP TABLE
D. SELECT

77. Which of the following statement is correct to insert a new record in the table student with given table structure:

Student

Name, Class, Rollno, Section

A. insert into student('Abhay', 'X', 1, 'A');
B. insert into student(name, class) values('Abhay', 'X');
C. insert into table student values('Abhay', 'X', 1, 'A');
D. insert values into student('Abhay', 'X', 1, 'A');

78. Evaluate the given postfix expression:
6 4 1 * 2 / +
A. 10 B. 8
C. 6 D. 7

79. Name the command when we want to use the database, d1:-
A. create database d1;
B. modify database d1;
C. update database d1;
D. use d1;

80. Match List-I with List-II

List-I	List-II
(*a*) Stack	(*i*) Insert at end and deletion from end
(*b*) Deque	(*ii*) Insert at end and deletion from front
(*c*) Binary File	(*iii*) Insertion and deletion from any end
(*d*) Queue	(*iv*) Stored in terms of bytes

Choose the correct answer from the options given below:

	(*a*)	(*b*)	(*c*)	(*d*)
A.	(*ii*)	(*i*)	(*iv*)	(*iii*)
B.	(*ii*)	(*i*)	(*iii*)	(*iv*)
C.	(*i*)	(*iii*)	(*iv*)	(*ii*)
D.	(*i*)	(*iii*)	(*ii*)	(*iv*)

81. In Binary search at each iteration a mid index is computed by taking average of first and last index of the part of list under consideration. What will be values at mid index if element 2 is to be searched from given list:

L = [2, 3, 5, 7, 10, 11, 12, 17, 19, 23, 29, 31, 37, 41, 43]

A. 19, 10, 3, 2 B. 17, 7, 3, 2
C. 12, 3, 2 D. 23, 10, 2

82. Which one of the following represent a valid combination for the measurement of the efficiency of an algorithm?

A. Processor and Memory
B. Complexity and Capacity
C. Time and Space
D. Data and Space

83. Match List-I with List-II

List-I	List-II
(*a*) Hub/Switch	(*i*) When one LAN is connected to the other LAN
(*b*) Router	(*ii*) Large number of computers in the building
(*c*) Modem	(*iii*) In the server room
(*d*) Server	(*iv*) Each building

Choose the correct answer from the options given below:

	(*a*)	(*b*)	(*c*)	(*d*)
A.	(*iv*)	(*iii*)	(*ii*)	(*i*)
B.	(*iv*)	(*i*)	(*iii*)	(*ii*)
C.	(*iv*)	(*i*)	(*ii*)	(*iii*)
D.	(*ii*)	(*iii*)	(*iv*)	(*i*)

84. The minimum and maximum number of comparisons done by linear search algorithm are:

A. 0 and *n* (where *n* is the total number of elements)
B. 1 and *n*–1 (where *n* is the total number of elements
C. 0 and *n*–1 (where *n* is the total number of elements
D. 1 and *n* (where *n* is the total number of elements)

85. For a list with *n* elements bubble sort takes .... passes to sort the elements in the list:

A. *n*+1
B. *n*
C. *n*–1
D. can't be determined

Directions (Qs. No. 86-90): *Data refers to unorganised facts that can be processed to generate meaningful result or information. Data are stored in computer in the electronic form in some storage devices such as HDD, SSD, Pen Drive, CD/DVD and memory card. There are two types of data, structured and unstructured. Structured data is where data stored in some format. Unstructured data are not stored in an organised format. There are some statistical technique to process the data. ICT technologies helps in the generation of large volume of data.*

Based on the above paragraph, answer the following questions:

86. What ICT stands for?

A. Information and Communication Technology
B. Information and Computing Technology
C. Internet and Computer Technology
D. Internet and Communication Technology

87. Which of the following is not Data storage device?

A. CD/DVD B. HDD
C. SSD D. CPU

88. Which of the following is an unstructured data?

A. Books data at shop
B. Business reports
C. Tabular data
D. Kitchen inventory data

89. Which of the following is a structure data?

A. Writing tweets
B. Recording a video

C. Marking attendance by teacher
D. Text document

90. Which of the following is a data processing data summerisation techniques?
A. mean squared error, max, min.
B. mean, median, mode, standard deviation
C. sum, average, max
D. count, left, right, power

Directions (Qs. Nos. 91-95): *Rohan has written a python code where he has created a function, searchword( ) to read a text file "notes.txt" and display words having length 4 or less than 4 characters. In writing code some parts are missing.*

Based on that answer questions.

```
def searchword( ):
count = 0
file = open("notes.txt", '_') # statement1
line = file. ................ # statement2
word = ................ # statement3
for c in word:
if ................ : # statement4
print(c)
................ # statement5
```

91. Mode of opening the file in #statement1 is:
A. a B. w
C. r D. ab

92. Fill in the blank in #statement2 to read the data from the file.
A. read( ) B. Read( )
C. readlines( ) D. read.lines( )

93. Fill in the blanks with #statement3 to read the data word by word
A. line.split B. line.word( )
C. split.word( ) D. line.split( )

94. Fill in the blank in # statement4 which display the word having lesser than or equal to 4 characters.
A. len(c) = 4 B. len(c) < = 4
C. len(c) < 4 D. len( ) < = 4

95. Fill in the blank in # statement5 to close the file:
A. close( ) B. File.close( )
C. close(File) D. file.close( )

96. Some operating system are required to handle multiple tasks called ....
A. Process B. Task
C. Jobs D. Queue

97. Write the output of the given code snippet:

```
L = ["One", "Two", "Three"]
L.append("Four")
L.append("Five")
X = L.pop( )
Y = L.pop( )
Z = L.pop( )
print (L, X, Y, Z)
```

A. ["One", "Two", "Three", "Four", "Five"]
B. [ ] "Five", "Four", "Three"
C. ["One", "Two"] Five, Four, Three
D. ["One", "Two"], Three, Four, Five

98. Match List-I with List-II

List-I	List-II
(*a*) Computer Network	(*i*) Used to set up a wired network
(*b*) Networking Devices	(*ii*) Used for conversion between electric signals and digital bits
(*c*) Network Interface Card	(*iii*) Used to connect multiple computers in different settings
(*d*) Modulator Demodulator	(*iv*) Allows computer to share data and resources among each other

Choose the correct answer from the options given below:

	(*a*)	(*b*)	(*c*)	(*d*)
A.	(*i*)	(*ii*)	(*iv*)	(*iii*)
B.	(*iv*)	(*iii*)	(*i*)	(*ii*)
C.	(*iii*)	(*iv*)	(*ii*)	(*i*)
D.	(*ii*)	(*i*)	(*iii*)	(*iv*)

99. Which is the correct expanded form of FOSS?
A. First Open Source Software
B. Free and Open Source Software

C. Fine and Open Source Services
D. Free and Open Source Services

100. Which of the following is not an advantage of RDBMS?

A. Reduced Data Redundancy
B. Data Isolation
C. Reduced Data Inconsistency
D. Controlled Data Sharing

MATHEMATICS

101. The value of the integral

$I = \int_{-1}^{1}(x + x^3 + x^5)dx$ is:

A. 2   B. −2
C. 0   D. 1

102. Which constraint correctly represents the situation "Mixture of x and y must be at least 8 units"?

A. $x + y > 8$ B. $x + y < 8$
C. $x + y \leq 8$ D. $x + y \geq 8$

103. A dice is thrown. If A is the event 'the number appearing is a multiple of 3 and B is the event 'the number appearing is even', then A and B are:

A. dependent events
B. independent events
C. $P(A \cap B) = \frac{1}{3}$
D. $P(B) = \frac{1}{3}$

104. The feasible region for the constrains $x \geq 0$, $x + y \leq 1$ and $x - y \leq 1$, is situated in:

(*a*) I and II Quadrant
(*b*) I Quadrant
(*c*) II and IV Quadrant
(*d*) IV Quadrant
(*e*) I, II, III and IV Quadrant

Choose the correct answer from the options given below:

A. (*a*) only
B. (*b*) and (*d*) only
C. (*b*) and (*c*) only
D. (*e*) only

105. Match List I with List II

List-I (Differential Equations)	List-II (Degree)
(*a*) $\left(\frac{dy}{dx}\right)^3 + yx = 0$	(*i*) 2
(*b*) $e^{\frac{dy}{dx}} + y^2 + y'' = 0$	(*ii*) 1
(*c*) $xyy'' + x(y')^2 - yy' = 0$	(*iii*) Not defined
(*d*) $(y'')^2 + y = 0$	(*iv*) 3

Choose the correct answer from the options given below:

	(*a*)	(*b*)	(*c*)	(*d*)
A.	(*iv*)	(*iii*)	(*ii*)	(*i*)
B.	(*i*)	(*ii*)	(*iii*)	(*iv*)
C.	(*ii*)	(*iii*)	(*iv*)	(*i*)
D.	(*iv*)	(*iii*)	(*i*)	(*ii*)

106. Area of the region bounded by the curve $x^2 = 4y$, x-axis and $x = 3$ is:

A. $\frac{9}{2}$ sq. units   B. $\frac{9}{4}$ sq. units
C. $\frac{9}{5}$ sq. units   D. $\frac{9}{8}$ sq. units

107. If a matrix has 24 elements, which of the following cannot be the possible order of the matrix?

A. 6×4 B. 12×12
C. 8×3 D. 1×24

108. Any function $f(x)$ is an increasing function in $[a, b]$ if:

(*a*) $\forall\, x_1, x_2 \in [a, b], f(x_1) \geq f(x_2)$ if $x_1 < x_2$
(*b*) $\forall\, x_1, x_2 \in [a, b], f(x_1) \geq f(x_2)$ if $x_1 > x_2$

(c) $\forall\ x_1, x_2 \in [a, b], f(x_1) \le f(x_2)$ if $x_1 < x_2$

(d) $\forall\ x_1, x_2 \in [a, b], f(x_1) < f(x_2)$ if $x_1 > x_2$

Choose the correct answer from the options given below:

A. (a), (d) only B. (b), (d) only

C. (b), (c) only D. (a), (c) only

109. The values of a for which, the function $f(x) = a^x$ is increasing on R are given by:

A. $0 < a < \infty$ B. $-\infty < a < \infty$

C. $1 < a < \infty$ D. $0 \le a < \infty$

110. If $\begin{vmatrix} 2 & 4 \\ 5 & 1 \end{vmatrix} = \begin{vmatrix} 2x & 4 \\ 6 & x \end{vmatrix}$, then x is equal to:

A. 1 B. $2\sqrt{3}$

C. $\pm\sqrt{3}$ D. $\pm 2\sqrt{3}$

111. If A and B are events such that P(A|B) = P(B|A), then:

A. A = B B. $A \cap B = \phi$

C. $A \subset B$ but $A \ne B$ D. P(A) = P(B)

112. The value of the integral $\int e^x \left(\frac{1}{x} - \frac{1}{x^2}\right) dx$ is:

A. $\frac{e^x}{x} + C$, where C is a constant

B. $\frac{e^{-x}}{x} + C$, where C is a constant

C. $e^x + C$, where C is a constant

D. $e^{-x} + C$, where C is a constant

113. Match List I with List II

List-I (Equation of curves)	List-II (Slope of tangent at x = 2)
(a) $y = x^3 - x$	(i) 8
(b) $y = (x - 2)^2$	(ii) 2/3
(c) $y = 2x^2 + 3$	(iii) 11
(d) $y = \sqrt{4x+1} - 7$	(iv) 0

Choose the correct answer from the options given below:

	(a)	(b)	(c)	(d)
A.	(ii)	(i)	(iv)	(iii)
B.	(i)	(ii)	(iv)	(iii)
C.	(iii)	(iv)	(i)	(ii)
D.	(iii)	(iv)	(ii)	(i)

114. The sum of the minor and the cofactor of the element 6 in the determinant

$$\Delta = \begin{vmatrix} 2 & 3 & 1 \\ 4 & 5 & 6 \\ 7 & 8 & 9 \end{vmatrix} \text{ is:}$$

A. –5 B. –10

C. 10 D. 0

115. If $(x + 1)e^y = 1$, then:

A. $\frac{d^2y}{dx^2} = y^2$ B. $\frac{d^2y}{dx^2} = \left(\frac{dy}{dx}\right)^2$

C. $\frac{d^2y}{dx^2} = -y^2$ D. $\frac{d^2y}{dx^2} = \frac{dy}{dx}$

116. Let $A = \begin{bmatrix} 1 & \cos\theta & 1 \\ -\cos\theta & 1 & \cos\theta \\ -1 & -\cos\theta & 1 \end{bmatrix}$ $0 \le \theta \le 2\pi$, then:

A. $|A| = 0$ B. $|A| \in [2, 4]$

C. $|A| \in (2, 4)$ D. $|A| \in (2, \infty)$

117. Which of the following statements is/are correct?

(a) $|x|$ is continuous every where in its domain.

(b) $|x|$ is differentiable every where in its domain.

(c) $|x|$ is continuous at every integral point.

(d) $|x|$ is discontinuous at every integral point.

Choose the correct answer from the options given below:

A. (a), (c) only B. (b), (d) only

C. (b), (c) only D. (a), (d) only

118. Vector in the direction of $\hat{i} + \hat{j} + \hat{k}$ with magnitude 5 units is:

A. $\frac{\hat{i} - \hat{j} + \hat{k}}{\sqrt{3}}$ B. $\frac{\hat{i} + \hat{j} + \hat{k}}{\sqrt{3}}$

C. $\frac{5(\hat{i} + \hat{j} + \hat{k})}{\sqrt{3}}$ D. $\frac{5}{3}(\hat{i} + \hat{j} + \hat{k})$

119. The general solution of the differential equation $ydx - (x + 2y^2)dy = 0$ is:

A. $x = 2y^2 + Cy$, C is a constant
B. $y = 2x^2 + Cy$, C is a constant
C. $y = 2x^2 + Cx$, C is a constant
D. $x = 2x^2 + Cy$, C is a constant

120. Which of the following is the correct equation to find the area of the shaded region, with reference to the figure given below?

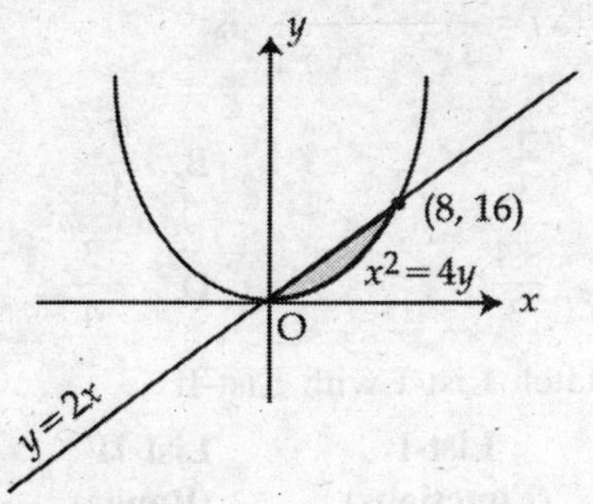

A. $A = 2\int_0^8 (2x - x^2)dx$

B. $A = 2\int_0^4 (2x - x^2)dx$

C. $A = 2\int_0^4 \left(2x - \frac{x^2}{4}\right)dx$

D. $A = \int_0^8 \left(2x - \frac{x^2}{4}\right)dx$

121. Corner points of the feasible region for a linear programming problem are (0, 2), (3, 0), (6, 0), (6, 8) and (0, 5). Let $F = 4x + 6y$ be the objective function. Then the minimum value of F occurs at:

A. (0, 2) only
B. (3, 0) only
C. The mid point of the line segment joining the points (0, 2) and (3, 0) only
D. Every point on the line segment joining the points (0, 2) and (3, 0)

122. The tangent to the curve $y = x^3 - 11x + 5$ at $x = 2$ is parallel to:

(*a*) $y = x + 1$ (*b*) $y = -x + 2$
(*c*) $2y = x + 3$ (*d*) $2y = 2x + 4$

Choose the correct answer from the options given below:

A. (*a*), (*b*) only B. (*b*), (*c*) only
C. (*a*), (*d*) only D. (*b*), (*d*) only

123. Consider a binary operation * on N defined as $a*b = a^3 + b^3$, choose the correct answer:

A. * is both associative and commutative
B. * is associative but not commutative
C. * is commutative but not associative
D. * is neither commutative nor associative

124. The value of $a + b + c + d$ if $\begin{bmatrix} 2a+b & a+2b \\ 2c+d & c+2d \end{bmatrix} = \begin{bmatrix} 8 & 4 \\ 3 & 3 \end{bmatrix}$ is:

A. 4 B. 2
C. 6 D. 8

125. The derivative of

$$\cos^{-1}\left(\frac{\sin x + \cos x}{\sqrt{2}}\right), -\frac{\pi}{4} < x < \frac{\pi}{4}$$

with respect to x is:

A. $\frac{1}{\sqrt{2}}$ B. 1

C. -1 D. $\frac{-1}{\sqrt{2}}$

126. If A is square matrix such that $A^2 = A$, then $(I + A)^3 - 8A$ is equal to:

A. I B. A
C. I – A D. 3A

127. Match List-I with List-II

List-I	**List-II**
(Function *y*)	**(Derivative $\frac{dy}{dx}$)**
(*a*) $y = \cos\sqrt{x}$	(*i*) $\frac{\sec(\tan\sqrt{x})\tan(\tan\sqrt{x})\sec^2\sqrt{x}}{2\sqrt{x}}$
(*b*) $y = \sqrt{\sin x}$	(*ii*) $-3x^2\cos(x^3)\sin(\sin(x^3))$
(*c*) $y = \sec(\tan\sqrt{x})$	(*iii*) $\frac{\cos x}{2\sqrt{\sin x}}$
(*d*) $y = \cos(\sin(x^3))$	(*iv*) $\frac{-1}{2\sqrt{x}}\sin\sqrt{x}$

Choose the correct answer from the options given below:

	(a)	(b)	(c)	(d)
A.	(i)	(iv)	(ii)	(iii)
B.	(iv)	(iii)	(i)	(ii)
C.	(iii)	(ii)	(iv)	(i)
D.	(ii)	(i)	(iii)	(iv)

128. The direction cosines of the normal to the plane $x - y + z = 4$ are:

A. $-\frac{1}{\sqrt{3}}, \frac{1}{\sqrt{3}}, \frac{1}{\sqrt{3}}$ B. $\frac{1}{\sqrt{3}}, \frac{1}{\sqrt{3}}, \frac{1}{\sqrt{3}}$

C. $\frac{1}{\sqrt{3}}, \frac{-1}{\sqrt{3}}, \frac{1}{\sqrt{3}}$ D. $\frac{-1}{\sqrt{3}}, \frac{-1}{\sqrt{3}}, \frac{1}{\sqrt{3}}$

129. The integral $I = \int e^x \left(\frac{1+\sin x}{1+\cos x}\right) dx$ is:

A. $e^x \tan x + C$, where C is a constant

B. $e^x \sec x + C$, where C is a constant

C. $e^x \tan\left(\frac{x}{2}\right) + C$, where C is a constant

D. $e^{-x} \tan\left(\frac{x}{2}\right) + C$, where C is a constant

130. The area lying between the curves $y^2 = 4x$ and $y = 2x$ is:

A. $\frac{2}{3}$ B. 1

C. $\frac{1}{3}$ D. $\frac{1}{4}$

131. The value(s) of x, for which the matrix

$$A = \begin{bmatrix} x-1 & 1 & 1 \\ 1 & x-1 & 1 \\ 1 & 1 & x-1 \end{bmatrix}$$ is singular, is/are:

A. 1   B. –1, 2

C. ± 1   D. 1, 2

132. If $A = [2\ -3\ 4]$ $B = \begin{bmatrix} 3 \\ 2 \\ 2 \end{bmatrix}$

$X = [1\ 2\ 3]$ $Y = \begin{bmatrix} 2 \\ 3 \\ 4 \end{bmatrix}$

then AB + XY =

A. [28]   B. [24]

C. 28   D. 24

133. The maximum value of the

$$f(x) = \frac{1}{4x^2 + 2x + 1}$$ is:

A. $\frac{4}{3}$ B. $\frac{3}{4}$

C. $\frac{-4}{3}$ D. $-\frac{3}{4}$

134. Match List-I with List-II

List-I (Functions)	**List-II (Range)**
(a) $\text{cosec}^{-1}x$	(i) $(0, \pi)$
(b) $\sec^{-1}x$	(ii) $\left[\frac{-\pi}{2}, \frac{\pi}{2}\right] - 0$
(c) $\tan^{-1}x$	(iii) $\left(-\frac{\pi}{2}, \frac{\pi}{2}\right)$
(d) $\cot^{-1}x$	(iv) $[0, \pi] - \left\{\frac{\pi}{2}\right\}$

Choose the correct answer from the options given below:

	(a)	(b)	(c)	(d)
A.	(iv)	(i)	(ii)	(iii)
B.	(iii)	(i)	(iv)	(ii)
C.	(ii)	(iv)	(iii)	(i)
D.	(i)	(ii)	(iii)	(iv)

135. The value of $\frac{9}{4}\sin^{-1}\frac{2\sqrt{2}}{3} + \frac{9}{4}\sin^{-1}\frac{1}{3}$ is:

A. $\frac{9}{4}$ B. $\frac{9\pi}{4}$

C. $\frac{\pi}{8}$ D. $\frac{9\pi}{8}$

136. The two events E and F are independent. If P(E) = 0.3 and P(E∪F) = 0.5, then P(E/F) – P(F/E) is:

A. $\frac{2}{7}$ B. $\frac{3}{35}$

C. $\frac{1}{70}$ D. $\frac{1}{7}$

137. If $\vec{a}+\lambda\vec{b}$ is perpendicular to $\vec{c}$, where $\vec{a} = -\hat{i}+2\hat{j}+\hat{k}, \vec{b} = 3\hat{i}+2\hat{j}+k$ and $\vec{c} = \hat{i}-\hat{j}$ then:

A. $\lambda = -1$ B. $\lambda = -3$

C. $\lambda = 1$ D. $\lambda = 3$

138. The Greatest Integer Function $f : R \to R$ given by $f(x) = [x]$, $x \in R$ and $[x]$, denotes the greatest integer less than or equal to x is:

A. one-one

B. onto

C. both one-one and onto

D. neither one-one nor onto

139. For $A = \begin{bmatrix} a_{11} & a_{12} & a_{13} \\ a_{21} & a_{22} & a_{23} \\ a_{31} & a_{32} & a_{33} \end{bmatrix}$ if M_{ij} and A_{ij} are the minor and the cofactor of a_{ij} respectively, then $|A|$ equals to:

(*a*) $a_{11}A_{11} + a_{12}A_{12} + a_{13}A_{13}$

(*b*) $a_{21}A_{12} + a_{22}A_{22} + a_{23}A_{32}$

(*c*) $a_{11}M_{11} - a_{12}M_{12} + a_{13}M_{13}$

(*d*) $a_{11}M_{11} + a_{12}M_{12} + a_{13}M_{13}$

Choose the correct answer from the options given below:

A. (*a*), (*b*) only B. (*a*), (*c*) only

C. (*c*), (*d*) only D. (*a*), (*c*), (*d*) only

140. The value of the integral $\int_{-1}^{1} |x|\, dx$ is:

A. 2 B. $\frac{1}{2}$

C. 1 D. 0

141. The probability that A speaks the truth is $\frac{4}{5}$. He throws a dice and reports that it is a five. The probability that it is actually a five is:

A. $\frac{4}{9}$ B. $\frac{1}{2}$

C. $\frac{2}{9}$ D. $\frac{5}{9}$

142. The linear programming problem : minimise $z = 3x + 2y$

subject to the constraints

$x + y \geq 8$,

$3x + 5y \leq 15$, $x \geq 0$, $y \geq 0$

has

A. one solution

B. two solutions

C. no feasible solution

D. infinitely many solutions

143. The general solution of the differential equation $\frac{dy}{dx} = \sin^{-1} x$ is:

A. $y = x\sin^{-1} x - \sqrt{1-x^2} + C$, where C is a constant

B. $y = x\sin^{-1} x + \sqrt{1+x^2} + C$, where C is a constant

C. $y = x\sin^{-1} x + \sqrt{1-x^2} + C$, where C is a constant

D. $y = -x\sin^{-1} x + \sqrt{1-x^2} + C$, where C is a constant

144. The distance of the point with position vector $\left(2\hat{i}+\hat{j}-\hat{k}\right)$ from the plane $\vec{r}\cdot\left(-2\hat{i}+\hat{j}+3\hat{k}\right) = 8$ is:

A. $\frac{7}{\sqrt{14}}$ B. $2\sqrt{14}$

C. $\sqrt{14}$ D. $\frac{\sqrt{14}}{7}$

145. The rate of change of the area of a equilateral triangle with respect to its side when its side = 2 is:

A. $\frac{\sqrt{3}}{4}$ B. $\sqrt{3}$

C. $\frac{\sqrt{3}}{2}$ D. $2\sqrt{3}$

146. The relation R in the set A = {1, 2, 3} given by R = {(1, 2), (2, 1)} is:

A. Reflexive
B. Symmetric
C. Reflexive but not symmetric
D. Equivalence Relation

147. The function f is given by

$$f(x) = \begin{cases} x^3 + 3 & , \text{if } x \neq 0 \\ 4 & , \text{if } x = 0 \end{cases}$$

Then number of points of discontinuity for this function is:

A. 0 B. 1
C. 2 D. 3

148. Which of the following functions satisfies Rolle's theorem?

A. $f(x) = x, x \in [1, 2]$
B. $f(x) = x^2, x \in [-1, 1]$
C. $f(x) = x^3, x \in [-1, 2]$
D. $f(x) = x^4, x \in [0, 2]$

149. Equation of a plane with intercept $\sqrt{3}$ on z-axis and parallel to XOY plane is:

A. $x = \sqrt{3}$ B. $z - \sqrt{3} = 0$

C. $x + \sqrt{3} = 0$ D. $z + \sqrt{3} = 0$

150. Two ropes are tied along the two diagonals of a cubic room. Ropes are inclined to each other at:

A. 45° B. 30°

C. $\cos^{-1}\left(\frac{1}{\sqrt{3}}\right)$ D. $\cos^{-1}\left(\frac{1}{3}\right)$

ANSWERS

1	2	3	4	5	6	7	8	9	10
B	D	A	D	C	C	A	B	D	C
11	**12**	**13**	**14**	**15**	**16**	**17**	**18**	**19**	**20**
B	B	D	D	C	B	B	C	B	B, D
21	**22**	**23**	**24**	**25**	**26**	**27**	**28**	**29**	**30**
A	B	A	A	A	C	B	A	C	B
31	**32**	**33**	**34**	**35**	**36**	**37**	**38**	**39**	**40**
A	B	A	A	D	B	B	A	C	C
41	**42**	**43**	**44**	**45**	**46**	**47**	**48**	**49**	**50**
B	A	B	D	D	C	B	A	B	A
51	**52**	**53**	**54**	**55**	**56**	**57**	**58**	**59**	**60**
D	A	B	D	B	C	C	A	D	A
61	**62**	**63**	**64**	**65**	**66**	**67**	**68**	**69**	**70**
B	A	C	B	D	B	D	C	B	C
71	**72**	**73**	**74**	**75**	**76**	**77**	**78**	**79**	**80**
A	B	C	D	C	D	B	B	D	C
81	**82**	**83**	**84**	**85**	**86**	**87**	**88**	**89**	**90**
B	C	B	D	C	A	D	B	C	B

91	92	93	94	95	96	97	98	99	100
C	A	D	B	D	C	C	B	B	B
101	**102**	**103**	**104**	**105**	**106**	**107**	**108**	**109**	**110**
C	D	B	B	A	B	B	C	C	C
111	**112**	**113**	**114**	**115**	**116**	**117**	**118**	**119**	**120**
*	A	C	D	B	B	D	C	A	D
121	**122**	**123**	**124**	**125**	**126**	**127**	**128**	**129**	**130**
D	C	C	C	C	C	B	C	C	C
131	**132**	**133**	**134**	**135**	**136**	**137**	**138**	**139**	**140**
B	A	A	C	D	C	D	D	B	C
141	**142**	**143**	**144**	**145**	**146**	**147**	**148**	**149**	**150**
A	C	C	C	B	B	B	B	B	D

Previous Paper (Solved)

GGSIPU—Bachelor of Computer Applications (BCA) Entrance Exam, 2022*

ENGLISH LANGUAGE AND COMPREHENSION

1. Identify the part with grammatical error in the following sentence:

He seldom or ever (A)/ goes out these days (B) / because he is (C)/ not keeping well. (D)

A. A B. B
C. C D. D

2. Choose the word, from the options, which is nearest in meaning to the underlined word in the sentence given below:

Rakesh is so garrulous that all his sober friends avoid his company.

A. Quarrelsome B. Talkative
C. Domineering D. Foolish

3. A person who believes that pleasure is the chief good is known as ________.

A. stoic B. hedonist
C. epicure D. sensual

4. Identify the part with grammatical error in the following sentence:

Considering about (A) /all the facts (B)/ he was offered (C)/ a bed by the hospital administration (D)

A. A B. B
C. C D. D

5. Identify the part with grammatical error in the following sentence:

I have never seen (A)/ a more complete (B)/ book on General Studies. (C)/ No error (D)

A. A B. B
C. C D. D

6. Choose the word from the options which is nearest in meaning to the underlined word in the sentence given below:

He is good looking but an insipid young man.

A. Arrogant B. Unscrupulous
C. Sick D. Lacking in spirit

7. Select the word or the phrase which is closest to the opposite in meaning of the underlined word or phrase in the sentence given below.

We should avoid making profligate use of scarce resources.

A. proper B. thrifty
C. extravagant D. effective

8. Anything written in a letter after it is signed is called as ________.

A. amendment B. postediting
C. postscript D. corrigendum

9. Identify the part with grammatical error in the following sentence:

India is a peace (A)/ loving nation which (B)/ has never attacked (C)/ on any country. (D)

A. A B. B
C. C D. D

10. Select the word or the phrase which is closest to the opposite in meaning of the underlined word or phrase in the sentence given below.

All thorough the evening, Rajesh looked very doleful.

A. Aggressive B. cheerful
C. tired D. involved

*Exam held on 18/06/2022.

Directions (Qs. No. 11–15): *Read the passage carefully and answer the questions that follow:*

The greatest thing, this age can be proud of, is the birth of Man in the consciousness of men. In his drunken orgies of power and national pride, man may flout and jeer at it. When organized national selfishness, racial antipathy and commercial self-seeking begin to display their ugly deformities in their nakedness, then comes the time for man to know that his salvation is not in political organizations and extended trade relations, not in any mechanical rearrangement of social system but in a deeper transformation of life, in the liberation of consciousness in love, in realization of God in man.

11. The author uses the phrase 'jeer at it'. It implies ______.
A. remorse for drinking
B. proud of national identity
C. derision at the birth of Man in the consciousness of man
D. derision at flouting

12. According to the author, this age can be proud of:
A. the birth of man
B. the orgies of power
C. the national identities
D. None of the above

13. According to the author, when will the man realize that his salvation is not in political organizations?
A. When he becomes aware of his nakedness
B. When his ugly deformities begin to display
C. Both (A) & (B)
D. Neither (A) nor (B)

14. Transformation of life and liberation of consciousness, according to the author, will lead to ______.
A. Revelations of God
B. Salvation
C. Both (A) & (B)
D. Conscious love

15. In the conception of the author salvation is ________.
A. social
B. political
C. mechanical
D. None of the above

MATHEMATICS

16. The sum of two numbers is 27 and product is 182. The numbers are ________.
A. 12 and 13 B. 13 and 14
C. 12 and 15 D. 13 and 11

17. $1 - \cos^2 A$ is equal to:
A. $\sin^2 A$ B. $\tan^2 A$
C. $1 - \sin^2 A$ D. $\sec^2 A$

18. What would be the value of A + B, if tan A = 1/2 and tan B = 1/3?
A. $\pi/3$ B. $\pi/4$
C. $\pi/2$ D. $\pi/3$

19. If p, q and r are the direction cosines of a line, which of the following is correct:
A. $p + q + r = 1$ B. $2p + 3q + r = 1$
C. $p^2 + q^2 + r^2 = 1$ D. $2p^2 + q^2 + r^2 = 2$

20. The first term and common difference for the A.P. 3, 1, –1, –3 is:
A. 1 and 3 B. –1 and 3
C. 3 and –2 D. 2 and 3

21. A box contains 10 black and 5 white socks. Two socks are pulled from the box one after another without replacement. The probability that both pulled socks are black will be:
A. 3/7 B. 1/5
C. 2/15 D. None of the above

22. The median of 6, 4, 2, 3, 4, 5, 5, 4 is ______.
A. 4 B. 5
C. 6 D. 3

23. Can two different vectors have the same magnitude?
A. Yes

B. No
C. Cannot be determined
D. None of the above

24. $\int_0^2 (x^2+3)dx$ equals to:

A. $\frac{22}{3}$ B. $\frac{25}{3}$
C. $\frac{26}{3}$ D. $\frac{28}{3}$

25. For any two matrices A and B, which of the following is true:

A. AB = BA
B. AB ≠ BA
C. AB = A + B
D. None of the above

26. Which of the following options is an example of Linear Programming problem?

A. Marketing
B. Financial investment
C. Manufacturing
D. All of the above

27. There are 10 questions in the examines to be answered in Yes or No. In how many ways, these questions may be answered?

A. 512 B. 252
C. 1024 D. 980

28. The number of tangents that can be drawn from (1, 2) to $x^2 + y^2 = 5$:

A. 1
B. 2
C. More than 2
D. No tangent can be drawn

29. The number of ways in which 5 students may be seated in a line:

A. 60 B. 100
C. 120 D. 30

30. A series has arithmetic mean as 49 and harmonic mean as 16. What will be the geometric mean of the same series?

A. 32 B. 28
C. 25 D. 16

31. The zeroes of $x^2 - 2x - 8$ are:

A. (2, –4) B. (4, –2)
C. (–2, –2) D. (–4, 4)

32. cos 2θ is equal to:

A. $\cos^2\theta - \sin^2\theta$
B. $2\cos^2\theta - 1$
C. $1 - 2\sin^2\theta$
D. All of the above

33. The magnitude of the vector $3i + 4j$ is:

A. 4 B. 5
C. 7 D. 3.5

34. The sum of n terms of an AP is given by $S_n = 3n + 2n^2$, then the common difference of the AP is

A. 4 B. 2
C. 6 D. None of these

35. The matrix $\begin{bmatrix} 2 & 0 & 0 \\ 0 & 4 & 0 \\ 0 & 0 & 6 \end{bmatrix}$ is a:

A. Identity matrix
B. Symmetric matrix
C. Skew symmetric matrix
D. Null matrix

36. The sum of two numbers is equal to thrice their difference. If the smaller of the numbers is 10, find the other number.

A. 15 B. 20
C. 40 D. None of these

37. If $y = ax^2 + b$, then the value of $\frac{dy}{dx}$ at $x = 6$ is equal to ______.

A. 12a
B. 24a
C. 2a
D. None of the above

38. The circumference of a circle exceeds its diameter by 16.8 cm. Find the circumference of the circle.

A. 12.32 cm B. 49.28 cm
C. 58.64 cm D. 26.64 cm

39. The optimal value of the objective function is attained at the points:
A. On X-axis
B. On Y-axis
C. Corner points of the feasible region
D. None of these

40. The scalar product of $4i + 2j - 3k$ and $6i - 4j + 2k$ will be ______.
A. 10
B. 28
C. 38
D. −10

41. What is the value of P if $\begin{vmatrix} 1 & 2 & P \\ 1 & 1 & 1 \\ 2 & 1 & -1 \end{vmatrix}$ is singular?
A. 1
B. 2
C. 3
D. 4

42. The differential equation of all parabola whose axis of symmetry is along the x-axis is of order
A. 3
B. 1
C. 2
D. None of the above

43. If $x = 2t^2$, $y = 4t^3$s, then $\dfrac{d^2y}{dx^2}$ is equal to ____.
A. $8t$
B. $6t$
C. $4t$
D. 6

44. Which of the following shows the relationship between Mean, Median and Mode:
A. Mode = 2 Median − 3 Mean
B. Mode = 2 Median + 3 Mean
C. Mode = 3 Median − 2 Mean
D. Mode = 3 Median + 2 Mean

45. The probability of getting a spade card from a deck of 52 cards is:
A. $\dfrac{1}{4}$
B. $\dfrac{1}{52}$
C. $\dfrac{1}{9}$
D. $\dfrac{3}{4}$

COMPUTER AWARENESS

46. What is the default file extension for all Word documents?
A. WRD
B. TXT
C. DOC
D. FIL

47. A _______ is approximately a million bytes.
A. Giga byte
B. Kilo byte
C. Mega byte
D. Tera byte

48. What does the acronym BIOS stand for?
A. Basic Input/Outer System
B. Basic Internal Output System
C. Basic Inner/Output System
D. Basic Input/Output System

49. Anything that is typed in a worksheet appears:
A. In the formula bar only
B. In the active cell only
C. In both active cell and formula bar
D. None of the above

50. Internal memory in a CPU is nothing but:
A. a set of register
B. a set of ALU
C. microprocessor
D. bus

51. C programming language was developed by:
A. Charles Babbage
B. Larry Wall
C. James Gosling
D. Dennis Ritchie

52. CD-ROM is an example of:
A. Primary memory
B. Read-Write memory
C. Cache memory
D. Read only memory

53. Information travels between components on the mother board through
A. Flash memory
B. CMOS
C. Bays
D. Buses

54. A processor having 16 bit address bus can access _______ locations in the RAM.
A. 32K B. 64K
C. 16K D. None of the above

55. What is the value of the binary number 101?
A. 3 B. 5
C. 6 D. 101

56. The operating system performs which of the following functions?
A. User interface
B. File system manipulation
C. Resource allocation
D. All of the above

57. Which of the following general-purpose software allows to do mathematical or financial calculation?
A. Word processing program
B. Spreadsheet program
C. Presentation program
D. Database program

58. What is the full form of PROM?
A. Programmable Read Only Memory
B. Program Read Output Memory
C. Program Read Only Memory
D. Primary Read Only Memory

59. A collection of various programs that helps to control your computer is called:
A. System software
B. Application software
C Microsoft Excel
D. Microsoft Word

60. What does ALU in computing denote?
A. Algorithm Logic Unit
B. Arithmetic Legal Unit
C. Arithmetic Layered Unit
D. Arithmetic Logic Unit

61. Which among the following is the smallest unit in an image on a computer screen?
A. Unit B. Pixel
C. Array D. Resolution

62. What type of device is a computer mouse?
A. Storage
B. Output
C. Input
D. Input/output

63. Which of the following is a very high speed semiconductor memory which can speed up the CPU?
A. Secondary memory
B. Main memory
C. Primary memory
D. Cache memory

64. What does MICR stand for?
A. Magnetic Ink Character Register
B. Magnetic Ink Code Reader
C. Magnetic Ink Code Register
D. Magnetic Ink Character Recognition

65. Memory unit that communicates directly with the CPU is called the:
A. main memory
B. secondary memory
C. auxiliary memory
D. None of the above

66. Storage that retains its data after the power is turned OFF is referred to as:
A. Volatile storage
B. Non-volatile storage
C. Sequential storage
D. Direct storage

67. What is the full form of URL?
A. Uniform Resource Locator
B. Uniform Random Locator
C. Unified Real Locator
D. Uniformly Read only Locator

68. Which of the following is known as father of computer?
A. Dennis Ritchie
B. Napier
C. Charles Babbage
D. Alan Turing

69. Which of the following is not a open source software?
A. Linux B. Microsoft Office
C. Mizilla Firefox D. Android

70. Database software is used to:
A. Generate report
B. Store contact list
C. Keep customer records
D. All of the above

71. Which one of the following is not an output device?
A. Projector B. Headphones
C. Plotter D. Joystick

72. What is the full name of DFD?
A. Data Flow Diagram
B. Data full Document
C. Data File Diagram
D. Data File Document

73. Of the following, which is the fastest?
A. CD-ROM B. RAM
C. Registers D. Cache

74. The part of a computer that coordinates all its functions, is called:
A. ROM program
B. System board
C. Arithmetic logic unit
D. Control unit

75. Operating system is a:
A. Application software
B. System software
C. Hardware
D. Language

GENERAL KNOWLEDGE—IT AND SCIENCE RELATED

76. The art and science of map making is called
A. Remote Sensing
B. Cartography
C. Photogrammetry
D. Mapping

77. Ultrasound waves are **not** used for the following purposes?
A. To locate its prey by a bat
B. To know the depth of sea bed by a ship
C. To diagnose defeat in internal organs of human body
D. To defeat aero plane in any air space

78. Indian's first satellite Aryabhatta was launched from:
A. Soviet Union B. USA
C. Israel D. India

79. First satellite to be placed in orbit by Indian made launch vehicle SLV3:
A. Aryabhatta B. Rohini
C. Bhaskara-I D. Insat

80. Internet in India was started by VSNL in the year:
A. 15 Aug, 1992 B. 15 Aug, 2000
B. 15 Aug, 1995 D. 26 Aug, 1997

81. Which of the following network protocols is described by GSM?
A. 2G B. 3G
C. 4G D. 5G

82. Which of the following is the first calculating device?
A. Abacus B. Calculator
C. Turing Machine D. Pascalin

83. What is the name of the anti-radiation missile developed by the Defence Research and Development Organization (DRDO)?
A. Rudram-1 B. Shaurya-1
C. Pralay-1 D. Pinaka-1

84. Satish Dhawan Space Centre (SDSC), SHAR is situated at:
A. Bengaluru B. Mahendragiri
C. Ahmedabad D. Sriharikota

85. Who among the following considered as the 'father of artificial intelligence'?
A. Charles Babbage

B. Lee De Forest
C. John McCarthy
D. JP Eckert

86. Which of the following is also called translator?
A. Data representation
B. MS-DOS
C. Operating System
D. Language Processor

87. Which one of the following is known as *Earth Summit*?
A. United Nations Framework Convention on Climate change
B. United Nations Conference on Environment and Development
C. Convention on Biological Diversity
D. None of the above

88. Which organization developed an Indian robot named *Vyom mitra*?
A. C-DAC, Pune B. ISRO
C. TIFR D. DRDO

89. Who is known as father of Indian Space Programme?
A. CV Raman
B. Vikram Sarabhai
C. APJ Kalam
D. Satish Dhawan

90. India's first unmanned lunar probe Chandrayan-1 was launched from:
A. Thiruvananthapuram
B. Wheeler island
C. Balasore
D. Sriharikota

91. Which space technology start-up has developed India's first in-orbit space debris monitoring and tracking system?
A. Digiantra Research and Technology
B. Pixel
C. GrowX
D. Astrome

92. Which country successfully tested a device deemed as the artificial sun?
A. USA
B. Japan
C. North Korea
D. China

93. Virtual currency *Bitcoin* is based on:
A. Block Chain Technology
B. Internet of Things
C. Artificial Intelligence
D. 3-D Printing

94. Which country has become the first nation to complete clinical trials of Covid-19 vaccine on humans?
A. China
B. United States
C. Russia
D. Australia

95. How much percentage of freshwater is available on earth?
A. 30% B. 3%
C. 0.3% D. 0.17%

96. Most commonly used material in making bulletproof jackets:
A. Formalin B. Coal-tar
C. Kevlar D. Fullerene

97. Select the example of application software of computer:
A. MS Word B. MS Excel
C. Both (A) and (B) D. MS-DOS

98. First nuclear reactor made in India:
A. CIRUS B. Dhruva
C. KAMINI D. Apsara

99. Who amongst the following is a pioneer in discovering the heating effect of electric current?
A. Isaac Newton
B. Galileo Galilei
C. James P. Joule
D. J.J. Thomson

100. Which Indian institute has developed an AI-based system to track social distancing?
A. I.I.Sc., Bengaluru
B. I.I.T., Kharagpur
C. I.I.T., Madras
D. N.I.T., Suratkal

ANSWERS

1	2	3	4	5	6	7	8	9	10
A	B	B	A	B	D	B	C	D	B
11	12	13	14	15	16	17	18	19	20
C	D	D	B	D	B	A	B	C	C
21	22	23	24	25	26	27	28	29	30
A	A	A	C	D	D	C	A	C	B
31	32	33	34	35	36	37	38	39	40
B	D	B	A	B	B	A	D	C	A
41	42	43	44	45	46	47	48	49	50
D	C	B	C	A	C	C	D	C	A
51	52	53	54	55	56	57	58	59	60
D	D	D	B	B	D	B	A	A	D
61	62	63	64	65	66	67	68	69	70
B	C	D	D	A	B	A	C	B	D
71	72	73	74	75	76	77	78	79	80
D	A	C	D	B	B	D	A	B	C
81	82	83	84	85	86	87	88	89	90
A	A	A	D	C	D	B	B	B	D
91	92	93	94	95	96	97	98	99	100
D	D	A	C	B	C	C	D	C	B

Previous Paper (Solved)

GGSIPU—Bachelor of Computer Applications (BCA) Entrance Exam, 2020*

ENGLISH LANGUAGE AND COMPREHENSION AND GENERAL KNOWLEDGE-IT AND SCIENCE RELATED

1. Which IT Company's nickname is 'The Big Blue'?

A. Apple B. Microsoft
C. IBM D. Samsung

2. Fill in the blanks with the appropriate option out of the four choices given below:

The man who has committed such a serious crime must .... punishment.

A. get the most severely
B. get the most severe
C. have got the most severely
D. got most severe

3. Web pages are written using ....

A. FTP B. HTTP
C. URL D. HTML

4. Which vitamin is abundant in citrus fruits?

A. Vitamin A B. Vitamin B
C. Vitamin C D. Vitamin D

5. Read the passage carefully and answer the questions that follow:

There are many types of protein molecules in the body, and each type is specific to its function. For example, proteins such as keratin and collagen give strength and elasticity to hair, as well as to skin and tendons; haemoglobin and myoglobin are the oxygen-binding proteins of the blood and the muscle, respectively; ovalbumin, the principal protein of egg white, is responsible for the setting and foaming properties of eggs. A particularly important group of proteins known as enzymes directs all the body cells to produce chemical reactions. These reactions provide the basis of every type of cell activity, including growth repair, the production of energy and the excretion of waste products.

The function of the enzymes is to ....

A. direct chemical reactions in body cells
B. bind oxygen in the blood
C. give strength and elasticity to hair
D. set and foam properties of egg

6. Another word for the CPU is ....

A. Execute B. Microprocessor
C. Micro chip D. Computer

7. In each of the following questions, an idiom or a phrase has been given, followed by four alternatives. Choose the one ***which best expresses the meaning*** of the given idiom/ phrase.

Pay one back in the same coin.

A. To provoke a person to quarrel
B. To offer another polite attention
C. To retaliate
D. To give a word of encouragement or praise to another

8. ROM stands for ....

A. Random Obsolete Memory
B. Read Only Memory
C. Read Memory Only
D. Real Obsolute Memory

*Exam held on 11/09/2020.

9. Mushroom belongs to:

A. Algae B. Fern
C. Fungi D. Plant

10. Which variety of glass is heat resistant?

A. bottle glass B. flint glass
C. hard glass D. pyrex glass

11. Read the passage carefully and answer the questions that follow:

There are many types of protein molecules in the body, and each type is specific to its function. For example, proteins such as keratin and collagen give strength and elasticity to hair, as well as to skin and tendons; haemoglobin and myoglobin are the oxygen-binding proteins of the blood and the muscle, respectively; ovalbumin, the principal protein of egg white, is responsible for the setting and foaming properties of eggs. A particularly important group of proteins known as enzymes directs all the body cells to produce chemical reactions. These reactions provide the basis of every type of cell activity, including growth repair, the production of energy and the excretion of waste products.

From the passage, it is clear that there are several types of proteins that ....

A. can create problems in our body
B. carry out specific tasks
C. are found in all organisms
D. have interchangeable functions

12. Air is a/an ....

A. Compound B. Element
C. Electrolyte D. Mixture

13. Which of the following is not a valid domain name?

A. www.google.com
B. www.yahoo.co.uk
C. www.fr.yahoo
D. www.ipu.ac.in

14. Which blood vessels have the smallest diameter?

A. Capillaries B. Arterioles
C. Venules D. Lymphatic

15. Which of the following is not a member of the vitamin B complex?

A. Thiamine B. Riboflavin
C. Folic acid D. Ascorbic acid

Directions (Qs. No. 16 and 17): *Fill in the blanks with the appropriate option out of the four choices given below:*

16. .... of the building collapse had everyone spellbound.

A. alarming report
B. reporting alarm
C. reported alarm
D. alarmed report

17. At the end of the play about women's liberation, the leading lady cautioned the audience not to judge womanhood by the way ....

A. she dresses B. she dressed
C. it dressed D. they dressed

18. Who invented Java?

A. James T Russel
B. J.M. Coetzee
C. Tim Burners Lee
D. James A Gosling

19. Which day is celebrated as World Computer Literacy Day?

A. December 2 B. December 4
C. December 6 D. December 8

20. What is the full form of PDF?

A. Portable device format
B. Portable document format
C. Portable disk format
D. Portable drive format

21. What is used to make computer chips?

A. Copper B. Steel
C. Silicon D. Iron

22. What is the characteristic of a reptile?

A. Cold blooded B. Warm Blooded
C. Non-Hearing D. Egg-laying

23. Which one is volatile memory in a computer system?

A. Hard Disk B. RAM
C. ROM D. Optical Drive

24. In each of the following questions, an idiom or a phrase has been given, followed by four alternatives. Choose the one ***which best expresses the meaning*** of the given idiom/ phrase.

Castles in the air.

A. romantic designs
B. perfect plans
C. ideal projects
D. imaginary unachievable plots

25. Choose the word wrongly spelt:

A. Teaser B. Teatotaller
C. Teething D. Tedious

26. Longhorn was the code name of:

A. Windows Vista B. Windows XP
C. Windows 7 D. Windows 10

27. In each of the following questions, choose the word ***most similar in meaning*** to the given word.

Livid

A. Complete B. Extravagant
C. Astute D. Angry

Directions (Qs. No. 28 and 29): *Read the passage carefully and answer the questions that follow:*

There are many types of protein molecules in the body, and each type is specific to its function. For example, proteins such as keratin and collagen give strength and elasticity to hair, as well as to skin and tendons; haemoglobin and myoglobin are the oxygen-binding proteins of the blood and the muscle, respectively; ovalbumin, the principal protein of egg white, is responsible for the setting and foaming properties of eggs. A particularly important group of proteins known as enzymes directs all the body cells to produce chemical reactions. These reactions provide the basis of every type of cell activity, including growth repair, the production of energy and the excretion of waste products.

28. Enzymes direct all the body cells to produce chemical reactions which provide ....

A. basis for every type of cell activity
B. growth and repair
C. production of energy and the excretion of waste
D. All the above

29. Which protein gives strength and elasticity to hair?

A. keratin B. myoglobin
C. ovalbumin D. None

30. Find out the ***correct spelling*** (A great writer)

A. Shakespeare B. Shakespear
C. Shakspiear D. Shakespier

31. Which of the gas is not known as green house gas?

A. Methane B. Nitrous oxide
C. Carbon dioxide D. Hydrogen

32. Read the passage carefully and answer the questions that follow:

There are many types of protein molecules in the body, and each type is specific to its function. For example, proteins such as keratin and collagen give strength and elasticity to hair, as well as to skin and tendons; haemoglobin and myoglobin are the oxygen-binding proteins of the blood and the muscle, respectively; ovalbumin, the principal protein of egg white, is responsible for the setting and foaming properties of eggs. A particularly important group of proteins known as enzymes directs all the body cells to produce chemical reactions. These reactions provide the basis of every type of cell activity, including growth repair, the production of energy and the excretion of waste products.

Proteins are classified according to ....

A. the number of molecules
B. their names
C. their functions
D. the part of the body they are found in

33. In which year Microsoft Office was launched?

A. 1969 B. 1979
C. 1990 D. 1999

34. Chemical formula for water is ....

A. $NaAlO_2$ B. H_2O
C. Al_2O_3 D. $CaSiCO_3$

35. Which of the following is a large blood vessel that carries blood away from the heart?

A. Vein B. Artery
C. Capillary D. Nerve

36. The longest and largest bone in the human body is ....

A. Spinal Cord B. Humerus
C. Fibula D. Femur

37. Viticulture is related with ....

A. Grapes B. Pine Apple
C. Orange D. Strawberry

38. In each of the following questions, choose the word ***most similar in meaning*** to the given word.

Scorn

A. Respect B. Laugh
C. Contempt D. Criticize

39. Fill in the blanks with the appropriate option out of the four choices given below:

The use of radar as well as two-way radio paging .... for state police to intercept most speeders.

A. make it possible
B. makes it possible
C. allows the possibility
D. makes possible

40. 1024 bit is equal to how many bytes?

A. 16 bytes B. 32 bytes
C. 64 bytes D. 128 bytes

MATHEMATICS

41. Which one of the following is a parametric form of a straight line?

A. $x = \cos(t),\ y = \sin(t),\ t \in \Re$
B. $x = t,\ y = t^2,\ t \in \Re$
C. $x = 2t,\ y = 3t,\ t \in \Re$
D. $x = \sqrt{t},\ y = t,\ t \in \Re$

42. $\lim\limits_{x \to 0} \dfrac{\sin^2 x}{x}$ is equal to:

A. 0 B. not defined
C. 1 D. –1

43. The radius of two circles, are 4 cm and 3 cm respectively. The diameter of the circle having area equal to the sum of the areas of the two circles (in cm) is:

A. 5 B. 7
C. 10 D. 14

44. If a random variable x follows the Poisson distribution such that $P(x = 1) = P(x = 2)$ then mean of the distribution is:

A. 0 B. 1
C. 2 D. 0.5

45. If $A = \begin{bmatrix} 2i & i \\ i & -i \end{bmatrix}$, then $|A| =$ ....

A. 2 B. 3
C. 4 D. 5

46. Differential coefficient of $\log x . \sin x$ with respect to x is:

A. $\sin x . \dfrac{1}{x}$
B. $\cos x . \sin x + \log x$
C. $\sin x . \dfrac{1}{x} + \log x . \cos x$
D. $\cos x . \left(-\dfrac{1}{x}\right) + \dfrac{1}{\log x}$

47. The value of $\int_1^4 \left(\sqrt{x} + \dfrac{1}{\sqrt{x}}\right) dx$ is:

A. $\dfrac{20}{3}$ B. $-\dfrac{20}{3}$
C. $\dfrac{10}{3}$ D. $\dfrac{15}{3}$

48. If ${}^{15}C_{3r} = {}^{15}C_{r+3}$, then r is equal to:

A. 5 B. 4
C. 3 D. 2

49. A circular wire of radius 42 cm is cut and bent into the form of a rectangle whose sides are in the ratio of 6 : 5. The smaller side of the rectangle is:

A. 30 cm B. 60 cm
C. 70 cm D. 80 cm

50. Find the value of $3^2 \times 3^3 \times \frac{1}{3^4} = ?$

A. 1 B. 3
C. 9 D. 27

51. If $P(A) = \frac{1}{4}$, $P(B) = \frac{1}{3}$, and $P(A \cup B) = \frac{1}{2}$, then P(A/B) is:

A. $\frac{1}{2}$ B. $\frac{1}{3}$
C. 1 D. $\frac{1}{4}$

52. What is the 31st term of the sequence: 1, 4, 7, 10, ... ?

A. 90 B. 91
C. 92 D. 93

53. If $\begin{bmatrix} a_{11} & a_{12} \\ a_{21} & a_{22} \\ a_{31} & a_{32} \end{bmatrix} A = \begin{bmatrix} b_{11} & b_{12} & b_{13} \\ b_{21} & b_{22} & b_{23} \\ b_{31} & b_{32} & b_{33} \end{bmatrix}$, then order of the matrix A is:

A. 2 × 2 B. 2 × 3
C. 3 × 2 D. 3 × 3

54. If $A = \begin{bmatrix} 0 & 1 \\ 0 & 0 \end{bmatrix}$ and I is a unit matrix of order two and a, b are arbitrary scalars, then $(aI + bA)^2$ will be:

A. $a^2I + ab\,A$ B. $a^2I + 2ab\,A$
C. $a^2I + b^2\,A$ D. None of these

55. The Taylor series expansion of e^{-x} is:

A. $1 + x + x^2 + ...$

B. $1 + x + \frac{x^2}{2!} + ...$

C. $1 - x + \frac{x^2}{2!} + ...$

D. $1 - x - x^2 - ...$

56. The Determinant of the matrix $\begin{bmatrix} 1 & \omega & \omega^2 \\ \omega & \omega^2 & 1 \\ \omega^2 & 1 & \omega \end{bmatrix}$ is (where ω is the cube root of unity):

A. 0 B. 1
C. ω D. ω^2

57. If $f(x) = e^x$ then $f^1(x) = ?$

A. e^{-x} B. e^x
C. ln x D. log x

58. If A and B are mutually exclusive events, then:

A. $P(A \cap B) = 1$
B. $P(A \cap B) = 0$
C. $P(A) = P(B)$
D. $P(A \cap B) = P(A)P(B)$

59. What is the order of the matrix with m rows and n columns?

A. $m + n$ B. $n \times n$
C. $m \times m$ D. $m \times n$

60. Find the value $\sqrt[3]{\sqrt{64}} = ?$

A. $\sqrt{2}$ B. 2
C. 4 D. 8

61. If $u = \sin^{-1}\left(\frac{y}{x}\right)$, then $x\frac{\partial u}{\partial x} + y\frac{\partial u}{\partial y}$ is equal to:

A. 0 B. u
C. $\frac{u}{2}$ D. $2u$

62. If tan(A + B) = p & tan(A – B) = q, then the value of tan 2A is:

A. $\frac{p+q}{p-q}$ B. $\frac{p-q}{1+pq}$
C. $\frac{1+pq}{1-p}$ D. $\frac{p+q}{1-pq}$

63. If $y = \sin x + \cos x - 5$, then $\frac{dy}{dx}$ is:

A. $\cos x - \sin x$
B. $\cos x + \sin x - 5$
C. $\sin x - \sec x$
D. $\sin x + \cos x + 5$

64. The value of $\lim_{x \to 0} \left(\frac{1+5x^2}{1+3x^2} \right)^{\frac{1}{x^2}}$ is:

A. e^4 B. e^3
C. e^2 D. None of these

65. The probability of drawing an ace or a spade or both from a deck of 52 cards is:

A. $\frac{4}{13}$ B. $\frac{1}{12}$
C. 1 D. $\frac{13}{4}$

66. If $x + \frac{1}{x} = 2\cos\theta$, then the value of $x^n + \frac{1}{x^n}$ is:

A. $2 \cos n\theta$ B. $-2 \cos n\theta$
C. $3 \cos \theta$ D. $2 \sin n\theta$

67. Coefficient of x in the expansion of $\left(x + \frac{2}{x} \right)^9$ is:

A. 1341 B. 3519
C. 216 D. 2016

68. The nth order derivative of $y = e^{3x}$ with respect to x is:

A. $3^{-n}e^{3x}$ B. $3^n e^{3x}$
C. $3^{-n}e^{-3x}$ D. $3^n e^{-3x}$

69. Find the value of $\frac{3^5}{3^5} = ?$

A. 1 B. 3
C. 9 D. 27

70. If $x = \log_2 3$ & $y = \log_{\frac{1}{2}} 5$, then:

A. $x > y$ B. $x < y$
C. $x = y$ D. None of these

COMPUTER AWARENESS

71. Firewall in computer is used for ....

A. Security
B. Data Transmission
C. Authentication
D. Monitoring

72. Word length of an i7 CPU is:

A. 4 bits B. 8 bits
C. 64 bits D. 24 bits

73. Which of the following is the first calculating device?

A. Abacus
B. Calculator
C. Turing Machine
D. Pascal

74. Which is not a function of Operating System?

A. Process Management
B. Memory Management
C. Web Server Management
D. File Mangement

75. Which of the following alphabet cannot be part of a hexadecimal digit?

A. A B. K
C. F D. E

76. Which is responsible for performing modulation/demodulation?

A. Receiver B. Transmitter
C. Router D. Modem

77. A program in execution is called ....

A. Process B. Instruction
C. Procedure D. Function

78. A computer program that converts assembly language to machine language is called ....

A. Compiler B. Interpreter
C. Assembler D. Comparator

79. Which among the following is not a logical gate?

A. NOR B. XO
C. AND D. NAND

80. What is full form of IP?

A. Interface Program
B. Internet Program

C. Internet Protocol
D. Interface Protocol

81. Which of the following four binary digits is equivalent to decimal number 12?
A. 1011 B. 1101
C. 1110 D. 1100

82. How many bits make a half byte?
A. 4 B. 2
C. 8 D. 6

83. Who among the following considered as the 'father of computer'?
A. Vint Cerf
B. Charles Babbage
C. Tim Berners Lee
D. None of these

84. Which of the following is not a valid bus in computer organization?
A. Data Bus B. Memory Bus
C. Address Bus D. System Bus

85. In which generation of computers, transistors were used?
A. First B. Second
C. Third D. Fourth

86. What is the Full form of URL?
A. Uniform Resource Locator
B. Uniform Resource Link
C. Uniform Registered Link
D. Unified Resource Link

87. Word processing, spreadsheet, and photo-editing are examples of ....
A. application software
B. system software
C. operating system software
D. platform software

88. The speed of a CPU is measured in ....
A. Hertz (Hz) B. Megahertz
C. Gigabytes D. Byte

89. Correcting errors in a program is called ....
A. Interpreting B. Translating
C. Debugging D. Compiling

90. Which of the following is the largest unit of storage?
A. Gigabyte B. Byte
C. Megabyte D. Kilobyte

91. Which of the following file extension used for Microsoft Word documents?
A. .txt B. .doc
C. .pdf D. .xls

92. Which gate is also known inverter gate?
A. AND B. OR
C. NOT D. XOR

93. Device drivers are examples of ....
A. Application software
B. System software
C. Utility software
D. These are type of hardware

94. What is called the part of CPU which coordinates all function of computer and other components?
A. ALU B. UPS
C. Motherboard D. Control unit

95. Which of the following is fastest Memory?
A. Cache B. Primary
C. Secondary D. HDD

96. Resolution of printer is measured in ....
A. Megabits B. Inches
C. Hertz D. DPI

97. Which among the following is not an input device?
A. Mouse B. Scanner
C. Keyboard D. Printer

98. What is the starting up of an operating system called?
A. Starting B. Entering
C. Booting D. Formatting

99. WAN stands for ....
A. Wired Area Network
B. Wide Area Network
C. Wide Array Net
D. Wireless Area Network

100. Who invented mechanical calculator called Pascaline?
A. Charles Babbage
B. Blaise Pascal
C. Alan Turing
D. Lee De Forest

ANSWERS

1	2	3	4	5	6	7	8	9	10
C	B	D	C	A	B	C	B	C	D
11	**12**	**13**	**14**	**15**	**16**	**17**	**18**	**19**	**20**
B	D	C	A	D	A	A	D	A	B
21	**22**	**23**	**24**	**25**	**26**	**27**	**28**	**29**	**30**
C	A	B	D	B	A	D	D	A	A
31	**32**	**33**	**34**	**35**	**36**	**37**	**38**	**39**	**40**
D	C	C	B	B	D	A	C	B	D
41	**42**	**43**	**44**	**45**	**46**	**47**	**48**	**49**	**50**
C	A	C	C	B	C	A	C	B	B
51	**52**	**53**	**54**	**55**	**56**	**57**	**58**	**59**	**60**
D	B	B	B	C	A	C	B	D	B
61	**62**	**63**	**64**	**65**	**66**	**67**	**68**	**69**	**70**
A	D	A	C	A	A	D	B	A	A
71	**72**	**73**	**74**	**75**	**76**	**77**	**78**	**79**	**80**
A	C	A	C	B	D	A	C	B	C
81	**82**	**83**	**84**	**85**	**86**	**87**	**88**	**89**	**90**
D	A	B	B	B	A	A	A	C	A
91	**92**	**93**	**94**	**95**	**96**	**97**	**98**	**99**	**100**
B	C	B	D	A	D	D	C	B	B

EXPLANATORY ANSWERS

42.
$$\lim_{x\to 0}\frac{\sin^2 x}{x} = \lim_{x\to 0}\frac{\sin x}{x}.\sin x$$
$$= 1.\lim_{x\to 0}\sin x$$
$$= 1.0$$
$$= 0$$

45. $A = \begin{bmatrix} 2i & i \\ i & -i \end{bmatrix}$

$$\therefore \quad |A| = \begin{bmatrix} 2i & i \\ i & -i \end{bmatrix}$$
$$= (2i)(-i) - i.i$$
$$= -2i^2 - i^2$$
$$= -3i^2$$
$$= -3(-1)$$
$$= 3$$

46. Let $y = \log x \,.\, \sin x$

Differentiating w.r.t. x, we get,

Then, $$\frac{dy}{dx} = \frac{\log x d(\sin x)}{dx} + \frac{\sin x d(\log x)}{dx}$$
$$= \log x.\cos x + \sin x.\frac{1}{x}$$
$$= \sin x.\frac{1}{x} + \log x.\cos x$$

47. Let, $$I = \int_1^4 \left(\sqrt{x} + \frac{1}{\sqrt{x}}\right) dx$$
$$= \left[\frac{x^{\frac{1}{2}+1}}{\frac{1}{2}+1} + \frac{x^{-\frac{1}{2}+1}}{-\frac{1}{2}+1}\right]_1^4$$

$$= \left[\frac{2}{3}x^{\frac{3}{2}} + 2x^{\frac{1}{2}}\right]_1^4$$

$$= \frac{2}{3}(4)^{\frac{3}{2}} + 2(4)^{\frac{1}{2}} - \frac{2}{3} - 2$$

$$= \frac{2}{3}(2)^3 + 2(2) - \frac{2}{3} - 2$$

$$= \frac{16}{3} + 4 - \frac{2}{3} - 2$$

$$= \frac{16}{3} - \frac{2}{3} + 2$$

$$= \frac{14}{3} + 2$$

$$= \frac{14+6}{3}$$

$$= \frac{20}{3}.$$

48. Given, ${}^{15}C_{3r} = {}^{15}C_{r+3}$

$\Rightarrow \quad 15 = 3r + r + 3$

$\Rightarrow \quad 15 - 3 = 4r$

$\Rightarrow \quad 12 = 4r$

$\Rightarrow \quad r = 3.$

49. Here, radius of a circular wire = 42 cm

$\therefore$ Circumference = $2\pi r$

$= 2 \times \frac{22}{7} \times 42$

$= 2 \times 22 \times 6$

$= 12 \times 22$

$= 264$ cm

Now, circular wire is bent into the form of a rectangle

$\therefore$ Let side of rectangles are $l = 6x$ and $b = 5x$

Then, perimeter = $2(l + b)$

$= 2(6x + 5x)$

$= 22x$

$\because$ Circumference = perimeter

$\therefore \quad 264 = 22x$

$\Rightarrow \quad x = \frac{264}{22}$

$= \frac{24}{2}$

$= 12$

Hence, the smaller side of the rectangle

$= 5x$

$= 5 \times 12$

$= 60$ cm.

50. $3^2 \times 3^3 \times \frac{1}{3^4} = 3^{2+3} \times 3^{-4}$

$= 3^5 \times 3^{-4}$

$= 3^{5-4}$

$= 3^1$

$= 3.$

51. Given,

$P(A) = \frac{1}{4}$, $P(B) = \frac{1}{3}$, and $P(A \cup B) = \frac{1}{2}$

$\because \quad P(A \cup B) = P(A) + P(B) - P(A \cap B)$

$\therefore \quad \frac{1}{2} = \frac{1}{4} + \frac{1}{3} - P(A \cap B)$

$\Rightarrow P(A \cap B) = \frac{7}{12} - \frac{1}{2}$

$= \frac{7-6}{12}$

$= \frac{1}{12}$

We know that,

$$P(A/B) = \frac{P(A \cap B)}{P(B)}$$

$$= \frac{\frac{1}{12}}{\frac{1}{3}}$$

$$= \frac{1}{12} \times \frac{3}{1}$$

$$= \frac{1}{4}.$$

52. Here, $a = 1$, $d = 4 - 1 = 3$

$\because \quad t_n = a + (n - 1)d$

$\therefore \quad t_{31} = a + (31 - 1)d$
$= 1 + 30 \times 3$
$= 1 + 90$
$= 91$

Hence, the 31st term = 91

54. Given, $A = \begin{bmatrix} 0 & 1 \\ 0 & 0 \end{bmatrix}$ and $I = \begin{bmatrix} 1 & 0 \\ 0 & 1 \end{bmatrix}$

$\therefore \ (aI + bA)^2 = a^2I^2 + b^2A^2 + 2I\ abA$

$$= a^2\begin{bmatrix} 1 & 0 \\ 0 & 1 \end{bmatrix}^2 + b^2\begin{bmatrix} 0 & 1 \\ 0 & 0 \end{bmatrix}^2 + 2ab\begin{bmatrix} 1 & 0 \\ 0 & 1 \end{bmatrix}\begin{bmatrix} 0 & 1 \\ 0 & 0 \end{bmatrix}$$

$$= a^2\begin{bmatrix} 1 & 0 \\ 0 & 1 \end{bmatrix} + b^2\begin{bmatrix} 0 & 0 \\ 0 & 0 \end{bmatrix} + 2ab\begin{bmatrix} 0 & 1 \\ 0 & 0 \end{bmatrix}$$

$= a^2I + 0 + 2ab\ A$
$= a^2I + 2ab\ A.$

56. Let $\Delta = \begin{vmatrix} 1 & \omega & \omega^2 \\ \omega & \omega^2 & 1 \\ \omega^2 & 1 & \omega \end{vmatrix}$

Applying $C_1 \to C_1 + C_2 + C_3$

Then, $\Delta = \begin{vmatrix} 1+\omega+\omega^2 & \omega & \omega^2 \\ \omega+\omega^2+1 & \omega^2 & 1 \\ \omega^2+1+\omega & 1 & \omega \end{vmatrix}$

$$= \begin{vmatrix} 1+\omega+\omega^2 & \omega & \omega^2 \\ 1+\omega+\omega^2 & \omega^2 & 1 \\ 1+\omega+\omega^2 & 1 & \omega \end{vmatrix}$$

$$= \begin{vmatrix} 0 & \omega & \omega^2 \\ 0 & \omega^2 & 1 \\ 0 & 1 & \omega \end{vmatrix}$$

expanding along $C_1 = 0$.

60. $\sqrt[3]{\sqrt{64}} = \sqrt[3]{8}$
$= (8)^{\frac{1}{3}}$
$= (2^3)^{\frac{1}{3}}$
$= 2.$

62. Given, $\tan(A + B) = p$

$\Rightarrow \dfrac{\tan A + \tan B}{1 - \tan A \tan B} = p$

and $\tan(A - B) = q$

$\Rightarrow \dfrac{\tan A - \tan B}{1 + \tan A \tan B} = q$

$\Rightarrow \tan 2A = \dfrac{2\tan A}{1 - \tan^2 A}$

$(\boldsymbol{p + q}) = \dfrac{\tan A + \tan B}{1 - \tan A \tan B} + \dfrac{\tan A - \tan B}{1 - \tan A \tan B}$

$$= \frac{\tan A + \tan^2 A \tan B + \tan B + \tan A \tan^2 B + \tan A - \tan^2 A \tan B - \tan B + \tan A \tan^2 B}{1 - \tan^2 A \tan^2 B}$$

$$= \frac{2\tan A + 2\tan A \tan^2 B}{1 - \tan^2 A \tan^2 B}$$

$$= \frac{2\tan A(1 + \tan^2 B)}{1 - \tan^2 A \tan^2 B}$$

$(\boldsymbol{p - q}) = \dfrac{\tan A + \tan B}{1 - \tan A \tan B} - \dfrac{\tan A - \tan B}{1 + \tan A \tan B}$

$$= \frac{\tan A + \tan^2 A \tan B + \tan B + \tan A \tan^2 B - \tan A + \tan^2 A \tan B + \tan B - \tan A \tan^2 B}{1 - \tan^2 A \tan^2 B}$$

$$= \frac{2\tan^2 A \tan B + 2\tan B}{1 - \tan^2 A \tan^2 B}$$

$$= \frac{2\tan B(1 + \tan^2 A)}{1 - \tan^2 A \tan^2 B}$$

$(\boldsymbol{1 - pq})$

$$= 1 - \left(\frac{\tan A + \tan B)}{1 - \tan A \tan B}\right)\left(\frac{\tan A - \tan B)}{1 - \tan A \tan B}\right)$$

$$= 1 - \left(\frac{\tan^2 A - \tan^2 B)}{1 - \tan^2 A \tan^2 B}\right)$$

$$= \frac{1-\tan^2 A\tan^2 B-\tan^2 A+\tan^2 B}{1-\tan^2 A\tan^2 B}$$

$$= \frac{(1+\tan^2 B)-\tan^2 A(1+\tan^2 B)}{1-\tan^2 A\tan^2 B}$$

$$= \frac{(1+\tan^2 A)(1+\tan^2 B)}{1-\tan^2 A\tan^2 B}$$

(1 + *pq*)

$$= 1+\left(\frac{\tan A+\tan B)}{1-\tan A\tan B}\right)\left(\frac{\tan A-\tan B)}{1-\tan A\tan B}\right)$$

$$= 1+\left(\frac{\tan^2 A-\tan^2 B)}{1-\tan^2 A\tan^2 B}\right)$$

$$= \frac{1-\tan^2 A\tan^2 B+\tan^2 A-\tan^2 B}{1-\tan^2 A\tan^2 B}$$

$$= \frac{(1+\tan^2 A)-\tan^2 B(1+\tan^2 A)}{1-\tan^2 A\tan^2 B}$$

$$= \frac{(1+\tan^2 A)(1-\tan^2 B)}{1-\tan^2 A\tan^2 B}$$

(1 – *p*)

$$= 1-\frac{\tan A+\tan B}{1-\tan A\tan B}$$

$$= \frac{1-\tan A\tan B-\tan A-\tan B}{1-\tan A\tan B}$$

$$= \frac{1-\tan A-\tan B(1+\tan A)}{1-\tan A\tan B}$$

Checking options:

(A) $$\frac{p+q}{p-q} = \frac{\dfrac{2\tan A(1+\tan^2 B)}{1-\tan^2 A\tan^2 B}}{\dfrac{2\tan B(1+\tan^2 A)}{1-\tan^2 A\tan^2 B}}$$

$$= \frac{2\tan A(1+\tan^2 B)}{2\tan B(1+\tan^2 B)}$$

$$= \frac{\tan A(1+\tan^2 B)}{\tan B(1+\tan^2 B)}$$

(B) $$\frac{p-q}{1+pq} = \frac{\dfrac{2\tan B(1+\tan^2 A)}{1-\tan^2 A\tan^2 B}}{\dfrac{(1+\tan^2 A)(1-\tan^2 B)}{1-\tan^2 A\tan^2 B}}$$

$$= \frac{2\tan B(1+\tan^2 A)}{(1+\tan^2 A)(1+\tan^2 B)}$$

$$= \frac{2\tan B}{1+\tan^2 B}$$

(C) $$\frac{1+pq}{1-p} = \frac{\dfrac{(1+\tan^2 A)(1-\tan^2 B)}{1-\tan^2 A\tan^2 B}}{\dfrac{1-\tan A-\tan B(1+\tan A)}{1-\tan A\tan B}}$$

$$= \frac{(1+\tan^2 A)(1-\tan^2 B)}{(1-\tan A\tan B)(1+\tan A\tan B)}$$

$$\times\frac{(1-\tan A\tan B)}{1-\tan A\tan B(1+\tan A)}$$

$$= \frac{(1+\tan^2 A)(1-\tan^2 B)}{(1+\tan A\tan B)[1-\tan A-\tan B(1+\tan A)]}$$

(D) $$\frac{p+q}{1-pq} = \frac{\dfrac{2\tan A(1+\tan^2 B)}{1-\tan^2 A\tan^2 B}}{\dfrac{(1+\tan^2 A)(1+\tan^2 B)}{1-\tan^2 A\tan^2 B}}$$

$$= \frac{2\tan A}{1-\tan^2 A}$$

$$= \tan 2A.$$

Hence, option (D) is correct.

63. Given, $y = \sin x + \cos x - 5$

Differentiating w.r.t. x, we get,

$$\frac{dy}{dx} = \frac{d(\sin x)}{dx}+\frac{d(\cos x)}{dx}-\frac{d(5)}{dx}$$

$$= \cos x - \sin x - 0$$

$$= \cos x - \sin x.$$

64. $\lim_{x\to 0}\left(\frac{1+5x^2}{1+3x^2}\right)^{\frac{1}{x^2}}$

$$\left[\lim_{x\to 0}(f(x))^{g(x)} = e^{\lim_{x\to 0}(g(x)(f(x)-1))}\right]$$

$$= e^{\lim_{x\to 0}\frac{2x^2}{1+3x^2}\cdot x^{\frac{1}{2}}} = e^{\lim_{x\to 0}\frac{2}{1+3x^2}} = e^2.$$

65. Here, $n(s) = 52$

Let E = Event of getting an ace or a spade or both

Then, $n(E) = 4 + 4 + 8 = 16$

$$[4C_1 + 4C_1 + 8C_1 = 4 + 4 + 8]$$

$$\therefore \quad P(E) = \frac{n(E)}{n(s)}$$

$$= \frac{16}{52}$$

$$= \frac{4}{13}.$$

67. Let $(r + 1)$th term contains x in the binomial expansion of $\left(x+\frac{2}{x}\right)^9$

Now, $T_{r+1} = {}^9C_r . x^{9-r}\left(\frac{2}{x}\right)^r$

$$= {}^9C_r\, x^{9-r}.\, 2^r .\, x^{-r}$$

$$= {}^9C_r .\, 2^r .\, x^{9-2r}$$

$\because$ T_{r+1} contains x

$\therefore$ $9 - 2r = 1$

$\Rightarrow$ $9 - 1 = 2r$

$\Rightarrow$ $r = \frac{8}{2} = 4$

$\therefore$ $T_{r+1} = {}^9C_4(2)^4 .\, x^{9-8}$

$$= {}^9C_4 .\, 16 .\, x$$

Coefficient of $x = {}^9C_4 .\, 16$

$$= \frac{\lfloor 9}{\lfloor 4 \lfloor 9-4}\times 16$$

$$= \frac{\lfloor 9}{\lfloor 4 \lfloor 5}\times 16$$

$$= \frac{9\times 8\times 7\times 6}{4\times 3\times 2\times 1}\times 16$$

$$= 9 \times 7 \times 2 \times 16$$

$$= 2016.$$

70. Given, $x = \log_2 3 = \frac{\log 3}{\log 2}$ and $y = \log_{\frac{1}{2}} 5$

$$= \frac{\log 5}{\log\frac{1}{2}}$$

$$= \frac{\log 5}{\log 1 - \log 2}$$

$$= \frac{\log 5}{0 - \log 2}$$

$$= -\frac{\log 5}{\log 2}$$

$$\because \frac{\log 3}{\log 2} > -\frac{\log 5}{\log 2}$$

$\therefore$ $x > y$.

Previous Paper (Solved)

Bachelor of Computer Applications (BCA) Entrance Exam, 2019*

MATHEMATICS

Directions (Qs. 1 to 46) : *Choose the most appropriate option.*

1. The following inequality is satisfied in which region:

$x\ (x + 2) \geq -4$

A. $(-\infty, \infty)$ B. $(0, \infty)$
C. $(-\infty, 0)$ D. $(-1, 1)$

2. Given that '!' represents the factorial operator, what is the right hand side of the expression below:

$1 + \sum_{k=1}^{n} k \times k! = ?$

A. $(k + 2)!$ B. $\frac{(k+2)!}{2}$

C. $(k + 1)!$ D. $\frac{(k+1)!}{2}$

3. $\sum_{k=1}^{n} \sin\left(\frac{k\pi}{3}\right) = ?$

A. $2\sin\left(\frac{n\pi}{3}\right)\sin\left(\frac{(n+1)\pi}{3}\right)$

B. $2\sin\left(\frac{n\pi}{6}\right)\sin\left(\frac{(n+1)\pi}{6}\right)$

C. $2\sin\left(\frac{n\pi}{3}\right)\sin\left(\frac{(n+1)\pi}{6}\right)$

D. $2\sin\left(\frac{n\pi}{6}\right)\sin\left(\frac{(n+1)\pi}{3}\right)$

4. Find $f \circ f \circ f$, where $f(x) = 1/(1 - x)$

A. $1/(1 - x)^3$ B. $(1 - x)^3$
C. x^3 D. x

5. $\lim_{x \to 1} \frac{x-1}{x^n - 1} = ?$

A. 0 B. 1
C. n D. $1/n$

6. Find a right triangle of maximum area with hypotenuse h.

A. The length of the legs is equal to $h/2$
B. The length of the legs is equal to $h/2^{½}$
C. The length of the legs is equal to $h/3^{½}$
D. The length of the legs is equal to $h/3$

7. $\int_0^{\pi/2} \cos^2 x\, dx = ?$

A. π B. $\pi/2$
C. $\pi/3$ D. $\pi/4$

8. Prakash gets paid three Rupees less than four times what Kalia gets paid. If the number of dollars that Kalia gets paid is represented by x, what does Prakash get paid?

A. $3 - 4x$ B. $3x - 4$
C. $4x - 3$ D. $4 - 3x$

9. Twice a number increased by 11 is equal to 32 less than three times the number. Find the number.

A. –21 B. 21/5
C. 43 D. 43/5

10. The sum of two consecutive even integers is 126. What are the integers?

A. 62, 64 B. 62, 63
C. 60, 66 D. 2, 63

11. Two trains leave two different cities 1,029 miles apart and head directly toward each other on parallel tracks. If one train is travelling at 45 miles per hour and the other at 53 miles per hour, how many hours will it take before the trains pass?

*Exam held on 25/05/2019. (Conducted by GGSIPU)

A. 9.5 B. 11
C. 11.5 D. 10.5

12. The sum of two integers is 36, and the difference is 6. What is the smaller of the two numbers?
A. 21 B. 15
C. 16 D. 18

13. Parth has a rectangular patio whose length is 5 m less than the diagonal and a width that is 7 m less than the diagonal. If the area of his patio is 195 m^2, what is the length of the diagonal?
A. 10 m B. 8 m
C. 16 m D. 20 m

14. Find the lesser of two consecutive positive even integers whose product is 168.
A. 12 B. 14
C. 10 D. 16

15. A photographer decides to reduce a picture she took in order to fit it into a certain frame. She needs the picture to be one-third of the area of the original. If the original picture was 4 inches by 6 inches, how many inches is the smaller dimension of the reduced picture if each dimension changes the same amount?
A. 2 B. 3
C. 4 D. 5

16. Mahesh scored 260 points during his junior year on the school basketball team. He scored 20% more points during his senior year. How many points did he score during his senior year?
A. 208 B. 52
C. 312 D. 345

17. The Dow Jones Industrial Average fell 2% today. The Dow began the day at 8,800. What was the Dow at the end of the day after the 2% drop?
A. 8,600 B. 8,976
C. 8,624 D. 8,720

18. There are 81 women teachers at Russell High. If 45% of the teachers in the school are women, how many teachers are there at Russell High?
A. 180 B. 36
C. 165 D. 205

19. Bikes are on sale for 30% off the original price. What per cent of the original price will the customer pay if he gets the bike at the sale price?
A. 130% B. 60%
C. 70% D. 97%

20. Find the next number in the following pattern:
320, 160, 80, 40, ...
A. 35 B. 30
C. 10 D. 20

21. The ratio of boys to girls at the dance was 3 : 4. There were 60 girls at the dance. How many boys were at the dance?
A. 45 B. 50
C. 55 D. 40

22. One inch equals 2.54 centimeters. The dimensions of a table made in Europe are 85 cm wide by 120 cm long. What is the width of the table in inches? Round to the nearest tenth of an inch.
A. 30 inches B. 215.9 inches
C. 33.5 inches D. 47.2 inches

23. Vihan has 5 pairs of pants and 8 shirts. How many different combinations can he make with these items?
A. 13 B. 24
C. 40 D. 21

24. Jihan earned scores of 85, 92 and 95 on his science tests. What does he need to earn on his next science test to have an average (arithmetic mean) of 93%?
A. 93 B. 100
C. 85 D. 96

25. The period of $|\sin(3x)|$ is:
A. 2 pi B. 2 pi/3
C. pi/3 D. 3 pi

26. The exam scores of all 500 students were recorded and it was determined that these scores were normally distributed. If Jane's score is 0.8 standard deviation above the mean, then how many, to the nearest unit, students scored above Jane?

A. 394 B. 250
C. 400 D. 106

27. The three solutions of the equation $f(x) = 0$ are 4, 8 and 11. Therefore, the Three solutions of the equation $f(2x) = 0$ are:
A. 2, 4 and 11/2 B. 8, 16 and 22
C. 4, 8 and 11 D. 2, 19/2 and 7/2

28. The graphs of the two linear equations $ax + by = c$ and $bx - ay = c$, where a, b and c are all not equal to zero.
A. are parallel
B. intersect at one point
C. intersect at two points
D. perpendicular

29. If $\log_x (1/8) = -3/2$, then x is equal to:
A. 4 B. –4
C. 1/4 D. 10

30. If $2^{3x-1} = 16$, then $x =$
A. 3/5 B. 5/3
C. 1 D. 4

31. If $x^2 + kx - 6 = (x - 2)(x + 3)$, then $k =$
A. 6 B. 3
C. 1 D. 0

32. The quadratic equation whose roots are at $x = 3$ and $x = 5$ is given by:
A. $(x - 3)(x - 5) = 1$
B. $(x + 3)(x + 5) - 9 = (x + 3)(x + 5) - 25$
C. $(x + 3)(x + 5) = 0$
D. $x^2 - 8x = -15$

33. If the domain of function f given by $f(x) = -x^2 + 6x$ is given by the interval [0, 6], then the range of f is given by the interval
A. [0, 9] B. [0, 6]
C. [0, 3] D. [3, 6]

34. The domain of $f(x) = 2 \log |x - 2|$ is given by the interval:
A. (–infinity, 2) U(2, + infinity)
B. (–2, + infinity)
C. (2, + infinity)
D. (–infinity, + infinity)

35. If x is an angle in standard position and its terminal side is in quadrant IV and is given by $y = -x$, then $\sin(x) =$
A. $2^{1/2}$ B. $1/2^{1/2}$
C. $-2^{1/2}$ D. $-1/2^{1/2}$

36. At 2:15 o'clock, the hour and minute hands of a clock (12 hours clock) form an angle of:
A. 30° B. 5°
C. $22\frac{1}{2}°$ D. $7\frac{1}{2}°$

37. Two high school classes took the same test. One class of 20 students made an average grade of 80%; the other class of 30 students made an average grade of 70%. The average grade for all students in both classes is:
A. 75% B. 74%
C. 72% D. 77%

38. The price of an article is cut by 10%. To restore it to its former value, the new price must be increased by:
A. 10% B. 9%
C. $11\frac{1}{9}\%$ D. 11%

39. If A and B are independent events, then $P(A \cup B)$ is:
A. P(A) . P(B) B. P(A) + P(B)
C. P(A | B) D. P(B | A)

40. An ellipse with center at the origin has a length of major axis 20 units. If the distance from center of ellipse to its focus is 5, then the equation of its directrix is:
A. $x = 18$ B. $x = 21$
C. $x = 10$ D. $x = 20$

41. Vectors $\vec{a} = \lambda\hat{i} + 2\hat{j} + \hat{k}$ and $\vec{b} = 5\hat{i} - 9\hat{j} + 2\hat{k}$ are perpendicular to each other. Then, λ is:
A. 11/6 B. 17/6
C. 16/5 D. 13/6

42. In a class, 40% of the students study math and science, 60% of the students study math. Then the probability of a student studying science given he/she is already studying math is:
A. 0.67 B. 0.31
C. 0.37 D. 0.81

43. During a fund-raiser, each of the 35 members of a group sold candy bars. If each member sold an average of six candy bars, how many total bars did the group sell?

A. 6 B. 41
C. 180 D. 210

44. Salesperson Rita drives 2,052 miles in six days, stopping at two towns each day. How many miles does she average between stops?

A. 171 miles
B. 342 miles
C. 684 miles
D. 1,026 miles

45. If a population of yeast cells grows from 10 to 320 in a period of five hours, what is the rate of growth?

A. It doubles its numbers every hour
B. It triples its numbers every hour
C. It doubles its numbers every two hour
D. It triples its numbers every two hour

46. If the length of a diagonal of a square is $(a + b)$, then the area of the square is:

A. $(a + b)^2$ B. $\frac{1}{2}(a+b)^2$

C. $a^2 + b^2$ D. $\frac{1}{2}(a^2+b^2)$

ENGLISH LANGUAGE AND COMPREHENSION

Directions (Qs. No. 47-52): *The questions are based on the text given below. Choose the most appropriate option.*

(*a*) For a long time, Americans tended to think that knowing English was sufficient for all their needs. As a result, Americans developed an image as the people who cannot say even the most rudimentary phrase in any other language. Fortunately, however, many business, political, and educational leaders are belatedly realizing that the whole world does not speak, English, and that even many of those who have learned English as a second language prefer to converse, to do business, and to negotiate in their native tongue.

(*b*) Not long ago learning a foreign language was considered to be merely a part of a liberal education or an intellectual exercise through the study of grammar and literature. It was automatically assumed that anyone studying a foreign language as a major field was going to be a teacher, an interpreter, or a translator and had no other career options. There is still a need for people in those professions. There is also a growing need for individuals who possess advanced skills in foreign languages and are trained in various technical areas. This is a result of increased activity in international business, the influx of large amounts of foreign capital to the United States, increased internationalization, and an expanded awareness of the need to conduct not only business but also diplomatic relations in the language of the host country.

(*c*) A second language is now becoming a vital part of the basic preparation for an increasing number of careers. Even in those cases where the knowledge of a second language does not help graduates obtain a first job, many report that their foreign language skills often enhance their mobility and improve their chances for promotion. In addition to any technical skills that foreign language students choose to develop, they also have further tangible advantages in the job market. In a recent study that sought to ascertain which college courses had been most valuable for people who were employed in the business world, graduates pointed not only to career-oriented courses such as business management but also to people-oriented subjects like psychology and to classes that had helped them to develop communication skills. Foreign language students, whose courses focus heavily on this aspect of learning, often posses outstanding communication skills, both written and oral. Furthermore, recent trends in the job marketplace indicate a revived recognition of the value of general liberal arts training in an employee's career preparation.

47. Which one of the following best states the main idea of the passage?
A. In recent years, fluency in a foreign language has become an important educational asset and a distinct advantage in the job market
B. People who study foreign languages are probably going to be teachers, interpreters, or translators
C. Foreign language skills are likely to improve an employee's chances for promotion
D. Increased internationalization in the American business world has necessitated the hiring of more foreign language speakers

48. The author argues that studying foreign languages is:
A. necessary for world travel
B. an internationalizing experience
C. merely one part of a liberal education
D. becoming crucial to career preparation

49. The second paragraph primarily serves to:
A. explain how the United States can obtain more foreign capital
B. tell the reader about the public view of foreign language study
C. explain how and why old widely held misconceptions should change
D. argue that many Americans have overlooked the power of a strong foreign language background

50. Which of the following statements would the author of this passage be LEAST likely to agree with?
A. The rise in demand for foreign language speakers in the job market is paralleled by the rise of international business
B. Knowledge of a second language does not always help students obtain a first job
C. Foreign language students still have many job options even without possessing another technical skill
D. The recent increase in demand for foreign language speakers in the job market is only temporary

51. The passage suggests which of the following about foreign language study in the past?
A. The lack of it held back American business
B. It seemed a frivolous part of a general liberal arts education
C. It was limited to European universities
D. It was as pertinent to any student as it is now

52. Of the following, the author's primary purpose in writing the passage most likely is to:
A. call attention to the increasing importance of foreign language studies in the job market
B. argue that foreign language studies are not the superficial exercise they once were thought to be
C. enlist students to study to become translators and foreign language teachers
D. debate the effects of internationalizing business

Directions (Qs. No. 53-65): *Choose the most appropriate option.*

53. Which of the following is most dissimilar to "abridge"?
A. shorten B. condense
C. digest D. span

54. Which of the following is most similar to "abaft"?
A. rear B. ahead
C. forward D. before

55. Which of the following is most dissimilar to "ban"?
A. prohibit B. forbid
C. abide D. interdict

56. Which of the following is most similar to "commune"?
A. loose B. dense
C. slack D. rare

57. Which of the following is most dissimilar to "deceptive"?
A. misleading B. delusory
C. true D. delusive

58. Which of the following is most similar to "extenuate"?
A. attenuate B. aggravate
C. heighten D. enhance

59. Although skinny as a rail, the young girl had a(n) .... appetite.
A. eager B. demanding
C. ravenous D. primal

60. Percival's .... approach to life caused him to miss the kind of .... experience his more frivolous peers enjoyed.
A. unhealthy, choleric
B. busy, understated
C. amiable, intense
D. utilitarian, ecstatic

61. Although conditions in Antarctica are quite ...., scientists and others who go there to work have managed to create a comfortable environment for themselves.
A. audacious B. inimical
C. felicitous D. incalculable

62. The famous daredevil was actually quite .... by temperament, as illustrated by the fact that he did not .... until he was two years old.
A. daring, tussle
B. arbitrary, contradict
C. careful, perambulate
D. mendacious, vocalize

63. After sitting in the sink for several days, the dirty, food-encrusted dishes became ....
A. malodorous B. prevalent
C. imposing D. perforated

64. Giulia soon discovered the source of the .... smell in the room: a week-old tuna sandwich that one of the children had hidden in the closet.
A. fastidious B. clandestine
C. laconic D. fetid

65. After making .... remarks to the President, the reporter was not invited to return to the White House pressroom.
A. hospitable B. enterprising
C. chivalrous D. irreverent

Directions (Qs. No. 66-68): *Choose the grammatically correct sentence.*

66. A. Out here, dry winds often blow in from the Arabian Peninsula, whipping up sheets of dust that plunge visibility down to near-zero.
B. Out here, dry winds often blowing in from the Arabian Peninsula, whipping up sheets of dust that plunging visibility down to near-zero.
C. Out here, dry winds often blowing in from the Arabian Peninsula, whipped up sheets of dust that plunged visibility down to near-zero.
D. Out here, dry winds often blow in from the Arabian Peninsula, whipped up sheets of dust that plunging visibility down to near-zero.

67. A. Heaton's six-year-old daughter, Emily, had once ask her father if she could ever be a real princess.
B. Heaton's six-year-old daughter, Emily, had once asked her father if she could ever be a real princess.
C. Heaton's six-year-old daughter, Emily, did once asked her father if she could ever be a real princess.
D. Heaton's six-year-old daughter, Emily, did once asked her father if she could ever been a real princess.

68. A. Within five minutes I was booked the flights.
B. I had book the flights within five minutes.
C. Within five minutes I had booked the flights.
D. I was booked the flight within five minutes.

COMPUTER AWARENESS

Directions (Qs. No. 69-113): *Choose the most appropriate option.*

69. Which type of printer is the most-often used shared network printer in organizations?
A. Inkjet B. Deskjet
C. Laser D. Daisy wheel

70. Which organization has produced standards commonly used for laptop expansion slots?
A. PCMCIA B. EIA
C. HP D. AMD

71. Which among the following transforms input data into output data?
A. ROM B. RAM
C. CPU D. Printer

72. Bitcoin was invented by an unknown person or group of people using the name:
A. Hal Finney B. Nick Szabo
C. Satoshi Nakamoto D. Dorian Nakamoto

73. Which among the following are not Objects in MS Access database?
A. Form B. Table
C. Query D. Pivot Table

74. Which among the following is a diagnostic tool(s)?
A. Speccy
B. HD Tune
C. Open Hardware Monitor
D. All of the above

75. Operating System is a type of ....
A. System software
B. Application software
C. Firmware
D. All of the above

76. Allocation of a resources in a time dependent manner to several program simultaneously called:
A. Time sharing
B. Multiprogramming
C. Multiprocessing
D. Virtual processing

77. Which protocol allows a user to log on to another computer and transfer information between it and his/her computer?
A. LAN B. FTP
C. ZigB D. WiFi

78. Dots per inch (dpi) refers to the resolution of which device?
A. Modem B. Printer
C. Keyboard D. None of the above

79. When you press a key on computer keyboard, ... notifies the system software.
A. Keyboard controller
B. Keyboard cpu
C. Keyboard bus
D. Keyboard arrow

80. Which among the following is a Supercomputer?
A. OLCF-4 B. MASSIVE Infinity
C. IBM HULK-6 D. WIN PACK-16

81. Which of the following is an android mobile operating system?
A. Pie B. Naught
C. Oreo D. All of the above

82. Which one of the following is a DTP package?
A. QuarkXPress B. ZDPress
C. MozillaP D. WRITEup

83. Alternative computer jargon for BUG is:
A. Glitch B. Worm
C. Virus D. All of the above

84. Which of the following is not an anti-virus software?
A. ESET NOD32 B. ZoneAlarm
C. Immunet D. AVB3

85. .... are client devices for making and receiving voice and video calls over the IP network.
A. EPBAX B. Softphones
C. VMphones D. TELEphones

86. Which of the following is a transmission media?
A. CAT6E cable B. RJ45
C. RJ11 D. MJ45

87. Interpreter is used as a translator for:
A. High level language
B. Low level language
C. C
D. COBOL

88. Which section in HTML contains generic information about the document?
A. Head B. Body
C. Title D. Style

89. Which among the following is often called the double precision format?
A. 128-bit B. 16-bit
C. 32-bit D. 64-bit

90. Which among the following is substituted for hardware and stored in ROM?
A. Package software
B. Firmware
C. Middleware
D. STACK

91. Which part of personal computer manages the computer's arithmetical, logical and control activities?
A. Assembler B. Microcontroller
C. Microprocessor D. Interpreter

92. Which of the following is a valid encoding format?
A. UTF-2 B. UTF-16
C. UTF-A D. UTF-4

93. A typical .... program obtains a remote reference to one or more remote objects on a server and then invokes methods on them.
A. Thread B. Virtual
C. Server D. Client

94. Which of the following computer language is used for artificial intelligence?
A. PROLOG B. C
C. FORTRAN D. COBOL

95. Which protocol provides e-mail facility among different hosts?
A. TFTP B. TELNET
C. SNMP D. SMTP

96. Which of the following is not a basic data type in C language?
A. char B. float
C. real D. int

97. The universal gate that can be used to implement any Boolean expression is called:
A. XOR B. NAND
C. AND D. OR

98. The symbols used in an assembly language are called:
A. Hex codes B. Byte codes
C. Mnemonics D. Bit codes

99. The .... is a windowing system for bitmap displays, common on Unix-like operating systems.
A. XT Windows system
B. X Window system
C. XP Windows system
D. WIN 10 system

100. A flat piece of film containing microphotographs of the pages of a newspaper, catalogue, or other document is called:
A. Microfiche B. Microsoft
C. Microlite D. Micronano

101. Which of the following irresponsible for holding the data, intermediate results and the results of ongoing processes or jobs?
A. Virtual storage
B. Internal storage
C. Auxiliary storage
D. Primary storage

102. .... regulate traffic between two dissimilar networks.
A. Switch B. Gateways
C. Router D. Hub

103. .... provide a way for the website to recognize you and keep track of your preferences.
A. Password B. Cookies
C. URL D. WWW

104. Which of these is a part of network identification?
A. OTP B. Password
C. UserID D. Biometric

105. Which of the following are (is) considered to be video component?
A. Color depth B. Refresh rate
C. Resolution D. All of the above

106. Which of the following represents one billion characters?
A. Gigabyte B. Terabyte
C. Petabyte D. Megabyte

107. Which among the following is a search engine?
A. Wolfram B. Firefox
C. Bing D. Jinx

108. Which among the following is a Dictionary attack software?
A. Aircrack-ng
B. HashPhantom
C. Shark View
D. LoopcrackXP

109. Which of the following memories has the shortest access time?
A. ROM
B. Cache memory
C. Magnetic bubble memory
D. Magnetic core memory

110. Who invented HTML?
A. Turing B. Tim Berner Lee
C. Steve Job D. Bill Gates

111. Which technology is used to verify the legitimacy or originality of paper documents, especially bank cheques?
A. QR codes B. MICR
C. Bar Codes D. All of the above

112. Which of the following is/are operating systems?
A. OS/2 B. JDK
C. AWS D. None of these

113. What does DMA stand for?
A. A Distinct Memory Access
B. Direct Memory Access
C. Direct Module Access
D. Direct Memory Allocation

GENERAL AWARENESS (IT/SCIENCE)

Directions (Qs. No. 114-150): *Choose the most appropriate option.*

114. Bluetooth is an example of:
A. LAN B. PAN
C. VPN D. All of the above

115. Which types of cables uses ST, SC, LC, or MT-RJ connectors?
A. UTP B. STP
C. Coaxial Cable D. Fiber Optic

116. IEEE 802.3 specification corresponds to which network among the following?
A. WI-MAX B. WI-FI
C. Ethernet D. Token Bus

117. Email spam, also known as:
A. unsolicited bulk email
B. email worm
C. email virus
D. email Trojan

118. Sasser and Conficker are examples of:
A. Worm
B. New Chipset of Intel
C. New Antivirus developed by Google
D. Search Engine

119. .... are set of rules and procedures to control the transmission over the internet.
A. DNS B. Protocols
C. IP address D. RFCs

120. TCP stands for ....
A. Transfer Center Protocol
B. Transmission Control Protocol
C. Transmission Center Protocol
D. Telephone Center Protocol

121. A protocol used for receiving email messages is called ....
A. URL B. Telnet
C. POP3 D. SMTP

122. .... routes the packets through the internet to go to their destination.
A. Protocol B. TCP
C. IP D. NIC

123. First computer network was ....
A. NSFNET B. FIRSTNET
C. ARPANET D. ORPHANET

124. A large number of networks interconnected physically is called ....
A. LAN B. WAN
C. Internet D. Network collection

125. In .... mode, the communication channel is used in both directions at the same time?
A. Full-duplex B. Simplex
C. Half-duplex D. None of these

126. Computers built before the First Generation of computers were:
A. Mechanical B. Electro-mechanical
C. Electrical D. None of these

127. Who is the founder of Wikipedia?
A. Jimmy Wales
B. Bill Moggridge
C. Nikesh Arora
D. Rob Stothard

128. The term Cyberknife is most closely associated with which among the following:
A. Software security
B. Robotic radiosurgery
C. MRI
D. Remote Hacking

129. Metals which chemically behave both as metals and non-metals is called:
A. Metalloids B. Alloys
C. Halloids D. Nanoparticles

130. .... was the first to observe Saturn with a telescope in 1610.
A. Christian Huygens
B. Jacques Cassini
C. Galileo Galilei
D. Johannes Kepler

131. What is the name of NASA Mars Rover?
A. Curiosity B. Prying
C. Marvel D. Wonder

132. In which city is located World's largest trade centre of diamond?
A. Surat B. Antwerp
C. Auckland D. Johannesburg

133. Horn Silver is composed of:
A. Silver Sulphide B. Silver Bromide
C. Silver Chloride D. Silver Iodide

134. Carbamide is commonly known as:
A. Fruit dye B. Urea
C. Explosive D. Cloth Dye

135. In a dry cell (battery), which of the following are used as electrolytes?
A. Ammonium chloride and Zinc chloride
B. Sodium chloride and Calcium chloride
C. Magnesium chloride and Zinc chloride
D. Ammonium chloride and Calcium chloride

136. Diffusion of light in the atmosphere takes place due to:
A. Carbon dioxide B. Dust particles
C. Helium D. Water vapours

137. A periscope works by the principle of:
A. Refraction
B. Total Internal reflection
C. Diffraction
D. Reflection and refraction

138. Titan is the largest natural satellite of planet:
A. Mercury B. Venus
C. Saturn D. Neptune

139. The oxide of Nitrogen used in medicine as anaesthetic is:
A. Nitrogen dioxide B. Nitric oxide
C. Nitrous oxide D. Nitrogen pentoxide

140. The concept of carbon credit originated from which one of the following?
A. Earth Summit, Rio de Janeiro
B. Kyoto Protocol
C. Montreal Protocol
D. None of the above

141. Workers of paint industry are exposed to which one of the following hazards?
A. Nickel pollution
B. Cadmium pollution
C. Strontium pollution
D. Lead pollution

142. Who gave the first evidence of the Big-Bang theory?
A. Edwin Hubble
B. Albert Einstein
C. S. Chandrasekhar
D. Stephen Hawking

143. Which one of the following is used as an explosive?
A. Phosphorus Trichloride
B. Mercuric oxide
C. Graphite
D. Nitroglycerine

144. Which gas is used to make light bulbs?
A. Freon B. Argon
C. Helium D. Ozone

145. Quartz is made of:
A. Silicon dioxide B. Calcium sulphate
C. Sodium silicate D. Calcium silicate

146. A .... is a device for measuring the power of incident electromagnetic radiation.
A. Platometer B. Electrometer
C. Bolometer D. Sphygmometer

147. Which one of the following types of Laser is used in Laser Printers?
A. Semiconductor laser
B. Excimer Laser
C. Dye Laser
D. Gas Laser

148. Two Flat mirrors are placed at an angle of 60° from each other. How many images will be formed of a Candle placed in between them?
A. 3 B. 4
C. 5 D. 6

149. Which among the following property of the matter is studied in "Rheology"?
A. Gravitation
B. Viscosity
C. Magnetic Properties
D. Entropy

150. How does the Isotope of Iodine, Iodine-135 plays an important role in Nuclear Power Generation?
A. It is used as a fuel supplement in some of the modern Nuclear Reactors
B. It is a bi-product of Nuclear Reaction which kills the neutrons and this inhibits the power formation
C. It is a moderator used actively in the Nuclear Reactors
D. It is an experimental substance for Nuclear Fusion

ANSWERS

1	2	3	4	5	6	7	8	9	10
A	C	B	D	D	B	D	C	C	A
11	**12**	**13**	**14**	**15**	**16**	**17**	**18**	**19**	**20**
D	B	D	A	A	C	C	A	C	D
21	**22**	**23**	**24**	**25**	**26**	**27**	**28**	**29**	**30**
A	C	*	B	B	C	A	D	A	B
31	**32**	**33**	**34**	**35**	**36**	**37**	**38**	**39**	**40**
C	D	A	D	D	C	B	C	A	D
41	**42**	**43**	**44**	**45**	**46**	**47**	**48**	**49**	**50**
C	A	D	A	A	B	A	D	D	D
51	**52**	**53**	**54**	**55**	**56**	**57**	**58**	**59**	**60**
B	A	D	A	C	B	C	A	C	D
61	**62**	**63**	**64**	**65**	**66**	**67**	**68**	**69**	**70**
B	C	A	D	D	A	B	C	C	C

71	72	73	74	75	76	77	78	79	80
C	C	D	D	A	A	B	B	A	A
81	**82**	**83**	**84**	**85**	**86**	**87**	**88**	**89**	**90**
D	A	D	D	B	A	A	A	D	B
91	**92**	**93**	**94**	**95**	**96**	**97**	**98**	**99**	**100**
C	B	D	A	D	C	B	C	B	A
101	**102**	**103**	**104**	**105**	**106**	**107**	**108**	**109**	**110**
D	B	B	C	D	A	C	A	B	B
111	**112**	**113**	**114**	**115**	**116**	**117**	**118**	**119**	**120**
B	A	B	B	D	C	A	A	B	B
121	**122**	**123**	**124**	**125**	**126**	**127**	**128**	**129**	**130**
C	C	C	C	A	B	A	B	A	C
131	**132**	**133**	**134**	**135**	**136**	**137**	**138**	**139**	**140**
A	B	C	B	A	B	B	C	C	B
141	**142**	**143**	**144**	**145**	**146**	**147**	**148**	**149**	**150**
D	A	D	B	C	C	A	C	B	B

EXPLANATORY ANSWERS

1. We have,

$$x(x + 2) \geq -4$$

$$x^2 + 2x + 4 \geq 0$$

$$(x + 1)^2 + 3 \geq 0$$

This is valid for all real value of x

Hence, $x \in (-\infty, \infty)$.

3. $\sum_{k=1}^{n} \sin \frac{k\pi}{3}$

$$= \sin\frac{\pi}{3} + \sin\frac{2\pi}{3} + \sin\frac{3\pi}{3} + \sin\frac{4\pi}{3} + \ldots \sin\frac{n\pi}{3}$$

$$= \sin\frac{\pi}{3} + \sin\left(\frac{\pi}{3}+\frac{\pi}{3}\right) + \sin\left(\frac{\pi}{3}+\frac{2\pi}{3}\right) +$$

$$\sin\left(\frac{\pi}{3}+\frac{3\pi}{3}\right) + \ldots \sin\left(\frac{\pi}{3}+(n-1)\frac{\pi}{3}\right)$$

$\because$ sin A + sin(A + B) + sin (A + 2B) + ... + sin(A + (n − 1)B)

$$= \frac{\sin\left\{A+(n-1)\frac{B}{2}\right\}\sin\frac{nB}{2}}{\sin\frac{B}{2}}$$

$$A = \frac{\pi}{3},\ B = \frac{\pi}{3},$$

$$= \frac{\sin\left\{\frac{\pi}{3}+(n-1)\frac{\pi}{6}\right\}\sin\frac{n\pi}{6}}{\sin\frac{\pi}{6}}$$

$$= 2\sin\left(\frac{n\pi}{6}\right)\sin\left(\frac{(n+1)\pi}{6}\right).$$

4. We have

$$f(x) = \frac{1}{1-x}$$

$$f \circ f \circ f = f \circ f\left(\frac{1}{1-x}\right)$$

$$= f\left[\frac{1}{1-\frac{1}{1-x}}\right]$$

$$= f\left(\frac{1-x}{1-x-1}\right)$$

$$= f\left(\frac{1-x}{-x}\right)$$

$$= \frac{1}{1 + \frac{1-x}{x}}$$

$$= \frac{x}{x + 1 - x}$$

$= x.$

5. $\lim_{x \to 1} \frac{x-1}{x^n - 1}, \frac{0}{0}$ form, Apply L's Hospital Rule

$$= \lim_{x \to 1} \frac{1}{n(x)^{n-1}}$$

$$= \frac{1}{n(1)^{n-1}}$$

$$= \frac{1}{n}.$$

7. $$\int_0^{\pi/2} \cos^2 dx = \frac{1}{2} \int_0^{\pi/2} (\cos 2x + 1) dx$$

$$= \frac{1}{2} \left[\frac{\sin 2x}{2} + x \right]_0^{\pi/2}$$

$$= \frac{1}{2} \left[\left\{ \frac{1}{2} \times \sin \pi + \frac{\pi}{2} \right\} - \left\{ \frac{1}{2} \sin 0 + 0 \right\} \right]$$

$$= \frac{1}{2} \left[\frac{\pi}{2} \right]$$

$$= \frac{\pi}{4}.$$

9. Let the number be x

Then,

$$2x + 11 = 3x - 32$$

$$x = 11 + 32$$

$$x = 43$$

Hence, the required number is 43.

10. Let the two consecutive even numbers are x and $x + 2$, then

$$x + (x + 2) = 126$$

$$2x + 2 = 126$$

$$2x = 124$$

$$x = 62$$

Hence, the required numbers are 62 and 64.

11. Required time $= \frac{\text{Total travelled distance}}{\text{Relative speed of both the train}}$

$$= \frac{1029}{45 + 53}$$

$$= \frac{1029}{98}$$

$= 10.5$ hours.

12. Let two numbers are x and y

Then, $x + y = 36$ ...(*i*)

$x - y = 6$ ...(*ii*)

After solving eq. (*i*) and eq. (*ii*), we get

$$x = \frac{36 + 6}{2} = \frac{42}{2} = 21$$

$$y = \frac{36 - 6}{2} = \frac{30}{2} = 15$$

Hence, the required smaller number is 15.

13. Let diagonal of rectangular patio = 'd' m

$\therefore$ length of rectangular patio = 'd – 5' m

width of rectangular patio = 'd – 7' m

Area of rectangular patio = $l \times b$

$$(d - 5) \times (d - 7) = 195$$

$$d^2 - 12d + 35 = 195$$

$$d^2 - 12d - 160 = 0$$

$$d^2 - 20d - 8d - 160 = 0$$

$$d(d - 20) - 8(d - 20) = 0$$

$$(d - 8)(d - 20) = 0$$

$\therefore d = 8$ (invalid)

$d = 20$ (valid)

Hence, the diagonal of rectangular patio is '20' m.

14. Let two consecutive positive integers are x and $x + 2$

Then,

$$x(x + 2) = 168$$

$$x^2 + 2x - 168 = 0$$

$$x^2 + 14x - 12x - 168 = 0$$

$$x(x + 14) - 12(x + 14) = 0$$

$$(x - 12)(x + 14) = 0$$

$\therefore$ $x = 12$ and $x = -14$ (invalid)

Hence, the required number is 12.

15. Area of the original picture

$= 4 \times 6$

$= 24$ square inches

Area of the reduced picture

$= \frac{1}{3} \times 24$

$= 8$ square inches

Let, each dimension reduces by x inches.

Then,

$$(4 - x)(6 - x) = 8$$
$$24 + x^2 - 10x = 8$$
$$x^2 - 10x + 16 = 0$$
$$(x - 8)(x - 2) = 0$$

$x = 8$ (invalid) and $x = 2$ (valid)

Hence, smaller dimension of the reduced picture $= 4 - x = 4 - 2 = 2$ inches.

16. Required points, he score during his senior year $= 120\% \times 260$

$$= \frac{120 \times 260}{100}$$
$$= 312.$$

17. Dow at the end of the day

$= 8800 \times 98\% = 8{,}624.$

18. Let there are 'x' teachers at Russell High

Then, $x \times 45\% = 81$

$$x = \frac{81 \times 100}{45}$$
$$= 180$$

Hence, there are '180' teachers at Russell High.

19. Let original price of bike = ₹ 100

Sale price of bike = ₹ 70 (30% off)

Required percentage $= \frac{70}{100} \times 100 = 70\%.$

20. 320 → 160 → 80 → 40 → **[20]**

(each step ÷2)

21. Let the number of boys and girls are $3x$ and $4x$ respectively.

Required No. of boys $= 60 \times \frac{3x}{4x} = 45.$

22. 1 inch = 2.54 cm

Width of the table = 85 cm

Width of the table in inch

$= \frac{85}{2.54} = 33.46 = 33.5$ inch.

24. Let Jihan scores x marks in science test

$$85 + 92 + 95 + x = 400 \times 93\%$$
$$272 + x = 372$$
$$x = 100.$$

25. We know, period of $\sin x = 2\pi$

If period of $\sin x$ is 2π then period of $\sin nx$ will be $\frac{2\pi}{n}$

Hence, required period is $\frac{2\pi}{3}$.

27. Required equation

$$f(x) = (x - 4)(x - 8)(x - 11)$$
$$f(2x) = (2x - 4)(2x - 8)(2x - 11)$$

Hence, solution of $f(2x)$ are

$$2x = 4 \Rightarrow x = 2$$
$$2x = 8 \Rightarrow x = 4$$
$$2x = 11 \Rightarrow x = \frac{11}{2}$$

28. We have,

$$ax + by = c$$
$$\text{Slope } (m_1) = -\frac{a}{b}$$
$$bx - ay = c$$
$$\text{Slope } (m_2) = -\left(\frac{b}{-a}\right)$$
$$= \frac{b}{a}$$

$\because m_1 \times m_2 = -\frac{a}{b} \times \frac{b}{a} = -1$

Hence, both linear equations are perpendicular.

29. $\log_x \frac{1}{8} = -\frac{3}{2}$

$$\frac{1}{8} = (x)^{-\frac{3}{2}}$$

$$\left(\frac{1}{x}\right)^{\frac{3}{2}} = \frac{1}{8}$$

$$\frac{1}{x} = \left(\frac{1}{8}\right)^{\frac{2}{3}}$$

$$\frac{1}{x} = \left(\frac{1}{2}\right)^{2}$$

$$\frac{1}{x} = \frac{1}{4}$$

$\therefore x = 4.$

30. $2^{3x-1} = 16$

$$2^{3x-1} = 2^4$$

On comparing both sides, we get

$$3x - 1 = 4$$

$$3x = 5$$

$$x = \frac{5}{3}.$$

31. $x^2 + kx - 6 = (x - 2)(x + 3)$

$x^2 + kx - 6 = x^2 + x - 6$

On comparing both sides, we get

$$k = 1$$

32. Required quadratic equation

$\Rightarrow x^2 - (\text{sum of roots})x + \text{product of roots} = 0$

$\Rightarrow x^2 - (3 + 5)x + 3 \times 5 = 0$

$\Rightarrow x^2 - 8x + 15 = 0$

$\Rightarrow x^2 - 8x = -15.$

33. We have, $f(x) = -x^2 + 6x = x(6 - x)$

Domain of $f(x) = [0, 6]$

$\therefore f(0) = 0, f(1) = 5, f(2) = 8, f(3) = 9, f(4) = 8, f(5) = 5, f(6) = 0,$

Co-domain of function $f(x) = [0, 9]$

$\because$ Range $\subseteq$ co-domain

$\therefore$ Range of the given function is $[0, 9]$.

34. We have $f(x) = 2 \log |x - 2|$

We know that, logarithm function $\log_a x$ is define for $a > 0$, $a \neq 1$ and $x > 0$

$\therefore |x - 2| > 0$

$\because 2 < e < 3$

This is valid for all real number

Hence, Domain of $f(x) = (-\infty, \infty)$.

36. 2 : 15

$$\text{Required Angle} = \frac{11 \text{ mm} - 60 \text{ HH}}{2}$$

$$= \frac{11 \times 15 - 60 \times 2}{2}$$

$$= \frac{165 - 120}{2}$$

$$= \frac{45}{2}$$

$$= 22\frac{1}{2}°.$$

37. Required Average of both the class

$$= \frac{20 \times 80\% + 30 \times 70\%}{20 + 30}$$

$$= \frac{1600 + 2100}{50}$$

$$= \frac{3700}{50}$$

$$= 74\%.$$

38. Required increase in new price

$$= \left(\frac{P}{100 - P}\right) \times 100\%$$

$$= \left(\frac{10}{100-10}\right) \times 100\%$$

$$= \frac{1}{9} \times 100$$

$$= 11\frac{1}{9}\%.$$

40. Centre of ellipse = (0, 0)

length of major axis $(2a)$ = 20 units

$$a = 10 \text{ units}$$

Focus $(ae, 0) = (05, 0)$

$$ae = 5$$

$$e = \frac{5}{a} = \frac{5}{10} = \frac{1}{2}$$

Equation of directrix is:

$$x = \frac{a}{e}$$

$$= \frac{10}{\left(\frac{1}{2}\right)}$$

$$= 20$$

41. We have,

$$\vec{a} = \lambda\hat{i} + 2\hat{j} + \hat{k}$$

$$\vec{b} = 5\hat{i} - 9\hat{j} + 2\hat{k}$$

$\because$ $\vec{a}$ and $\vec{b}$ are perpendicular, then

$$\vec{a}.\vec{b} = 0$$

$$\left(\lambda\hat{i} + 2\hat{j} + \hat{k}\right)\left(5\hat{i} - 9\hat{j} + 2\hat{k}\right) = 0$$

$$5\lambda - 18 + 2 = 0$$

$$5\lambda - 16 = 0$$

$$\lambda = \frac{16}{5}.$$

42. We have,

$$P(M \cap S) = 40\% = \frac{2}{5}$$

$$P(M) = 60\% = \frac{3}{5}$$

$$P(S/M) = \frac{P(S \cap M)}{P(M)}$$

$$= \frac{\left(\frac{2}{5}\right)}{\left(\frac{3}{5}\right)}$$

$$= \frac{2}{3}$$

$$= 0.666$$

$$= 0.67.$$

43. Total bars sold by the group = 35 × 6 = 210.

44. Required average between stops

$$= \frac{2052}{6 \times 2}$$

$$= \frac{2052}{12}$$

= 171 miles.

46. Diagonal of square $\sqrt{2}\,a = a + b$

$$a = \frac{a+b}{\sqrt{2}}$$

Area of the square $= (a)^2 = \left(\frac{a+b}{\sqrt{2}}\right)^2$

$$= \frac{(a+b)^2}{2}$$

$$= \frac{1}{2}(a+b)^2.$$

Previous Paper (Solved)

BACHELOR OF COMPUTER APPLICATIONS (BCA) Entrance Exam–2018*

1. Complete the following sequence:
ACEG, IKMO,______, YACE
A. QSVX B. PRTV
C. QSUW D. UVSQ

2. If the code for NAME is 13261422, then what will be the code for TEAM?
A. 1426227 B. 7222614
C. 7142622 D. 7262214

3. If the ratio of an external angle and an internal angle of a regular polygon is 1:17, the number of sides of the regular polygon is:
A. 18 B. 12
C. 36 D. 20

4. Which among the following neighboring countries of India is the largest producer of Opium in the World?
A. Maldives B. Sri Lanka
C. Pakistan D. Afghanistan

5. Which portal was launched to make online complaints of sexual harassment in the workplace for women employees?
A. Help-Box B. She-Box
C. Empower-Box D. None of these

6. Given the equation $x^2 - y^2 = (x - y)(x + y)$, where x and y are matrices of order $n \times n$, which of the following is true?
A. Both x and y are invertible and x and y commute with each other
B. x and y commute with each other
C. x and y are invertible
D. None of these

7. Tuticorin is:
A. From where Agni 5 was launched
B. Birth place of former president Abdul Kalam
C. Where Rajeev Gandhi was assassinated
D. Town in Tamil Nadu where Sterlite Copper Company is located

8. Garbine Muguruza winner of Women's Single Match in Wimbledon (2017) Tennis Tournament belongs to which country?
A. United States of America
B. Israel
C. Spain
D. Switzerland

9. Simplify the expression: $b - [b - (a + b) - \{b - (b - a + b)\} + 2a]$
A. a B. $4a$
C. 0 D. $2a$

10. Who has been named TIME Person of the year 2017?
A. The Silence Breakers
B. Prime Minister Narendra Modi
C. President Donald Trump
D. President Xi Jinping

11. Which actress has received National Award for best acting in 2018?
A. Sonam Kapoor
B. Deepika Padukone
C. Divya Dutta
D. Sridevi

12. Here are some words translated from an artificial language.
Tamceno means sky blue
Cenorax means blue cheese
Aplmitl means star bright
Which word could mean "bright sky"?
A. Cenotam B. Raxmitl
C. Aplceno D. Mitltam

* Based on Memory.

13. Many times we read in financial newspapers about 'FII'. What is the full form of FII?
A. Final Investment in India
B. Formal Investment in India
C. Foreign Investment in India
D. Foreign Institutional Investment

14. I am facing South. I turn right and walk 20 m. Then I turn right again and walk 10 m. Then I turn left and walk 10 m and then turning right walk 20 m. Then, I turn right again and walk 60 m. In which direction am I from the starting point?
A. West B. North-West
C. North-East D. North

15. If both the President and the Vice President are unavailable, who among the following would discharge the functions?
A. Prime Minister
B. Lok Sabha Speaker
C. Chief Justice of India
D. Any person nominated by President or Vice President

16. Om Prakash Rawat is:
A. India's envoy to Pakistan
B. Chief of Army Staff
C. Deputy Governor of RBI
D. Chief Election Commissioner

17. Two ships are anchored in the sea on opposite sides of a lighthouse. The angle of elevation of the top of the lighthouse observed from the two ships is 30° and 45° respectively. If the lighthouse is 100 m high, the distance between the two ships is:
A. 273 m B. 173 m
C. 300 m D. 200 m

18. In a circle with radius 21 cm, an arc subtends an angle of 72° at the centre. The length of the arc is:
A. 26.4 cm B. 21.6 cm
C. 13.2 cm D. 19.8 cm

19. Deficiency of red cells in blood causes:
A. Osteoporosis B. Anemia
C. Tuberculosis D. Chronic infection

20. Which Indian Olympian boxer won her fifth gold at the 2017 Asian Championships?
A. Kavita Goyat
B. Mary Kom
C. Sarjubala Devi
D. Laishram Sarita Devi

21. Fact 1: Kamal has four vehicles.
Fact 2: Two of the vehicles are red.
Fact 3: One of the vehicles is a minivan.
If the first three statements are facts, then which of the following statements must also be a fact?
I. Kamal has a red minivan.
II. Kamal has three cars.
III. Kamal's favourite colour is red.
A. I only
B. II and III only
C. None of the statements is a known fact
D. II only

22. Laissez Faire policy is adopted in:
A. Open Economic System
B. Mixed Economic System
C. Regulated Economic System
D. Controlled Economic System

23. Who is the Chief Justice of India?
A. Dipak Misra
B. None of these
C. T.S. Thakur
D. Jagdish Singh Khehar

24. In a certain code, SIKKIM is written as THLJJL, how is TRAINING written in that code?
A. UBQHOHOI B. UQBHOHOF
C. UQBOHIOF D. SBQHOHOF

25. In a certain language, "You are great" means "Water is cold". "They are poor" means "rain is heavy" and "poor not great" means "heavy never cold". Which word stands for "rain"?
A. poor B. not
C. you D. they

26. If the 3rd of a month falls on Friday, what day will it be on the 4th day after the 21st of this month?

A. Saturday B. Monday
C. Friday D. Thursday

27. If A is an invertible matrix and $A^2 - A + I = 0$, then the inverse of A is:
A. I – A B. I + A
C. $I + A^2$ D. $I - A^2$

28. The lengths of three perpendiculars from a point inside an equilateral triangle on the three sides are 16 cm, 25 cm and 28 cm. The area of the triangle (in cm^2) will be:
A. $1587\sqrt{3}$ B. 1587
C. 2116 D. $2116\sqrt{3}$

29. Name the first city of India to roll out the supply of ultra-clean Bharat Stage VI grade fuel.
A. Mumbai
B. Faridabad
C. New Delhi
D. Hyderabad

30. Fill in the blank with the most appropriate option.

He is .... honour to this profession.
A. an B. none of these
C. a D. the

31. In the question below two statements are followed by three conclusions numbered I, II and III. Taking the two statements given as true, read all the conclusions and select the conclusions that follow from the given statement.

Statements:
I. All roads are trees.
II. No tree is soap.

Conclusions:
I. No soap is a road.
II. Some trees are roads.
III. No road is a soap.

A. Only III B. Only I
C. Only II D. I, II and III

32. Which Article is related with "Abolition of Untouchability"?
A. Article 20 B. Article 18
C. Article 19 D. Article 17

33. Choose the most suitable word for the phrase: 'That which cannot be avoided':
A. Inevitable
B. Unaccountable
C. Impregnable
D. Untenable

34. Choose the most suitable word for the phrase: 'One who lives off another':
A. Hospitable B. Inhospitable
C. Incognito D. Parasite

35. Choose the word that is spelt incorrectly:
(*i*) Transgression (*ii*) Grammer (*iii*) Concussion (*iv*) Paucity
A. (*iii*) B. (*ii*)
C. (*i*) D. (*iv*)

36. Choose the word that is spelt incorrectly:
(*i*) Pernicious (*ii*) Obnoctious (*iii*) Scintillating (*iv*) Serendipity
A. (*iii*) B. (*ii*)
C. (*i*) D. (*iv*)

37. Complete the following sequence:

5G7, 7H10, 10I14, 14J19, ...
A. 18K21 B. 16K20
C. 19K25 D. 17K21

38. Choose the pair that best represents a similar relationship to the one expressed in the original pair of words — DEPRESSED : SAD
A. progressive : regressive
B. towering : cringing
C. exhausted : tired
D. neat : considerate

39. Mohan is 18th from either end of a row of boys. How many boys are there in that row?
A. 26 B. 32
C. 24 D. 35

40. Find the slope of the tangent to the curve in the XY plane given by
$x = t^2 + 3t - 8$, $y = 2t^2 - 2t - 5$ at $t = 2$.

A. $\frac{2}{7}$ B. $\frac{6}{7}$

C. $\frac{2}{5}$ D. $\frac{5}{6}$

41. Which state launches India's first social audit law?

A. Tamil Nadu
B. Kerala
C. Meghalaya
D. West Bengal

42. A and B can together complete a piece of work in 4 days. If A alone can complete the same work in 12 days, in how many days can B alone complete that work?

A. 7 days B. 6 days
C. 4 days D. 5 days

43. Find the value of x from the equation $6^{x^2+3x} = \frac{1}{36}$:

A. 2 B. –1 and –2
C. 1 D. Both 1 and 2

44. The frequency distribution of the age of 130 persons is given as:

Age	Number of persons
0–30	15
30–50	25
50–60	40
60–100	50

What is the minimum age of the oldest 20 per cent of the persons?

A. 80.8 B. 80
C. 90 D. 79.2

45. $\int_{-1}^{1} x^3(x^4+1)^3\,dx$ equals:

A. 2 B. 0
C. 1 D. 3

46. The functions f and g are defined as $f = \{(2,4), (6,10), (8,2)\}$ and $g = \{(4,6), (10,6), (2,6)\}$.

Then fog and gof will be:

A. $fog = \{(10,4),(4,10),(10,2)\}$ and $gof = \{(6,2), (2,6), (6,8)\}$
B. $fog = \{(4,10),(10,4),(2,10)\}$ and $gof = \{(2,6), (6,2), (8,6)\}$
C. $fog = \{(4,8),(2,2),(6,6)\}$ and $gof = \{(8,4), (2,2), (6,10)\}$
D. They do not exist

47. Evaluate $\int (x^6 + x^3 + 1)\,d(x^3)$:

A. $\frac{x^6}{2} + \frac{x^5}{4} + x^4 + C$

B. $\frac{x^9}{3} + \frac{x^6}{2} + x^3 + C$

C. $\frac{x^3}{4} + \frac{x^7}{3} + x^6 + C$

D. $\frac{x^7}{3} + \frac{x^4}{4} + x + C$

48. The value of $\begin{vmatrix} x & a & x+a \\ y & b & y+b \\ z & c & z+c \end{vmatrix}$ is:

A. 0 B. a
C. 1 D. $a + b$

49. The maximum value of $f(x) = \sin x + \sqrt{3}\cos x$ occurs when x equals:

A. π B. $\frac{\pi}{2}$

C. $\frac{\pi}{6}$ D. $\frac{\pi}{4}$

50. The value of $\lim_{x\to 0}\left(\frac{1+5x^2}{1+3x^2}\right)^{\frac{1}{x^2}}$ is:

A. e^4 B. e^3
C. e^2 D. None of these

51. If $\sin\left(\sin^{-1}\frac{1}{2} + \cos^{-1} x\right) = 1$ then the value of x is:

A. 1 B. 0

C. $\frac{2}{3}$ D. $\frac{1}{2}$

52. The value of x if $\begin{pmatrix} x+y+z \\ x+z \\ y+z \end{pmatrix} = \begin{pmatrix} 9 \\ 5 \\ 7 \end{pmatrix}$ is:

A. 2
B. 1
C. 3
D. 4

53. Find the value of k, if the area of the triangle is 12 square units with vertices (0,0), (k,0) and (4,3):

A. $k = 0$
B. $k = 9$
C. $k = 8$
D. $k = 6$

54. A bag contains 2 red, 3 green and 2 blue balls. Two balls are drawn at random. What is the probability that none of the balls drawn is blue?

A. $\frac{2}{7}$
B. $\frac{10}{21}$
C. $\frac{11}{21}$
D. None of these

55. Choose the option that best explains the phrase:

'A tall order'

A. summon
B. long list of demands
C. major problem
D. difficult task

56. Choose the most suitable antonym for the word:

DESPONDENT

A. Revengeful
B. Cheerful
C. Peaceful
D. Correspondent

57. Choose the most suitable antonym for the word:

BELLIGERENT

A. Friendly
B. Stupid
C. Intelligent
D. Literate

58. Choose the most suitable antonym for the word:

JEOPARDY

A. Feline
B. Safety
C. Tilt
D. Endanger

59. Choose the most suitable antonym for the word:

WANE

A. Humble
B. Small
C. Emaciated
D. Wax

60. Choose the most suitable word for the phrase:

'A single cure for all diseases'

A. Utopia
B. Panacea
C. Antidote
D. Panic

61. Choose the correct spelling:

A. Embarassment
B. Embarasment
C. Embarrassment
D. Embarrasment

62. Choose the correct meaning for the idiom:

through and through

A. make a circular argument
B. completely
C. to make a hole
D. to see the hidden meaning

63. Choose the correct meaning for the idiom:

hue and cry

A. loud noise
B. colorful drawing
C. mourn quietly
D. to plead

64. Choose the correct meaning for the idiom:

null and void

A. to clear a jungle
B. not binding
C. empty space
D. to begin work

65. Choose the correct meaning for the idiom:

storm in a teacup

A. danger signal
B. excitement over something trivial
C. great noise
D. unexpected event

66. Choose the correct meaning for the word:

SAVANT

A. Grasslands
B. Very learned
C. Indecent
D. Severe criticism

67. Choose the correct meaning for the word:

EMANCIPATE

A. Argue
B. Waste away
C. Liberate
D. Antiseptic

68. Choose the correct meaning for the word: CONCISE

A. Elaborate B. Revise
C. Convince D. Terse

69. Choose the correct meaning for the word: ABHORRENT

A. Loquacious B. Yellowish
C. Torrential D. Detestable

70. ABCD is a parallelogram, if the coordinates of A, B and C are (4, 6), (2, 8) and (0, –4) respectively, what is the coordinate of D?

A. (6, –4) B. (2, –6)
C. (4, –4) D. (2, –4)

71. Sagarbandhu, the CSR initiative for helping the fishermen in Gujarat, is the CSR initiative of which company?

A. HUL
B. Tata Power
C. Indian Oil Limited
D. RIL

72. Sultan Azlan Shah Cup is related to which of the following Sports?

A. Badminton B. Table Tennis
C. Cricket D. Hockey

73. Which of the following organization/ agency has established a fund known as 'Investor Protection Fund'?

A. BSE
B. Inter connected Stock Exchange (ISE)
C. SEBI
D. Ministry of Finance

74. Headquarters of the SAARC is located at?

A. Jakarta B. Kathmandu
C. New Delhi D. Manila

75. Which is the first industry using plasma technology for the disposal of hazardous waste for the conservation of the environment and natural resources?

A. Steel Authority of India Limited (SAIL)
B. Madras Rubber factory (MRF)
C. Madras Fertilizers Limited (MFL)
D. Bharat Sanchar Nigam Limited (BSNL)

76. The Telecom company, Nokia originally belongs to which country?

A. USA B. Finland
C. Sweden D. Denmark

77. The angle between the planes $x - y + 2z = 9$ and $2x + y + z = 7$ is:

A. 75° B. 90°
C. 45° D. 60°

78. The world's smallest country is:

A. Maldives B. Peru
C. Bhutan D. Vatican City

79. The minimum distance of the point (3, –5, 12) from x-axis is

A. 11 B. 13
C. 12 D. None of these

80. India is the largest emitter of which harmful gas in 2017?

A. Nitrous oxide B. Carbon monoxide
C. Sulphur trioxide D. Sulphur dioxide

81. In India the Parliament is made up of ....:

I. Lok Sabha
II. Rajya Sabha
III. President
IV. Vice President
V. Lok Sabha Speaker

A. Only I and II
B. I, II and III
C. I, II and V
D. All I, II, III, IV and V

82. On a railway line there are 20 stops. A ticket is needed to travel between any two stops. How many different tickets can be prepared to cater to all the travel possibilities?

A. 380 B. 760
C. 190 D. 72

83. The first pair of two numbers follows some paired relationship, using a similar analogy to that of the first pair, find the missing number in the second pair:

63: 80 :: 15:

A. 24 B. 12
C. 13 D. 42

84. One morning after sunrise Vikram and Shailesh were standing in a lawn with their backs toward each other. Vikram's shadow fell exactly towards the left-hand side. In which direction was Shailesh facing?

A. West B. North
C. East D. South

Directions (Qs. 85-89): *Read the following passage carefully and answer the questions given below in the context of the passage.*

Conflict had existed between Spain and England since the 1570s. England wanted a share of the wealth that Spain had been taking from the lands it had claimed in the Americas.

Elizabeth I, Queen of England, encouraged her staunch admiral of the navy, Sir Francis Drake, to raid Spanish ships and towns. Though these raids were on a small scale, Drake achieved dramatic success, adding gold and silver to England's treasury and diminishing Spain's supremacy.

Religious differences also caused conflict between the two countries. Whereas Spain was Roman Catholic, most of England had become Protestant. King Philip II of Spain wanted to claim the throne and make England a Catholic country again. To satisfy his ambition and also to retaliate against England's theft of his gold and silver, King Philip began to build his fleet of warships, the Spanish Armada, in January 1586.

Philip intended his fleet to be indestructible. In addition to building new warships, he marshaled 130 sailing vessels of all types and recruited more than 19,000 robust soldiers and 8,000 sailors.

Although some of his ships lacked guns and others lacked ammunition, Philip was convinced that his Armada could withstand any battle with England.

The martial Armada set sail from Lisbon, Portugal, on May 9, 1588, but bad weather forced it back to port. The voyage resumed on July 22 after the weather became more stable.

The Spanish fleet met the smaller, faster, and more maneuverable English ships in battle off the coast of Plymouth, England, first on July 31 and again on August 2. The two battles left Spain vulnerable, having lost several ships and with its ammunition depleted. On August 7, while the Armada lay at anchor on the French side of the Strait of Dover, England sent eight burning ships into the midst of the Spanish fleet to set it on fire. Blocked on one side, the Spanish ships could only drift away, their crews in panic and disorder. Before the Armada could regroup, the English attacked again on August 8.

Although the Spaniards made a valiant effort to fight back, the fleet suffered extensive damage. During the eight hours of battle, the Armada drifted perilously close to the rocky coastline. At the moment when it seemed that the Spanish ships would be driven onto the English shore, the wind shifted, and the Armada drifted out into the North Sea. The Spaniards recognized the superiority of the English fleet and returned home, defeated.

85. Sir Francis Drake added wealth to the treasury and diminished Spain's ....

A. territory
B. unrestricted growth
C. treaties
D. unlimited power

86. The two battles left the Spanish fleet ....

A. defeated
B. triumphant
C. open to change
D. open to attack

87. The .... Armada set sail on May 9, 1588.

A. warlike B. independent
C. complete D. isolated

88. The Armada was .... on one side.

A. alone B. closed off
C. circled D. damaged

89. King Philip recruited many .... soldiers and sailors.

A. timid B. warlike
C. accomplished D. strong

Direction (Qs. 90-92): *Read the information given in and on the basis of the information, answer the questions.*

At a small company, parking spaces are reserved for the top executives: CEO, president, vice-president, secretary, and treasurer with the spaces lined up in that order. The parking lot guard can tell at a glance if the cars are parked correctly by looking at the colour of the cars. The cars are yellow, green, purple, red, and blue, and the executive's names are Alice, Bert, Cheryl, David, and Enid.

- The car in the first space is red.
- A blue car is parked between the red car and the green car.
- The car in the last space is purple.
- The secretary drives a yellow car.
- Alice's car is parked next to David's.
- Enid drives a green car.
- Bert's car is parked between Cheryl's and Enid's.
- David's car is parked in the last space.

90. Who is the CEO?

A. Alice B. David
C. Bert D. Cheryl

91. Who is the secretary?

A. Enid B. Alice
C. David D. Cheryl

92. What colour is the vice president's car?

A. yellow B. green
C. blue D. purple

Direction (Qs. 93-97): *Read the information given in and on the basis of the information, answer the questions.*

A TV channel is going to telecast 6 soppy soaps over the week – Sob, Cry, Weep, Wail, Lament and Moan. One of these will be telecast each day from Monday to Saturday, with Sunday being a fun day. The conditions specified by the Boss are as follows:

- Sob must be telecast earlier in the week than Lament.
- Weep must be telecast on Tuesday
- Wail must be telecast on the day immediately before or immediately after the day on which Cry is telecast

93. If Wail is to be featured on Thursday, the latest day on which Sob can be telecast is:

A. Monday B. Friday
C. Tuesday D. Wednesday

94. If Cry is telecast on Thursday, the earliest day on which Lament can be featured is:

A. Monday B. Friday
C. Tuesday D. Wednesday

95. If Moan is to be telecast on Friday, Sob must be telecast on:

A. Monday B. Thursday
C. Tuesday D. Wednesday

96. If Moan is to be telecast on Thursday, which of the following is strictly true?

A. Lament must be telecast on Wednesday
B. Wail must be telecast exactly two days after Lament is telecast
C. Sob must be telecast on Wednesday
D. Cry must be telecast on Saturday

97. Which of the following soaps can be telecast on Monday?

A. Lament B. Weep
C. Moan D. Cry

Direction (Qs. 98-100): *Read the information given below and answer the questions that follow:*

Six persons are sitting in a circle. A is facing B. B is to the right of E and left of C. C is to the left of D. F is to the right of A. Now, D exchanges his seat with F and E with B.

98. Who is sitting to the left of D?

A. D B. E
C. B D. A

99. Who will be sitting to the left of C?

A. E B. B
C. A D. F

100. Who will be sitting opposite to A?

A. D B. E
C. B D. F

ANSWERS

1	2	3	4	5	6	7	8	9	10
C	B	C	D	B	B	D	C	C	A
11	**12**	**13**	**14**	**15**	**16**	**17**	**18**	**19**	**20**
D	D	D	C	C	D	A	A	B	B
21	**22**	**23**	**24**	**25**	**26**	**27**	**28**	**29**	**30**
C	A	A	B	D	A	A	A	C	A
31	**32**	**33**	**34**	**35**	**36**	**37**	**38**	**39**	**40**
D	D	A	D	B	B	C	C	D	B
41	**42**	**43**	**44**	**45**	**46**	**47**	**48**	**49**	**50**
C	B	B	D	B	B	B	A	C	C
51	**52**	**53**	**54**	**55**	**56**	**57**	**58**	**59**	**60**
D	A	C	B	D	B	A	B	D	B
61	**62**	**63**	**64**	**65**	**66**	**67**	**68**	**69**	**70**
C	B	A	B	B	B	C	D	D	B
71	**72**	**73**	**74**	**75**	**76**	**77**	**78**	**79**	**80**
B	D	B	B	A	B	D	D	B	D
81	**82**	**83**	**84**	**85**	**86**	**87**	**88**	**89**	**90**
B	A	A	D	D	D	A	B	D	D
91	**92**	**93**	**94**	**95**	**96**	**97**	**98**	**99**	**100**
B	B	B	D	A	A	C	D	A	B

EXPLANATORY ANSWERS

1.

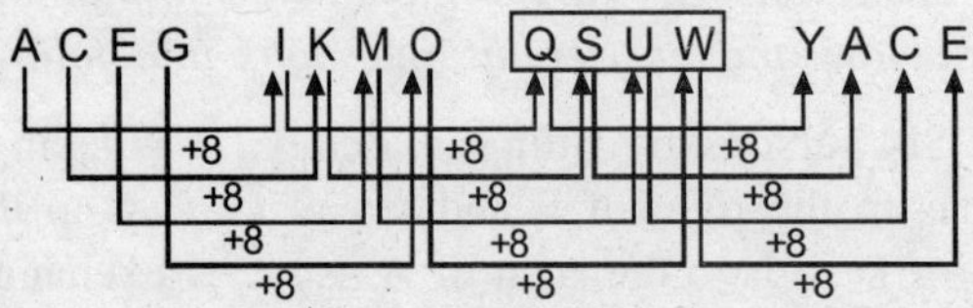

Hence, QSUW will come at the missing place.

2. In a certain code language, each letter of the given word is coded into the opposite letter's. Number position in the English alphabet.

As, N A M E is coded as

↓ ↓ ↓ ↓

M Z N V (opposite letter)

↓ ↓ ↓ ↓

13 26 14 22

Similarly,

T E A M

↓ ↓ ↓ ↓

G V Z N (opposite letter)

↓ ↓ ↓ ↓

7 22 26 14

3. $1x + 17x = 180°$

$\Rightarrow \quad 18x = 180 \quad \Rightarrow \quad x = 10°$

External angle $= 10°$

$\therefore$ No. of sides $= \dfrac{360°}{10} = 36.$

9. $b - [b - (a + b) - \{b - (b - a + b)\} + 2a]$

$= b - [b - a - b - \{b - b + a - b\} + 2a]$

$= b - [b - a - b - b + b - a + b + 2a]$

$= b - b = 0.$

17.

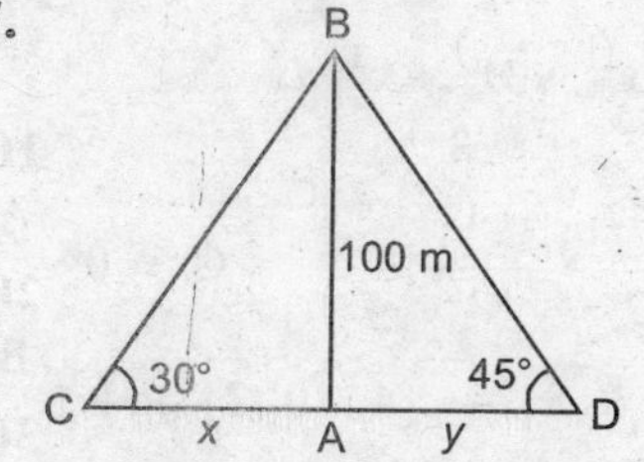

In Δ ABC, $\tan 30° = \dfrac{100}{x}$

$$\Rightarrow \quad \frac{1}{\sqrt{3}} = \frac{100}{x} \Rightarrow x = 100\sqrt{3}$$

In Δ ABD,

$$\tan 45° = \frac{100}{y}$$

$$\Rightarrow \quad 1 = \frac{100}{y} \quad \Rightarrow \quad y = 100$$

$$\therefore \quad x + y = 100\sqrt{3} + 100$$
$$= 100\left(\sqrt{3}+1\right)$$
$$= 100(1.73 + 1)$$
$$= 2.73 \times 100 = 273.$$

18. Length of arc $= \dfrac{\theta}{360} \times 2\pi r$

$$= \frac{72}{360} \times 2 \times \frac{22}{7} \times 21$$
$$= \frac{1}{5} \times 2 \times 66$$
$$= \frac{132}{5} = 26.4 \text{ cm.}$$

24. In a certain code,

S I K K I M is written as
+1↓ −1↓ +1↓ −1↓ +1↓ −1↓
T H L J J L

Similarly,

T R A I N I N G is written as
+1↓ −1↓ +1↓ −1↓ +1↓ −1↓ +1↓ −1↓
U Q B H O H O F

25. In a certain language

"You are great" means "water is cold"

"They are poor" means "rain is heavy"

and "poor not great" means "heavy never cold"

The word "they" stands for "rain".

26. $\because$ 3rd of the month is Friday.

$\therefore$ 4th day after 21st = 21 + 4 = 25

Friday is 3, 10, 17, 24

$\therefore$ 4th day after 21st day = Saturday.

27. $A^2 - A + I = 0$

Multiply by A^{-1}, we get

$$A^2 \cdot A^{-1} - A \cdot A^{-1} + I \cdot A^{-1} = 0A^{-1}$$
$$A - I + A^{-1} = 0$$
$$A^{-1} = I - A.$$

28.

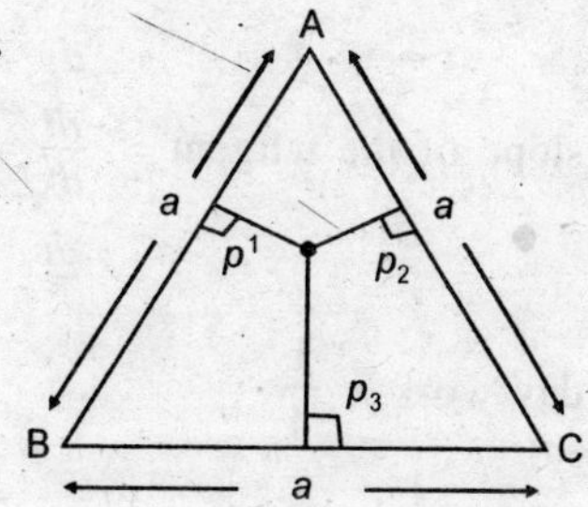

Side of equilateral triangle 'a'

$$= \frac{2}{\sqrt{3}}\left(p_1 + p_2 + p_3\right)$$
$$= \frac{2}{\sqrt{3}}(16+25+28) = \frac{69 \times 2}{\sqrt{3}} = \frac{138}{\sqrt{3}}$$

Area of equilateral triangle $= \dfrac{\sqrt{3}}{4}a^2$

$$= \frac{\sqrt{3}}{4} \times \frac{138}{\sqrt{3}} \times \frac{138}{\sqrt{3}}$$
$$= \frac{69 \times 69}{\sqrt{3}} \times \frac{\sqrt{3}}{\sqrt{3}}$$
$$= \frac{4761\sqrt{3}}{3} = 1587\sqrt{3} \text{ cm}^2.$$

37.

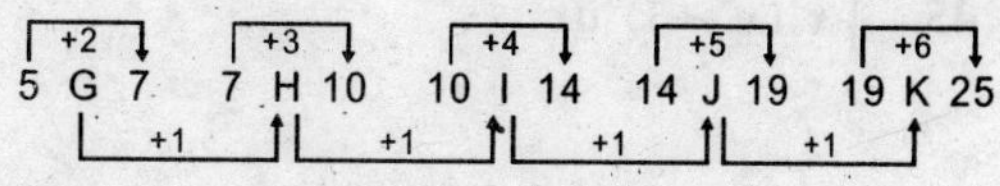

Hence, 19 k 25 will come at missing place.

39. → Mohan ← 18th

$\because$ Mohan's place is 18th from left and right

$\therefore$ Total no. of boys in that row

$= 18 + 18 - 1 = 35$

40. $\because \quad x = t^2 + 3t - 8$

$$\Rightarrow \frac{dx}{dt} = 2t + 3$$

$$= 2 \times 2 + 3 = 7 \quad [\because t = 2 \text{ given}]$$

Again, $y = 2t^2 - 2t - 5$

$$\frac{dy}{dt} = 4t - 2$$

$$= 4 \times 2 - 2 = 6 \quad [\because t = 2 \text{ given}]$$

$$\therefore \text{Required slope of the tangent} = \frac{\frac{dy}{dt}}{\frac{dx}{dt}} = \frac{6}{7}.$$

42. (A + B)'s 1 day work $= \frac{1}{4}$

A's 1 day work $= \frac{1}{12}$

B's 1 day work $= \frac{1}{4} - \frac{1}{12} = \frac{2}{12} = \frac{1}{6}$

Hence, B alone complete that work in 6 days.

43. $6^{x^2+3x} = \frac{1}{36}$

$$\Rightarrow 6^{x^2+3x} = (6)^{-2}$$
$$\Rightarrow x^2 + 3x = -2$$
$$\Rightarrow x^2 + 3x + 2 = 0$$
$$\Rightarrow x^2 + 2x + x + 2 = 0$$
$$\Rightarrow x(x + 2) + 1(x + 2) = 0$$
$$\Rightarrow (x + 2)(x + 1) = 0$$
$$\Rightarrow x = -2, -1$$

Hence, the value of $x = -1$ and -2.

45. $\int_{-1}^{1} x^3(x^4+1)^3\,dx$

$$= \int_{-1}^{1} x^3(x^{12}+3x^8+3x^4+1)\,dx$$

$$= \int_{-1}^{1} (x^{15}+3x^{11}+3x^7+x^3)\,dx$$

$$= \left[\frac{x^{16}}{16}+\frac{3x^{12}}{12}+\frac{3x^8}{8}+\frac{x^4}{4}\right]_{-1}^{1} + C = 0.$$

46. Let, $f : \{2, 6, 8\} \rightarrow \{4, 10, 2\}$ and

$g : \{4, 10, 2\} \rightarrow \{2, 6\}$

Clearly, Co-domain of f is same as Domain of g.

Then $fog(4) = f(g(4)) = f(6) = 10$

$fog(10) = f(g(10)) = f(2) = 4$

$fog(2) = f(g(2)) = f(6) = 10$

$\therefore \quad fog = \{(4, 10), (10, 4), (2, 10)\}$

$gof(2) = g(f(2)) = g(4) = 6$

$gof(6) = g(f(6)) = g(10) = 2$

$gof(8) = g(f(8)) = g(2) = 6$

$\therefore \quad gof(2) = \{(2, 6),(6, 2), (8, 6)\}$

Hence, $fog = \{(4, 10), (10, 4), (2, 10)\}$ and $gof = \{(2, 6), (6, 2), (8, 6)\}$.

47. $\int (x^6+x^3+1)\,d(x^3)$

Let, $x^3 = t$

$$\therefore \int (t^2+t+1)\,dt = \frac{t^3}{3}+\frac{t^2}{2}+t+C$$

$$= \frac{x^9}{3}+\frac{x^6}{2}+x^3+C$$

48. $\begin{bmatrix} x & a & x+a \\ y & b & y+b \\ z & c & z+c \end{bmatrix}$

$= x[b(z + c) - c(y + b)] - a[y(z + c) - z(y + b)] + (x + a)(yc - zb)$

$= x[bz + bc - cy - bc] - a[yz + cy - yz - bz] + (xyc - xbz + acy - azb)$

$= xbz - cxy - acy + abz + cxy - bxz + acy - abz$

$= 0.$

49. $\because \quad f(x) = \sin x + \sqrt{3}\cos x$

Let, $\quad y = \sin x + \sqrt{3}\cos x$

$$\frac{dy}{dx} = \cos x - \sqrt{3}\sin x$$

For maximum value,

$$\frac{dy}{dx} = 0$$

$$\Rightarrow \quad \cos x - \sqrt{3}\sin x = 0$$

$$\Rightarrow \quad \sqrt{3}\sin x = \cos x$$

$$\Rightarrow \quad \tan x = \frac{1}{\sqrt{3}} = \tan\frac{\pi}{6}$$

$$\Rightarrow \quad x = \frac{\pi}{6}.$$

50. $\lim_{x\to 0}\left(\frac{1+5x^2}{1+3x^2}\right)^{\frac{1}{x^2}}$

$$\left[\lim_{x\to 0}(f(x))^{g(x)} = e^{\lim_{x\to 0}(g(x)(f(x)-1))}\right]$$

$$= e^{\lim_{x\to 0}\frac{2x^2}{1+3x^2}\cdot x^2} = e^{\lim_{x\to 0}\frac{2}{1+3x^2}} = e^2.$$

51. $\sin\left(\sin^{-1}\frac{1}{2} + \cos^{-1}x\right) = 1$

$$\Rightarrow \quad \sin^{-1}\frac{1}{2} + \cos^{-1}x = \frac{\pi}{2}$$

$$\Rightarrow \quad \sin^{-1}\frac{1}{2} = \frac{\pi}{2} - \cos^{-1}x$$

$$\Rightarrow \quad \sin^{-1}\frac{1}{2} = \sin^{-1}x$$

$$\Rightarrow \quad x = \frac{1}{2}.$$

52. $\begin{bmatrix} x+y+z \\ x+z \\ y+z \end{bmatrix} = \begin{bmatrix} 9 \\ 5 \\ 7 \end{bmatrix}$

$\because \quad x + y + z = 9 \quad \ldots(i)$

$x + z = 5 \quad \ldots(ii)$

$y + z = 7 \quad \ldots(iii)$

From (*i*) and (*iii*)

$$x = 9 - 7 = 2.$$

53.

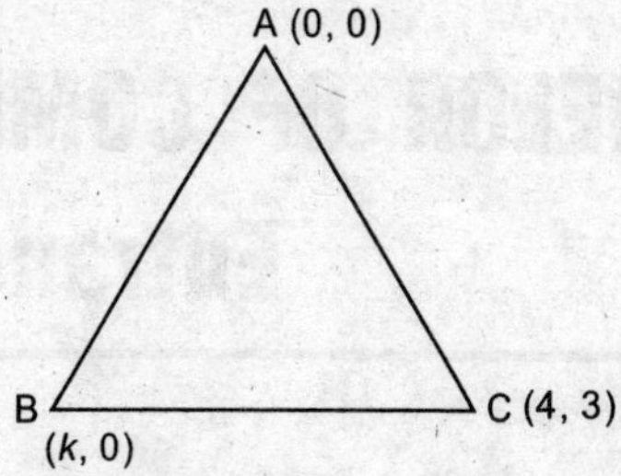

Area of triangle

$$= \frac{1}{2}\left[x_1(y_2 - y_3) + x_2(y_3 - y_1) + x_3(y_1 - y_2)\right]$$

$$\Rightarrow \quad 12 = \frac{1}{2}[0(0-3) + k(3-0) + 4(0-0)]$$

$$\Rightarrow \quad 24 = 3k$$

$$\Rightarrow \quad k = 8.$$

54. Required probability $= \frac{^5C_2}{^7C_2}$

$$= \frac{\frac{5\times 4\times 3!}{3!\times 2!}}{\frac{7\times 6\times 5!}{5!\times 2!}} = \frac{10}{21}.$$

82. $2 \times {}^{20}C_2 = 2\times\frac{20\times 19\times 18!}{18!\times 2!}$

$= 2 \times 10 \times 19 = 380.$

83.

63	:	80	: :	15	:	24
↓		↓		↓		↓
$8^2 - 1$		$9^2 - 1$		$4^2 - 1$		$5^2 - 1$

Hence, the missing number in the second pair = 24.

84. $\because$ Vikram's shadow fell exactly towards left-hand side in the morning. It means. Vikram was standing in North direction facing.

$\therefore$ They were standing with their backs towards each other.

Hence, direction of Shailesh facing was in South.

97. $\because$ Weep is fixed at Tuesday, Before Lament Sob would be telecast and immediately after or before Wail would be telecast,

So Moan soaps can be telecast on Monday.

Previous Paper (Solved)

BACHELOR OF COMPUTER APPLICATIONS (BCA) Entrance Exam–2017

1. What geometric figure does the equation $x^2 + y - 5x + 10 = 0$ represent?
A. Straight Line B. Circle
C. Parabola D. None of these

2. Which of the following has emerged as India's best university in a countrywide National Institute Ranking Framework (NIRF) of educational institutes released recently?
A. IISc., Bangalore
B. University of Delhi
C. JNU, New Delhi
D. BHU, Varanasi

3. Which of the following is the 'First Green Train Corridor' inaugurated by the Railway Minister in July, 2016?
A. Rameshwaram – Munamadurai
B. Kalka – Shimla Junction
C. Delhi – Varanasi
D. Jammu – Katra

4. The matrix A of order $n \times n$ is given by $A = I - X(X'X)^{-1} X'$ where I is an identity matrix and X′ is the transpose of X. What can you conclude about the order of X?
A. X has n rows
B. X has n columns
C. X has n rows and n columns
D. None of these

5. Among the options given choose the word that is spelt incorrectly:
(*i*) Tiptoing (*ii*) Tippling
(*iii*) Tattletale (*iv*) Contiguous
A. (*i*) B. (*ii*)
C. (*iii*) D. (*iv*)

6. Leukaemia is:
A. Cancer of the blood
B. Deformation of bones in human body
C. A disease which makes bones brittle
D. Cancer of glands

7. Which bank has launched a unique credit card 'UNNATI' for which any customer with a balance of at least ₹ 25000 in his/her savings account with the bank would be eligible?
A. HDFC Bank
B. ICICI Bank
C. Axis Bank
D. SBI

8. Find the word closest in meaning to the word "LOQUACITY"
A. misery
B. fantasy
C. repetition
D. talkativeness

9. The area enclosed between the curves $y^2 = x$ and $y = x$ is:
A. $\frac{2}{3}$ B. $\frac{1}{2}$
C. $\frac{1}{3}$ D. $\frac{1}{6}$

10. The domain and range respectively of the function $f(x) = \sqrt{x^2 + 1}$ are:
A. $(-\infty, -1] \cup [1, \infty]$ and $[1, \infty]$
B. $(-\infty, \infty)$ and $(-\infty, -1] \cup [1, \infty)$
C. $(-\infty, -1] \cup [1, \infty]$ and $(-\infty, -1] \cup [1, \infty)$
D. $(-\infty, \infty)$ and $[-\infty, -1] \cup [1, \infty)$

11. Match the following:

Person	Field
(*a*) Bhavish Aggarwal	(*i*) Ola
(*b*) Binny Bansal	(*ii*) Bandhan Bank
(*c*) Chandra Shekhar Ghosh	(*iii*) Yes Bank
(*d*) Rana Kapoor	(*iv*) Flipkart

	(*a*)	(*b*)	(*c*)	(*d*)
A.	(*ii*)	(*iii*)	(*i*)	(*iv*)
B.	(*i*)	(*ii*)	(*iii*)	(*iv*)
C.	(*i*)	(*iv*)	(*ii*)	(*iii*)
D.	(*iii*)	(*ii*)	(*i*)	(*iv*)

12. Two dice are tossed once. The probability of getting an even number on the first die or a total of 8 is:

A. $\frac{1}{36}$ B. $\frac{3}{36}$

C. $\frac{11}{36}$ D. None of the above

13. $\sum_{i=1}^{n}(X_i - A)^2$ equals:

A. $\sum_{i=1}^{n} X_i^2 - 2A\sum_{i=1}^{n} X_i + A^2$

B. $\sum_{i=1}^{n} X_i^2 - 2nA\sum_{i=1}^{n} X_i + nA^2$

C. $\sum_{i=1}^{n} X_i^2 - 2A\sum_{i=1}^{n} X_i + nA^2$

D. $\sum_{i=1}^{n} X_i^2 - 2nA\sum_{i=1}^{n} X_i + n^2A^2$

14. Choose the option that fits the blank to complete the sentence.

There are .... views on the issue of giving bonus to employees.

A. Independent B. Divergent

C. Modest D. Adverse

15. UDAY is:

A. Scheme related to urban youth

B. A plan for the development of urban infrastructure

C. Plan to aid ailing electricity distribution companies

D. Scheme for the development of university infrastructure

16. The idiom "mind your P's and Q's" means:

A. behave politely and follow social conventions

B. spell correctly

C. write legibly and correctly

D. ignore minor details

17. In the following question, two statements numbered I and II are given.

There may be cause and effect relationship between the two statements. These two statements may be the effect of the same cause or independent causes. These statements may be independent causes without having any relationship. Read both the statements in the question and mark your answer accordingly.

I. The school authority has started special coaching classes for XII Std. Students after school hours.

II. The parents of the XII Std. Students have withdrawn their wards from private coaching classes.

A. Statement I is the cause and statement II is its effect

B. Statement II is the cause and statement I is its effect

C. Both the statements I and II are independent causes

D. Both the statements I and II are effects of some common causes

18. The derivative of the function $y = \sqrt{x}(x+1)^5 e^x$ at $x = 1$ is:

A. $128e$ B. 4

C. $32e$ D. $96e$

19. The question given below is followed by two statements, I and II. Study the information given in the two statements and assess whether the statements are sufficient to answer the question and choose the appropriate option from among the choices given below.

What percentage of questions were attempted by Ramya in the exam?

I. 30% of the questions are attempted by both Ramya and Swathi.

II. The number of questions attempted by Ramya but not by Swathi is $\left(\frac{5}{8}\right)^{th}$ of the total number of questions attempted by Ramya.

A. The question can be answered by using one of the statements alone but not by the other.
B. The question can be answered by using either statement alone.
C. The question can be answered by using both the statements together, but cannot be answered by using either statement alone.
D. The question cannot be answered even by using both the statements together.

20. What is the rank of India on the 2016 Global Hunger Index (GHI) released by the International Food Policy Research Institute (IFPRI)?

A. 80 B. 55
C. 97 D. 30

21. The idiom "at a stone's throw" means:

A. make a correct choice
B. a short distance
C. aim accurately
D. pelt stones at the enemy

22. Examine the statements I, II and III and answer.

I. The mean, median and mode of any set of numbers are smaller than the maximum number in the set.

II. The standard deviation of a set of numbers is always positive.

III. In a set of numbers, the number of elements that are smaller than the mean is always equal to the number of elements that are larger than the mean.

A. I and II are true
B. I and III are true
C. II and III are true
D. I, II and III are true

23. All of the following categories are covered under priority sector except one. Identify that one.

A. Social Infrastructure
B. Micro, Small and Medium Enterprises (MSME)
C. Consumer Finance
D. Renewable Energy

24. Choose the option that fits the blank to complete the sentence.

Man who has committed such an .... crime must get the most severe punishment.

A. Injurious B. Uncharitable
C. Unworthy D. Abominable

25. Find the word closest in meaning to the word "AUDACIOUS":

A. Useless B. Bold
C. Foolish D. Necessary

26. Among the options given, choose the word that is spelt incorrectly:

(*i*) Aggressive (*ii*) Counterfiet
(*iii*) Arrival (*iv*) Serendipity

A. (*i*) B. (*ii*)
C. (*iii*) D. (*iv*)

27. Which state has the lowest sex ratio in India as per Census 2011?

A. Haryana B. Sikkim
C. Uttar Pradesh D. Punjab

28. The following question consists of a question followed by two statements numbered I and II given below it. You have to decide whether the data provided in the statements are sufficient to answer the question. Read both the statements and give the answer.

If X's age is exactly twice of Y's age, what is X's age?

I. Eight years ago X's age was exactly three times Y's age.

II. Ten years from now, X's age will be exactly 1.5 times Y's age.

A. The data in the statement I alone is sufficient to answer the question, but the data in statement II alone is not sufficient to answer the question
B. The data in the statement II alone is sufficient to answer the question, but the data in statement I alone is not sufficient to answer the question
C. Data in both statement I and statement II together are necessary to answer the question
D. The data either in statement I alone or in statement II alone is sufficient to answer the question

29. In the following question, two statements numbered I and II are given.

There may be cause and effect relationship between the two statements. These two statements may be the effect of the same cause or independent causes. These statements may be independent causes without having any relationship. Read both the statements in the question and mark your answer accordingly.

I. There has been a steady increase in the per capita income of people in India in recent years.
II. There is a substantial increase in the literacy rate of India.

A. Statement I is the cause and statement II is its effect
B. Statement II is the cause and statement I is its effect
C. Both the statements I and II are independent causes
D. Both the statements I and II are effects of some common causes

30. The most suitable antonym for the word "Affectation" will be:

A. Revengeful B. Affectionate
C. Concentration D. Artlessness

31. A and B are two independent events where $P(A \cup B) = 0.7$ and $P(A) = 0.4$. What is the value of P(B)?

A. 0.3 B. 0.5
C. 0.6 D. 0.7

32. Headquarters of International Red Cross is situated at:

A. Paris B. The Hague
C. Geneva D. Vienna

33. The courier charges for sending packages to a certain destination are ₹ 65 for the first 250 gms and ₹ 10 for each additional 100 grams of part thereof. If the charge for a package is ₹ 155, what could be its weight in grams?

A. 1155 B. 1145
C. 1040 D. 950

34. Bob Dylan, the Nobel prize winner for Literature in 2016 is a:

A. sportsperson B. philanthropist
C. songwriter D. novelist

35. Four boys Monu, Baba, Tilu and Addi are standing on a ladder. Monu is further up the ladder than Baba. Baba is in between Monu and Tilu. If Addi is further up than Monu, then who is the second boy from the bottom?

A. Monu
B. Baba
C. Tilu
D. Cannot be determined

36. A, B, C, D, E and 0 are matrices of order $n \times n$. It is known that $A \cdot B = A \cdot C$ and $D \cdot E = 0$.

Examine the statements I and II and choose the correct option.

I. $B = C$ II. $D = 0$ or $E = 0$

A. I is true B. II is true
C. I and II are true D. None of these

37. Exchange rate in India is determined by:

A. RBI
B. Forces of Demand and Supply
C. IMF
D. Finance ministry

38. In the following question, some symbols have been used for certain mathematical operations as indicated below: × for "greater than"; © for "not less than"; ÷ for "not equal to"; ϕ for "equal to"; + for "not greater than"; Δ for "less than". Using these symbols, choose the correct alternative for the following question:

If $p \times q \; \Delta \; r$, it follows that:

A. $r + q © p$ B. $p © q + r$
C. $q © p \times r$ D. $p \; \phi \; r \; \Delta \; q$

39. In the diagram provided, ASB is a quarter circle and PQRS is a rectangle with sides PQ = 8 and PS = 6.

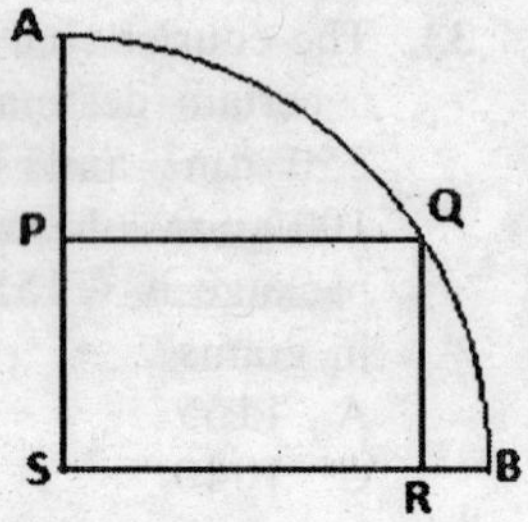

What is the length of the arc AQB?

A. 5π B. 10π
C. 14π D. 14

40. Find the word closest in meaning to the word "FUDDLE"

A. Focus B. Confuse
C. Cheat D. Fudge

41. The word "Magniloquent" means:

A. Mean-minded B. Humorous
C. Miserly D. Boastful

42. In the following question, some symbols have been used for certain mathematical operations as indicated below: × for "greater than"; © for "not less than"; ÷ for "not equal to"; ϕ for "equal to"; + for "not greater than"; Δ for "less than". Using these symbols, choose the correct alternative for the following question.

If $p \Delta q \Delta r$, it does not imply that:

A. $p \times r \times q$ B. $p \; \Delta \; r \times q$
C. $r \times q \times p$ D. $q \times p \; \Delta \; r$

43. The shape of the curve $y = x^2 - 8x + 18$ is best represented by the sketch:

A.

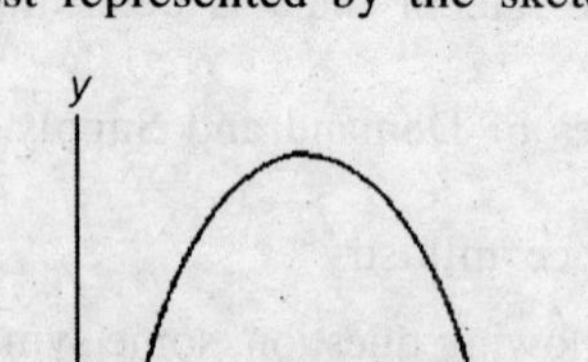

B.

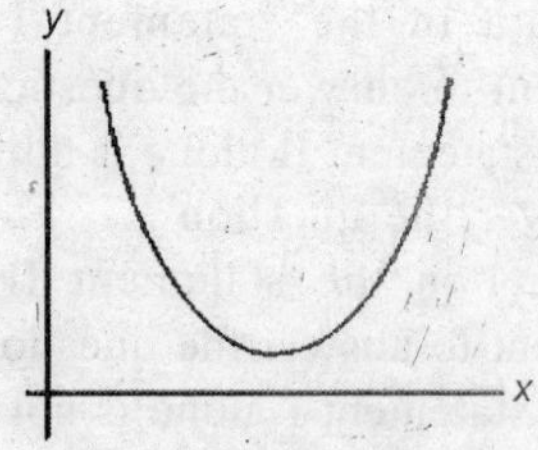

C.

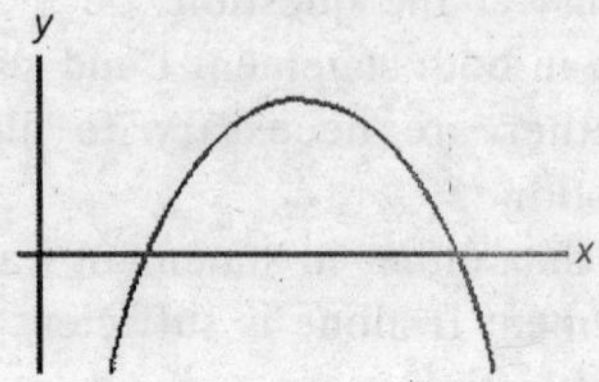

D.

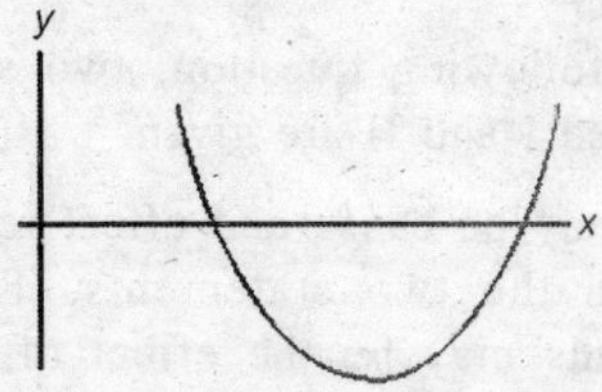

44. Which of the following is/are true:

(*i*) Qatar is the largest exporter of LNG (Liquefied Natural Gas)
(*ii*) Saudi Arabia is the largest exporter of Petroleum oil.
(*iii*) Qatar and Saudi Arabia are the members of GCC (Gulf Cooperation Council)
(*iv*) Qatar is host of FIFA World Cup 2022

A. (*i*), (*ii*) and (*iii*) only
B. (*i*), (*ii*) and (*iv*) only
C. (*ii*), (*iii*) and (*iv*) only
D. All of the above

45. Four equal circles are drawn about the four corners of a square so that each touches two of the others. If each side of the square is 14 cm, then the area of the square not covered by the circles is:

A. 44 sq. cm B. 42 sq. cm
C. 54 sq. cm D. 52 sq. cm

46. Which among the following is the longest bridge over water in India:

A. Dhola Sadiya Bridge
B. Mahatma Gandhi Setu
C. Bandra Worli Sea Link
D. Vikramshila Setu

47. Two equal circles of maximum possible size are cut out of a rectangular card of size 16 cm by 8 cm. What is the approximate area of the card paper left after removing the circles?

A. 13 cm^2 B. 27 cm^2
C. 54 cm^2 D. 104 cm^2

48. MPC is a:

A. Parliamentary committee that looks after civil matters
B. Committee that formulates monetary policy of India
C. A big multinational company
D. Multilateral forum that decides policy on common interest for member countries

49. Among the options given, choose the word that is spelt incorrectly:

(*i*) Picnicking (*ii*) Fraudulent
(*iii*) Froliking (*iv*) Filing

A. (*i*) B. (*ii*)
C. (*iii*) D. (*iv*)

50. Half the people on a bus get off at each stop after the first, and no one gets on after the first stop. If only one person gets off at stop number 7, how many people got on to the bus at the first stop?

A. 128 B. 64
C. 32 D. 16

51. A cube of edge 6 cm is melted and smaller cubes of edge 2 cm each are formed. How many such cubes are possible?

A. 21 B. 22
C. 27 D. 26

52. Choose the option that fits the blank to complete the sentence.

Although he never learnt to read, his exceptional memory and enquiring mind eventually made him a very .... man.

A. Dedicated B. Erudite
C. Pragmatic D. Benevolent

53. Bank rate is:

A. The interest rate at which a nation's central bank lends money to domestic banks.
B. The interest rate at which a bank lends money to its customers.
C. The interest rate at which a bank lends money to nation's central bank.
D. The interest rate at which a nation's central bank lends money to foreign banks.

54. Choose the correct word or phrase to complete the English grammar question.

I'll .... their cat while they are away on holiday.

A. be looking into B. be looking at
C. be looking after D. be looking over

55. The idiom "face the music" means:

A. conduct a choir
B. work as a music director
C. accept difficult or unpleasant consequences
D. attend a music concert

56. If TRIANGLE is coded as SSHBMHKF in a certain code. SQUARE should be coded as:

A. RRIASF B. RRTBQF
C. RPVBSF D. RPVBSD

57. Look at this series: F2, ___, D8, C16, B32,... What number should fill the blank?

A. A16 B. G4
C. E4 D. E3

58. Choose the option that fits the blank to complete the sentence.

Rajeev failed in the examination because none of his answers were .... to the questions asked.

A. Allusive B. Revealing
C. Pertinent D. Referential

59. Which bank recently introduced a range of Gender neutral titles (Mx, Ind, M, Mre, Msr, Myr, PR, Sai, Ser and Misc) for transgender and other customers who don't identify as male or female.

A. Citibank
B. Standard Chartered
C. Barclays
D. HSBC

60. The domain of $f(x) = \ln(2 - x) + \ln(3 - x)$ is given by:

A. $(-\infty, 2)$ B. $(2, 3)$
C. $(-\infty, 3)$ D. $(-\infty, 2)$

61. Among the options given, choose the word that is spelt incorrectly:

(*i*) Infinity (*ii*) Foundling
(*iii*) Mimiking (*iv*) Arguable

A. (*i*) B. (*ii*)
C. (*iii*) D. (*iv*)

62. The system of linear equations:

$$(4d - 1)x + y + z = 0$$
$$-y + z = 0 \text{ and } (4d - 1)z = 0$$

has a trivial solution, if d equals:

A. 1/2 B. 1/4
C. 3/4 D. 1

63. The following question consists of a question followed by two statements numbered I and II given below it. You have to decide whether the data provided in the statements are sufficient to answer the question. Read both the statements and give the answer.

Among five boys A, B, C, D, E and F, who is the tallest?

I. D is taller than A and C.
II. B is shorter than E but taller to D.

A. Data in the statement I alone is sufficient to answer the question, but the data in statement II alone is not sufficient to answer the question
B. The data in the statement II alone is sufficient to answer the question, but the data in statement I alone is not sufficient to answer the question
C. Data in both statement I and statement II together are necessary to answer the question
D. The data either in statement I alone or in statement II alone is sufficient to answer the question

64. Rate of interest on savings account is determined by:

A. RBI
B. Ministry of Finance
C. Indian Bank Association
D. Individual Banks

65. There are 3 Mathematics, 4 Physics and 1 Chemistry books and they are placed in a shelf. The probability that the books of the same subject is placed together is:

A. $\frac{3}{140}$ B. $\frac{1}{40}$
C. $\frac{9}{70}$ D. $\frac{1}{18}$

66. The current budget allocation for national skill development is:

A. 100 Crores B. 500 Crores
C. 1000 Crores D. 2000 Crores

67. Which one of the following is NOT true about 'BrahMos'?

A. It is a supersonic cruise missile
B. Its full range is 290 km
C. It's a joint venture between India and France
D. It was test fired from Bay of Bengal off Visakhapatnam

68. N.K. Singh Committee was constituted to recommend the Government of India in the field of:

A. Goods and Services Taxes (GST)
B. Fiscal Responsibility and Budget Management Act
C. Power sharing between the center and state
D. Judicial Activism

69. The river Satluj originates in

A. Jammu and Kashmir
B. Himachal Pradesh
C. Uttarakhand
D. Tibet

70. The idiom "the sword of Damocles" means:

A. the sharpest sword in the world
B. an imminent danger
C. the sword presented to Damocles
D. have a sharp tongue

71. The most suitable antonym for the word "Abet" will be:

A. Gamble B. Deter
C. Pray D. Release

72. FMCG stands for:
A. Fast Multiplying Consumer Goods
B. Fast Moving Consumer Goods
C. Fast and More Consumed Goods
D. Free Market Consumption Goods

73. Which team was defeated by India to claim eleventh junior hockey world cup 2016?
A. Germany B. Australia
C. Netherlands D. Belgium

74. If the system of equations $3x - 2y + z = 0$, $kx - 14y + 15z = 0$, $x + 2y + 3z = 0$ has a nontrivial solution then $k =$
A. 9 B. 29
C. 39 D. 19

75. If there is a loss of 11 per cent in selling an article at ₹ 178, at what price should it be sold to earn a profit of 11 per cent?
A. 200 B. 232
C. 222 D. 242

76. The most suitable antonym for the word "Temerity" will be:
A. Caution B. Bold
C. Sourness D. Preparedness

77. Which of the following has launched 'Dulari Kanya' a special scheme to check infant mortality in the state?
A. Himachal Pradesh
B. Haryana
C. Uttar Pradesh
D. Arunachal Pradesh

78. Choose the correct word or phrase to complete the English grammar question.

He made his children .... their homework every afternoon.
A. do B. to do
C. studied D. to study

79. The value of $9^{\frac{1}{3}} \times 9^{\frac{1}{9}} \times 9^{\frac{1}{27}} \times$ ....
A. 9 B. 1
C. 3 D. None of these

80. Consider the circle $x^2 + y^2 = 14x$. The point (6, –7) is:
A. On the circle
B. In the circle
C. Outside the circle
D. Cannot be ascertained

81. Ms. Harita Kaur has the distinction of being the first Indian woman
A. to be inducted in Indian Army
B. Doctor to create test tube baby
C. Pilot to fly an aircraft solo in the IAF
D. Ambassador to a foreign country

82. 'Ace against Odds' is the autobiography of:
A. P. Gopichand B. Saina Nehwal
C. M.S. Dhoni D. Sania Mirza

83. GST Bill 2014 is related to which of the following constitutional amendments?
A. 100 B. 115
C. 121 D. 122

Directions (Qs. No. 84-87): *Five friends, Amol, Mandar, Piyu, Shashi and Reena attended Sagar's birthday party, where they partook of the sumptuous snacks and dinner. Each of the five friends gifted Sagar a different article – a fountain pen, a cellphone, a shirt, a jacket and an I-Pod and Sagar, in return gifted each of them a different article – a video game, a sweater, a perfume, a calculator and a pair of sunglasses. The following is additional information about the gifts given by the friends and the gifts received from Sagar.*

- Amol gifted the shirt and received the video game in return.
- Shashi did not gift the I-Pod, but received the perfume in return.
- Mandar did not gift an electronic item and received the calculator in return.
- The person who gifted the jacket received the sweater in return and Reena received the pair of sunglasses.

84. Who among the following gifted the jacket?
A. Mandar B. Shashi
C. Reena D. None of these

85. Which of the following statements is true?
A. Two of the friends who did not gift electronic items, received electronic items in return
B. Piyu gifted the jacket and Shashi gifted the I-Pod
C. Shashi neither gifted nor did he receive an electronic item
D. The person who gifted the cellphone received the calculator in return

86. Which of the following is the correct combination of friend, article gifted and article received in return?
A. Piyu-Fountain Pen-Sunglasses
B. Shashi-I-Pod-Perfume
C. Reena-I-Pod-Sunglasses
D. None of these

87. Which of the following is false?
A. Only one friend whose name does not start with a vowel, received an electronic item in return.
B. The friend whose name appears last in alphabetical order, gifted an electronic item and received a non-electronic item in return
C. In alphabetical order the friend who gifted the I-Pod appears before atleast two other friends
D. The friend whose name in alphabetical order appears in the middle neither gifted nor received an electronic item

Directions (Qs. No. 88-91): *Answer the question on the basis of the information given below.*

Mr. Suzuki, a car dealer, sold cars of only two brands, A and B, in the previous year. This year, he introduced a new brand, C. The number of cars of brand A and brand B sold in the previous year were in the ratio 3 : 2, and the ratio of the number of cars sold in the previous year to that sold in this year is 2 : 3 for brand A and 2 : 5 for brand B. Further, the number of cars of brand C sold this year forms 81% of the total number of cars sold this year.

88. Find the number of cars of brand C sold this year, given that a total of 24 cars of brand A were sold in the previous year.
A. 324 B. 648
C. 162 D. 243

89. What is the percentage increase in the total number of cars sold this year when compared to the total number of cars sold in the previous year?
A. 400% B. 600%
C. 900% D. 1000%

90. In the next year, Mr. Suzuki wants to increase sales by 80%, compared to the total sales this year, by keeping the sales of each of A, B and C at the same level as that in this year and introducing a new brand D. By what per cent will the number of cars of brand D (to be sold next year) be more than the total number of cars sold last year?
A. 400% B. 600%
C. 900% D. 700%

91. If a total of 380 cars were sold this year, and the sales of C this year were nil, instead of 81% of total sales, then how many cars of brand A were sold in the previous year?
A. 140 B. 120
C. 100 D. 160

Directions (Qs. No. 92-96): *Answer on the basis of the information given below.*

Five roommates – Randy, Sally, Terry, Uma and Vernon – each do one housekeeping task – mopping, sweeping, laundry, vacuuming, or dusting – one day a week, Monday through Friday.

- Vernon does not vacuum and does not do his task on Tuesday
- Sally does the dusting, and does not do it on Monday or Friday
- The mopping is done on Thursday
- Terry does his task, which is not vacuuming, on Wednesday
- The laundry is done on Friday, and not by Uma
- Randy does his task on Monday

92. When does Sally do the dusting?
A. Friday B. Monday
C. Tuesday D. Wednesday

93. What task does Terry do on Wednesday?
A. Vacuuming B. Dusting
C. Mopping D. Sweeping

94. What day is the vacuuming done?
A. Friday B. Monday
C. Tuesday D. Wednesday

95. What task does Vernon do?
A. Vacuuming B. Dusting
C. Mopping D. Laundry

96. What day does Uma do her task?
A. Monday B. Tuesday
C. Wednesday D. Thursday

Directions (Qs. No. 97-100): *Read the following passage and answer questions that follow.*

In economics as in most other disciplines, we use models to illustrate complex subjects, such as relationships between the economy and the environment. In using these models, however, we should also be sensitive to their limitations. Models are simplified characterizations of reality. For example, although a road map, by design, leaves out a lot, it is a useful guide to reality. The map shows how various locations relate to each other and gives an overall perspective. It cannot, however, capture the unique details which characterize any particular location. The map highlights only those characteristics that are crucial for the purpose at hand. Through simplification, less is held in view so that more can be understood of what is retained. Models allow us to rigorously study issues which are interrelated and global in scale, but through their selectivity, models may yield conclusions that are wrong. What is omitted may turn out, in retrospect, to be crucial in understanding a particular dimension. Models are therefore useful abstractions that should always be viewed with scepticism.

97. "A map gives an overall perspective" means:
A. a map simplifies reality
B. a map highlights important characteristics
C. a map provides a complete picture
D. a map provides a useful guide to reality

98. Models simplify reality because:
A. their conclusions may be wrong
B. what they omit may be crucial
C. more can be understood of what is included
D. they should be viewed with scepticism

99. Which of these statements follow from the above:
(*i*) A model is a map.
(*ii*) A map is a model.
(*iii*) Models characterize reality.
(*iv*) Maps are used in economics.
A. (*i*) B. (*iii*)
C. (*ii*) and (*iii*) D. (*iv*)

100. Models are used to:
A. show buildings
B. make maps
C. illustrate relationships
D. hide limitations

ANSWERS

1	2	3	4	5	6	7	8	9	10
C	A	A	A	A	A	D	D	D	B
11	**12**	**13**	**14**	**15**	**16**	**17**	**18**	**19**	**20**
C	D	C	B	C	A	A	A	C	C
21	**22**	**23**	**24**	**25**	**26**	**27**	**28**	**29**	**30**
B	A	C	D	B	B	A	D	B	D
31	**32**	**33**	**34**	**35**	**36**	**37**	**38**	**39**	**40**
B	C	B	C	B	D	B	B	A	B
41	**42**	**43**	**44**	**45**	**46**	**47**	**48**	**49**	**50**
D	C	B	D	B	A	B	B	C	A

51	52	53	54	55	56	57	58	59	60
C	B	A	C	C	B	C	C	D	A
61	**62**	**63**	**64**	**65**	**66**	**67**	**68**	**69**	**70**
C	B	C	D	A	C	C	B	D	B
71	**72**	**73**	**74**	**75**	**76**	**77**	**78**	**79**	**80**
B	B	D	B	C	A	D	A	C	C
81	**82**	**83**	**84**	**85**	**86**	**87**	**88**	**89**	**90**
C	D	D	D	A	C	C	A	C	D
91	**92**	**93**	**94**	**95**	**96**	**97**	**98**	**99**	**100**
B	C	D	B	D	D	D	C	C	C

EXPLANATORY ANSWERS

1. $x^2 + y - 5x + 10 = 0$

$$y + x^2 - 2 \times x \times \frac{5}{2} + \left(\frac{5}{2}\right)^2 - \left(\frac{5}{2}\right)^2 + 10 = 0$$

$$\left(x - \frac{5}{2}\right)^2 + y + \frac{15}{4} = 0$$

$$\left(x - \frac{5}{2}\right)^2 = -\left(y - \frac{15}{4}\right)$$

This is equation of parabola.

2. Union human resources development (HRD) minister Prakash Javadekar released the India Rankings of National Institutional Ranking Framework (NIRF) in New Delhi under nine categories – overall, universities, engineering, colleges, management, pharmacy, medical, architecture, and law this year. The Indian Institute of Science, Bangalore and Delhi's Miranda House are India's best university and college this year, according to the countrywide government ranking of educational institutions.

3. The nation's first Green Rail Corridor, a 114-km long Rameswaram-Munamadurai stretch in Tamil Nadu which ensures zero toilet discharge on rail tracks, inaugurated by Railways Minister Suresh Prabhu in July, 2016.

Trains in the section have been equipped with bio-toilets ensuring zero discharge of human waste on the rail tracks.

4. From matrix properties

$$X'\cdot X = X^{-1}\cdot X = I$$

Now, $A = I - X(X'\cdot X)^{-1}X^{1}$

$A = I - X(I)^{-1}X'$

$A = I - X(I)^{-1}\cdot X'$

Again, matrix A has n rows.

So, X has n number of rows.

5. Correct word is tiptoing. It mean to move or go on tiptoe, as with caution or stealth.

6. Leukaemia is a cancer which starts in blood-forming tissue, usually the bone marrow. It leads to the over-production of abnormal white blood cells, the part of the immune system which defends the body against infection.

7. Aiming to bring more users in the digital fold, the State Bank of India has launched 'Unnati' (credit) card for its customers holding an account with a minimum balance of ₹ 25,000.

SBI Unnati Credit Card is an entry-level credit card for first-time users. If you are looking for your first credit card, this could be a good fit for you. The card charges an annual fee of ₹ 499 which is **waived off for the first four years**. The **reward rate** of the card is **0.25%.** The card charges a low-interest rate of 2.50% per month.

9. Point of intersection of $y^2 = x$ and $y = x$

$$y^2 = y \Rightarrow y^2 - y = 0$$

$$y(y-1) = 0 \Rightarrow y = 0 \text{ and } 1$$

Area enclosed by the curve:

$$A = \left|\int_0^1 (y - y^2)\cdot dy\right|$$

$$= \left|\frac{y^2}{2} - \frac{y^3}{3}\right|_0^1$$

$$= \frac{1}{2} - \frac{1}{3} = \frac{1}{6}.$$

10. $y = f(x) = \sqrt{x^2+1}$

Domain of $f(x)$:

Function $\sqrt{x^2+1}$ is defined for all x, so, domain = $(-\infty, \infty)$

Range of $f(x)$:

$$y = \sqrt{x^2+1}$$

$$y^2 = x^2 + 1$$

$$x = \sqrt{y^2-1}$$

This is defined for $(-\infty, -1] \cup [1, \infty)$

Hence, correct option is (B).

11. (*i*) **Bhavish Aggarwal** (born 28 August, 1985 in Ludhiana, Punjab) is an Indian entrepreneur and co-founder of Ola Cabs. In January, 2011 he co-founded Ola Cabs with Ankit Bhati in Mumbai. In 2015 Aggarwal and Bhati were the youngest to be included in that year's list of richest Indians.

(*ii*) **Binny Bansal** is an Indian software engineer and Internet entrepreneur. In 2007, he co-founded the e-commerce platform Flipkart with Sachin Bansal (not related) and was serving as the Chief Operating Officer until 11 January, 2016 and was promoted to Chief Executive Officer. In January, 2017 he was promoted to Group CEO .

(*iii*) **Chandra Shekhar Ghosh** born in 1960 at Bishalgarh in Tripura India, is the founder and chairman managing director of Bandhan, the first micro finance company to receive banking license in India. Ghosh started his first venture named Bandhan Konnagar an NGO in November, 2001 with a capital of INR 200000 ($3200) and three employees at Kolkata, West Bengal. The NGO provided finance to small and marginal women entrepreneurs in areas not assisted by banks. In 2009, Ghosh registered Bandhan as an NBFC (Non Banking Finance Company) with the Reserve Bank of India.

In 2014, the Reserve Bank of India granted an approval for banking license to Bandhan.

(*iv*) **Rana Kapoor** (born 9 September, 1957) is an Indian billionaire, and the founder, managing director and CEO of Yes Bank, an Indian private sector bank, with its registered office in Mumbai.

12. In tossing of two dice,

Sample space $n(s) = 6 \times 6 = 36$

Sample event (E_1) of getting even number of first dice = (2,1), (2,2), (2,3), (2,4), (2,5), (2,6), (4,1), (4,2), (4,3), (4,4), (4,5), (4,6), (6,1), (6,2), (6,3), (6,4), (6,5), (6,6)

$$n(E_1) = 18$$

Same event of getting a total 8(E_2)

= (2,6), (3,5), (4,4), (5,3), (6,2)

$$n(E_2) = 5$$

Common event $(E_1 \cap E_2)$

= (2,6), (4,4), (6,2)

$$n(E_1 \cap E_2) = 3$$

Hence, required probability

$$= \frac{18+5-3}{36} = \frac{20}{36}.$$

13. $\sum_{i=1}^{n} (X_i - A)^2$

$$= \sum_{i=1}^{n} X_i^2 - 2A\cdot\sum_{i=1}^{n} X_i + (A^2 + A^2 + A^2 \ldots + n \text{ times})$$

$$= \sum_{i=1}^{n} X_i^2 - 2A\sum_{i=1}^{n} X_i + nA^2.$$

15. The government's Ujjwal Discom Assurance Yojna (UDAY) Scheme to aid ailing electricity distribution companies (discoms) has a better chance of succeeding than the previous financial restructuring plan.

Under UDAY, state governments will take over 75 per cent of the debt held by their discoms as of September 30, 2015. Half the debt will be taken over in 2015-16 and 25 per cent in 2016-17. The balance 25 per cent of the debt is to be serviced through state government-guaranteed bonds issued by the discoms.

16. **Mind your Ps and Qs** is an English language expression meaning "mind your manners", "mind your language", "be on your best behaviour" or similar.

17. As the coaching classes started in the school so, there is no need for private coaching for the student of class-XII.

Here, coaching classes has been started for student XII by the school authority. As a effect of that parents of the students have withdrawn their wards from private coaching classes.

Hence, statement I is cause and statement II is its effect.

18.
$$y = \sqrt{x}(x+1)^5 \cdot e^x$$
$$y = e^x \cdot (x)^{\frac{1}{2}}(x+1)^5$$
$$= e^x \cdot \left(x^{\frac{1}{10}}\right)^5 (x+1)^5$$
$$= e^x \cdot \left(x \cdot x^{\frac{1}{10}} + x^{\frac{1}{10}}\right)^5$$
$$\Rightarrow \quad y = e^x \left(x^{\frac{11}{10}} + x^{\frac{1}{10}}\right)^5$$
$$y' = e^x \left(x^{\frac{11}{10}} + x^{\frac{1}{10}}\right)^5 + e^x \cdot 5\left(x^{\frac{11}{10}} + x^{\frac{1}{10}}\right)^4 \cdot \left(\frac{11}{10}x^{\frac{1}{10}} + \frac{1}{10}x^{\frac{-9}{10}}\right)$$
$$y' \text{ at } x = 1 = e(1+1)^5 + e \cdot 5(1+1)^4 \times \left(\frac{11}{10} + \frac{1}{10}\right)$$
$$= 2^5 \cdot e + 5e \cdot 2^4 \cdot \frac{12}{10}$$
$$= 32e + 96e = 128e.$$

19. From both statements I & II, we can find the solution.

Let total number of questions = 100

30% of questions are attempted by both Ramya and Swathi.

Number of questions attempted by both

$$= 100 \times \frac{30}{100} = 30.$$

Again, Let number of questions attempted by Ramya = P.

Then from question,

$$P \times \frac{5}{8} + 30 = P$$
$$P - \frac{5}{8}P = 30$$
$$\frac{3P}{8} = 30$$
$$P = 80$$

Hence, per cent of question attempted by Ramya in the exam = 80%.

20. India has been ranked low 97th among the 118 countries surveyed in 2016 Global Hunger Index (GHI). In 2016 GHI, India has scored low 28.5 on a 0-100 point scale of the index.

It describes India's hunger situation as serious. The index was released by the International Food Policy Research Institute (IFPRI).

21. *At a stone's throw* is a short distance. The phrase *at a stone's throw* is taken from the idea that a stone may only be thrown to a short distance.

22. I. The **mean** (or average) of a set of data values is the sum of all of the data values divided by the number of data values. That is:

$$\text{Mean} = \frac{\text{Sum of all data values}}{\text{Number of data values}}$$

Symbolically,

$$\bar{x} = \frac{\sum x}{n}$$

where $\bar{x}$ (read as 'x bar') is the mean of the set of x values,

Σx is the sum of all the x values, and

n is the number of x values.

Median: The **median** of a set of data values is the middle value of the data set when it has been arranged in ascending order. That is, from the smallest value to the highest value.

Mode: The **mode** of a set of data values is the value(s) that occurs most often.

The mode has applications in printing. For example, it is important to print more of the most popular books; because printing different books in equal numbers would cause a shortage of some books and an oversupply of others.

Thus, Mean, Median and Mode of any set of numbers are smaller than the maximum number in the set.

II. The formula for standard deviation:

$$s = \sqrt{\frac{1}{N-1}\sum_{i=1}^{N}(x_i - \bar{x})^2}$$

As you can see, you need to take the square root of the above expression in order to find the standard deviation and we know that we cannot have a negative number inside the square root.

23. **Priority Sector Lending** is an important role given by the Reserve Bank of India (RBI) to the banks for providing a specified portion of the bank lending to few specific sectors like agriculture and allied activities, micro and small enterprises, poor people for housing, students for education and other low income groups and weaker sections. This is essentially meant for an all round development of the economy as opposed to focusing only on the financial sector.

Priority Sector includes the following categories:

(*i*) Agriculture
(*ii*) Micro, Small and Medium Enterprises
(*iii*) Export Credit
(*iv*) Education
(*v*) Housing
(*vi*) Social Infrastructure
(*vii*) Renewable Energy

27. Sex ratio is used to describe the number of females per 1000 of males. In the Population Census of 2011 it was revealed that the population ratio in India 2011 is 943 females per 1000 of males. Haryana has the lowest sex ratio (877) in Indian states while in union territory Daman & Diu has lowest sex ratio of 618. Kerala has the highest sex ratio of 1084 in the all Indian states, while Puducherry has the highest sex ratio among the all Union territories.

28. Age of X = 2 × (Age of Y) $\Rightarrow$ $x = 2y$

I. Eight years ago, their age's are:

$$x - 8 = 3(y - 8)$$
$$3y - x = 24 - 8$$
$$3y - x = 16$$
$$3y - 2y = 16 \Rightarrow y = 16$$
$$\therefore \quad x = 32 \text{ years}$$

II.
$$x + 10 = 1.5\,(y + 10)$$
$$2y + 10 = 1.5y + 15$$
$$0.5y = 15 - 10 = 5$$
$$y = 10$$
$$\therefore \quad x = 20 \text{ years.}$$

Hence, either I or II are sufficient to give the answer.

29. When there is increase in the literacy rate of India, there has been steady increase in the per capita income of people in India in recent years.

31. As, A and B are two independent events then, $P(A \cap B) = P(A) \cdot P(B)$

Now, $P(A \cup B) = P(A) + P(B) - P(A \cap B)$

$$P(A \cup B) = P(A) + P(B) - P(A) \cdot P(B)$$
$$0.7 = 0.4 + P(B) - 0.4 \cdot P(B)$$
$$0.7 - 0.4 = 0.6 \cdot P(B)$$
$$P(B) = \frac{0.3}{0.6} = \frac{1}{2} = 0.5.$$

32. The ICRC is part of the International Red Cross and Red Crescent Movement along with the International Federation of Red Cross and Red Crescent Societies (IFRC) and 190 National Societies. It is the oldest and most honoured organization within the movement and one of the most widely recognized organizations in the world, having won three Nobel Peace Prizes in 1917, 1944, and 1963. The **International Committee of the Red Cross (ICRC)** is a humanitarian institution based in Geneva, Switzerland.

33. $₹\ 155 = ₹\ 65 + \frac{x}{100} \times 10$

$90 = \frac{x}{10} \quad \Rightarrow \quad x = 900$

Total weight = 250 + 900 = 1150 gram

Thus, upto 1150 gram, charge could be ₹ 155

Hence, weight could be = 1145 gram.

34. Bob Dylan has won the 2016 Nobel Prize in literature. The prolific musician is the first Nobel winner to have forged a career primarily as a singer-songwriter. Dylan earned the prize "for having created new poetic expressions within the great American song tradition," according to the citation by the Swedish Academy, the committee that annually decides the recipient of the Nobel Prize.

35.

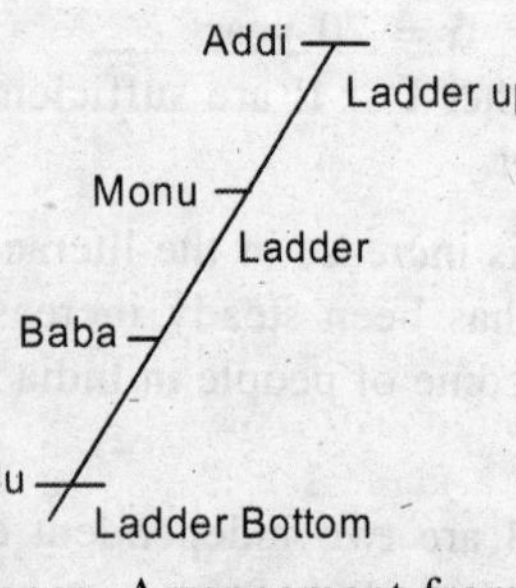

Hence, Arrangement from bottom to top are:

Tilu, Baba, Monu, Addi.

37. The major determinants of exchange rates are the supply and demand for currencies. Exchange rates rise and fall based on the underlying economic conditions that prompt traders, investors and others to want more of a particular currency. Import and export companies, speculators, bankers and central banks all have a need for buying currencies, and their interaction with each other creates the supply and demand for foreign exchange.

38.

Symbol	**Mathematical Symbol**
×	>
©	≥
÷	≠
ϕ	=
+	≤
Δ	<

then, $p \times q \ \Delta \ r \rightarrow p > q < r$

From option

A. $r + q \text{ © } p \ \rightarrow \ r \leq q \geq p$ {False}

B. $p \text{ © } q + r \ \rightarrow \ p \geq q \leq r$ {May be true}

C. $q \text{ © } p \times r \ \rightarrow \ q \geq p > r$ {False}

D. $p \ \phi \ r \ \Delta \ q \ \rightarrow \ p = r < q$ {False}

Hence, correct alternative is $p \text{ © } q + r$.

39.

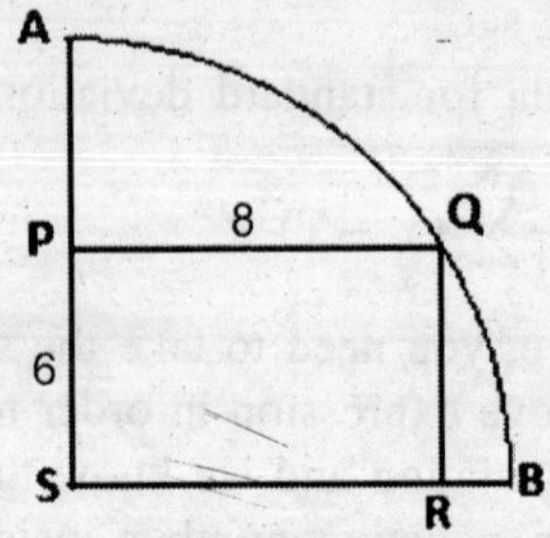

Here, radius of the circle

= Diagonal of the rectangle

$= \sqrt{(PQ)^2 + (PS)^2} = \sqrt{(8)^2 + (6)^2}$

$= \sqrt{64 + 36} = \sqrt{100} = 10$

Now, perimeter of the circle with centre 'S' and radius r = 10 units

$= 2 \times \pi \times 10 = 20\pi$

So, Arc AQB $= \frac{20\pi}{4} = 5\pi$.

42.

Symbol	**Mathematical Symbol**
×	>
©	≥
÷	≠
ϕ	=
+	≤
Δ	<

Now, $p \Delta q \Delta r \rightarrow p < q < r$

From option

A. $p \times r \times q \quad \rightarrow p > r > q$ {False}

B. $p \Delta r \times q \quad \rightarrow p < r > q$ {False}

C. $r \times q \times p \quad \rightarrow r > q > p$ {True}

D. $q \times p \Delta r \quad \rightarrow q > p < r$ {False}

Hence, option (C) is true.

43. $y = x^2 - 8x + 18$

$y = \{x^2 - 8x + 16\} + 2$

$y = (x - 4)^2 + 2$

Now, from table:

x	$(x - 4)^2$	$(x - 4)^2 + 2 = y$
−2	$(-6)^2 = 36$	$36 + 2 = 38$
−1	$(-5)^2 = 25$	$25 + 2 = 27$
0	$(-4)^2 = 16$	$16 + 2 = 18$
1	$(-3)^2 = 9$	$9 + 2 = 11$
2	$(-2)^2 = 4$	$4 + 2 = 6$
4	$0^2 = 0$	$+ 2 = 2$
6	$(2)^2 = 4$	$4 + 2 = 6$
7	$(3)^2 = 9$	$9 + 2 = 11$
8	$(4)^2 = 16$	$16 + 2 = 18$

On plotting, we get

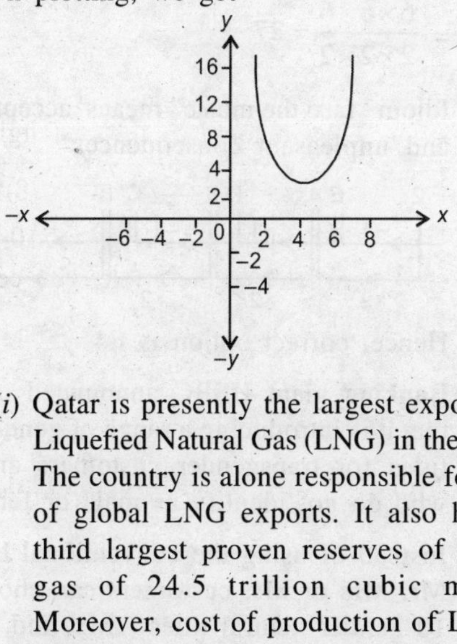

44. (*i*) Qatar is presently the largest exporter of Liquefied Natural Gas (LNG) in the world. The country is alone responsible for 32% of global LNG exports. It also has the third largest proven reserves of natural gas of 24.5 trillion cubic meters. Moreover, cost of production of LNG in Qatar is the lowest in the world. However, there is a new contender for the top spot now, Australia.

(*ii*) Saudi Arabia with 16 per cent of the world's proved oil reserves, is the largest exporter of total petroleum liquids in the world, and maintains the world's largest crude oil production capacity at roughly 12 million barrels per day.

(*iii*) The **Cooperation Council for the Arab States of the Gulf** known as the **Gulf Cooperation Council** is a regional intergovernmental political and economic union consisting of all Arab states of the Persian Gulf, except for Iraq. Its member states are Bahrain, Kuwait, Oman, Qatar, Saudi Arabia, and the United Arab Emirates. The Charter of the Gulf Cooperation Council was signed on 25 May 1981, formally establishing the institution.

45.

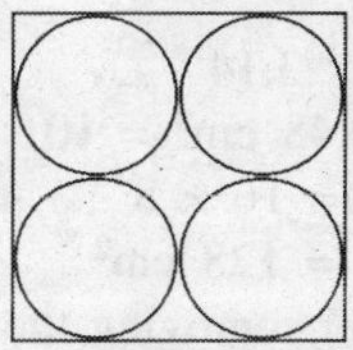

Area of the square $= (14)^2 = 196$ cm^2

Area of the 4 circles $= 4 \times \frac{22}{7} \times \frac{7}{2} \times \frac{7}{2}$

$= 22 \times 7 = 154$ cm^2

Hence, area of the square not covered by the circles $= 196 - 154 = 42$ cm^2.

46. The **Dhola-Sadiya Bridge**, also referred to as the **Bhupen Hazarika Setu** is a beam bridge in India, connecting the northeast states of Assam and Arunachal Pradesh. The bridge spans the Lohit River, a major tributary of the Brahmaputra River, from the village of Dhola (Tinsukia District) in the south to Sadiya to the north. The bridge is the first permanent road connection between the northern Assam and eastern Arunachal Pradesh.

At 9.15 kilometres (5.69 mi) in length, it is the longest bridge in India. However, the New Ganga Bridge Project under construction in the Indian state of Bihar, is expected to become the longest bridge in India upon its estimated completion in December 2020, with a length of 9.8 kilometres (6.1 mi).

47. 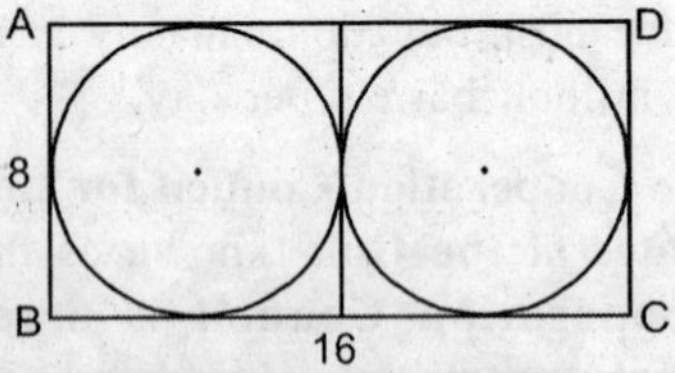

Largest circle cut out from rectangular card will have diameter = width of the rectangle

So, $\frac{\text{Diameter of the circle}}{2} = \text{radius}$

$$\text{radius} = \frac{8}{2} = 4 \text{ cm}$$

Now, Area of two equal circles

$= 2 \times \pi(4)^2$

$= 32\pi$

$= 32 \times 3.14$

$= 100.48 \text{ cm}^2 = 101 \text{ cm}^2$

Area of the rectangle $= 16 \times 8$

$= 128 \text{ cm}^2$

Area of paper left after removing the circles

$= 128 - 101 = 27 \text{ cm}^2$.

48. The **Monetary Policy Committee** of India is a committee of the Reserve Bank of India that is responsible for fixing the benchmark interest rate in India. The committee comprises six members - three officials of the Reserve Bank of India and three external members nominated by the Government of India. They need to observe a "silent period" seven days before and after the rate decision for "utmost confidentiality". The Governor of Reserve Bank of India is the chairperson ex officio of the committee. Decisions are taken by majority with the Governor having the casting vote in case of a tie. The current mandate of the committee is to maintain 4% annual inflation until March 31, 2021 with an upper tolerance of 6% and a lower tolerance of 2%.

50. Let total number of people at first stop = n and let, denote first stop by S_0.

Then,

Stop	No. of people get down
S_0	0
S_1	$\frac{x}{2}$
S_2	$\frac{x}{4}$
S_3	$\frac{x}{8}$
S_4	$\frac{x}{16}$
S_5	$\frac{x}{32}$
S_6	$\frac{x}{64}$

Now, number of person get down at 7th stop

$= \frac{x}{128}$

From question, $\frac{x}{128} = 1$

$\therefore \quad x = 128$

Thus, number of people at first stop = 128.

51. Number of such cubes possible

$= \frac{6\times6\times6}{2\times2\times2} = 27.$

55. Idiom "face the music" means accept difficult and unpleasant consequences.

57. 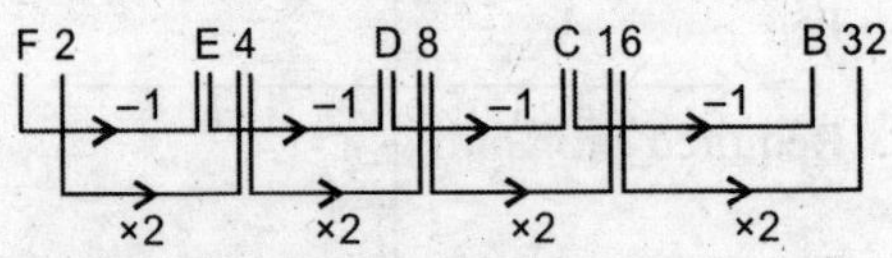

Hence, correct option is E4

59. Banking giant HSBC announced on Friday that it is introducing a range of gender neutral titles for transgender customers and others who do not identify as male or female.

Instead of using the conventional honorifics Mr, Mrs or Ms, customers can choose from 10 gender neutral titles - Mx, Ind, M, Mre, Msr, Myr, Pr, Sai, Ser and Misc.

60. $f(x) = \ln(2 - x) + \ln(3 - x)$

Domain: $2 - x > 0 \quad \therefore \quad x < 2$

and $\quad 3 - x > 0 \qquad \therefore\ x < 3$

Domain = $(-\infty, 2)$.

61. Correct word is Mimicking. Mimicking means to imitate or copy in action, speech, etc., often playfully or derisively.

62. From Cramer's rule

System of linear equation has a trivial solution, if $\Delta = 0$

$$\begin{vmatrix} 0 & 0 & (4d-1) \\ (4d-1) & 1 & 1 \\ 0 & -1 & 0 \end{vmatrix} = 0$$

$$\therefore \quad -(4d-1)(4d-1) = 0$$

$$(4d-1)^2 = 0$$

$$\therefore \quad d = \frac{1}{4}.$$

63. From statement I & II, we get that:

Tallest ↗ E > B > D > A > B
or
↘ E > B > D > B > A

Hence, data in both statement I & II together are necessary to answer the question.

64. Banks are generally free to determine the interest rate they will pay for deposits and charge for loans, but they must take the competition into account, as well as the market levels for numerous interest rates and Fed policies.

65. Required probability = $\dfrac{3!\,4!\,3!\,1!}{(3+4+1)!} = \dfrac{3}{140}$.

68. The Government had constituted a Committee in May, 2016 to review the Fiscal Responsibility and Budget Management (FRBM) Act under the Chairmanship of Shri N.K. Singh, former Revenue and Expenditure Secretary and former Member of Parliament. The Committee consisted of Dr. Urjit R. Patel, Governor, Reserve Bank of India (RBI), Shri Sumit Bose, former Finance Secretary, Dr. Arvind Subramanian, Chief Economic Adviser and Dr. Rathin Roy, Director, National Institute of Public Finance & Policy (NIPFP) as members.

The Committee had wide ranging Terms of Reference (ToR) to comprehensively review the existing FRBM Act in the light of contemporary changes, past outcomes, global economic developments, best international practices and to recommend the future fiscal framework and roadmap for the country.

69. The **origin** of the **Sutlej River** is located close to Lake Rakhastal in **Tibet** in the vicinity of the Kailash Mountain Range. The **Sutlej River** usually runs according to a west to southwest itinerary moving into India via the Shipki La Pass located in Himachal Pradesh.

70. The sword of Damocles hangs over (one's) head means One is faced with imminent danger or trouble.

73. India defeated Belgium 2-1 in the final of Junior Hockey World Cup 2016 to win the title for second time. India had earlier won the title in 2001.

India have become the first nation to win the hockey junior World Cup at home. At the Major Dhyan Chand Stadium, India beat Belgium 2-1 to win their second world title after 15 years.

74.
$$3x - 2y + z = 0 \qquad \text{....}(i)\ ] \times 3$$
$$x + 2y + 3z = 0 \qquad \text{...}(ii)\ ] \times 1$$
$$4x + 4z = 0 \qquad \text{...(A)}$$

$$\begin{array}{r} 9x - 6y + 3z = 0 \\ x + 2y + 3z = 0 \\ - \quad - \quad - \quad \\ \hline 8x - 8y = 0 \end{array}$$

$$x - y = 0$$
$$x = y$$
$$4y + 4z = 0$$
$$y + z = 0$$
$$y = -z$$
$$\Rightarrow \quad z = -y$$
$$kx - 14y + 15z = 0$$
$$kx - 14x + 15(-y) = 0$$
$$\Rightarrow \quad kx - 14x - 15x = 0$$
$$x(k - 14 - 15) = 0$$
$$k - 29 = 0$$
$$k = 29.$$

75. Loss % = 11%

Selling price = ₹ 178

$$\text{Cost price} = \text{Selling price} \times \frac{100}{(100-11)}$$

$$= 178 \times \frac{100}{89} = ₹\ 200$$

Now, Cost price = ₹ 200

Profit % = 11%

$$\text{Selling price} = \text{Cost price} \times \left(\frac{\text{Profit}+100}{100}\right)$$

$$= 200 \times \left(\frac{11+100}{100}\right)$$

$$= 200 \times \frac{111}{100} = 222$$

Hence, correct option is (C).

77. The Arunachal Pradesh government has launched a special scheme "Dulari Kanya" to check infant mortality in the state on the occasion of the 68th Republic Day on January 26, 2017. As per the scheme, the government will deposit ₹ 20,000 in the bank account of a girl child, born in any government hospital. It would be paid along with the accrued interest after she attains 18 years of her age.

79. $9^{\frac{1}{3}} \times 9^{\frac{1}{9}} \times 9^{\frac{1}{27}} \times ....\infty$

$= 9^{\frac{1}{3}+\frac{1}{9}+\frac{1}{27}+......\infty}$

$\frac{1}{3}+\frac{1}{9}+\frac{1}{27}+.....$ are in G.P.

where $a = \frac{1}{3}$ and c.r. = $\frac{1}{3}$

$$s_\infty = \frac{a}{1-r} = \frac{\frac{1}{3}}{1-\frac{1}{3}} = \frac{\frac{1}{3}}{\frac{2}{3}} = \frac{1}{2}$$

$$\therefore \quad 9^{\frac{1}{2}} = 3^{2\times\frac{1}{2}} = 3^1 = 3.$$

81. Flight Lt. **Harita Kaur Deol** (10 November, 1971 – 24 December, 1996) was a pilot with the Indian Air Force. She was the first woman pilot to fly solo in the Indian Air Force. The flight was on 2 September, 1994 in an Avro HS-748, when she was 22 years old . Hailing from Chandigarh in a Sikh family, in 1993, she became one of the first seven women cadets inducted into the Air Force as Short Service Commission (SSC) officers.

Sadly, she died in an aircrash near Nellore on 24 December 1996, at age 24. She was one of 24 Air Force personnel to die when an Indian Air Force Avro aircraft crashed near the Bukkapuram village in Prakasam district of Andhra Pradesh.

82. **Ace Against Odds** is the 2016 biography of the Indian professional tennis player Sania Mirza. The book is her official biography chronicling her journey to becoming one of India and world's top female tennis player. The book also contains some memorable encounters of the player on and off the court and the people and relationships that have contributed to her growth as a person and a sportsperson.

84–87.

Person	Gift given	Gift received
Amol	Shirt	Video Game
Shashi	Cellphone	Perfume
Mandar	Fountain Pen	Calculator
Piyu	Jacket	Sweater
Reena	I–Pod	Sunglasses

84. Piyu has gifted the Jacket.

85. Amol and Mandar have gifted shirt and fountain pen and got a return gift video game & calculator. Thus Amol and Mandar received electronic gift but given non-electronic gift.

86. Reena has gifted I-Pod and received sunglasses as return gift.

87. I-Pod is gifted by Reena and in alphabetical order Reena has appeared after Amol, Mandar and Piyu.

88-91. Number of cars of brand A sold previous year = 24.

So, number of cars of brand B sold previous year = $24\times\frac{2}{3}$ = 16.

Number of cars sold by brand A in this year

= $24\times\frac{3}{2}$ = 36.

Number of cars sold by brand B in this year

= $16\times\frac{5}{2}$ = 40.

88. Let total number of cars sold this year is x.

Then, $(36 + 40 + x) \times \frac{81}{100} = x$

$(76 + x)81 = 100x$

$76 \times 81 = (100 - 81)x$

$x = \frac{76\times81}{19} = 324.$

89. Increase in total number of cars sold

= (324 + 76) – (24 + 16)

= 360

Percentage increase = $\frac{360\times100}{40}$ = 900%.

90. Increase in sales in next year = 80%

= $400 \times \frac{80}{100}$ = 320 cars

Car D sales in next year = 320 cars

Previous year car (A + B) sold = 24 + 16

= 40 cars

Percentage increase = $\left(\frac{320-40}{40}\right)\times100$

$= \frac{280}{40}\times100$

= 700%.

91. Let, number of cars of brand A sold in previous year was x and number of cars of brand B sold in previous year was y

then, from question,

$2x = 3y$

or, $y = \frac{2x}{3}$

Number of cars of brand A sold in previous year = x

Then, number of cars of brand A sold in this year = $\frac{3x}{2}$

Again, number of cars of brand B sold in previous year $y = \frac{2x}{3}$

Number of cars of brand B sold in this year

$= \frac{5y}{2} = \frac{2x\times5}{3\times2} = \frac{5x}{3}$

From question, $\frac{3x}{2}+\frac{5x}{3} = 380$

$\Rightarrow \frac{9x+10x}{6} = 380 \Rightarrow \frac{19x}{6} = 380$

$x = \frac{380\times6}{19}$ = 120 cars.

92-96.

Day	Task	Person
Monday	Vacuuming	Randy
Tuesday	Dusting	Sally
Wednesday	Sweeping	Terry
Thursday	Mopping	Uma
Friday	Laundry	Vernon

92. Sally do the dusting on Tuesday.

93. Terry do the Sweeping on Wednesday.

94. Vacuuming is done in Monday by Randy.

95. Vernon do Laundry on Friday.

96. Uma do his task mopping on Thursday.

YOUR SPACE

QUANTITATIVE ABILITY

1 Arithmetical Mathematics

PROBLEM BASED ON NUMBERS

MULTIPLE CHOICE QUESTIONS

1. Three numbers are in the ratio of 5 : 4 : 3. The difference of the largest and the smallest numbers is exceeds by 24. The middle number is:

A. 18 B. 24
C. 30 D. 48

2. Three consecutive numbers such that twice the first, 3 times the second and 4 times the third together make 182. The numbers are:

A. 18, 19 and 20 B. 19, 20 and 21
C. 20, 21 and 22 D. 21, 22 and 23

3. There is a number of two digits, the sum of whose digits is 9. If the digits of that number are reversed, the new number is $\frac{3}{8}$th of the original number, then the original number is:

A. 27 B. 45
C. 54 D. 72

4. The sum of three numbers is 68. If the ratio between first and second is 2 : 3 and that between second and third is 5 : 3, then the second number is:

A. 20 B. 30
C. 18 D. None of these

5. The sum of the digits of a number less than 100 is 6. If the digits be interchanged, the resulting number will be less by 18 than the original number, the number is:

A. 51 B. 15
C. 24 D. 42

ANSWERS

1	2	3	4	5
D	B	D	B	D

SOME SELECTED EXPLANATORY ANSWERS

1. Let the numbers be $5x$, $4x$ and $3x$.

Then $5x - 3x = 24$

$\Rightarrow$ $2x = 24$ or $x = 12$

$\therefore$ Middle number is $4 \times 12 = 48$

2. Let three consecutive numbers be x, $x + 1$, $x + 2$.

$\therefore 2x + 3(x + 1) + 4(x + 2) = 182$

$\Rightarrow$ $2x + 3x + 3 + 4x + 8 = 182$

$\Rightarrow$ $9x = 182 - 11 = 171$

$\therefore$ $x = \frac{171}{9} = 19$

Required numbers are 19, 20 and 21.

3. Let the two digits be x and y and the number be $10x + y$.

Then $x + y = 9$ ...(1)

and $10y + x = \frac{3}{8}(10x + y)$

$\Rightarrow 80y + 8x = 30x + 3y$

$\Rightarrow 77y - 22x = 0$

$\Rightarrow 7y - 2x = 0$

or $2x - 7y = 0$ ...(2)

Multiplying equation (1) by (2), we get

$2x + 2y = 18$ ...(3)

Subtract (3) from (2),

$-9y = -18 \quad \therefore y = 2$

From (1), $x = 9 - y = 9 - 2 = 7$

Hence, the original number is 72.

4.

	First		Second		Third
	2	:	3	:	3
			5		3
$\Rightarrow$	2	:	3	:	$\frac{3}{5}\times 3$
or	10	:	15	:	9

Let the three numbers be $10x$, $15x$ and $9x$.

Then, $10x + 15x + 9x = 68$

$\Rightarrow 34x = 68 \qquad \therefore x = \frac{68}{34} = 2$

The numbers are 20, 30, 18,

i.e., second number = 30.

5. Let the digits be x and y and the number be $10x + y$

According to the given conditions,

$x + y = 6$

$10y + x = 10x + y - 18$

$\Rightarrow 9y - 9x = -18$ or $x - y = 2$

Adding (1) and (2),

$2x = 8 \quad \therefore \quad x = 2$

Subtracting (2) from (1),

$2y = 4 \quad \therefore \quad y = 2$

Hence, the required number is 42.

H.C.F. & L.C.M.

Solved Examples

Example 1: *Find the H.C.F. of 120, 240 and 300.*

Solution: I. Factor method:

$120 = 2 \times 2 \times 2 \times 3 \times 5$

$240 = 2 \times 2 \times 2 \times 2 \times 3 \times 5$

$300 = 2 \times 2 \times 3 \times 5 \times 5$

Clearly, the common factors are $2 \times 2 \times 3 \times 5$.

$\therefore$ H.C.F. = 60.

Example 2: *Find the LCM of 3.6, 4.5 and 6.3.*

Solution: $36 = 2^2 \times 3^2$

$45 = 3^2 \times 5$

$63 = 3^2 \times 7$

L.C.M. $= 2^2 \times 3^2 \times 5 \times 7 = 1260$

$\therefore$ Required L.C.M. = 126.0 = 126

Alternative Method:

$3.6 = \frac{36}{10}$, $4.5 = \frac{45}{10}$,

$6.3 = \frac{63}{10}$

Required L.C.M. $= \frac{\text{LCM of 36, 45 and 63}}{\text{HCF of 10, 10 and 10}}$

$= \frac{1260}{10} = 126.$

Example 3: *Find the least perfect square number which is divisible by 2, 3, 4, 5, 6.*

Solution: The least number divisible by 2, 3, 4, 5, 6 is clearly their LCM which is 60.

Since $60 = 2 \times 2 \times 3 \times 5$.

Multiply it by 3×5 to make it a perfect square.

Hence, the required least perfect square number

$= 60 \times 15 = 900.$

Example 4: *Find the least number which is a multiple of 5, but when it is divided by 18, 21 and 24, the remainders are 7, 10 and 13 respectively.*

Solution: $18 - 7 = 21 - 10 = 24 - 13 = 11$, constant

L.C.M. of 18, 21, 24 = 504

$\therefore$ Required number = 504 M – 11, will be a multiple of 5 for M = 4

$= 504 \times 4 - 11$

$= 2016 - 11 = 2005.$

MULTIPLE CHOICE QUESTIONS

1. The H.C.F. of 1233, 726, 531 and 345 is:
A. 5 B. 3
C. 4 D. 2

2. The L.C.M. of 18, 28, 35, 60 and 100 is:
A. 6300 B. 6200
C. 6400 D. 6500

3. If the H.C.F. of two numbers is 5, their L.C.M. is 165 and one of the number is 55, then the other number is:
A. 5 B. 15
C. 75 D. 2475

4. The smallest number of 4 digits which when divided by 6, 8, 12 and 20 leaves remainder 5 in each case is:
A. 1285 B. 1200
C. 1085 D. 1080

5. The greatest number of 6 digits which is exactly divisible by 27, 45, 60, 72 and 96 is:
A. 998000 B. 989980
C. 997920 D. 999999

6. Four bells ring at an interval of 8, 12, 15 and 18 second respectively. All the four begin to ring together. How many times will they ring together in one hour excluding the one at the start?
A. 10 times B. 20 times
C. 30 times D. 40 times

7. Three different persons buy some notebooks for ₹ 92.50, ₹ 129.50 and ₹ 166.50. The maximum price of the notebook is:
A. ₹ 15.50 B. ₹ 18.50
C. ₹ 21.50 D. ₹ 23.50

8. The circumferences of the front wheel and hind wheel of a cart are $5\frac{1}{2}$ m and $14\frac{2}{3}$ m respectively. A mark is put at the point of contact of each wheel with the ground. Find the distance travelled by the cart so that the mark points on each wheel touch the ground together again:
A. 22 m B. 44 m
C. 66 m D. 88 m

ANSWERS

1	2	3	4	5	6	7	8
B	A	B	C	C	A	B	B

SOME SELECTED EXPLANATORY ANSWERS

3. Other number $= \frac{\text{H.C.F.} \times \text{L.C.M.}}{\text{First number}}$

$= \frac{5 \times 165}{55} = 15$

4. Smallest number of 4 digits = 1000
LCM of the given number = 120
When 1000 is divided by 120 gives remainder = 40
Required number
= 1000 + (120 – 40) + Common remainder
= 1080 + 5 (1085

8. L.C.M. of $5\frac{1}{2}$ and $14\frac{2}{3}$

i.e., $\frac{11}{2}$ and $\frac{44}{3}$

i.e., $\frac{\text{L.C.M. of 11 and 44}}{\text{H.C.F. of 2 and 3}}$

$= \frac{44}{1} = 44$

∴ Required distance = 44 m

6

TIME WORK, PIPE AND CISTERN

Solved Examples

Example 1: *A can complete a piece of work in 8 days, whereas A and B together can complete the same work in 6 days. How long will it take for B alone to complete the work?*

Solution: A's one day's work = $\frac{1}{8}$

(A + B)'s one day's work = $\frac{1}{6}$

B's one day's work = $\left(\frac{1}{6}-\frac{1}{8}\right) = \frac{1}{24}$

∴ B can complete the work in 24 days.

Example 2: *Two pipes A and B can separately, fill a cistern in 8 hours and 12 hours respectively while a third pipe C can empty it in 24 hours. In what time will the cistern be full, if all the pipes are opened together?*

Solution: In 1 hour, the pipe A fills $\frac{1}{8}$ th of the cistern.

In 1 hour, the pipe B fills $\frac{1}{12}$ th of the cistern.

In 1 hour, the pipe C can empty $\frac{1}{24}$ th of the cistern.

Net filling of the cistern in 1 hour

$$= \left(\frac{1}{8}+\frac{1}{12}\right)-\frac{1}{24}$$

$$= \frac{5}{24}-\frac{1}{24} = \frac{4}{24} = \frac{1}{6}$$

So, the cistern will be full in 6 hours.

MULTIPLE CHOICE QUESTIONS

1. If 36 binders bind 900 books in 10 days, how many binders will be required to bind 1,200 books in 12 days?

A. 30 B. 32
C. 40 D. 42

2. If A can complete a work in 30 days and B can complete the same work in 25 days, then in how many days will 'A' and 'B' together complete the work?

A. $\frac{11}{150}$ days B. $\frac{150}{11}$ days
C. 55 days D. $\frac{1}{55}$ days

3. If 100 men can do 100 jobs in 100 days, then 1 man can do one job in:

A. 1 day B. 100 days
C. 50 days D. 10 days

4. Ajit can complete a job in 4 days, Manoj can complete the same job in 6 days and Ravi can complete it in 12 days. In how many days will Ajit, Manoj and Ravi together complete the same job?

A. 2 days B. 3 days
C. $\frac{1}{2}$ day D. 1 day

5. A and B can finish a work in 16 days while A alone can do the same work in 24 days. Therefore B alone can finish the same work in ...... days.

A. 24 B. 36
C. 48 D. 56

6. A, B and C undertake to complete a piece of work for ₹ 1,950. A works for 8 days, B for 9 days and C for 12 days to complete the work. If their daily wages are in the ratio of 3 : 5 : 4, what does C get?

A. ₹ 400 B. ₹ 750
C. ₹ 675 D. ₹ 800

7. Two taps A and B can fill a cistern in 30 minute and 45 minute respectively. There is third exhaust tap C at the bottom of the tank. If all the taps are opened at the same time the cistern will be full in 45 minute. In what time can exhaust tap C empty the cistern when full?

A. 10 min B. 15 min
C. 18 min D. 20 min

8. Two taps A and B can separately fill a cistern in 24 minute and 30 minute respectively. Both the pipes are opened together. Find when the pipe B must be turned off so that the cistern may be full in 18 minute.

A. $6\frac{1}{2}$ min B. $6\frac{3}{4}$ min
C. 7 min D. $7\frac{1}{2}$ min

9. Efficiency of B is 80% of A. If both can complete a work in 24 days, in how many days B alone will complete the same work?

A. 54 B. 50
C. 49 D. 56

10. The efficiency of A is twice that of B. A completes a work in 9 days less than taken by B. In how many days A alone will complete this work?

A. 12 days B. 10 days
C. 9 days D. 13 days

11. If 3 men or 6 boys can finish a work in 20 days, then 6 men and 8 boys finish twice the work in:

A. 9 days B. 11 days
C. 3 days D. 12 days

12. 6 boys and 4 girls together complete a work in 5 days. The same work is done in 5 days by 10 boys. How many girls would be required if only the girls can finish this work in 5 days?

A. 20 B. 10
C. 15 D. 12

13. A man and a boy can complete digging in 40 days. The ratio of their speed of digging is 8 : 5. How many days the boys alone will take to do this work?

A. 68 days B. 52 days
C. 104 days D. 80 days

14. 104 men are employed to complete a work in 56 days working 8 hours per day. After 30 days $\frac{2}{5}$th work is finished. How many more men should be employed to finish the remaining work within time working 9 hours per day?

A. 52 B. 54
C. 56 D. 58

15. 5 persons prepare an admission list in 8 days working 7 hours per day. If two more persons are included to finish the work in 4 days, how much hours per day they should do the work?

A. 10 hours B. 9 hours
C. 12 hours D. 8 hours

16. A and B take 15 days and 10 days respectively to complete a job. Both of them together started the job, but after 2 days B have to leave the job due to any reason and the remaining work was finished by A. In how many days the job was completed?

A. 10 days B. 8 days
C. 12 days D. 15 days

17. A work can be finished in 100 days by some persons, but due to the absence of 10 persons, the work is finished in 110 days. How many persons were employed initially?

A. 100 B. 110
C. 55 D. 56

18. The efficiencies of two workmen A and B are in the ratio of 5 : 4. If A can do a piece of work in 12 hours, then B can do it in:

A. 18 hours B. 16.5 hours
C. 16 hours D. 15 hours

19. A pipe can fill a cistern in 12 hours and another pipe can empty completely filled cistern in 18 hours. If both the pipes are opened together, the cistern will be filled in:

A. 30 hours B. 36 hours
C. 40 hours D. 44 hours

ANSWERS

1	2	3	4	5	6	7	8	9	10
C	B	B	A	C	D	A	D	A	C
11	**12**	**13**	**14**	**15**	**16**	**17**	**18**	**19**	
D	B	C	C	A	C	B	D	B	

SOME SELECTED EXPLANATORY ANSWERS

1. less books, less number of binders (direct)
more days, less number of binders (indirect)

$$\left.\begin{array}{ll}\text{books} & 900:1{,}200\\ \text{days} & 12:10\end{array}\right\} :: 36 : x$$

Compounding the ratio,
$(900 \times 12) : (1{,}200 \times 10) = 36 : x$

$$\Rightarrow \quad x = \frac{1{,}200 \times 10 \times 36}{900 \times 12} = 40$$

Hence, 40 binders will be required.

2. A's work for one day $= \frac{1}{30}$

B's work for one day $= \frac{1}{25}$

(A + B)'s work for one day $= \frac{1}{30} + \frac{1}{25} = \frac{11}{150}$

$\therefore$ A and B together can complete the work in $\frac{150}{11}$ days.

3. 100 men can do 100 jobs in days = 100
$\therefore$ 1 man can do 100 jobs in days
= 100 × 100 days
$\therefore$ 1 man can do 1 job in days

$$= \frac{100 \times 100}{100} \text{ days} = 100 \text{ days.}$$

4. Ajit's one day's work $= \frac{1}{4}$

Manoj's one day's work $= \frac{1}{6}$

Ravi's one day's work $= \frac{1}{12}$

(Ajit + Manoj + Ravi)'s one day's work

$$= \frac{1}{4} + \frac{1}{6} + \frac{1}{12} = \frac{1}{2}$$

$\therefore$ Ajit, Manoj and Ravi together can complete the work in 2 days.

7. Taps (A + B)'s one minute work

$$= \frac{1}{30} + \frac{1}{45} = \frac{5}{90} = \frac{1}{18}$$

Taps (A + B + C)'s one minute work $= \frac{1}{45}$

$\therefore$ Exhaust tap C's one minute work

$$= \frac{1}{45} - \frac{1}{18} = -\frac{1}{10}$$

Thus, tap C can empty $\frac{1}{10}$th of tank in 1 minute.

Tap C can empty the full tank in 10 minute.

9.

	A		B		A + B
Efficiency	100		80		
	5	:	4	:	9
			E_1	:	E_2
			D_1	:	$D_2 = 24$

$\therefore \quad D_1E_1 = D_2E_2$

$\Rightarrow \quad 4 \times D_1 = 9 \times 24$

$\therefore \quad D_1 = \frac{9 \times 24}{4} = 54$ days.

10. Let A completes this work in x days.
Then B completes this work in $(x + 9)$ days.

	A		B
Efficiency	2	:	1
Days	x	:	$x + 9$

$\Rightarrow \quad 2 : 1 :: x + 9 : x$

$\Rightarrow \quad 2 \times x = (x + 9) : x$

$2 \times x = (x + 9) \times 1$

$2x = x + 9 \quad \therefore x = 9.$

11. 3 men's work = 6 boy's work
$\therefore$ 6 men's work = 12 boy's work
6 men's + 8 boy's work = (12 + 8) boy's work
i.e., 20 boy's work
Now, 6 boys can do the work in 20 days.

$\therefore$ 20 boys can do the work in $\frac{20 \times 6}{20}$ days

i.e., 6 days
$\therefore$ 20 boys can do twice the work in 12 days.
Thus, 6 men and 8 boys finish twice the work in 12 days.

12. $(6B + 4G) \times 5 = 10B \times 5$

$6B + 4G = 10B$

$4B = 4G$ *i.e.*, $1B = 1G$

Thus, the work of 1 boy = The work of 1 girl
The work of 10 boys = The work of 10 girls
Hence the required number of girls = 10.

13. M : B = 8 : 5 Efficiency
$\therefore$ M : B = 5 : 8 No. of days
Let the number of days be $5x$ and $8x$. Then

$$\frac{1}{5x}+\frac{1}{8x} = \frac{1}{40}$$

$$\frac{8+5}{40x} = \frac{1}{40} \qquad \therefore\ x = 13$$

Hence the required number of days
= 8 × 13 = 104.

14. Formule : $\frac{M_1D_1H_1}{W_1} = \frac{M_2D_2H_2}{W_2}$

$$\Rightarrow \frac{104\times30\times8}{\frac{2}{5}} = \frac{M_2\times(56-30)\times9}{\left(1-\frac{2}{5}\right)}$$

$$\Rightarrow M_2 = \frac{3}{5}\times\frac{5}{2}\times\frac{104\times30\times8}{26\times9} = 160$$

Required number of men = 160 – 104 = 56.

15. $M_1D_1H_1 = M_2D_2H_2$

$\Rightarrow$ 5 × 8 × 7 = (5 + 2) × 4 × H_2

$$\Rightarrow H_2 = \frac{5\times8\times7}{7\times4} = 10 \text{ hours.}$$

16. Let A alone finish the remaining job in T days. Then

$$\frac{2}{15}+\frac{2}{10}+\frac{T}{15} = 1$$

$$\Rightarrow \frac{T}{15} = 1-\left(\frac{2}{15}+\frac{2}{10}\right) = 1-\frac{1}{3} = \frac{2}{3}$$

$$\therefore T = \frac{2}{3}\times15 = 10.$$

Hence the required number of days
= 2 + 10 = 12.

17. $M_1D_1 = M_2D_2$

$\Rightarrow$ M_1 × 100 = (M_1 – 10) × 110

$\Rightarrow$ $10M_1$ = 1100 $\therefore$ M_1 = 110.

18. $E_1 : E_2 :: D_2 : D_1$

$$D_2 = \frac{E_1D_1}{E_2} = \frac{5\times12}{4} = 15 \text{ hours.}$$

19. $$\frac{1}{12}-\frac{1}{18} = \frac{1}{T}$$

or $$\frac{T}{12}-\frac{T}{18} = 1$$

$$\Rightarrow \frac{3T-2T}{36} = 1$$

$\therefore$ T = 36 hours.

SPEED, TIME AND DISTANCE

Solved Examples

Example 1: *In how much time will a car cover a distance of 4,500 m with a speed of 45 km/hour?*

Solution: $$\text{Time} = \frac{\text{Distance}}{\text{speed}}$$

$$= \frac{4.5}{45} = 0.1 \text{ hour (or 6 min.)}$$

($\because$ 4,500 m = 4.5 km)

Example 2: *A man travels a certain distance at the rate of 70 km/hour and returns the same point at the rate of 55 km/hour. What is his average speed of journey?*

Solution: Using formula,

$$\text{Average speed} = \frac{2xy}{x+y} = \frac{2\times70\times55}{70+55}$$

= 61.6 km/hour.

Example 3: *A train 270 m long passes a standing man in 24 sec. What is the speed of the train?*

Solution: Required speed = $\frac{270}{24}$ m/sec

$$= \frac{270}{24}\times\frac{18}{5} \text{ km/hour}$$

= 40.5 km/hour.

MULTIPLE CHOICE QUESTIONS

1. A man travels a certain distance at the rate of 10 km per hour and returns the same point at the rate of 15 km per hour. His average rate for the whole journey is:

A. 12 km/hour B. $12\frac{1}{2}$ km/hour
C. 13 km/hour D. None of these

2. Walking at the rate of 4 km an hour, a man covers a distance in 2 hrs. 45 min. Running at a speed of 11 km per hour, the man will cover this much distance in:

A. $\frac{1}{2}$ hour B. 1 hour
C. $1\frac{3}{4}$ hour D. 2 hours

3. If a person takes as much time in running 20 metre as a car takes in covering 50 m; the distance covered by the person during the time car covers 1 km is:

A. 100 m B. 140 m
C. 400 m D. 500 m

4. A motorist travels a distance of 10 km at a speed of 50 km/hour in the onward journey and 60 km/hour while returning. His average speed is:

A. $54\frac{6}{11}$ km/hr B. 55 km/hr
C. $55\frac{6}{11}$ km/hr D. 54 km/hr

5. On a tour a man travels at the rate of 35 km an hour for the first 160 km, then travels the next 160 km at the rate of 45 km an hour. What is the average speed in km per hour for the first 320 km of the tour?

A. $39\frac{1}{4}$ B. $39\frac{1}{2}$
C. $39\frac{1}{16}$ D. $39\frac{3}{8}$

6. X and Y are 15 km apart. X can walk at the speed of 14 km/hr and Y at the speed of 16 km/hr. They start walking towards each other at 7 a.m. At what time will they meet:

A. 7.15 a.m. B. 7.30 a.m.
C. 7.45 a.m. D. 8.00 a.m.

7. A train 600 metre long is running with a speed of 54 km/hr. In what time will it pass a tunnel 200 metre long?

A. 48 sec B. 50 sec
C. $53\frac{1}{3}$ sec D. $55\frac{1}{4}$ sec

8. A man travels 3/4th of the distance of his journey by bus, 1/6th by rickshaw and 4 km on foot. How many km does he travel in the journey?

A. 40 km B. 46 km
C. 48 km D. 50 km

9. A man walks from his house at an average speed of 5 km/hr and reaches his office 6 minute late. If he walks at an average speed of 6 km/hr he reaches 2 minute early. What is the distance of the office from his house?

A. 4 km B. 4.5 km
C. 5.0 km D. 5.5 km

10. If a man can row 30 km downstream and 18 km upstream, each in 3 hours, what is the speed of boat in still water?

A. 8 km/hr B. 10 km/hr
C. 12 km/hr D. 15 km/hr

ANSWERS

1	2	3	4	5	6	7	8	9	10
A	B	C	A	D	B	C	C	A	A

SOME SELECTED EXPLANATORY ANSWERS

1. Using formula,

Average speed = $\left(\frac{2\times10\times15}{10+15}\right)$ km/hr

= 12 km/hr

2. 2 hours 45 min. = $2\frac{3}{4}$ hours = $\frac{11}{4}$ hours

Distance covered by man = speed × time

= $4\times\frac{11}{4}$ = 11 km

So, the time taken by man to cover 11 km distance when speed in 11 km/hr. is

= $\frac{11}{11}$ = 1 hour

3. Clearly, 20 : 50 = x : 1,000, x being the distance covered the person.

So, $x = \frac{20}{50}\times1{,}000$ = 400 m

4. Using formula,

Average speed = $\frac{2\times50\times60}{50+60}$

= $\frac{6{,}000}{110}$ = $54\frac{6}{11}$ km/hour

5. Using formula,

Average speed = $\frac{2\times35\times45}{35+45}$

= $\frac{3{,}150}{80}$ = $39\frac{3}{8}$ km/hour

6. X and Y are moving towards each other, so their relative speed

= (14 + 16) km/hour

= 30 km/hour

Time taken = $\frac{\text{Distance}}{\text{Speed}}$

= $\frac{15}{30}$ hour = $\frac{1}{2}$ hour

Since, they start at 7 a.m., they will meet at 7.30 a.m.

7. Speed of train = $\left(54\times\frac{5}{18}\right)$ m/sec

= 15 m/sec

In passing a tunnel, train will have to cover a distance of (200 + 600) m *i.e.,* 800 m.

∴ Time it will take to pass = $\frac{800}{15} = 53\frac{1}{3}$ sec.

8. Let the total distance be x km. Then,

$$\frac{3}{4}x+\frac{1}{6}x+4 = x$$

$$\Rightarrow \frac{9x+2x+48}{12} = x$$

$$\Rightarrow 11x + 48 = 12x \quad \therefore \; x = 48 \text{ km}$$

9. Let the distance of office from the house be x km.

Difference of two timings = 6 + 2 = 8 min.

= $\frac{8}{60}$ hour = $\frac{2}{15}$ hour

Then, $\frac{x}{5}-\frac{x}{6} = \frac{2}{15}$

$$\Rightarrow \frac{6x-5x}{30} = \frac{2}{15}$$

$$\therefore \quad x = \frac{2\times30}{15} = 4 \text{ km}$$

10. Let speed of boat = x km/hr and speed of stream = y km/hr

Then, $\frac{30}{x+y} = 3$

and $\frac{18}{x-y} = 3$

⇒ $3x + 3y = 30$ ...(*i*)

and $3x - 3y = 18$ ...(*ii*)

Adding (*i*) and (*ii*),

$6x = 48 \quad \therefore x = 8$

∴ Speed of boat in still water is 8 km/hr.

PERCENTAGE

Solved Examples

Example 1: *35% of a number is 315. What is the number?*

Solution: Let the number be x. Then,

$$35\% \text{ of } x = 315$$

or $$\frac{35}{100}x = 315$$

$\therefore$ $$x = \frac{315 \times 100}{35} = 900$$

Thus, the required number is 900.

Example 2: *Mohan spent 20% of his income on food, 30% on house rent and 25% on clothes. If he saved ₹ 750, then find his income.*

Solution: $$750 = I\left(1 - \frac{20+30+25}{100}\right)$$

$$= \frac{I[100-(20+30+25)]}{100}$$

$\Rightarrow$ $$I = \frac{750 \times 100}{100-75}$$

$$= 750 \times \frac{100}{25} = ₹\ 3,000$$

Example 3: *Rakesh spends 20% on food, 25% of the rest on education and 10% of the remaining on house rent. If still he has ₹ 120 with him, find his income.*

Solution: Formula:

$$\text{Income} = \frac{\text{Saving} \times 100 \times 100 \times 100}{(100-20)(100-25)(100-10)}$$

$$= \frac{120 \times 100 \times 100 \times 100}{80 \times 75 \times 90}$$

$$= ₹\ \frac{20,000}{9} = ₹\ 2,222.22$$

MULTIPLE CHOICE QUESTIONS

1. What percent is 25 paise of ₹ 100?

A. 250% B. 25%
C. 2.5% D. 0.25%

2. In a co-educational school 35% of the students are boys. If there are 416 girls in the school, the number of boys in the school is:

A. 220 B. 224
C. 228 D. 230

3. In an examination a candidate has to secure 40% of the marks to pass. If a candidate secures 190 marks and fails by 10 marks, the total number of marks in the examination is:

A. 600 B. 500
C. 400 D. 360

4. If Ram's salary is 50% more than Shyam's, how much percent is Shyam's salary less than Ram's salary?

A. 33.5% B. $33\frac{1}{3}\%$
C. 50% D. 15%

5. Surinder appears in an examination, in which a student has to secure 36% of the marks to pass. If he secures 198 marks and fails by 18 marks, find the total marks in examination:

A. 800 B. 600
C. 700 D. 900

6. If 2 litre of water are evaporated on boiling 8 litre of sugar solution containing 6% of sugar, the % of sugar in the remaining solution is:

A. 0.6% B. 0.8%
C. 6% D. 8%

7. The population of a city is 15,00,000. It increases by 10% during 1st year, decreases by 20% in 2nd year and increases by 30% in the 3rd year. The population after 3 years is:

A. 17,16,000 B. 17,50,000
C. 16,50,000 D. 16,00,000

8. A man spends 80% of his income. His income is increased by 20% and his expenditure is also increased by 15%. What is the % increase/decrease in his savings?

A. 40% increase B. 10% decrease

C. 5% increase D. 20% decrease

9. If the price of sugar is increased by 1%, what percentage should be the reduction in the consumption so that there is no extra expenditure:

A. 1% B. 10%

C. $\frac{101}{100}\%$ D. $\frac{100}{101}\%$

10. The ratio of boys and girls in a school is 3 : 2. 20% boys and 25% girls get scholarship. How many students do not get scholarship?

A. 22% B. 40%

C. 60% D. 78%

ANSWERS

1	2	3	4	5	6	7	8	9	10
B	B	B	B	B	D	A	A	D	D

SOME SELECTED EXPLANATORY ANSWERS

1. Required % = $\frac{25}{100} \times 100 = 25\%$

2. Let the total number of students = x

% of boys = 35,

$\therefore$ % of girls = 100 − 35 = 65%

So, 65% of x = 416

or $\frac{65}{100} \times x = 416$

$\therefore$ $x = \frac{416 \times 100}{65} = 640$

Hence, no. of boys = 35% of 640

$= \frac{35}{100} \times 640 = 224$

3. Let the total marks in the examination = x

Pass marks = 190 + 10 = 200

So, 40% of x = 200

or $\frac{40}{100} \times x = 200$

$\therefore$ $x = \frac{200 \times 100}{40} = 500$

4. Let Ram's salary = ₹ 100

Then,

Shyam's salary = ₹ 100 + 50% of 100

$= ₹100 + \frac{50}{100} \times 100 = ₹\,150$

$\therefore$ Ram's salary is ₹ 50 less from Shyam's salary.

Required percentage $= \frac{50}{150} \times 100 = 33\frac{1}{3}\%$

6. Sugar in 8 litre of solution = sugar in (8 − 2) *i.e.,* 6 litre of solution

So, 6% of 8 = x% of 6

or $\frac{6}{100} \times 8 = \frac{x}{100} \times 6$

$\therefore$ $x = \frac{6 \times 8}{6} = 8\%$

7. Required population

$= \frac{15,00,000 \times (100+10)(100-20)(100+30)}{100 \times 100 \times 100}$

= 17,16,000

8. Let the monthly income be ₹ 100. Then, the man spends ₹ 80 and saves ₹ 20.

His increased income = ₹ 120

His increased expenditure = ₹ 80 + 15% of ₹ 80

$= ₹\,80 + ₹\frac{15}{100} \times 80 = ₹\,92$

New savings = ₹ 120 − ₹ 92 = ₹ 28

% increase in savings $= \frac{28-20}{20} \times 100 = 40\%$

10. Let number of boys = $3x$ and number of girls = $2x$

Total number of students = $3x + 2x = 5x$

Students who get scholarship

$$= \frac{3x \times 20}{100} + \frac{2x \times 25}{100} = \frac{110x}{100} = \frac{11x}{10}$$

Number of students who do not get scholarship

$$= 5x - \frac{11x}{10} = \frac{39x}{10}$$

$$\therefore \text{Required Percentage} = \frac{39x}{10} \times \frac{1}{5x} \times 100 = 78$$

Alternative Method:

Let the number of students be 100. Then

B	:	G	Total
3	:	2	5
↓ × 20		↓ × 20	↓ × 20

Note : 20% of 60 + 25% of 40

= 12 + 10 = 22

∴ Required percentage = 100 – 22 = 78

PROFIT AND LOSS

Solved Examples

Example 1: *A person buys an article at $\frac{3}{4}$ of its value and sells it for 20% more than its value. What is his gain %?*

Solution: Let the value of the article = ₹ x

∴ The person buys it for ₹$\frac{3}{4}x$

and sells it for ₹ $(x + 20\%$ of $x)$

i.e., $\left(x + \frac{20}{100}x\right) = ₹\frac{6x}{5}$

$$\text{Gain} = \frac{6}{5}x - \frac{3}{4}x = \frac{24x - 15x}{20} = \frac{9}{20}x$$

$$\text{Gain \%} = \frac{\frac{9}{20}x}{\frac{3}{4}x} \times 100 = 60\%$$

Example 2: *Manu buys a radio at 20% discount of its value and sells it for 20% more than its value. What will be his profit %?*

Solution: Let List price of radio be ₹ x.

C.P. of radio = ₹ $(x - 20\%$ of $x)$

$$= ₹\left(x - \frac{x}{5}\right) = ₹\frac{4}{5}x$$

S.P. of radio = ₹ $(x + 20\%$ of $x)$

$$= ₹\left(x + \frac{x}{5}\right) = \frac{6}{5}x$$

$$\text{Profit} = \frac{6}{5}x - \frac{4}{5}x = \frac{2}{5}x$$

$$\text{Profit\%} = \frac{\frac{2}{5}x}{\frac{4}{5}x} \times 100 = 50\%$$

MULTIPLE CHOICE QUESTIONS

1. Surabhi sold a washing machine for ₹ 9,499 at a gain of 15%. Find the cost price of the washing machine:

A. ₹ 8,000 B. ₹ 8,100
C. ₹ 8,260 D. ₹ 8,300

2. A fruit seller buys mangoes at the rate of 15 for ₹ 12 and sells them at the rate of ₹ 15 per dozen. Find his gain %:

A. 25.65% B. 32.25%
C. 51.35% D. 56.25%

3. Raj Kumar sold 2 calculators for ₹ 990 each. On one calculator he gained 10% and on the other he lost 10%; find his gain or loss in the transaction:

A. no loss-no gain B. 1% gain
C. 1% loss D. 5% loss

4. Mickey sells an article to Minnie at a profit of 20% and Minnie sells it to Meha at a profit of 25%. If Meha pays ₹ 450 for it, the cost price for Mickey is:

A. ₹ 300 B. ₹ 325
C. ₹ 350 D. ₹ 375

5. A shopkeeper buys 2 varieties of rice, one costing him ₹ 26 per kg and another ₹ 30.50 per kg. He mixes them in the ratio of 3 : 4 and this blended variety of rice is sold off at rate of ₹ 30 per kg. Gain % is:

A. 2% B. 3%
C. 4% D. 5%

6. Mudit purchases 5 shirts and 10 trousers for ₹ 5,000. He sells the shirts at 15% profit and trousers at 10% loss. Thus he gets ₹ 375 as profit. The cost of one shirt is:

A. ₹ 650 B. ₹ 675
C. ₹ 700 D. ₹ 725

7. Shobit marks his goods 25% above cost price, but allows 17.5% discount for cash payment. If he sells the article for ₹ 825, find the cost price of the article:

A. ₹ 800 B. ₹ 810
C. ₹ 820 D. ₹ 823

8. The selling price of two cows is ₹ 500 each. There is a gain of 20% on one and a loss of 10% on the other. Total gain or loss is:

A. $1\frac{5}{9}\%$ B. $3\frac{4}{5}\%$
C. 1.44% D. $2\frac{6}{7}\%$

9. By selling an article in ₹ 480, the loss is 20%. The selling price for gaining 20% is:

A. ₹ 720 B. ₹ 600
C. ₹ 620 D. ₹ 700

10. Mohan sells a radio at 10% profit. If the purchasing price would be 10% less and selling price ₹ 132 less, then there is a loss of 10% to him. The purchasing price of the radio is:

A. ₹ 264 B. ₹ 728
C. ₹ 1,200 D. ₹ 2,100

ANSWERS

1	2	3	4	5	6	7	8	9	10
C	D	C	A	D	C	A	D	A	C

SOME SELECTED EXPLANATORY ANSWERS

1. Cost Price = $₹\frac{100}{100+15}\times 9{,}499$ = ₹ 8,260

2. C.P. of 15 mangoes = ₹ 12

∴ C.P. of 1 mango = $₹\frac{12}{15}$

∴ C.P. of 12 mangoes = $₹\frac{12}{15}\times 12 = ₹\frac{48}{5}$

= ₹ 9.60

Given, S.P. of 12 mangoes = ₹ 15

$$\text{Gain} = ₹\left(15-\frac{48}{5}\right) = ₹\frac{27}{5} = ₹\,5.40$$

$$\text{Gain\%} = \frac{5.40}{9.60}\times 100 = 56.25\%$$

3. $$\text{Loss\%} = \left(\frac{\text{Common loss and gain}}{10}\right)^2 = \left(\frac{10}{10}\right)^2 = 1$$

4. Cost Price for Mickey = $₹450\times\frac{100}{120}\times\frac{100}{125}$

= ₹ 300

Another Method:

Since it is a case of successive profit,

resultant profit = $x+y+\frac{xy}{100}$,

formula for x% and y% profit

$$= 20+25+\frac{20\times 25}{100} = 50\%$$

∴ C.P. = $₹450\times\frac{100}{150}$ = ₹ 300

5. Let the shopkeeper boys 3 kg of the 1st variety and 4 kg of the 2nd variety of rice.

C.P. of 3 kg of rice at the rate ₹ 26 per kg

= ₹ 26 × 3 = ₹ 78

C.P. of 4 kg of rice at the rate of ₹ 30.50 per kg = ₹ 30.50 × 4 = ₹ 122

∴ C.P. of 7 kg of rice = ₹ 78 + ₹ 122 = ₹ 200

S.P. of 7 kg of rice = ₹ 30 × 7 = ₹ 210

Gain = ₹ 210 – ₹ 200 = ₹ 10

$\therefore \quad \text{Gain } \% = \frac{10}{200} \times 100 = 5\%$

6. Let the cost of one shirt be ₹ x.

Then, total S.P.

$= 5x\left(\frac{115}{100}\right) + (5{,}000 - 5x)\left(\frac{90}{100}\right)$

= 5,375 (given)

$\Rightarrow \quad 5\frac{3}{4}x + 4{,}500 - 4\frac{1}{2}x = 5{,}375$

$\Rightarrow \quad \frac{5}{4}x = 875 \quad \therefore x = 700$

∴ Cost of one shirt = ₹ 700.

7. $\text{Market Price} = ₹\,825 \times \frac{100}{100 - 17.5}$

$= ₹\ 825 \times \frac{100}{82.5} = ₹\ 1000$

$\text{C.P.} = ₹\ 1000 \times \frac{100}{100 + 25} = ₹\ 800$

8. $\text{Percentage gain or loss} = \frac{100(P-L) - 2PL}{200 + P - L}$

$= \frac{100(20-10) - 2 \times 20 \times 10}{200 + 20 - 10}$

$= \frac{1{,}000 - 400}{210} = \frac{600}{210} = \frac{20}{7}$ positive

$\therefore$ Total percentage gain $= \frac{20}{7}\%$ or $2\frac{6}{7}\%$

9. 100 – 20 = 80

When SP ₹ 80 then CP = ₹ 100

When SP ₹ 480 then CP $= \frac{100}{80} \times 480 = ₹\ 600$

Again 100 + 20 = ₹ 120

When CP ₹ 100 then SP ₹ 120

When CP ₹ 600 then SP $= \frac{120}{100} \times 600 = ₹\ 720$

∴ SP = ₹ 720

10. Let purchasing price be ₹ 100.

Then selling price = ₹ 100 + 10 = ₹ 110

New purchasing price = 100 – 10 = ₹ 90

and new selling price $= 90\left(1 + \frac{10}{100}\right)$

$= 90 \times \frac{11}{10} = ₹\ 99$

Difference in the two selling prices = 110 – 99 = ₹ 11

When difference is ₹ 11, then P.P. = ₹ 100

When difference is ₹ 132, then P.P.

$= \frac{100}{11} \times 132 = ₹\ 1{,}200$

RATIO, PROPORTION AND VARIATION

MULTIPLE CHOICE QUESTIONS

1. What should be added to each of the numbers 12, 30, 40 and 86, so that they are in proportion:

A. 6 B. 4

C. – 6 D. – 4

2. The mean proportional to $6 + \sqrt{27}$ and $6 - \sqrt{27}$ is:

A. 3 B. 9

C. 10 D. $\sqrt{10}$

3. If $x : y = 9 : 11$, the value of $\frac{5x + 3y}{3x + 5y}$ is:

A. 45 : 55 B. 18 : 22

C. 37 : 41 D. 39 : 41

4. The ratio of males and females of a village is 5 : 3. If there are 800 males in the village, females are :

A. 240 B. 480
C. 840 D. 488

5. In a mixture of 60 litre, the ratio of ethanol to ether is 4 : 1. How much ether must be added to the mixture to make this ratio 2 : 1?

A. 10 litre B. 12 litre
C. 18 litre D. 24 litre

6. A mixture of 45 litre of spirit and water, contains 20% of water in it. How much water must be added to it make the water 25% in the new mixture?

A. 5 litre B. 3 litre
C. 4 litre D. 6 litre

ANSWERS

1	2	3	4	5	6
A	A	D	B	B	B

SOME SELECTED EXPLANATORY ANSWERS

1. Let x be added to each of the numbers. Then,

$(12 + x) : (30 + x) :: (40 + x) : (86 + x)$

$\Rightarrow (86 + x)(12 + x) = (30 + x)(40 + x)$

$\Rightarrow 1{,}032 + 86x + 12x + x^2 = 1{,}200 + 30x + 40x + x^2$

$\Rightarrow 28x = 168 \therefore x = 6$

2. Mean proportion $= \sqrt{(6+\sqrt{27})(6-\sqrt{27})}$

$= \sqrt{36-27} = \sqrt{9} = 3$

3. $\dfrac{5x+3y}{3x+5y} = \dfrac{5\left(\frac{x}{y}\right)+3}{3\left(\frac{x}{y}\right)+5}$, dividing both num. and denom. by y

$= \dfrac{5\left(\frac{9}{11}\right)+3}{3\left(\frac{9}{11}\right)+5}, = \dfrac{\frac{45+33}{11}}{\frac{27+55}{11}} = \dfrac{78}{82} = \dfrac{39}{41}$

4. $5 : 3 = 800 : x$, where x represent females of the village.

$\therefore \quad x = \dfrac{800 \times 3}{5} = 480$

5. Quantity of ethanol in the mixture

$= \dfrac{4}{5} \times 60 = 48$ litre

Quantity of ether in the mixture

$= \dfrac{1}{5} \times 60 = 12$ litre

Let x litre of ether be added to mixture to get the desired ratio. Then,

$\dfrac{48}{12+x} = \dfrac{2}{1} \Rightarrow 24 + 2x = 48$

$\Rightarrow \quad 2x = 24 \qquad \therefore x = 12$

$\therefore$ 12 litre of ether is to be added.

6. Quantity of water in the mixture

$= \dfrac{20}{100} \times 45$ litre $= 9$ litre

Quantity of spirit in the mixture

$= \dfrac{80}{100} \times 45$ litre $= 36$ litre

Let x litre of water be added to make the water 25% in the new mixture. Then,

$\dfrac{9+x}{36} = \dfrac{25}{75} \quad \therefore x = 3$ litre

INTEREST

Solved Examples

Example 1: *What sum of money will produce ₹ 2,430 interest in 3 years at 3% simple interest?*

Solution: We have,

$$\text{S.I.} = \frac{\text{PRT}}{100}$$

Here, S.I. = ₹ 2,430, R = 3%, T = 3 years

So, $P = \frac{\text{SI} \times 100}{\text{R} \times \text{T}} = ₹\frac{2{,}430 \times 100}{3 \times 3} = ₹\,27{,}000$

Example 2: *In what time does a money becomes double at simple interest rate of 5% per annum?*

Solution: Let the money be ₹ 100.

After T years, it becomes ₹ 200, so interest = ₹ 100

$\therefore$ Time, $T = \frac{100 \times (\text{S.I.})}{\text{Principal} \times \text{Rate}} = \frac{100 \times (100)}{100 \times 5}$

= 20 years

Example 3: *A sum of ₹ 300 amounts to ₹ 420 in 4 years. What will it amount to if rate of interest is increased by 2%?*

Solution: Rate of interest before increase

$$= \frac{100 \times 120}{300 \times 4} = 10\%$$

$\therefore$ New rate of interest = 12%

S.I. with new rate of interest

$$= \frac{300 \times 12 \times 4}{100} = ₹\,144$$

Amount = ₹ 300 + ₹ 144 = ₹ 444

Example 4: *What annual instalment will discharge a debt of ₹ 1,326 due in 4 years at 7% simple interest?*

Solution: Let the annual payment be ₹ x. Then,

Amount of x for 3 years = $x + \frac{x \times 7 \times 3}{100}$

Amount of x for 2 years = $x + \frac{x \times 7 \times 2}{100}$

Amount of x for 1 year = $x + \frac{x \times 7 \times 1}{100}$

The three payments along with last payment of ₹ x will discharge the debt.

According to question,

$$\left(x + \frac{21x}{100}\right) + \left(x + \frac{14x}{100}\right) + \left(x + \frac{7x}{100}\right) + x = 1{,}326$$

or $442x = 1{,}32{,}600$

$\therefore$ $x = 300$

Hence, annual payment = ₹ 300

Example 5: *Find the compound interest on ₹ 8,000 at the rate of 5% p.a. for 2 years.*

Solution: Amount = ₹ $\left[8{,}000 \times \left(1 + \frac{5}{100}\right)^2\right]$

$\therefore$ Amount = ₹ $\left[8{,}000 \times \frac{21}{20} \times \frac{21}{20}\right]$

= ₹ 8,820

Compound interest = ₹ 8,820 – ₹ 8,000 = ₹ 820

MULTIPLE CHOICE QUESTIONS

1. In how many years will a sum of ₹ 1,500 yield an interest of ₹ 1,080 at 12 per cent per annum?

A. 5 years B. $5\frac{1}{4}$ years

C. $5\frac{1}{2}$ years D. 6 years

2. The principal which yields an interest of ₹ 2,500 in $2\frac{1}{2}$ years at 10% per annum at simple interest is:

A. ₹ 8,000 B. ₹ 9,000

C. ₹ 10,000 D. ₹ 11,000

3. A sum of ₹ 7,800 is lent out in 2 parts in such a way that the interest on one part at 10% for 5 years is equal to that on the other part at 9% for 6 years. The sum lent out at 10% is:

A. ₹ 4,050 B. ₹ 3,750

C. ₹ 4,500 D. ₹ 3,300

4. The simple interest on a sum of money is $\frac{1}{16}$ of the principal and the number of years is equal to the rate percent per annum. The rate percent per annum is:

A. $2\frac{1}{2}\%$ B. $2\frac{1}{3}\%$

C. $2\frac{1}{6}\%$ D. $6\frac{1}{4}\%$

5. What is the compound interest on ₹ 6,250 at 4% p.a. compounded annually for 3 years?

A. ₹ 780.40
B. ₹ 789.00
C. ₹ 788.80
D. ₹ 780.40

6. At what rate percent compound interest ₹ 800 amounts to ₹ 926.10 in $1\frac{1}{2}$ years interest compounded semi-annually?

A. 8% p.a. B. 10% p.a.
C. 12% p.a. D. 14% p.a.

7. A sum of money doubles itself at compound interest, compounded annually in 15 years. In how many years will it become 8 times, the remaining rate the same?

A. 40 years B. 45 years
C. 50 years D. 55 years

8. A loan ₹ 50,440 at 5% compound interest is to be paid in three equal annual instalments. What will be the amount of each annual instalment?

A. ₹ 18,522 B. ₹ 2,089
C. ₹ 2,689 D. ₹ 9,522

ANSWERS

1	2	3	4	5	6	7	8
D	C	A	A	D	B	B	A

SOME SELECTED EXPLANATORY ANSWERS

1. Here, P = ₹ 1,500; R = 12%; S.I. = ₹ 1,080

$$\text{Time, T} = \frac{₹\,1{,}080 \times 100}{₹\,1{,}500 \times 12} = 6 \text{ years}$$

3. $$\frac{\text{I part} \times 5 \times 10}{100} = \frac{\text{II part} \times 9 \times 6}{100}$$

or $$\frac{\text{I part}}{\text{II part}} = \frac{9 \times 6}{5 \times 10} = \frac{27}{25}$$

∴ $$\text{I part} = \frac{7{,}800}{27+25} \times 27 = ₹\,4{,}050$$

and II part = ₹ 7,800 − ₹ 4,050
= ₹ 3,750

4. Time = R years, P = the sum in ₹

$$\frac{P}{16} = \frac{P \times R \times R}{100}$$

or $$R^2 = \frac{100}{16}$$

or $$R = \frac{10}{4} = 2\frac{1}{2}\% \text{ p.a.}$$

5. $$\text{Amount} = ₹\,6{,}250 \times \left(1 + \frac{4}{100}\right)^3$$

$$= ₹\,6{,}250 \times \left(\frac{26}{25}\right)^3$$

= ₹ 7,030.40

∴ Compound Interest
= ₹ 7,030.40 − ₹ 6,250
= ₹ 780.40

8. Let the annual instalment be ₹ a. Then,

$$a\left[\left(\frac{100}{100+5}\right) + \left(\frac{100}{100+5}\right)^2 + \left(\frac{100}{100+5}\right)^3\right] = 50{,}440$$

$$\Rightarrow a\left[\frac{100}{105}\left\{1 + \frac{100}{105} + \left(\frac{100}{105}\right)^2\right\}\right] = 50{,}440$$

$$\Rightarrow a = ₹\,18{,}522$$

DISCOUNT

MULTIPLE CHOICE QUESTIONS

1. A suitcase of ₹ 240 is sold for ₹ 202. The rate of discount is:

A. $15\frac{5}{6}\%$ B. $15\frac{5}{8}\%$

C. $18\frac{41}{50}\%$ D. $18\frac{5}{8}\%$

2. A merchant allows a discount of 15% on the clothes purchased. Manohar purchases clothes worth ₹ 470. The money he will give is:

A. ₹ 70.50 B. ₹ 399.50

C. ₹ 469 D. ₹ 270

3. A trader allows 10% trade discount and 20% cash discount. If the list price is ₹ 500, then selling price is:

A. ₹ 360 B. ₹ 350

C. ₹ 355 D. ₹ 340

4. A retailer gains 20% after allowing 10% discount on the cost price. If the cost price is ₹ 100, then selling price is:

A. ₹ 120 B. ₹ 108

C. ₹ 95 D. ₹ 115

5. The printed price of an electric fan is ₹ 500. It is sold at 10% discount. But due to change of season the shopkeeper, declares 10% additional discount. The sale price of the fan is:

A. ₹ 455 B. ₹ 405

C. ₹ 450 D. ₹ 400

6. The true discount of ₹ 12,100 due to two years, hence at 10% per annum compound interest is:

A. ₹ 1,000 B. ₹ 1,100

C. ₹ 2,100 D. ₹ 1,200

ANSWERS

1	2	3	4	5	6
A	B	A	B	B	C

SOME SELECTED EXPLANATORY ANSWERS

1. Amount of Discount

$= \text{List price} - \text{Selling price}$

$= 240 - 202 = ₹\ 38$

$$\text{Rate of Discount} = \frac{\text{Discount} \times 100}{\text{List Price}}$$

$$= \frac{38 \times 100}{240} = \frac{95}{6}$$

$$= 15\frac{5}{6}$$

i.e., Discount $= 15\frac{5}{6}\%$

2. Cost price = ₹ 470

Rate of Discount = 15%

$$\text{Amount of Discount} = \frac{470 \times 15}{100}$$

$$= \frac{141}{2}$$

$= ₹\ 70.50$

$\therefore$ Amount Due $= 470 - 70.50$

$= ₹\ 399.50$

3. Selling Price

$$= \text{List price}\left(1-\frac{10}{100}\right)\left(1-\frac{20}{100}\right)$$

$$= 500 \times \frac{9}{10} \times \frac{4}{5} = ₹\ 360$$

Alternative Method:

List price	500
Less : Trade Discount @ 10%	
$\left(\frac{500 \times 10}{100}\right)$	50
	450
Less : Cash Discount @ 20%	
$\left(\frac{450 \times 20}{100}\right)$	90
	360

4. $\text{Selling Price} = \text{Cost Price}\left(1+\frac{20}{100}\right)\left(1-\frac{10}{100}\right)$

$$= 100\left(1+\frac{1}{5}\right)\left(1-\frac{1}{10}\right)$$

$$= 100 \times \frac{6}{5} \times \frac{9}{10} = ₹\ 108$$

5. $\text{Sale price} = \text{Printed price}\left(1-\frac{d_1}{100}\right)\left(1-\frac{d_2}{100}\right)$

$$= 500\left(1-\frac{10}{100}\right)\left(1-\frac{10}{100}\right)$$

$$= 500 \times \frac{9}{10} \times \frac{9}{10}$$

$$= ₹\ 405$$

6. $\text{Present value} = \frac{12{,}100}{\left(1+\frac{10}{100}\right)^2}$

$$= ₹\ 10{,}000$$

$\therefore$ True Discount = ₹ 12,100 – ₹ 10,000

= ₹ 2,100

AVERAGE

MULTIPLE CHOICE QUESTIONS

1. The heights of 7 buildings are 12 m, 13 m, 14 m, 15 m, 16 m, 17 m and 18 m. The average height of 7 buildings is:

A. 15 m B. 16 m
C. 17 m D. 18 m

2. The average height of 10 students is computed as 153 cm. But it was found later on that 151 cm was wrongly read as 141 cm. The correct average height is:

A. 155 cm B. 154 cm
C. 152 cm D. 151 cm

3. In a school 85 boys and 35 girls appeared in an examination. The average marks of the boys were found to be 40% whereas the average marks of the girls were 60%. The average marks percentage of the school is:

A. $50\frac{3}{5}$ B. 45
C. $45\frac{5}{6}$ D. 60

4. If the average of 5 observations x, $x + 2$, $x + 4$, $x + 6$, $x + 8$ is 11, then the average of the last three observations is:

A. 11 B. 13
C. 15 D. 17

5. The average age of 8 persons is 87 years. Of these the age of oldest is 2 years more than the one next. If these two persons are ignored, then the average age of the remaining 6 persons is 85 years. The age of the oldest person is (in years):

A. 90 B. 94
C. 96 D. 98

ANSWERS

1	2	3	4	5
A	B	C	B	B

SOME SELECTED EXPLANATORY ANSWERS

1. Average height

$$= \frac{12+13+14+15+16+17+18}{7}$$

$$= \frac{105}{7} = 15 \text{ m}$$

2. Wrong average = $\bar{x}$ = 153 cm

Wrong sum of heights,

$$\Sigma x = n\bar{x} = 10 \times 153 = 1{,}530 \text{ cm}$$

Correct sum of heights

$$\Sigma' x = \Sigma x - 141 + 151$$
$$= 1{,}530 + 10 = 1{,}540 \text{ cm}$$

∴ Correct average height,

$$\bar{x}' = \frac{\Sigma' x}{n} = \frac{1{,}540}{10} = 154 \text{ cm}$$

3. Let the maximum marks be 100

Then average marks of boys = 40

and average marks of girls = 60

$$\therefore \text{ Required average} = \frac{85\times40+35\times60}{85+35}$$

$$= \frac{3{,}400+2{,}100}{120}$$

$$= \frac{5{,}500}{120} = 45\frac{5}{6}$$

4. $$\bar{x} = \frac{x+(x+2)+(x+4)+(x+6)+(x+8)}{5} = 11$$

$$\Rightarrow \quad 5x + 20 = 11 \times 5 = 55$$

$$\therefore \quad x = \frac{55-20}{5} = \frac{35}{5} = 7$$

This average of the last three numbers

$$= \frac{(x+4)+(x+6)+(x+8)}{3}$$

$$= \frac{(7+4)+(7+6)+(7+8)}{3}$$

$$= \frac{11+13+15}{3} = \frac{39}{3} = 13$$

5. Let $x_1, x_2, x_3, x_4, x_5, x_6, x_7, x_8$ be the ages of 8 persons where x_8 is the age of the oldest person.

Thus, total of ages of the 8 persons

$$= 8 \times 87 = 696$$

Total of ages of the 6 persons

$$= 6 \times 85 = 510$$

$$\therefore \quad x_7 + x_8 = 696 - 510 = 186 \quad ...(i)$$

$$\text{But} \quad x_8 - x_7 = 2 \text{ (given)} \quad ...(ii)$$

Adding these two equations

$$2x_8 = 188$$

$$\therefore \quad x_8 = \frac{188}{2} = 94 \text{ years}$$

PARTNERSHIP

MULTIPLE CHOICE QUESTIONS

1. A, B and C share the profit in the ratio of 3 : 5 : 7. If the gain is ₹ 2,040, then C's share is :

A. ₹ 360
B. ₹ 600
C. ₹ 840
D. ₹ 120

2. Mishra, Sharma and Shukla started a business with ₹ 47,000. Mishra puts ₹ 5,000 more than Sharma and Sharma ₹ 3,000 more than Shukla. The share of Mishra out of the profit of ₹ 14,100 will be:

A. ₹ 3,600 B. ₹ 4,500
C. ₹ 6,000 D. ₹ 6,300

3. A, B and C are three partners in a business. The profit share of A is $\frac{3}{16}$ of the profit and

B's share is $\frac{1}{4}$ of the profit. If C receives ₹ 243, then the amount received by B will be:

A. ₹ 90 B. ₹ 96
C. ₹ 108 D. ₹ 120

4. A starts a business with ₹ 5,000. After 4 months B joins him with a sum of ₹ 4,000. In the end of the year there is a profit of ₹ 8,970. The share of A in the profit will be:

A. ₹ 3,120 B. ₹ 4,020
C. ₹ 5,850 D. ₹ 6,360

5. A, B and C share the profit in the ratio of 2 : 3 : 7. If the average gain is ₹ 8,000, then B's share is:

A. ₹ 2,000 B. ₹ 1,000
C. ₹ 1,500 D. ₹ 3,000

ANSWERS

1	2	3	4	5
C	C	C	C	A

SOME SELECTED EXPLANATORY ANSWERS

1. C's share $= \frac{7}{3+5+7} \times 2{,}040 = ₹\ 840$

2. Let Shukla's capital = ₹ x

Then Sharma's capital = ₹ $(x + 3{,}000)$

and Mishra capital = ₹ $(x + 3{,}000 + 5{,}000)$

$\Rightarrow x + (x + 3{,}000) + (x + 3{,}000 + 5{,}000) = 47{,}000$

$\Rightarrow 3x = 47{,}000 - 11{,}000 = 36{,}000$

$\therefore x = ₹\ 12{,}000$

Thus, capitals of Mishra, Sharma and Shukla are:

₹ 20,000; ₹ 15,000; ₹ 12,000

$\therefore$ Profit sharing ratio = 20 : 15 : 12, Sum = 47

$\therefore$ Profit of Mishra $= \frac{20}{47} \times 14{,}100 = ₹\ 6{,}000$

3. Let the profit be ₹ 1. Then

$$A : B : C = \frac{3}{16} : \frac{1}{4} : \left[1 - \left(\frac{3}{16} + \frac{1}{4}\right)\right]$$

$$= \frac{3}{16} : \frac{1}{4} : \frac{9}{16}$$

$$= \frac{3}{16} : \frac{4}{16} : \frac{9}{16}, \text{ i.e., } 3 : 4 : 9$$

When C's share is ₹ 9, then B's share = ₹ 4

When C's share is ₹ 243, then B's share

$$= \frac{4 \times 243}{9} = ₹\ 108$$

4. ₹ 5,000 × 12 = ₹ 60,000 for A

₹ 4,000 × (12 − 4) = ₹ 32,000 for B

Ratio of profit sharing = 60,000 : 32,000 or 60 : 32 or 15 : 8

$\therefore$ A's share $= \frac{15}{15+8} \times 8{,}970 = 15 \times 390 = ₹\ 5850$

5. B's share $= \frac{3}{2+3+7} \times 8{,}000 = \frac{3 \times 8{,}000}{12} = ₹\ 2{,}000$

STOCK AND SHARES

MULTIPLE CHOICE QUESTIONS

1. The 6% stock at 125 which can be purchased to get an annual income of ₹ 4,320 will be:

A. ₹ 24,000 B. ₹ 48,000
C. ₹ 36,000 D. ₹ 72,000

2. The rate of interest obtained by investing in 8% stock at ₹ 160 will be:

A. $2\frac{1}{2}\%$ B. 5%
C. $7\frac{1}{2}\%$ D. 10%

3. The investment required in "5% stock at 102" to obtain an annual income of ₹ 600 will be:

A. ₹ 6,120 B. ₹ 12,240
C. ₹ 9,120 D. ₹ 12,000

4. Ramesh holds ₹ 2,100 of 3% stock. He sells them at ₹ 121 and invests the proceeds in 5% stock. Thereby, his income increases by ₹ 14. The market price of 5% stock is:

A. ₹ 125 B. ₹ 135
C. ₹ 155 D. ₹ 165

5. Mohan invests ₹ 3,467.25 in a company paying 4% per annum when its ₹ 35 shares are selling for ₹ 51.75 each. His annual income will be:

A. ₹ 93.80 B. ₹ 39.80
C. ₹ 98.30 D. ₹ 39.08

ANSWERS

1	2	3	4	5
D	B	B	D	A

SOME SELECTED EXPLANATORY ANSWERS

1. $\text{Stock} = \frac{\text{Income} \times 100}{\text{Rate}}$

$= \frac{4,320 \times 100}{6} = ₹\ 72,000$

2. ∵ On an investment of ₹ 160, interest = ₹ 8

∴ On an investment of ₹ 100, interest

$= \frac{8 \times 100}{160} = ₹\ 5$

3. $\text{Investment} = \frac{\text{Income} \times \text{Market Value}}{\text{Rate}}$

$= \frac{600 \times 102}{5} = ₹\ 12,240$

4. Income from ₹ 100 stock = ₹ 3

Income from ₹ 2,100 stock $= \frac{3 \times 2,100}{100} = ₹\ 63$

The income from new stock = 63 + 14 = ₹ 77

The cost of ₹ 100 stock = ₹ 121

The cost of ₹ 2,100 stock $= \frac{121 \times 2,100}{100}$

$= ₹\ 2,541$

When the income is ₹ 77, then cost = ₹ 2,541

When the income is ₹ 5, then cost

$= \frac{2,541 \times 5}{77} = ₹\ 165$

5. Market value of a share of ₹ 35 = ₹ 51.75

∴ No. of such shares purchased by ₹ 3,467.25

$= \frac{3467.25}{51.75} = 67$

Face value of 67 shares = 35 × 67 = ₹ 2,345

Hence, divided @ 4% of the face value

$= 2,345 \times \frac{4}{100} = ₹\ 93.80$

PROBLEM ON AGE

Solved Examples

Example 1: *The ratio of ages of Kavya and Neha is 4 : 5. After 12 years, this ratio will become 5 : 6. What will be the age of Kavya after 2 years?*

Solution: Let the age of Kavya be $4x$ years and age of Neha be $5x$ years.

Age of Kavya after 12 years = $(4x + 12)$ years

Age of Neha after 12 years = $(5x + 12)$ years

Hence, $$\frac{4x+12}{5x+12} = \frac{5}{6}$$

$\Rightarrow$ $24x + 72 = 25x + 60$ $\quad \therefore x = 12$

Present age of Kavya = $4 \times 12 = 48$ years

Thus, age of Kavya after 2 years

= $48 + 2 = 50$ years

Example 2: *The age of a father is four times the age of his son. If the age of father is x years, find the age of his son after 8 years.*

Solution: Age of the father = x years

$\therefore$ Age of the son = $\frac{1}{4}x$ years

$\therefore$ Age of the son after 8 years = $\left(\frac{x}{4}+8\right)$ years

MULTIPLE CHOICE QUESTIONS

1. A father's age is four times that of his son. Eight years before, the father's age was sixteen times that of the son. Father's age is:

A. 40 years B. 35 years
C. 42 years D. 36 years

2. A is older than B by 5 years. Seven years hence, thrice A's age shall be equal to four times that of B. The present age of A is:

A. 13 years B. 8 years
C. 9 years D. 7 years

3. The ages of Ram and Mohan are in the ratio of 5 : 7 and the difference between them is 12 years. The ages (in years) of Ram and Mohan are respectively:

A. 30, 42 B. 42, 30
C. 15, 21 D. 21, 15

4. The ages of A and B are in the ratio of 9 : 4. 7 years hence, the ratio of their ages will be 5 : 3. The age of A is:

A. 8 years B. 18 years
C. 26 years D. 52 years

5. The ratio between the present ages of X and Y is 4 : 5. The ratio between the present age of X and the age of Y before 3 years is 7 : 8. The ratio between the present age of X and his age after 7 years will be:

A. 5 : 4 B. 8 : 7
C. 7 : 8 D. 4 : 5

6. The ratio between Rahim's and Karim's ages two years ago was 3 : 2 and at present it is 7 : 5. The present age of Karim is:

A. 10 years B. 14 years
C. 12 years D. 16 years

7. The sum of the ages of Ram and Shyam is 40 years. 5 years hence, the ratio of their ages will be 3 : 7. The age of Ram is:

A. 10 years B. 30 years
C. 15 years D. 25 years

8. The ratio of ages of the mother and her daughter is 12 : 5. The difference of their ages is 28 years. The ratio between the present age of the mother and the age of the daughter 4 years after will be:

A. 2 : 1 B. 1 : 2
C. 3 : 2 D. 2 : 3

9. The ratio of present ages of Mahesh and Dinesh is 7 : 8. If 4 years ago the ratio of their ages be 5 : 6, then present age of Dinesh is:

A. 10 years B. 12 years
C. 14 years D. 16 years

10. Six years back Seema was half that of Rupa in age. Four years hence, the respective ratio of their ages would be 3 : 5. The present age of Rupa is:

A. 46 years B. 40 years
C. 32 years D. 16 years

ANSWERS

1	2	3	4	5	6	7	8	9	10
A	A	A	B	D	A	A	A	D	A

SOME SELECTED EXPLANATORY ANSWERS

1. Let the age of the son = x years

Then age of the father = $4x$ years

Before 8 years,

Son's age = $x - 8$

Father's age = $4x - 8$

$4x - 8 = 16(x - 8)$

$\Rightarrow \quad 4x - 8 = 16x - 128$

$\Rightarrow \quad 12x = 120 \quad \therefore x = 10$

Thus, father's age = $4 \times 10 = 40$ years

2. Let the age of A be x years

$\therefore$ the age of B = $(x - 5)$ years

Seven years hence,

Age of A = $x + 7$

Age of B = $(x - 5) + 7$

$3(x + 7) = 4(x - 5 + 7)$

$\therefore \quad 3x + 21 = 4x - 20 + 28 = 4x + 8$

$\Rightarrow \quad 3x + 21 = 4x - 20 + 28 = 4x + 8$

$\therefore \quad x = 13$

3. Let the ages of Ram and Mohan be $5x$ and $7x$

Then, $7x - 5x = 12 \Rightarrow 2x = 12 \therefore x = 6$

Age of Ram = $5 \times 6 = 30$ years

Age of Mohan = $7 \times 6 = 42$ years

4. Let the ages of A and B be $9x$ and $4x$.

Then $\dfrac{9x+7}{4x+7} = \dfrac{5}{3}$

$\Rightarrow \quad 3(9x + 7) = 5(4x + 7)$

$\Rightarrow \quad 27x + 21 = 20x + 35$

$\Rightarrow \quad 7x = 35 - 21 = 14 \quad \therefore x = 2$

Hence, age of A = $9 \times 2 = 18$ years.

5. Let the present ages of X and Y be $4x$ and $5x$

$\therefore \quad \dfrac{4x}{5x-3} = \dfrac{7}{8}$

$\Rightarrow \quad 8 \times 4x = 7(5x - 3)$

$\Rightarrow \quad 32x = 35x - 21$

$\Rightarrow \quad 3x = 21 \quad \therefore x = 7$

Thus, age of X = $4 \times 7 = 28$ years

Age of X after 7 years = $28 + 7 = 35$ years

$\therefore$ Required ratio = $\dfrac{28}{35} = \dfrac{4}{5}$ or 4 : 5

6. Let the present ages of Rahim and Karim be $7x$ and $5x$.

Then $\dfrac{7x-2}{5x-2} = \dfrac{3}{2}$

$\Rightarrow \quad 14x - 4 = 15x - 6$

$\Rightarrow \quad x = 2$

$\Rightarrow$ The present age of Karim is $5 \times 2 = 10$ years

7. Let the ages of Ram and Shyam 5 years hence be $3x$ and $7x$.

The sum of their present ages

$= (3x - 5) + (7x - 5) = 40$

$\Rightarrow \quad 10x = 40 + 10 = 50 \quad \therefore x = 5$

Hence, age of Ram = $3 \times 5 - 5 = 15 - 5$

= 10 years.

8. Let the ages of mother and her daughter be $12x$ and $5x$.

Then, $12x - 5x = 28 \Rightarrow x = \dfrac{28}{7} = 4$

$\therefore$ Present age of the mother

$= 12 \times 4 = 48$ years

and age of daughter after 4 years

$= 5x + 4$

$= 5 \times 4 + 4 = 24$

$\therefore$ Required ratio = $\dfrac{48}{24} = \dfrac{2}{1}$, *i.e.*, 2 : 1

9. Let present ages of Mahesh and Dinesh be $7x$ and $8x$.

4 years ago,

Mahesh's age = $7x - 4$

Dinesh's age = $8x - 4$

$\therefore \quad \dfrac{7x-4}{8x-4} = \dfrac{5}{6}$

$\Rightarrow \quad 6(7x - 4) = 5(8x - 4)$

$\Rightarrow \quad 42x - 24 = 40x - 20$

$\Rightarrow \quad 2x = 4 \quad \therefore x = 2$

$\therefore$ Dinesh's present age $= 8 \times 2 = 16$ years.

10. Let the present ages of Seema and Rupa be x and y. Six years back,

Seema's age $= x - 6$

Rupa's age $= y - 6$

$$(x-6) = \frac{1}{2}(y-6)$$

or $\quad 2x - y = 6 \quad ...(i)$

Four years hence,

Seema's age $= x + 4$

Rupa's age $= y + 4$

$$\frac{x+4}{y+4} = \frac{3}{5}$$

$5x + 20 = 3y + 12$

$5x - 3y = -8 \quad ...(ii)$

Multiply equation (*i*) by 3,

$6x - 3y = 18 \quad ...(iii)$

Subtract eq. (*iii*) from eq. (*ii*),

$x = 26$

Substitute this value of x in (*i*),

$y = 2x - 6 = 2 \times 26 - 6$

$= 52 - 6 = 46.$

ALLIGATION, MIXTURE

MULTIPLE CHOICE QUESTIONS

1. In a mixture of 60 litre, the ratio of ethanol to ether is 4 : 1. The quantity of ether to be added to the mixture to make this ratio 2 : 1 will be:

A. 10 litre B. 12 litre
C. 18 litre D. 24 litre

2. The price of a variety of a commodity is ₹ 5 per kg and that of another is ₹ 8 per kg. The ratio in which two varieties should be mixed so that the price is ₹ 7 per kg will be:

A. 1 : 2 B. 2 : 1
C. 3 : 1 D. 8 : 5

3. A confectioner sells the milk after mixing some water in it at the same rate at which he bought. If he gains 25% in this way, the quantity of water mixed with per litre of milk is:

A. 0.25 litre B. 2.5 litre
C. 1.5 litre D. 0.35 litre

4. A milk seller bought some milk at the rate of ₹ 16 per litre. He mixed water $\frac{1}{4}$th of it and sold the mixture at the cost price. Assuming the price of water as ₹ 0.00 per litre. The gain % is:

A. 16%
B. 20%
C. 25%
D. None of these

5. Ramesh has ₹ 3,600. He invests a part of it at 3% per annum and the remaining at 5% higher rate of simple interest. He gets in all ₹ 540 at the end of 3 years. The sum invested at 3% per annum is:

A. ₹ 1,440 B. ₹ 2,000
C. ₹ 2,160 D. ₹ 2,200

ANSWERS

1	2	3	4	5
B	A	A	C	C

SOME SELECTED EXPLANATORY ANSWERS

1. The quantity of ethanol $= \frac{4}{5} \times 60 = 48$ litre

The quantity of ether $= \frac{1}{5} \times 60 = 12$ litre

$\therefore \quad \frac{48}{12+x} = \frac{2}{1}$

$\Rightarrow \quad 48 = 2(12 + x)$

$\Rightarrow \quad 48 = 24 + 2x$

$\Rightarrow \quad 2x = 48 - 24 = 24$

$\therefore \quad x = 12$

2.

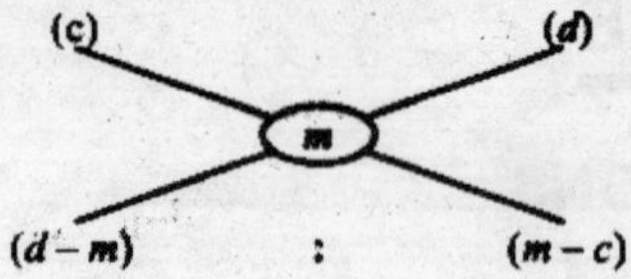

Required ratio $= \frac{d-m}{m-c} = \frac{\text{cheaper variety}}{\text{dearer variety}}$

$= \frac{8-7}{7-5}$

$= \frac{1}{2}$ *i.e.,* 1 : 2

3. Let the cost price of 1 litre milk = ₹ 100

Profit on 1 litre = ₹ 25 ...(1)

Suppose he mixes x litre of water in 1 litre milk.

Then selling price of $(1 + x)$ litre milk

$= (1 + x) \times 100$

and Profit = Selling Price – Cost Price

$= 100 (1 + x) - 100$

$= 100x$ ...(2)

Comparing (1) and (2),

$100x = 25$

$\therefore \quad x =$ ₹ 0.25

4. Suppose he bought 1 litre of milk,

Cost price = ₹ 16/litre

Mixture = Milk + Water

$= 1 + \frac{1}{4} = \frac{5}{4}$

Cost price of the mixture = ₹ 16

Selling price of the mixture $= \frac{5}{4} \times 16 =$ ₹ 20

$\therefore$ Gain % $= \frac{20-16}{16} \times 100$

$= \frac{4}{16} \times 100 = 25\%$

5. Average rate of interest $= \frac{100 \times 540}{3{,}600 \times 3} = 5$

By Rule of Alligation :

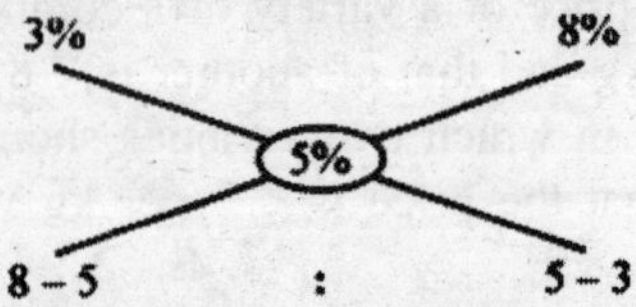

Investment at 3% per annum

$= \frac{3}{3+2} \times 3{,}600 =$ ₹ 2,160

CLOCK AND CALANDER

MULTIPLE CHOICE QUESTIONS

1. How many times the hands of a clock are at right angle in a day?

A. 24 B. 16

C. 44 D. 48

2. At what angle the hands of a clock are inclined at 15 minute past 5?

A. $58\frac{1}{2}°$ B. 64°

C. $67\frac{1}{2}°$ D. $72\frac{1}{2}°$

3. What angle do the hands of a clock form at 20 past 7?

A. 70° B. 80°
C. 90° D. 100°

4. What will be the time when the hour hand makes an angle of 50° with the minute hand?

A. 1.15 hrs B. 1.20 hrs
C. 1.10 hrs D. 1.25 hrs

5. What is the time when the hands of the clock make an angle of 90° with each other?

A. 3.10 hrs B. 3.30 hrs
C. 3.20 hrs D. 3.25 hrs

6. What angle is formed when the hour hand is at 6.00 and the minute hand is at 12.00?

A. 100° B. 120°
C. 180° D. 90°

7. The angle subtended by the small hand of the clock in 20 minutes will be:

A. 10° B. 15°
C. 20° D. 25°

8. There are 5 Saturday in a month. The first day of the month will be:

A. Sunday B. Friday
C. Wednesday D. Monday

9. The first day of a year is Sunday what day of the week lies on the first day of the next year?

A. Saturday B. Friday
C. Monday D. Thursday

10. December 3, 1990 is Sunday; what day of the week will fall on Jan. 3, 1991?

A. Tuesday B. Wednesday
C. Thursday D. Friday

11. If 7th day of a month is a 3 days before Friday, then the 19th day of the same month will be:

A. Sunday B. Monday
C. Wednesday D. Friday

ANSWERS

1	2	3	4	5	6	7	8	9	10
C	C	D	A	B	C	A	B	C	B
11									
A									

SOME SELECTED EXPLANATORY ANSWERS

1. It is clear from the properties of the clock that both hands of a clock are at right angle twice in every hour, except at 3.00 o'clock and 9.00 o'clock. At 3.00 o'clock and 9.00 o'clock the positions are identical. So, they are at right angle 22 times in 12 hrs. Thus, in 24 hrs they are 22 × 2 = 44 times at right angles.

2. Whan the minute hand is at 3 and hour hand is slightly ahead of 5, only then the time is 15 past 3. The angle through which the four hand shifts in 15 minute = $15\times\frac{1}{2}^\circ = 7\frac{1}{2}^\circ$

Hence, angle at 15 minute past 5

$$= 60 + 7\frac{1}{2}^\circ = 67\frac{1}{2}^\circ$$

3. The hands of a clock form an angle of 100° at 20 past 7.

4. When the hour hand makes an angle of 50°, the time is 1.15 hrs.

5. The time is 3.30 hrs, when the hands make an angle of 90°.

6. An angle of 180° is formed when the hour hand is at 6.00 and the minute hand is at 12.00.

7. The small hand of the clock rotates 0.5° in one minute.

Hence, required angle = 20 × 0.5° = 10°.

8. In a month of 31 days, there are 4 weeks + 3 days.

The three days may be

Thursday, Friday, Saturday

Friday, Saturday, Sunday
Saturday, Monday, Tuesday

The first day of the week may be
Thursday, *Friday* or Saturday

9. The answer depends on the year.
If the year is an ordinary year then next day.
If the year is a leap year then beyond 2 days.
Thus, possible answers are *Monday* or Tuesday.

10. No. of days from Dec. 3, 1990 to Jan. 3, 1991
= 31

No. of odd days in this period = 3

Hence, the required day is 3 days beyond Sunday, *i.e.,* Wednesday.

11. *Tuesday,* Wednesday, Thursday, Friday
7th day of the month = Tuesday
14th day of the month = Tuesday

15,	16,	17,
Wednesday,	Thursday,	Friday,
Saturday,	*Sunday*	
18,	19	

2 Logarithms and Exponents

THE EXPONENTIAL SERIES

If x is any real number (whether rational or irrational), then

1. $e^x = 1 + \frac{x}{1!} + \frac{x^2}{2!} + \frac{x^3}{3!} + ...$

   The series on the right hand side of the above relation is called the exponential series.

2. $e^{-x} = 1 - \frac{x}{1!} + \frac{x^2}{2!} - \frac{x^3}{3!} + \frac{x^4}{4!} - ....$

3. $e^x + e^{-x} = 2\left[1 + \frac{x^2}{2!} + \frac{x^4}{4!} + ...\right]$

4. $e^x - e^{-x} = 2\left[\frac{x}{1!} + \frac{x^3}{3!} + \frac{x^5}{5!} + ...\right]$

5. $e = 1 + \frac{1}{1!} + \frac{1}{2!} + \frac{1}{3!} + \frac{1}{4!} + ...$

6. $e^{-1} = 1 - \frac{1}{1!} + \frac{1}{2!} - \frac{1}{3!} + \frac{1}{4!} - ....$

7. $e + e^{-1} = 2\left[1 + \frac{1}{2!} + \frac{1}{4!} + ...\right]$

8. $e - e^{-1} = 2\left[\frac{1}{1!} + \frac{1}{3!} + \frac{1}{5!} + ...\right]$

9. For $a > 0$, $a^x = e^{x \log_e a}$

   $= 1 + \frac{x \log_e a}{1!} + \frac{x^2 (\log_e a)^2}{2!} + \frac{x^3 (\log_e a)^3}{3!} + ...$

The Logarithmic Series

The expansion of $\log_e (1 + x)$ in ascending powers of x is given by

1. $\log(1 + x) = x - \frac{x^2}{2} + \frac{x^3}{2} - \frac{x^4}{4} + ...$ to ∞,

   where $-1 < x \le 1$.

   The series on the right hand side is called the logarithmic series which holds for $|x| < 1$.

2. $\log(1 - x) = -\left(x + \frac{x^2}{2} + \frac{x^3}{3} + ... \text{ to } \infty\right)$,

   where $-1 \le x < 1$.

3. $\frac{1}{2}\log\left(\frac{1+x}{1-x}\right) = x + \frac{x^3}{3} + \frac{x^5}{5} + ...$

   where $-1 < x < 1$.

4. $\log 2 = 1 - \frac{1}{2} + \frac{1}{3} - \frac{1}{4} + ...$ to ∞.

   This series is called *Libnitz series.*

Solved Examples

Example 1: *Find the coefficient of x^n in*

$$1 + \frac{a+bx}{1!} + \frac{(a+bx)^2}{2!} + ... + \frac{(a+bx)^n}{n!} + ...$$

Solution: $1 + \frac{a+bx}{1!} + \frac{(a+bx)^2}{2!} + ... + \frac{(a+bx)^n}{n!} + ...$

$= e^{a+bx}, = e^a \cdot e^{bx},$

$= e^a\left[1 + bx + \frac{b^2x^2}{2!} + \frac{b^3x^3}{3!} + ... + \frac{b^nx^n}{n!} + ...\right]$

$\therefore$ The required coefficient of $x^n = \frac{e^a b^n}{n!}$.

Example 2: *For what value of x,*

$\log 2 + \log(x + 2) - \log(3x - 5) = \log 3$.

Solution: log 2 + log (x + 2) – log (3x – 5) = log3

$\Rightarrow \quad \log\frac{2(x+2)}{3x-5} = \log 3 \Rightarrow \frac{2(x+2)}{3x-5} = 3$

$\Rightarrow \quad 2x + 4 = 9x - 15$

$\Rightarrow \quad -7x = -19 \therefore x = \frac{19}{7}$

Example 3: *Find the value of* $\log_{b^3} a^2 . \log_{c^3} b^2 . \log_{a^3} c^2$.

Solution: Given expression may be written as,

$$= \frac{\log_{10} a^2}{\log_{10} b^3} \cdot \frac{\log_{10} b^2}{\log_{10} c^3} \cdot \frac{\log_{10} c^2}{\log_{10} a^3}$$

$$\left(\text{Using } \log_a m = \frac{\log_b m}{\log_b a}\right)$$

$$= \frac{2\log_{10} a}{3\log_{10} b} \cdot \frac{2\log_{10} b}{3\log_{10} c} \cdot \frac{2\log_{10} c}{3\log_{10} a}$$

$$= \frac{2}{3} \times \frac{2}{3} \times \frac{2}{3} = \frac{8}{27}$$

Example 4: *If* $\frac{\log(2x-1)}{\log x} = 2$, *find x.*

Solution: $\frac{\log(2x-1)}{\log x} = 2$

$\Rightarrow \quad \log (2x - 1) = 2 \log x = \log x^2$

$\Rightarrow \quad 2x - 1 = x^2$

$\Rightarrow \quad x^2 - 2x + 1 = 0$

$\Rightarrow \quad (x - 1)^2 = 0 \quad \therefore x = 1$

MULTIPLE CHOICE QUESTIONS

1. The value of $2^{\log_{2\sqrt{2}} 27}$ is:

A. 27 B. $\frac{1}{9}$

C. 9 D. $\frac{1}{27}$

2. The value of $\log_{11}\left[\frac{121\sqrt{14,641}}{\sqrt[3]{1,331}}\right]$ is:

A. 3 B. 4

C. 11 D. 12

3. The value of the expression $\log 18^{3/2} + 3 \log (2 \times 2) - 2 \log (3 \times 2)$ is:

A. $\log 96\sqrt{2}$ B. $\log 45\sqrt{3}$

C. 0 D. 1

4. The value of $\sqrt{\left(\frac{1}{\sqrt{27}}\right)^2 - \frac{\log_5 13}{\log_5 81}}$ is:

A. $3\sqrt{3}$ B. $\frac{1}{\sqrt{27}}\sqrt{1-\frac{27}{4}\log_3 13}$

C. 1 D. 0

5. The value of $\log_7\left[\log_7\sqrt{7\sqrt{7\sqrt{7}}}\right]$ is:

A. 7 B. log 7

C. $\log_7\sqrt{7}$ D. $1 - 3\log_7 2$

6. Evaluate $\log_{\sqrt{q}} p^2 \cdot \log_{\sqrt{r}} q^2 \cdot \log_{\sqrt{p}} r^2$:

A. 1 B. log pqr

C. 64 D. log (p/q/r)

7. Find x, if:

$\log_{10} x \times \log_{10} 64 = \log_{10} 8 \times \log_{10} 256$:

A. 16 B. 32

C. 64 D. 128

8. If $\log_{10}(x - 9) + \log_{10} x = 1$, then x equals to:

A. 9 B. 1

C. 0 D. 10

9. If $\log_{27}\left(\log_4\sqrt{x^9}\right) = \frac{2}{3}$, then x equals to:

A. 3 B. 8

C. 4 D. 16

10. If $a^x = b^y = ab$, the value of $\frac{1}{x}+\frac{1}{y}$ is:

A. a B. 1

C. b D. ab

11. If $\log_4 \log_3 \log_2 x = 0$, the value of x is:

A. 6 B. 8

C. 12 D. 16

12. If $\log\left(\frac{x-y}{3}\right) = \frac{1}{2}(\log x + \log y)$, then $x^2 + y^2$ is equal to:

A. $9xy$ B. x^2y^2
C. $6xy$ D. $11xy$

13. If $\log_{16}(\log_2 a) = \log_4 b$, then 2^{b^2} is:

A. a B. $\frac{1}{a}$
C. a^2 D. $\frac{1}{a^2}$

14. The value of $\log_{10}125$, (given $\log_{10}2 = 0.30$), is:

A. 2.05 B. 2.10
C. 2.15 D. 2.21

15. $\log_{10}\frac{26}{51} + \log_{10}\frac{119}{91} - \log_{10}\frac{13}{32} - \log_{10}\frac{64}{39}$ is equal to:

A. 0 B. 1
C. 2 D. 3

16. The expansion $e^x = 1 + \frac{x}{1!} + \frac{x^2}{2!} + \frac{x^3}{3!} + \ldots$ to ∞ is valid for

A. $-1 < x < 1$
B. all real x
C. $-1 \le x \le 1$
D. $0 < x < 1$

17. $\frac{1}{2!} - \frac{1}{3!} + \frac{1}{4!} - \frac{1}{5!} + \ldots$ equals

A. log 2 B. log e
C. e D. e^{-1}

18. Co-efficient of x^4 in the expansion of $\frac{1-3x+x^2}{e^x}$ is

A. $\frac{25}{24}$ B. $\frac{24}{25}$
C. $\frac{4}{25}$ D. $\frac{5}{24}$

19. $\dfrac{1+\frac{1}{2!}+\frac{1}{4!}+\frac{1}{6!}+\ldots}{1+\frac{1}{3!}+\frac{1}{5!}+\frac{1}{7!}+\ldots}$ is equal to

A. $\frac{e^2+1}{e^2-1}$ B. $\frac{e^2-1}{e^2+1}$
C. $e^2 + 1$ D. $e^2 - 1$

20. $e^{\log_e x}$ is equal to

A. x B. e
C. 1 D. None of these

ANSWERS

1	2	3	4	5	6	7	8	9	10
C	A	A	B	D	C	A	D	D	B
11	**12**	**13**	**14**	**15**	**16**	**17**	**18**	**19**	**20**
B	D	A	B	A	B	D	A	A	A

SOME SELECTED EXPLANATORY ANSWERS

2. $\sqrt{14,641} = 121$, $\sqrt[3]{1,331} = 11$

$\therefore$ Given expression $= \log_{11}\left(\frac{121\times121}{11}\right)$

$= \log_{11} 11^3 = 3\log_{11} 11 = 3$

4. $\sqrt{\left(\frac{1}{\sqrt{27}}\right)^2 - \frac{\log_5 13}{\log_5 81}}$

$= \sqrt{\frac{1}{27} - \log_{81} 13}$ $\left[\because \text{Using } \log_a m = \frac{\log_b m}{\log_b a}\right]$

$= \frac{1}{\sqrt{27}}\sqrt{1 - 27\log_{3^4} 13}$

$= \frac{1}{\sqrt{27}}\sqrt{1 - \frac{27}{4}\log_3 13}$ $\left[\because \text{Using } \log_{a^b} x = \frac{1}{b}\log_a x\right]$

5. $\log_7\left[\log_7\sqrt{7\sqrt{7\sqrt{7}}}\right]$

$= \log_7\left[\log_7\sqrt{7\sqrt{7^{3/2}}}\right]$

$= \log_7\left[\log_7\sqrt{7^{1+3/4}}\right]$

$= \log_7\left[\log_7 7^{7/8}\right]$

$= \log_7\frac{7}{8} = \log_7 7 - \log_7 8$

$= 1 - 3\log_7 2$

6. Given expression

$$= \frac{\log p^2}{\log\sqrt{q}}\cdot\frac{\log q^2}{\log\sqrt{r}}\cdot\frac{\log r^2}{\log\sqrt{p}}$$

$$= \frac{2\log p}{\frac{1}{2}\log q}\cdot\frac{2\log q}{\frac{1}{2}\log r}\cdot\frac{2\log r}{\frac{1}{2}\log p}$$

$= 4 \times 4 \times 4 = 64$

7. $\frac{\log_{10} x}{\log_{10} 8} = \frac{2\log_{10} 16}{2\log_{10} 8}$

$\Rightarrow \quad \log_8 x = \log_8 16 \qquad \therefore x = 16$

8. $\log_{10}(x - 9) + \log_{10} x = 1$

$\Rightarrow \quad \log_{10}(x - 9)\,x = 1$

$\Rightarrow \quad (x - 9)\,x = 10^1 = 10$

$\Rightarrow \quad x^2 - 9x - 10 = 0$

$\Rightarrow \quad (x - 10)(x + 1) = 0 \quad \therefore x = -1, 10$

Since $x = -1$ is not possible, $x = 10$

9. $\log_{27}\left(\log_4\sqrt{x^9}\right) = \frac{2}{3}$

$\Rightarrow \quad \log_4\sqrt{x^9} = 27^{2/3}$

$\Rightarrow \quad \log_4 x^{9/2} = (3^3)^{2/3} = 3^2 = 9$

$\Rightarrow \quad x^{9/2} = 4^9$

$\Rightarrow \quad x^{9/2} = (16)^{9/2} \quad \therefore x = 16$

11. $\log_4\log_3\log_2 x = 0 \Rightarrow \log_3\log_2 x = 4^0 = 1$

$\Rightarrow \log_2 x = 3^1 = 3 \Rightarrow x = 2^3 = 8$

12. $\log\left(\frac{x-y}{3}\right) = \frac{1}{2}(\log x + \log y)$

$\Rightarrow \quad \log\left(\frac{x-y}{3}\right) = \frac{1}{2}\log xy$

$\Rightarrow \quad 2\log\left(\frac{x-y}{3}\right) = \log xy$

$\Rightarrow \quad \log\left(\frac{x-y}{3}\right)^2 = \log xy$

$\Rightarrow \quad \left(\frac{x-y}{3}\right)^2 = xy$

($\because$ log is a one-one function)

$\Rightarrow \quad \frac{x^2 + y^2 - 2xy}{9} = xy \Rightarrow x^2 + y^2 = 11xy$

14. $\log_{10} 125 = \log_{10} 5^3$

$= 3\log_{10} 5$

$= 3\log_{10}\left(\frac{10}{2}\right)$

$= 3\log_{10} 10 - 3\log_{10} 2$

$= 3 - 3 \times 0.30 = 3 - 0.90 = 2.10$

15. Given expression

$$= \log_{10}\frac{13\times2}{17\times3} + \log_{10}\frac{17\times7}{13\times7} - \log_{10}\frac{13}{32} - \log_{10}\frac{32\times2}{13\times3}$$

$$= \log_{10}\left[\frac{13\times2+17\times7}{17\times3\times13\times7}\times\frac{32}{13}\times\frac{13\times3}{32\times2}\right] = \log_{10} 1$$

$= 0$

3 Linear and Quadratic Equation

REMEMBER

1. An equation of the form $ax^2 + bx + c = 0$, $a \neq 0$ in which the highest power of x is 2 and a, b, c are any three numbers free from x but $a \neq 0$ is called a *quadratic equation* or second *degree equation* in x.
2. A quadratic equation is satisfied by two values of x, *i.e.*, there are two roots of the quadratic equation.
3. The formula for solving a quadratic equation $ax^2 + bx + c = 0$ is:

$$x = \frac{-b \pm \sqrt{b^2 - 4ac}}{2a}$$

where $b^2 - 4ac$ is called *discriminant.*

(*i*) If $b^2 - 4ac > 0$, the two roots are real and different.

(*ii*) If $b^2 - 4ac = 0$, the two roots are real and equal.

(*iii*) If $b^2 - 4ac < 0$, the two roots are imaginary.

(*iv*) If $b^2 - 4ac$ is a perfect square and a, b, c are rational, the two roots are rational.

(*v*) If $b^2 - 4ac$ is not a perfect square and a, b, c, are rational, then the two roots are irrational.

4. *Linear Equations in two variables* : The equation of the form $ax + by + c = 0$, where a, b, c are real constants, is called a linear equation in two variables x and y. Two equations

$$a_1x_1 + b_1y_1 + c_1 = 0$$

and $$a_2x + b_2y + c_2 = 0$$

which satisfy the same values of x and y are called linear simultaneous equations in two variables.

Important Rule:

(*i*) The solution is unique, if $\frac{a_1}{a_2} \neq \frac{b_1}{b_2}$.

(*ii*) The solutions are infinite, if $\frac{a_1}{a_2} = \frac{b_1}{b_2} = \frac{c_1}{c_2}$.

(*iii*) No solution, if $\frac{a_1}{a_2} = \frac{b_1}{b_2} \neq \frac{c_1}{c_2}$.

The equation $a_1x - b_1y = c$ and $a_2x^3 + b_2y^3 = c_2$ say are non-linear simultaneous equations in x and y.

Solved Examples

Example 1: *Solve the equation:*

$$2(x - 3) = 9 + 3(x - 9)$$

Solution: $2(x - 3) = 9 + 3(x - 9)$

or $2 \times x - 2 \times 3 = 9 + 3 \times x - 3 \times 9$

or $2x - 6 = 9 + 3x - 27$

or $2x - 3x = 9 - 27 + 6$

or $-x = -12$

$\therefore$ $x = 12$

Example 2: *Find two numbers whose sum is 64, and whose difference is 16.*

Solution: Let the smaller number be x.

Then another number $= 64 - x$

Difference, $(64 - x) - x = 16$

$\Rightarrow$ $64 - 2x = 16$

$\Rightarrow$ $-2x = 16 - 64 = -48$

$\therefore \qquad x = \dfrac{-48}{-2} = 24$

$\therefore$ Second number = 64 – 24 = 40.

Example 3: *Solve:* $x^2 + (1 - p)x - p = 0.$

Solution: $x^2 + (1 - p)x - p = 0$

$\Rightarrow \quad x^2 + x - px - p = 0$

$\Rightarrow \quad x(x + 1) - p(x + 1) = 0$

$\Rightarrow \quad (x + 1)(x - p) = 0$

$\Rightarrow \quad x + 1 = 0$

or $\quad x - p = 0$

$\therefore \quad x = -1$

or $\quad x = p$

Thus, the two roots of the quardratic equation are –1 and p.

Example 4: *If the equations* $4x + 7y = 10$ *and* $10x + ky = 25$ *represent coincident lines, then find value of k.*

Solution: Since the two lines $y = -\dfrac{4}{7}x + \dfrac{10}{7}$, $y = -\dfrac{10}{k}x + \dfrac{25}{k}$ represent coincident lines.

$$-\frac{10}{k} = -\frac{4}{7}$$

$$\therefore \quad k = \frac{70}{4} = \frac{35}{2}$$

Example 5: *If the quadratic equation* $2x^2 + 3x + p = 0$ *has equal roots, then find the value of p.*

Solution: Since the given equation has equal roots,

$b^2 - 4ac = 0$

or $\quad 3^2 - 4.2.p = 0$

or $\quad 9 - 8p = 0$

$\therefore \quad p = \dfrac{9}{8}$

MULTIPLE CHOICE QUESTIONS

1. The value of x in the equation $\dfrac{x+2}{x-1} = \dfrac{5}{2}$ is:

A. 3 B. 7
C. 5 D. 9

2. 32 is divided into two parts such that if the larger is divided by the smaller, the quotient is 2 and the remainder is 5. The larger part is:

A. 9 B. 18
C. 23 D. 27

3. If the sum of the roots of the equation $qx^2 + 2x + 3q = 0$ is equal to their product, then the value of q is:

A. $-\dfrac{2}{3}$ B. $\dfrac{3}{2}$
C. 3 D. – 6

4. If $(x - 2)(x + 6) \geq 0$, then the solution set is:

A. $\{x : x \geq 2\}$
B. $\{x : x \leq 6\}$
C. $\{x : x \leq -6\}$
D. $\{x : x \geq 2 \text{ or } x \leq -6\}$

5. If α, β are the roots of the quadratic equation $4x^2 - 4x + 1 = 0$, then $\alpha^3 + \beta^3$ is equal to:

A. $\dfrac{1}{4}$ B. $\dfrac{1}{8}$
C. 16 D. 32

6. If the roots of the equation:

$$\lambda^2 + 8\lambda + \mu^2 + 6\mu = 0$$

are real, then μ lies between:

A. –2 and 8 B. –3 and 6
C. –8 and 2 D. –6 and 3

7. The values of x satisfying the equation $5^{2x} - 5^{x+3} + 125 = 5^x$ are:

A. 0 and 2 B. –1 and 3
C. 0 and –3 D. 0 and 3

8. Two students while solving a quadratic equation in x, one copied the constant term incorrectly and got the roots 3 and 2; while the other copies the constant term and coefficient of x^2 as –6 and 1 respectively. The correct roots are:

A. 3, –2 B. –3, 2
C. –6, –1 D. 6, –1

9. For a given value of k, the product of roots of $x^2 - 2kx + 3k^2 - 4 = 0$ is 5. The roots may be characterised as:

A. integral
B. rational but not integral
C. irrational
D. imaginary

10. If the roots of the equation $x^2 - 6x + 10 = 0$ are α and β, then $\alpha^2 + \beta^2$ is:
A. –16 B. 4
C. 60 D. 16

11. Total salary of A and B is equal. If A gets 65% allowance of his basic salary and B gets 80% of his basic salary. If the basic salary of B is ₹ 1,100, then the basic salary of A is:
A. ₹ 1,200 B. ₹ 1,980
C. ₹ 1,800 D. ₹ 1,100

12. The length of a field is twice its breadth. If the length is reduced by 5 metre and breadth is increased by 3 metre, the area remains as before. The length of the field is:
A. 15 m B. 30 m
C. 12 cm D. 25 m

13. A student starts for a hostel 24 km away from his house on bicycle. If he increases his speed by 2 km per hour, he reaches 2 hours early. His speed in km/hour is:
A. 8 B. 6
C. 4 D. 3

14. Ravi, after giving away 80% of his pocket money to Komal and 6% of the remaining to Kavita, has ₹ 47 left with him. The money with Ravi in the beginning was:
A. ₹ 200 B. ₹ 250
C. ₹ 500 D. ₹ 700

15. The solution of the simultaneous linear equations $2x - 3y = 3$ and $4x - y = 11$ is:
A. $x = 1, y = 1$ B. $x = 3, y = 2$
C. $x = 2, y = 3$ D. $x = 3, y = 1$

ANSWERS

1	2	3	4	5	6	7	8	9	10
A	C	A	D	A	C	D	D	D	D
11	**12**	**13**	**14**	**15**					
A	B	C	B	D					

SOME SELECTED EXPLANATORY ANSWERS

1.
$$\frac{x+2}{x-1} = \frac{5}{2}$$
$$2(x + 2) = 5(x - 1)$$
$$2x + 4 = 5x - 5$$
$$2x - 5x = -5 - 4$$
$$-3x = -9$$
$$x = \frac{-9}{-3} = 3$$

2. Let smaller number = x

∴ larger number = $32 - x$

According to the condition given,

larger number = 2 × smaller number + 5

$\Rightarrow$ $(32 - x) = 2 \times x + 5$

$\Rightarrow$ $3x = 32 - 5 = 27$

∴ $x = 9$

$\Rightarrow$ larger number = $32 - 9 = 23$

3.
$$\alpha + \beta = \alpha\beta$$
or $\frac{-2}{q} = \frac{3q}{q} = 3$

$\Rightarrow$ $q = \frac{-2}{3}$

4. $(x - 2)(x + 6) \geq 0$

$\Rightarrow$ $(x - 2) \geq 0$ and $(x + 6) \geq 0$

$\Rightarrow$ $x \geq 2$ and $x \geq -6$

Also $(x - 2)(x + 6) \geq 0$

$\Rightarrow$ $(x - 2) \leq 0$ and $(x + 6) \leq 0$

$\Rightarrow$ $x \leq 2$ and $x \leq -6$

5. $\alpha + \beta = \frac{4}{4} = 1, \alpha\beta = \frac{1}{4}$

∴ $\alpha^3 + \alpha^3 = (\alpha + \beta)^3 - 3\alpha\beta(\alpha + \beta)$

$$= 1^3 - 3 \times \frac{1}{4} \times 1 = 1 - \frac{3}{4} = \frac{1}{4}$$

6. $\lambda^2 + 8\lambda + \mu^2 + 6\mu = 0$ (quadratic in λ)

Since roots are real,

$$b^2 - 4ac \geq 0$$

or $8^2 - 4(\mu^2 + 6\mu) \geq 0$

$\Rightarrow$ $\mu^2 + 6\mu - 16 \leq 0$

$\Rightarrow$ $(\mu + 8)(\mu - 2) \leq 0$

$\Rightarrow$ $\mu \geq -8$ and $\mu \leq 2$

or $\mu \leq -8$ and $\mu \geq 2$

It means μ lies between -8 and 2.

7. $5^{2x} - 5^{x+3} + 125 = 5^x$

or $5^{2x} - 5^x(125 + 1) + 125 = 0$

or $5^x(5^x - 125) - 1(5^x - 125) = 0$

or $(5^x - 1)(5^x - 125) = 0$

$\therefore$ $5^x - 1 = 0$

or $5^x - 125 = 0$

or $5^x = 1 = 5^0$

$\therefore$ $x = 0$

or $5^x = 125 = 5^3$

$\therefore$ $x = 3$

8. Suppose the correct equation be

$$ax^2 + bx + c = 0$$

Taking c and the correct roots α and β, wrong roots as 3 and 2.

$\therefore$ $\alpha + \beta = 3 + 2 = 5$ ...(*i*)

Also $a = 1$ and $c = -6$,

$\alpha\beta = c/a = -6$ ...(*ii*)

Solving, we get the correct roots are 6 and -1.

9. By hypothesis,

$$3k^2 - 4 = 5$$

or $3k^2 = 9$

$\Rightarrow$ $k^2 = 3$

$$\text{Disc.} = 4k^2 - 4(3k^2 - 4)$$

$$= -8 < 0$$

Hence, roots are imaginary.

10. $x^2 - 6x + 10 = 0$ ...(1)

$\therefore$ $x - (\alpha + \beta)x + \alpha\beta = 0$ ...(2)

{$\because$ α, β are the roots of (1)

Comparing (1) and (2),

$$\alpha + \beta = 6 \text{ and } \alpha\beta = 10$$

$\therefore$ $\alpha^2 + \beta^2 = (\alpha + \beta)^2 - 2\alpha\beta$

$= 6^2 - 2 \times 10$

$= 36 - 20 = 16$

11. Let the basic salary of A = x

$\therefore$ A's total salary

$= x + 65\%$ of x

$$= x + x \times \frac{65}{100} = x + \frac{65x}{100} \quad ...(i)$$

B's total salary

$= 1,100 + 80\%$ of $1,100$

$$= 1,100 + \frac{80 \times 1,100}{100}$$

$= 1,100 + 880 = 1,980$ ...(*ii*)

A's total salary = B's total salary (given)

$$\Rightarrow \quad x + \frac{65x}{100} = 1,980$$

$\Rightarrow$ $100x + 65x = 1,980 \times 100$

$\Rightarrow$ $165x = 1,980 \times 100$

$$\therefore \quad x = \frac{1,980 \times 100}{165}$$

$= ₹\ 1,200$

12. Let the breadth of the field = x metre

$\therefore$ length of the field = $2x$ metre

and area of the room = $2x \times x = 2x^2$ metre^2 ...(*i*)

New area = $(2x - 5)(x + 3) = 2x^2 + x - 15$ ...(*ii*)

Comparing (*i*) and (*ii*),

$$2x^2 = 2x^2 + x - 15$$

$\Rightarrow$ $x - 15 = 0$

$\therefore$ $x = 15$

Hence, length = $2 \times 15 = 30$ metre

11. Let the speed of the student be x km/hour

$\therefore$ Time taken to cover 24 km

$$= \frac{24}{x} \text{ hour} \quad ...(1)$$

When speed is $(x + 2)$ km/hour

Then time taken to cover 24 km

$$= \frac{24}{x+2} \text{ hours} \quad ...(2)$$

According to the condition given,

$$\frac{24}{x} - \frac{24}{x+2} = 2$$

$\Rightarrow \quad 24(x + 2) - 24x = 2x(x + 2)$

$\Rightarrow \quad 24x + 48 - 24x = 2x^2 + 4x$

$\Rightarrow \quad 2x^2 + 4x - 48 = 0$

$\Rightarrow \quad x^2 + 2x - 24 = 0$

$\Rightarrow \quad (x + 6)(x - 4) = 0$

$\therefore \quad x = -6 \text{ or } x = 4$

neglecting negative value, the speed of the student is 4 km/hour.

14. Let the pocket money be x

$$\therefore \quad 80\% \text{ of } x = \frac{80x}{100} = \frac{4x}{5}$$

$$\text{Balance} = x - \frac{4x}{5} = \frac{x}{5}$$

$$\text{Again } 6\% \text{ of } \frac{x}{5} = \frac{6}{100} \times \frac{x}{5} = \frac{3x}{250}$$

$$\text{The amount left with Ravi} = \frac{x}{5} - \frac{3x}{250} = 47$$

$$\Rightarrow \quad \frac{50x - 3x}{250} = 47 \Rightarrow \frac{47x}{250} = 47$$

$\therefore \quad x =$ ₹ 250

15. $2x - 3y = 3$ ...(1)

$4x - y = 11$ ...(2)

Multiply equation (2) by (3), which gives

$12x - 3y = 33$ ...(3)

Subtracting equation (1) from (3), we get

$10x = 30$

$\therefore \quad x = 3$

Substituting this value of x in (2), we have

$4 \times 3 - y = 11$

$\therefore \quad y = 12 - 11 = 1$

4 Sequences and Series

SEQUENCE

A sequence is a function whose domain is the set N of natural numbers.

Series: If $a_1, a_2, a_3, a_4, ..., a_n, ...$ is a sequence, then the expression $a_1 + a_2 + a_3 + a_4 + a_5 + ... + a_n + ...$ is a series.

A series is finite or infinite according as the number of terms in the corresponding sequence is finite or infinite.

Arithmetic Progression (A.P.)

A sequence is called an arithmetic progression if the difference of a term and the previous term is always same, *i.e.*, $a_{n+1} - a_n$ = constant (= d) for all $n \in$ N.

The constant difference, generally denoted by d is called the common difference.

The nth term of the A.P., $a, a + d, a + 2d, ...$ a_n is

$$a_n = a + (n - 1)d.$$

Sum to *n* Terms of an A.P.

The sum S_n of n terms of an A.P. with first term 'a' and common difference 'd' is given by

$$S_n = \frac{n}{2}[2a+(n-1)d]$$

or

$$S_n = \frac{n}{2}[a+l]$$

where l = last term = $a + (n - 1)d$.

The nth term,

$$a_n = S_n - S_{n-1}$$

Arithmetic Mean (A.M.)

If three terms are in A.P. the middle term is called the A.M. between the other two.

Single A.M. Between two numbers *a* and *b*

If A is the arithmetic mean between a and b, then a, A, b are in A.P.

$$\therefore \quad A = \frac{a+b}{2}$$

If $x_1, x_2 ...., x_n$ are n numbers then their A.M. is given by $\frac{x_1+x_2+...+x_n}{n}$.

Insertion of *n* arithmetic means between any two given numbers

The numbers $A_1, A_2, ..., A_n$ are said to be n arithmetic means between any two given numbers a and b if $a, A_1, A_2, ..., A_n, b$ are in A.P. Obviously $b - t_{n+2} = a + (n + 1) d$,

$$\therefore \quad d = \frac{b-a}{n+1} \text{ and so } A_1 = a+\frac{b-a}{n+1},$$

$$A_2 = a+\frac{(b-a)}{n+1}, \; A_3 = a+\frac{3(b-a)}{n+1},....,$$

$$A_n = \frac{n(b-a)}{n+1}.$$

Geometric Progression

A sequence of non-zero number is called a *geometric progression* (abbreviated as G.P.) if the ratio of a term and the term preceding to it is always a constant quantity.

The constant ratio is called the *common ratio* of the G.P.

The *n*th or General Term of a G.P.

The nth term of a G.P. with first term a and common ratio r is given by $a_n = ar^{n-1}$.

Sum of *n* terms of a G.P.

The sum of n terms of a G.P. with first term 'a' and common ratio 'r' is given by:

$$S_n = a\left(\frac{r^n-1}{r-1}\right) \text{ or } S_n = a\left(\frac{1-r^n}{1-r}\right),\ r \neq 1.$$

Sum of an Infinite G.P.

The sum of an infinite G.P. with first term a and common ratio $r(-1 < r < 1$; *i.e.*, $|r| < 1)$ is:

$$S = \frac{a}{1-r}$$

If $r \geq 1$, then the sum of an infinite G.P. tends to infinity.

Geometric Mean (G.M.)

If a, b, c are in G.P., then b is called *geometric mean* between a and c.

Single geometric mean between *a* and *b*

If G be the geometric mean between a and b, then a, G, b are in G.P.

$$\therefore \quad G = \sqrt{(ab)}$$

If $a_1, a_2, ..., a_n > 0$, then their geometric mean is given by $(a_1 . a_2 . a_3 ... a_n)^{1/n}$.

Insertion of n geometric means between any two given positive numbers

Let a and b be two given positive real numbers and $G_1, G_2, ..., G_n$ be the n G.Ms. to be inserted between them.

$\therefore a, G_1, G_2, ..., G_n, b$ are in G.P.

Let r be the common ratio of this G.P.

$$\text{Then, } b = ar^{n+1} \Rightarrow r = \left(\frac{b}{a}\right)^{\frac{1}{n+1}}$$

$$\therefore G_1 = ar = a\left(\frac{b}{a}\right)^{\frac{1}{n+1}},\ G_2 = ar^2 = a\left(\frac{b}{a}\right)^{\frac{1}{n+2}},$$

$$... G_n = ar^n = a\left(\frac{b}{a}\right)^{\frac{n}{n+2}}.$$

Harmonic Progression

A sequence $a_1, a_2, a_3, ... a_n, ...$ of non-zero numbers is called a Harmonic Progression if the sequence $\frac{1}{a_1}, \frac{1}{a_2}, \frac{1}{a_3}, ..., \frac{1}{a_n}, ...$ is an A.P.

Harmonic Mean

If a and b are two non-zero numbers then harmonic mean of a and b denoted by H is given by

$$H = \frac{1}{2}\left(\frac{1}{a}+\frac{1}{b}\right) \text{ or } H = \left(\frac{2ab}{a+b}\right)$$

If a, H, b are in H.P., then H is called single harmonic mean between a and b.

If $a_1, a_2, a_3, ..., a_n$ be n non-zero numbers, then their harmonic mean H is given by

$$\frac{1}{H} = \frac{1}{2}\left(\frac{1}{a_1}+\frac{1}{a_2}+...+\frac{1}{a_n}\right).$$

Insertion of *n* Harmonic Means between any two given numbers

Let a and b be any two given numbers and $H_1, H_2, ... H_n$ be n harmonic means between them.

$\therefore a, H_1, H_2, ..., H_n, b$ are in H.P.

$$\therefore \frac{1}{a}, \frac{1}{H_1}, \frac{1}{H_2}, ... \frac{1}{H_n}, \frac{1}{b} \text{ are in A.P.}$$

Let d be the common difference of this A.P., then $(n+2)^{th}$ term $= \frac{1}{b} = \frac{1}{a}+(n+2-1)d$

$$\Rightarrow \quad d = \frac{a-b}{ab(n+1)}$$

$$\therefore \quad \frac{1}{H_1} = \frac{1}{a}+\frac{a-b}{ab(n+1)} \Rightarrow H_1 = \frac{ab(n+1)}{bn+a}.$$

$$\text{Similarly, } \frac{1}{H_2} = \frac{1}{a}+2d,\ \frac{1}{H_3}\frac{1}{a}+3d,...$$

$\therefore H_2, H_3, ..., H_n$ can be calculated.

Properties of AM, GM and HM between two given Number, *a* and *b*

$$A = \frac{a+b}{2},\ G = \sqrt{ab}$$

$$\text{and} \quad H = \frac{2ab}{a+b}$$

These three means possess the following properties:

Prop. I : $A > G > H$

Prop. II : A, G, H form a GP, *i.e.*, $G^2 = AH$

Prop. III : The equation having a and b as its roots is $x^2 - 2Ax + G^2 = 0$.

Solved Examples

Example 1: *If the sum of n terms of an AP is $S_n = 3n^2 + 2n$, then find the value of d.*

Solution: Formula :

$$S_n = An^2 + Bn \Rightarrow A = 3$$

$$\Rightarrow \quad d = 2A = 2 \times 3 = 6.$$

Example 2: *If $x > 1$, $y > 1$, $z > 1$ are in G.P., then $\frac{1}{1+\log x}, \frac{1}{1+\log y}, \frac{1}{1+\log z}$ are in A.P., prove.*

Solution: Since x, y, z are in G.P.

$$y^2 = xz$$

$$\Rightarrow \quad \log y^2 = \log (xz)$$

$$\Rightarrow \quad 2 \log y = \log x + \log z$$

$$\Rightarrow \quad 2(1 + \log y) = (1 + \log x) + (1 + \log z)$$

$\Rightarrow 1 + \log x,\ 1 + \log y,\ 1 + \log z$ are in A.P.

$\Rightarrow \frac{1}{1+\log x}, \frac{1}{1+\log y}, \frac{1}{1+\log z}$ are in H.P.

Example 3: *A GP consists of 2n terms. If the sum of the terms occupying the odd places is S_1 and that of the terms in the even places is S_2, then S_2 / S_1 dependent on r.*

Solution: We have :

$$S_1 = a + ar^2 + ar^4 + \ldots + ar^{2n-2}$$

$$S_2 = ar + ar^3 + ar^5 + \ldots + ar^{2n-1}$$

Clearly, $S_2/S_1 = r$, which depends on r.

MULTIPLE CHOICE QUESTIONS

1. If the sum of first n positive integers is $\frac{1}{5}$ times the sum of their squares, then n equals:
A. 5 B. 6
C. 7 D. 8

2. If $\log_3 2$, $\log_3 (2^x - 5)$ and $\log_3 (2^x - 7/2)$ are in A.P., then x is equal to:
A. 2 B. 3
C. 4 D. 2, 3

3. If a, b, c, are in A.P., b, c, d are in G.P., c, d, e are in H.P., then a, c, e will be in:
A. A.P. B. G.P.
C. H.P. D. None of these

4. The value of 0.423 is:
A. $\frac{419}{999}$ B. $\frac{419}{990}$
C. $\frac{423}{1000}$ D. None of these

5. The following consecutive terms $\frac{1}{1+\sqrt{x}}, \frac{1}{1-x}, \frac{1}{1-\sqrt{x}}$ of a series are in:
A. H.P. B. G.P.
C. A.P. D. A.P., G.P.

6. $\log_3 2$, $\log_6 2$, $\log_{12} 2$ are in:
A. A.P.
B. G.P.
C. H.P.
D. None of these

7. The fourth, seventh and tenth terms of a GP are p, q, r respectively, then:
A. $p^2 = q^2 + r^2$
B. $q^2 = pr$
C. $p^2 = qr$
D. $pqr + pq + 1 = 0$

8. In a GP of postive terms, any term is equal to the sum of the next two terms. Then the common ratio of the GP is:
A. 2 cos 18° B. sin 18°
C. cos 18° D. 2 sin 18°

9. If $\log (x + z) + \log (x - 2y + z) = 2 \log (x - z)$, then x, y, z are in:
A. H.P. B. G.P.
C. A.P. D. None of these

10. If $< a_n >$ is an arithmetic sequence, then

$$\Delta = \begin{vmatrix} a_m & a_n & a_p \\ m & n & p \\ 1 & 1 & 1 \end{vmatrix} \text{ equals:}$$

A. 1 B. – 1
C. 0 D. None of these

11. If $a_1, a_2, a_3, \ldots$ is an A.P. such that $a_1 + a_5 + a_{10} + a_{15} + a_{20} + a_{24} = 225$, then $a_1 + a_2 + a_3 + \ldots + a_{23} + a_{24}$ is equal to:

A. 909 B. 75

C. 750 D. 900

12. The value of $2.\overline{357}$ is:

A. $\frac{2355}{1001}$ B. $\frac{2355}{999}$

C. $\frac{2355}{1111}$ D. None of these

13. The third term of a GP is 4. The product of first five terms is:

A. 4^3

B. 4^5

C. 4^4

D. None of these

14. The second, third and sixth terms of an A.P. are consecutive terms of a G.P. The common ratio of the G.P. is:

A. 1 B. – 1

C. 3 D. – 3

15. If x, y, z are in G.P. and $x + 3, y + 3, z + 3$ are in H.P., then:

A. $y = 2$ B. $y = 3$

C. $y = 1$ D. $y = 0$

ANSWERS

1	2	3	4	5	6	7	8	9	10
C	D	B	B	C	C	B	D	A	C
11	**12**	**13**	**14**	**15**					
D	B	B	C	B					

SOME SELECTED EXPLANATORY ANSWERS

1.
$$\Sigma n = \frac{1}{5}\Sigma n^2$$
$$\Rightarrow \quad \frac{n(n+1)}{2} = \frac{1}{5}\cdot\frac{n(n+1)(2n+1)}{6}$$
$$\Rightarrow \quad n = 7$$

2. The terms are in A.P., hence

$$2 \log_3 (2^x - 5) = \log_3 2 + \log_3\left(2^x - \frac{7}{2}\right)$$
$$\Rightarrow \quad (2^x - 5)^2 = 2\times\left(2^x - \frac{7}{2}\right)$$
$$\Rightarrow \quad (y - 5)^2 = 2\left(y - \frac{7}{2}\right), \text{ where } y = 2^x$$
$$\Rightarrow \quad y = 4 \text{ or } 8$$
$$\Rightarrow \quad 2^x = 4 \text{ or } 8 - 2^2 \text{ or } 2^3$$
$$\therefore \quad x = 2 \text{ or } 3$$

3. We have $2b = a + c$, $c^2 = bd$ and $d = \frac{2ce}{c+e}$

$$\Rightarrow \quad c^2 = \left(\frac{a+c}{2}\right) d = \left(\frac{a+c}{2}\right)\left(\frac{2ce}{c+e}\right)$$
$$\Rightarrow \quad c^2 = ae$$

$\therefore$ *a, c, e* are in G.P.

4. $S = 0.42323232\ldots$
$$= 0.4 + 0.023 + 0.00023 + \ldots$$
$$= 0.4 + 23 \times 10^{-3} + 23 \times 10^{-5} + \ldots$$
$$= 0.4 + \frac{23\times10^{-3}}{1-10^{-2}}$$
$$= 0.4 + \frac{23}{990} = \frac{419}{990}$$

5. Here $\frac{1}{1-x} - \frac{1}{1+\sqrt{x}} = \frac{\sqrt{x}}{1-x}$

Also, $\frac{1}{1-\sqrt{x}} - \frac{1}{1-x} = \frac{\sqrt{x}}{1-x}$

Hence, the terms are in A.P.

6. Consider $\log_2 3$, $\log_2 6$, $\log_2 12$

We have
$$\log_2 6 = \log_2 (3 \times 2) = 1 + \log_2 3$$
$$\log_2 12 = \log_2 (2^2 \times 3) = 2 + \log_2 3$$

Since $\log_2 3$, $1 + \log_2 3$ and $2 + \log_2 3$ are in A.P., we have

$\log_2 3$, $\log_2 6$ and $\log_2 12$ are in A.P.

$\Rightarrow \dfrac{1}{\log_2 3}, \dfrac{1}{\log_2 6}, \dfrac{1}{\log_2 12}$ are in H.P.

$\Rightarrow \log_3 2, \log_6 2, \log_{12} 2$ are in H.P.

7. Let A = first term, R = common ratio

Then $p = AR^3$, $q = AR^6$

and $r = AR^9$

$\therefore \quad (AR^6)^2 = (AR^3)(AR^9)$

$\Rightarrow \quad q^2 = pr$

8. $a_n = a_{n+1} + a_{n+2}$

$\Rightarrow \quad a_1 r^{n-1} = a_1 r^n + a_1 r^{n+1}$

$\Rightarrow \quad r^{-1} = 1 + r$

$\Rightarrow \quad r^2 + r - 1 = 0$

$\Rightarrow \quad r = \dfrac{\sqrt{5}-1}{2} \qquad (\because r > 0)$

$= 2 \sin 18°$

9. $\log(x + z) + \log(x - 2y + z) = 2\log(x - z)$

$\Rightarrow (x + z)(x - 2y + z) = (x - z)^2$

$\Rightarrow \quad xy + yz = 2xz$

$\Rightarrow \quad \dfrac{1}{z} + \dfrac{1}{x} = \dfrac{2}{y}$

$\Rightarrow$ x, y, z are in H.P.

10. $a_m = a + (m - 1)d \quad ...(i)$

$a_n = a + (n - 1)d \quad ...(ii)$

$a_p = a + (p - 1)d \quad ...(iii)$

Multiply (*i*) by $(n - p)$, (*ii*) by $(p - m)$ and (*iii*) by $(m - n)$ and add,

$a_m(n - p) + a_n(p - m) + a_p(m - n) = 0$

Expanding along the first row, we have

$\Delta = a_m(n - p) + a_n(p - m) + a_p(m - n)$

$= 0$

11. We have

$a_1 + a_5 + a_{10} + a_{15} + a_{20} + a_{24} = 225$

$\Rightarrow (a_1 + a_{24}) + (a_5 + a_{20}) + (a_{10} + a_{15}) = 225$

$\Rightarrow \quad 3(a_1 + a_{24}) = 225$

$\Rightarrow \quad a_1 + a_{24} = \dfrac{225}{3}$

$\Rightarrow a_1 + a_2 + a_3 + ... + a_{24} = \dfrac{24}{2}(a_1 + a_{24})$

$= 12 \times \dfrac{225}{3} = 900$

12. $2.\overline{357} = 2 + 0.357357357357...$

$= 2 + 0.357 + 0.000357 + 0.000000357 + ...$

$= 2 + \dfrac{357}{10^3} + \dfrac{357}{10^6} + \dfrac{357}{10^9} + ...$

$= 2 + \dfrac{\frac{357}{10^3}}{1 - \frac{1}{10^3}} = 2 + \dfrac{357}{999} = \dfrac{2355}{999}$

13. Let a be the first term and r be the common ratio. Then

$ar^2 = 4$ (given)

$\therefore$ Product of first five terms

$= a\ ar\ ar^2\ ar^3\ ar^4 = (ar^2)^5 = 4^5$

14. Let a be the first term and d be the common difference of the A.P. Then $a + d$, $a + 2d$, $a + 5d$ are in G.P.,

$\Rightarrow \quad (a + 2d)^2 = (a + d)(a + 5d)$

$\Rightarrow 4d^2 + 4ad = 6ad + 5d^2 \Rightarrow d = -2a$

So, the terms are $-a$, $-3a$, $-9a$ which are in G.P. with common ratio 3.

15. x, y, z are in G.P. $\Rightarrow y^2 = xz$

$x + 3$, $y + 3$, $z + 3$ are in H.P.

$\Rightarrow \quad y + 3 = \dfrac{2(x+3)(z+3)}{(x+3)+(z+3)}$

$\Rightarrow \quad y + 3 = \dfrac{2[xz + 3(x+z) + 9]}{[(x+z)+6]}$

$\Rightarrow \quad y + 3 = \dfrac{2[y^2 + 3(x+z) + 9]}{[x+z+6]}$

Obviously, $y = 3$ satisfies it.

5 Binomial Theorem

THE FACTORIAL FUNCTION

For any natural number n (*i.e.*, $n \in N$), factorial of n, denoted by $n!$ or $\underline{|n}$ is defined as

$$n! = n(n-1)(n-2) \dots 3\cdot2\cdot1$$

0! is defined as = 1.

Thus $n!$ is defined only for whole numbers.

Remarks: $n! = n.(n-1)! = n(n-1)\cdot(n-2)!$ etc.

The notation ${}^nC_r$, *i.e.*, $C(n, r)$

$${}^nC_r = \frac{n!}{(n-r)!r!}, \text{ where } 0 < r < n, \text{ and } n, r \in N$$

(*i*) ${}^nC_0 = {}^nC_n = 1$ and ${}^nC_r = 0$ for $r > n$

(*ii*) ${}^nC_{n-r} = {}^nC_r$

(*iii*) ${}^nC_r = {}^nC_s$ iff $r = s$ or $r + s = n$

(*iv*) ${}^nC_r = \dfrac{n(n-1)(n-2)\dots(n-r+1)}{r!}$

$$\therefore {}^nC_1 = \frac{n}{1} = n, \; {}^nC_2 = \frac{n(n-1)}{2!}, \text{ etc.}$$

Greatest value of ${}^nC_r$

${}^nC_r$ is greatest for $r = \dfrac{n}{2}$, if n is even and is greatest for $r = \dfrac{n-1}{2}$ or for $r = \dfrac{n+1}{2}$, if n is odd. These value of ${}^nC_r$ will be equal if n is odd.

Binomial Theorem: (Statement for positive integral index). For any positive integral n and $x, y \in C$,

$$(x+y)^n = {}^nC_0x^n + {}^nC_1x^{n-1}y + {}^nC_2x^{n-2}y^2 + \dots + {}^nC_rx^{n-r}y^r + \dots + {}^nC_n y^n. \quad \dots(i)$$

$$\text{Also } (1+x)^n = {}^nC_0 + {}^nC_1x + {}^nC_2x^2 + \dots + {}^nC_rx^r + \dots + {}^nC_n x^n. \quad \dots(ii)$$

where ${}^nC_0, {}^nC_1, \dots, {}^nC_n$ are called binomial coefficients and ${}^nC_r = \dfrac{n!}{r! \times (n-r)!}$ ...(*iii*)

Replacing y by $-y$ in (*i*), we get

$$(x-y)^n = {}^nC_0x^n - {}^nC_1x^{n-1}y + {}^nC_2x^{n-2}y^2 + \dots + (-1)^r x^{n-r}y^r + \dots + (-1)^n\,{}^nC_n y^n \quad \dots(iv)$$

The last term is positive or negative according as n is even or odd respectively.

Note: (*a*) Adding (*i*) and (*iv*), we get

$(x+y)^n + (x-y)^n$

$= 2[x^n + {}^nC_2x^{n-2}y^2 + \dots]$ ...(*v*)

= 2 (sum of terms of odd number)

The last term is ${}^nC_ny^n$ or ${}^nC_{n-1}xy^{n-1}$ according as n is even or odd respectively.

(*b*) Subtracting (*iv*) from (*i*), we get

$(x+y)^n - (x-y)^n$

$= 2[{}^nC_1x^{n-1}y + {}^nC_3x^{n-3}y^3 + \dots]$ ...(*vi*)

= 2 [sum of terms of even number].

The last term is ${}^nC_{n-1}xy^{n-1}$ or ${}^nC_ny^n$ according as n is even or odd respectively.

Some important points to remember

In the binomial expansion of $(x+y)^n$, where n is a positive integer

(*i*) The number of terms in the expansion is $(n+1)$.

(*ii*) In each term of the expansion, the sum of the exponents (powers of x and y) is n (*i.e.*, each term is of degree n).

(*iii*) The binomial coefficients of terms at the same positions from the beginning and from the end are equal since ${}^nC_r = {}^nC_{n-r}$.

PROPERTIES OF BINOMIAL THEOREM

(*i*) The number of terms in the expansion of $(x + y)^n$ is $n + 1$.

(*ii*) In each term, the sum of the indices of x and y is n.

(*iii*) **General term:** In the expansion (1), $(r + 1)^{th}$ term, *i.e.*, the general term denoted by T_{r+1} is given by

$T_{r+1} = {}^nC_r x^{n-r} y^r$.

(*iv*) **Middle term (s):**

(*a*) If n is even, the number of terms in the expansion (1) is $n + 1$, which is an odd number.

$\therefore$ there is only one middle term $\left(\frac{n}{2}+1\right)$th term.

$\therefore$ The middle term $= \left(\frac{n}{2}+1\right)$th term

$= {}^nC_{n/2}\, x^{n/2}\, y^{n/2}$.

Example: If $n = 8$, then the middle term is $\left(\frac{8}{2}+1\right)$th term = 5th term, *i.e.*, T_5.

And is given by $T_5 = {}^8C_4 x^{8-4} y^4 = 70x^4y^4$

(*b*) If n is odd, the number of terms in the expansion (1) will be even.

Thus there will be two middle terms in the expansion, *i.e.*, $\frac{1}{2}(n+1)$ th and $\frac{1}{2}(n+3)$ th terms.

i.e., middle terms are

$T_{(n+1)/2} = {}^nC_{(n-1)/2}\, x^{(n+1)/2} \cdot y^{(n-1)/2}$.

and $T_{(n+3)/2} = {}^nC_{(n+1)/2}\, x^{(n-1)/2}\, y^{(n+1)/2}$.

Example: If $n = 7$, then the number of terms in the expansion of $(x + y)^7$ is $7 + 1 = 8$.

$\therefore$ The middle terms are 4th and 5th terms (*i.e.*, T_4 and T_5) are given by

$T_4 = {}^7C_3\, x^{7-3}\, y^3 = 35x^4y^3$ and

$T_5 = {}^7C_4\, x^{7-4}\, y^4 = 35x^3y^4$.

PROPERTIES OF BINOMIAL COEFFICIENTS

(*i*) $C_0 + C_1 + C_2 + ... + C_n = 2^n$

(*ii*) $C_0 + C_2 + C_4 + ... = C_1 + C_3 + C_5 + ... = 2^{n-1}$

(*iii*) $C_1 + 2C_2 + 3C_3 + ... + {}^nC_n = n.2^{n-1}$

(*iv*) $C_1 - 2C_2 + 3C_3 - ... = 0$

(*v*) $C_0 + 2C_1 + 3C_2 + ... + (n + 1)\, C_n = (n + 1)\, 2^{n-1}$

(*vi*) $C_0C_r + C_1C_{r-1} + ... + C_{n-r}C_n = \dfrac{(2n)!}{(n-r)!\,(n+r)!}$

(*vii*) $C_0^2 + C_1^2 + C_2^2 + ... + C_n^2 = \dfrac{(2n)!}{(n!)^2}$

(*viii*) $C_0^2 - C_1^2 + C_2^2 - C_3^2 + ...$

$$= \begin{cases} 0, & \text{if } n \text{ is odd} \\ (-1)^{n/2}\, {}^nC_{n/2}, & \text{if } n \text{ is even} \end{cases}$$

Some Important equations

(*i*) $(1 - x)^{-1} = 1 + x + x^2 + x^3 + ... + x^r + ...$

(*ii*) $(1 + x)^{-1} = 1 - x + x^2 - x^3 + ... + (-1)^r x^r + ...$

(*iii*) $(1 - x)^{-2} = 1 + 2x + 3x^2 + 4x^3 + ... + (r + 1)\, x^r + ...$

(*iv*) $(1 + x)^{-2} = 1 - 2x + 3x^2 - 4x^3 + ... + (-1)^r (r + 1)\, x^r + ...$

Solved Examples

Example 1: *Use Binomial Theorem to find $(999)^3$.*

Solution: $(999)^3 = (10^3 - 1)^3$

$= (10^3)^3 - {}^3C_1\, (10^3)^2 + {}^3C_2\, (10^3) - {}^3C_3$

$= 10^3\, [10^6 - 3(10^3 - 1)] - 1$

$= 10^3\, (1000000 - 2997) - 1$

$= 1000 \times 997003 - 1 = 997002999$

Example 2: *Find the middle term or terms in the expansion of*

(*i*) $\left(\frac{x}{a} - \frac{a}{x}\right)^{10}$ (*ii*) $\left(3x - \frac{x^3}{6}\right)^9$

Solution:

(*i*) In this case the number of terms in the expansion are $10 + 1 = 11$, so the middle term is T_6

$\therefore \quad T_6 = {}^{10}C_5 \left(\frac{x}{a}\right)^5 \left(-\frac{a}{x}\right)^5 = -252$

(*ii*) In this case the number of terms in the expansion are 9 + 1 = 10, so the middle terms are T_5 and T_6.

Now $T_5 = {}^9C_4(3x)^{9-4}\left(-\frac{x^3}{6}\right)^4$

$= \frac{9.8.7.6}{4.3.2}\cdot 3^5 \cdot \frac{x^{17}}{6^4} = \frac{189}{8}x^{17}$

$T_6 = {}^9C_5(3x)^{9-5}\left(-\frac{x^3}{6}\right)^5 = -\frac{21}{16}x^{19}.$

Example 3: *Find the coefficient of x^4 in the expansion of $(2 - x + 3x^2)^6$.*

Solution: Put $(2 - x + 3x^2)^6 = [2 - x(1 - 3x)]^6$

$= 2^6 - {}^6C_1 . 2^5\, x(1 - 3x) + {}^6C_1 . 2^4 . x^2(1 - 3x)^2 - {}^6C_3 . 2^3 . x^3 (1 - 3x)^3 + {}^6C_4 . 2^2 . x^4 (1 - 3x)^4 - {}^6C_5 . 2 . x^5 (1 - 3x)^5 + x^6 (1 - 3x)^6$

Coefficient of x^4 occurs in 3rd, 4th and 5th terms

= 15.16.9 + 20.8.9 + 15.4

= 2160 + 1440 + 60

= 3660.

MULTIPLE CHOICE QUESTIONS

1. The number of integral terms in the expression of

$\left(5^{\frac{1}{2}} + 7^{\frac{1}{8}}\right)^{1024}$ is

A. 127 B. 129
C. 131 D. 133

2. If the sum of the co-efficients in the expansion of $(a + b)^n$ is 1024, then the greatest co-efficient in the expansion is

A. 252 B. 352
C. 452 D. 552

3. If the sum of the co-efficients in the expansion of $(1 + 2x)^n$ is 6561, the greatest term in the expansion for $x = \frac{1}{2}$ is

A. 3rd B. 4th
C. 5th D. None of these

4. The positive integer just greater than $(1 + 0.0001)^{1000}$ is

A. 2 B. 3
C. 4 D. None of these

5. The number $101^{100} - 1$ is divisible by

A. 100 B. 1000
C. 10000 D. All of them

6. The remainder when 2^{2003} is divisible 17 is

A. 1 B. 2
C. 8 D. None of these

7. The digit at unit's place in the number $17^{1995} + 11^{1995} - 7^{1995}$ is

A. 0 B. 1
C. 2 D. 3

8. The sum to $(n + 1)$ terms of the series

$\frac{C_0}{2} - \frac{C_1}{3} + \frac{C_2}{4} - \frac{C_3}{5} + ...$ is

A. $\frac{1}{n+1}$ B. $\frac{1}{n+2}$

C. $\frac{1}{n(n+1)}$ D. $\frac{1}{(n+1)(n+2)}$

9. If $|x| = 1$, then the co-efficient of x^n in the expansion of $(1 + x + x^2 + ...)^2$ is

A. n B. $n - 1$
C. $n + 2$ D. $n + 1$

10. If a_1, a_2, a_3, a_4 are the co-efficients of any four consecutive terms in the expansion of $(1 + x)^n$, then $\frac{a_1}{a_1 + a_2} + \frac{a_2}{a_3 + a_4}$ is equal to

A. $\frac{a_2}{a_2 + a_3}$ B. $\frac{1}{2}\cdot\frac{a_2}{a_2 + a_3}$

C. $\frac{2a_2}{a_2 + a_3}$ D. $\frac{2a_3}{a_2 + a_3}$

11. The remainder when 5^{99} is divided by 13 is

A. 6 B. 8
C. 9 D. 10

12. If the co-efficient of x^7 and x^8 in $\left[2+\frac{x}{3}\right]^n$ are equal then n is

A. 15 B. 25

C. 45 D. 55

13. The value of $\frac{1}{n!}+\frac{1}{2!\,(n-2)!}+\frac{1}{4!\,(n-4)!}+....$

A. $\frac{2^{n-1}}{(n-1)!}$ B. $\frac{2^{n-1}}{n!}$

C. $\frac{2^n}{n!}$ D. None of these

14. The approximate value of $(7.995)^{\frac{1}{3}}$ correct to four decimal places is

A. 1.9995 B. 1.9996

C. 1.9990 D. 1.9991

15. The co-efficient of the term independent of x in the expansion of

$$\left(\frac{x+1}{x^{\frac{2}{3}}-x^{\frac{1}{3}}+1}-\frac{x-1}{x-x^{\frac{1}{2}}}\right)^{10}$$ is

A. 210 B. 105

C. 70 D. 112

ANSWERS

1	2	3	4	5	6	7	8	9	10
B	A	C	B	D	C	B	C	D	C
11	**12**	**13**	**14**	**15**					
B	D	B	B	A					

SOME SELECTED EXPLANATORY ANSWERS

6. We have $2^{2000} = \left(2^4\right)^{500} = (17-1)^{500}$

$= {}^{500}C_0.17^{500} - {}^{500}C_1 17^{499} + ... - {}^{500}C_{499}.17 + (-1)^{500}.$

$= 17m + 1$ where m is some positive integer.

$\therefore \quad 2^{2003} = 8\,(2^{2000}) = 8\,(17m+8)$

$= 17\,(8m) + 8$

$\therefore$ Required remainder is 8.

9. Given $\left(1+x+x^2+....\right)^2$

$= \left\{(1-x)^{-1}\right\}^2 = (1-x)^{-2}$

Now coefficient of x^n in $(1-x)^{-r}$ is ${}^{n+r-1}C_{r-1}$

$\therefore$ Coefficient of x^n in $(1-x)^{-2}$ is ${}^{n+2-1}C_{2-1}$

$= {}^{n+1}C_1 = n+1.$

13. Given $\frac{1}{n!}+\frac{1}{2!(n-2)!}+\frac{1}{4!(n-4)!}+....$

$$= \frac{1}{n!}\left[\frac{n!}{n!}+\frac{n!}{2!(n-2)!}+\frac{n!}{4!(n-4)!}+....\right]$$

$$= \frac{1}{n!}\left({}^nC_0+{}^nC_2+{}^nC_4+....\right)$$

$$= \frac{2^{n-1}}{n!}.$$

6 Permutations And Combinations

COMBINATIONS

A group of r things (r can be equal to n also) chosen out of given n things is called a combination. Here the order of things is not taken into consideration.

Important Formulae of Combination

1. The number of combinations of r dissimilar things chosen out of n things is denoted by ^nC_r and is given by:

$$^nC_r = \frac{n!}{r!(n-r)!}$$

$$= \frac{n(n-1)(n-2)......(n-r+1)}{1.2.3....r}$$

2. $^nC_r = {^nC_{n-r}}$
3. $^nC_r + {^nC_{r-1}} = {^{n+1}C_r}$
4. $^nC_r + {^nC_{r+1}} = {^{n+1}C_{r+1}}$
5. $^nC_1 + {^nC_2} + ... + {^nC_n} = 2^n - 1$

   This is the number of combinations of n things in which at least one thing is selected.
6. The number of *combinations* of $(p + q + r)$ things when p are alike of one kind q are alike of second kind, and r are alike of third kind, is
   $(p - 1)(q - 1)(r - 1) - 1$.
7. The number of *combinations* of n distinct things taken r at a time when p-particular *thing always taken is* $^{(n-p)}C_{(r-p)}$.
8. The number of *combinations* of n distinct things taken r at a time when *p-particular things* never taken is:
   $^{(n-p)}C_r$.
9. The number of *ways* to make a selection by taking some or all of $p_1 + p_2 + ... + p_r$ things, when p_1 are alike of one kind, p_2 are alike of second kind, ..., p_r are alike of rth kind, is given by:
   $[(p_1 + 1)(p_2 + 1) ... (p_r + 1) - 1]$.
10. The number of *combinations* of n distinct things taken r at a time when anything or object may be repeated any number of times is:
    $^{n+r-1}C_r$ = Coeff. of x^r in the expansion of $(1 - x)^n$.

Permutations

A group of r or all things chosen out of the given n things and arranged in a definite order is called a *permutation*.

The number of permutations of r things out of the given n thigns is denoted by ^nP_r or $P(n, r)$.

Circular Permutations

When the objects are arranged in a circle then it is called a circular permutation.

Important Rules

(*i*) The number of circular permutations of n different things taken r at a time is $\frac{^nP_r}{r}$.

(*ii*) The number of ways of permuting n distinct objects along a circle is $(n - 1)!$

(*iii*) The number of ways of arranging n distinct objects along a circle when clockwise and anti-clockwise arrangements are considered alike is $\frac{1}{2}(n - 1)!$.

Solved Examples

Example 1: *There are three roads from A to B and four roads from B to C. In how many ways a person can go to place C from place A via place B?*

Solution:

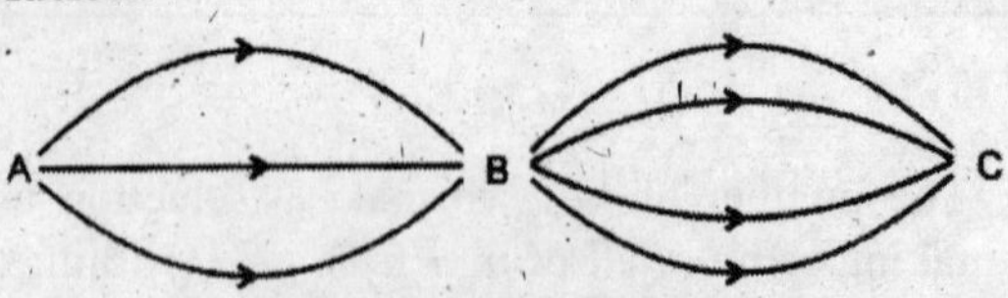

Number of ways from A to B = 3

Number of ways from A to B = 3

and number of ways from B to C = 4

∴ Required number of ways = 3 × 4 = 12

[By multiplication rule]

Example 2: *In how many ways the letters BLEEDE can be rearranged?*

Solution: Required number of different arrangements

$$= \frac{6!}{3!} = \frac{6\times5\times4\times3\times2\times1}{3\times2\times1}$$

$$= 6 \times 5 \times 4 = 120.$$

Example 3: *If a polygon has 27 diagonals, then how many sides does it have?*

Solution: A n-sided polygon has ${}^nC_2 - n = \frac{n(n-3)}{2}$ diagonals.

$\therefore \quad \frac{n(n-3)}{2} = 27$

$\Rightarrow \quad n(n-3) = 54 \Rightarrow n^2 - 3n - 54 = 0$

$\therefore \quad n = 9$

Example 4: *If ${}^nP_r = 120$, ${}^nC_r = 20$, then what are the values of n and r?*

Solution: $r! = \frac{{}^nP_r}{{}^nC_r} = \frac{120}{20} = 6 = 3!$

$\therefore \quad r = 3$

Now $\quad {}^nP_r = 120$

$\Rightarrow \quad {}^nP_3 = 120 = 6 \times 5 \times 4 = {}^6P_3$

$\therefore \quad n = 6$

Example 5: *Find the number of ways in which 5 boys and 5 girls can sit in a ring.*

Solution: Given that total members to sit in a ring = 10

∴ Number of ways of sitting = (10 – 1)! = 9!

MULTIPLE CHOICE QUESTIONS

1. The number of triangles that are formed by choosing the vertices from a set of 12 points, seven of which lie on the same straight line, is:

   A. 175 B. 715
   C. 75 D. 185

2. Out of 18 points in a plane, no three are in the same straight line except five points which are collinear. The number of straight lines which can be formed joining them, is:

   A. 133
   B. 144
   C. 145
   D. None of these

3. A, B, C and D are four non-coplanar points. The number of planes that can be drawn passing through any three of these points, is:

   A. 3 B. 4
   C. 5 D. 6

4. If ${}^nC_r + {}^nC_{r+1} = {}^{n+1}C_x$, then x is:

   A. $r - 1$ B. r
   C. n D. $r + 1$

5. The digits 4, 5, 6, 7, 8 are written in every possible order. The number of numbers greater than 56,000 is:

   A. 98 B. 90
   C. 96 D. 70

6. the sum of all numbers greater than 1,000 formed by using digits 1, 3, 5, 7 no digit being repeated in any number is:

   A. 72,215 B. 83,911
   C. 1,06,656 D. 1,14,712

7. There are 10 lamps in a hall. Each one of them can be switched on independently. The number of ways in which the hall can be illuminated, is:

   A. 10 ! B. 1,023
   C. 2^{10} D. 100 !

8. There are 10 true-false questions. The number of ways in which they can be answered is:
A. 10 !
B. 10^2
C. 2^{10}
D. 100 !

9. The number of all possible selections when a student can make for answering one or more questions out of eight given questions in a paper when each question have an alternative is:
A. ${}^8C_1 + {}^8C_2 + {}^8C_3 + ... + {}^8C_8$
B. 2×2^8
C. 3^8
D. $3^8 - 1$

10. The number of 3-digit numbers which can be formed from the digit 1, 2, 3, 4 and 5 if repetitions of digits is allowed, is:
A. 15
B. 125
C. 5 !
D. 3 !

11. The number of ways in which a team of eleven players can be selected from 22 players always including 2 of them and excluding 4 of them is:
A. ${}^{16}C_5$
B. ${}^{16}C_{11}$
C. ${}^{16}C_9$
D. ${}^{20}C_9$

12. The number of divisors of 9,600 including 1 and 9,600 is:
A. 46
B. 58
C. 48
D. 60

13. In a college examination, a candidate is required to attempt 6 out of 10 questions which are divided into two sections each containing 5 questions. Further, the candidate is not permitted to attempt more than 4 questions from either of the section. The number of ways in which he can make up a choice of 6 questions, is:
A. 15
B. 60
C. 100
D. 200

14. A class is composed of two brothers and six other boys. In how many ways can all the boys be seated at a round table so that the two brothers are not seated besides each other?
A. 720
B. 1,440
C. 3,600
D. 4,320

15. On a railway route, there are 15 stations. The number of different tickets required in order that it may be possible to book a passenger from every station to every other (one way), is:
A. $\frac{15!}{2!}$
B. 15!
C. $\frac{15!}{13!}$
D. $\frac{15!}{13!2!}$

16. An examination paper contains 8 questions of which 4 have 3 possible answers, 3 have 2 possible answers each and the remaining one question has 5 possible answers. The total number of possible answers to all the questions, is:
A. 3,240
B. 94
C. 78
D. 2,880

ANSWERS

1	2	3	4	5	6	7	8	9	10
D	B	B	D	B	C	B	C	D	B
11	**12**	**13**	**14**	**15**	**16**				
C	C	D	C	D	D				

SOME SELECTED EXPLANATORY ANSWERS

1. No. of triangles = ${}^{12}C_3 - {}^7C_3 = 185$.

2. The number of straight lines = ${}^{18}C_2 - ({}^3C_2 - 1)$ $= 144$.

3. Number of planes passing through any three of given four points.
A, B, C, D = ${}^4C_3 = {}^4C_{4-3} = {}^4C_1 = 4$

4. We have
$${}^{n+1}C_x = {}^nC_r + {}^nC_{r+1} = {}^{n+1}C_{r+1}$$
or $x = r + 1$.

5. A number would be less than 56,000 only if either 4 occurs in the first place or 5, 4 occurs on the first two places.

Hence, required number of ways

$= 5! - 4! - 3!$

$= 120 - 24 - 6 = 90.$

6. As each digit occurs 3! times in unit place, ten's place, hundred's place and thousand's place. Hence, required sum

$= 3!\ [1 + 3 + 5 + 7][1 + 10 + 100 + 1{,}000]$

$= 6[16][1{,}111] = 96[1{,}111] = 1{,}06{,}656.$

7. For each bulb there are two choices; either switched on or off.

$\therefore$ Required number $= 2^{10} - 1 = 1{,}023.$

8. Since each questions can be answered in two ways.

$\therefore$ Required number

$= 2 \times 2 \times 2 \times 2 \times 2 \times 2 \times 2 \times 2 \times 2 \times 2$

$= 2^{10}.$

9. Since a student can solve every question in 3 ways–either he can attempt the first alternative or a second or he does not attempt it.

Hence, required number $= 3^8 - 1.$

10. Since each place out of unit, ten, hundred can be filled up in 5 ways.

Hence, required number of ways

$= 5 \times 5 \times 5 = 125.$

11. Leaving 4 from 22, we must select 9 from the reamining $22 - 4 - 2 = 16$.

Hence, number of selection $= {}^{16}C_9$.

12. As $9{,}600 = 2^7 \times 3 \times 5^2$

$\therefore$ Number of divisors

$= (7 + 1) \times (1 + 1) \times (2 + 1) = 48.$

13. Required number of ways

$= {}^5C_4.{}^5C_2 + {}^5C_3.{}^5C_3 + {}^5C_2.{}^5C_4$

$= 50 + 100 + 50 = 200.$

14. Required number of ways $= (6 - 1)! \times {}^6P_2$

$= 5! \times 30 = 120 \times 30 = 3{,}600.$

15. Here desired number of tickets $= {}^{15}C_2 = \dfrac{15!}{13!2!}$

16. Required number of possible answers

$= 4^3 \times 3^2 \times 5$

$= 64 \times 9 \times 5 = 2{,}880.$

7 Matrices and Determinants

Matrices (Def.): A system of mn numbers (real or complex) arranged in a rectangular array of m rows and n columns is called a matrix of order $m \times n$ or an $m \times n$ matrix. Such an array is enclosed by [ ] or ( ). Each of the mn numbers constituting the matrix, is called an element or an entry of the matrix.

Examples:

(*i*) $A = \begin{bmatrix} 3 & 5 & -4 \\ 0 & 1 & 9 \end{bmatrix}$ is a matrix, having 2 rows and 3 columns. Its order is 2×3 and it has 6 elements.

(*ii*) $B = \begin{bmatrix} 5+3i & 4 & \sqrt{2} & -1 \\ 1 & i & -3 & 2 \\ 6 & 0 & 5 & 7 \end{bmatrix}$ is a matrix, having 3 rows and 4 columns. Its order is 3×4 and it has 12 elements.

How to represent a matrix?

An element occurring in the ith row and j^{th} column of a matrix A will be called the $(i, j)^{th}$ element of A, denoted by a_{ij}. In general, an $m \times n$ matrix A may be written as

$$A = \begin{bmatrix} a_{11} & a_{12} & a_{13} & \dots & a_{1n} \\ a_{21} & a_{22} & a_{23} & \dots & a_{2n} \\ \dots & \dots & \dots & \dots & \dots \\ a_{i1} & a_{i2} & a_{i3} & a_{i4} & a_{i5} \\ \dots & \dots & \dots & \dots & \dots \\ a_{m1} & a_{m2} & a_{m3} & \dots & a_{mn} \end{bmatrix} = \left[a_{ij}\right]_{m\times n}$$

TYPES OF MATRICES

Row Matrix

A matrix having only one row and any number of columns is known as a row matrix or a row vector.

Column Matrix

A matrix having only one column and any number of rows is known as a column matrix or a column vector.

Null (or zero) matrix: If all the elements of a matrix are equal to zero, then it is called a null matrix.

Square Matrix

A matrix which has the same number of rows and columns, is called a square matrix.

Any matrix of order $(n \times n)$ is called a square matrix of order n or an n rowed square matrix.

Any matrix of order $m \times n$, where $m \neq n$, is called a rectangular matrix.

Singular and non-singular square matrix

A square matrix is singular or non-singular according to the corresponding determinant of the matrix is zero or non-zero. It is non-zero if the matrix is invertible. (Invertibility of a matrix is explained later.)

Diagonal Matrix

A square matrix in which every non-diagonal elements are zero, is called a diagonal matrix.

If $A = [a_{ij}]_{n \times n}$ be a diagonal matrix, ($a_{ij} = 0$, when $i \neq j$). We can also write A as

$A = \text{diag}\,[a_{11}, a_{22}, a_{33} \dots, a_{nn}]$.

Scalar Matrix

A square matrix in which every non-diagonal element is zero and all diagonal elements are equal, is known as a scalar matrix.

Unit Matrix or Identity Matrix: A square matrix in which all its diagonal elements are equal to 1 and all other elements are equal to zero is called a **unit matrix or identity matrix**.

A unit matrix of order n will be denoted by I_n or simply by I.

Thus, a square matrix $[a_{ij}]_{n \times n}$ is a unit matrix, if

$$a_{ij} = \begin{cases} 0 & \text{when } i \neq j; \\ 1 & \text{when } i = j. \end{cases}$$

Equal Matrices

Two matrices A and B are said to be equal, written as A = B, if they are of the same order and their corresponding elements are equal.

PROPERTIES OF MATRIX ADDITION

(*i*) **Matrix Addition is Commutative:** If A and B be two $m \times n$ matrices, then A + B = B + A.

(*ii*) **Matrix Addition is Associative:** If A, B and C be three $m \times n$ matrices, then (A + B) + C = A + (B + C).

(*iii*) If A is an $m \times n$ matrix and O is an $m \times n$ null matrix, then

A + O = O + A = A

Note: The null matrix O of order $m \times n$ is the *additive identity* in the set of all $m \times n$ matrices.

Negative of a Matrix

Let $A = [a_{ij}]_{m \times n}$, obtained by replacing each element of A with its corresponding additive inverse.

PROPERTIES OF SCALAR MULTIPLICATION

1. If A and B are two matrices of the same order and k is a scalar, then $k(A + B) = (kA + kB)$.
2. If A is any matrix and k_1, k_2 are any scalars, then

   (*i*) $(k_1 + k_2)\,A = k_1A + k_2A$

   (*ii*) $k_1\,(k_2A) = (k_1k_2)\,A$

Transpose of a Matrix: Let A be an $m \times n$ matrix. Then the matrix of order $n \times m$ obtained by changing its rows into columns and columns into rows is called the transpose of A and is denoted by A′ or A^T. Thus,

(*i*) if the order of A is $m \times n$, then, the order of A′ is $n \times m$.

(*ii*) $(i, j)^{th}$ element of A = $(j, i)^{th}$ element of A′.

Properties of transpose of matrices

1. For any matrix A, (A′)′ = A
2. If A and B are two matrices of the same order, then (A + B)′ = A′ + B′.
3. If A is any matrix and k is a scalar, then $(kA)' = kA'$.

Some important results of transposed matrices

(*i*) (A + B)′ = A′ + B′

(*ii*) $(kA)' = kA'$, where k is constant

(*iii*) (AB)′ = B′A′.

Symmetric Matrix: A square matrix A is said to be symmetric if A′ = A.

Thus a square matrix $A = [a_{ij}]$ is symmetric if $a_{ij} = a_{ji}$ for all values of i and j.

Skew-symmetric Matrix: A square matrix A is said to be skew-symmetric if A′ = –A.

Thus a square matrix $A = [a_{ij}]$ is skew-symmetric if $a_{ij} = -a_{ji}$ for all values of i and j.

Properties of symmetric and skew-symmetric matrices

1. (*i*) the sum of two symmetric matrices is always symmetric.

   (*ii*) the sum of two skew-symmetric matrices is always skew-symmetric.
2. Let A be a square matrix and k be a scalar.

   (*i*) If A is symmetric, then kA is symmetric;

   (*ii*) If A is skew-symmetric, then kA is skew-symmetric.
3. If A is any square matrix, then

   (*i*) (A + A′) is symmetric and

   (*ii*) (A – A′) is skew-symmetric.
4. Every square matrix is uniquely expressible as the sum of a symmetric matrix and a skew-symmetric matrix.

5. Every diagonal element of a skew-symmetric matrix is zero.

where the first matrix on right hand side is symmetric and the second one is skew-symmetric.

PROPERTIES OF MATRIX MULTIPLICATION

(*i*) **Associative Law for multiplication:** If A, B and C be three matrices of order $m \times n$, $n \times p$ and $p \times q$ respectively, then (AB)C = A(BC).

(*ii*) **Distributive Law:** If A, B, C be three matrices of order $m \times n$, $n \times p$ and $n \times p$ respectively, then

A. (B + C) = A.B + A.C.

(*iii*) Matrix multiplication is not commutative in general, *i.e.,* A.B ≠ B.A (in general).

(*iv*) The product of two non-zero matrices can be a zero matrix.

Determinant: Corresponding to each square matrix

$$A = \begin{bmatrix} a_{11} & a_{12} & a_{13} & \cdots & a_{1n} \\ a_{21} & a_{22} & a_{23} & \cdots & a_{2n} \\ \cdots & \cdots & \cdots & \cdots & \cdots \\ a_{n1} & a_{n2} & a_{n3} & \cdots & a_{nn} \end{bmatrix},$$

there is an associated expression, which is called the *determinant* of A, denoted by det A or |A|, written as

$$\det A = |A| = \begin{vmatrix} a_{11} & a_{12} & a_{13} & \cdots & a_{1n} \\ a_{21} & a_{22} & a_{23} & \cdots & a_{2n} \\ \cdots & \cdots & \cdots & \cdots & \cdots \\ a_{n1} & a_{n2} & a_{n3} & \cdots & a_{nn} \end{vmatrix}$$

A matrix is an arrangement of numbers and so it has no fixed value, while each determinant has a fixed value.

A determinant having n rows and n columns is knonw as a determinant of order n.

Thus, the determinants of non-square matrices are not defined.

Minor of an element: The minor M_{ij} of an element a_{ij} of a square matrix A is the determinant of the matrix that remains after deleting the i-th row and j-th column in given matrix A.

Cofactor of an element: The cofactor C_{ij} of an element a_{ij} of a square matrix A is $(-1)^{i+j}$ times the determinant of the matrix that reamins after deleting the i-th row and j-th column in the given matrix A.

Example: Find the minors and co-factors of the elements of the determinant

$$\Delta = \begin{vmatrix} a_{11} & a_{12} & a_{13} \\ a_{21} & a_{22} & a_{23} \\ a_{31} & a_{32} & a_{33} \end{vmatrix}$$

Let M_{ij} denote the minor of a_{ij} in Δ.

Now, a_{11} occurs in 1st column. So, in order to find the minor of a_{11}, we delete the 1st row and 1st column of Δ. The minor M_{11} of a_{11} is given by

$$M_{11} = \begin{vmatrix} a_{22} & a_{23} \\ a_{32} & a_{33} \end{vmatrix} = (a_{22}a_{33} - a_{32}a_{23}).$$

Similarly, we have:

$$M_{12} = \begin{vmatrix} a_{21} & a_{23} \\ a_{31} & a_{33} \end{vmatrix} = (a_{21}a_{33} - a_{31}a_{23})$$

$$M_{13} = \begin{vmatrix} a_{21} & a_{22} \\ a_{31} & a_{32} \end{vmatrix} = (a_{21}a_{32} - a_{31}a_{22})$$

$$M_{21} = \begin{vmatrix} a_{12} & a_{13} \\ a_{32} & a_{33} \end{vmatrix} = (a_{12}a_{33} - a_{32}a_{13})$$

Similarly, we may obtain the minor of each one of the remaining elements.

Now, if we denote the co-factor of a_{ij} by c_{ij}, then

$C_{11} = (-1)^{1+1} . M_{11} = M_{11} = (a_{22}a_{33} - a_{32}a_{23})$;

$C_{12} = (-1)^{1+2} . M_{12} = -M_{12} = (a_{31}a_{23} - a_{21}a_{33})$;

$C_{13} = (-1)^{1+3} . M_{13} = M_{13} = (a_{21}a_{32} - a_{31}a_{22})$

$C_{21} = (-1)^{2+1} . M_{21} = -M_{21} = (a_{32}a_{13} - a_{12}a_{33})$.

Similarly, the co-factor of each one of the remaining elements of Δ can be determined.

PROPERTIES OF DETERMINANTS

(*i*) The value of the determinant does not change when rows and columns are interchanged.

(*ii*) If all the elements of a rwo (column) are zero, then the value of the determinant is zero.

(*iii*) The interchange of any two rows (columns) of the determinant changes its sign.

(*iv*) If all the elements of a row (column) of a determinant are multiplied by a *non-zero* constant, then the value of the determinant gets multiplied by the same constant.

(*v*) If all the elements of a row (column) are *proportional (identical)* to the elements of some other row (column), then the value of the determinant is zero.

(*vi*) If each element of any row (column) is sum of two numbers, the determinant can be expressed as the sum of two determinants of the same order.

(*vii*) The value of a determinant remains unaltered under an operation of the form

$R_i \to R_i + pR_j = qR_k,\ j, k \neq i$

and $C_i \to C_i + pC_j + qC_k,\ j, k \neq i.$

SOME MORE PROPERTIES

(*i*) If a determinant $\Delta(x)$ becomes zero on putting $x = \alpha$, then $(x - \alpha)$ is a factor of $\Delta(x)$.

(*ii*) Determinant, which have all elements equal to zero except the diagonal elements, is equal to the product of the diagonal elements.

Solution of System of Linear Equations in Three variables by Cramers Rule: Solution of three linear equations in three unknown

$$a_1x_1 + b_1x_2 + c_1x_3 = d_1$$
$$a_2x_1 + b_2x_2 + c_2x_3 = d_2$$
$$a_3x_1 + b_3x_2 + c_3x_3 = d_3$$

is given by $x_1 = \frac{D_1}{D}$, $x_2 = \frac{D_2}{D}$ and $x_3 = \frac{D_3}{D}$.

Where $D = \begin{vmatrix} a_1 & b_1 & c_1 \\ a_2 & b_2 & c_2 \\ a_3 & b_3 & c_3 \end{vmatrix}$, $D_1 = \begin{vmatrix} d_1 & b_1 & c_1 \\ d_2 & b_2 & c_2 \\ d_3 & b_3 & c_3 \end{vmatrix}$,

$D_2 = \begin{vmatrix} a_1 & d_1 & c_1 \\ a_2 & d_2 & c_2 \\ a_3 & d_3 & c_3 \end{vmatrix}$ and $D_3 = \begin{vmatrix} a_1 & b_1 & d_1 \\ a_2 & b_2 & d_2 \\ a_3 & b_3 & d_3 \end{vmatrix}$, provided that $D \neq 0$.

Conditions for Consistency and Inconsistency

(*i*) If $D \neq 0$ and out of D_1, D_2, D_3 at least one is $\neq 0$, then the system of equation is consistent and has a unique solution.

(*ii*) If $D = 0$ and also $D_1 = D_2 = D_3 = 0$, then the given system of equation is consistent and has infinite number of solutions.

(*iii*) If $D = 0$ and at least one of D_1, D_2, D_3 is non-zero, then the given system of equation is inconsistent.

MULTIPLE CHOICE QUESTIONS

1. If $M(\theta) = \begin{bmatrix} \cos\theta & \sin\theta \\ -\sin\theta & \cos\theta \end{bmatrix}$, then $M(\alpha)\,M(\beta)$ is equal to

A. $M(0)$
B. $M(\alpha\beta)$
C. $M(\alpha + \beta)$
D. $M(\alpha - \beta)$

2. If the product of matrices

$A = \begin{bmatrix} \cos^2\theta & \cos\theta\sin\theta \\ \cos\theta\sin\theta & \sin^2\theta \end{bmatrix}$

$B = \begin{bmatrix} \cos^2\phi & \cos\phi\sin\phi \\ \cos\phi\sin\phi & \sin^2\phi \end{bmatrix}$

is a null matrix, then θ and ϕ differ by

A. an odd multiple of π
B. an even multiple of π
C. an odd multiple of $\frac{\pi}{2}$
D. an even multiple of $\frac{\pi}{2}$

3. If $D = \text{diag}(d_1, d_2, d_3, \ldots, d_n)$, where $d_i \neq 0$ for all $i = 1, 2, \ldots, n$ then D^{-1} is equal to

A. D
B. $\text{diag}\left(d_1^{-1}, d_2^{-1}, \ldots, d_n^{-1}\right)$
C. I_n
D. None of these

4. If $X = \begin{bmatrix} 3 & -4 \\ 1 & -1 \end{bmatrix}$, the value of X^n is

A. $\begin{bmatrix} 3n & -4n \\ n & -n \end{bmatrix}$ B. $\begin{bmatrix} 2+n & 5-n \\ n & -n \end{bmatrix}$

C. $\begin{bmatrix} 3^n & (-4)^n \\ 1^n & (-1)^n \end{bmatrix}$ D. None of these

5. The matrix, $A = \begin{bmatrix} 2 & -2 & -4 \\ -1 & 3 & 4 \\ 1 & -2 & -3 \end{bmatrix}$ is

A. non-singular B. idempotent
C. nilpotent D. orthogonal

6. If $A = \begin{bmatrix} 1 & 0 \\ 0 & 1 \end{bmatrix}$, $B = \begin{bmatrix} 0 & 1 \\ -1 & 0 \end{bmatrix}$ and

$C = \begin{bmatrix} \cos\theta & \sin\theta \\ -\sin\theta & \cos\theta \end{bmatrix}$, then which of the following is true?

A. $C = A\cos\theta - B\sin\theta$
B. $C = A\sin\theta + B\cos\theta$
C. $C = A\sin\theta - B\cos\theta$
D. $C = A\cos\theta + B\sin\theta$

7. The inverse of the matrix

$\begin{bmatrix} 2 & -5 & 1 \\ 8 & 6 & 7 \\ \lambda & -10 & 2 \end{bmatrix}$ does not exist if λ equals to

A. 0 B. 2
C. 4 D. 5

8. The characteristic roots of the matrix

$A = \begin{bmatrix} 8 & -6 & 2 \\ -6 & 7 & -4 \\ 2 & -4 & 3 \end{bmatrix}$ are

A. 0, 3, 15 B. 0, – 3, – 15
C. 0, 3, – 15 D. 0, – 3, 15

9. The rank of

$A = \begin{bmatrix} 6 & 1 & 3 & 8 \\ 4 & 2 & 6 & -1 \\ 10 & 3 & 9 & 7 \\ 16 & 4 & 12 & 15 \end{bmatrix}$ is

A. 4 B. 3
C. 2 D. 1

10. The transformation matrix $\begin{bmatrix} 1 & 0 & 0 \\ 0 & 0 & 1 \\ 0 & 1 & 0 \end{bmatrix}$ represents

A. Rotation about x-axis by 90°
B. Reflection about $y = z$
C. Reflexion about x-axis
D. None of these

11. The matrix $\begin{bmatrix} 1 & 5-i & 3 \\ 5+i & 2 & 3i \\ 3 & -3i & 0 \end{bmatrix}$ is

A. Symmetric B. Skew-Symmetric
C. Hermitian D. Skew-Hermitian

12. The eigen values of the matrix

$\begin{bmatrix} 2 & 2 & 1 \\ 1 & 3 & 1 \\ 1 & 2 & 2 \end{bmatrix}$ are

A. 1, 3, 1 B. 2, 3, 2
C. 5, 1, 1 D. 3, 5, 2

13. Given that $xyz = -1$, the value of the determinant

$\begin{vmatrix} x & x^2 & 1+x^3 \\ y & y^2 & 1+y^3 \\ z & z^2 & 1+z^3 \end{vmatrix}$ is

A. 0 B. Positive
C. Negative D. None of these

14. If the value of the determinant $\begin{vmatrix} a & 1 & 1 \\ 1 & b & 1 \\ 1 & 1 & c \end{vmatrix}$ is positive, then

A. $abc > 1$ B. $abc > -8$
C. $abc < -8$ D. $abc > -2$

15. If $\omega = \dfrac{(-1+\sqrt{3}i)}{2}$, then the value of

$\begin{vmatrix} 1 & 1 & 1 \\ 1 & \omega & \omega^2 \\ 1 & \omega^2 & \omega \end{vmatrix}$ is

A. $3\sqrt{3}i$ B. $-3\sqrt{3}i$
C. $-\sqrt{3}i$ D. $\sqrt{3}i$

16. If $\Delta = \begin{vmatrix} \cos\alpha & -\sin\alpha & 1 \\ \sin\alpha & \cos\alpha & 1 \\ \cos(\alpha+\beta) & -\sin(\alpha+\beta) & 1 \end{vmatrix}$, then

A. $\Delta \in [1-\sqrt{2}, 1+\sqrt{2}]$

B. $\Delta \in [-1, 1]$

C. $\Delta \in [-\sqrt{2}, \sqrt{2}]$

D. None of these

17. If $a_1, a_2, a_3, \ldots, a_m, \ldots$ are in G.P., then the determinant

$$\Delta = \begin{vmatrix} \log a_n & \log a_{n+1} & \log a_{n+2} \\ \log a_{n+3} & \log a_{n+4} & \log a_{n+5} \\ \log a_{n+6} & \log a_{n+7} & \log a_{n+8} \end{vmatrix}$$ is equal to

A. 0 B. 1

C. 2 D. None of these

18. $\Delta_r = \begin{vmatrix} 2r & x & n(n+1) \\ 6r^2-1 & y & n^2(2n+3) \\ 4r^3-2nr & z & n^3(n+1) \end{vmatrix}$, then $\sum_{r=1}^{n} \Delta_r$ is independent of

A. x, y, z only B. x, y, z and n

C. x only D. None of these

19. Let a, b, c be positive real numbers. The following system of equations in x, y, and z

$$\frac{x^2}{a^2}+\frac{y^2}{b^2}-\frac{z^2}{c^2} = 1, \quad \frac{x^2}{a^2}-\frac{y^2}{b^2}+\frac{z^2}{c^2} = 1,$$

$$-\frac{x^2}{a^2}+\frac{y^2}{b^2}+\frac{z^2}{c^2} = 1$$ has

A. no solution

B. unique solution

C. infinitely many solutions

D. finitely many solutions

20. The system of linear equations

$x + y + z = 2$

$2x + y - z = 3$

$3x + 2y + kz = 4$ has unique solutions if

A. $k \neq 0$ B. $-1 < k < 1$

C. $-2 < k < 1$ D. $k = 0$

ANSWERS

1	2	3	4	5	6	7	8	9	10
C	C	B	D	B	D	C	A	A	B
11	**12**	**13**	**14**	**15**	**16**	**17**	**18**	**19**	**20**
C	C	A	B	B	A	A	B	B	A

SOME SELECTED EXPLANATORY ANSWERS

4. Given $X = \begin{bmatrix} 3 & -4 \\ 1 & -1 \end{bmatrix}$

$$\Rightarrow \quad X^2 = \begin{bmatrix} 3 & -4 \\ 1 & -1 \end{bmatrix}\begin{bmatrix} 3 & -4 \\ 1 & -1 \end{bmatrix}$$

$$= \begin{bmatrix} 5 & -8 \\ 2 & -3 \end{bmatrix}$$

Putting $n = 2$ in all the given option, *i.e., (a), (b)* and *(c)*, it is seen that none of them talies. Thus *(d)* is the required choice.

5. Given $A = \begin{bmatrix} 2 & -2 & -4 \\ -1 & 3 & 4 \\ 1 & -2 & 3 \end{bmatrix}$

$$\Rightarrow \quad A^2 = \begin{bmatrix} 2 & -2 & -4 \\ -1 & 3 & 4 \\ 1 & -2 & 3 \end{bmatrix}\begin{bmatrix} 2 & -2 & -4 \\ -1 & 3 & 4 \\ 1 & -2 & 3 \end{bmatrix}$$

$$\Rightarrow \quad A^2 = \begin{bmatrix} 2 & -2 & -4 \\ -1 & 3 & 4 \\ 1 & -2 & -3 \end{bmatrix} = A$$

Hence, A is idempotent.

6. By closely inspecting and w.r.t. $A=\begin{bmatrix}1 & 0\\ 0 & 1\end{bmatrix}$

and $B=\begin{bmatrix}0 & 1\\ -1 & 0\end{bmatrix}$ we conclude that

$$A\cos\theta + B\sin\theta = \begin{bmatrix}1 & 0\\ 0 & 1\end{bmatrix}\cos + \begin{bmatrix}0 & 1\\ -1 & 0\end{bmatrix}\sin\theta$$

$$= \begin{bmatrix}\cos\theta & \sin\theta\\ -\sin\theta & \cos\theta\end{bmatrix} = C$$

11. All the elements of the given matrix are of the form $a_{ji} = \bar{a}_{ij}$.

12. Let $A = \begin{bmatrix}2 & 2 & 1\\ 1 & 3 & 1\\ 1 & 2 & 2\end{bmatrix}$

The characteristic equation of A is

$|A - \lambda I| = 0$

$$\Rightarrow \begin{vmatrix}2-\lambda & 2 & 1\\ 1 & 3-\lambda & 1\\ 1 & 2 & 2-\lambda\end{vmatrix} = 0$$

$\Rightarrow (\lambda - 1)^2 (\lambda - 5) = 0$

$\Rightarrow \lambda = 1, 1, 5.$

19. Let $\frac{x^2}{a^2} = X, \frac{y^2}{b^2} = Y, \frac{z^2}{c^2} = Z.$

Then the given system of equation reduces to

$X + Y - Z = 1$
$X - Y + Z = 1$
$-X + Y + Z = 1$

The coefficient matrix is

$$A = \begin{bmatrix}1 & 1 & -1\\ 1 & -1 & 1\\ -1 & 1 & 1\end{bmatrix}$$

Here $|A| \neq 0$, so the given system of equations has unique solution.

20. The given system will have unique solution if $|A| \neq 0$

$$\Rightarrow \begin{vmatrix}1 & 1 & 1\\ 2 & 1 & -1\\ 3 & 2 & k\end{vmatrix} \neq 0$$

$$\Rightarrow 1\begin{vmatrix}1 & -1\\ 2 & k\end{vmatrix} - 1\begin{vmatrix}2 & -1\\ 3 & k\end{vmatrix} + 1\begin{vmatrix}2 & 1\\ 3 & 2\end{vmatrix} \neq 0$$

$\Rightarrow (k + 2) - (2k + 3) + (4 - 3) \neq 0$

$\Rightarrow -k \neq 0 \Rightarrow k \neq 0.$

8 Set, Relation and Function

SETS

A well defined class or collection of objects is called a set and these objects are called elements of the set.

Finite and Infinite Sets

If the number of elements in a set is finite, then the set is called a finite set and if the number of elements in the set is infinite, then the set is called an infinite set.

Null Set

A set containing no element is called a null set.

Non-Empty Set

Any set which is not a null / void / empty set.

Singleton Set

Which contains one element only, *e.g.*, {0}, {1}, {Ram}.

Equivalent Sets

Two sets are equivalent if the number of elements in one set is equal to the number of elements in the other set, *e.g.*, {1, 2, 3} is equivalent to {*a*, *b*, *c*}.

Equal Sets (A = B)

If every element of set 'A' is in set 'B' and vice-versa.

Set of Sets/Family of Sets/Class of Sets

When the elements of a set are sets themselves.

e.g., $A = \{\{\phi\}, \{2\}, \{1\}, \{1, 2\}\}$,

$B = \{\phi\}$ because ϕ itself is a set called as null set.

Subset ($A \subseteq B$)

If every element of 'A' is an element of 'B', then 'A' is a subset of 'B'.

Proper Subset ($A \subset B$)

'A' is a proper subset of 'B', if all the elements of 'A' are elements of 'B' but not vice-versa. *e.g.*,

if $A = \{1, 2, 3, 4\}$, and

$B = \{A, B, 1, 2, 3, 4, 5\}$, then $A \subset B$

i.e., A is a proper subset of B if $A \subset B$ but $B \not\subset A$.

i.e., A is a proper subset of B if $A \subset B$ but $B \neq A$.

Improper Subset ($A \subseteq B$)

i.e., A is an improper subset of 'B', if A = B, *i.e.*, all the elements of A are elements of B and vice-versa.

Super Set ($A \supset B$)

{*i.e.*, A contains B}. If B is a sub-set of A, then A is called a super set of B.

Universal Set (U)

If a set contains all the sets under consideration, then it is called universal set.

Largest non-empty set of which all the sets under consideration, is universal set.

Power Set (P(A))

P(A) is the "power set of A" if P(A) contains all the possible subsets of A.

Thus power set is a "set of sets" or "class of sets", *e.g.*, if A = {2, 3, 4} then

$P(A) = \{\{\phi\}, \{2\}, \{3\}, \{4\}, \{2, 3\}, \{2, 4\}, \{3, 4\}, \{2, 3, 4\}\}$

Disjoint set

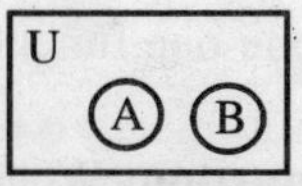

If two sets A and B do not have any common element, then A and B are disjoint sets, *i.e.*, $(A \cap B) = \phi$.

Representation of Sets

(*a*) **Rester Method or Tabular Method**
Here we list out all the elements as such within curly brackets, *e.g.*,
$A = \{1, 2, 3, 4, 5, ..., n)$

(*b*) **Property of Set Builder Method**
By starting all the properties of the elements in the set, which will define all the elements of the set but nothing else, *e.g.*,
$A = \{2, 4, 6, 8\}$ is written as
$A = \{x : x \text{ is even natural number} \leq 8\}$

Cartesian Product (A × B)

Let A and B be two sets, then the set of all the ordered pairs of the form (a, b) such that $a \in A$ and $b \in B$ is $A \times B$ (read as A cross B).

Symbolically,

$$A \times B = \{(a, b) / a \in A \text{ and } b \in B\}$$

Complement of A Set (A^C or A')

Complement of a set is always with respect to one of its universal sets or super sets.

If X is an universal set of A, then the set of all the elements which are in X but not in A is A^c, *i.e.*, complement of A with respect to X.

Symbolically,

$$A' \text{ or } A^c = (X \setminus A), \text{ i.e., } (X - A)$$

Results on Number of Elements in Sets

If A, B and C are finite sets, and U be the finite universal set, then

(*i*) $n(A \cup B) = n(A) + n(B) - n(A \cap B)$

(*ii*) $n(A \cup B) = n(A) + n(B) \Leftrightarrow$ A, B are disjoint non-void sets.

(*iii*) $n(A - B) = n(A) - n(A \cap B)$
i.e., $n(A - B) + n(A \cap B) = n(A)$

(*iv*) $n(A \Delta B)$ = No. of elements which belong to exactly one of A or B
$= n[(A - B) \cup (B - A)]$
$= n(A - B) + n(B - A)$
$[\because (A - B) \text{ and } (B - A) \text{ are disjoint}]$
$= n(A) - n(A \cap B) + n(B) - n(A \cap B)$
$= n(A) + n(B) - 2n(A \cap B)$

(*v*) $n(A \cup B \cup C) = n(A) + n(B) + n(C) - n(A \cap B) - n(B \cap C) - n(A \cap C) + n(A \cap B \cap C)$

(*vi*) No. of elements in exactly two of the sets A, B, C $= n(A \cap B) + n(B \cap C) + n(C \cap A) - 3n(A \cap B \cap C)$

(*vii*) No. of elements in exactly one of the sets A, B, C $= n(A) + n(B) + n(C) - 2n(A \cap B) - 2n(B \cap C) - 2n(A \cap C) + 3n(A \cap B \cap C)$

(*viii*) $n(A' \cup B') = (n(A \cap B)') = n(U) - n(A \cap B)$

(*ix*) $n(A' \cap B') = (n(A \cap B)') = n(U) - n(A \cap B)$

(*x*) $n(A' \cap B') = n(A \cup B)' = n(U) - n(A \cup B)$

RELATION

Let there be two sets A and B, then a "relation R from set A to set B" is a sub-set of A × B.

A is called 'Domain of R'

B is called 'Co-domain of R'

And the set of the corresponding second entries in the ordered pairs comprising the relation R is called the 'Range of R'.

Inverse Relation (R^{-1})

Let R be a relation from A to B (*i.e.*, from set A to set B), then the inverse relation R^{-1} (which will be from set B to set A) is defined by

$$R^{-1} = \{(b, a) : (a, b) \in R\}$$

(*i*) **Reflexive relation**
If "a R a" holds good for all $a \in A$.

(*ii*) **Symmetric relation**
Here "a R b" implies "b R a". This means R is symmetric, if
$(a, b) \in R \Rightarrow (b, a) \in R$ for all $a, b \in A$.

(*iii*) **Transitive relation**
If "a R b" and "b R c" together imply "a R c".
A relation R is transitive on set A if
$(a, b) \in R$ and $(b, c) \in R \Rightarrow (a, c) \in R$
for all $a, b, c \in A$.

(*iv*) **Equivalence relation**
If a relation is reflexive and symmetric as well as transitive, it is called an "equivalence relation".

FUNCTIONS

Cartesian Product of 2 sets A and B (A × B)

Cartesian Product of two sets A and B denoted by A × B is the set of all ordered pairs (a, b) such that $a \in$ A and $b \in$ B.

Symbolically,

A × B = $\{(a, b) : a \in A \text{ and } b \in B\}$

Function

Let X and Y be two non-empty sets. A subset f of X × Y is called a function from X into Y iff (*i.e.*, if and only if) for each $x \in$ X, there exists a unique y in Y such that $(x, y) \in f$.

Representation of Function

A function from a set X into a set Y is denoted as

$f : X \longrightarrow Y$ or as $X \xrightarrow{f} Y$.

Domain and co-domain: If f be the function defined from the set X into the set Y, then the set X is called domain of the function f denoted by (D_f) or dom (f) and the set Y is called co-domain of the function f.

Image: The unique element y in Y assigned to $x \in$ X is called the image of x under f or value of f at x. It is denoted by $f(x)$. It is also written as:

Pre-image: If y is image of x, then x is called a pre-image of y.

Inverse Image of B $\forall$ B $\subset$ Y: (Read — Inverse image of B where B is a sub-set of Y)

If B $\subset$ Y, then the set $\{x \in X : f(x) \in B\}$ is called the inverse image of B under f and is denoted as f^{-1} [B].

"Onto" and "Into" functions: Onto function is also known as surjection or surjective mapping.

If range of f is the set Y, *i.e.*, range = co-domain, then f is called *onto function*. However, if range of f is a proper subset of the set Y, then f is said to be an *into function*.

Two-one / Many-one function: If two or more elements in X have the same image in Y, then f is called a two-one or many-one function, respectively.

One-one function: Also known as "Injection Function" or "Injective Mapping".

If different elements in X have different images in Y then f is a one-one function.

Hence, if f is a one-one function, it means $f(x_1) = f(x_2) \Rightarrow x_1 = x_2$.

One-one onto function: When for each $x \in$ X, there is a unique $f(x) \in$ Y and for each $f(x) \in$ Y there is a unique $x \in$ X, then the function is an "one-one onto function".

In case of an inverse function,

dom (f^{-1}) = range (f)

where f^{-1} is the inverse of the function f.

Solved Examples

Example 1: *If A = {1, 2, 3, 4}, define relation on A which have properties of being*

(i) reflexive, transitive but not symmetric

(ii) symmetric but netither reflexive nor transitive

(iii) reflexive, symmetric and transitive.

Solution:

(*i*) Let R_1 = {(1, 1), (2, 2), (3, 3), (4, 4), (1, 3), (3, 4), (1, 4)}, This relation is reflexive, transitive but not symmetric.

(*ii*) Let R_2 = {(1, 3), (3, 1)}
Here R_2 is symmetric but neither reflexive nor transitive.

(*iii*) Let R_3 = {(1, 1), (2, 2), (3, 3), (4, 4), (1, 2), (2, 1)}.
Here R_3 is reflexive, symmetric and transitive.

Example 2: *If A = {1, 3, 5, 7, 11, 13, 15, 17}, B = {2, 4, 6, ..., 18} and N is the univeral set, then find A′ ∪ ((A ∪ B) ∩ B′).*

Solution: We have

(A ∪ B) ∩ B′ = A [∵ A, B are disjoint sets]

∴ A′ ∪ ((A ∪ B) ∩ B′) = A′ ∪ A = N.

Example 3: *Three relations R_1, R_2 and R_3 are defined on set A = {a, b, c} as follows:*

(i) R_1 = {(a, a), (a, b), (a, c), (b, b), (b, c), (c, a), (c, b), (c, c)}

(ii) R_2 = {(a, b), (b, a), (a, c), (c, a)}

(iii) R_3 = {(a, b), (b, c), (c, a)}

Find whether each of R_1, R_2 and R_3 is reflexive, symmetric and transitive.

Solution:

(*i*) **Reflexive:** Clearly, $(a, a), (b, b), (c, c), \in R_1$.
So, R_1 is reflexive on A.

Symmetric: We observe that $(a, b) \in R_1$ but $(b, a) \notin R_1$.
So, R_1 is not symmetric on A.
Transitive: We find that $(b, c) \in R_1$ and $(c, a) \in R_1$ but $(b, a) \notin R_1$. So, R is not transitive on A.

(*ii*) **Reflexive:** Since (a, a), (b, b) and (c, c) are not in R_2. So, it is not a reflexive relation on A.
Symmetric: We find that the ordered pairs obtained by interchanging the components of ordered pairs in R_2 are also in R_2. So, R_2 is a symmetric relation on A.
Transitive: Clearly $(a, b) \in R_2$ and $(b, a) \in R_2$ but $(a, a) \in R_2$.

(*iii*) **Reflexive:** Since none of (a, a), (b, b) and (c, c) is an element of R_3. So, R_3 is not reflexive on A.
Symmetric: Clearly, $(b, c) \in R_3$ but $(c, b) \notin R_3$. So, R_3 is not symmetric on A.
Transitive: Clearly, $(a, b) \in R_3$ and $(b, c) \in R_3$ but $(a, c) \notin R_3$.
So, R_3 is not transitive on A.

Example 4: *If A × B = {(a, 1), (a, 5), (a, 2), (b, 2), (b, 5), (b, 1), find B × A.*

Solution: Clearly, B × A can be obtained from A × B by interchanging the entries (or components) or ordered pair in A × B.

$\therefore$ B × A = {(1, a), (5, a), (2, a), (3, a), (5, b), (1, b)}

MULTIPLE CHOICE QUESTIONS

1. If A = {1, 3, 5, 7, 9, 11, 13, 15, 17}, B = {2, 4, ..., 18} and N is the universal set, then A′ ∪ ((A B) B′) is

A. A B. N
C. B D. None of these

2. If X = $\{4^n - 3n - 1 | n \in N\}$ and Y = $\{9(n-1) | n \in N\}$, then X ∪ Y is equal to

A. X B. Y
C. N D. None of these

3. Let A = $\{x, y) \mid y = e^x, x \in R\}$
B = $\{(x, y) \mid y = e^x, x \in R\}$, then

A. A ∩ B = ϕ B. A ∩ B ≠ ϕ
C. A ∪ B = R^2 D. None of these

4. Suppose $A_1, A_2, ..., A_{30}$ are thirty sets each with five elements and $B_1, B_2, ..., B_n$ are n sets each with three elements such that $\bigcup_{i=1}^{30} A_i = \bigcup_{i=1}^{n} B_i$ = S. If each element of S belongs to exactly ten of the A_i's and exactly 9 of the B_i's, then the value of n is

A. 15 B. 135
C. 45 D. 90

5. If sets A and B are defined as

$$A = \left\{(x, y) \mid y = \frac{1}{x},\ x \neq 0,\ x \in R\right\}$$

B = $\{(x, y) \mid y = -x, x \in R\}$, then

A. A ∩ B = A B. A ∩ B = B
C. A ∪ B = ϕ D. None of these

6. A set contains n elements. The power set contains

A. n elements B. 2^n elements
C. n^2 elements D. None of these

7. If A = {1, 2, 3} and B = {3, 8}, then (A ∪ B) × (A ∩ B) is

A. {(3, 1), (3, 2), (3, 3), (3, 8)}
B. {(1, 3), (2, 3), (3, 3), (8, 3)}
C. {(1, 2), (2, 2), (3, 3), (8, 8)}
D. {(8, 3), (8, 2), (8, 1), (8, 8)}

8. The number of subsets of a set containing n elements is

A. n B. $2^n - 1$
C. n^2 D. 2^n

9. The symmetric difference of A and B is

A. (A – B) ∩ (B – A)
B. (A – B) ∪ (B – A)
C. (A ∪ B) – (B ∩ A)
D. {(A – B) – A} ∪ (A – B) – B}

10. If A = {1, 2, 3}, B = {4, 5, 6} and C = {1, 2}, then (A – B) × (A ∩ C) is

A. {(1, 3), (1, 5)}
B. {(2, 1), (2, 2), (2, 3)}
C. {(1, 2), (1, 3), (1, 5)}
D. None of these

11. If R is a relation from a finite set A having m elements to a finite set B having n elements, then the number of relations from A to B is

A. 2^{mn} B. $2^{mn} - 1$
C. $2mn$ D. m^n

12. Let R be a relation on a set A such that R = R^{-1}, then R is

A. reflexive B. symmetric
C. transitive D. None of these

13. Let R_1 be a relation defined by $R_1 = \{(a, b) \mid a \le b, a, b \in R\}$. Then R_1 is

A. an equivalence relation on R
B. reflexive, transitive but not symmetric
C. symmetric, transitive but not reflexive
D. neither transitive nor reflexive but symmetric

14. The relation R = {(1, 1), (2, 2), (3, 3), (1, 2), (2, 3), (1, 3)} on set A = {1, 2, 3} is

A. reflexive but not symmetric
B. reflexive but not transitive
C. symmetric and transitive
D. neither symmetric nor transitive

15. Let $P = \{(x, y) \mid x^2 + y^2 = 1, x, y \in R\}$. Then P is

A. reflexive B. symmetric
C. transitive D. antisymmetric

16. If R be a relation < from A = {1, 2, 3, 4} to B = {1, 3, 5}, *i.e.*, $(a, b) \in R \Leftrightarrow a < b$, then R o R^{-1} is

A. {(1, 3), (1, 5), (2, 3), (2, 5), (3, 5), (4, 5)}
B. {(3, 1), (5, 1), (3, 2), (5, 2), (5, 3), (5, 4)}
C. {(3, 3), (3, 5), (5, 3), (5, 5)}
D. {(3, 3), (3, 4), (4, 5)}

17. Let A = {p, q, r{. Which of the following is not an equivalence relation on A?

A. $R_1 = \{(p, q), (q, r), (p, r), (p, p)\}$
B. $R_2 = \{(r, q), (r, p), (r, r), (q, q)\}$
C. $R_3 = \{(p, p), (q, q), (r, r), (p, p)\}$
D. None of these

18. Let R be a relation on the set N of natural numbers defined by nR$m \Leftrightarrow n$ is a factor of m (*i.e.*, $n|m$). Then R is

A. reflexive and symmetric
B. transitive and symmetric
C. equivalence
D. reflexive, transitive but not symmetric

19. Let X = {1, 2, 3, 4, 5} and Y = {1, 3, 5, 7, 9}. Which of the following is/are relations from X to Y?

A. $R_1 = \{(x, y) \mid y = 2 + x, x \in X, y \in Y\}$
B. $R_2 = \{(1, 1), (2, 1), (3, 5), (9, 4)\}$
C. $R_3 = \{(1, 5), (2, 7), (4, 7), (7, 2)\}$
D. $R_4 = \{(1, 3), (2, 5), (2, 4), (7, 9)\}$

20. Let R = {(1, 3), (2, 2), (3, 2) and S = {(2, 1), (3, 2), (2, 3)} be two relations on set A = {1, 2, 3}. Then RoS =

A. {(1, 3), (2, 2), (3, 2), (2, 1), (2, 3)}
B. {(3, 2), (1, 3)}
C. {(2, 3), (3, 2), (2, 2)}
D. {(2, 3), (3, 2)}

21. Let A and B be two finite sets having m and n elements, respectively. Then the total number of mappings from A to B is

A. mn B. 2^{mn}
C. m^n D. n^m

22. Then total number of injective mappings from a set with m elements to a set with n elements, $m \le n$, is

A. m^n B. n^m
C. $\frac{n!}{(n-m)!}$ D. $n!$

23. If $f(x) = \cos(\log_e x)$, then $f(x) f(y) - \frac{1}{2}[f(x/y), f(x y)]$ is equal to

A. 0 B. $\frac{1}{2}f(x) f(y)$
C. $f(x + y)$ D. None of these

24. Let $f(x)$ be defined on [–2, 2] and is given by

$$f(x) = \begin{cases} -1, & -2 \le x \le 0 \\ x-1, & 0 < x \le 2 \end{cases}$$

and $g(x) = f(|x|) + |f(x)|$. Then $g(x)$ is equal to

A. $\begin{cases} -x, & -2 \le x < 0 \\ 0, & 0 \le x < 1 \\ x-1, & 1 \le x \le 2 \end{cases}$

B. $\begin{cases} -x, & -2 \le x < 0 \\ 0, & 0 \le x < 1 \\ 2(x-1), & 1 \le x \le 2 \end{cases}$

C. $\begin{cases} -x & -2 \le x < 0 \\ x-1 & 0 \le x \le 2 \end{cases}$

D. None of these

25. Let $f : R \to R$ be a function defined by $f(x) = \cos(5x + 2)$. Then f is

A. injective B. surjective
C. bijective D. None of these

26. If $f(x) = \dfrac{3x+2}{5x-3}$, then

A. $f^{-1}(x) = f(x)$ B. $f^{-1}(x) = -f(x)$
C. $(fof)(x) = -x$ D. $f^{-1}(x) = -\dfrac{1}{19} f(x)$

27. If $f(x) = \dfrac{x-1}{x+1}$, then $f(2x)$ is

A. $\dfrac{f(x)+1}{f(x)+3}$ B. $\dfrac{3f(x)+1}{f(x)+3}$
C. $\dfrac{f(x)+3}{f(x)+1}$ D. $\dfrac{f(x)+3}{3f(x)+1}$

28. If $f(x) = \log\left(\dfrac{1+x}{1-x}\right)$ and $g(x) = \dfrac{3x+x^3}{1+3x^2}$, then $fog(x)$ equals

A. $-(f)(x)$ B. $3f(x)$
C. $[f(x)]^3$ D. None of these

29. The number of bijective functions from set A to itself when A contains 106 elements is

A. 106 B. $(106)^2$
C. 106! D. 2^{106}

30. Let $f : R \to R$ be a function defined by $f(x) = \dfrac{e^{|x|} - e^{-x}}{e^x + e^{-x}}$. Then

A. f is a bijection
B. f is an injection only
C. f is a surjection only
D. f is neither an injection nor a surjection

ANSWERS

1	2	3	4	5	6	7	8	9	10
B	B	B	C	C	B	B	D	B	D
11	**12**	**13**	**14**	**15**	**16**	**17**	**18**	**19**	**20**
A	B	B	A	B	C	D	D	A	C
21	**22**	**23**	**24**	**25**	**26**	**27**	**28**	**29**	**30**
D	C	A	B	D	A	B	B	C	D

9 Limit and Continuity

DEFINITION OF LIMIT

A quantity l is said to be the limit of a function $f(x)$ at $x = a$, written as $\lim_{x \to a} f(x) = l$, if for a given small positive number $\in$ there exists a number δ such that $|f(x) - l| < \in$ for every $|x - a| < \delta$.

Existence of A Limit at A Point

$\lim_{x \to a} f(x)$ exists only if $\lim_{x \to a+0} f(x)$ and $\lim_{x \to a-0} f(x)$ both exist and are equal, *i.e.*, both right and left hand limits exist and are equal. This common value is known as the limit of the function $f(x)$ as $x \to a$.

Working Methods of Finding Limit on the Right and Left

(*i*) To find the limit on the right we put $a + h$ for x in $f(x)$ and then take the limit as $h \to 0$. Thus

$$\lim_{x \to a+0} f(x) = \lim_{h \to 0} f(a+h).$$

(*ii*) To find the limit on the left we put $a - h$ for x in $f(x)$ and then take the limit as $h \to 0$. Thus

$$\lim_{x \to a-0} f(x) = \lim_{h \to 0} f(a-h).$$

Some Important Limits

(*i*) $\lim_{n \to \infty} \left(1 + \frac{1}{n}\right)^n = e;$

(*ii*) $\lim_{n \to 0} (1+n)^{1/n} = e;$

(*iii*) $\lim_{x \to 0} \left(\frac{\sin x}{x}\right) = 1;$

(*iv*) $\lim_{x \to 0} \left(\frac{\tan x}{x}\right) = 1;$

(*v*) $\lim_{x \to 0} \left[\frac{\log_e(1+x)}{x}\right] = 1;$

(*vi*) $\lim_{x \to 0} \left(\frac{e^x - 1}{x}\right) = 1;$

(*vii*) $\lim_{x \to 0} \left(\frac{a^x - 1}{x}\right) = \log_e a;$

(*viii*) $\lim_{x \to a} \left(\frac{x^n - a^n}{x - a}\right) = na^{n-1};$

where n is an integer, $n \neq 0$.

Some Important Expansions

(*i*) $\sin x = x - \frac{x^3}{3!} + \frac{x^5}{5!} - \ldots$ to ∞;

(*ii*) $\cos x = 1 - \frac{x^2}{2!} + \frac{x^4}{4!} - \ldots$ to ∞;

(*iii*) $\tan x = x + \frac{x^3}{3} + \frac{2}{15}x^5 + \ldots$ to ∞;

(*iv*) $\tan^{-1} x = x - \frac{x^3}{3} + \frac{x^5}{5} - \frac{x^7}{7} + \ldots$ to ∞;

(*v*) $\log_e(1+x) = x - \frac{1}{2}x^2 + \frac{1}{3}x^3 - \frac{1}{4}x^4 + \ldots$ to ∞, where $|x| < 1$;

(*vi*) $\log_e(1-x) = -x - \frac{1}{2}x^2 - \frac{1}{3}x^3 - \frac{1}{4}x^4 - \ldots$ to ∞, where $|x| < 1$;

(*vii*) $e^x = 1 + x + \frac{x^2}{2!} + \frac{x^3}{3!} + \ldots$ to $\infty \sum_{n=0}^{\infty} \left(\frac{x^n}{n!}\right)$

(*viii*) $a^x = 1 + x(\log_e a) + \frac{x^2}{2!}(\log_e a)^2 + \ldots$ to ∞;

(*ix*) $(1 - x)^{-1} = 1 + x + x^2 + \ldots + x^r + \ldots$ to ∞.

DEFINITION OF CONTINUITY

A function $f(x)$ is continuous at a point $x = a$ if

$$\lim_{x \to a-0} f(x) = \lim_{x \to a+0} f(x) = f(a)$$

i.e., $\lim_{x \to a} f(x)$ exists and is equal to the value of the function $f(x)$ at $x = a$.

Continuity in An Interval

A function $f(x)$ is said to be continuous in the closed interval $[a, b]$ if it is continuous at every point in this interval and the continuity at the end points is defined as $f(x)$ is continuous at $x = a$ if

$$\lim_{x \to a+0} f(x) = f(a)$$

and at $x = b$, if

$$\lim_{x \to b-0} f(x) = f(b)$$

Discontinuity

A function which is not continuous at a point is said to have a discontinuity at that point.

Differentiability

If $f(x)$ be a function defined on an interval $[a, b]$ and $x_0 \in \,]a, b[$ then $f(x)$ is said to be derivable (or differentiable) at $x = x_0$ if

$$\lim_{x \to x_0} \frac{f(x) - f(x_0)}{x - x_0}$$

or $\lim_{h \to 0} \frac{f(x_0 + h) - f(x_0)}{h}$ exists and is denoted by $f'(x_0)$ or $Df\,(x_0)$.

Right-Hand Derivative

$\lim_{h \to 0} \frac{f(x_0 + h) - f(x_0)}{h}$, $h > 0$ is called the right hand or progressive derivative of $f(x)$ at $x = x_0$ and is denoted by

$$Rf'(x_0) \text{ or by } f'(x_0 + 0).$$

Left-Hand Derivative

$\lim_{h \to 0} \frac{f(x_0 - h) - f(x_0)}{-h}$, $h > 0$ is called the left hand or regressive derivative of $f(x)$ at $x = x_0$ and is denoted by

$$Lf'(x_0) \text{ or by } f'(x_0 - 0).$$

Differentiability at the end points of $[a, b]$ and in $[a, b]$:

A function $f(x)$ is said to be differentiable at $x = a$ if $Rf'(a)$ exists and is equal to $f'(a)$.

Similarly a function $f(x)$ is said to be differentiable at $x = b$ if $Lf'(b)$ exists and is equal to $f'(b)$.

Also a function $f(x)$ is said to be differentiable in $[a, b]$ if and only if it is differentiable at every point of $]a, b[$ and is differentiable at the end points of $[a, b]$.

Indeterminate Forms and L-Hospital's Rule

$\frac{0}{0}, \frac{\infty}{\infty}, \infty - \infty, 0 \times \infty, 1^\infty, 0^\infty, \infty^0$ are indeterminate forms.

If a function takes the form $\frac{0}{0}$ or $\frac{\infty}{\infty}$ at $x = a$, then L-Hospital's Rule applies.

L-Hospital's Rule

If $\phi(x)$ and $\Psi(x)$ are functions of x such that

$$\phi(a) = 0$$

and $\Psi(a) = 0$

or $\phi(a) = \Psi(a) = \infty$

Then $\operatorname{Lim}_{x \to a} \frac{\phi(x)}{\Psi(x)} = \operatorname{Lim}_{x \to a} \frac{\phi'(x)}{\Psi'(x)}$

Solved Examples

Example 1: *If $f(a) = 2$, $f'(a) = 1$, $g(a) = -1$, $g'(a) = 2$, then evaluate*

$$\operatorname{Lt}_{x \to a} \frac{g(x)f(a) - g(a)f(x)}{x - a}$$

Solution: $\text{Lt}_{x \to a} \dfrac{g(x)f(a) - g(a)f(x)}{x - a}$, of the form 0/0

$$= \text{Lim}_{x \to a} \frac{\frac{d}{dx}[g(x)f(a) - g(a)f(x)]}{\frac{d}{dx}[x - a]}$$

by De L. Hospital's rule

$$= \text{Lim}_{x \to a} \frac{g'(x)f(a) - g(a)f'(x)}{1}$$

$= g'(a)\, f(a) - g(a)\, f'(a)$

$= (2)\,(2) - (-1)\,(1) = 5.$

Example 2: *A function f(x) is defined by*

$f(x) = 1 + x$, if $x \le 2$

$= 5 - x$, if $x \ge 2$

Is the function f(x) differentiable at x = 2?

Solution: $Rf'(2) = \text{Lim}_{h \to 0} \dfrac{f(2+h) - f(2)}{h}$

$$= \text{Lim}_{h \to 0} \frac{\{5 - (2+h)\} - (5 - 2)}{h}$$

$[\because f(x) = 5 - x, \text{ if } x \ge 2 - 1]$

And $L\, f'(2) = \text{Lim}_{h \to 0} \dfrac{f(2-h) - f(2)}{-h}$

$$= \text{Lim}_{h \to 0} \frac{\{1 + (2-h) - (1+2)\}}{-h}$$

$[\because f(x) = 1 + x, \text{ if } x \le 2]$

$\therefore \quad Rf'(2) \ne Lf'(2)$

i.e., $f(x)$ is not differentiable at $x = 2$.

MULTIPLE CHOICE QUESTIONS

1. $\lim_{x \to 27} \dfrac{x^{1/3} - 3}{x - 27}$ is equal to

A. 3 B. $\dfrac{1}{3}$

C. 27 D. $\dfrac{1}{27}$

2. If $\lim_{x \to 0} (1 + x)^{1/x} = e$, then $\lim_{x \to \infty} \left(\dfrac{n}{1+n}\right)^{2n}$ is

A. e B. e^2

C. $1/e$ D. $1/e^2$

3. If $f(x) = \dfrac{\sin^2 ax}{x^2}$, when $x \ne 0$

$= P$, when $x = 0$

is discontinuous at $x = 0$, then for what value of P, $f(x)$ will be continuous at $x = 0$?

A. 1 B. 2

C. a D. a^2

4. If $f(x) = 2$, $x \le 3$

$= ax + b$ $3 < x < 5$

$= 7$, $x \ge 5$

is continuous, then

A. $a = 2, b = 5$ B. $a = 3, b = -8$

C. $a = -3, b = 8$ D. $a = 5, b = 7$

5. Let $f(x) = \cos x$, then

A. $f(x)$ is continuous at $x \in R$ excepting odd multiple of $\dfrac{\pi}{2}$

B. $f(x)$ is continuous at $x \in R$ excepting even multiple of $\dfrac{\pi}{2}$

C. $f(x)$ is continuous at $x \in R$ excepting $x = 0$

D. $f(x)$ is always a continuous function.

6. If $f(x) = \dfrac{1}{1 + 2^{1/x}}$, then at $x = 0$ the function is

A. Continuous

B. Discontinuous, because $\lim_{x \to 0^+} f(x)$ does not exist.

C. Discontinuous, because $\lim_{x \to 0^-} f(x) \ne \lim_{x \to 0^+} f(x)$

D. Discontinuous, because $\lim_{x \to 0} f(0) \ne f(0)$

7. $\lim_{x \to 0} \left(\dfrac{1 + 2x}{1 - 2x}\right)^{\frac{1}{x}}$ is given by

A. e^2 B. e^3

C. e^4 D. e^5

8. $\lim_{x\to 0} \dfrac{\log(3+x)-\log 3}{\sqrt{1+x}-1} =$

A. 1/2 B. 1/3

C. $\dfrac{2}{3}$ D. $\dfrac{3}{2}$

9. If $\lim_{x\to 0} kx \operatorname{cosec} x = \lim_{x\to 0} x \operatorname{cosec} kx$, then $k =$

A. 2 B. – 3

C. ± 1 D. ± 3

10. $\lim_{x\to 0} \dfrac{2^x - 1}{(1+x)^{1/2} - 1} =$

A. log 3 B. log 4

C. $\log\sqrt{3}$ D. None of these

11. If $f(x) = \begin{cases} \dfrac{e^{[x]+x}-1}{[x]+x}, & x \neq 0 \\ 1 & x = 0 \end{cases}$ then

A. $f(x)$ is continuous at $x = 0$

B. $f(x)$ is discontinuous at $x = 0$

C. $\lim_{x\to 0^+} f(x) = 1$

D. Both B and C

12. Let $f(x) = \begin{cases} \dfrac{\sqrt{1+ax}-\sqrt{1-ax}}{x} & -1 \le x < 0 \\ \dfrac{2x+1}{x-2}, & 0 \le x \le 1 \end{cases}$

If $f(x)$ is continuous in the interval [–1, 1], then a equals

A. 1 B. –2

C. 1/2 D. –1/2

13. If $f(x) = x \sin 1/x$, $x \neq 0$, then the value of the function at $x = 0$, so that the function is continuous at $x = 0$, is

A. 1 B. –1

C. 0 D. indeterminate

14. Let $f(x) = \begin{cases} \dfrac{1-\sin \pi x}{1+\cos 2\pi x} & \text{if } x < 1/2 \\ \dfrac{a}{\sqrt{2x-1}} & \text{if } x = 1/2 \\ \sqrt{4+\sqrt{2x-1}} - 2 & \text{if } x > 1/2 \end{cases}$

Determine the value of a, if positive, so that the function is continuous at $x = 1/2$

A. 1/2 B. 1/3

C. 1/4 D. 1/5

15. If $f(x) = \begin{cases} \dfrac{x^2+3x+p}{2(x^2-1)} & x \neq 1 \\ 5/4 & x = 1 \end{cases}$ is continuous at $x = 1$, then

A. P = 1 B. P = –2

C. P = 3 D. P = –4

ANSWERS

1	2	3	4	5	6	7	8	9	10
D	D	D	B	D	C	C	C	C	B
11	**12**	**13**	**14**	**15**					
D	D	C	C	D					

SOME SELECTED EXPLANATORY ANSWERS

3. $\lim_{x\to 0} f(x) = \lim_{x\to 0} a^2\left(\dfrac{\sin ax}{ax}\right)^2 = a^2 \times 1 = a^2$

$\therefore f(x)$ is continuous,

if $f(0) = f(0) = \lim_{x\to 0} f(x) \Rightarrow p = a^2$

5. Given function is $f(x) = \cos x$

Let $a \in R$

$\because \lim_{x\to a^-} f(x) = \lim_{h\to 0} f(a-h) = \lim_{h\to 0} \cos(a-h)$

$= \lim_{h\to 0} [\cos a \cdot \cos h + \sin a \cdot \sinh] = \cos a$

$\lim_{x\to a^+} f(x) = \lim_{h\to 0}(a+h) = \lim_{h\to 0}\cos(a+h)$

$= \lim_{h\to 0}[\cos a\cdot\cos h - \sin a \sinh] = \cos a.$

Also $f(a) = \cos a$

7. $\lim_{x\to 0}\left(\frac{1+2x}{1-2x}\right)^{\frac{1}{x}} = \frac{\lim_{x\to 0}(1+2x)^{\frac{1}{x}}}{\lim_{x\to 0}(1-2x)^{\frac{1}{x}}}$

$= \frac{\lim_{x\to 0}\left[(1+2x)^{\frac{1}{2x}}\right]^2}{\lim_{x\to 0}\left[(1-2x)^{\frac{-1}{2x}}\right]^{-2}} = \frac{e^2}{e^{-2}} = e^4$

9. $\lim_{x\to 0} kx \operatorname{cosec} x = \lim_{x\to 0} x \operatorname{cosec} kx$

$\Rightarrow k\cdot\lim_{x\to 0}\frac{x}{\sin x} = \frac{1}{k}\lim_{x\to 0}\frac{kx}{\sin kx}$

$\Rightarrow k = \frac{1}{k} \Rightarrow k = \pm 1$

10. $\lim_{x\to 0}\frac{2^x - 1}{(1+x)^{1/2} - 1}$

$= \lim_{x\to 0}\frac{2^x\cdot\log 2}{\frac{1}{2}(1+x)^{-1/2}} \left\{\because \lim_{x\to a}\frac{f(x)}{g(x)} = \lim_{x\to a}\frac{f'(x)}{g'(x)}\right\}$

$= 2\log 2 = \log 4$

13. For $f(x)$ to be continuous at $x = 0$, we must have $f(0)$ $\lim_{x\to 0} f(x)$

$\Rightarrow f(0) = \lim_{x\to 0} x.\sin\frac{1}{x} = 0 \times$ a finite quantity

$= 0$

Hence, $f(0) = 0$

10 Differentiation

SOME STANDARD RESULTS

Function		Differential Coefficient
1. $y = f(x)$	$\Rightarrow$	$\frac{dy}{dx} = \lim_{\delta x \to 0} \frac{f(x+\delta x) - f(x)}{\delta x}$
2. $y = x^n$	$\Rightarrow$	$\frac{dy}{dx} = nx^{n-1}$
3. $y =$ constant	$\Rightarrow$	$\frac{dy}{dx} = 0$
4. $y = c\,f(x)$	$\Rightarrow$	$\frac{dy}{dx} = c\frac{d}{dx}f(x)$
5. $y = e^x$	$\Rightarrow$	$\frac{dy}{dx} = e^x$
6. $y = a^x = e^{x \log a}$	$\Rightarrow$	$\frac{dy}{dx} = a^x \log a$
7. $y = \sin x$	$\Rightarrow$	$\frac{dy}{dx} = \cos x$
8. $y = \cos x$	$\Rightarrow$	$\frac{dy}{dx} = -\sin x$
9. $y = \tan x$	$\Rightarrow$	$\frac{dy}{dx} = \sec^2 x$
10. $y = \cot x$	$\Rightarrow$	$\frac{dy}{dx} = -\text{cosec}^2 x$
11. $y = \sec x$	$\Rightarrow$	$\frac{dy}{dx} = \sec x \tan x$
12. $y = \text{cosec } x$	$\Rightarrow$	$\frac{dy}{dx} = -\text{cosec } x . \cot x$
13. $y = f_1(x) + f_2(x)$	$\Rightarrow$	$\frac{dy}{dx} = \frac{d}{dx}f_1(x) + \frac{d}{dx}f_2(x)$
14. $y = f_1 f_2$	$\Rightarrow$	$\frac{dy}{dx} = f_1 \cdot \frac{d}{dx}(f_2) + f_2 \cdot \frac{d}{dx}(f_1)$
15. $y = \frac{f_1}{f_2}$	$\Rightarrow$	$\frac{dy}{dx} = \frac{\frac{d}{dx}(f_1)\cdot f_2 - f_1 \frac{d}{dx} f_2}{f_2^2}$
16. $y = \sin^{-1} x$	$\Rightarrow$	$\frac{dy}{dx} = \frac{1}{\sqrt{(1-x^2)}}$
17. $y = \cos^{-1} x$	$\Rightarrow$	$\frac{dy}{dx} = \frac{1}{\sqrt{(1-x^2)}}$
18. $y = \tan^{-1} x$	$\Rightarrow$	$\frac{dy}{dx} = \frac{1}{1+x^2}$
19. $y = \cot^{-1} x$	$\Rightarrow$	$\frac{dy}{dx} = -\frac{1}{1+x^2}$
20. $y = \sec^{-1} x$	$\Rightarrow$	$\frac{dy}{dx} = \frac{1}{x\sqrt{(x^2-1)}}$
21. $y = \text{cosec}^{-1} x$	$\Rightarrow$	$\frac{dy}{dx} = -\frac{1}{x\sqrt{(x^2-1)}}$

Function of a function: If y is a function of u and u is a function of x, then derivative of y wrt x is obtained as

$$\frac{dy}{dx} = \frac{dy}{du} \cdot \frac{du}{dx}$$

Parametric equations: Sometimes both x and y are expressed in terms of a third variable, usually called a parameter. In such cases we always find the value of $dy/dx = (dy/dt) . (dt/dx)$.

SECOND ORDER DERIVATIVES

Let $y = f(x) \therefore \dfrac{dy}{dx} = f'(x)$

differentiating w.r.t. 'x' $\dfrac{d}{dx}\left(\dfrac{dy}{dx}\right) = \dfrac{d}{dx}(f'(x))$

$$\Rightarrow \frac{d^2y}{dx^2} = f''(x)$$

We also denote

$$y' = f'(x) = \frac{dy}{dx}$$

and $$y'' = f''(x) = \frac{d^2y}{dx^2}$$

nth Derivatives of Some Special Functions

(i) $D^n a^x = (\log a)^n a^x$

(ii) $D^n e^{ax+b} = a^n e^{ax+b}$

(iii) If $m > n$, then

$D^n (ax+b)^m = m(m-1)(m-2) \ldots\ldots (m-n+1) a^n (ax+b)^{m-n}$

$$= \frac{m!}{(m-n)} a^n (ax+b)^{m-n}$$

If $m < n$, then $D^n (ax+b)^m = 0$

And if $m = n$, then $D^n (ax+b)^n = a^n \,.\, n!$

(iv) $D^n (ax+b)^{-1} = (-1)^n n!\, a^n (ax+b)^{-n-1}$

(v) $D^n \log (ax+b) = \dfrac{(-1)^n (n-1)!\, a^n}{(ax+b)^n}$

(vi) $D^n \sin (ax+b) = a^n \sin (ax + b + n\pi/2)$

(vii) $D^n \cos (ax+b) = a^n \cos (ax + b + n\pi/2)$

(viii) $D^n \{e^{ax} \sin(bx+c)\}$

$$= (a^2+b^2)^{n/2} \times e^{ax} \sin\left\{bx+c+n\tan^{-1}\left(\frac{b}{a}\right)\right\}$$

(ix) $D^n \{e^{ax} \cos (ax+c)\}$

$$= (a^2+b^2)^{n/2} \times e^{ax} \cos\left\{bx+c+n\tan^{-1}\left(\frac{b}{a}\right)\right\}$$

LEIBNITZ'S THEOREM

If u and v are any two functions of x such that their required differential coefficients exist, then the nth differential coefficient of uv is given by

$D^n (uv) = (D^n u) \,.\, v + {}^nC_1 (D^{n-1} u) \,.\, (Dv) + {}^nC_2 (D^{n-2} u)(D^2 v) + \ldots + u (D^n v)$.

Solved Examples

Example 1: *If $f(x) = \log_x (\ln x)$, then evaluate $f'(x)$ at $x = e$. Here $\ln x$ means natural logarithm of x, i.e., $\log_e x$.*

Solution: We have $f(x) = \log_x (\log_e x) = \log_x y$, where $y = \log_e x$

$$= \log_e y \cdot \log_x e = \frac{\log_e y}{\log_e x}$$

Then $$f'(x) = \frac{\frac{1}{y}\cdot\frac{dy}{dx}\cdot\log_e x - \frac{1}{x}\cdot\log_e y}{(\log_e x)^2}$$

$$\Rightarrow \quad f'(e) = \frac{1\cdot\frac{1}{e}\cdot 1 - \frac{1}{e}\cdot 0}{(1)^2} = e^{-1}$$

Example 2: *Differentiate x^x*

Solution: Let $y = x^x$

Taking logarithms on both sides, we get

$$\log y = x \,.\, \log x.$$

Now differentiating both the sides w.r.t. "x", we get

$$\frac{1}{y}\frac{dy}{dx} = x\cdot\frac{1}{x} + 1\cdot\log x = 1 + \log x,$$

$$dy/dx = y(1+\log x) = x^x (1 + \log x)$$

$$= x^x (\log e + \log x)$$

$$= x^x \log (x\,e)$$

Example 3: *Find the derivative of $\sec^{-1}\left(\dfrac{1}{2x^2-1}\right)$ w.r.t $\sqrt{(1-x^2)}$ at $x = \dfrac{1}{2}$.*

Solution: Let $y = \sec^{-1}\left(\frac{1}{2x^2-1}\right)$ and $z = \sqrt{(1-x^2)}$

then $y = \cos^{-1}(2x^2 - 1)$

Whence putting $x = \cos\theta$, we get

$y = \cos^{-1}(2\cos^2\theta - 1)$ and $z = \sin\theta$

$\Rightarrow$ $y = \cos^{-1}(\cos 2\theta)$ and $z = \sin\theta$

$\Rightarrow$ $y = 2\theta$ and $z = \sin\theta$

$\therefore$ $\frac{dy}{d\theta} = 2$ and $\frac{dz}{d\theta} = \cos\theta$

$\Rightarrow$ $\frac{dy}{dz} = \frac{2}{(\cos\theta)} = \frac{2}{x}$

$\Rightarrow$ $\left[\frac{dy}{dz}\right]$ at $x = \frac{1}{2}$ is 4.

MULTIPLE CHOICE QUESTIONS

1. If $y = \tan^{-1}\frac{2x}{1-x^2}$, then the value of $\frac{dy}{dx}$ is

A. $\frac{1}{1+x^2}$ B. $\frac{2}{1+x^2}$

C. $\frac{1-x^2}{1+x^2}$ D. $\frac{1+x^2}{1-x^2}$

2. If $y = x^{x^{x\ldots\infty}}$, then $x\cdot\frac{dy}{dx}$ is

A. $\frac{x^2}{1+y\cdot\log x}$ B. $\frac{y^2}{1+y\cdot\log x}$

C. $\frac{x^2}{1-y\cdot\log x}$ D. $\frac{y^2}{1-y\cdot\log x}$

3. $\frac{d^n}{dx^n}[\log(ax+b)]$ is equal to

A. $\frac{(-1)^n n! a^n}{(ax+b)^n}$

B. $\frac{(-1)^{n-1}(n-1)!\cdot a^n}{(ax+b)^{n+1}}$

C. $\frac{(-1)^{n+1}(n-1)!\cdot a^{n-1}}{(ax+b)^{n+1}}$

D. $\frac{(-1)^{n-1}(n-1)!\cdot a^n}{(ax+b)^n}$

4. Differentiate u with respect to v where $u = e^x.\cos x$ and $v = e^x \sin x$.

A. $\frac{\cos x - \sin x}{\cos x + \sin x}$ B. $\frac{\sin x + \cos x}{\sin x - \cos x}$

C. 1 D. 0

5. If $y = x^5\cdot e^{x^2}\cdot\sqrt{\sin x}, \frac{dy}{dx} =$

A. $x^5\cdot e^{x^2}\cdot\sqrt{\sin x}\cdot\left[\frac{5}{x}+2x+\frac{1}{2}\cot x\right]$

B. $x^5\cdot e^{x^2}\cdot\sqrt{\sin x}\cdot\left[\frac{5}{x}-2x-\frac{1}{2}\cot x\right]$

C. $x^5\cdot e^{x^2}\cdot\sqrt{\sin x}\cdot\left[\frac{5}{x}-2x+\frac{1}{2}\cot x\right]$

D. None of these

6. Differentiate $x^x + (\sin x)^x$ with respect to x

A. $x^x(1 + \log x) + (\sin x)^x [x\cot x + \log(\sin x)]$

B. $x^x(1 + \log x) - (\sin x)^x [x\cot x + \log(\sin x)]$

C. $x^x(1 + \log x) + (\sin x)^x [x\cot x - \log(\sin x)]$

D. $x^x(1 + \log x) - (\sin x)^x [x\cot x - \log(\sin x)]$

7. If $y = \frac{\cos\alpha}{\cos x}+\frac{\sin\alpha}{\sin x}$, then $\frac{d^2y}{dx^2} =$

A. $\cos\alpha.\sec x[1 + 2\tan^2 x] + \sin\alpha.\text{cosec } x [1 + 2\cot^2 x]$

B. $\sin x.\sec x[1 + 2\tan^2 x] + \cos\alpha.\sec x [1 + 2\cot^2 x]$

C. $\cos\alpha.\sec x[1 - 2\tan^2 x] + \sin\alpha.\text{cosec } x [1 - 2\cot^2 x]$

D. None of these

8. The nth derivative of the function $y = a_0 + a_1x + a_2x^2 + \ldots\ldots + a_nx^n$ is

A. $n\ .\ an$ B. $n\ .\ an!$

C. $n!\ .\ a_n$ D. $-n!\ a^n$

9. If $y = A\cos nx + B\sin nx$, then $\dfrac{d^2y}{dx^2} =$

A. $-y$ B. n^2y
C. $-n^2y$ D. None of these

10. The differential coefficient of $\sin^{-1}\dfrac{1-x}{1+x}$ w.r.t. $\sqrt{x}$ is

A. $\dfrac{3}{2\sqrt{x}}$ B. $\dfrac{\sqrt{x}}{\sqrt{1-x}}$
C. $2\sqrt{x}$ D. None of these

11. If $y = \dfrac{x}{2}\sqrt{a^2+x^2} + \dfrac{a^2}{2}\log(x+\sqrt{x^2+a^2})$, then $\dfrac{dy}{dx} =$

A. $\sqrt{x^2+a^2}$ B. $\dfrac{1}{\sqrt{x^2+a^2}}$
C. $2\sqrt{x^2+a^2}$ D. $\dfrac{2}{\sqrt{x^2+a^2}}$

12. If $y = (x^x)^x$, then $\dfrac{dy}{dx} =$

A. $(x^x)^x(1+2\log x)$ B. $(x^x)^x(1+\log x)$
C. $x(x^x)^x(1+2\log x)$ D. $x(x^x)^x(1+\log x)$

13. If $y = \dfrac{\tan x + \cot x}{\tan x - \cot x}$, then $\dfrac{dy}{dx} =$

A. $2\tan 2x\sec 2x$ B. $\tan 2x\sec 2x$
C. $-\tan 2x\sec 2x$ D. $-2\tan 2x\sec 2x$

14. If $y = \sqrt{\sin x + \sqrt{\sin x + \sqrt{\sin x + ...\infty}}}$, then

A. $(2y-1)\dfrac{dy}{dx} = \sin x$

B. $(2y-1)\dfrac{dy}{dx} = -\sin x$

C. $(2y-1)\dfrac{dy}{dx} = -\cos x$

D. $(2y-1)\dfrac{dy}{dx} = \cos x$

15. $\dfrac{d}{dx}\{(\sin x)^{\log x}\} =$

A. $(\sin x)^{\log x}\left[\dfrac{1}{x}\log\sin x + \cot x\right]$

B. $(\sin x)^{\log x}\left[\dfrac{1}{x}\log\sin x + \cot x\log x\right]$

C. $(\sin x)^{\log x}\left[\dfrac{1}{x}\log\sin x + \log x\right]$

D. None of these

16. $\dfrac{d}{dx}\left[\log\sqrt{\sin\sqrt{e^x}}\right] =$

A. $\dfrac{1}{4}e^{x/2}\cot(e^{x/2})$ B. $\dfrac{1}{4}e^x\cot(e^x)$

C. $\dfrac{1}{2}e^{x/2}\cot(e^{x/2})$ D. None of these

17. If $y = x^2 e^{mx}$, where m is a constant, then $\dfrac{d^3y}{dx^3} =$

A. $me^{mx}(m^2x^2 + 6mx + 6)$
B. $me^{mx}(m^2x^2 + 2mx + 2)$
C. $2m^3xe^{mx}$
D. None of these

18. If $y = \dfrac{a^{\cos^{-1}x}}{1+a^{\cos^{-1}x}}$ and $z = a^{\cos^{-1}x}$, then $\dfrac{dy}{dx} =$

A. $-\dfrac{1}{1+a^{\cos^{-1}x}}$ B. $\dfrac{1}{1-a^{\cos^{-1}x}}$

C. $\dfrac{1}{(1+a^{\cos^{-1}x})^2}$ D. None of these

19. The derivative of the function $\cot^{-1}[(\cos 2x)^{1/2}]$ at $x = \dfrac{\pi}{6}$ is

A. $(2/3)^{1/2}$ B. $(1/3)^{1/2}$
C. $3^{1/2}$ D. $6^{1/2}$

20. If $y = (\tan x)^{(\tan x)^{\tan x}}$, then at $x = \dfrac{\pi}{4}$, $\dfrac{dy}{dx} =$

A. 1 B. -1
C. 2 D. None of these

ANSWERS

1	2	3	4	5	6	7	8	9	10
B	D	D	A	A	A	A	C	C	D
11	**12**	**13**	**14**	**15**	**16**	**17**	**18**	**19**	**20**
A	C	D	D	D	A	A	C	A	C

SOME SELECTED EXPLANATORY ANSWERS

1. $y = \tan^{-1}\dfrac{2x}{1-x^2} = 2\tan^{-1} x$

$\therefore \dfrac{dy}{dx} = \dfrac{2}{1+x^2}$

3. Using TST : $8\dfrac{d^n}{dx^n}[\log(ax+b)]$

$= \dfrac{(-1)^{n-1}(n-1)!\cdot a^n}{(ax+b)^n}$

8. Let $y = a_0 + a_1x + a_2x^2 + ...a_nx^n$.

$\dfrac{dy}{dx} = a_1x + 2a_2x + 3a_3x^2 + ...n.a_n.x^{n-1}$

$\dfrac{d2y}{dx^2} = 2a_2 + 2.3a_3x + ...n.(n-1)a_n.x^{n-1}$

$\dfrac{d^ny}{dx^n} = n(n-1)(n-2)\ ....3.2.1.a_nx^0 = n!a_n$.

9. $y = A\cos(nx) + B\sin(nx)$

$\therefore \dfrac{dy}{dx} = -nA\sin(nx) + nB\cos(nx)$

Again $\dfrac{d^2y}{dx^2} = -n^2A\cos(nx) - n^2B\sin(nx)$

$= -n^2[A\cos(nx) + B\sin(nx)] \Rightarrow \dfrac{d^2y}{dx^2} = -n^2y$

10. Let $y = \sin^{-1}\dfrac{1-x}{1+x} \Rightarrow \dfrac{dy}{dx} = \dfrac{-1}{\sqrt{x}(1+x)}$ ...(*i*)

and $z = \sqrt{x} \Rightarrow \dfrac{dz}{dx} = \dfrac{1}{2\sqrt{x}}$ ...(*ii*)

By (*i*) and (*ii*) $\dfrac{dy}{dz} = \dfrac{dy/dx}{dz/dx} = \dfrac{-2}{1+x}$

12. $y = (x^x)^x \Rightarrow \log_e y = x\log_e(x)^x$

$\Rightarrow \dfrac{1}{y}\dfrac{dy}{dx} = \log(x)^x + x\dfrac{1}{(x)^x}(x^x)(1+\log_e x)$

$\therefore \dfrac{dy}{dx} = x(x^x)^x[1 + 2\log_e x]$

13. $y = \dfrac{\tan x + \cot x}{\tan x - \cot x} = \dfrac{1+\tan^2 x}{1-\tan^2 x} = -\sec 2x$

$\Rightarrow \dfrac{dy}{dx} = -2\sec 2x\tan 2x$

15. Let $y = (\sin x)^{\log x} \Rightarrow \log_e y = \log_e x\log_e\sin x$

$\Rightarrow \dfrac{dy}{dx} = (\sin x)^{\log_e x}\left[\dfrac{1}{x}\log_e\sin x + \cot x\log_e x\right]$

16. $\dfrac{d}{dx}\left[\log\sqrt{\sin\sqrt{e^x}}\right] = \dfrac{d}{dx}\left[\dfrac{1}{2}\log(\sin\sqrt{e^x})\right]$

$= \dfrac{1}{2}\cot\sqrt{e^x}\dfrac{1}{2\sqrt{e^x}} = \dfrac{1}{4}e^{x/2}\cot(e^{x/2})$

18. $y = \dfrac{a^{\cos^{-1}x}}{1+a^{\cos^{-1}x}},\ z = a^{\cos^{-1}x}$

$\Rightarrow y = \dfrac{z}{1+z} \Rightarrow \dfrac{dy}{dx} = \dfrac{(1+z)1-z(1)}{(1+z)^2} = \dfrac{1}{(1+z)^2}$

$= \dfrac{1}{(1+a^{\cos^{-1}x})^2}$

19. $\dfrac{dy}{dx} = -\dfrac{1}{1+\cos 2x}\cdot\dfrac{1}{2\sqrt{\cos 2x}}(-2\sin 2x)$

Now substitute $x = \dfrac{\pi}{6}$, then $\dfrac{dy}{dx} = \sqrt{\dfrac{2}{3}}$

$\left[\because \cos 2x = \dfrac{1}{2} \text{ and } \sin 2x = \dfrac{\sqrt{3}}{2}\right]$

11 Application of Derivatives

Equation of tangent: The equation of tangent at the point $P(x_1, y_1)$ on the curve $y = f(x)$ is

$$y - y_1 = \left[\frac{dy}{dx}\right]_{(x_1, y_1)} (x - x_1)$$

If the tangent at the point $P(x, y)$ on the curve $y = f(x)$ makes an angle ψ with the positive direction of the axis of x, then

$$\tan \psi = dy/dx$$

and is called the **gradient** (or slope) of the curve at $P(x, y)$.

Tangent parallel to the axis of *x*: At the point where the tangent is **parallel** to the axis of x,

$$\frac{dy}{dx} = 0.$$

Tangent perpendicular to the axis of *x*: At the point where the tangent is perpendicular to the axis of x,

$$dx/dy = 0$$

Equation of normal: The equation of the **normal** at the point $P(x_1, y_1)$ on the curve $y = f(x)$ is

$$(y - y_1)\left[\frac{dy}{dx}\right]_{(x_1, y_1)} + (x - x_1) = 0$$

Angle of Intersection of Two Curves

Def. The angle of intersection of two curves is defined as the angle between the tangents to the two curves at their point of intersection.

If θ is the angle of intersection of the two curves at the point of intersection, then

$$\theta = \tan^{-1}\left|\frac{m_1 - m_2}{1 + m_1 m_2}\right|$$

where $m_1 = \tan \psi_1$ and $m_2 = \tan \psi_2$

where ψ_1 and ψ_2 are the angles which the tangents to the two curves at their point of intersection make with the positive direction of the axis of x.

Condition for the two curves to touch: The two curves having slope m_1 and m_2 respectively **touch** each other at their point of intersection if

$$m_1 = m_2.$$

Condition of orthogonal intersection of two curves: The two curves having slope m_1 and m_2 respectively **intersect orthogonally** (*i.e.,* at right angles) at their point of intersection if

$$m_1 m_2 = -1.$$

Lengths of Tangent, Normal, Subtangent and Subnormal

(*i*) Length of Tangent

$$= \left|\frac{y\sqrt{[1 + (dy/dx)^2}}{dy/dx}\right|$$

(*ii*) Length of Normal

$$= |y[1 + (dy/dx)^2]^{1/2}|$$

(*iii*) Length of Sub-tangent

$$= |y/(dy/dx)|$$

(*iv*) Length of Sub-normal

$$= |y(dy/dx)|.$$

Intercept of Tangent on The Axex

(*i*) Intercept of a tangent on the axis of x

$$= |x - y\ (dx/dy)|$$

(*ii*) Intercept of a tangent on the axis of y

$$= |y - x\ (dy/dx)|$$

Monotonic Function (Def.): A function $f(x)$ in an interval I is said to be **monotonic** if it follows any of the following properties:

I. Increasing if $x_1 < x_2 \Rightarrow f(x_1) < f(x_2)$
II. Non-decreasing if $x_1 < x_2 \Rightarrow f(x_1) \leq f(x_2)$
III. Decreasing if $x_1 < x_2 \Rightarrow f(x_1) > f(x_2)$
IV. Non-increasing if $x_1 < x_2 \Rightarrow f(x_1) \geq f(x_2)$.

Tests for Monotonicity : (First Derivative Test)

I. In an interval I, $f(x)$ is
II. Increasing if $f'(x) > 0$
III. Non-decreasing if $f'(x) \geq 0$
IV. Decreasing if $f'(x) < 0$
V. Non-increasing if $f'(x) \leq 0$

Maxima and Minima: $f(x)$ has maximum at x_0 if in some interval

$$I =]x_0 - h, x_0 + h[$$

for all $x \in I, f(x) < f(x_0)$

and $f'(x)$ has minimum at x_0 if in some interval

$$I =]x_0 - h, x_0 + h[$$

for all $x \in I$ if $f(x) > f(x_0)$.

Critical Points: All such points where $f'(x) = 0$ or $f(x)$ is continuous but not differentiable are called **critical points.** So maximum or minimum can exist only at critical points.

Methods of Testing for Maxima or Minima

(*i*) **First derivative test**

Let x_0 be a critical point, then

	$f'(x_0 - h)$	$f'(x_0 + h)$	
Result	> 0	< 0	max. at x_0
	< 0	> 0	min. at x_0
	> 0	> 0	neither maxima
	< 0	< 0	nor minima

where h is taken as very small positive number.

(*ii*) **Second derivative test:** If $f(x)$ has derivative, at x_0 and $f'(x_0) = 0$, then

$f''(x_0) > 0 \Rightarrow f(x)$ has minima at x_0,

$f''(x_0) < 0 \Rightarrow f(x)$ has maxima at x_0.

Derivative as a rate measure: Let $y = f(x)$ be a relation between two variables x and y. If δx be a small change in x and δy be the corresponding change in y, then $\delta y/\delta x$ represents the average rate of change in y with respect to x in the interval $(x, x + \delta x)$ and $\lim_{\delta x \to 0} \frac{\delta y}{\delta x} = \frac{dy}{dx}$, called **instantaneous rate** of change of y with respect to x.

Velocity and Acceleration: If s is the distance moved by a particle in time t, *s.t.s.* $= f(t)$, then the **velocity** v and the **acceleration** a of the particle at any instant t are given by

$$v = \frac{ds}{dt}$$

and $$a = \frac{dv}{dt} = \frac{d^2 s}{dt^2}$$

Approximation and Error

We have $\lim_{\delta x \to 0} \frac{\delta y}{\delta x} = \frac{dy}{dx}$.

$\therefore$ For smaller values of δx, we have $\frac{\delta y}{\delta x} = \frac{dy}{dx}$ (approximately)

i.e., $$\delta y = \left(\frac{dy}{dx}\right)\delta x \text{ (appr.)}$$

Thus corresponding to a small error δx in the value of x, the approximate error in the value of y is $\frac{dy}{dx}\delta x$, *i.e.*,

$$\delta y = \left(\frac{dy}{dx}\right)\delta x.$$

Percentage error: Let δx be an error in the variable x, then $\delta x/x$ is called the **relative error** in x and $(\delta x/x) \times 100$ is called the **percentage error** in x.

Rolle's Theorem: If function $f(x)$ is such that

(*i*) $f(x)$ is continuous in the closed interval $[a, b]$.

(*ii*) $f(x)$ is differentiable at every point in the open interval $]a, b[$.

(*iii*) $f(a) = f(b)$, then there exists at least one value of x, say c, where $a < c < b$, such that $f'(c) = 0$.

Lagrange's Mean Value Theorem

If a function $f(x)$ is such that

(*i*) $f(x)$ is continuous in the closed interval $[a, b]$.

(*ii*) $f(x)$ is differentiable at every point in the open interval $]a, b[$, then there exists at least one value c of x lying in the open interval $]a, b[$, such that

$$\frac{f(b)-f(a)}{b-a} = f'(c)$$

Law of Exponential Growth: The growth (increase) in some variable x is said to be according to the law of exponential,

if the rate of change in $x \propto x$

$$dx/dt = \lambda x$$

$$dx/x = \lambda\ dt = x = ce^{\lambda t}.$$

Solved Examples

Example 1: *Find the equation of the tangent to the curve $y = x^3 + 1$ at the point (1, 2).*

Solution: Curve is $y = x^3 + 1$

Differentiating, $\dfrac{dy}{dx} = 3x^2$

$\therefore$ value of $\dfrac{dy}{dx}$ at $(1, 2) = 3(1)^2 = 3$

$\therefore$ Required equation of tangent is

$$y - 2 = \left(\frac{dy}{dx}\right)_{(1,2)} (x-1)$$

or $\quad y - 2 = 3(x - 1)$ or $3x - y = 1$.

Example 2: *The perimeter of a rectangle is 40 cms. Find the length of sides when its area is maximum.*

Solution: Let the lengths of the sides be x and y cms.

Then perimeter of the rectangle

$= 2(x + y) = 40$ cm. (given)

$\therefore \quad y = 20 - x$ cms. ...(I)

$\therefore$ If A be the area of the rectangle, then $A = xy = x(20 - x) = 20x - x^2$

$\therefore \quad \dfrac{dA}{dx} = 20 - 2x, \quad \dfrac{d^2A}{dx^2} = -2 = -\text{ve}$

$\therefore \quad (dA/dx) = 0 \Rightarrow 20 - 2x = 0$ or $x = 10$

And (d^2A/dx^2) being $-$ve, A is maximum when $x = 10$ and then from (1), $y = 10$.

$\therefore$ Rectangle with max. area and perimeter = 40 cms is a square whose each side is 10 cms long.

MULTIPLE CHOICE QUESTIONS

1. If m be the slope of a tangent to the curve $e^{2y} = 1 + 4x^2$, then

A. $m < 1$ B. $|m| > 1$
C. $|m| \leq 1$ D. None of these

2. The values of k for which the function $f(x) = kx^3 - 9x^2 + 9x + 3$ may be increasing on R are.

A. $k > 3$ B. $k < 3$
C. $k \leq 3$ D. None of these

3. The number of values of x where the function $f(x) = \cos x + \cos\left(\sqrt{2}x\right)$ attains its maximum is

A. 2 B. 1
C. 0 D. infinite

4. The local maximum value of $f(x) = \dfrac{\log x}{x}$ is

A. 1 B. e
C. $1/e$ D. None of these

5. If the radius of a circle increases from 3 cm to 3.2 cm., then the increase in the area of the circle is

A. 1.2π cm^2 B. 6π cm^2
C. 12π cm^2 D. None of these

6. The function $f(x) = x^2$ is increasing in the interval

A. $(-1, 1)$ B. $(-\infty, \infty)$
C. $(0, \infty)$ D. $(-\infty, 0)$

7. The maximum and minimum values of the function $f(x) = 3x^4 - 8x^3 + 12x^2 - 48x + 25$ in the interval [1, 3] are

A. 16, –39 B. –16, 39
C. –16, –39 D. None of these

8. If $x + y = 10$, then the maximum value of xy is

A. 20 B. 30
C. 25 D. None of these

9. The slope of the tangent to the curve $x = t^2 + 3t - 8$, $y = 2t^2 - 2t - 5$ at the point (2, –1) is

A. $-\frac{6}{7}$ B. $-\frac{6}{7}$
C. $\frac{11}{7}$ D. None of these

10. The maximum value of $f(x) = \sin x + \cos x$ is

A. $\frac{1}{\sqrt{3}}$ B. –2
C. 1 D. $\sqrt{2}$

ANSWERS

1	2	3	4	5	6	7	8	9	10
C	A	C	C	A	C	A	C	B	D

SOME SELECTED EXPLANATORY ANSWERS

1. We have, $e^{2y} = 1 + 4x^2 \Rightarrow e^{2y} \cdot 2\frac{dy}{dx} = 8x$

$$\Rightarrow \frac{dy}{dx} = \frac{4x}{e^{2y}} = \frac{4x}{1+4x^2}$$

$\therefore$ Slope of tangent = m

$$= \frac{4x}{1+4x^2} \Rightarrow |m| = \frac{4|x|}{1+4|x|^2} \leq 1$$

3. The maximum value of $f(x) = \cos x + \cos(\sqrt{2x})$ is 2, which occurs at $x = 0$. Also, there is no value of x for which this value will be attained again.

5. The area of a circle is $A = \pi R^2$

$$\therefore \frac{dA}{dt} = 2\pi R\frac{dR}{dt} = 1.2\pi \text{ cm}^2$$

12 Integration and Area Under Curve

Anti-Derivative (or Primitive): The inverse operation of Differentiation is called Integration.

If $$\frac{d}{dx}\{f(x)\} = \phi(x)$$

then $f(x)$ is called integral or anti-derivative or primitive of $\phi(x)$.

Integrand and Integral: The function $f(x)$ whose integral is required is called the integrand and the function F(x), obtained by integration is called the integral.

STANDARD FORMULAE

1. $\int x^n dx = \frac{x^{n+1}}{n+1}, (n \neq -1)$

2. $\int \frac{1}{2} dx = \log x$

3. $\int e^x dx = e^x$

4. $\int a^x dx = \frac{a^x}{\log_e a}$

5. $\int \sin x \, dx = -\cos x$

6. $\int \cos x \, dx = \sin x$

7. $\int \sec^2 x \, dx = \tan x$

8. $\int \text{cosec}^2 x \, dx = -\cot x$

9. $\int \sec x \tan x \, dx = \sec x$

10. $\int \text{cosec}\, x \cot x \, dx = -\text{cosec}\, x$

11. $\int \frac{1}{\sqrt{(1-x^2)}} dx = \sin^{-1} x$

12. $\int \frac{-1}{\sqrt{(1-x^2)}} dx = \cos^{-1} x$

13. $\int \frac{1}{1+x^2} dx = \tan^{-1} x$

14. $\int \frac{-1}{1+x^2} dx = \cot^{-1} x$

15. $\int \frac{1}{x\sqrt{(x^2-1)}} dx = \sec^{-1} x$

16. $\int \frac{-1}{x\sqrt{(x^2-1)}} dx = \text{cosec}^{-1} x$

Standard Integral of Hyperbolic Function

(*i*) $\int \sinh x \, dx = \cosh x$

(*ii*) $\int \cosh x \, dx = \sinh x$

(*iii*) $\int \text{sech}^2 x \, dx = \tanh x$

(*iv*) $\int \text{cosech}^2 \, dx = -\coth x$

(*v*) $\int \text{sech}\, x \tanh x \, dx = \text{sech}\, x$

(*vi*) $\int \text{cosech}\, x \coth x \, dx = -\text{cosech}\, x$

Extended Forms of Fundamental Formulae

$$\int \frac{1}{a^2+x^2} dx = \frac{1}{a}\tan^{-1}\left(\frac{x}{a}\right)$$

$$\int \frac{dx}{\sqrt{(a^2-x^2)}} = \sin^{-1}\left(\frac{x}{a}\right)$$

$$\int \frac{dx}{x\sqrt{(x^2-a^2)}} = \frac{1}{a}\sec^{-1}\left(\frac{x}{a}\right)$$

$$\int \frac{dx}{\sqrt{(a^2+x^2)}} = \sinh^{-1}\frac{x}{a}$$

$$\int \frac{dx}{\sqrt{a^2+x^2}} = \log[x+\sqrt{a^2+x^2}]$$

$$\int \frac{dx}{\sqrt{(x^2-a^2)}} = \cosh^{-1}\frac{x}{a}$$

$$\int \frac{dx}{\sqrt{(x^2-a^2)}} = \log[x+\sqrt{(x^2-a^2)}]$$

$$\int \sqrt{[(a^2-x^2)]}dx = \frac{1}{2}x\sqrt{(a^2-x^2)} + \frac{1}{2}a^2\sin^{-1}(x/a)$$

$$\int \sqrt{(a^2+x^2)}\,dx = \frac{1}{2}x\sqrt{(a^2+x^2)} + \frac{1}{2}a^2\log[x+\sqrt{(a^2+x^2)}]$$

$$\int \sqrt{(x^2-a^2)}\,dx = \frac{1}{2}x\sqrt{(x^2-a^2)} - \frac{1}{2}a^2\log[x+\sqrt{(x^2-a^2)}]$$

$$\int \frac{dx}{x^2-a^2} = \frac{1}{2a}\log\left(\frac{x-a}{x+a}\right), x>a.$$

$$\int \frac{dx}{a^2-x^2} = \frac{1}{2a}\log\left(\frac{a+x}{a-x}\right), \text{ when } x<a.$$

Integration by parts. The integration of the product of two functions is evaluated by the method of *integration by parts.*

The integral of the product of two functions u and v is given by

$$\int (u.v)\,dx = u.\int v\,dx - \int\left[\frac{d}{dx}(u).\int v\,dx\right]dx$$

i.e., $\int$ (first function) . (second function) dx
= (first function) . (integral of second function)
– $\int$ [(diff. coeff. of first) . (integral of second)] dx.

Solved Examples

Example 1: *Integrate the following*

(*i*) $\int \frac{(1+x)^2}{x^3}dx$ (*ii*) $\int \sqrt{1+\cos 2x}\,dx$

Solution:

(*i*) $$\int \frac{(1+x)^2}{x^3}dx = \int\left(\frac{1+2x+x^2}{x^3}\right)dx$$

$$= \int\left(\frac{1}{x^3}+\frac{2}{x^2}+\frac{1}{x}\right)dx$$

$$= \int x^{-3}dx + 2\int x^{-2}dx + \int \frac{1}{x}dx$$

$$= \frac{x^{-2}}{(-2)} + 2.\frac{x^{-1}}{(-1)} + \log x$$

$$= -\frac{1}{2x^2} - \frac{2}{x} + \log x + c$$

(*ii*) $$\int \sqrt{(1+\cos 2x)}dx$$

$$= \int \sqrt{(1+2\cos^2 x-1)}dx$$

$$= \sqrt{2}.\int \cos x\,dx = \sqrt{2}.\sin x + C$$

Example 2: *Integrate the following*

(*i*) $\int \frac{dx}{(x+1)^2-4}$ (*ii*) $\int \frac{x^4\,dx}{(x-1)(x^2+1)}$

Solution:

(*i*) $$\int \frac{dx}{(x+1)^2-4} = \int \frac{dx}{(x+3)(x-1)}$$

$$= \int\left[\frac{1}{4(x-1)} - \frac{1}{4(x+3)}\right]dx$$

$$= \frac{1}{4}[\log(x-1) - \log(x+3)]$$

$$= \frac{1}{4}[\log(x-1)/(x+3)]+c$$

(ii) $$\frac{x^4 dx}{(x-1)(x^2+1)} = x+1+\frac{1}{(x-1)(x^2+1)}$$

$$= x+1+\frac{1}{2(x-1)}-\frac{(x+1)}{2(x^2+1)}$$

∴ The given integral

$$= \int\left[x+1+\frac{1}{2(x-1)}-\frac{1}{2(x^2+1)}-\frac{1}{2(x^2+1)}\right]dx$$

$$= \frac{1}{2}x^2+x+\frac{1}{2}\log(x-1)-\frac{1}{4}\log(x^2+1)$$

$$-\frac{1}{2}\tan^{-1}x+c.$$

MULTIPLE CHOICE QUESTIONS

1. $\int\frac{1}{\sqrt{x^2-a^2}}dx$ is equal to

A. $\log_e\{x-\sqrt{x^2-a^2}\}$

B. $\log_e\{x+\sqrt{x^2-a^2}\}$

C. $\log_e\{x^2-\sqrt{x^2-a^2}\}$

D. $\log_e\{x^2+\sqrt{x^2-a^2}\}$

2. $\int\frac{\log(\sec^{-1}x)}{x\sqrt{x^2-1}}dx$ is equal to

A. $\sec^{-1}x\cdot\log(e\cdot\sec^{-1}x)$

B. $e\cdot\sec^{-1}x.\log(\sec^{-1}x)$

C. $\sec^{-1}x\cdot\log\left(\frac{\sec^{-1}x}{e}\right)$

D. None of these

3. $\int\frac{1}{1+4\cos^2 x}dx$ is equal to

A. $\frac{1}{\sqrt{2}}\tan^{-1}(\sqrt{2}\tan x)$

B. $\frac{1}{\sqrt{5}}\tan^{-1}\left(\frac{\tan x}{\sqrt{5}}\right)$

C. $\frac{1}{\sqrt{3}}\tan^{-1}(\sqrt{3}\tan x)$

D. $\frac{1}{\sqrt{5}}\tan^{-1}(\sqrt{3}\tan x)$

4. $\int e^x(\sin x+\cos x)\,dx$ is equal to

A. $e^x . \cos x$ B. $e^x . \sin x$

C. $-e^x . \sin x$ D. $-e^x . \cos x$

5. $\int e^{3\log x}(x^4+1)^{-1}dx =$

A. $\frac{1}{3}\log(x^4+1)+c$

B. $\frac{1}{4}\log(x^4+1)+c$

C. $\frac{1}{2}\log(x^4-1)+c$

D. None of these

6. $\int e^{\sin x}(x\cos x-\sec x\cdot\tan x)\cdot dx =$

A. $xe^{\sin x}+e^{\sin x}\sec x+c$

B. $xe^{\sin x}-e^{\sin x}.\tan x+c$

C. $xe^{\cos x}+e^{\cos x}\tan x+c$

D. $x.e^{\sin x}-e^{\sin x}+\sec x+c$

7. $\int\frac{\sin x\cos x}{3\sin^2 x+5\cos^2 x}dx =$

A. $\frac{1}{4}\log[3\sin^2 x+5\cos^2 x]+c$

B. $-\frac{1}{4}\log[3\sin^2 x+5\cos^2 x]+c$

C. $\frac{1}{4}\log[3\sin^2 x-5\cos^2 x]+c$

D. $-\frac{1}{4}\log[3\sin^2 x-3\cos^2 x]+c$

8. $\int \tan^{-1}\sqrt{\frac{1-x}{1+x}}\,dx =$

A. $\frac{1}{2}\cos^{-1}x+\frac{1}{2}\sin(\cos^{-1}x)+c$

B. $\frac{1}{2}x\cos^{-1}x-\frac{1}{2}\sin(\cos^{-1}x)+c$

C. $\frac{1}{2}\cos^{-1}x-\frac{1}{2}\sin(\cos^{-1}x)+c$

D. $\frac{1}{2}x\cos^{-1}x+\frac{1}{2}\sin(\cos^{-1}x)+c$

9. $\int \frac{e^{\frac{x}{2}}}{\sqrt{e^{-x}-e^{x}}}dx =$

A. $\cos^{-1}(e^x)+c$ B. $\sin^{-1}(e^x)+c$
C. $\cos^{-1}(e^{-x})+c$ D. $\sin^{-1}(e^{-x})+c$

10. $\int \frac{\sec^2 x\,dx}{(\tan x+1)(2\tan x+3)} =$

A. $\log(\tan x+1)-\log(2\tan x+3)+c$
B. $\log(x+\tan x)-\log(x+2\tan x)+c$
C. $\log(\tan x-1)+\log(2\tan x-3)+c$
D. $\log(x-\tan x)+\log(x-2\tan x)+c$

11. $\int_0^{\pi/2}\log\cos x\,dx$ is equal to

A. $\log 2$ B. $\pi\log 2$

C. $-\frac{\pi}{2}\log 2$ D. $\frac{\pi}{2}\log 2$

12. $\int_0^{\pi/2}\frac{1}{9+16\cos^2 x}dx$ is equal to

A. $\frac{\pi}{10}$ B. $\frac{\pi}{20}$

C. $\frac{\pi}{30}$ D. $\frac{\pi}{40}$

13. $\int_0^{\frac{\pi}{2}}\frac{\sqrt{\tan x}}{\sqrt{\tan x}+\sqrt{\cot x}}dx =$

A. $\frac{\pi}{2}$ B. $\frac{\pi}{3}$

C. $\frac{\pi}{4}$ D. $\frac{\pi}{12}$

14. $\int_0^3\frac{x^2}{\sqrt{x+1}}dx =$

A. $\frac{70}{13}$ B. $\frac{71}{14}$

C. $\frac{73}{15}$ D. $\frac{76}{15}$

15. $\int_0^{\frac{\pi}{2}}\frac{\sin x-\cos x}{1-\sin x.\cos x}dx =$

A. 1 B. 2
C. 3 D. 0

16. The area of the region bounded by the curve $y^2 = 16x$ and lines $x = 4$, $x = 1$ above the x-axis is

A. $\frac{36}{5}$ sq. units B. $\frac{47}{3}$ sq. units

C. $\frac{56}{3}$ sq. units D. $\frac{59}{7}$ sq. units

17. The area between parabola $y^2 = 4x$ and its latus-rectum, is

A. $\frac{2}{3}$ sq. units B. $\frac{8}{3}$ sq. units

C. $\frac{16}{3}$ sq. units D. $\frac{32}{3}$ sq. units

18. The area bounded by $y = \sin x$, the x-axis and the ordinates $x = 0$, $x = 2\pi$, is

A. 4 sq. units B. 6 sq. units
C. 8 sq. units D. 10 sq. units

19. The area of region bounded by the curves $y = x^2 + 2$, $y = x$, $x = 0$ and $x = 3$, is

A. 8.5 sq. units B. 9.5 sq. units
C. 10.5 sq. units D. 11.5 sq. units

20. The area enclosed by the two curves $y^2 = x + 1$ and $y^2 = -x + 1$, is

A. $\frac{2}{3}$ sq. units B. $\frac{3}{5}$ sq. units

C. $\frac{4}{3}$ sq. units D. $\frac{8}{3}$ sq. units

ANSWERS

1	2	3	4	5	6	7	8	9	10
B	C	B	B	B	D	B	B	B	A
11	**12**	**13**	**14**	**15**	**16**	**17**	**18**	**19**	**20**
C	C	C	D	D	C	B	A	C	D

SOME SELECTED EXPLANATORY ANSWERS

5. $\int e^{3\log x}\cdot(x^4+1)^{-1}dx$

$= \int e^{\log x^3}\cdot\dfrac{dx}{x^4+1} = \int\dfrac{x^3}{x^4+1}dx$

$= \dfrac{1}{4}\int\dfrac{4x^3}{x^4+1}dx = \dfrac{1}{4}\log(x^4+1)+c$

6. Let I = $\int e^{\sin x}[(x\cos x)-\sec x.\tan x]\,dx$

$= \int x.e^{\sin x}\cdot\cos x\,dx - \int e^{\sin x}.\sec x.\tan x.dx$

Integrating by parts, we get

$I = \left(x.e^{\sin x}-\int e^{\sin x}.dx\right)-\left(e^{\sin x}.\sec x-\int e^{\sin x}.dx\right)$

$= x.e^{\sin x} - e^{\sin x} + \sec x + c$

9. Let $I = \int\dfrac{e^{\frac{x}{2}}}{\sqrt{e^{-x}-e^{x}}}dx$

Multiply Numetator and Denominator by $e^{x/2}$

$\therefore \quad I = \int\dfrac{e^x}{\sqrt{1-e^{2x}}}dx$

Substitute $e^x = t$ $\qquad e^x\,dx = dt$

$\therefore \quad I = \int\dfrac{dt}{\sqrt{1-t^2}} = \sin^{-1} t + c$

$= \sin^{-1}(e^x) + c$

10. Let $I = \int\dfrac{\sec^2 x}{(\tan x+1)(2\tan x+3)}dx$

Substitute $\tan x = t$ $\qquad \sec^2 x\,dx = dt$

$I = \int\dfrac{dt}{(t+1)(2t+3)}dx$

$= \int\left[\dfrac{1}{t+1}+\dfrac{-2}{2t+3}\right]dt$

$= \log(t+1)-\dfrac{2\log(2t+3)}{2}+c$

$= \log(t+1) - \log(2t+3) + c$

$= \log(\tan x + 1) - \log(2\tan x + 3) + c$

19. Equation of parabola is $y = x^2 + 2$

The line $y = x$ passes through origin

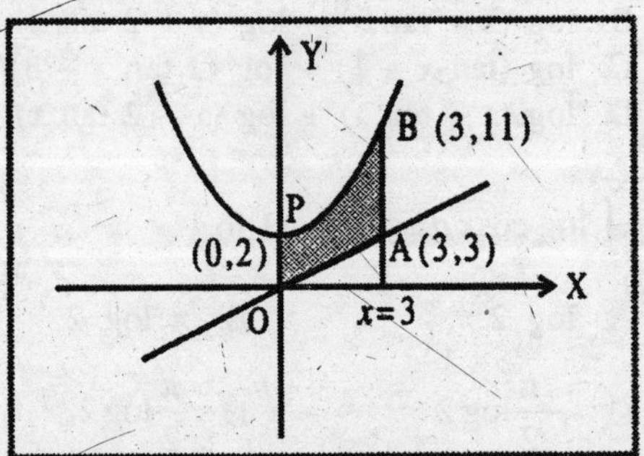

$\therefore$ Required area = Area under the parabola − Area under the line

$= \int_0^3(x^2+2)dx - \int_0^3 x\,dx = \left[\dfrac{x^3}{3}+2x\right]_0^3 - \left(\dfrac{x^2}{3}\right)_0^3$

$= (9+6)-\left(\dfrac{9}{2}\right) = 15-\dfrac{9}{2}$

$= \dfrac{21}{2} = 10.5$ sq. units.

13 Straight Line and Circle

Distance Formula:

(*i*) The distance between the points (x_1, y_1) and $(x_2, y_2) = \sqrt{[(x_2 - x_1)^2 + (y_2 - y_1)^2]}$

(*ii*) The distance of the point (x_1, y_1) from the origin $= \sqrt{(x_1^2 + y_1^2)}$.

Section Formulae:

The coordinates (x, y) of a point R which divides the join of two given points $P(x_1, y_1)$ and $Q(x_2, y_2)$ in the ratio $m_1 : m_2$ are

(I) $$x = \frac{m_1 x_2 + m_2 x_1}{m_1 + m_2}$$

$$y = \frac{m_1 y_2 + m_2 y_1}{m_1 + m_2}$$

if R divides join of P and Q internally

(II) $$x = \frac{m_1 x_2 - m_2 x_1}{m_1 - m_2}$$

$$y = \frac{m_1 y_2 - m_2 y_1}{m_1 - m_2}$$

if R divides join of P and Q externally.

(III) Co-ordinates of any point dividing the join of (x_1, y_1) and (x_2, y_2) in the ratio $\lambda : 1$, are

$$\left(\frac{\lambda x_2 + x_1}{\lambda + 1}, \frac{\lambda y_2 + y_1}{\lambda + 1}\right)$$

(IV) Co-ordinates of the middle point of (x_1, y_1), and (x_2, y_2), are

$$\left(\frac{x_1 + x_2}{2}, \frac{y_1 + y_2}{2}\right)$$

Co-ordinates of Standard points connected with a triangle, the coordinates of whose vertices are $A(x_1, y_1)$, $B(x_2, y_2)$ and $C(x_3, y_3)$

(I) Centroid: It is the point of intersection of the medians of a triangle and divides each median in the ratio 2 : 1 [*i.e.*, 2 from the vertex A(say) and 1 from the side BC]. Its coordinates are

$$\left[\frac{1}{3}(x_1 + x_2 + x_3), \frac{1}{3}(y_1 + y_2 + y_3)\right]$$

(II) Circumcentre: It is the point of intersection of the right bisectors of the sides of the triangle.

(III) Incentre: It is the point of intersection of the internal bisectors of the angles of a triangle. It is also the centre of the circle which touches the sides of the triangle internally. Its coordinates are

$$\left(\frac{ax_1 + bx_2 + cx_3}{a + b + c}, \frac{ay_1 + by_2 + cy_3}{a + b + c}\right)$$

where a = BC, b = CA, c = *AB*.

(IV) Orthocentre: It is the point of intersection of the altitudes of the triangle, *i.e.*, the lines through the vertices and perpendicular to the opposite sides.

(V) Ex-centres of a triangle: Let ABC be a triangle. There are three ex-centres. Let us denote the ex-centre opposite to vertex A, *i.e.*, touching extended sides AB and AC and the side BC from outside, by E_A. Then

$$E_A = \left(\frac{-ax_1 + bx_2 + cx_3}{-a + b + c}, \frac{-ay_1 + by_2 + cy_3}{-a + b + c}\right)$$

Other ex-centres, *i.e.*, E_B and E_C can be found like-wise.

Area of a triangle: The area of a triangle whose vertices are (x_1, y_1), (x_2, y_2) and (x_3, y_3) is

$$\frac{1}{2}[x_1(y_2-y_3)+x_2(y_3-y_1)+x_3(y_1-y_2)]$$

or $$\frac{1}{2}\begin{vmatrix} x_1 & y_1 & 1 \\ x_2 & y_2 & 1 \\ x_3 & y_3 & 1 \end{vmatrix}$$

Condition of collinearity of three points: Three points (x_1, y_1), (x_2, y_2) and (x_3, y_3) are collinear if the area of the triangle formed by these three points is zero. Hence the condition of collinearity is

$$x_1(y_2 - y_3) + x_2(y_3 - y_1) + x_3(y_1 - y_2) = 0$$

or $$\begin{vmatrix} x_1 & y_1 & 1 \\ x_2 & y_2 & 1 \\ x_3 & y_3 & 1 \end{vmatrix} = 0$$

Area of a quadrilateral: The area of a quadrilateral whose vertices are (x_1, y_1), (x_2, y_2), (x_3, y_3) and (x_4, y_4) is

$$\frac{1}{2}[(x_1y_2+x_2y_3+x_3y_4+x_4y_1) -(x_2y_1+x_3y_2+x_4y_3+x_1y_4)]$$

Note: If the area of a quadrilateral is zero, then its four vertices lie in a straight line.

LOCUS OF A POINT

The path traced out by a moving point which moves under some given geometrical conditions is called the locus of the point.

SLOPE OF A LINE

The slope of a line joining two points $A(x_1, y_1)$ and $B(x_2, y_2)$ is denoted by m and is given by $m = \frac{y_2-y_1}{x_2-x_1} = \tan\theta$, where θ is the angle which the line makes with the positive direction of x-axis.

STRAIGHT LINE

1. **Equations of straight lines in different forms:**
   (*i*) Equation of the line cutting off an intercept c on the positive side of y-axis and making an angle θ with the positive direction (anticlock wise) of x-axis is $y = mx + c$, where $m = \tan\theta$ is called the slope of the line.
   (*ii*) Equation of the line in general form is $ax + by + c = 0$
   (*iii*) Any line through the origin is $y = mx$.
   (*iv*) Equation of a line passing through (x_1, y_1) and having slope m is $y - y_1 = m(x - x_1)$
   (*v*) Equation of a line passing through (x_1, y_1) and (x_2, y_2) is given by
   $$y - y_1 = \frac{y_2-y_1}{x_2-x_1}(x-x_1)$$
   (*vi*) Equation of the line in double intercept form is $\frac{x}{a}+\frac{y}{b}=1$
2. Angle between the lines $y = m_1x + c_1$ and $y = m_2x + c_2$ is $\theta = \tan^{-1}\left(\frac{m_1 \sim m_2}{1+m_1m_2}\right)$, where $m_1 \sim m_2$ means either $m_1 - m_2$ or $m_2 - m_1$ as the case may be. If the two lines are parallel, then $m_1 = m_2$ and if perpendicular then $m_1m_2 = -1$.
3. Equation of any straight line parallel (||) to $ax + by + c = 0$ is $ax + by + \lambda = 0$, where λ is any constant.
4. Equation of any straight line perpendicular ($\perp$) to $ax + by + c = 0$ is $bx - ay + \lambda = 0$.
5. Length of the perpendicular from (a, b) to the line $ax + by + c = 0$ is $\left|\frac{a\alpha+b\beta+c}{\sqrt{(a^2+b^2)}}\right|$.
6. General equation of a line through the intersection of two given lines $a_1x + b_1y + c_1 = 0$ (*i.e.*, P = 0) and $a_2x + b_2y + c_2 = 0$ (*i.e.*, Q = 0) is $P + \lambda Q = 0$, *i.e.*, $(a_1x + b_1y + c_1) + \lambda(a_2x + b_2y + c_2) = 0$.
7. **Distance between parallel lines:** Find the perpendicular distance of each line from the origin and retain their signs. Let them be p_1, p_2. The required distance between them is $p_1 - p_2$, *i.e.*, either $p_1 - p_2$ or $p_2 - p_1$.

8. Equations of the bisectors of the angles between two lines

Let the two lines be given by

$a_1x + b_1y + c_1 = 0$ and $a_2x + b_2y + c_2 = 0$

Then the equations of the bisectors of the angles between these two lines are

$$\left|\frac{a_1x+b_1y+c_1}{\sqrt{(a_1^2+b_1^2)}}\right| = \pm\left|\frac{a_2x+b_2y+c_2}{\sqrt{(a_2^2+b_2^2)}}\right|.$$

General Equation of Second Degree

The general equation of second degree is

$$ax^2 + 2hxy + by^2 + 2gx + 2fy + c = 0 \quad ...(i)$$

The condition that the above equation (*i*) may represent a *pair of straight line* is

$$abc + 2fgh - af^2 - bg^2 - ch^2 = 0 \quad ...(ii)$$

or $$\begin{vmatrix} a & h & g \\ h & b & f \\ g & f & c \end{vmatrix} = 0$$

The equation to the pair of lines joining the origin to the points of intersection of the line $lx + my + n = 0$ and the curve

$$ax^2 + 2hxy + by^2 + 2gx + 2fy + c = 0$$

It is obtained by making the equation of the curve homogeneous with the help of the equation of the line.

CIRCLE

Equation of the circle in various forms:

Standard Form:

Let $p(x, y)$ be any point on the circle whose centre is origin and radius is '*r*'. Join OP, then $|OP| = r$.

$$\therefore \quad \sqrt{(x-0)^2+(y-0)^2} = r$$

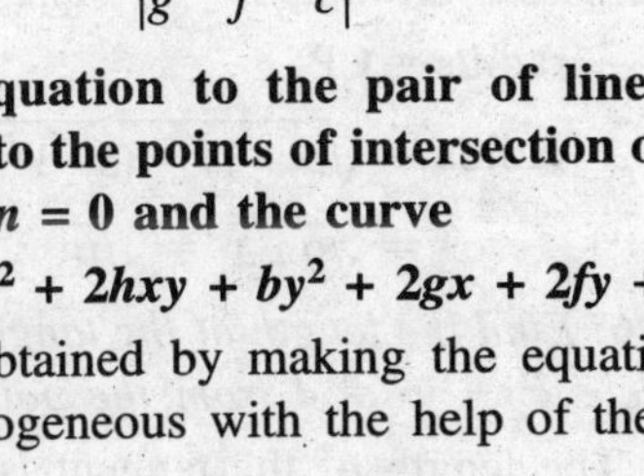

$x^2 + y^2 = r^2$ (By squaring), which is equation of a circle in standard form.

Corollory: The circle is real if $r^2 > 0$. If $r^2 < 0$, then no point in the plane satisfies the equation $x^2 + y^2 = r^2$

Central Form:

Let $p(x, y)$ by any point on the circle whose centre is $c(h, k)$ and radius is r.

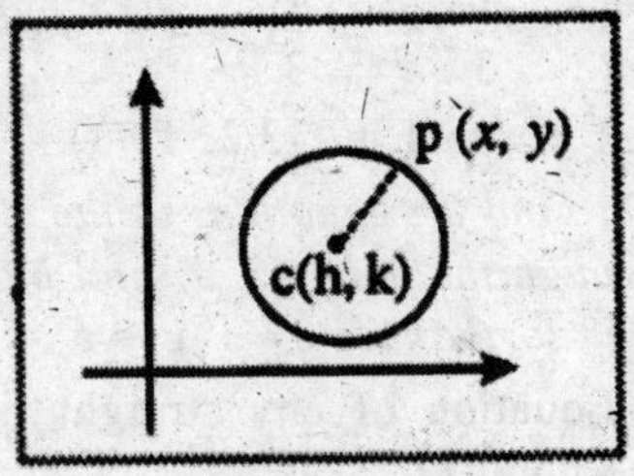

Join CP, then $|CP| = r$

$$\therefore \quad \sqrt{(x-h)^2+(y-k)^2} = r$$

Squaring, $(x - h)^2 + (y - k)^2 = r^2$, which is the required equation

$\therefore$ central form of a circle is $(x - h)^2 + (y - k)^2 = r^2$

General Form:

The equation of the circle (h, k) and radius '*r*' is - $(x - h)^2 + (y - k)^2 = r^2 \Rightarrow x^2 - 2xh + h^2 + y^2 - 2ky + k^2 = r^2$

$$\Rightarrow x^2 + y^2 - 2hx - 2ky + (h^2 + k^2 - r^2) = 0$$

Which can be written in the form $x^2 + y^2 + 2gx + 2fy + c = 0$ where $h = -g$, $k = -f$ and $h^2 + k^2 - r^2 = c$

$\therefore$ General form of a circle is $x^2 + y^2 + 2gx + 2fy + c = 0$

The centre and radius of the circle $x^2 + y^2 + 2gx + 2fy + c = 0$ are

$$C = (h, k) = (-g, -f)$$

and $\quad r = \sqrt{g^2+f^2-c}, \; g^2 + f^2 \geq c$

Note: The equation $ax^2 + ay^2 + 2gx + 2fy + c = 0$ $a \neq 0 \Rightarrow x^2 + y^2 + \frac{2g}{a}x + \frac{2f}{a}y + \frac{c}{a} = 0$

This represents a circle with centre at $\left(\frac{-g}{a}, \frac{-f}{a}\right)$

and radius $= \sqrt{\frac{g^2}{a^2}+\frac{f^2}{a^2}-\frac{c}{a}}$.

Solved Examples

Example 1: *Find the centroid of the triangle whose angular points are (2, 2), (7, 4) and (4, 7).*

Solution: If $(\bar{x}, \bar{y})$ be the required centroid, then

$$\bar{x} = \frac{1}{3}\Sigma x_1 = \frac{1}{3}(2+7+4) = \frac{13}{3}$$

and $$\bar{y} = \frac{1}{3}\Sigma y_1 = \frac{1}{3}(2+4+7) = \frac{13}{3}$$

∴ Required centroid is (13/3, 13/3).

Example 2: *Find the equations to the straight lines passing through the point (2, 3) and inclined at an angle of 45° to the line 3x + y – 5 = 0.*

Solution: Equation of any straight line passing through the point (2, 3) is

$$y - 3 = m(x - 2) \quad ...(1)$$

Line DE is given by

$$3x + y - 5 = 0$$

⇒ Slope of line DE = –(3/1) = –3.

But the angle between the lines is (± 45°)

$$\Rightarrow \tan(\pm 45°) = \frac{m-(-3)}{1+m(-3)}; \Rightarrow m = -(1/2) \text{ or } 2$$

Putting the values of m in (1), required equations of the stright lines are $x + 2y - 8 = 0$ and $2x - y - 1 = 0$.

Example 3: *Determine the equation of bisectors of the angles between the lines*

$$4x^2 - 16xy - 7y^2 = 0.$$

Solution: Here $a = 4$; $2h = -16$, $b = -7$

∴ Required equation of bisectors is

$$\frac{x^2 - y^2}{a-b} = \frac{xy}{h}$$

or, $$\frac{x^2 - y^2}{4-(-7)} = \frac{xy}{-8}$$

or, $$8x^2 + 11xy - 8y^2 = 0.$$

Example 4: *Find the equation of a circle with centre (–5, 4) and radius 3.*

Solution: The required circle is given by

$$[x - (-5)]^2 + [y - 4]^2 = 3^2.$$

$$\therefore \quad x^2 + 10x + 25 + y^2 - 8y + 16 = 9$$

$$\therefore \quad x^2 + y^2 + 10x - 8y + 32 = 0.$$

Example 5: *Find the equation of the circle two of whose diameters are x = 4 and y = 3 and passing through (1, 1).*

Solution: The diameters are $x = 4$ and $y = 3$.

The centre C = (4, 3)

The circle passes through P = (1, 1).

⇒ radius = CP

$$\therefore \quad \text{radius} = \sqrt{(4-1)^2+(3-1)^2}$$

$$= \sqrt{9+4} = \sqrt{13}.$$

Example 6: *Find the length of the tangent, segment to the circle $x^2 + y^2 = 4$ from the point (2, 6).*

Solution: The length of the tangent is

$$PT = \sqrt{S_1}$$

$$PT = \sqrt{(2)^2+(6)^2-4}$$

$$= \sqrt{4+36-4} = \sqrt{36}$$

$$= 6 \text{ units.}$$

MULTIPLE CHOICE QUESTIONS

1. The point which divides the join of (1, 2) and (3, 4) externally in the ratio 1 : 1

A. lies in the 1st quadrant

B. lies in the IInd quadrant

C. lies in the IIIrd quadrant

D. cannot be found

2. Slope of any line parallel to x-axis is

A. 1 B. –1

C. 0 D. not defined

3. The vertices of a triangle are (0, 0), (3, 0) and (0, 4). Its orthocentre is at

A. (0, 0) B. $\left(1, \frac{4}{3}\right)$

C. $\left(\frac{3}{2}, 2\right)$ D. None of these

4. The medians of a triangle meet at (0, –3) and two vertices are at (–1, 4) and (5, 2). Then the third vertex is at

A. (4, 15) B. (–4, –15)
C. (–4, 15) D. (4, –15)

5. The area of a triangle is 5. Two of the vertices are (2, 1) and (3, –2). The thrid vertex lies on $y = x + 3$. The co-ordinates of the third vertex are given by

A. $\left(-\frac{7}{2}, \frac{13}{2}\right)$ and $\left(\frac{3}{2}, -\frac{3}{2}\right)$

B. $\left(-\frac{3}{2}, \frac{3}{2}\right)$ and $\left(\frac{7}{2}, \frac{13}{2}\right)$

C. $\left(\frac{3}{2}, \frac{9}{2}\right)$

D. $\left(\frac{13}{2}, \frac{9}{2}\right)$

6. If $u = a_1x + b_1y + c_1 = 0$

$v = a_2x + b_2y + c_2 = 0$ and $\frac{a_1}{a_2} = \frac{b_1}{b_2} = \frac{c_1}{c_2}$, the curve $u + kv = 0$ is

A. the same straight line
B. different straight line
C. it is not a straight line
D. None of these

7. The points $(-a, -b)$, (0, 0), (a, b) and (a^2, ab) are

A. collinear
B. vertices of a parallelogram
C. vertices of a rectangle
D. None of these

8. If the lines $4x + 3y = 1$, $y = x + 5$ and $5y + bx = 3$ are concurrent, then the value of b is

A. 1 B. 3
C. 6 D. 0

9. The straight lines $x + y = 0$, $3x + y - 4 = 0$ and $x + 3y - 4 = 0$ form a triangle which is

A. isosceles B. equilateral
C. right angled D. None of these

10. Two points $(a, 0)$ and $(0, b)$ are joined by a straight line. Another point on this line is

A. $(3a, -2b)$ B. (a^2, ab)
C. $(-3a, 2b)$ D. (a, b)

11. If $y = 2x$ be a chord of the circle $x^2 + y^2 = 10x$, then the equation of the circle whose diameter lies on this line is

A. $x^2 + y^2 - 2x + 4y = 4$
B. $x^2 + y^2 + 2x + 4y = 3$
C. $x^2 + y^2 - 2x + 4y = 0$
D. $x^2 + y^2 - 2x - 4y = 0$

12. Radius of the circle $16x^2 + 16y^2 - 8x + 32y - 144 = 0$ is

A. $\frac{1}{3}\sqrt{274}$ B. $\frac{1}{4}\sqrt{161}$

C. $\frac{1}{5}\sqrt{274}$ D. $\frac{1}{6}\sqrt{274}$

13. Find the equation of the circle concentric with the circle $x^2 + y^2 - 6x - 2y + 4 = 0$ and passing through the point (1, 2).

A. $x^2 + y^2 - 6x + 2y - 5 = 0$
B. $x^2 + y^2 - 6x + 2y + 5 = 0$
C. $x^2 + y^2 + 6x + 2y - 5 = 0$
D. $x^2 + y^2 - 6x - 2y + 5 = 0$

14. The angle between the tangent drawn from the point (–1, 7) to the circle $x^2 + y^2 = 25$ is

A. $\frac{\pi}{2}$ B. $\frac{\pi}{3}$

C. $\frac{\pi}{4}$ D. $\frac{\pi}{6}$

15. If one end of the diameter of the circle $x^2 + y^2 - 4x - 2y - 5 = 0$ is (3, 4), the co-ordinates of the other end are.

A. (1, –2) B. (–1, 2)
C. (–1, –2) D. (1, 2)

16. The circle $x^2 + y^2 - 8x + 4y + 4 = 0$ touches.

A. x-axis
B. y-axis
C. both the axis
D. neither x-axis nor y-axis

17. Find the equation of the circle passing through (0, 0), (2, 0) and (0, –9)

A. $x^2 + y^2 + 2x - 9y = 0$
B. $x^2 - y^2 + 2x - 9y = 0$
C. $x^2 + y^2 - 2x + 9y = 0$
D. $x^2 - y^2 - 2x - 9y = 0$

18. The circum circle of the triangle with vertices (0, 0), (5, 0) and (0, –6) is:
A. $x^2 + y^2 - 5x + 6y = 0$
B. $x^2 + y^2 + 5x - 6y = 0$
C. $x^2 + y^2 - 5x - 6y = 0$
D. $x^2 + y^2 + 5x + 3y = 0$

19. The tangent to the circle $x^2 + y^2 - 8x - 10y - 8 = 0$ parallel to the line $5x - 12y = 2$ is
A. $5x + 12y - 131 = 0$
B. $5x - 12y + 131 = 0$
C. $5x + 12y - 121 = 0$
D. $5x - 12y + 121 = 0$

20. Equation of the circle having normal at (3, 3) as the line $y = x$ and passing through (2, 2) is
A. $x^2 + y^2 + 5x + 5y + 12 = 0$
B. $x^2 + y^2 + 5x - 5y + 12 = 0$
C. $x^2 + y^2 - 5x - 5y + 12 = 0$
D. $x^2 + y^2 - 5x + 5y + 12 = 0$

ANSWERS

1	2	3	4	5	6	7	8	9	10
D	C	A	B	B	A	A	C	A	A
11	**12**	**13**	**14**	**15**	**16**	**17**	**18**	**19**	**20**
D	B	D	A	A	B	C	A	B	C

SOME SELECTED EXPLANATORY ANSWERS

12. Equation of circle is $16x^2 + 16y^2 - 8x + 32y - 144 = 0$

$$\Rightarrow x^2+y^2-\frac{1}{2}x+2y-9=0$$

Here, $g = -\frac{1}{4}$, $f = 1$, $c = -9$

$$\therefore \quad \text{Radius} = \sqrt{g^2+f^2-c}$$

$$= \sqrt{\frac{1}{16}+1+9}$$

$$= \sqrt{\frac{161}{16}} = \frac{1}{4}\sqrt{161}.$$

15. We have $x^2 + y^2 - 4x - 2y - 5 = 0$. Here $g = -2, f = -1$. If one end is (x_1, y_1) the other end of the diameter is given by $(-2g - x_1; -2f - y_1)$

$\therefore$ One end $(3, 4) = (x_1, y_1)$

$\therefore$ other end $= (4 - 3, 2 - 4) = (1, -2)$

16. The given equation is $x^2 + y^2 - 8x + 4y + 4 = 0$

clearly $f^2 = c$, *i.e.*, $2^2 = 4$

$\therefore$ circle touches y-axis.

17. We have equation of the circle passing through the points (0, 0), $(a, 0)$ and $(0, b)$ is $x^2 + y^2 - ax - by = 0$.

$\therefore$ Required equation of circle is $x^2 + y^2 - 2x + 9y = 0$

19. The given equation of circle is

$$x^2 + y^2 - 8x - 10y - 8 = 0 \quad ...(i)$$

Its centre is (4, 5) and radius is 7

Let the tangent to the circle (i) parallel to the line

$$5x - 12y = 2 \text{ is } 5x - 12y + k = 0$$

$\therefore$ Perpendicular length from the centre (4, 5) of the circle (i) to the line (ii) = radius of the circle.

$$\therefore \quad \frac{5(4)-12(5)+k}{\sqrt{5^2+12^2}} = 7 \Rightarrow k = 131.$$

14 Vector

VECTOR

A directed line segment is called a vector:

Kinds of Vectors

(*i*) **Unit Vector:** The vector whose magnitude is one unit is called the unit vector.

(*ii*) **Co-planar Vectors:** A system of vectors is said to be coplanar, if their supports are parallel to the same plane.

Note that two vectors are always coplanar.

(*iii*) **Negative of a Vector:** The vector which has the same magnitude as the vector $\vec{a}$ but opposite direction is called the negative of $\vec{a}$ and is denoted by $-\vec{a}$. Thus, if $\overrightarrow{OP} = -\vec{a}$

(*iv*) **Reciprocal of a vector:** A vector having the same direction as that of a given vector $\vec{a}$ but magnitude equal to the reciprocal of the given vector is known as the reciprocal of $\vec{a}$ and is denoted by $\vec{a}^{-1}$. Thus, if $|\vec{a}| = a, |\vec{a}^{-1}| = 1/a$.

Scalar or Dot Product of Two Vectors

Definition: The scalar or dot product of two vectors $\vec{a}$ and $\vec{b}$ is defined to be the scalar $ab \cos \theta$, where $a = |\vec{a}|$, $b = |\vec{b}|$ and θ is the angle between the direction of the vectors, $\vec{a}$ and $\vec{b}$.

Algebraic Properties of Scalar or Dot Product

(I) Commutative : $\vec{a}\cdot\vec{b} = \vec{b}\cdot\vec{a}$

(II) Associative w.r.t. scalar n:

$$\vec{a}\cdot n\vec{b} = (n\vec{a})\cdot\vec{b} = n(\vec{a}\cdot\vec{b})$$

(III) Distributive Law:

$$\vec{a}\cdot(\vec{b}+\vec{c}) = \vec{a}\cdot\vec{b}+\vec{a}\cdot\vec{c}$$

Some Important Applications

(I) $\vec{a}\cdot(-\vec{b}) = (-\vec{a}\cdot\vec{b})$

(II) $(\vec{a}+\vec{b})^2 = \vec{a}^2+\vec{b}^2+2\vec{a}\cdot\vec{b}$

(III) $(\vec{a}-\vec{b})^2 = \vec{a}^2+\vec{b}^2-2\vec{a}\cdot\vec{b}$

(IV) $(\vec{a}+\vec{b})(\vec{a}-\vec{b}) = \vec{a}^2-\vec{b}^2$

(V) $(\vec{a}+\vec{b}+\vec{c}...)\cdot(\vec{l}+\vec{m}+\vec{n}...)$

$$= (\vec{a}\cdot\vec{l}+\vec{a}\cdot\vec{m}+\vec{a}\cdot\vec{n}+...)+(\vec{b}\cdot\vec{l}+\vec{b}\cdot\vec{m}+\vec{b}\cdot\vec{n}+...)+(\vec{c}\cdot\vec{l}+\vec{c}\cdot\vec{m}+\vec{c}\cdot\vec{n}+...)+...$$

(VI) If $\vec{i}, \vec{j}, \vec{k}$ be the orthonormal trid of unit vectors, then

$$\hat{i}^2 = \hat{i}.\hat{i} = 1 = \hat{i}^2 = \hat{k}$$

and $\quad \hat{i} = \hat{j} = 0 = \hat{j}\cdot\hat{k} = \hat{k}\cdot\hat{i}$

(VII) If θ be the angle between the vectors $\vec{a}$ and $\vec{b}$, then $\cos\theta = \dfrac{\vec{a}\cdot\vec{b}}{ab}$

where $a = |\vec{a}|$ and $b = |\vec{b}|$

Vector or Cross Product of Two Vectors

The vector or cross product of two vectors $\vec{a}$ and $\vec{b}$ is defined as

$$\vec{a}\times\vec{b} = (|\vec{a}||\vec{b}|\sin\theta)\hat{n}$$

or $\vec{a}\times\vec{b} = (a\ b\ \sin\theta)\ \hat{n}$

where θ is the angle between the vectors $\vec{a}$ and $\vec{b}$, and $\hat{n}$ is a unit vector perpendicular to both $\vec{a}$ and $\vec{b}$ such that $\vec{a}$, $\vec{b}$, $\hat{n}$ form a right handed triad of vectors.

Geometrical Interpretation of Cross Product

(*i*) If two non-parallel and non-null vectors $\vec{a}$ and $\vec{b}$ be represented along two adjacent sides of a parallelogram then $|\vec{a}\times\vec{b}|$ represents the area of that parallelogram.

(*ii*) The area of the triangle whose adjacent sides are represented by the vectors $\vec{a}$ and $\vec{b}$ is $\frac{1}{2}|\vec{a}\times\vec{b}|$.

(*iii*) If two diagonals of a parallelogram be represented by $\vec{a}$ and $\vec{b}$, then its area will be $\frac{1}{2}|\vec{a}\times\vec{b}|$.

Laws of Vector Product

(I) $(\vec{a}\times\vec{b}) = -(\vec{b}\times\vec{a})$,

where $\vec{a}$ and $\vec{b}$ are any vectors.
i.e., vector product is **not commutative.**

(II) $m(\vec{a}\times\vec{b}) = (m\vec{a})\times\vec{b} = \vec{a}\times(m\vec{b})$,

where $\vec{a},\vec{b}$ are vectors and *m* is a scalar, *i.e.*, vector product is **associative** with respect to a scalar.

(III) $\vec{a}\times(\vec{b}+\vec{c}) = (\vec{a}\times\vec{b})+(\vec{a}\times\vec{c})$

where $\vec{a},\vec{b},\vec{c}$ are any three vectors.
i.e., vector product is **distributive** with respect to vector addition.

(IV) Vector products of $\hat{i}, \hat{j}, \hat{k}$

If $\hat{i}, \hat{j}, \hat{k}$ be the orthonormal triad of unit vectors, then

$\hat{i}\times\hat{j} = \hat{k} = -\hat{j}\times\hat{i}$

$\hat{j}\times\hat{k} = \hat{i} = -\hat{k}\times\hat{j}, \hat{k}\times\hat{i} = \hat{j} = -\hat{i}\times\hat{k}.$

(V) Angle between two vectors

The angle θ between two vectors $\vec{a}$ and $\vec{b}$ is given by

$$\sin\theta = \frac{|\vec{a}\times\vec{b}|}{|a||b|}$$

Scalar Triple Product

Let $\vec{a}$, $\vec{b}$, $\vec{c}$ be three vectors. Then the scalar $(\vec{a}\times\vec{b})\cdot\vec{c}$ is called the scalar triple product and is written as $[\vec{a}\ \vec{b}\ \vec{c}]$ or $[\vec{a}, \vec{b}, \vec{c}]$.

Geometrical Interpretation of Scalar Triple Product

If three coterminous edges of a parallelopiped are represented by vectors $\vec{a}$, $\vec{b}$ and $\vec{c}$ respectively both in magnitude and direction, then the volume of the parallelopiped is $[\vec{a}\ \vec{b}\ \vec{c}]$, *i.e.*, the scalar triple product of the vectors $\vec{a}$, $\vec{b}$ and $\vec{c}$.

Properties of Scalar Triple Product

(I) $(\vec{a}\times\vec{b})\cdot\vec{c} = (\vec{b}\times\vec{c})\cdot\vec{a} = (\vec{c}\times\vec{a})\cdot\vec{b}$

(II) $(\vec{a}\times\vec{b})\cdot\vec{c} = \vec{a}\cdot(\vec{b}\times\vec{c})$

(III) $(\vec{a}\times\vec{b})\cdot\vec{c} = -(\vec{b}\times\vec{a})\cdot\vec{c} = -\vec{c}\cdot(\vec{b}\times\vec{a})$

(IV) **A.** Scalar triple product is zero when two of the three vectors are equal.

B. Scalar triple product is zero when two of the three vectors are parallel.

(V) Condition for three vectors to be coplanar: If three non-parallel and non-zero vectors $\vec{a},\vec{b},\vec{c}$ are **coplanar**, then their scalar triple product is zero, *i.e.*, **[*abc*] = 0.**

Expression of Scalar Triple Product in Determinant Form

If $\vec{a} = a_1\hat{i}+a_2\hat{j}+a_3\hat{k}, \vec{b} = b_1\hat{i}+b_2\hat{j}+b_3\hat{k}$

$\vec{c} = c_1\hat{i}+c_2\hat{j}+c_3\hat{k}$, then

$$[\vec{a}\ \vec{b}\ \vec{c}] = \begin{vmatrix} a_1 & a_2 & a_3 \\ b_1 & b_2 & b_3 \\ c_1 & c_2 & c_3 \end{vmatrix}$$

Scalar Product of Four Vectors

Definition

For four vectors $\vec{a}, \vec{b}, \vec{c}, \vec{d}$, the expression $(\vec{a}\times\vec{b})\cdot(\vec{c}\times\vec{d})$ is termed as the scalar product of four vectors and is given by

$$(\vec{a}\times\vec{b})\cdot(\vec{c}\times\vec{d}) = \begin{vmatrix} \vec{a}\vec{c} & \vec{a}\vec{d} \\ \vec{b}\vec{c} & \vec{b}\vec{d} \end{vmatrix}$$

$$= (\vec{a}\cdot\vec{c})(\vec{b}\cdot\vec{d}) - (\vec{a}\cdot\vec{d})(\vec{b}\cdot\vec{c}).$$

Vector Product of Four Vectors

Definition

The expression $(\vec{a}\times\vec{b})\times(\vec{c}\times\vec{d})$ is called the vector product of four vectors $\vec{a}, \vec{b}, \vec{c}, \vec{d}$.

Note:

1. $(\vec{a}\times\vec{b})\times(\vec{c}\times\vec{d}) = [\vec{a}\ \vec{b}\ \vec{d}]\,\vec{c} - [\vec{a}\ \vec{b}\ \vec{c}]\,\vec{d}$

   [Considering $\vec{a}\times\vec{b}$ as one single vector.]

2. $(\vec{a}\times\vec{b})\times(\vec{c}\times\vec{d}) = [\vec{a}\ \vec{c}\ \vec{d}]\,\vec{b} - [\vec{b}\ \vec{c}\ \vec{d}]\,\vec{a}$

   [Considering $\vec{c}\times\vec{d}$ as one single vector]

3. $\because\ [\vec{a}\ \vec{b}\ \vec{d}]\,\vec{c} - [\vec{a}\ \vec{b}\ \vec{c}]\,\vec{d}$

   $= [\vec{a}\ \vec{c}\ \vec{d}]\,\vec{b} - [\vec{b}\ \vec{c}\ \vec{d}]\,\vec{a}$

   $\therefore\ [\vec{a}\ \vec{b}\ \vec{c}]\,\vec{d}$

   $= [\vec{b}\ \vec{c}\ \vec{d}]\,\vec{a} - [\vec{c}\ \vec{a}\ \vec{d}]\,\vec{b} + [\vec{a}\ \vec{b}\ \vec{d}]\,\vec{c}$

   $= [\vec{b}\ \vec{c}\ \vec{d}]\,\vec{a} + [\vec{c}\ \vec{a}\ \vec{d}]\,\vec{b} + [\vec{a}\ \vec{d}\ \vec{b}]\,\vec{c}$

   $$\therefore\ \vec{d} = \frac{[\vec{b}\ \vec{c}\ \vec{d}]}{[\vec{a}\ \vec{b}\ \vec{c}]}\vec{a} + \frac{[\vec{c}\ \vec{a}\ \vec{d}]}{[\vec{a}\ \vec{b}\ \vec{c}]}\vec{b} + \frac{[\vec{a}\ \vec{b}\ \vec{d}]}{[\vec{a}\ \vec{b}\ \vec{c}]}\vec{c}$$

   Let us write $\vec{r}$ in place of $\vec{d}$ every where.

   $$\vec{r} = \frac{[\vec{b}\ \vec{c}\ \vec{r}]}{[\vec{a}\ \vec{b}\ \vec{c}]}\vec{a} + \frac{[\vec{c}\ \vec{a}\ \vec{r}]}{[\vec{a}\ \vec{b}\ \vec{c}]}\vec{b} + \frac{[\vec{a}\ \vec{b}\ \vec{r}]}{[\vec{a}\ \vec{b}\ \vec{c}]}\vec{c}$$

Thus any vector $\vec{r}$ can be written as a linear combination of any three non-coplanar vectors $\vec{a}, \vec{b}, \vec{c}$.

Solved Examples

Example 1: *Find k, if the vectors $\overline{a} = \hat{i} - 2\hat{j} + \hat{k}$, $\overline{b} = k\hat{i} - 5\hat{j} + 3\hat{k}$, $\overline{c} = 5\hat{i} - 9\hat{j} + 4\hat{k}$ are coplanar.*

Solution: We know that if the vectors $\overline{a}, \overline{b}, \overline{c}$ are coplanar then $[\overline{a}\ \overline{b}\ \overline{c}] = 0$.

$$\therefore\quad \begin{vmatrix} 1 & -2 & 1 \\ k & -5 & 3 \\ 5 & -9 & 4 \end{vmatrix} = 0$$

$\Rightarrow\ 1(-20 + 27) + 2(4k - 15) + 1(-9k + 25) = 0$

$\Rightarrow\ 7 + 8k - 30 - 9k + 25 = 0 \Rightarrow -k + 2 = 0$

$\Rightarrow\ -k = -2 \Rightarrow k = 2$

Example 2: *If two adjacent sides of a ΔABC are given by $2\overline{i} - 3\overline{j} + \overline{k}$ and $\overline{i} + 2j - 4\overline{k}$, find its third side.*

Solution: For a triangle ABC, we have

$\overline{AB} + \overline{BC} + \overline{CA} = \overline{O}$

$\therefore\quad \overline{BC} = -(\overline{AB} + \overline{CA})$

$= -(2\overline{i} - 3\overline{j} + \overline{k} + \overline{i} + 2\overline{j} - 4\overline{k})$

$= -(3\overline{i} - \overline{j} - 3\overline{k})$

$= -3\overline{i} + \overline{j} + 3\overline{k}.$

Example 3: *If $\overline{a} = 3\hat{i} + 2\hat{j} - \hat{k}$; $\overline{b} = 4\hat{i} - 5\hat{j} - 3\hat{k}$, $\overline{c} = \hat{i} + \hat{j} + \hat{k}$ find $[\overline{a}\ \overline{b}\ \overline{c}]$.*

Solution: $[\overline{a}\ \overline{b}\ \overline{c}] = \begin{vmatrix} 3 & 2 & -1 \\ 4 & -5 & 3 \\ 1 & 1 & 1 \end{vmatrix}$

$= 3\,(-5 - 3) - 2\,(4 - 3) - 1\,(4 + 5)$

$= 3\,(-8) - 2\,(1) - 1\,(9)$

$= -24 - 2 - 9 = -35$

MULTIPLE CHOICE QUESTIONS

1. $\bar{a}, \bar{b}, \bar{c}, \bar{d}$ are the position vectors of the points A, B, C and D respectively such that $2\bar{a}-\bar{d} = 4\bar{c}-3\bar{b}$, then the lines AB and CD are
A. parallel
B. perpendicular
C. intersect each other
D. None of these

2. Find the ratio in which the segment joining the points (3, 5, 6) and (4, 6, –3) is divided by *yz*-plane
A. internally in the ratio 2 : 1
B. externally in the ratio 3 : 2
C. internally in the ratio 4 : 5
D. externally in the ratio 3 : 4

3. Find $[\bar{a}, \bar{b}, \bar{c}]$ if $\bar{a} = \hat{i}+2\hat{j}-3\hat{k}$, $\bar{b} = 2\hat{i}-\hat{j}+\hat{k}$ and $\bar{c} = \hat{i}+\hat{j}-\hat{k}$
A. 11　　B. –12
C. –15　　D. 17

4. The position vector of a point which divides the join of the points $2\bar{a}-3\bar{b}$ and $3\bar{a}-2\bar{b}$ externally in the ratio 2 : 3 is:
A. $-3\bar{b}$　　B. $4\bar{b}$
C. $-5\bar{b}$　　D. $6\bar{b}$

5. Find the area of the tirangle whose vertices have the position vectors $\bar{a}=2\hat{i}+2\hat{j}+\hat{k}$, $\bar{b}=3\hat{i}+2\hat{k}$ and $\bar{c}=\hat{i}+2\hat{j}+2\hat{k}$
A. $\sqrt{2}$ sq. units　　B. $\sqrt{3}$ sq. units
C. $\sqrt{5}$ sq. units　　D. $\sqrt{7}$ sq. units

6. If A ≡ (3, –2, 2) and B ≡ (5, 1, –3) are any two points, find $\overline{AB}$ in terms of $\hat{i}, \hat{j}, \hat{k}$.
A. $2\hat{i}+3\hat{j}-5\hat{k}$　　B. $2\hat{i}-3\hat{j}+4\hat{k}$
C. $\hat{i}+2\hat{j}-3\hat{k}$　　D. $2\hat{i}+\hat{j}-5\hat{k}$

7. The volume of the parallelopiped whose edges are $-6\hat{i}+\lambda\hat{k}$, $2\hat{i}-\hat{k}$ and $2\hat{i}+\hat{j}-10\hat{k}$ is 130 cub. units, find the value of λ..
A. –31　　B. –61
C. –51　　D. –67

8. The position vector of the mid-point M of seg. BA where p.v.'s of A and B are given by $3\bar{i}+2\bar{j}+8\bar{k}$ and $\hat{i}-8\hat{j}-2\hat{k}$ is:
A. $2\hat{i}-3\hat{j}+3\hat{k}$　　B. $2\hat{i}+3\hat{j}-\hat{k}$
C. $\hat{i}-3\hat{j}+2\hat{k}$　　D. None of these

9. $\bar{a}=\hat{i}+2\hat{j}-3\hat{k}$ and $\bar{b}=2\hat{i}+3\hat{j}+5\hat{k}$ are the diagonals of a parallelogram. Find the area of the parallelogram.
A. $\frac{\sqrt{359}}{2}$ sq. units　　B. $\frac{\sqrt{423}}{2}$ sq. units
C. $\frac{\sqrt{455}}{2}$ sq. units　　D. $\frac{\sqrt{483}}{2}$ sq. units

10. If A ≡ (2, 3, –3) and B ≡ (5, –1, 2), find the vector having magnitude 5 units along $\overline{AB}$
A. $\frac{1}{\sqrt{2}}(3\hat{i}-4\hat{j}+5\hat{k})$　　B. $\frac{1}{\sqrt{2}}(2\hat{i}+3\hat{j}-5\hat{k})$
C. $\frac{1}{\sqrt{3}}(\hat{i}+2\hat{j}+\hat{k})$　　D. $\frac{1}{\sqrt{3}}(\hat{i}-2\hat{j}-\hat{k})$

11. If $\bar{a}=5\hat{i}-3\hat{j}+4\hat{k}$, $\bar{b}=\hat{i}-2\hat{j}+\hat{k}$, $\bar{c}=3\hat{i}+5\hat{j}$ then find $\bar{a}\cdot(\bar{b}\times\bar{c})$
A. 8　　B. 10
C. 14　　D. 20

12. If A(1, 2, 3), B(2, 3, 4), C(*p*, *q*, 6) are three collinear points, find *p* and *q*.
A. 3, 4　　B. 4, 5
C. 5, 6　　D. 6, 7

13. If $\bar{a}, \bar{b}, \bar{c}$ are position vectors of A, B and C where A ≡ (1, 3, 0), B ≡ (2, 5, 0), C ≡ (4, 2, 0) and $\bar{c}=x\bar{a}+y\bar{b}$, find *x* and *y*.
A. $x = -15, y = 9$　　B. $x = -16, y = 10$
C. $x = 17, y = -11$　　D. $x = 18, y = -12$

14. Find λ, if the vectors $\bar{a}=\hat{i}-2\hat{j}+\hat{k}$, $\bar{b}=\lambda\hat{i}-5\hat{j}+3\hat{k}$, $\bar{c}=5\hat{i}-9\hat{j}+4\hat{k}$ are coplanar.
A. λ = 1　　B. λ = 2
C. λ = –2　　D. λ = 3

15. The position vectors of the centroid of the ΔABC when the position vectors of the vertices are (1, 3, 0) (2, 1, 1), (0, –1, 0) is:
A. (1, –1, 2) B. (2, 1, –1)
C. (1, 1, 1) D. None of these

16. Find the value of x such that the four points A(3, 2, 1), B(4, x, 5), C(4, 2, –2) and D(6, 5, –1) are coplanar
A. $x = 3$ B. $x = 5$
C. $x = 7$ D. $x = -1$

17. Find the volume of the parallelopiped if $\overline{a} = 4\hat{i}$, $\overline{b} = 5\hat{j}$ and $\overline{c} = 6\hat{k}$ are coterminous edges of the parallelopiped.
A. 98 cub. units B. 100 cub. units
C. 110 cub. units D. 120 cub. units

18. Find the unit vector along $\overline{PQ}$ if P(–2, 2, 3) and Q(–1, 4, 5)
A. $\frac{1}{2}(\hat{i}-\hat{j}+2\hat{k})$ B. $\frac{1}{2}(2\hat{i}+\hat{j}-\hat{k})$
C. $\frac{1}{3}(2\hat{i}+2\hat{j}+\hat{k})$ D. $\frac{1}{3}(\hat{i}+2\hat{j}+2\hat{k})$

19. For what value of k, the vectors $2\hat{i}+2\hat{j}-3\hat{k}$, $3\hat{i}+k\hat{j}+2\hat{k}$ and $\hat{i}+2\hat{j}+3\hat{k}$ are coplanar.
A. 20/3 B. 30/7
C. 40/9 D. 50/13

20. Find the volume of the tetrahedron whose vertices are A(2, 6, 3), B(4, –3, 2), C(5, 4, 1) and D(7, 3 4).
A. $\frac{25}{3}$ cub. units B. $\frac{46}{3}$ cub. units
C. $\frac{50}{3}$ cub. units D. $\frac{53}{3}$ cub. units

ANSWERS

1	2	3	4	5	6	7	8	9	10
C	D	C	C	B	A	B	A	D	A
11	**12**	**13**	**14**	**15**	**16**	**17**	**18**	**19**	**20**
B	B	B	B	C	B	D	D	C	C

SOME SELECTED EXPLANATORY ANSWERS

11. We have, $\overline{a} = 5\hat{i}-3\hat{j}+4\hat{k}$, $\overline{b} = \hat{i}-2\hat{j}+\hat{k}$, $\overline{c} = 3\hat{i}+5\hat{j}$

$$\therefore \overline{a}\cdot(\overline{b}\times\overline{c}) = [\overline{a}\ \overline{b}\ \overline{c}] = \begin{vmatrix} 5 & -3 & 4 \\ 1 & -2 & 1 \\ 3 & 5 & 0 \end{vmatrix}$$

$= 5(0 - 5) + 3(0 - 3) + 4(5 + 6)$

$= -25 - 9 + 44 = 10$

14. Since the vectors $\overline{a}\ \overline{b}\ \overline{c}$ are coplanar, we have $[\overline{a}\ \overline{b}\ \overline{c}] = 0$.

$$\therefore \begin{vmatrix} 1 & -2 & 1 \\ \lambda & -5 & 3 \\ 5 & -9 & 4 \end{vmatrix} = 0$$

$\Rightarrow 1(-20 + 27) + 2(4\lambda - 15) + 1(-9p + 25) = 0$

$\Rightarrow 7 + 8\lambda - 30 - 9\lambda + 25 = 0$

$\Rightarrow -\lambda = -2 \Rightarrow \lambda = 2$

15. Let A(1, 3, 0), B(2, 1, 1) and C(0, –1, 0) be the given points. Let G($(\overline{x}, \overline{y}, \overline{z})$ be the centroid. Then

$$\overline{x} = \frac{1+2+0}{3},\quad \overline{y} = \frac{3+1-1}{3},\quad \overline{z} = \frac{0+1+0}{3}$$

$\Rightarrow \overline{x} = 1, \overline{y} = 1, \overline{z} = 1/3.$

17. Volume of a parallelopiped whose three coterminous edges are $\overline{a}\ \overline{b}\ \overline{c} = [\overline{a}\ \overline{b}\ \overline{c}]$

$= \overline{a}\times\overline{b}\cdot\overline{c} = 4\hat{i}\times 5\hat{j}\cdot 6\hat{k} = 120\hat{i}\times\hat{j}\cdot\hat{k}$

$= 120\hat{k}\cdot\hat{k} = 120$ cub. units $[\because \hat{i}\times\hat{j} = \hat{k}]$

15 Trigonometry

Solved Examples

Example 1: *If* $\tan\theta = \frac{4}{3}$, *what is the value of* $\sqrt{\frac{1-\sin\theta}{1+\sin\theta}}$?

Solution: If $\tan\theta = \frac{4}{3}$, then $\sin\theta = \frac{4}{5}$

$$\sqrt{\frac{1-\sin\theta}{1+\sin\theta}} = \sqrt{\frac{1-\frac{4}{5}}{1+\frac{4}{5}}} = \sqrt{\frac{1}{9}} = \frac{1}{3}.$$

Example 2: *If* $\cos y° = \sin(y° + 20°)$, *find the least positive value of y.*

Solution: $\cos y° = \sin(90° - y°)$

$\therefore$ $\sin(90° - y°) = \sin(y° + 20°)$

or $90° - y° = y° + 20°$

$\Rightarrow$ $2y° = 70°$ or $y = 35°$.

Example 3: *If* $A = 29°$, *find the value of* $\sin^4 A + \cos^4 A + 2\sin^2 A\cos^2 A$.

Solution: Since $\sin^4 A + \cos^4 A + 2\sin^2 A\cos^2 A = (\sin^2 A + \cos^2 A)^2 = 1$ for all values of A

Hence the value of the given expression is 1.

Example 4: *A vertical tower stands on a horizontal plane, and from a point on the ground at a distance of 30 metres from the foot of the tower, the angle of elevation is 60°. The height of the tower is... ($\sqrt{3} = 1.73$).*

Solution: From the adjoining figure, the height of the tower MP is given by

$$\frac{h}{30} = \tan 60°$$

$$= \sqrt{3} = 1.73$$

$\therefore$ $h = 30 \times (1.73)$

$= 51.9$ m

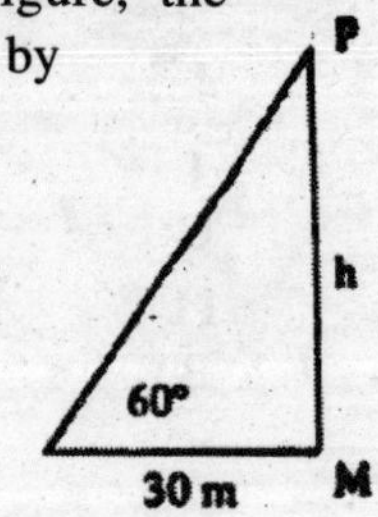

MULTIPLE CHOICE QUESTIONS

1. On the same side of the tower two objects are located. Observed from the top of the tower, their angles of depressions are 45° and 60°. If the height of the tower is 300 m, the distance between the two objects is:

A. $100(2-\sqrt{3})$m B. $300(2-\sqrt{3})$m

C. $100(3-\sqrt{3})$m D. $300(3-\sqrt{3})$m

2. If $\cos\theta = \frac{3}{5}$, the value of $\sqrt{\frac{\sec\theta - \operatorname{cosec}\theta}{\sec\theta + \operatorname{cosec}\theta}}$ is

A. $\sqrt{7}$ B. $\frac{1}{\sqrt{7}}$

C. $\frac{2}{\sqrt{7}}$ D. $\frac{3}{\sqrt{7}}$

3. What is the value of $\frac{\cot\alpha\tan\beta(\tan\alpha + \cot\beta)}{\cot\alpha + \tan\beta}$?

A. 1 B. $\sin\alpha\sin\beta$

C. $\cos\alpha\cos\beta$ D. $\cot\alpha\tan\beta$

4. The angle of elevation of the top of a pillar is 30°, and on approaching 20 m nearer it is 60°. Find the height of the pillar.

(Given $\sqrt{3}$ = 1.732)

A. 10.73 m B. 173.2 m
C. 1.732 m D. 17.32 m

5. The value of $\frac{\cot(90° - A)}{\text{cosec}^2 A} \cdot \frac{\sec A \cot^3 A}{\sin^2(90° - A)}$

A. sec A B. tan A
C. $\sec^2$ A D. $\tan^2$ A

6. The angles of depression of the top and the bottom of a 7 m tall building from the top of a tower are 45° and 60° respectively. The height of the tower is:

A. $\frac{7}{2}(\sqrt{3}-1)$ m

B. $\frac{7\sqrt{3}}{2}(\sqrt{3}+1)$ m

C. $7(\sqrt{3}+1)$ m

D. $7(\sqrt{3}+2)$ m

7. What is the value of $\cos^2 22\frac{1}{2}° + \cos^2 67\frac{1}{2}° + \cos^2 112\frac{1}{2}° + \cos^2 157\frac{1}{2}°$

A. 4 B. 2
C. $2\frac{1}{2}$ D. 3

8. If $\sin \alpha = \frac{12}{13}\left(0 < \alpha < \frac{\pi}{2}\right)$ and $\cos \beta = -\frac{3}{5}\left(\pi < \beta < \frac{3}{2}\pi\right)$, then the value of $\sin(\alpha + \beta)$ is

A. $-\frac{56}{65}$ B. $\frac{16}{65}$

C. $\frac{56}{65}$ D. $-\frac{16}{65}$

9. If $x = 8a \cos^3 \theta$, $y = 8b \sin^3 \theta$, what is the vlaue of $\left(\frac{x}{a}\right)^{\frac{2}{3}} + \left(\frac{y}{b}\right)^{\frac{2}{3}}$

A. 1 B. 2
C. 4 D. 8

10. ABC is a triangle, and BD is perpendicular to AC produced: Find BD if A = 30°, C = 120° and AC = 20

A. $5\sqrt{3}$ B. $10\sqrt{3}$
C. $6\sqrt{2}$ D. $8\sqrt{3}$

11. If $\cos(\alpha + \beta) = \frac{4}{5}$ and $\sin(\alpha - \beta) = \frac{5}{13}$ where α, β lie between 0° and 45°, then the value of tan 2α is

A. $\frac{56}{33}$ B. $\frac{46}{33}$

C. $\frac{14}{33}$ D. $\frac{16}{33}$

12. A ladder is placed against the wall such that it just reaches the top of the wall. The foot of the ladder is 1.5 m away from the wall and the ladder is inclined at an angle of 60° with the ground. The height of the wall is ($\sqrt{3}$ = 1.73)

A. 2.695 B. 2.785
C. 2.595 D. 2.545

13. Find the numerical value of $3\tan^2 30° + \frac{1}{4}\sec 60° + 5\cot^2 45° - \frac{2}{3}\sin^2\theta = 3\cos\theta$?

A. $3\frac{1}{2}$ B. $4\frac{1}{2}$

C. 5 D. 6

14. The angle of elevation of the top of a tower from a point on the ground is 30°. After walking 30 m towards the tower, the angle of elevation becomes 60°. The height of the tower is:

A. $15\sqrt{3}$ m B. $20\sqrt{3}$ m
C. $30\sqrt{3}$ m D. $10\sqrt{3}$ m

15. If $x \tan(180° + A) \tan(90° + A) \sin(-A) = \sin(180° - A) \cot(90° - A) \cos(360° - A)$, find the value of x.

A. sin A
B. cos A
C. tan A
D. cot A

16. The angle of elevation of the top and the foot of a flagstaff fixed on a wall are 60° and 45° to a man standing on the other end of a road 30 m wide, the height of the flagstaff is:

A. $30(\sqrt{3}-1)$
B. $10(\sqrt{3}+1)$
C. $30(\sqrt{3}+1)$
D. $30\sqrt{3}$

17. Find the value of cot (90° – A) cot A cos (90° – A) tan (90° – A)

A. sec A B. sin A
C. cos A D. tan A

18. $4\tan^{-1}\frac{1}{5}-\tan^{-1}\frac{1}{239}$ is equal to

A. π B. $\frac{\pi}{2}$
C. $\frac{\pi}{3}$ D. $\frac{\pi}{4}$

19. $\tan^{-1}\left(\frac{x}{y}\right)-\tan^{-1}\left(\frac{x-y}{x+y}\right)$ is

A. $\frac{\pi}{2}$ B. $\frac{\pi}{3}$
C. $\frac{\pi}{4}$ D. None of these

20. The solution of

$$\sin^{-1}\left(\frac{2a}{1+a^2}\right)-\cos^{-1}\left(\frac{1-b^2}{1+b^2}\right)$$

$$=\tan^{-1}\left(\frac{2x}{1-x^2}\right) \text{ is}$$

A. $\frac{a-b}{1-ab}$ B. $\frac{1+ab}{a-b}$
C. $\frac{ab-1}{a+b}$ D. $\frac{a-b}{1+ab}$

21. The value of

$$\tan\left[\cos^{-1}\left(\frac{4}{5}\right)+\tan^{-1}\left(\frac{2}{3}\right)\right] \text{ is}$$

A. $\frac{6}{17}$
B. $\frac{7}{16}$
C. $\frac{17}{6}$
D. None of these

22. If $\sin^{-1}x + \sin^{-1}y + \sin^{-1}z = \frac{3\pi}{2}$, the value of

$$x^{100}+y^{100}+z^{100}-\frac{9}{x^{101}+y^{101}+z^{101}} \text{ is}$$

A. 0 B. 1
C. 2 D. 3

ANSWERS

1	2	3	4	5	6	7	8	9	10
C	B	A	D	A	B	B	A	C	B
11	**12**	**13**	**14**	**15**	**16**	**17**	**18**	**19**	**20**
A	C	D	A	A	A	C	D	C	D
21	**22**								
C	A								

SOME SELECTED EXPLANATORY ANSWERS

6. Let the height of tower is h metre then, In ΔABC

$$\tan 45° = \frac{AB}{BC}$$

$$1 = \frac{h-7}{x} \qquad [\because \tan 45° = 1]$$

$$x = h - 7 \qquad ...(1)$$

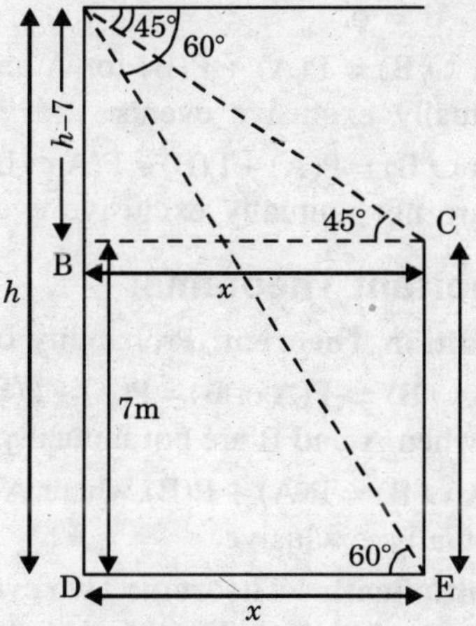

Again, In ΔADE,

$$\tan 60° = \frac{AD}{DE}$$

$$\frac{h}{x} = \sqrt{3} \qquad [\because \tan 60° = \sqrt{3}]$$

$$h = x\sqrt{3} \qquad ...(2)$$

Put $x = h - 7$ from equation (1) to (2), we get

$$h = (h-7)\sqrt{3}$$

$$h = \sqrt{3}h - 7\sqrt{3}$$

$$h(\sqrt{3}-1) = 7\sqrt{3}$$

$$h = \frac{7\sqrt{3}}{\sqrt{3}-1}$$

After Rationalization, we get

$$h = \frac{7\sqrt{3}}{\sqrt{3}-1} \times \frac{\sqrt{3}+1}{\sqrt{3}+1}$$

$$h = \frac{7\sqrt{3}(\sqrt{3}+1)}{(\sqrt{3})^2-(1)^2} = \frac{7\sqrt{3}}{2}(\sqrt{3}+1)$$

Hence, the height of tower is $\frac{7\sqrt{3}}{2}(\sqrt{3}+1)$ m.

7. $\cos^2 112\frac{1°}{2} = \cos^2\left(90° + 22\frac{1}{2}\right) = \sin^2 22\frac{1°}{2}$

$\cos^2 157\frac{1°}{2} = \cos^2\left(90° + 67\frac{1°}{2}\right) = \sin^2 67\frac{1°}{2}$

9. $2\cos = \left(\frac{x}{a}\right)^{\frac{1}{3}}$ and $2\sin\theta = \left(\frac{y}{b}\right)^2$

squaring and adding

$$4(\cos^2\theta + \sin^2\theta) = \left(\frac{x}{a}\right)^{\frac{2}{3}} + \left(\frac{y}{b}\right)^{\frac{2}{3}} = 4$$

10. $\angle ABC = 30° \Rightarrow AC = BC = 20$

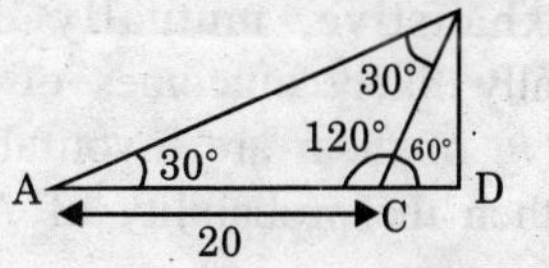

$$\therefore \qquad BD = BC \sin 60° = 20 \times \frac{\sqrt{3}}{2}$$

$$= 10\sqrt{3}$$

15. $x(\tan A)(-\cot A)(-\sin A) = \sin A \tan A (\cos A)$

$\Rightarrow x \sin A = \sin^2 A$ or $x = \sin A$

20. $\sin^{-1}\left(\frac{2a}{1+a^2}\right) - \cos^{-1}\left(\frac{1-b^2}{1+b^2}\right)$

$$= \tan^{-1}\left(\frac{2x}{1-x^2}\right)$$

$$\Rightarrow 2\tan^{-1} a - 2\tan^{-1} b = 2\tan^{-1} x$$

$$\Rightarrow \tan^{-1} x = \tan^{-1}\left(\frac{a-b}{1+ab}\right)$$

$$\Rightarrow x = \frac{a-b}{1+ab}.$$

16 Probability

1. **Event.** An *event* is an occurrence. Presence of a tail when a coin is tossed is an event.
2. **Mutually Exclusive Events.** If two or more events have no point in common, *i.e.*, they cannot occur simultaneously, the event are said to be mutually exclusive events. A head and tail are two mutually exclusive events of a coin. There are six mutually exclusive event in case of a dice, because only one event at a time can occur.
3. **Exhaustive events.** All possible outcome of an experiment are called exhaustive events.
4. **Definition of probability.** If there are n exhaustive, mutually exclusive and equally likely outcomes of an experiment and m of them are fovourable to an event A, then the probability of A is defined as the ratio $\frac{m}{n}$

$$\Rightarrow \quad P(A) = \frac{\text{favourable events}}{\text{total number of events}}$$

5. Odds in favour and odds against an event. If '*a*' of the outcomes are favourable to an event A and '*b*' of the outcomes are *against* it as a result of an experiment, then we say that odds are 'a' to 'b' in favour of A, or odds are 'b' to 'a' against A.
6. P(A) and $P(\bar{A})$ are the probabilities of occurrence and non-occurrence of an event A, then

   $P(A) + P(\bar{A}) = 1$ i.e.,

   $P(\bar{A}) = 1 - P(A)$
7. If A and B are two mutually exclusive events, then $P(A \cap B) = 0$. This means that A and B cannot occur simultaneously, *i.e.*, $A \cap B = \phi$.
8. $P(A \cup B) = P(A) + P(B)$ for A and B to be mutually exclusive events.
9. $P(A \cup B) = P(A) + P(B) - P(A \cap B)$ if A and B are not mutually exclusive events.

Two Important Theorems:

(*i*) **Addition Theorem:** Probability of A or B $P(A \cup B) \Rightarrow P(A \text{ or } B) = P(A) + P(B) - P(A \cap B)$ when A and B are not mutually exclusive

$P(A \cup B) = P(A) + P(B)$ where A and B are mutually exclusive.

(*ii*) **Multiplicative Theorem:** Two events A and B are mutually independent if and only if $P(A \cap B) \Rightarrow P(A \text{ and } B) = P(A) \times P(B)$. Provided $P(A) \neq 0$, $P(B) \neq 0$.

Solved Examples

Example 1: *If two coins are tossed once, what is the probability that at least one head occur?*

Solution: There are four outcomes

H, H; H, T; T, H, T, T

∴ P [at least one head] = ¾

Example 2: *Compare the chance of throwing 4 with one dice and 8 with two dice.*

Solution: There are 6 possible ways in which the dice can fall and of these one is favourable to an event.

$$\therefore \text{ P(throwing 4 with one die)} = \frac{1}{6}$$

Again when two dice are thrown there are 36 exhausive cases and a sum 8 can happen in 5 cases namely

(3, 5); (5, 3); (4, 4); (2, 6) and (6, 2).

$\therefore$ P (getting a sum eight) $= \dfrac{5}{36}$

$\therefore$ Ratio is $\dfrac{1}{6}:\dfrac{5}{36} \Rightarrow 6:5.$

Example 3: *A bag contains 6 white, 7 red and 8 black balls. Three balls are drawn at random. What is the chance that a white, red and a black ball is drawn?*

Solution: $\dfrac{6_{c_1} \times 7_{c_1} \times 8_{c_1}}{21_{c_3}} = \dfrac{6\times7\times8\times3\times2\times1}{21\times20\times19}$

$= \dfrac{29}{95}.$

MULTIPLE CHOICE QUESTIONS

1. Assuming that for a husband-wife couple the chance of their child being a boy or a girl are the same, the probability of their two children being a boy and a girl is:

A. $\frac{1}{2}$ B. 1

C. $\frac{1}{4}$ D. $\frac{1}{8}$

2. A cricket team has 15 members, of whom only 5 can bowl. If the names of the 15 members are put into a hat and 11 are drawn at random, then the chance of obtaining an eleven containing at least 3 bowlers is:

A. $\frac{7}{13}$ B. $\frac{11}{15}$

C. $\frac{12}{13}$ D. $\frac{12}{15}$

3. 8 coins are tossed simultaneously. The probability of getting at least 6 heads is:

A. 57/64 B. 229/256

C. 7/64 D. 37/256

4. From a pack of cards, two are drawn, the first being replaced before the second is drawn. The probability that the first is a diamond and the second is a king will be:

A. 13/4 B. 5/52

C. 1/52 D. 52

5. A number is chosen at random among the first 120 natural numbers. What is the probability of the number chosen being a multiple of 5 or 15?

A. 1/5 B. 1/8

C. 1/6 D. 1/15

6. Three dice are rolled. What is the probability of getting different faces?

A. $\frac{1}{3}$ B. $\frac{1}{4}$

C. $\frac{5}{9}$ D. $\frac{4}{9}$

7. What is the probability that three persons selected at random will be born on different days of the week?

A. $\frac{48}{49}$ B. $\frac{2}{3}$

C. $\frac{30}{49}$ D. $\frac{36}{49}$

8. The probability of having a king and a queen when the two cards are drawn at random from a pack of 52 cards, is:

A. $\frac{16}{663}$ B. $\frac{8}{663}$

C. $\frac{4}{663}$ D. $\frac{2}{663}$

9. A card is drawn from an ordinary pack and a gambler bets that it is either a spade or an ace. The odds against his winning are:

A. 9 : 4 B. 9 : 5

C. 9 : 6 D. 9 : 8

10. The probability that is leap year, selected at random, will contain 53 Sundays, is:

A. $\frac{1}{3}$ B. $\frac{2}{7}$

C. $\frac{3}{7}$ D. $\frac{4}{3}$

11. Which one of the following is not a fundamental approach of probability?

A. Classical B. Empirical

C. Subjective D. None of these

12. A bag, contains 5 white, 5 black, 7 yellow and 8 red balls the probability of getting a red ball when a ball is drawn at random is:

A. $\frac{8}{25}$ B. $\frac{1}{6}$

C. $\frac{1}{4}$ D. $\frac{7}{24}$

13. The probability of drawing a king of red colour from a pack of 52 cards is:

A. $\frac{1}{13}$ B. $\frac{1}{26}$

C. $\frac{1}{52}$ D. None of these

14. The probability that a non-leap year should have fifty-three Sundays is:

A. $\frac{1}{7}$ B. $\frac{2}{7}$

C. $\frac{3}{7}$ D. None of these

15. Probability of not getting a total of 7 in a single throw with two dice is:

A. $\frac{1}{9}$ B. $\frac{5}{6}$

C. $\frac{7}{18}$ D. $\frac{1}{8}$

16. A doctor is to visit a patient once in the month of November. The probability that he visits on date which is a multiple of 5 or 6 is:

A. $\frac{11}{30}$ B. $\frac{11}{31}$

C. $\frac{10}{30}$ D. $\frac{10}{31}$

17. A coin is tossed thrice. The probability of getting exactly one head or one tail is:

A. $\frac{3}{8}$ B. $\frac{5}{8}$

C. $\frac{4}{8}$ D. $\frac{6}{8}$ or $\frac{3}{4}$

18. P(A) = 0.4, then odds in favour of the event A are:

A. 2 : 3 B. 2 : 5

C. 3 : 2 D. 5 : 4

19. If $P(A \cap B) = 0$, then events A and B are:

A. mutually exclusive

B. equally likely

C. dependent

D. independent

20. The probability of getting a total 8 or at least 9 or less than 8 with two dice is:

A. $\frac{5}{36}$ B. $\frac{10}{36}$

C. $\frac{21}{36}$ D. 1

ANSWERS

1	2	3	4	5	6	7	8	9	10
C	D	D	C	A	C	C	B	A	B
11	**12**	**13**	**14**	**15**	**16**	**17**	**18**	**19**	**20**
D	A	B	A	B	C	D	A	A	D

EXPLANATORY ANSWERS

1. Clearly, $P(B) = \frac{1}{2} = P(G)$

Hence, required probability

$$= P(BG) = P(B)P(G)$$

$$= \frac{1}{2} \times \frac{1}{2} = \frac{1}{4}$$

3. Required probability

$$= {}^8C_6\left(\frac{1}{2}\right)^6 \cdot \left(\frac{1}{2}\right)^2 + {}^8C_7\left(\frac{1}{2}\right)^7 \cdot \left(\frac{1}{2}\right) + {}^8C_8\left(\frac{1}{2}\right)^8$$

$$= \frac{1}{256}(28+8+1) = \frac{37}{256}$$

4. Required probability $= \frac{^{13}C_1}{^{52}C_1} \cdot \frac{^4C_1}{^{52}C_1}$

$$= \frac{13}{52} \cdot \frac{4}{52} = \frac{1}{52}$$

6. The exhaustive number of cases $= 6^3 = 216$. The number of cases when all the three faces are distinct $= {}^6P_3 = 120$

$\therefore$ Required probability $= \frac{120}{216} = \frac{5}{9}$

7. Let A, B and C be three persons selected at random. If A can be born on any one of the day of the 7 days of the week.

However, B and C should have been born on different days.

Therefore, the required probability

$$= \frac{7}{7} \times \frac{6}{7} \times \frac{5}{7} = \frac{30}{49}.$$

10. A leap year contains 366 days and therefore 52 weeks and 2 days.

Clearly there are 52 Sundays in 52 weeks.

So, for remaining two days

Probability of Sunday $= \frac{2}{7}$

$\therefore$ Required probability $= \frac{2}{7}$

12. We have,

Total balls $= 5 + 5 + 7 + 8$

$= 25$

Total sample space to select a ball

$= {}^{25}C_1 = 25$

Favourable case to select a red ball from 8 balls

$= {}^8C_1 = 8$

Required probability $= \frac{8}{25}$.

14. In a non leap year,

There are 52 week + 1 days

In 52 week, we are confirm that here will we 52 Sundays

So required probability that the 1 day which is left is Sunday $= \frac{1}{7}$.

15. Total case $= 6 \times 6 = 36$

total favourable case, that the sum of two dice is 7 = {(1, 6)(2, 5)(3, 4)(4, 3)(5, 2)(6, 1)}

$= 6$

Probability that the sum is 7 $= \frac{6}{36} = \frac{1}{6}$

Required probability which is not getting the sum 7 $= 1 - \frac{1}{6} = \frac{5}{6}$.

17 Mensuration

1. A land measure unit is an *are*. One *are* measures an area equal to 100 m^2. One *Hectare* means 100 ares and is therefore equal to 10000 m^2. Whenever the area of a plane or that of a solid is given in Hectares and Ares? This must be converted into m^2.
2. *Planes* are two dimenstionals and occupy surface area.
3. *Perimeter.* The lengths of all the sides of a polygon is called a perimeter of the polygon. The perimeter of a circle is called the circumference.
4. *Rectangle.* If the length and breadth of the rectangle be '*l*' and '*b*' and '*d*' be the length of the diagonal, then P (perimeter) = 2 (l + b).

   A (surface area or area) = $l \times b$

   D (diogonal) = $\sqrt{l^2 + b^2}$

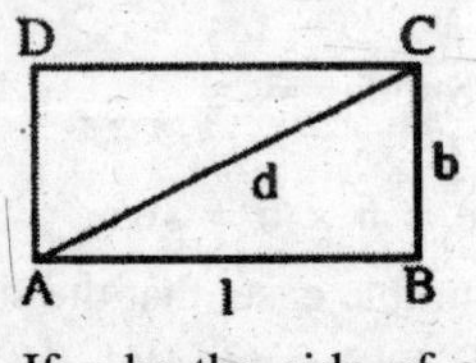

5. *Square.* If x be the side of a square, then

   $P = 4x$ or $x = \frac{1}{4}P$

   $A = x^2$ or $x = \sqrt{A}$

   D (diogonal) = $\sqrt{2}x$

   or $D^2 = 2A$

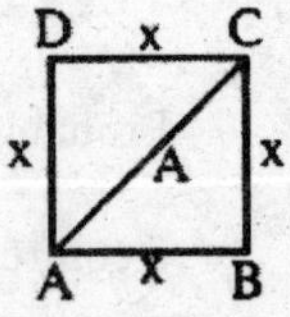

6. *Rhombus.* If x be the side the rhombus, all its side are equal and diagonal bisect at right angle.

   $P = 4x$ or $x = \frac{1}{4}P$

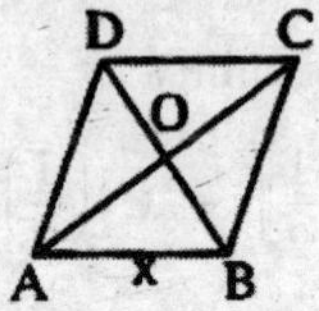

   $A = \frac{1}{2} \times$ Product of the diagonals

   $= \frac{1}{2} \times AC \times BD$

7. *Triangle.* This is a polygon with minimum number of sides *i.e.,* three

   (*i*) Area of any triangle = $\frac{1}{2} \times$ base $\times$ height

   (*ii*) Area of a triangle when its sides are given as a, b, c.

   $= \sqrt{s(s-a)(s-b)(s-c)}$

   where = $s = \frac{1}{2}(a + b + c)$.

   (*iii*) Area of an equilateral triangle

   $= \frac{\sqrt{3}}{4} \times (\text{side})^2$.

   (*iv*) Area of an isoceles triangle whose base is '*b*' and equal sides are '*a*' each

   $= \frac{1}{4} \times b \times \sqrt{4a^2 - b^2}$

   Note: If a regular hexagon (6 equal side polygon) is inscribed in a circle of radius x. The area of the hexagon is equal to six time the area of the equilateral triangle of side x.

8. Area of four walls of a room = 2 × height × (length + breadth) = $2h(l + b)$

9. *Circle.* It is a polygon with maximum number of sides. Given the perimeter, the circle is the plane with maximum area.
10. What is π? This is ratio of the circumference of the circle with its diameter remain constant. Its approximate value is $\frac{22}{7}$ or 3.1416.

Thus $\pi = \frac{\text{Circumference}}{\text{diameter}}$

11. Circumference of a circle = $2\pi r$

Area = πr^2 or $r = \sqrt{\frac{\text{Area}}{\pi}}$

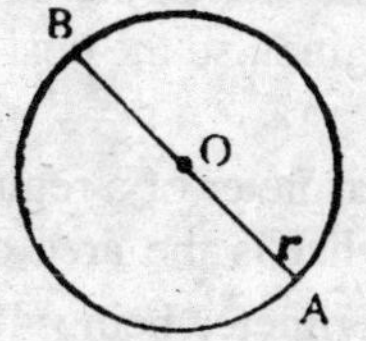

12. The radius R of a circle whose area is equal to the sum of the areas of series of a circles with radii r_1, r_2, r_3 etc. is equal to

$$R = \sqrt{r_1^2 + r_2^2 + r_3^2 + ...}$$

For example, the radius of a circle whose area is equal to the sum of the areas of two circles of radii 6 cms. and 8 cms. is = $\sqrt{6^2 + 8^2}$ cm. = 10 cm.

13. *Volume of Solids.* A solid occupies space and the space it occupies is known as its volume. A sphere, a cube are the examples of solids. It is measured in cubic units.
14. CUBOID. OA, OB, OC are called three coterminous edges of the cuboid and may be considered as length, breadth and height *i.e.*, '*l*', '*b*', '*h*'.

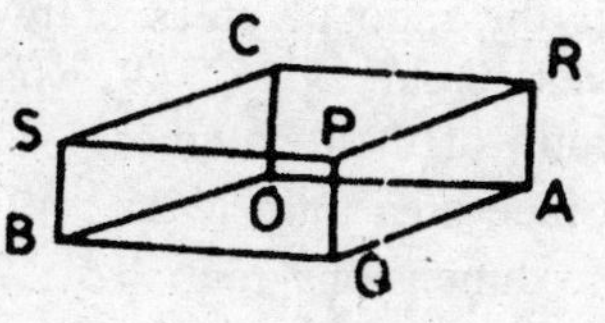

(*i*) Surface area = $2 \times (lb + bh + lh)$

(*ii*) Volume = $l \times b \times h$

(*iii*) Diagonal = $\sqrt{l^2 + b^2 + h^2}$

Note: If we want to find the quantity of paint required for painting the wooden or iron box or iron sheet required for making a box, formula (*i*) is used. In order to find, how much space a box can occupy or how much a box can contain, formula (*ii*) can be used. Formula (*iii*) be used to find the length of the longest pole which can be placed in a big hall.

15. CUBE. A cube has all its edges equal say '*e*' be its length. All its faces are square faces. It has 12 edges.

(*i*) Perimeter = 12 × edge

(*ii*) Area = 6 × (edge)^2

(*iii*) Volume = (edge)^3 or edge = (volume)$^{1/3}$

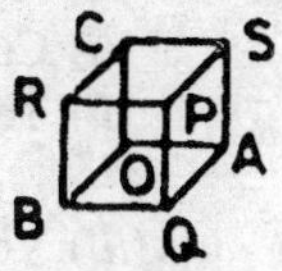

(*iv*) Diagonal = $\sqrt{3}$ × edge.

(*v*) Edge 'E' of a cube whose volume, is equal to the sum of volume : of cubes of edges e_1, e_2, e_3, ... is given by $E = (e_1^3 + e_2^3 + e_3^3 + ...)^{1/3}$

16. *SPHERE.* A rubber ball is an example of a sphere. If the radius of the sphere is *r*, then

(*i*) Surface area = $4\pi r^2$

(*ii*) Volume = $\frac{4}{3}\pi r^3$

(*iii*) Area of the solid hemisphere = $3\pi r^2$.

(*iv*) Radius 'R' of the sphere whose volume is equal to the sum of the volumes of spheres with radii r_1, r_2, r_3, ... is given by $R = (r_1^3 + r_2^3 + r_3^3 + ...)^{1/3}$

17. *CYLINDER.* When a rectangle is revolved about one of its side, a solid so formed is a cylinder.

(*i*) Curved surface of the cylinder
= base circumference × height
= $2\pi r \times h$

(*ii*) Total surface of a closed cylinder
= $2\pi r\,(r + h)$

(*iii*) Volume = based area × height
= $\pi r^2 \times h$

(*iv*) Height of the cylinder

$$= \frac{\text{Volume of cylinder}}{\text{base area of cylinder}}$$

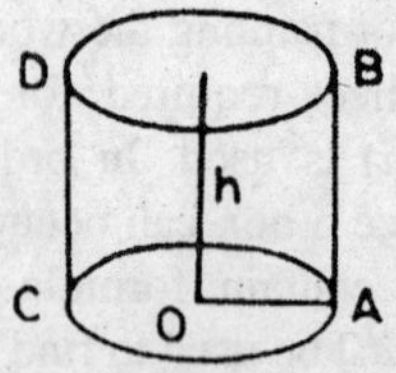

18. *CONE.* When a right angle triangle is revolved about one of its side a solid so formed is a cone. If r be the base radius, h the height and l, the slant height, then $l = \sqrt{r^2 + h^2}$

(*i*) Curved surface area = πrl

(*ii*) Total surface area = $\pi r(l + r)$

(*iii*) Volume = $\frac{1}{3}\pi r^2 h$

Note: Volume of the cone = $\frac{1}{3}$ volume of the cylinder

$$\therefore \quad \frac{\text{Volume of cone}}{\text{Volume of cylinder}} = \frac{1}{3}$$

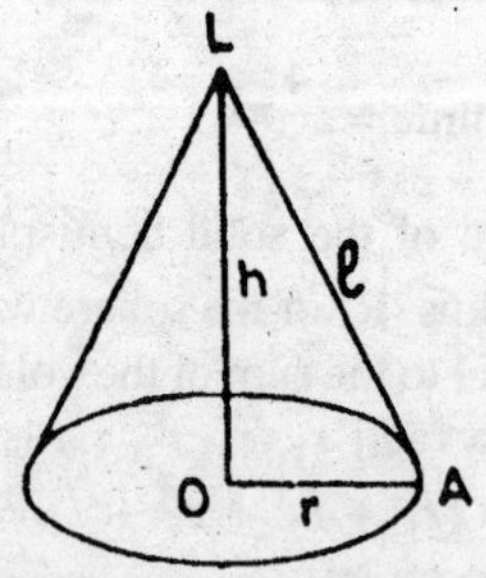

For example, if a conical vessel can hold 20 litres of milk, then a cylindrical vessel can hold 3 × 20, *i.e.,* 60 litres of milk.

19. If it is to find the canvas required for making the conical tent with given dimensions, formula (*i*) is used. How much iron sheet is required to construct a conical vessel, formula (*ii*) is used. To find the capacity of the cone, formula (*iii*) is used.

20. *Very Important Note*

If the ratio of the two similar planes or solids are as $x : y$, then their areas are as $x^2 : y^2$ and volumes are $x^3 : y^3$. This is explained by the following examples.

(*i*) If the sides of a rectangle are doubled, what percent of its area is increased?

Now it is very clear that the area of the corresponding rectangle becomes four times the original and thus the increase is 3 times or 300%.

(*ii*) If the cost of levelling the field in the form of a square is ₹ 25, what is the cost of levelling another square field whose side is three time the side of the first.

Since the area of the other field is 9 times the original, so the cost is ₹ (25 × 9), *i.e.,* ₹ 225.

(*iii*) The perimeter of a regular hexagon is 48 cm., what is the area of the hexagon.

The perimeter being 48 cm, so the side of the hexagon is (48 ÷ 6), *i.e.,* 8 cm. Hence the area of the hexagon is

$$6 \times \frac{\sqrt{3}}{4} \times (8)^2 \text{ cm}^2 \text{ or } 96\sqrt{3} \text{ cm}^2.$$

(*iv*) The perimeter of a cube is 36 cm. What is its volume?

Now side of the cube = $\frac{1}{12} \times 36$ cm. = 3 cm.

$\therefore$ Volume = 3^3 cm^3 or 27 cm^3.

(*v*) The weight of an iron ball of radius 2 cm is 25 grams. What is the weight of another similar sphere whose radius is 6 cm.

Since the radius of the other sphere is 3 times the first the volume is 27 times the first. Now weights are proportional to their volume, so the weight of the other sphere is 27 × 25 grams or 675 grams.

(*vi*) If the ratio of areas of two cylindrical vessels are as 25 : 49, what will be the ratio of their volumes?

Since area ratio is 25 : 49

$\therefore$ dimensions ratio = 5 : 7

or Volume ratio = 125 : 343

Solved Examples

Example 1: *The length of the room is* $5\frac{1}{2}$ *metres and width* $3\frac{3}{4}$ *metres, find the cost of paving the floor by slabs at the rate of ₹ 800 per m².*

Solution: Area of the floor of the room $= 5\frac{1}{2} \times 3\frac{3}{4}$ m²

$$= \frac{165}{8} \text{ m}^2$$

Cost for paving the floor = ₹ $\frac{165}{8} \times 800$

= ₹ 16500.

Example 2: *The area of a square field is 6050 m²; find the length of the diagonal.*

Solution: Area = (Diagonal)²

$\therefore$ Diagonal $= \sqrt{2 \times \text{Area}}$ meters

$= \sqrt{2 \times 6050}$ m

$= \sqrt{12100}$ m

= 110 m

Example 3: *How many bricks 20 cm. by 10 cm. will be needed to pave the floor of a room 25 m. long and 16 m. wide?*

Solution: Area of the room = 25 m. × 16 m.

= 400 m²

Area of the brick = 20 cm. × 10 cm.

$= \frac{1}{5}$ m $\times \frac{1}{10}$ m $= \frac{1}{50}$ m²

$\therefore$ Number of bricks required $= \left(400 \div \frac{1}{50}\right) = 20{,}000$.

Example 4: *The material of a cone is converted into the shape of the cylinder of equal radius. If the height of the cylinder is 5 cm, what is the height of the cone?*

Solution: Volume of the cone

= Volume of the cylinder

$\therefore \quad \frac{1}{3}\pi r^2 h = \pi r^2 \times 5$

$\therefore \quad h = 15$ cm.

Example 5: *Three solid spheres of gold whose radii are 1 cm, 6 cm and 8 cm respectively are melted into a single solid sphere. Find the radius of the sphere.*

Solution: According to the formula, radius of the new sphere is

$= (1^3 + 6^3 + 8^3)^{1/3}$

$= (729)^{1/3} = 9.$

Example 6: *A solid spherical ball is prepared by melting a cone and cylinder having the same height and same base radius equal to r. Find the radius of the sphere.*

Solution: Volume of the sphere of radius R

= Vol. of cone + Vol. of cylinder

$$\therefore \quad \frac{4}{3}\pi R^3 = \frac{1}{3}\pi r^2 h + \pi r^2 h \qquad (\because r = h)$$

$\therefore \quad R = r.$

Hence the radius of the sphere is the same as the base radius of the other two solids.

Example 7: *Cone, a hemisphere and a cylinder stand on equal bases and have the same height. What is the ratio of their respective volumes?*

Solution: Let the radius of the cone, hemisphere and cylinder be *r*.

$\therefore$ height of the hemisphere is also *r*.

$$\therefore \quad V_1 : V_2 : V_3 = \frac{1}{3}\pi r^2 \cdot r : \frac{2}{3}\pi r^3 : \pi r^2 r$$

$$= \frac{1}{3} : \frac{2}{3} : 1$$

or 1 : 2 : 3.

Example 8: *How many spherical bullets can be made out of a metre cube, if there is no loss in the process, given that the diameter of the sphere is 2 cm.?*

Solution: No. of spherical bullets

$$= \frac{\text{Volume of the cube}}{\text{Volume of the sphere}}$$

$$= \frac{(100 \text{ cm})^3}{\frac{4}{3} \times \frac{22}{7} \times r^3} = \frac{10^6 \times 7 \times 3}{88}$$

= 238636.36.

MULTIPLE CHOICE QUESTIONS

1. The perimeter of a rectangular field is 480 m and the ratio between the length and breadth is 5 : 3. Find the area in hectare.

A. 135 B. 1.35
C. 13.5 D. 13500

2. The area of a rectangular field is 3600 m^2. The ratio of its length and breadth is 16 : 9. Find its perimeter.

A. 250 m B. 1250 m
C. 500 m D. 750 m

3. Find the length of the wire required to go 15 times round a square field containing 69696 m^2.

A. 15840 m B. 16840 m
C. 15820 m D. 15640 m

4. The area of the floor of a room is 20 m^2, that of a longer wall 15 m^2 and of the shorter wall 12 m^2. Find the volume of the room.

A. 45 m^3 B. 10 m^3
C. 60 m^3 D. 40 m^3

5. Find the cost of fencing a circular field at the rate of 50 P. per metre if its area is 13860 m^2.

$$\left(\pi = \frac{22}{7}\right)$$

A. ₹ 660 B. ₹ 540
C. ₹ 700 D. ₹ 800

6. The radii of the two circular field is in the ratio 3 : 5. The area of the first field is what per cent less than the area of the second?

A. 50% B. 60%
C. 40% D. 64%

7. If all the sides of a triangle be increased by 200 per cent. What is the corresponding increase in its area?

A. 300% B. 400%
C. 600% D. 800%

8. The edges of three iron cubes are 6 cm, 8 cm, 10 cm respectively. A new cube was made by melting them. Find the edge of the new cube.

A. 8 cm B. 12 cm
C. 14 cm D. 10 cm

9. The length of the room is 6 m, width 4 m and 3 m high. How many boxes will it hold if each box occupies 1.5 cubic metres of space?

A. 64 B. 48
C. 54 D. 60

10. If the length of a rectangle is increased by 50% and its breadth is decreased by 25%, what is the change percent in its area?

A. 12.5% increase B. 10% increase
C. 25% increase D. 20% decrease

11. A reservoir is 45 metres long and 12 metres broad. How many kilo litres of water must be poured into it to raise the water level by 2 metres. [1 cube metric can contain 1 kilolitre]

A. 540 B. 1280
C. 1080 D. 1380

12. A cubic metre of a certain metal is hammered to form a fine sheet so as to cover one hectare of land. What is the thickness of the sheet?

A. 1 cm B. 0.1 cm
C. 0.01 cm D. 0.001 cm

13. A conical flask of radius r and height h is full of water. It is emptied into another cylindrical flask of radius x r. If this flask becomes full, what is its height?

A. $3x^2h$ B. $\frac{h}{3x^2}$
C. $\frac{3h}{x^2}$ D. $\frac{3x^2}{h}$

14. It is required to construct a conical circus tent of radius 21 m and 35 m slant high. The width of the canvas cloth is 3 metre, what will be the length of the cloth which shall do the need full.

A. 700 m B. 1250 m
C. 776.5 m D. 770 m

15. Two sphere have volumes in the ratio 64 : 729. If 160 ml paint is required fot painting the surface area of the smaller sphere, how much paint is required to paint the larger one?

A. 729 ml B. 750 ml
C. 216 ml D. 810 ml

16. Find the volume of the right circular conical tent whose vertical height is 8 m and area of whose base is 156 m^2.

A. 225 m^3 B. 396 m^3
C. 416 m^3 D. 516 m^3

17. A solid cone is melted and converted into a cylindrical shape of equal radius. Find the height of the cone if the height of cylinder is 5 cm.

A. 15 cm B. 1 cm
C. 45 cm D. 25 cm

18. From a right circular cylinder with height 10 cm and radius of base 6 cm, a right circular cone of the same height and base is removed. Find the volume of the remaining solid.

A. 744 cm^3 B. 814 cm^3
C. 654 cm^3 D. 754 cm^3

19. A hollow sphere of internal and external radii 2 cm. and 4 cm. is melted into a solid of base radius 4 cm. Find the height of the cone.

A. 12 cm B. 7 cm
C. 14 cm D. 21 cm

20. The radius of a circle is 20 cm. The radii (in centimeters) of three concentric circles drawn in such a manner that the whole area is divided into four equal parts, are

A. $20\sqrt{2},\ 20\sqrt{3},\ 20$

B. $\frac{10\sqrt{3}}{3},\ \frac{10\sqrt{2}}{3},\ \frac{10}{3}$

C. $10\sqrt{3},\ 10\sqrt{2},\ 10$

D. 17, 14, 10

21. A surveyor in his field book has drawn the plot as shown in the given figure. The area of the plot is

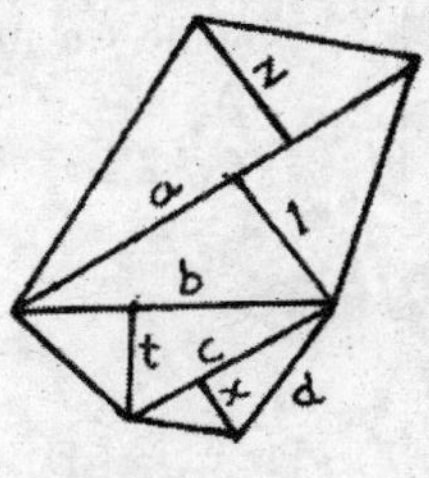

A. $\frac{1}{2}(az+by+ct+dx)$

B. $\frac{1}{2}(bt+cx+ay+az)$

C. $\frac{1}{2}(cx+bt+by+az)$

D $\frac{1}{2}(d+t)(c+x)+\frac{1}{2}(a+b)(y+z)$

22. The area of a quadrilateral of sides *a, b, c, d* inscribed in a circle is $\left(s=\frac{a+b+c+d}{2}\right)$

A. $\sqrt{s(s-a)(s-b)(s-c)(s-d)}$

B. $\sqrt{(s-a)(s-b)(s-c)(s-d)}$

C. $s(s-a)\sqrt{(s-b)(s-c)(s-d)}$

D. $s\sqrt{(s-a)(s-b)(s-c)(s-d)}$

23. ABCD is a square, ΔOAB is equilateral OL $\perp$ CD. The area of the quadrilateral OALB is

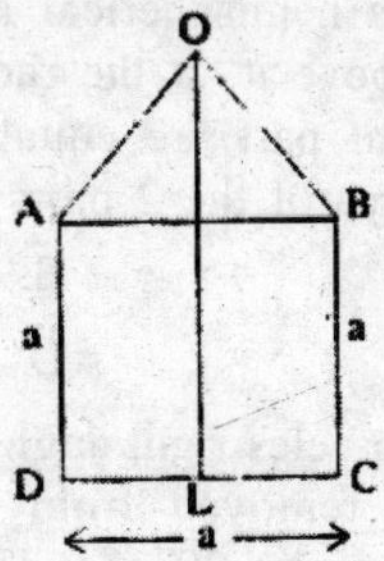

A. $\frac{a^2}{8}(2+\sqrt{3})$ B. $2a^2$

C. $a^2+\frac{\sqrt{3}}{2}a^2$ D. $\frac{a^2}{2}+\frac{\sqrt{3}}{4}a^2$

24. ABC is a triangle with perimeter *p* and $\angle A = \frac{\pi}{3}$. A circle of radius *r* with centre O is drawn to touch BC at P, AB produced at Q and AC produced at R. The area of the portion bounded by AQ, AR and the arc QPR is

A. $\frac{1}{3}(rp-\pi r^2)$ B. $\frac{1}{3}r(p-\pi r)$

C. $\frac{1}{3}rp-\frac{1}{2}\pi r^2$ D. $\frac{1}{2}rp-\frac{1}{3}\pi r^2$

25. A sphere is placed in an inverted conical vessel of base radius 3 cm and slant height 5 cm and it is observed that the base of the cone touches the sphere. The ratio of the volume of the sphere of that of the cone is

A. 2 : 7 B. 3 : 8
C. 4 : 9 D. 5 : 11

26. A tent is formed in this shape of a prism of *n* sides surmounted by a pyramid. If the length of each side is 'a' and the height of the prism is h and the height of the pyramid is H, then the capacity of the tent will be

A. $(h + 3H) \dfrac{na^2}{12} \cot\dfrac{\pi}{n}$

B. $(3h + H) \dfrac{na^2}{12} \cot\dfrac{\pi}{n}$

C. $(3h + H) \dfrac{na^2}{24} \cot\dfrac{\pi}{n}$

D. $(h + 3H) \dfrac{na^2}{24} \cot\dfrac{\pi}{n}$

27. A solid is hemispherical at the bottom and conical above it. If the radius and height of the conical part are equal, the ratio of the surface area of the 2 parts is

A. $\sqrt{2}:1$ B. $\sqrt{3}:1$
C. 1 : 1 D. $1:\sqrt{3}$

28. If four isosceles right angled triangles of side 5 m are removed from the corners of a rectangular plot 20 m × 10 m, then the area of the remaining portion (in m^2) is

A. 156.0 B. 156.5
C. 150.0 D. 150.6

29. The measurements in a field book are recorded as under

	To B	
	500	
	300	
To C 100	100	To D....
	0	
	From A	

The reading to D is missing in the field book. But the area of this field is mentioned as 40,000 m^2. Then the missing value (in m) should be

A. 60 B. 50
C. 40 D. 30

30. The diameter of two cones are equal and their slant heights are in the ratio 5 : 4. If the curved surface of the smaller cone 200 cm^2, then the curved surface of the bigger cone (in cm^2) is

A. 200 B. 250
C. 400 D. 500

31. If the radius of the base and the height of a right circular cone are increased by 20%, then the percentage increase in volume is approximately

A. 60 B. 68
C. 73 D. 78

32. From four corners of a rectangular iron sheet of 24 m × 30 cm, four squares of side 6 cm are cut. The remaining 2 portions of the sheet is formed into an open box. The internal volume (in cm^3) of the box is

A. 4300 B. 2592
C. 2542 D. 1296

33. If the volumes of a cone and a hemisphere having the same base are equal, then the height of the cone will be x times the radius of the base of the hemisphere, where x is

A. 1 B. 2
C. 3 D. π

34. An iron pipe is 3.5 m long, its external and internal diameters are 8 cm and 6 cm respectively. The volume (in cc) of the pipe is (given π = 22/7)

A. 7700 B. 1100
C. 770 D. 77

35. Within a rectangular garden 10 m wide and 20 m long, we wish to pave a walk around the borders of uniform width so as to leave an area of 96 square meters for flowers. How wide (in meter) should the walk be?

A. 1 B. 2
C. 2.1 D. 2.5

ANSWERS

1	**2**	**3**	**4**	**5**	**6**	**7**	**8**	**9**	**10**
B	A	A	C	A	D	D	B	B	A
11	**12**	**13**	**14**	**15**	**16**	**17**	**18**	**19**	**20**
C	C	B	D	D	C	A	D	C	C

21	22	23	24	25	26	27	28	29	30
B	A	D	D	B	A	A	C	A	B
31	**32**	**33**	**34**	**35**					
C	B	C	D	B					

SOME SELECTED EXPLANATORY ANSWERS

20. Since the area of each part is $\frac{1}{4}$ of the whole, the areas of the four circles (including the given one) must be
$\pi . 400$ cm^2, $\pi . 300$ cm^2, $\pi . 200$ cm^2 and $\pi . 100$ cm^2 which is valid only if the radii of the concentric circles be
$10\sqrt{3}$, $10\sqrt{2}$ and 10.

21. Area of the plot = sum of the areas of triangles.

23. Area of quadrilateral

$$\text{OALB} = \Delta\text{OAB} + \Delta\text{ALB}$$

$$= \frac{\sqrt{3}}{4}a^2 + \frac{1}{2}a^2$$

(Area of ΔALB = area of half the square ABCD)

24. Required area = Area of quadrilateral AQOR – area of the sector QOR

Now BL = BQ and CL = CR

$\therefore$ p = AB + BC + AC
= (AB + BL) + (LC + AC)
= AQ + AR

Required area

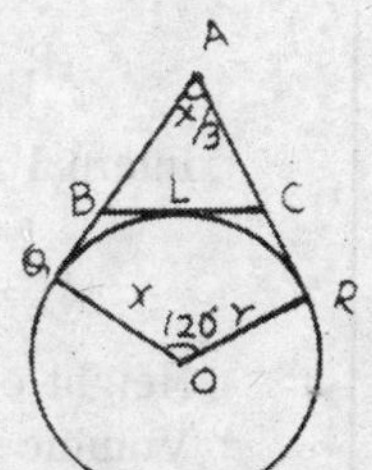

$$= \left(\frac{1}{2}\text{AQ} \times r + \frac{1}{2}\text{AR} \times r\right) - \frac{120}{360} \times \pi r^2$$

$$= \frac{1}{2}(\text{AQ} + \text{AR}) \times r - \frac{1}{3}\pi r^2$$

$$= \frac{1}{2}pr - \frac{1}{3}\pi r^2$$

25. AC = AD = 3
OD = OA – AD = 2
OC^2 = AO^2 – AC^2 = 25 – 9 = 16

$\therefore$ OC = 4
OL = 4 – r

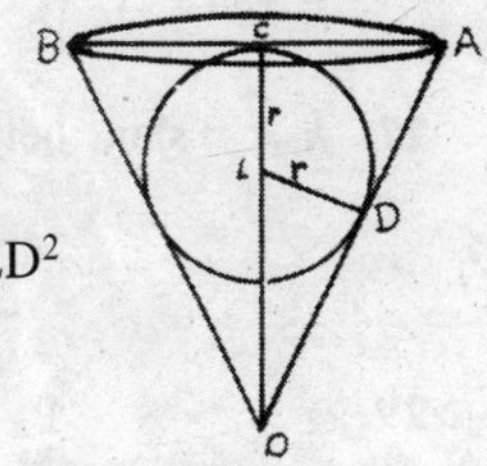

In ΔOLD,

$$\text{OL}^2 = \text{OD}^2 + \text{LD}^2$$

$$\Rightarrow (4 - r)^2 = 2^2 + r^2$$

$$\Rightarrow r = \frac{3}{2}$$

Volume of the sphere $= \frac{4}{3}\pi\left(\frac{3}{2}\right)^3 = \frac{9}{2}\pi$

Volume of the cone $= \frac{1}{3}\pi \cdot 3^2 \cdot 4 = 12\pi$

Required ratio $= \frac{9}{2}\pi : 12\pi$

$= 3 : 8$

26. $\because$ The base of n side prism and pyramid is a n side polygon.

$\therefore$ The area of n side polygon of

$$= \frac{na^2}{4} \times \cot\left(\frac{\pi}{n}\right)$$

Volume of prism = Area of base × height

$$= \frac{na^2}{4} \times \cot\left(\frac{\pi}{n}\right) \times h$$

Volume of pyramid $= \frac{1}{3}$ × Area of base × height

$$= \frac{1}{3} \times \frac{na^2}{4} \times \cot\frac{\pi}{n} \times \text{H}$$

Capacity of the tent = Volume of prism + Volume of pyramid

$$= \frac{na^2}{4}\cot\left(\frac{\pi}{n}\right) \times h + \frac{1}{3} \times \frac{na^2}{4}\left(\frac{\pi}{n}\right) \times \text{H}$$

$$= \frac{na^2}{4}\cot\left(\frac{\pi}{n}\right)\left[h+\frac{H}{3}\right]$$

$$= \frac{na^2}{4}\cot\left(\frac{\pi}{n}\right)\left[\frac{3h+H}{3}\right]$$

$$= (3h+H)\frac{na^2}{12}\cot\left(\frac{\pi}{n}\right).$$

27. $h = r$ slant height of the cone $= \sqrt{2}\, r$

$\therefore \quad 2\pi r^2 : \pi r.\ \sqrt{2}\, r$

$\Rightarrow \quad \sqrt{2} : 1$

29.

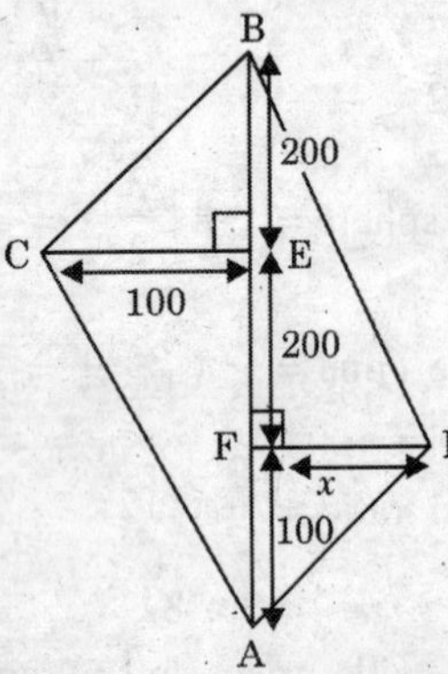

Let the reading of D is x m

Then, Area of the field book

$$= \frac{1}{2}(CE + FD) \times AB$$

$$= \frac{1}{2}(100 + x) \times 500$$

$$= 250\ (100 + x)$$

Given that

Area of the field book = 40,000 m^2

Then,

$$250(100 + x) = 40{,}000$$

$$100 + x = 160$$

$$x = 160 - 100$$

$$x = 60.$$

30. Radii of two cones = r and r

Slant height = $5x$ and $4x$

$\pi r.4x = 200 \Rightarrow \pi rx = 50$

$\therefore \quad 5\pi\ rx = 5 \times 50 = 250$

31. Let r and h be the radius and height of the cone, then $\frac{6}{5}r$ and $\frac{6}{5}h$ be the radius and height of the new cone.

$$\text{Increase in volume} = \frac{1}{3}\pi r^2 h\left(\frac{6^3}{5^3}-1\right)$$

$$= \frac{1}{3}\pi r^2 h\left(\frac{91}{125}\right)$$

$$\text{Percentage increase} = \frac{91}{125}\times 100\%$$

$= 73\%$ approximately.

32. $\sqrt{3}x = \sqrt{300} \Rightarrow x = 10$

Surface area = $6x^2 = 600$

33. $\pi rl = 2\pi r \times 3 \Rightarrow l = 6$

34.

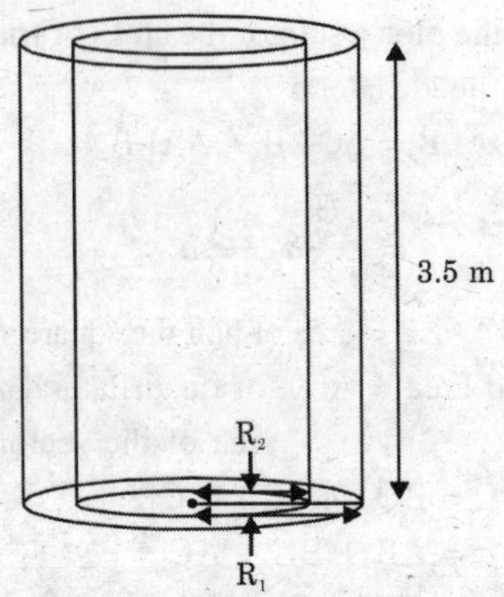

We have, external radius

$$(R_1) = \frac{8}{2} = 4 \text{ cm}$$

Internal radius

$$(R_2) = \frac{6}{2} = 3 \text{ cm}$$

Height of the pipe (h) = 3.5 m

Volume of the pipe (Hollow cylinder)

$$= \pi(R_1^2 - R_2^2)h$$

$$= \frac{22}{7}((4)^2 - (3)^2) \times 3.5$$

$$= \frac{22}{7}(16 - 9) \times 3.5$$

$$= 22 \times (0.5) \times 7 = 77 \text{ m}^3.$$

35. $(20 - 2x)(10 - 2x) = 96$ only if $x = 2$.

18 Statistics

Statistics : Statistics is the science which deals mainly with collection, presentation and interpretation of numerical data.

Measures of Central Tendency : Certain methods which reduce the given data to a single representative figure is called the measure of central tendency.

The commonly used measures of central tendency are *the mean*, *the median* and *the mode.*

Means:

1. *The arithmetic mean* of a set of n numbers is

$$\overline{X} = \frac{x_1 + x_2 + ... + x_n}{n} = \frac{\sum x}{n}$$

If the numbers occur f_1, f_2, ..., f_n times, respectively, then

$$\overline{X} = \frac{f_1x_1 + f_2x_2 + ... + f_nx_n}{f_1 + f_2 + ... + f_n} = \frac{\sum fx}{\sum f}$$

If the numbers are associated with a *weighting factor* $w_i \geq 0$, then

$$\overline{X} = \frac{w_1x_1 + w_2x_2 + ... + w_nx_n}{w_1 + w_2 + ... + w_n} = \frac{\sum wx}{\sum w}$$

2. *The geometric mean* of a set of n numbers is

$\overline{G} = \sqrt[n]{x_1x_2....x_n}$

If the numbers occur f_1, f_2, ... f_n times, respectively

then $\overline{G} = \sqrt[n]{x_1^{f_1} x_2^{f_2} ....x_n^{f_n}}$

where $n = f_1 + f_2 + ... + f_n$.

3. *The harmonic mean* of a set of n numbers is

$$\overline{H} = \frac{1}{\left(\frac{1}{n}\right)\left(\frac{1}{x_1} + \frac{1}{x_2} + ... + \frac{1}{x_n}\right)} = \frac{n}{\sum\left(\frac{1}{x}\right)}$$

If the numbers occur f_1, f_2, ..., f_n times, respectively, then

$$\overline{H} = \frac{1}{\left(\frac{1}{n}\right)\left(\frac{f_1}{x_1} + \frac{f_2}{x_2} + ... + \frac{f_n}{x_n}\right)} = \frac{n}{\sum\left(\frac{f}{x}\right)}$$

where $n = f_1 + f_2 + ... + f_n$.

4. *The quadratic mean* of a set of n numbers is

$$\overline{Q} = \sqrt{\frac{x_1^2 + x_2^2 + ... + x_n^2}{n}} = \sqrt{\frac{\sum x^2}{n}}$$

5. *Relation*

$$\overline{H} \leq \overline{G} \leq \overline{X}$$

Median : If the data of a series are arranged in ascending or descending order of magnitude, the value of the middle term is called the *median*.

If n is the number of terms, the median is the $\left(\frac{n+1}{2}\right)$th term in case n is *odd*.

If n is even then the average of the two middle terms is given by the median.

In case of grouped data, the median is given by the formula

$$\text{Median} = L + \frac{(U - L)}{f} \times \left(\frac{n}{2} - C\right) = L + \frac{\frac{n}{2} - C}{f} \times i$$

Where L and U are respectively the lower and upper limit of the median class.

f is the frequency of the median class.

C is cumulative frequency of the class preceding the median class.

i is the class interval and n is the total frequency.

Mode: For ungrouped data (discrete distribution)

Mode = The value of the item which occurs most frequently.

For grouped data (continuous distribution)

$$\text{Mode} = L + \frac{f_m - f_1}{(f_m - f_1) + (f_m - f_2)} \times (U - L)$$

$$= L + \frac{f_m - f_1}{2f_m - f_1 - f_2} \times h$$

Where U and L are upper and lower limit

h is width of the modal class

f is the frequency of the modal class.

f_1 is the frequency of the class preceding the modal class.

f_2 is the frequency of the class following the modal class.

Relation between Mean, Median and Mode :

$$\text{Median} = \text{Mode} + \frac{2}{3}(\text{Mean} - \text{Mode})$$

approximately.

or Mode = 3 Median – 2 Mean.

approximately.

Average or Mean Deviation : It is defined as the arithmetic average of the absolute values of the deviations, *i.e.*, all deviations taken positive, from the mean, mode or median.

(i) The deviation from the arithmetic mean $\overline{X}$ of each number x_j in a set of numbers $x_1, x_2, ..., x_n$ is $D_j = x_j - \overline{X}$, $j = 1, 2, ..., n$.

(ii) The mean deviation of the same set is

$$\overline{D} = \frac{|x_1 + x_2 + ... + x_n - n\overline{X}|}{n} = \frac{\sum |x_j - \overline{X}|}{n}$$

Where $|x_j - X|$ is the absolute value of Dj.

If the numbers occur $f_1, f_2, ..., f_n$ times, then $n = f_1 + f_2 + ... + f_n$ and

$$\overline{D} = \frac{f_1|x_1 - \overline{X}| + f_2|x_2 - \overline{X}| + ... + f_n|x_n - \overline{X}|}{n}$$

$$= \frac{\sum f\,|n - \overline{X}|}{n}$$

Standard Deviation : The standard deviation in a set of number $x_1, x_2, ..., x_n$ is

$$\sigma = \sqrt{\frac{(x_1 - \overline{X})^2 + (x_2 - \overline{X})^2 + ... + (x_n - \overline{X})^2}{n}}$$

$$= \sqrt{\frac{\sum (x_j - \overline{X})^2}{n}}$$

If the numbers occurs $f_1, f_2, ..., f_n$ times, then $n = f_1 + f_2 + ... + f_n$ and

$$\sigma = \sqrt{\frac{f_1(x_1 - \overline{X})^2 + f_2(x_2 - \overline{X})^2 + ...+ f_n(x_n - \overline{X})^2}{n}}$$

$$= \sqrt{\frac{\sum f_n(x - \overline{X})^2}{n}}$$

Variance: The square of standard deviation is called the variance (σ^2).

$$\therefore\ \sigma^2 = \frac{\sum (x - \overline{X})^2}{n} \quad \text{or} \quad \sigma^2 = \sum f(x - \overline{X})^2$$

7. *The covariance of two sets X* $(x_1, x_2, ..., x_n)$, the arithmetic means of which are $\overline{X}$ and $\overline{Y}$, respectively, is

$$\sigma_{xy} = \frac{\sum (x - \overline{X})(y - \overline{Y})}{n}$$

MULTIPLE CHOICE QUESTIONS

1. If the means of a set of observations $x_1, x_2, ..., x_n$ is $\overline{X}$, then the mean of the observations $x_i + 2i$; $i = 1, 2, 3, ..., n$ is

A. $\overline{X}+2$ B. $\overline{X}+2n$

C. $\overline{X}+(n+1)$ D. $\overline{X}+n$

2. The weighted AM of first n natural numbers whose weights are equal to the corresponding numbers is equal to

A. $2n + 1$ B. $\frac{1}{2}(2n+1)$

C. $\frac{1}{3}(2n+1)$ D. $\frac{2n+1}{6}$

3. 10 is the mean of a set of 7 observations and 5 is the mean of a set of 3 observations. The mean of the combined set is given by

A. 15 B. 10

C. 8.5 D. 7.5

4. Out of 50 students in a class, 10 were of the age of 10 years, 14 were of the age of 11 years and the remaining of 12 years. Then AM of students is

A. 11.5 B. 11.24

C. 11.32 D. None of these

5. The GM of the series 1, 2, 4, 8, 16, ..., 2^n is,

A. $2^{\frac{n+1}{2}}$ B. 2^{n+1}

C. $2^{n/2}$ D. 2^n

6. If G_1, G_2 are the geometric means of the series of observations and G is the GM of the ratios of the corresponding observations then G is equal to

A. $\frac{G_1}{G_2}$ B. $\log G_1 - \log G_2$

C. $\frac{\log G_1}{\log G_2}$ D. $\log (G_1.G_2)$

7. If a variable takes values 0, 1, 2, ..., n with frequencies 1, $^nC_1$, $^nC_2$, ..., ^nC_n, then the AM is

A. n B. $\frac{2^n}{n}$

C. $n + 1$ D. $\frac{n}{2}$

8. The mean of the series $x_1, x_2, ..., x_n$ is $\overline{X}$. If x_2 is replaced by λ, then the new mean is

A. $\overline{X}-x_2+\lambda$ B. $\frac{\overline{X}-x_2-\lambda}{n}$

C. $\frac{(n-1)\overline{X}+\lambda}{n}$ D. $\frac{n\overline{X}-x_2+\lambda}{n}$

9. In a college of 100 teachers, the mean age is 30 years and in another college of 50 teachers, the mean age is 60. The mean age of the teachers of two colleges taken together is

A. 40 B. 42

C. 45 D. None of these

10. In any discrete series (when all values are not same) the relationship between M.D. about mean and S.D is

A. M.D. = S.D. B. M.D. $\geq$ S.D.

C. M.D. $<$ S.D. D. M.D. $\leq$ S.D.

11. Quartile deviation of the following data 32, 45, 28, 72, 63, 59, 60 is

A. 14.5 B. 15

C. 15.5 D. 16

12. The mean deviation from the mean of the AP a, $a + d$, $a + 2d$, ..., $a + 2nd$ is

A. $n (n + 1) d$ B. $\frac{n(n+1)d}{2n+1}$

C. $\frac{n(n+1)d}{2n}$ D. $\frac{n(n-1)}{2n+1}d$

13. The standard deviation of Q. 12 is

A. $\frac{n(n+1)}{3}d^2$ B. $\sqrt{\frac{n(n+1)}{3}}\,d$

C. $\frac{n(n-1)}{3}d^2$ D. $\sqrt{\frac{n(n-1)}{3}}\,d$

14. The standard deviation of 4, 5, 6, 7, ..., 13 is x, then the standard deviation of 14, 15, 16, ..., 23 is

A. 2
B. $10x$
C. $x + 10$
D. $x+\sqrt{10}$

15. The mean of five observations is 15 and their variance is 9.2. If three observations are 16, 17 and 19, the other two are

A. 10, 11
B. 11, 12
C. 12, 13
D. None of these

ANSWERS

1	2	3	4	5	6	7	8	9	10
C	C	C	C	A	A	D	D	A	D
11	**12**	**13**	**14**	**15**					
C	B	B	A	B					

SOME SELECTED EXPLANATORY ANSWERS

3. Given $n_1 = 7,\ \overline{X}_1 = 10,\ n_2 = 3,\ \overline{X}_2 = 5$

$$\therefore \text{Combined mean} = \frac{n_1\overline{X}_1 + n_2\overline{X}_2}{n_1+n_2}$$

$$= \frac{7\times10+3\times5}{7+3} = \frac{85}{10} = 8.5.$$

4. Required AM

$$= \frac{10\times10+14\times11+\{50-(10+14)\}\times12}{10+14+\{50-(10+14)\}}$$

$$= \frac{10\times10+14\times11+26\times12}{10+14+26}$$

$$= \frac{566}{50} = 11.32.$$

5. GM of the series 1, 2, 4, 8, ..., 2^n

$$= \{1.2.4.8....2^n\}^{1/n}$$

$$= \{2^1.2^2.2^3.....2^n\}^{1/n}$$

$$= \left\{2^{\frac{n(n+1)}{2}}\right\}^{1/n} = 2^{\frac{n+1}{2}}.$$

13. We have

$$\sigma^2 = \frac{1}{2n+1}\sum_{r=0}^{2n}\{(a+rd)-(a+nd)\}^2$$

$$= \frac{2d^2}{2n+1}(1^2+2^2+....+n^2)$$

$$= \frac{n(n+1)}{3}d^2$$

$$\therefore\ \sigma = \sqrt{\frac{n(n+1)}{3}}.d.$$

GENERAL INTELLIGENCE & REASONING

1. LETTER SERIES

In letter series, the letters follow a definite order. The given series of letters can be in natural order or in reverse order or combination of both. The letters may be skipped or repeated or consecutive. The given series may be single or may even comprise of two different series merged at alternate positions. While attempting questions on letter series one should note the pattern of alphabet series.

Alphabets in natural series are :

A B C D E F G H I J K L M N O P Q R S T U V W X Y Z

A	E	J	O	T	Y
↓	↓	↓	↓	↓	↓
1st	5th	10th	15th	20th	25th

Alphabets in reverse series are :

Z Y X W V U T S R Q P O N M L K J I H G F E D C B A

Z	V	Q	L	G	B
↓	↓	↓	↓	↓	↓
1st	5th	10th	15th	20th	25th

Note : On reaching Z, the series restarts from A and on reaching A, it restarts from Z.

EXERCISE

Directions : *In each of the following series determine the order of the letters. Then from the given options select the one which will complete the given series.*

1. B Y C X D W E ?
(*a*) S (*b*) T
(*c*) U (*d*) V

2. B A F E J I P O ? U
(*a*) V (*b*) T
(*c*) S (*d*) Q

3. B A D C ? H G J I
(*a*) EF (*b*) FE
(*c*) FG (*d*) DF

4. ADG, XVT, BEH, WUS, ?
(*a*) VTR (*b*) CFI
(*c*) DFJ (*d*) STU

5. GMSY, IOUA, KQWC, ?
(*a*) MSYE (*b*) NSYE
(*c*) MTYE (*d*) MSYF

6. ADG, GJM, ?, SVY
(*a*) MPS (*b*) MQR
(*c*) MQS (*d*) SPM

7. XYZ, UVW, ?, OPQ
(*a*) RST (*b*) STU
(*c*) QRS (*d*) TUV

8. JOBS, KMEO, LKHK, ?, NGNC
(*a*) MJLH (*b*) LIKG
(*c*) MIKG (*d*) MNGM

9. AZ, GT, MN, ?, YB
(*a*) KF (*b*) TS
(*c*) RX (*d*) SH

10. BMY, DNW, FOU, ?
(*a*) HPT (*b*) HPS
(*c*) HQS (*d*) GPS

11. AZ, CX, EV, ?
(*a*) HU (*b*) GS
(*c*) GT (*d*) HT

12. DMP, FLN, HKL, JJJ, ?
(*a*) MIH (*b*) III
(*c*) LIH (*d*) MII

13. ECA, JHF, OMK, ?, YWU
(*a*) TRP (*b*) LNP
(*c*) QPN (*d*) RPT

14. ABP, CDQ, EFR, ?
(*a*) GHS (*b*) HGS
(*c*) GHR (*d*) GHT

15. BEH, KNQ, TWZ, ?
(*a*) IJL (*b*) BDF
(*c*) CFI (*d*) ADG

EXPLANATORY ANSWERS

1. (*d*) : There are two alternate series.

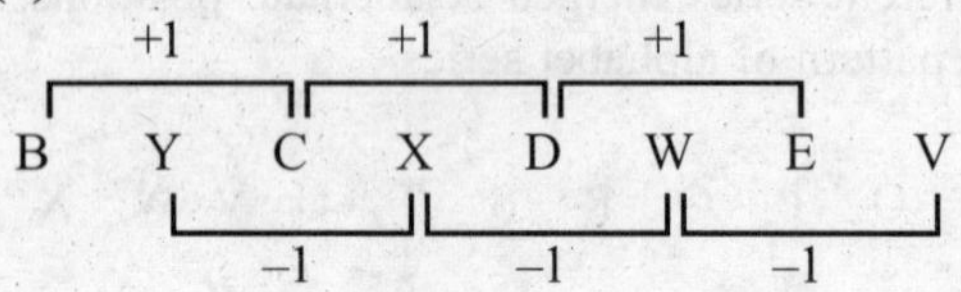

Series I : BCDE (natural order)
Series II : YXWV (reverse order)

2. (*a*) : Each vowel (AEIOU) is preceded by the letter that comes next to it in the natural alphabetical series.

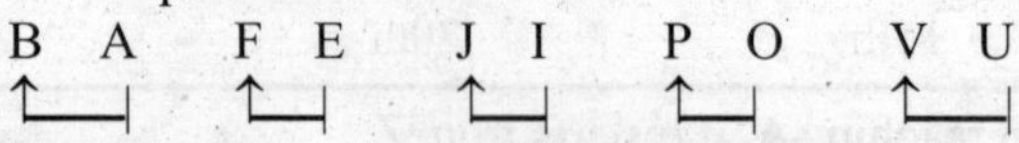

3. (*b*) : The letters in natural series are divided into sections of two letters each. The letters in each section are written backward.
BA DC FE HG JI.

4. (*b*) : There are two alternate series.

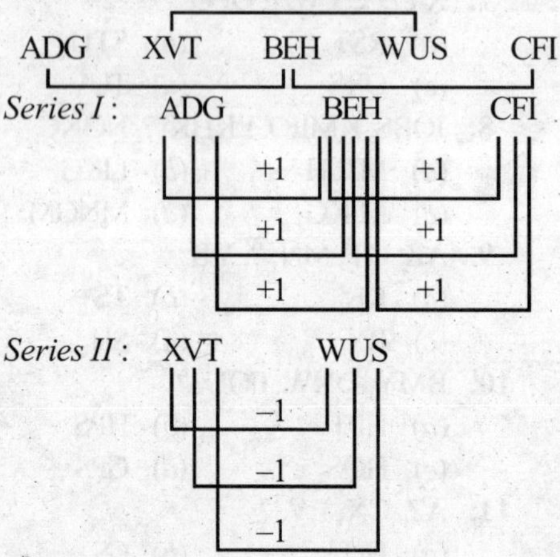

5. (*a*) : The series is formed by moving each letter two steps forward from one group to the next.

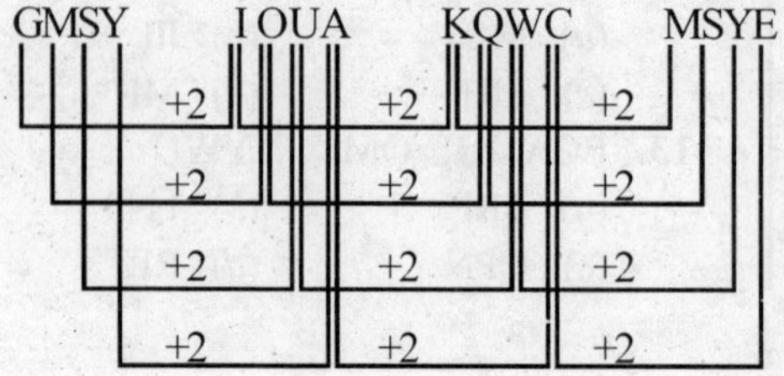

(The series restarts from A on reaching Z)

6. (*a*) : In each group of three letters the alphabet is in the succession of +3. The next group begins with the last alphabet of the previous group.

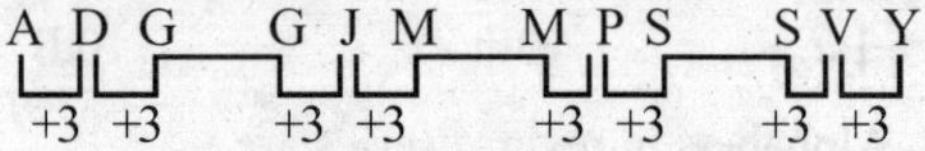

7. (*a*) : The alphabet from one group to the next are in recession of –3, *i.e.,*

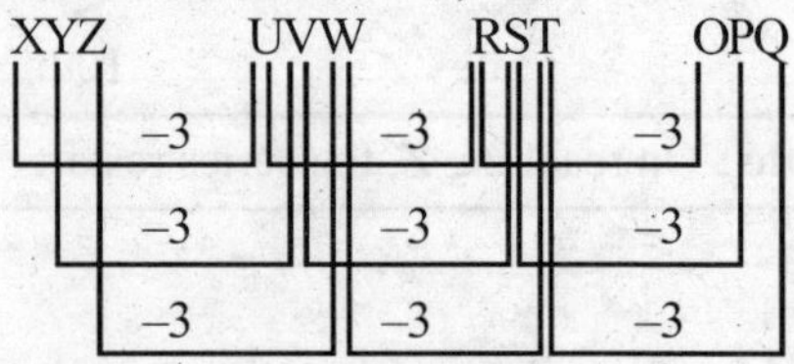

8. (*c*) : The alphabets in each group follow the pattern +1, –2, +3 and –4 respectively from one group to the next group.

9. (*d*) : The letters in one group correspond to the letters in the next group in the manner +6, –6 respectively, *i.e.,*

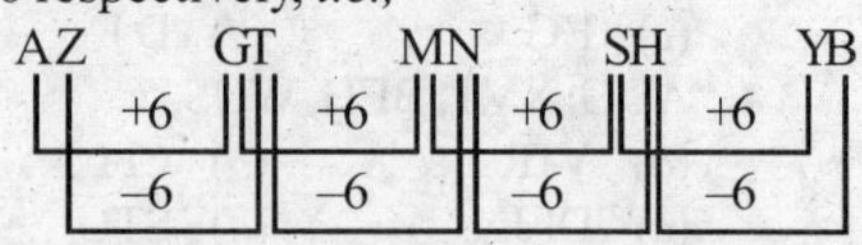

10. (*b*) : The letters in one group correspond to the letters in the next group in the manner +2, +1, -2 respectively, *i.e.,*

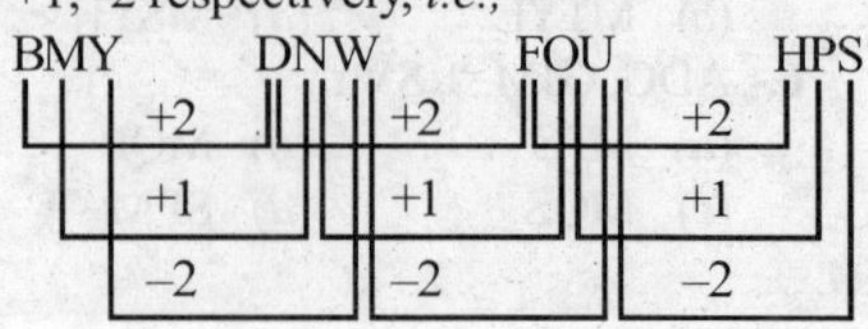

11. (*c*) **:** The letters in each group correspond to the letters in the next group in the manner +2, –2 respectively, *i.e.,*

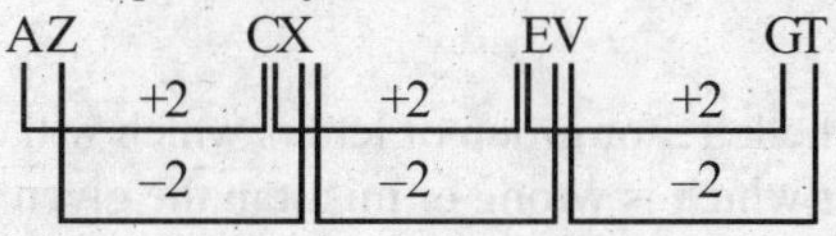

12. (*c*) **:** The alphabets in each group correspond to the alphabets in the next group in the manner +2, –1, –2 respectively, *i.e.,*

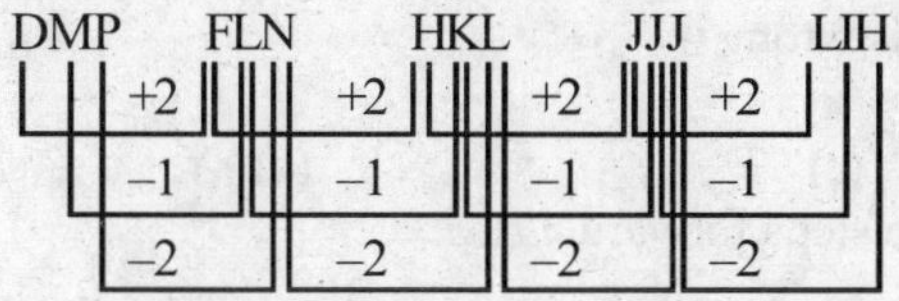

13. (*a*) **:** The alphabets in each group are moved five steps forward, *i.e.,*

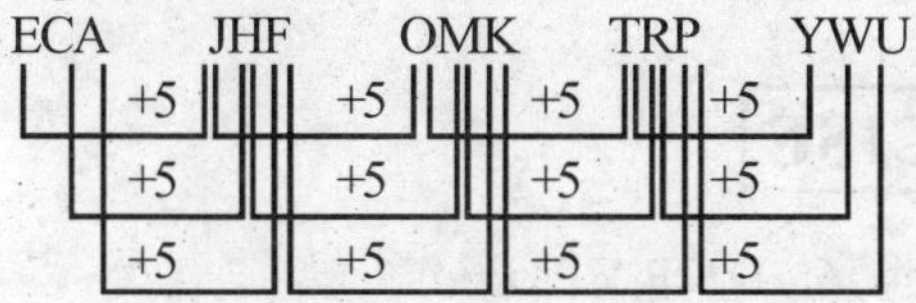

14. (*a*) **:** The letters in one group correspond to the letters in the next group in the manner +2, +2, +1 respectively, *i.e.,*

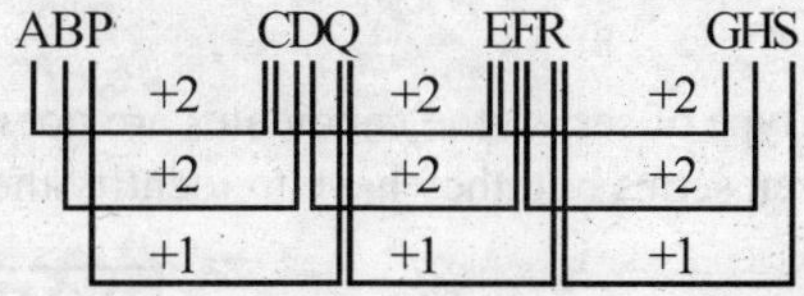

15. (*c*) **:** All the letters in each group are moved nine steps forward.

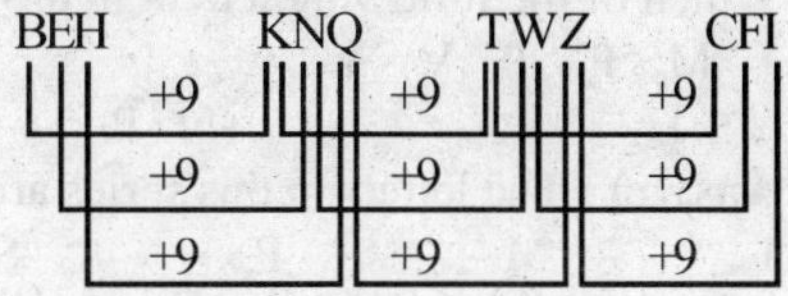

2. WRONG LETTER SERIES

In this type of series, the candidates are not required to find the letter or group of letters which will complete the given series but, they have to identify the letter or number which is wrong or misfit in the given series.

SOLVED EXAMPLE

1. Which of the following letters in the given series is wrong?
J M P T V Y
(*a*) J (*b*) P (*c*) T (*d*) Y

Ans. (*c*) : The letters in this series are moved three steps forward, *i.e.*,

J → M → P → S → V → Y
(+3 +3 +3 +3 +3)

Letter 'T' should have been 'S'.

EXERCISE

Directions : *Which letter(s) in each of the following series is wrong or is misfit in the series?*

1. AEHOU
(*a*) U (*b*) O
(*c*) H (*d*) E

2. CHMSWB
(*a*) C (*b*) S
(*c*) B (*d*) W

3. XSNICY
(*a*) Y (*b*) C
(*c*) S (*d*) I

4. ZAWBXC
(*a*) D (*b*) C
(*c*) X (*d*) W

5. MLONQPR
(*a*) R (*b*) O
(*c*) Q (*d*) L

6. DKRYFL
(*a*) L (*b*) D
(*c*) R (*d*) Y

7. LNQTWZCF
(*a*) C (*b*) Q
(*c*) L (*d*) F

8. XW, DC, CB, NM, PQ
(*a*) NM (*b*) CB
(*c*) PQ (*d*) XW

9. BEINSAI
(*a*) A (*b*) E
(*c*) S (*d*) I

10. ZTPKHF
(*a*) Z (*b*) P
(*c*) T (*d*) F

EXPLANATORY ANSWERS

1. (*c*) : The series is made with vowels only. AEIOU. I should be in place of H.

2. (*b*) : The letters in the series are moved five steps forward.

C → H → M → R → W → B
(+5 +5 +5 +5 +5)

R should be in place of S
(The series restarts from A on reaching Z)

3. (*b*) : The pattern in the series is –5, *i.e.*,

X → S → N → I → D → Y
(–5 –5 –5 –5 –5)

D should be in place of C.

4. (*d*) : There are two alternate series

```
         +1        +1
      ┌────────┐┌────────┐
Z   A    Y    B    X    C
└────────┘└────────┘
    –1        –1
```

Series I : ZYX (reverse series)

Series II : ABC (natural series)

Y should be in place of W.

5. (*a*) : Two consecutive letters are written backwards.

ML ON QP SR

S should be in place of R.

6. (*a*) : The pattern in this series in moving the letters seven steps forward.

```
D    K    R    Y    F    M
└────┘└───┘└───┘└───┘└───┘
  +7   +7   +7   +7   +7
```

M should be in place of L.

7. (*c*) : The pattern in the series is +3

```
K    N    Q    T    W    Z    C    F
└────┘└───┘└───┘└───┘└───┘└───┘└───┘
  +3   +3   +3   +3   +3   +3   +3
```

K should be in place of L.

8. (*c*) : The series is made with any two consecutive letters written backwards.

XW DC CB NM QP
← ← ← ← ←

Q should come before P in the series.

9. (*c*) : The difference between the letters is increased by one at each step.

```
B    E    I    N    T    A    I
└────┘└───┘└───┘└───┘└───┘└───┘
  +3   +4   +5   +6   +7   +8
```

T should be in place of S.

10. (*b*) : The difference between the letters is decreased by one at each step.

```
Z    T    O    K    H    F
└────┘└───┘└───┘└───┘└───┘
  –6   –5   –4   –3   –2
```

O should be in place of P.

3. REPEAT SERIES

In this type of series, small letters of the alphabet are used to make a set of letters which are repeated. The candidate has to find the set of letters which will fit the blanks left in the given series in such a manner that one section of the series is further repeated in the same manner.

SOLVED EXAMPLE

1. Which of the following groups of letters will complete the given series?
ba-b-aab-a-b
(*a*) baab (*b*) abba (*c*) abaa (*d*) babb
Ans. (*b*) : The series is baab, baab, baab. Here the section 'baab' is repeated in the series.

Solving steps **:** The candidate has to look for clues to solve such series pattern. 'aab' in the Series indicates that 'b' in this series is preceded by two 'a' so, the first blank and the last blank will be filled by 'a'. Now the first set is formed, *i.e.*, 'baab' in the beginning. This set is repeated, so the second and third blanks will have 'b' filling them. Now, solve the exercise given below to know the different ways in which these series are formed.

EXERCISE

Directions : *Which of the following groups of letters will complete the given series?*

1. ab---b-bbaa-
(*a*) babba (*b*) abaab
(*c*) abbab (*d*) baaab

2. aa-ab--aaa-a
(*a*) baaa (*b*) abab
(*c*) aaab (*d*) aabb

3. -baa-aab-a-a
(*a*) baab (*b*) abab
(*c*) aaba (*d*) aabb

4. -a cca-ccca-acccc-aaa
(*a*) ccaa (*b*) acca
(*c*) caac (*d*) caaa

5. c-bbb--abbbb-abbb-
(*a*) abccb (*b*) bacbb
(*c*) aabcb (*d*) abacb

6. ac-cab-baca-aba-acac
(*a*) bcbb (*b*) aacb
(*c*) babb (*d*) acbc

7. --aba--ba-ab
(*a*) abbab (*b*) bbaba
(*c*) baabb (*d*) abbba

8. --babbba-a--
(*a*) bbaba (*b*) babbb
(*c*) baaab (*d*) ababb

9. k-mk-lmkkl-kk-mk
(*a*) lklm (*b*) lkmk
(*c*) lkmm (*d*) lkml

10. abc-d-bc-d-b-dd
(*a*) decdb (*b*) dadac
(*c*) cdabe (*d*) bacde

11. b-abbc-bbca-bcabb-ab
(*a*) acba (*b*) acaa
(*c*) cacc (*d*) cabc

12. aca-ac--a-ac
(*a*) babc (*b*) aaac
(*c*) cacc (*d*) caca

13. ba-cb-b-bab-?
(*a*) acbb (*b*) bcaa
(*c*) cabb (*d*) bacc

14. ab-aa-caab-aab-a
(*a*) bcbc (*b*) bbca
(*c*) cbcc (*d*) caba

15. -bbcaa-bcaa-bc-a-bca
(*a*) bacab (*b*) abbab
(*c*) abcba (*d*) bcaab

16. a-bccb-ca-cca-baab-c
(*a*) accab (*b*) abcaa
(*c*) bacaa (*d*) ababc

17. b-dabbcd-b-c-ab
(*a*) cabd (*b*) bcad
(*c*) dcba (*d*) acbd

18. a-ba-caacb-bc-
(*a*) acbb (*b*) cbab
(*c*) cbaa (*d*) cbba

19. c-baa-aca-cacab-acac-bca
(*a*) acbaa (*b*) cbaac
(*c*) bccab (*d*) bbcaa

20. -bcc-ac-aabb-ab-cc
(*a*) bacab (*b*) abaca
(*c*) aabca (*d*) bcaca

21. ab-ccca-bccc-bbcc-
(*a*) abbc (*b*) bbac
(*c*) bbca (*d*) cabc

22. -cbc-a-bcaac-ca
(*a*) aaba (*b*) caab
(*c*) bcab (*d*) aacb

23. ab-ba--ba-
(*a*) abba (*b*) baab
(*c*) baba (*d*) abab

24. yx-yx-yxz-xzy-zyxz
(*a*) zzyx (*b*) xxzy
(*c*) yyzx (*d*) yzxz

25. xxxy-y-xxy-yxx-
(*a*) xyxy (*b*) yxyx
(*c*) yyxx (*d*) xxyy

EXPLANATORY ANSWERS

1. (*d*) : The series is abbaab, abbaab.
2. (*c*) : The series is aaaaba, aaaaba.
3. (*b*) : The series is aba, aba, aba, aba.
4. (*d*) : The series is c,a,cc,aa, ccc, aaa, cccc, aaaa.
5. (*a*) : The series is cabbbb, cabbbb, cabbbb.
6. (*b*) : The series is acac, abab, acac, abab, acac.
7. (*a*) : The series is ab, ab, ab, ab, ab, ab.
8. (*b*) : The series is bababb, bababb.
9. (*d*) : The series is klmk, klmk, klmk, klmk.
10. (*b*) : The series is abcdd, abcdd, abcdd.
11. (*d*) : The series is bcab, bcab, bcab, bcab, bcab.
12. (*c*) : The series is ac, ac, ac, ac, ac, ac.
13. (*d*) : The series is babc, babc, babc.
14. (*c*) : The series is abca, abca, abca, abca.
15. (*b*) : The series is abbca, abbca, abbca, abbca.
16. (*d*) : The series is aabcc, bbcaa, ccabb, aabcc.
17. (*a*) : The series is bcdab, bcdab, bcdab.
18. (*c*) : The series is acbabca, acbabca.
19. (*a*) : The series is cabaac, acabca, cabaac, acabca.
20. (*a*) : The series is bbccaa, ccaabb, aabbcc.
21. (*b*) : The series is abbccc abbccc.
22. (*d*) : The series is acbca acbca acbca.
23. (*d*) : The series is ab ab ab ab ab.
24. (*a*) : The series is yxz yxz yxz yxz yxz yxz.
25. (*b*) : The series is xxx yyy xxx yyy xxx.

4. NUMBER SERIES

In this type of series, the set of given numbers in a series are related to one another in a particular pattern or manner. The relationship between the numbers may be (i) consecutive odd/even numbers; (ii) consecutive prime numbers; (iii) squares/cubes of some numbers with/without variation of addition or subtraction of some number; (iv) sum/product/difference of preceding numbers; (v) addition/subtraction/multiplication/division by some number; and (vi) many more combinations of the relationships given above.

EXERCISE

Directions : *In the following questions, select the number(s) from the given options for completing the given series.*

1. 7776, 1296, 216, 36, 6, ?
(*a*) 6 (*b*) 0
(*c*) 3 (*d*) 1

2. 29282, 2662, 242, 22, ?
(*a*) 1 (*b*) 2
(*c*) 0 (*d*) 11

3. 1, 2, 2, 4, 16, ?, 65536
(*a*) 276 (*b*) 64
(*c*) 256 (*d*) 198

4. 3, 5, 9, 15, 23, ?, 45
(*a*) 37 (*b*) 35
(*c*) 31 (*d*) 33

5. 7, 21, 35, 49, 63, ?
(*a*) 70 (*b*) 77
(*c*) 81 (*d*) 108

6. 10, 14, 23, 39, 64, ?, 149
(*a*) 78 (*b*) 128
(*c*) 103 (*d*) 100

7. 6, 24, 29, 116, 121, ?, 489
(*a*) 468 (*b*) 484
(*c*) 243 (*d*) 363

8. 5, 50, 45, 450, 445, ?, 4445
(*a*) 4450 (*b*) 4600
(*c*) 4550 (*d*) 4500

9. 6.25, 9, 12.25, 16, 20.25, 25, 30.25?
(*a*) 36 (*b*) 32
(*c*) 28.25 (*d*) 40.25

10. 243, 5, 81, 15, 27, 45, 9, ?
(*a*) 5 (*b*) 15
(*c*) 135 (*d*) 27

11. 2, 7, 14, 23, ?, 47
(*a*) 31 (*b*) 38
(*c*) 28 (*d*) 34

12. 0, 1, 8, 27, 64, ?
(*a*) 125 (*b*) 128
(*c*) 256 (*d*) 121

13. 37, 47, 58, ?, 79, 95
(*a*) 71 (*b*) 69
(*c*) 68 (*d*) 67

14. 4, –8, 14, –22, 32, ?
(*a*) –44 (*b*) 42
(*c*) –42 (*d*) 44

15. 6, 7, 9, 11, 15, 15, 24, 19, ?
(*a*) 32 (*b*) 34
(*c*) 36 (*d*) 37

EXPLANATORY ANSWERS

1. (*d*) : The numbers in this sequence are divided by 6 each time.

2. (*b*) : The numbers in the series are divided by 11 at each step.

3. (*c*) : The number in the series is product of all the numbers preceding it.

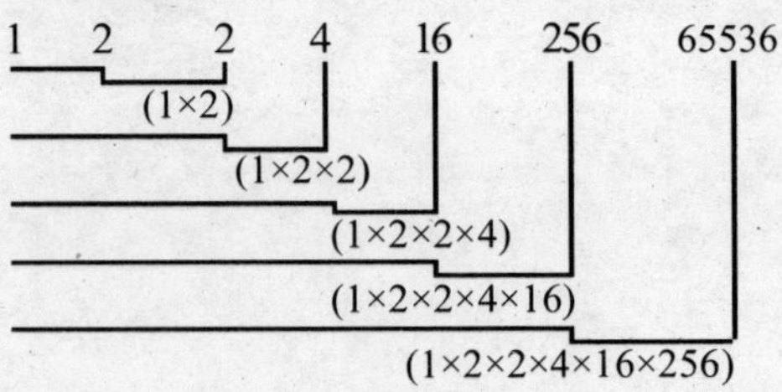

4. *(d)* : The difference between consecutive numbers increases by 2 at each step.

3 5 9 15 23 33 45

+2 +4 +6 +8 +10 +12

5. *(b)* : The series is multiplication of 7 by odd numbers starting from 3.

7 21 35 49 63 77

× 3, × 5, × 7, × 9, × 11

6. *(d)* : The number plus the square of numbers in natural order starting from 2 gives the next number in the series.

10 14 23 39 64 100 149

$+2^2$ $+3^2$ $+4^2$ $+5^2$ $+6^2$ $+7^2$

7. *(b)* : The sequence in the series is ×4, +5, which is repeated.

8. *(a)* : The sequence in the series is ×10, –5, which is repeated.

9. *(a)* : There are two alternate series :

+6 +8 +10

6.25 9 12.25 16 20.25 25 30.25 36

+7 +9 +11

Series I : 6.25, 12.25, 20.25, 30.25 (sequence is +6, +8, +10)

Series II : 9, 16, 25, 36 (sequence is +7, +9, +11)

10. *(c)* : There are two alternate series :

÷ 3 ÷ 3 ÷ 3

243 5 81 15 27 45 9 135

×3 ×3 ×3

Series I : 243, 81, 27, 9 (division by 3)

Series II : 5, 15, 45, 135 (multiplication by 3)

11. *(d)* : The difference between two consecutive numbers is increasing by 2 starting from 5.

2 7 14 23 34 47

+5 +7 +9 +11 +13

12. *(a)* : The numbers are cubes of numbers in natural order.

13. *(a)* : The sum of the digits of the number is added to the number to obtain the next number in the series.

37 47 58 71 79 95

+(3+7) +(4+7) +(5+8) +(7+1) +(7+9)

14. *(a)* : Alternate numbers are marked positive and negative, but the difference between their magnitude increases by 2 at each step.

4 – 8 14 – 22 32 – 44

4 6 8 10 12

15. *(c)* : There are two alternate series :

+3 +6 +9 +12

6 7 9 11 15 15 24 19 36

+4 +4 +4

Series I : 6, 9, 15, 24, 36 (sequence is +3, +6, +9, +12)

Series II : 7, 11, 15, 19 (addition of 4 at each step)

5. WRONG NUMBER SERIES

In this type of series, the given series may be complete but what needs to be identified is the number in the given completed series which is disturbing the sequential pattern of that series and does not fit in with the relationship shared between the other numbers.

EXERCISE

Directions : *In the given series find the number which is wrong.*

1. 5, 25, 120, 625, 3125, 15625
(*a*) 15625 (*b*) 625
(*c*) 120 (*d*) 5

2. 4, 8, 11, 22, 18, 36, 24, 50
(*a*) 8 (*b*) 22
(*c*) 36 (*d*) 24

3. 2, 4, 12, 24, 72, 142, 432
(*a*) 432 (*b*) 12
(*c*) 142 (*d*) 72

4. 2, 3, 4, 4, 6, 8, 9, 12, 16
(*a*) 3 (*b*) 9
(*c*) 6 (*d*) 12

5. 97, 91, 86, 83, 79, 77, 76, 76
(*a*) 86 (*b*) 76
(*c*) 91 (*d*) 83

6. 7, 11, 11, 9, 15, 7, 19, 5, 23, 1
(*a*) 5 (*b*) 7
(*c*) 1 (*d*) 9

7. 3, 7, 12, 28, 48, 118, 192, 448
(*a*) 12 (*b*) 118
(*c*) 28 (*d*) 7

8. 10, 100, 1100, 11000, 111000, 1210000
(*a*) 1210000 (*b*) 11000
(*c*) 100 (*d*) 111000

9. 24576, 6144, 1536, 386, 96, 24
(*a*) 386 (*b*) 6144
(*c*) 96 (*d*) 1536

10. 11, 13, 15, 17, 19, 23, 29, 31, 37
(*a*) 13 (*b*) 23
(*c*) 15 (*d*) 31

11. 36, 43, 49, 54, 60, 61, 63, 64
(*a*) 60 (*b*) 63
(*c*) 54 (*d*) 43

12. 3, 10, 41, 206, 1236, 8660
(*a*) 10 (*b*) 41
(*c*) 206 (*d*) 1236

13. 17, 25, 37, 50, 65, 82, 101
(*a*) 25 (*b*) 17
(*c*) 101 (*d*) 65

14. 12, 20, 38, 42, 56, 72
(*a*) 20 (*b*) 38
(*c*) 56 (*d*) 72

15. 5, 6, 11, 22, 42, 88, 176
(*a*) 5 (*b*) 42
(*c*) 176 (*d*) 11

EXPLANATORY ANSWERS

1. (*c*) : The numbers in the series are multiplied by 5 to get the next number.
∴ 125 should be in place of 120.

2. *(d)* : Two numbers form a pair. The first number increases by 7 for the next pair and the second number is the double of first number.

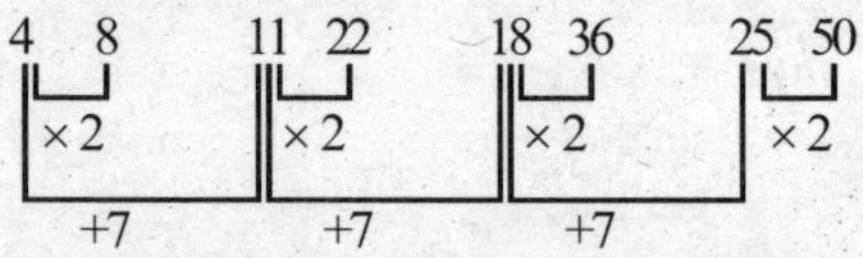

∴ 25 should be in place of 24.

3. (c) : There are two alternate series and in each series, the numbers are multiplied by 6 to get the next number.

×6 ×6 ×6

2 4 12 24 72 144 432

×6 ×6

∴ 144 should be in place of 142.

4. (b) : There are three alternate series and in each series, the numbers are multiplied by 2 to get the next number.

×2 ×2

2 3 4 4 6 8 8 12 16

×2 ×2

×2 ×2

Series I : 2, 4, 8 *Series II* : 3, 6, 12

Series III : 4, 8, 16

∴ 8 should be in place of 9.

5. (d) : The difference between the consecutive numbers in the series decreases by 1 at each step.

97 91 86 82 79 77 76 76

−6 −5 −4 −3 −2 −1 −0

∴ 82 should be in place of 83.

6. (c) : There are two alternate series :

+4 +4 +4 +4

7 11 11 9 15 7 19 5 21 3

−2 −2 −2 −2

Series I : 7, 11, 15, 19, 23 (addition of 4)

Series II : 11, 9, 7, 5, 3 (subtraction of 2)

∴ 3 should be in place of 1.

7. (b) : There are two alternate series and in each series, the numbers are multiplied by 4 to get the next number.

×4 ×4 ×4

3 7 12 28 48 112 192 448

×4 ×4 ×4

∴ 112 should be in place of 118.

8. (d) : The numbers in this series are multiplied by 10 and 11 alternately is, *i.e.,* ×10, ×11.

10 100 1100 11000 121000 1210000

×10 ×11 ×10 ×11 ×10

∴ 121000 should be in place of 111000.

9. (a) : The numbers in this series are divided by 4 to get the next number.

24576 6144 1536 384 96 24

÷4 ÷4 ÷4 ÷4 ÷4

∴ 384 should be in place of 386.

10. (c) : The series comprises of prime numbers in increasing order. Only 15 is an exception.

11. (a) : The difference between two consecutive numbers is decreasing by 1 at each step.

36 43 49 54 58 61 63 64

+7 +6 +5 +4 +3 +2 +1

∴ 58 should be in place of 60.

12. (d) : The sequence followed in this series is :

$3 \times 3 + 1 = 10$, $10 \times 4 + 1 = 41$

$41 \times 5 + 1 = 206$, $206 \times 6 + 1 = 1237$; and

$1237 \times 7 + 1 = 8660$

∴ 1237 should be in place of 1236.

13. (a) : The numbers in the series are 1 plus the squares of numbers in natural order starting from 4.

17 26 37 50 65 82 101

↓ ↓ ↓ ↓ ↓ ↓ ↓

$4^2 + 1$ $5^2 + 1$ $6^2 + 1$ $7^2 + 1$ $8^2 + 1$ $9^2 + 1$ $10^2 + 1$

∴ 26 should be in place of 25.

14. (b) : The sequence followed in this series is :

$3 \times 4 = 12$, $4 \times 5 = 20$, $5 \times 6 = 30$,

$6 \times 7 = 42$, $7 \times 8 = 56$, $8 \times 9 = 72$

∴ 30 should be in place of 38.

15. (b) : The numbers in the series are the sum of all the numbers preceding them.

5 6 11 22 44 88 176

$(5+6)$

$(5+6+11)$

$(5+6+11+22)$

$(5+6+11+22+44)$

$(5+6+11+22+44+88)$

∴ 44 should be in place of 42.

6. WORD ANALOGY

In Analogy Tests, the relationship between two given words is established and then applied to the other words. The type of relationship may vary, so while attempting such questions the first step is to identify the type of relationship, which can be any one of the following.

EXERCISE

Directions : *In the questions given below one term is missing. Based on the relationship of the two given words find the missing term from the given options.*

1. HUNGER : FOOD : : THIRST : ?
(*a*) Water (*b*) Drink
(*c*) Tea (*d*) Coffee

2. HUNTER : GUN : : WRITER : ?
(*a*) Book (*b*) Pen
(*c*) Poem (*d*) Page

3. WOOL : SHEEP : : SILK : ?
(*a*) Saree (*b*) String
(*c*) Silkworm (*d*) Moth

4. FOOD : STOMACH : : FUEL : ?
(*a*) Engine (*b*) Automobile
(*c*) Rail (*d*) Aeroplane

5. WATER : SAND : : OCEAN : ?
(*a*) Island (*b*) River
(*c*) Desert (*d*) Waves

6. ADULT : BABY : : FLOWER : ?
(*a*) Seed (*b*) Bud
(*c*) Fruit (*d*) Butterfly

7. WRITER : READER : : PRODUCER : ?
(*a*) Creator (*b*) Contractor
(*c*) Creature (*d*) Consumer

8. ENTRANCE : EXIT : : LOYALTY : ?
(*a*) Treachery (*b*) Patriotism
(*c*) Fidelity (*d*) Reward

9. MOTHER : MATERNAL : : FATHER : ?
(*a*) Eternal (*b*) Detrimental
(*c*) Paternal (*d*) Formidable

10. PEARL : NECKLACE : : FLOWER : ?
(*a*) Plant (*b*) Garden
(*c*) Petal (*d*) Bouquet

11. ALPHABET : WORD : : WORD : ?
(*a*) Sound (*b*) Music
(*c*) Sentence (*d*) Dictionary

12. LIFE : DEATH : : HOPE : ?
(*a*) Cry (*b*) Pain
(*c*) Despair (*d*) Sad

13. GOOD : BAD : : VIRTUE : ?
(*a*) Blame (*b*) Sin
(*c*) Despair (*d*) Vice

14. BIRD : FLY : : SNAKE : ?
(*a*) Timid (*b*) Clatter
(*c*) Crawl (*d*) Hole

15. CAT : MOUSE : : BIRD : ?
(*a*) Cage (*b*) Trap
(*c*) Eagle (*d*) Worm

16. STATE : EXILE
(*a*) Police : Arrest
(*b*) Judge : Convict
(*c*) Constitution : Amendment
(*d*) Church : Excommunicate

17. CAPRICIOUSNESS : RELIABILITY
(*a*) Extemporaneous : Predictability
(*b*) Unreliable : Inhuman
(*c*) Tenacious : Practicality
(*d*) Arbitrary : Whimsical

18. LOATH : COERCION
(*a*) Detest : Caressing
(*b*) Irritate : Caressing
(*c*) Irate : Antagonism
(*d*) Reluctant : Persuasion

19. SCALES : FISH
(*a*) Lady : Dress (*b*) Tree : Leaves
(*c*) Bird : Feather (*d*) Skin : Man

20. TREE : SAPLING
(*a*) Hut : Mansion
(*b*) Giant : Dwarf
(*c*) Horse : Foal
(*d*) Ant : Elephant

21. CHALK : BLACKBOARD
(*a*) Door : Handle
(*b*) Table : Chair
(*c*) Ink : Paper
(*d*) Type : Paint

22. PRIMEVAL : MEDIEVAL
(*a*) Dinosaur : Dragon
(*b*) Gorilla : Soldier
(*c*) Evolution : Revelation
(*d*) Thorn : Rose

23. TRILOGY : NOVEL
(*a*) Rice : Husk
(*b*) Milk : Cream
(*c*) Fabric : Weaving
(*d*) Serial : Episode

24. PEDANT : ERUDITION
(*a*) Prude : Modesty
(*b*) Blunt : Politician
(*c*) Diplomats : Tactless
(*d*) Enemy : Friendly

25. FURY : IRE
(*a*) Convulsion : Spasm
(*b*) Amusement : Happiness
(*c*) Joke : Laugh
(*d*) Dispassion : Emotion

EXPLANATORY ANSWERS

1. *(a)* : Hunger is satiated by food, thirst by water.

2. *(b)* : Weapon of a hunter is a gun, weapon of a writer is a pen.

3. *(c)* : Wool is obtained from sheep, silk is obtained from silkworm.

4. *(a)* : Food is consumed in stomach, fuel is consumed in engine.

5. *(c)* : The related words are near opposites.

6. *(b)* : The youngone of an adult is a baby and that of a flower is a bud.

7. *(d)* : A writer aims to please the readers by his writings, a producer aims to please the consumers by his products.

8. *(a)* : The related words are opposites.

9. *(c)* : Relations on the mother's side are maternal and on the father's side paternal.

10. *(d)* : Many pearls make a necklace, many flowers make a bouquet.

11. *(c)* : More than one alphabet make a word, more than one word make a sentence.

12. *(c)* : The related words are opposites.

13. *(d)* : The related words are opposites.

14. *(c)* : Birds fly, snakes crawl.

15. *(d)* : Cat chases the mouse, bird chases the worm.

16. *(d)* : Punishment of leaving the State is exile, punishment of leaving the Church is excommunication.

17. *(c)* : The related words are antonyms.

18. *(d)* : Loathing is the result of constant coersion, reluctance is the result of constant persuasion.

19. *(d)* : Covering of the fish is scales, covering of man is skin.

20. *(c)* : Young tree is a sapling, young horse is a foal.

21. *(c)* : Chalk is used to write on blackboard, ink is used to write on paper.

22. *(a)* : The related words represent almost the same time period and answer option represents almost the same sized creatures.

23. *(d)* : Trilogy is section of a novel, episode is a section of a serial.

24. *(a)* : The related words are synonyms.

25. *(b)* : Fury causes ire, amusement causes happiness.

7. NUMBER ANALOGY

In number analogy also, the relationship between the given numbers is detected and then applied to the second part to find the missing numbers. This relationship between the numbers can be based on any of the following patterns : *(i)* numbers can be odd/even/prime numbers; *(ii)* numbers can be multiples of one number; *(iii)* numbers can be squares/cubes of different numbers; *(iv)* some numbers can be added to/subtracted from/multiplied to/divided into the first number to get the second number; *(v)* the second number can be the sum/product/difference of the digits of first number; and *(vi)* combinations of any mathematical calculations given above can apply to the relationship between the two given numbers.

EXERCISE

Directions : *In the following questions, select the number from the given options which follows the same relationship as shared between the first two numbers.*

1. 1 : 11 : : 2 : ?
(*a*) 20 (*b*) 22
(*c*) 24 (*d*) 44

2. $\frac{1}{7} : \frac{1}{14} :: \frac{1}{9} : ?$
(*a*) $\frac{1}{88}$ (*b*) $\frac{1}{80}$
(*c*) $\frac{1}{81}$ (*d*) $\frac{1}{18}$

3. 0.16 : 0.0016 : : 1.02 : ?
(*a*) 10.20 (*b*) 0.102
(*c*) 0.0102 (*d*) 1.020

4. 663 : 884 : : 221 : ?
(*a*) 332 (*b*) 554
(*c*) 773 (*d*) 442

5. 16 : 0.16 : : ?
(*a*) 2 : 0.02 (*b*) 7 : 0.007
(*c*) 1.3 : 0.13 (*d*) 0.01 : 0.001

6. $3 : \frac{1}{3} :: ?$
(*a*) 6 : 12 (*b*) 5 : 2/15
(*c*) 8 : 1/8 (*d*) 9 : 27

7. 65 : 13 : : 180 : ?
(*a*) 93 (*b*) 36
(*c*) 133 (*d*) 102

8. 125 : 27 : : 343 : ?
(*a*) 729 (*b*) 64
(*c*) 216 (*d*) 512

9. 357 : 73 : : ?
(*a*) 429 : 94
(*b*) 201 : 21
(*c*) 138 : 38
(*d*) 93 : 39

10. 731 : 902 : : 655 : ?
(*a*) 646 (*b*) 800
(*c*) 793 (*d*) 556

11. 162 : 9 : : 310 : ?
(*a*) 33 (*b*) 27
(*c*) 16 (*d*) 4

12. 13 : 17 : : 15 : ?
(*a*) 19 (*b*) 11
(*c*) 21 (*d*) 16

13. 225 : 15 : : 256 : ?
(*a*) 26 (*b*) 16
(*c*) 20 (*d*) 28

14. 46 : 48 : : 54 : ?
(*a*) 59 (*b*) 40
(*c*) 67 (*d*) 62

15. 33 : 36 : : 21 : ?
(*a*) 9 (*b*) 18
(*c*) 25 (*d*) 32

EXPLANATORY ANSWERS

1. (b) : The first number is repeated to obtain the second number.

2. (d) : The first fraction is multiplied by half to obtain the second fraction.

$$\frac{1}{7} : \frac{1}{14} :: \frac{1}{9} : \frac{1}{18}$$

$\times \frac{1}{2}$; $\times \frac{1}{2}$

3. (c) : The decimals are divided by 100.

0.16 : 0.0016 :: 1.02 : 0.0102

$\div 100$; $\div 100$

4. (d) : The digits at tens and hundreds place is same but the digit at the units place is half the other identical digits.

663 : 884 :: 221 : 442

5. (a) : Of the two related numbers, the second number is the result of first number divided by 100.

16 : 0.16 :: 2 : 0.02

$\div 100$; $\div 100$

6. (c) : Of the two related numbers, the second number is the part fraction of the first number, *i.e.* 3 is related to one-third $\left(\frac{1}{3}\right)$.

Similarly, 8 will be related to one-eighth $\left(\frac{1}{8}\right)$.

7. (b) : The first number is divided by 5 to get the second number.

65 : 13 :: 180 : 36

$\div 5$; $\div 5$

8. (a) : The numbers are cubes of different odd numbers.

125 : 27 :: 343 : 729

5^3 ; 3^3 ; 7^3 ; 9^3

9. (a) : The central digit of the first number is left out and the corner digits written in reverse order to get the second number.

357 : 73 :: 429 : 94

10. (a) : The sum of the digits of both the numbers is same.

$731 : 902 \rightarrow 7 + 3 + 1$
$= 9 + 0 + 2$ *i.e.* $11 = 11$

$655 : 646 \rightarrow 6 + 5 + 5$
$= 6 + 4 + 6$ *i.e.* $16 = 16$

11. (d) : The sum of the digits of the first number is the second number.

162 : 9 :: 310 : 4

$1 + 6 + 2$; $3 + 1 + 0$

12. (a) : First number plus 4 gives the second number.

13 : 17 :: 15 : 19

$+4$; $+4$

13. (b) : The root of first number is the second number.

225 : 15 :: 256 : 16

$\sqrt{225}$; $\sqrt{256}$

14. (b) : The product of the digits of first number is multiplied by 2 to get the second number.

46 : 48 :: 54 : 40

$(4 \times 6)\, 2$; $(5 \times 4)\, 2$

15. (a) : The square of the sum of the digits of the first number is the second number.

33 : 36 :: 21 : 9

$(3 + 3)^2$; $(2 + 1)^2$

8. ODD ONE OUT

In this type of classification, four words are given out of which three are almost same in matter or meaning and only one word is different from the common three. One has to find out the word which is different from the rest.

EXERCISE

Directions : *In each of the following questions, three words are alike in some manner. Spot the odd one out.*

1. (*a*) Green (*b*) Red (*c*) Colour (*d*) Orange

2. (*a*) Stable (*b*) Hole (*c*) Canoe (*d*) Sty

3. (*a*) Nose (*b*) Eyes (*c*) Skin (*d*) Teeth

4. (*a*) Venus (*b*) Moon (*c*) Pluto (*d*) Mars

5. (*a*) Happy (*b*) Gloomy (*c*) Lively (*d*) Cheerful

Directions : *Three of the following four in each question are alike in a certain way and so form a group. Select the group of letters that does not belong to that group.*

6. (*a*) ACE (*b*) LOR (*c*) GIK (*d*) VXZ

7. (*a*) TSR (*b*) LKJ (*c*) PQO (*d*) HGF

8. (*a*) EF LM (*b*) KJ SR (*c*) XW HG (*d*) ED YX

9. (*a*) JOPK (*b*) BOPC (*c*) QOPR (*d*) TOPS

10. (*a*) DfH (*b*) MoQ (*c*) UwY (*d*) InO

Directions : *In each of the following questions, there are four options. Three numbers, in these options, are alike in certain manner. Only one number does not fit in. Choose the one which is different from the rest.*

11. (*a*) 1948 (*b*) 2401 (*c*) 966 (*d*) 1449

12. (*a*) 182 (*b*) 169 (*c*) 130 (*d*) 158

13. (*a*) 129 (*b*) 130 (*c*) 131 (*d*) 132

14. (*a*) 3215 (*b*) 9309 (*c*) 4721 (*d*) 2850

15. (*a*) 1776 (*b*) 2364 (*c*) 1976 (*d*) 3776

Directions : *In the following questions select the pair which is different from the other three.*

16. (*a*) Chair - Furniture
(*b*) Shirt - Garment
(*c*) Necklace - Jewellery
(*d*) Bogie - Engine

17. (*a*) Crayon - Paper
(*b*) Pencil - Lead
(*c*) Pen - Ink
(*d*) Brush - Paint

18. (*a*) War - Peace
(*b*) Real - Natural
(*c*) Premiere - First
(*d*) Wrath - Anger

19. (*a*) Finger - Thimble
(*b*) Head - Cap
(*c*) Waist - Tiara
(*d*) Foot - Shoe

20. (*a*) Day - Night
(*b*) Clever - Foolish
(*c*) Clear - Blurred
(*d*) Arrive - Come

Directions : *In the following questions, which of the following pair of letters is different from the other three?*

21. (*a*) FGH - HIJ (*b*) PQR - RST (*c*) MNO - OPQ (*d*) CDE - DEF

22. (*a*) JuM - jUm (*b*) iLo - Ilo (*c*) PSa - psA (*d*) ZeX - zEx

23. (*a*) NQT - JMP (*b*) CFI - RUX (*c*) ADG - FGH (*d*) SVY - ORU

24. (*a*) DXD - XDX (*b*) KUK - UKU (*c*) FHF - EHE (*d*) RSR - SRS

25. (*a*) AYT - BZU (*b*) FNG - EMF (*c*) RWO - QVN (*d*) HJD - GIC

EXPLANATORY ANSWERS

1. *(c)* : All others are types of colour.

2. *(c)* : Canoe is a boat. Others are resting places of birds/animals.

3. *(d)* : All others are sense organs.

4. *(b)* : All others are planets.

5. *(b)* : All others are expressions of joy.

6. *(b)* : The sequence in each group is +2. Only option (*b*) has sequence in +3, *i.e.,*

ABCDE (+2 +2) LMNOPQR (+3 +3)
GHIJK (+2 +2) VWXYZ (+2 +2)

7. *(c)* : The sequence of alphabet in each group is in reverse order. Only option (*c*) has sequence in disturbed order.

8. *(a)* : Two consecutive alphabet in each group are in reverse sequence (–1), *i.e.,*

KJ SR; XW HG; ED YX
–1 –1 –1 –1 –1 –1

Only in option (*a*) the sequence is in natural order (+1), *i.e.,*

E F (+1) L M (+1)

9. *(d)* : In each group, letters 'OP' are common. The two corner alphabet are in natural order (+1); *i.e.,*

JOPK (+1) ; BOPC (+1) ; QOPR (+1)

Only in option (*d*) they are in reverse order (–1); *i.e.,*

TOPS (–1)

10. *(d)* : In other groups, only the alphabet in the centre is of lower case. In this option letter 'L' on the left is also in lower case.

11. *(a)* : Other numbers are divisible by 7.

12. *(d)* : Other numbers are multiples of 13.

13. *(c)* : 131 is a prime number.

14. *(b)* : In other numbers, no digit is repeated.

15. *(b)* : In other numbers, the last two digits are same.

16. *(d)* : Bogie is a part of train which is a type of conveyance. Chair, Shirt and Necklace are types of furniture, garment and jewellery respectively.

17. *(a)* : The medium used for writing with pencil is lead, with pen it is ink and with brush, it is paint. With crayon it should be wax.

18. *(a)* : The pair of words are opposite. Other pairs are synonyms.

19. *(c)* : Tiara is worn on the head.

20. *(d)* : Other words are opposite to each other.

21. *(d)* : In all other groups, the letters are in natural series and the last letter of first part is the first letter of the second part.

22. *(b)* : In all other groups, only the vowel is in lower case in the first part and in second part the case is reversed.

23. *(c)* : In all other groups, the letters jump two letters in between them.

24. *(c)* : In all other groups, the single letter in first part is repeated in the second and vice versa.

25. *(a)* : In all other groups, the letters in the first part are one step forward than the corresponding letters in the second part.

9. CODING AND DECODING

Coding is a secretive language which is used to change the representation of the actual term/word/value. This coded language can be framed by *(i)* moving the letters one or more steps forward or backward; *(ii)* substituting numbers for letters and vice–versa; *(iii)* writing the letters of the given word in reverse order in part or in whole; and *(iv)* replacing the letters in their natural series by the same positioned letters in their reverse series.

There is variety in ways of coding. Coding language is not only for words and numbers but also for hiding a group of words, statements or even sentences. This form of coding pattern may appear to be confusing but after solving only a few questions it is very easy to understand. Questions based on this coding pattern require no moving of steps or straining efforts of calculations, but only quick tallying or comparing ability. The codes can be letters or numbers.

EXERCISE

Directions : *In the following questions select the right option which indicates the correct code for the word or letter given in the question.*

1. If MUSK is coded as 146816, then ZERO will be coded as :

(*a*) 113811 (*b*) 122912
(*c*) 15915 (*d*) 2651815

2. If BAD is coded as 7, HIS as 9, LOW will be coded as :

(*a*) 50 (*b*) 8
(*c*) 23 (*d*) 5

3. In a certain code LIBERATE is written as 56403170, TRIBAL will be written in the same code as :

(*a*) 734615 (*b*) 736415
(*c*) 136475 (*d*) 034615

4. In certain military code, SYSTEM is written as SYSMET, and NEARER as AENRER, what will be the code for FRACTION?

(*a*) CRAFNOIT (*b*) FRCAITNO
(*c*) CARFNOIT (*d*) FRACNOIT

5. If CRUDE is written as BSTED, then MOIST will be coded as :

(*a*) NNJRU (*b*) LNHRS
(*c*) NPJTU (*d*) LPHTS

6. In a certain code ALPACA is written as ACAPLA. How will ANIMAL be written in that code?

(*a*) LAMINA (*b*) ALAMIN
(*c*) LAMNIA (*d*) AAMLIN

7. In a certain code FINGER is written as DGLECP. What will be the code for KIDNEY?

(*a*) IGBLCW (*b*) IGCLBW
(*c*) IBCGLE (*d*) IGBKCV

8. In a certain code QUESTION is written as NXBVQLLQ. How will REPLY be coded?

(*a*) YHMOV (*b*) OBMVI
(*c*) VHSOB (*d*) OHMOV

9. If in a certain code SKEW is coded as PNCY, then what will JXQV will stand for?

(*a*) MUTS (*b*) MUST
(*c*) MTSU (*d*) STUM

10. In a certain code LONDON is written as MPOEPO. What will IVOHSZ mean in the same code?

(*a*) HUNGRY (*b*) HUNDRY
(*c*) GRUNHY (*d*) HONDUS

11. In a certain code language 8514 is a code for HEAD, 3945 for RIDE and 057 for BEG. What will be the code for GRADE?

(*a*) 71345 (*b*) 73415
(*c*) 74135 (*d*) 73145

12. If MOTHERLAND is coded as 9501623748, how will DREAM be coded?

(*a*) 82697 (*b*) 86297
(*c*) 82769 (*d*) 82679

13. If OATH is coded in a certain language as TEYL, then how will WORD be coded?

(*a*) BWRH (*b*) HRWB
(*c*) BSWH (*d*) CSXI

14. If FINANCE is coded as GKQESIL, then how will BANK be coded in the same manner?

(*a*) CBOL (*b*) CDRP
(*c*) CCQO (*d*) CCPN

15. PLANNING is coded in a certain language as UFFHSCSA. How will AUTHORITY be coded in the same language?

(*a*) FOYBTLNND
(*b*) FYOTBNNLT
(*c*) FBOYTLNTN
(*d*) FBOYTNLTN

EXPLANATORY ANSWERS

1. *(b)* : The coded number signifies the position of the alphabet in its reverse order of the alphabetical series (ZYXW...)

M U S K → MUSK
↓ ↓ ↓ ↓
14th 6th 8th 16th → 146816

Similarly,

Z E R O → ZERO
↓ ↓ ↓ ↓
1st 22nd 9th 12th → 122912

2. *(d)* : The coded number is the sum of number digits signifying the position of the alphabet in the natural order.

B A D
↓ ↓ ↓
2nd 1st 4th *i.e.,* 2 + 1 + 4 = 7

Similarly,

H I S
↓ ↓ ↓
8th 9th 19th *i.e.,* 8 + 9 + 19 = 36
further, 3 + 6 = 9

Also,

L O W
↓ ↓ ↓
12th 15th 23rd *i.e.,* 12 + 15 + 23 = 50
further, 5 + 0 = 0

3. *(b)* : The letters of the word TRIBAL are picked from LIBERATE. So will be the coded numbers.

L I B E R A T E → given word
5 6 4 0 3 1 7 0 → codes

Similarly,

T R I B A L → word to be coded
7 3 6 4 1 5 → answer codes

4. *(c)* : The word is divided into two equal parts and the letters of each part are written in reverse order.

SYS TEM SYS MET NEA RER AEN RER

Similarly,

FRAC TION CARF NOIT

5. *(d)* : The code is formed by moving the letters one step backwards and one step forward alternately.

CRUDE BSTED
−1 +1 −1 +1 −1

Similarly,

MOIST LPHTS
−1 +1 −1 +1 −1

6. *(a)* : The letters of the word are written backwards.

ALPACA ACAPLA

Similarly,

7. *(a)* : The word is coded by moving the letters two steps backwards.

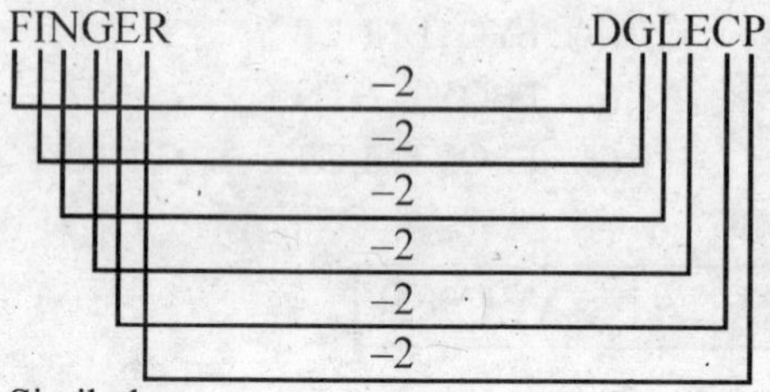

Similarly,

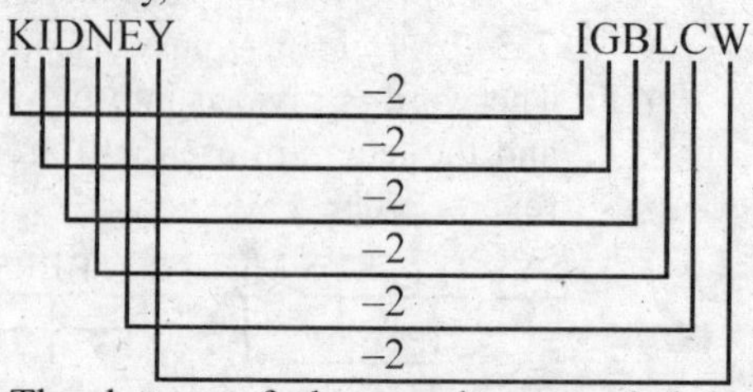

8. *(d)* : The letters of the word are coded by moving three steps backward and three steps forward alternately.

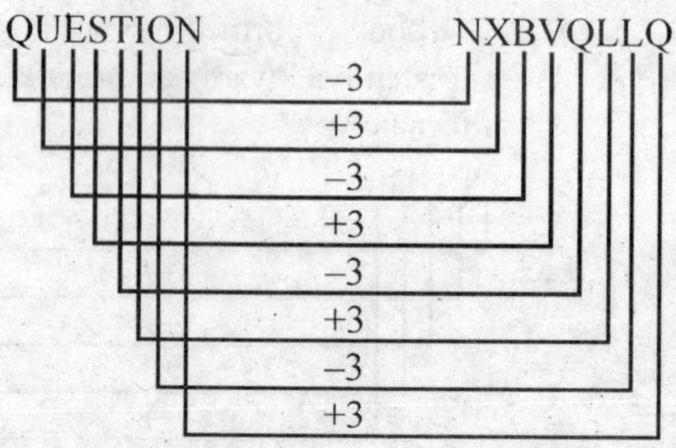

Similarly,

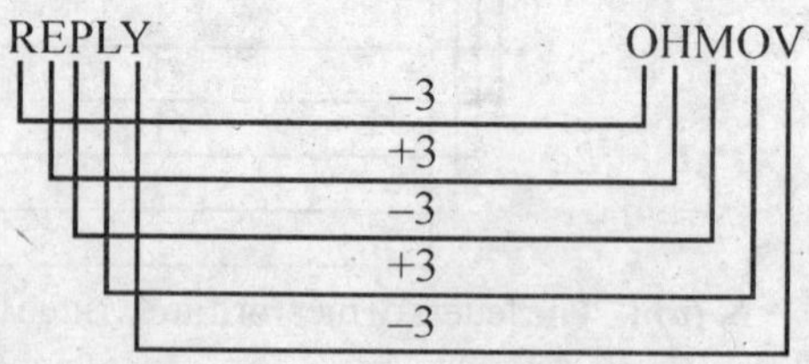

9. *(b)* : The letters are decoded by moving the letters +3, –3, +2 and –2 steps respectively.

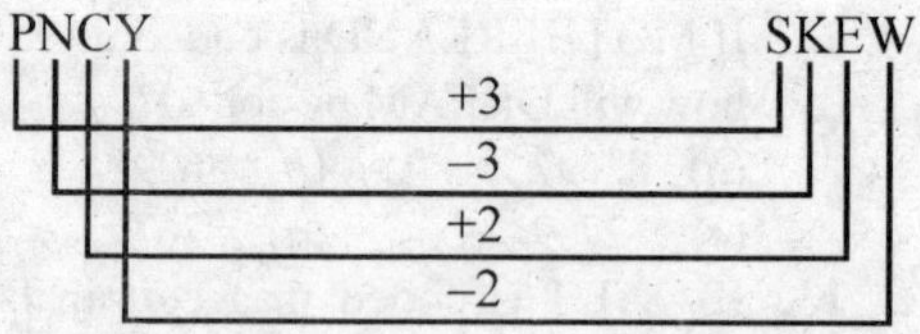

Similarly,

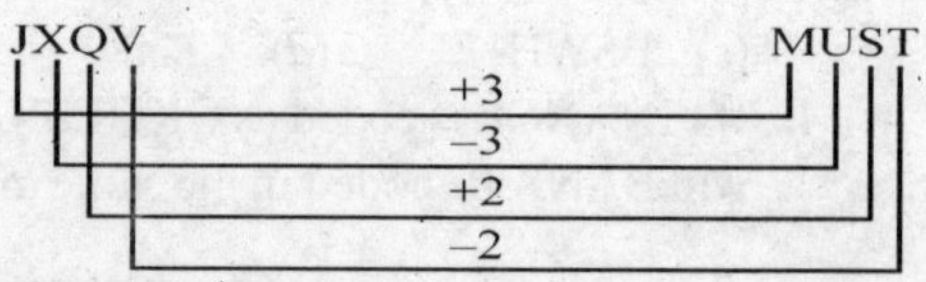

10. *(a)* : The letters of the coded word are moved one step backward.

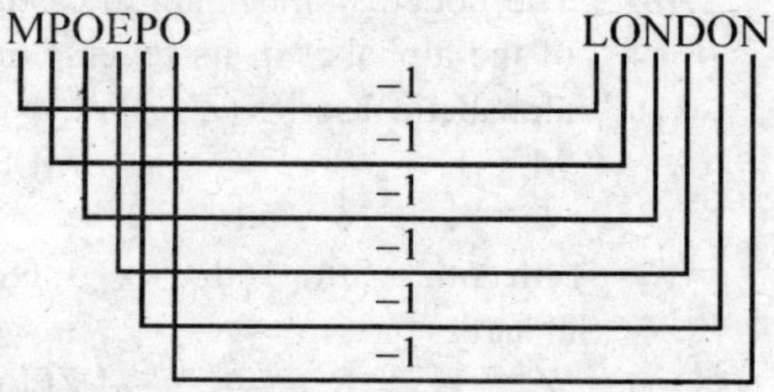

Similarly,

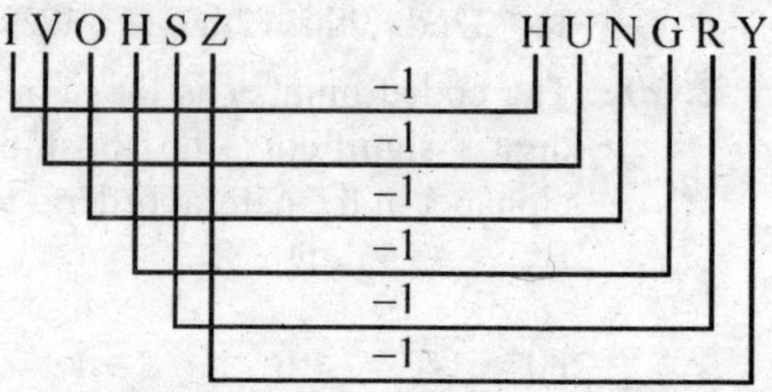

11. *(d)* : The word GRADE is framed by letters in the given words. So, in order to find the code for GRADE select the respective number codes.

H E A D R I D E B E G → letters
8 5 1 4 3 9 4 5 0 5 7 → codes

So,

G R A D E →letters
7 3 1 4 5 →answer codes

12. *(d)* : The letters of the word are coded by numbers. So to find the code for DREAM select the respective numbers.

M O T H E R L A N D → letters
9 5 0 1 6 2 3 7 4 8 → codes

So, D R E A M → letters
8 2 6 7 9 → answer codes

13. *(c)* : The letters are coded by moving five and four steps forward alternately.

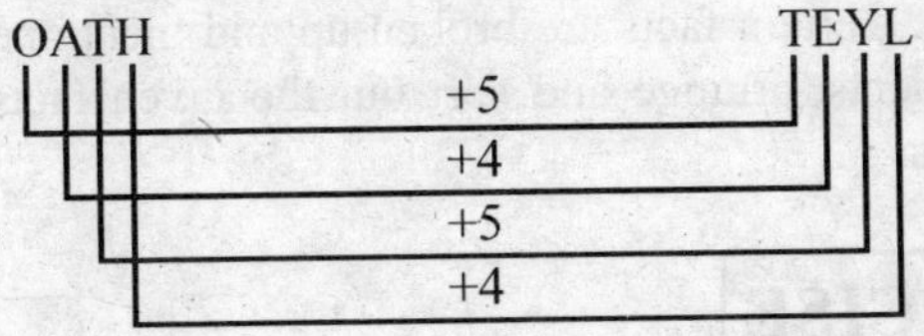

Similarly,

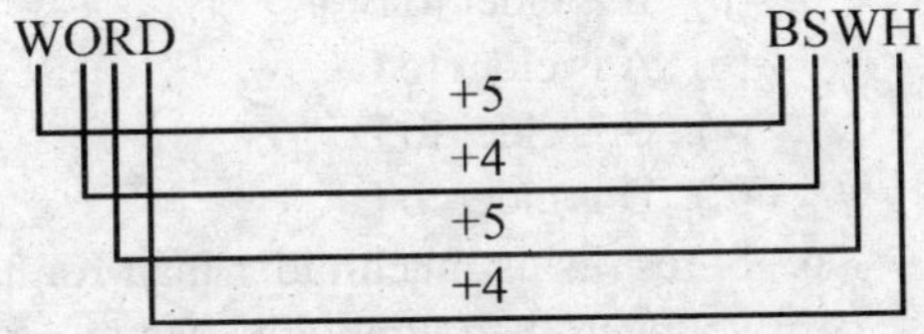

14. *(c)* : The letters of the word are coded by moving one step ahead and increasing the difference by one.

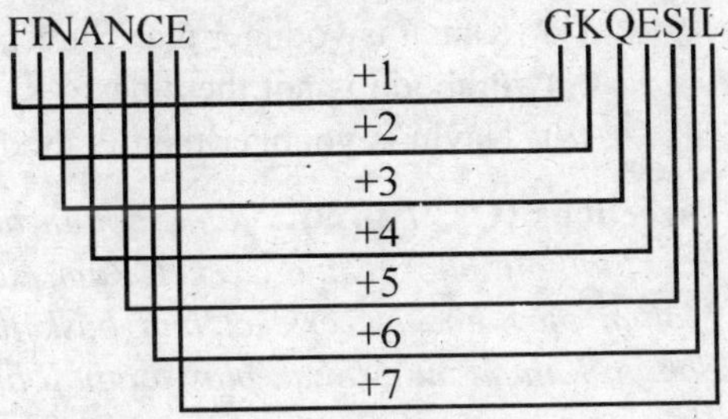

Similarly,

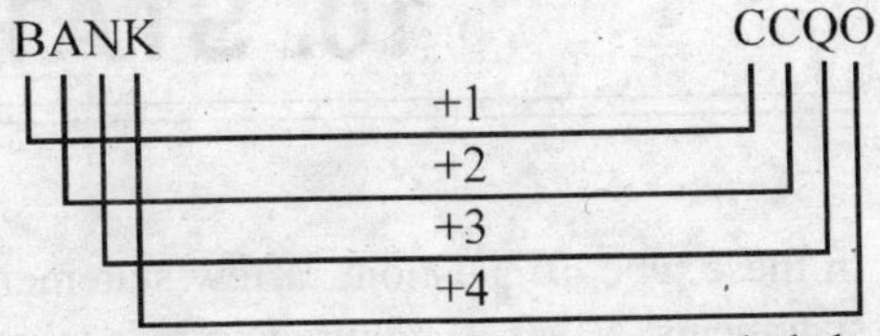

15. *(a)* : The letters of the word are coded by moving five steps forward and six steps backward alternately.

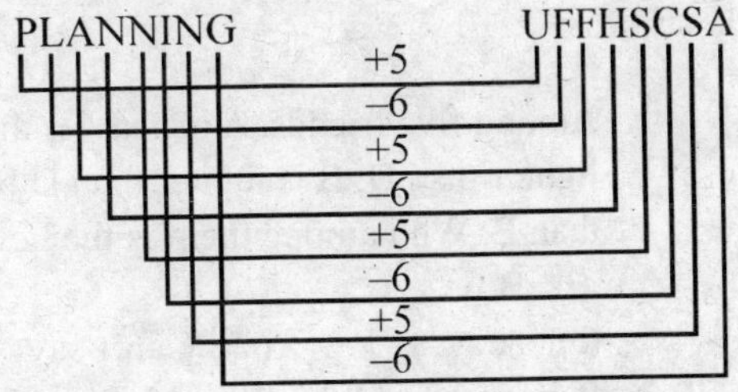

Similarly,

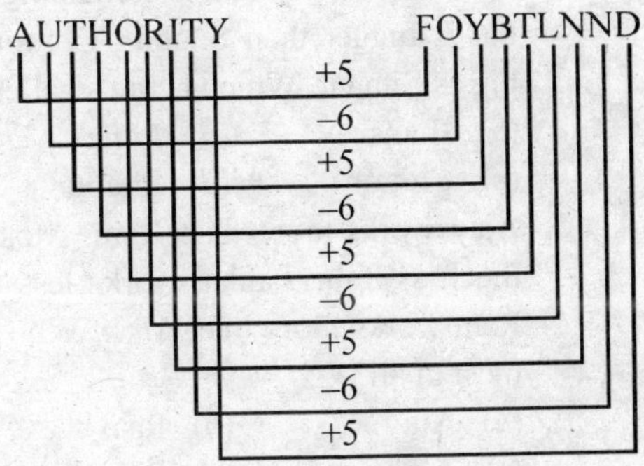

10. STATEMENT ANALYSIS

In these type of questions, a few statements are given. Certain facts are broken up and mentioned in these statements. What is required is to analyse the statements, arrange and sort out the given facts and then answer the questions related to the given statements.

EXERCISE

1. Among five friends, A is heavier than B; C is lighter than D; B is lighter than D but heavier than E. Who among them is the heaviest?
(*a*) B (*b*) C
(*c*) A (*d*) Can't say

2. Pune is bigger than Jhansi, Sitapur is bigger than Chittor. Raigarh is not as big as Jhansi, but is bigger than Sitapur. Chittor is not as big as Sitapur. Which is the smallest?
(*a*) Jhansi (*b*) Pune
(*c*) Chittor (*d*) Sitapur

3. Ajay works more than Ram. Alok works as much as Raju. Pankaj works less than Alok. Ram works more than Alok. Who works the most of all?
(*a*) Ajay (*b*) Ram
(*c*) Alok (*d*) Raju

4. Among five friends P, Q, R, S and T, who is the youngest? To arrive at the answer which of the following information given in the statements (A) and (B) is sufficient?
(A) R is younger than P and T.
(B) S is younger than Q.
(*a*) Only A alone is sufficient
(*b*) Either A or B is sufficient
(*c*) Both A and B together are needed
(*d*) Both A and B together are not sufficient

5. A is elder to B while C and D are elder to E who lies between A and B. If C be elder to B, which one of the following statements is necessarily true?
(*a*) E is elder to B
(*b*) A is elder to C
(*c*) C is elder to D
(*d*) D is elder to C

6. Suresh is as much older than Kamal as he is younger than Prabodh. Navin is as old as Kamal. Which of the following statements is wrong?
(*a*) Suresh is older than Navin
(*b*) Kamal is younger than Suresh
(*c*) Prabodh is not the oldest
(*d*) Navin is younger than Prabodh

Directions (Qs. 7 to 9) : *Ram, Sohan and Mohan play football, hockey and cricket. Ram, Ramesh and Mohan play hockey, cricket and basketball. Ram, Sohan, Rahim and Mohan play football and cricket. Now answer the following questions based on the above statements :*

7. Which game is played by all the boys?
(*a*) Football (*b*) Hockey
(*c*) Cricket (*d*) Basketball

8. Which two boys play all the games?
(*a*) Ram, Sohan (*b*) Ram, Ramesh
(*c*) Sohan, Mohan (*d*) Ram, Mohan

9. Who does not play football?
(*a*) Ramesh (*b*) Sohan
(*c*) Rahim (*d*) Mohan

Directions (Qs. 10 to 12) : *Read the following directions and answer the questions given below :*

There are five persons in a group. Out of these two are men. Only three persons know swimming, of which one is a man. There is a couple, of which the husband knows swimming. A is the younger sister of D and B is the husband of E. C is a swimming champion.

10. Who is the other man in the group?
(*a*) C (*b*) B
(*c*) A (*d*) D

11. The two women who know how to swim are:
(*a*) A and C (*b*) C and D
(*c*) D and E (*d*) A and E

12. The two persons who do not know how to swim are :
(*a*) B and D (*b*) D and E
(*c*) A and E (*d*) A and D

Directions (Qs. 13 to 15) : *Read the following statements and answer the questions given below :*

Rajat, Sushil and Nagesh play football, hockey and cricket. Rajat, Ramu and Nagesh play hockey, cricket and basketball. Rajat, Sushil, Mayank and Nagesh play football and cricket.

13. Which game is played by all the boys?
(*a*) Hockey (*b*) Basketball
(*c*) Football (*d*) Cricket

14. Who does not play football?
(*a*) Rajat (*b*) Nagesh
(*c*) Sushil (*d*) Ramu

15. Which of the following two boys play all the games?
(*a*) Nagesh, Rajat (*b*) Mayank, Ramu
(*c*) Ramu, Nagesh (*d*) Sushil, Mayank

EXPLANATORY ANSWERS

1. (*d*) : The five friends in descending order of weight are : A/D, B/C, E or A/D, B, C/E. Either A or D is the heavìest.

2. (*c*) : The order of cities in descending order of size is : Pune, Jhansi, Raigarh, Sitapur, Chittor.

3. (*a*) : On the basis of doing work, the descending order will be : Ajay, Ram, Alok/Raju, Pankaj.

4. (*d*) : Statements are not inter-related.

5. (*a*) : The order in descending seniority will be : A/C/D, E, B.

6. (*c*) : On the basis of age the descending order will be : Prabodh, Suresh, Kamal/Navin.

Chart for Answers 7 to 9

Boy	*Games Played*
Ram	Football, Hocky, Cricket, Basketball
Sohan	Football, Hockey, Cricket
Mohan	Football, Hockey, Cricket, Basketball
Ramesh	Hockey, Cricket, Basketball
Rahim	Football, Cricket.

7. (*c*) **8. (*d*)** **9. (*a*)**

For Answers 10 to 12 the information chart will be :

A. Woman ((younger sister of D); knows swimming.
B. Man (husband of E); knows swimming
C. Woman; Swimming champion
D. Man (brother of A)
E. Woman (wife of B)

From the couple B & E, B (husband) knows swimming. C is a swimming champion. Three persons know how to swim of which only B is a man. So, the two women who know how to swim are C and A (the younger sister of D). There are two men in the group of five. One is B and the other will be D.

10. (*d*) **11. (*a*)** **12. (*b*)**

Chart for Answers 13 to 15

Boy	*Games Played*
Rajat	— Football, Hockey, Cricket, Basketball
Sushil	— Football, Hockey, Cricket, Basketball
Nagesh	— Football, Hockey, Cricket, Basketball
Ramu	— Hockey, Cricket, Basketball
Mayank	— Football, Cricket

13. (*d*) **14. (*d*)** **15. (*a*)**

11. PLACE ARRANGEMENT

Place arrangement generally refers to the positioning of persons or objects in a manner indicated by set of information given. One has to understand the order of placement and then attempt questions following the given information.

EXERCISE

Directions : *In the following questions, understand the arrangement pattern and then select the right answer from the given options :*

1. Five boys are sitting in a row. Raghu is not adjacent to Shyam or Amit. Ajay is not adjacent to Shyam. Raghu is adjacent to Mayank. If Mayank is at the middle in the row, then Ajay is adjacent to whom out of the following?

(*a*) Amit (*b*) Raghu
(*c*) Mayank (*d*) Shyam

2. Mini is to the right of Rajni but to the left of Ananta. Saya is to the right of Mini but to the left of Jaya. Who is on the extreme left if all the girls are facing North?

(*a*) Jaya (*b*) Mini
(*c*) Rajni (*d*) Saya

3. O, P, Q, R, S and T are standing on a bench according to their height. P is taller than O but shorter than S. Only S is taller than T. R is shorter than P but taller than Q. Who is the shortest?

(*a*) O (*b*) Q
(*c*) P (*d*) Cannot be said

4. Five personalities are living in a multistoried building. Mr. Effortless lives in a flat above Mr. Active, Mr. Charge lives in a flat below Mr. Diligent, Mr. Active lives in a flat above Mr. Diligent and Mr. Behaved lives in a flat below Mr. Charge. Who lives in the topmost flat?

(*a*) Mr. Charge (*b*) Mr. Diligent
(*c*) Mr. Effortless (*d*) Mr. Behaved

5. Six friends are sitting in a circle and playing cards. Kenny is to the left of Danny. Michael is in-between Bob and John. Roger is in between Kenny and Bob. Who is sitting to the right of Michael?

(*a*) Danny (*b*) John
(*c*) Kenny (*d*) Bob

6. Four girls A, B, C and D are sitting in a circle. B and C are facing each other. Which of the following is definitely true?

(*a*) A is to the left of C
(*b*) D is to the left of C
(*c*) A and D are facing each other
(*d*) A is not between B and C

7. Brijesh, Jayesh, Amar and Praveer are playing a game of cards. Amar is to the right of Jayesh who is to the right of Brijesh. Who is to the right of Amar?

(*a*) Brijesh
(*b*) Praveer
(*c*) Brijesh or Praveer
(*d*) Jayesh

8. In a pile of 10 books there are 3 of History, 3 of Hindi, 2 of Maths, and 2 of English. Taking from above there is an English book between a History and Maths book, a History book between a Maths and an English book, a Hindi book between an English and a Maths book, a Maths book between two Hindi books, and two Hindi books between a Maths and a History book. Book of which subject is at the sixth position from the top?

(*a*) English (*b*) Hindi
(*c*) History (*d*) Maths

9. Five persons A, B, C, D and E are sitting in a row facing you such that D is on the left of C and B is on the right of E. A is on the right of C and B is on the left of D. If E occupies a corner position, then who is sitting in the centre?

(*a*) A (*b*) B
(*c*) C (*d*) D

10. Six friends A, B, C, D, E and F are standing in a circle. B is between F and C; A is between E and D; F is to the left of D. Who is between A and F?

(*a*) C (*b*) B
(*c*) D (*d*) E

EXPLANATORY ANSWERS

1. *(b)* : The order of sitting is :
Amit, Shyam, Mayank, Ajay, Raghu
or
Ajay, Raghu, Mayank, Amit, Shyam

2. *(c)* : The order in which the girls are positioned is :
Rajni, Mini, Ananta, Saya, Jaya
or
Saya, Jaya, Ananta
or
Saya, Ananta, Jaya

3. *(d)* : In descending order of height, the standing positions are :

S		S
T		T
P	*or*	P
R		R
O		Q
Q		O

Either O or Q is the shortest. The informa-tion given is not enough to clarify the answer.

4. *(c)* : The personalities living in flats in multi-storied building are in order given below :
Mr. Effortless
Mr. Active
Mr. Diligent
Mr. Charge
Mr. Behaved

5. *(d)* : The order in which the friends are sitting is :

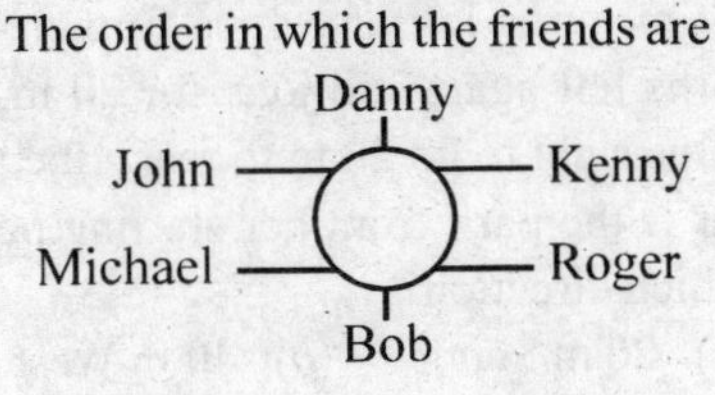

6. *(c)* : The sitting positions are :

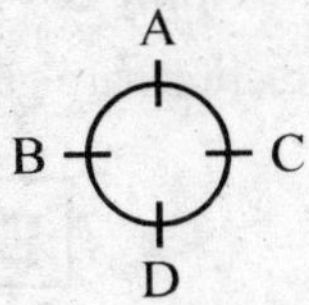

or

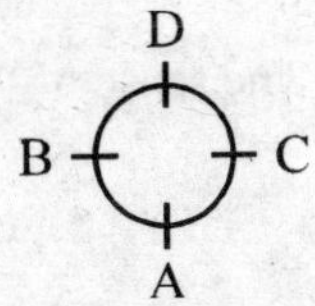

7. *(b)* : The order from left to right is :
Brijesh, Jayesh, Amar, Praveer

8. *(b)* : The pile of books is in the order :
1st — History
English
Maths
History
English
6th — Hindi
Maths
Hindi
Hindi
10th — History

9. *(d)* : Sitting order while facing us is :
A, C, D, B, E

10. *(c)* : The pattern of standing is :

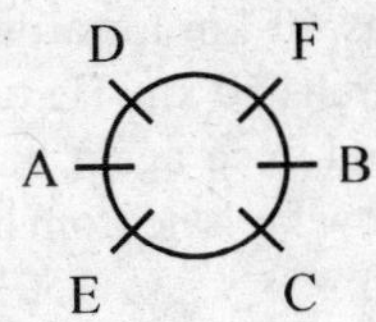

12. DIRECTION SENSE

In these type of tests, the directions in questions needs to be perceived. Such questions are based on the direction chart.

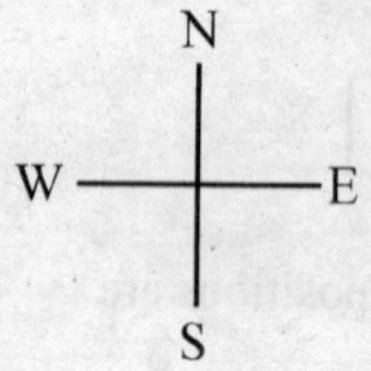

N = North S = South E = East W = West

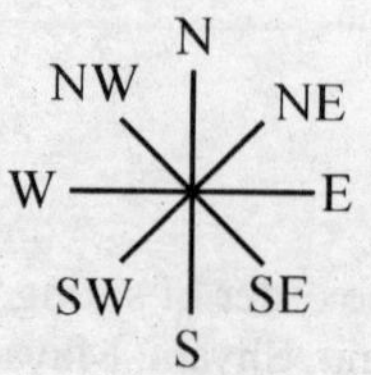

The sense of the different directions are guided by the left and right turns or angular turns.

EXERCISE

Directions : *In the following questions, select the right answer from the given options to depict the correct direction/distance.*

1. Kittu walks towards East and then towards South. After walking some distance he turns towards West and then turns to his left. In which direction is he walking now?
(*a*) North (*b*) South
(*c*) East (*d*) West

2. A person is driving towards West. What sequence of directions should he follow so that he is driving towards South?
(*a*) left, right, right
(*b*) right, right, left
(*c*) left, left, left
(*d*) right, right, right

3. Richa drives 8 km to the South, turns left and drives 5 km. Again, she turns left and drives 8 km. How far is she from her starting point?
(*a*) 3 km (*b*) 5 km
(*c*) 8 km (*d*) 13 km

4. Dingi runs 40 km towards North then turns right and runs 50 km. He turns right and runs 30 km, and once again turns right and runs 50 km. How far is he from his starting point?
(*a*) 90 km (*b*) 50 km
(*c*) 10 km (*d*) 5 km

5. If North is called North-West, North-West is called West, West is called South-West and so on. What will South-East be called?
(*a*) East (*b*) West
(*c*) North-East (*d*) South-East

6. A man travels 100 km towards South. From there he turns right and travels 100 km and again turns right to travel 50 km. Which direction is he in from his starting point?
(*a*) North (*b*) North-East
(*c*) East (*d*) South-West

7. A train runs 120 km in West direction, 30 km in South direction and then 80 km in east direction before reaching the station. In which direction is the station from the train's starting point?
(*a*) South-West (*b*) North-West
(*c*) South-East (*d*) South

8. Facing the West direction, Priya jogs for 20 m, turns left and goes further 40 m. She turns left again and jogs for 20 m. Then she turns right to go 20 m to reach the park. How far is the park from her starting point and in which direction?
(*a*) 20 m South (*b*) 40 m West
(*c*) 60 m South (*d*) 100 m East

9. If all the directions are rotated, *i.e.,* if North is changed to West and East to North and so on, then what will come in place of North-West?
(*a*) South-West (*b*) North-East
(*c*) East-North (*d*) East-West

10. A and B start together from one point. They walk 10 km towards North. A turns left and covers 5 km whereas B turns right and covers 3 km. A turns left again and covers 15 km whereas B turns right and covers his 15 km. How far is A from B?
(*a*) 18 km (*b*) 10 km
(*c*) 5 km (*d*) 8 km

EXPLANATORY ANSWERS

1. (*b*) :

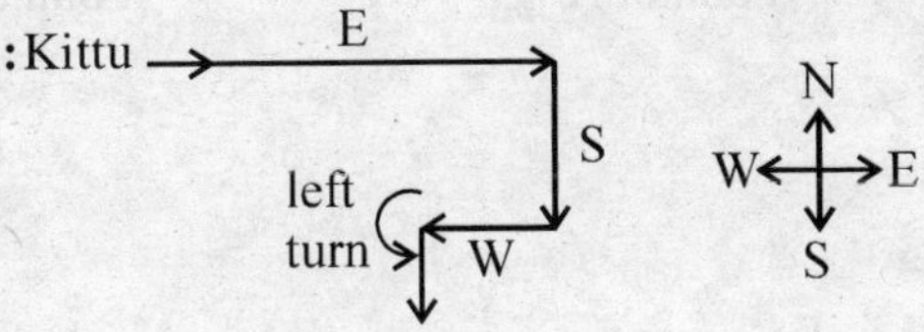

2. (*d*) :

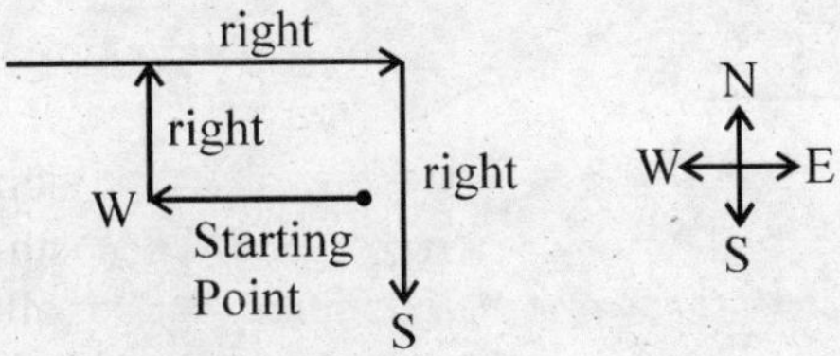

3. (*b*) :

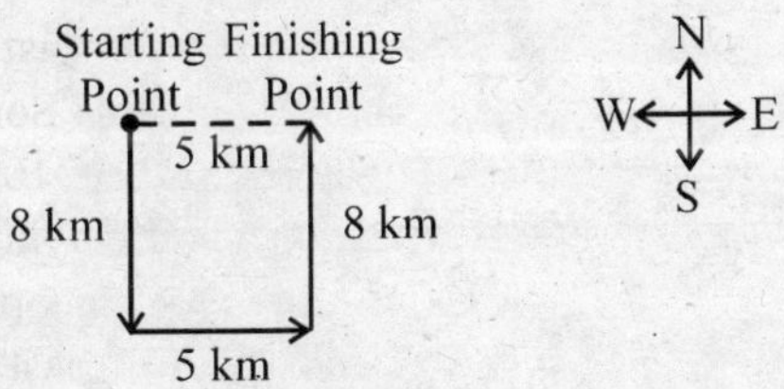

4. (*c*) :

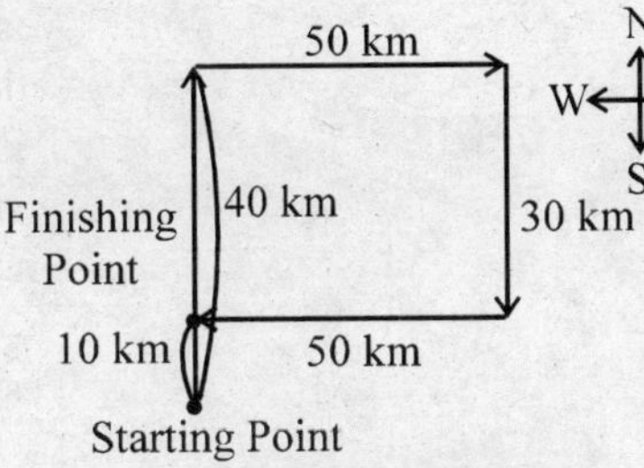

5. (*a*) : **Original Directions**

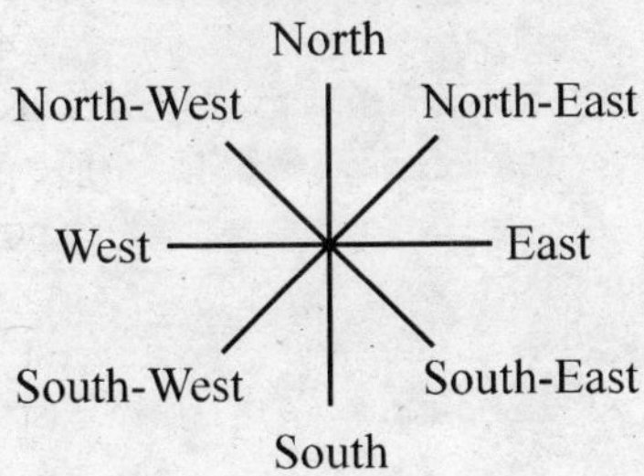

Changed Directions

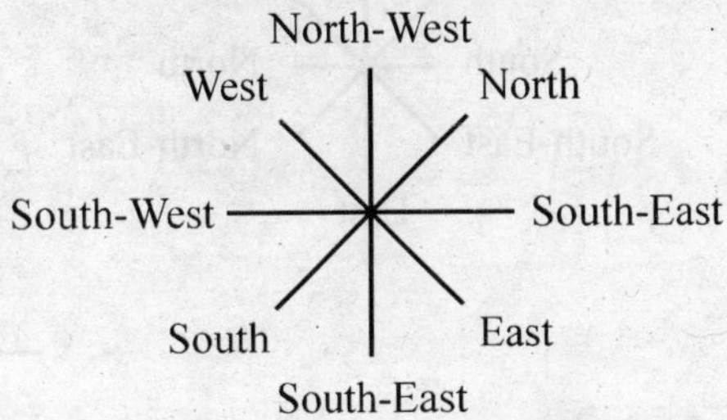

6. (*d*) :

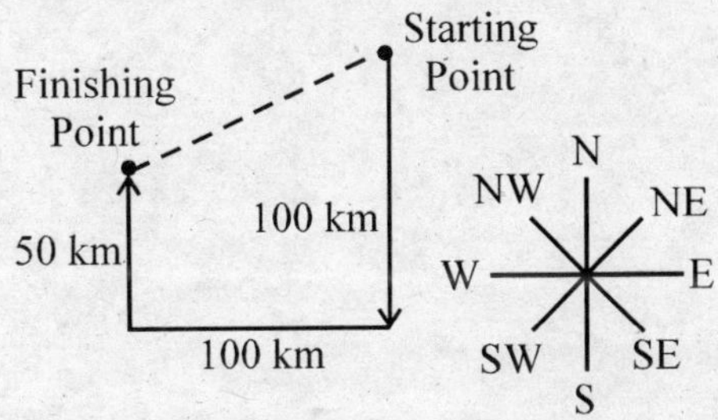

7. (*a*) :

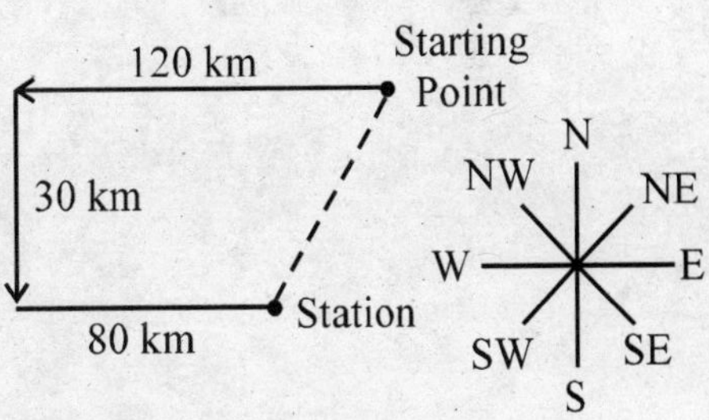

8. (*c*) : (40 + 20) = 60 metres South

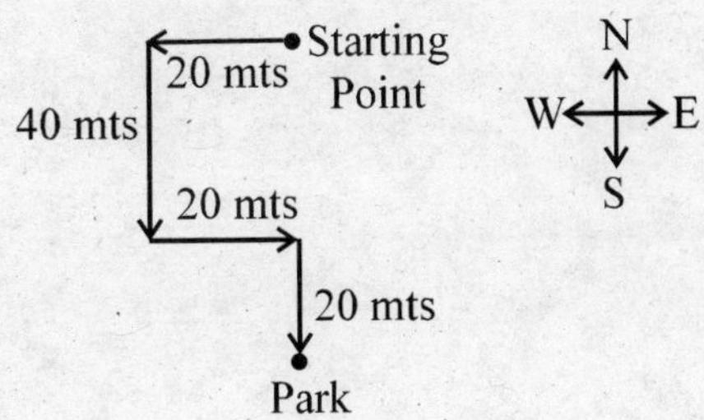

9. ***(a)*** **: Original Directions**

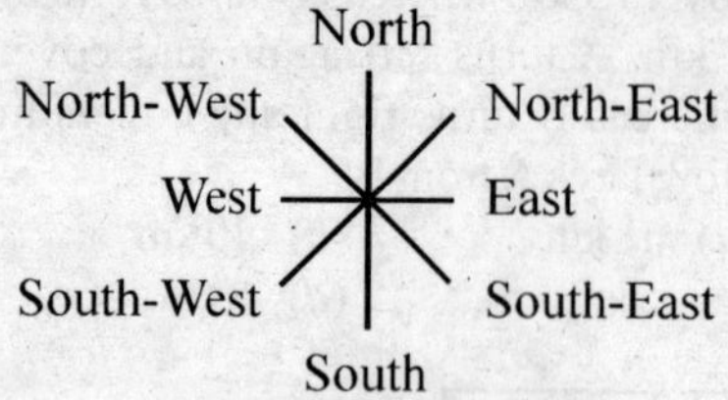

Changed Directions

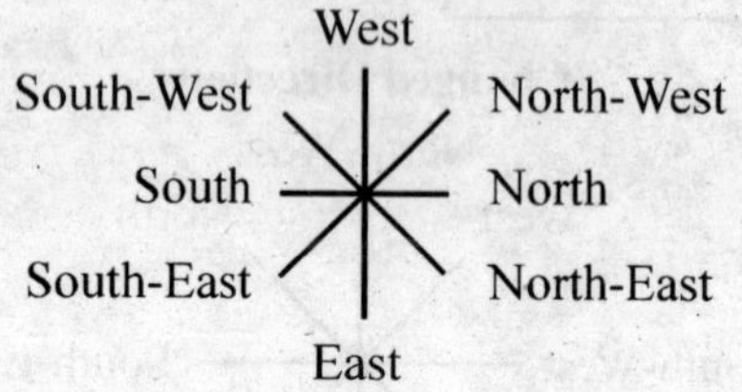

10. ***(d)*** **:**

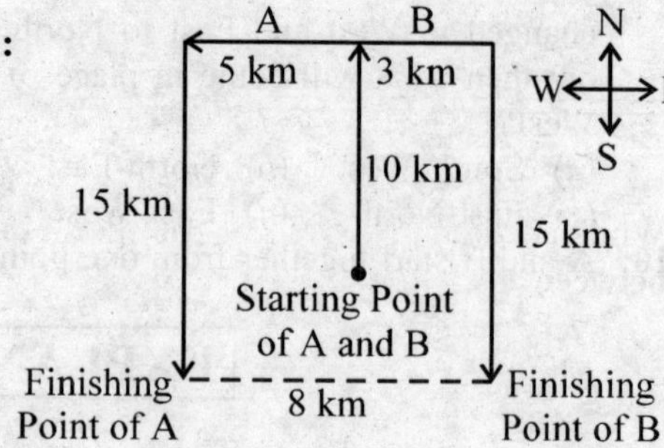

13. BLOOD RELATIONSHIPS

While attempting questions on blood relations, one should be clear of all the relation patterns that can exist between any two individuals. These type of questions are given mainly to test one's relationship ability.

Very well-known relations are :

Mother	Grandmother	Father	Grandfather	Son	Grandson
Daughter	Granddaughter	Brother	Brother-in-law	Sister	Sister-in-law
Niece	Father-in-law	Nephew	Mother-in-law	Uncle	Son-in-law
Aunt	Daughter-in-law	Husband	Cousin	Wife	

The patterns of some relationships which help in solving questions in these tests are :

Father's *or* Mother's Father	—	Grandfather (Paternal *or* Maternal)
Father's *or* Mother's Mother	—	Grandmother (Paternal *or* Maternal)
Father's *or* Mother's Son	—	Brother
Father's *or* Mother's Daughter	—	Sister
Father's Brother	—	Paternal Uncle
Father's Sister	—	Paternal Aunt
Mother's Brother	—	Maternal Uncle
Mother's Sister	—	Maternal Aunt
Uncle *or* Aunt's Son *or* Daughter	—	Cousin
Son's Wife	—	Daughter-in-law
Daughter's Husband	—	Son-in-law
Husband's *or* Wife's Brother	—	Brother-in-law
Husband's *or* Wife's Sister	—	Sister-in-law
Brother's Wife	—	Sister-in-law
Sister's Husband	—	Brother-in-law
Brother's Son	—	Nephew
Brother's Daughter	—	Niece

EXERCISE

Directions : *In each of the following questions keenly study the relationship mentioned between the persons, and then from the given options select the right relationship as the answer.*

1. A lady said, "The person standing there is my grandfather's only son's daughter". How is the lady related to the standing person?

(*a*) Sister (*b*) Mother
(*c*) Aunt (*d*) Cousin

2. Ajay is the brother of Vijay. Mili is the sister of Ajay. Sanjay is the brother of Rahul and Mehul is the daughter of Vijay. Who is Sanjay's Uncle?

(*a*) Rahul (*b*) Ajay
(*c*) Mehul (*d*) Data inadequate

3. A man introduced the boy coming with him as "He is son of the father of my wife's daughter". What relation did the boy bear to the man?

(*a*) Son-in-law (*b*) Son
(*c*) Brother (*d*) Father

4. If Amit's father is Billoo's father's only son and Billoo has neither a brother nor a

daughter, what is the relationship between Amit and Billoo?
(a) Uncle — Nephew
(b) Father — Daughter
(c) Father — Son
(d) Cousins

5. Pointing to a woman in the photograph a man said, "She is the daughter of my grandmother's only son." How is the woman related to the man?
(a) Mother (b) Daughter
(c) Sister-in-law (d) Sister

6. Pointing to a photograph, a woman said, "She is the only daughter of my mother's father." How is the woman related to the person in the photograph?
(a) Mother
(b) Grandmother
(c) Daughter
(d) Cannot be determined

7. Ram is the brother of Shyam and Mahesh is the father of Ram. Jagat is the brother of Priya and Priya is daughter of Shyam. Who is the uncle of Jagat ?
(a) Shyam (b) Mahesh
(c) Ram (d) Data insufficient

8. Introducing a man, a woman said, "His wife is the only daughter of my father". How is the man related to the woman?
(a) Husband (b) Father
(c) Father-in-law (d) Brother

9. If Maya is the only daughter of Richa's grandmother's brother, how is Maya's daughter related to Richa?
(a) Niece (b) Cousin
(c) Aunt (d) Mother

10. Pointing to a woman, a man said, "Her husband's mother is the wife of my father's only son". How is the man related to the woman?
(a) Son (b) Brother-in-law
(c) Uncle (d) Father-in-law

EXPLANATORY ANSWERS

1. (a) :

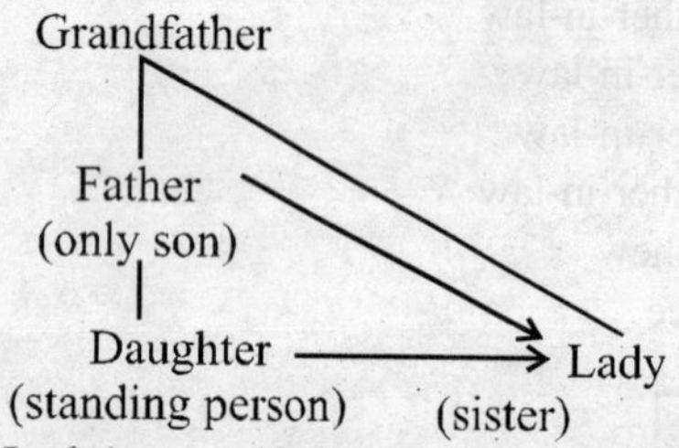

Lady's grandfather's son is lady's father and father's daughter will only be lady's sister.

2. (d) :

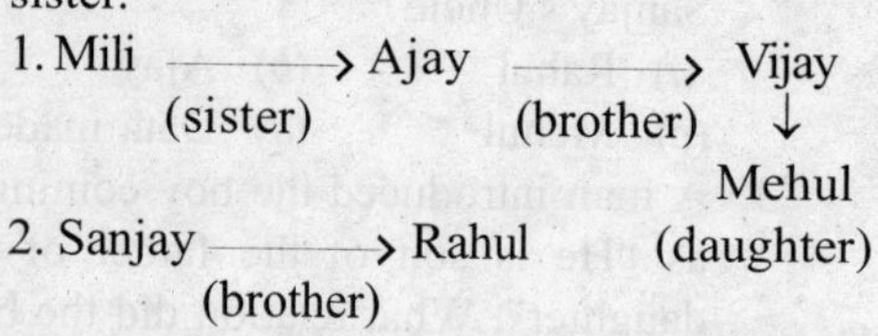

There are two sets of relationship. Information given is incomplete and no relation can be established between the two sets.

3. (b) : The relationship chart based on problem is :

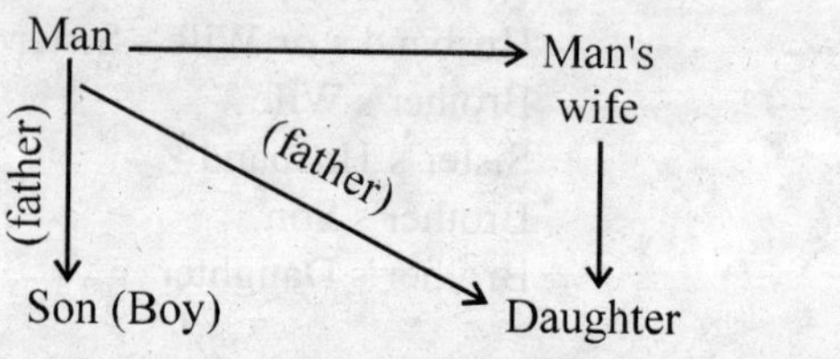

'Father of the man's wife's daughter' is the man himself and the boy in question is the man's son.

4. (c) : The relationship chart based on problem is :

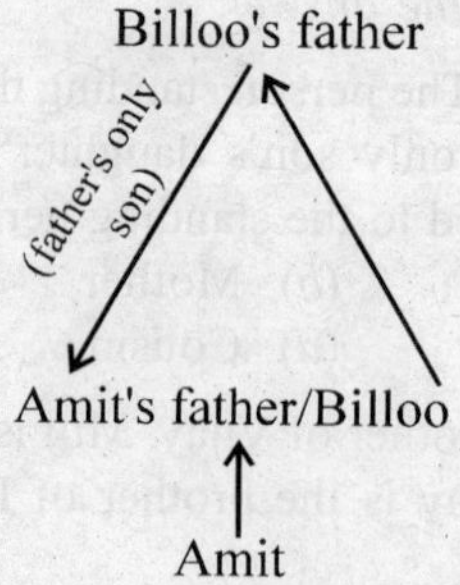

Amit's father is Billoo's father's only son means Billoo is the only son in question also, he is the father of Amit. It must be noted that Billoo has no brother which means he is single and also, when he has no daughter, Amit is his only son.

5. (*d*) :

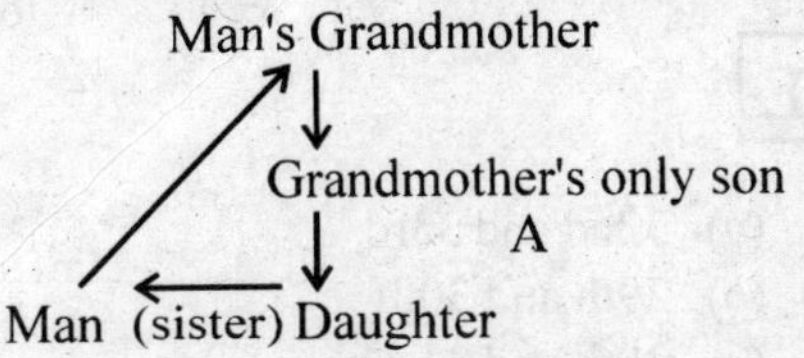

'My grandmother's only son' is the father of the man, and 'daughter of my grandmother's only son' is the sister of the man.

6. (*c*) :

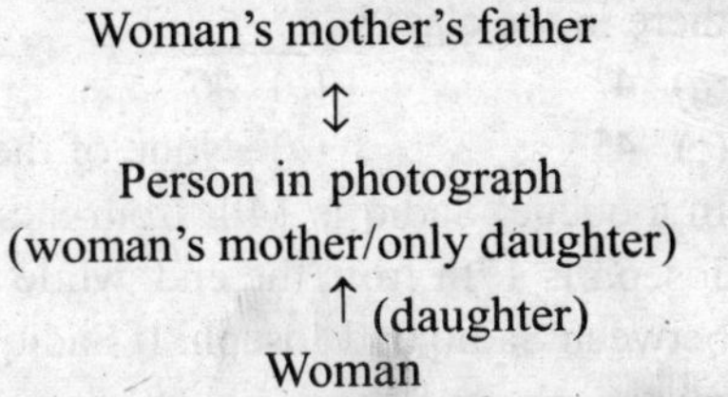

'Only daughter of my mother's father' is the person in the photograph and she is also the mother of the woman. So, the woman is the daughter of the person in the photograph.

7. (*c*) :

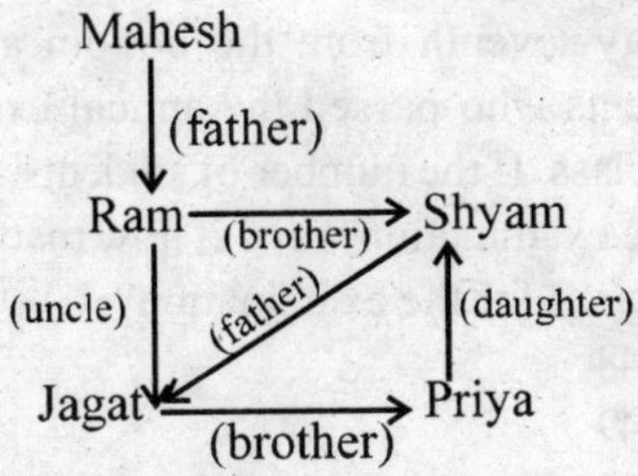

Jagat is brother of Priya and Priya is daughter of Shyam. So Shyam is also the father of Jagat. Ram is the brother of Shyam. So, Jagat's father's brother Ram is the uncle of Jagat.

8. (*a*) :

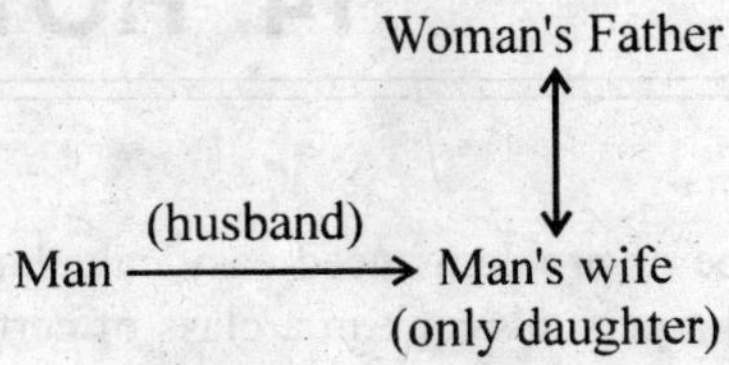

'Only daughter of my father' is the woman herself and the man is her husband.

9. (*b*) :

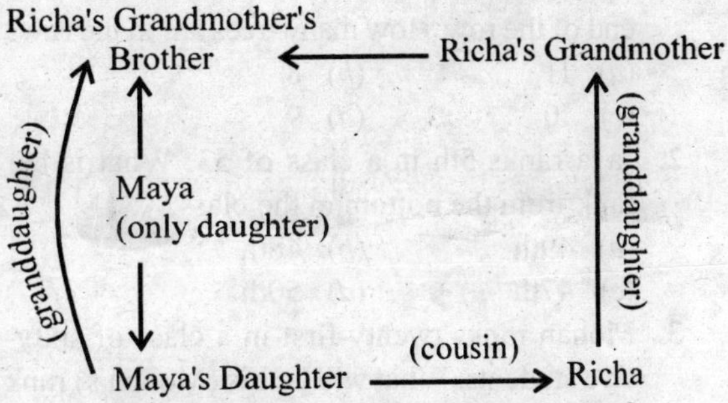

Both Maya's Daughter and Richa are granddaughters of a brother and a sister respectively. So Maya's daughter is the cousin of Richa.

10. (*d*) :

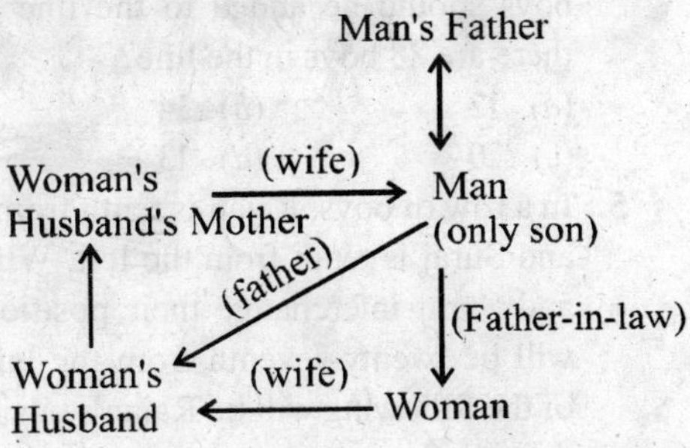

'My father's only son' is the man himself. 'Her husband's mother' is the wife of the man and so the man is the father of the woman's husband. As the woman is the wife of man's son, the man is the father-in-law of the woman.

14. ROWS AND RANKS

These type of problems need easy calculations to find out the number of objects in a row, lane or queue or to find a person's rank in a class of certain number of students; or to find the total number of students.

EXERCISE

1. In a row of trees, one tree is fifth from either end of the row. How many trees are in the row?
(*a*) 11 (*b*) 8
(*c*) 10 (*d*) 9

2. Jaya ranks 5th in a class of 53. What is her rank from the bottom in the class?
(*a*) 49th (*b*) 48th
(*c*) 47th (*d*) 50th

3. Mohan ranks twenty-first in a class of sixty-five students. What will be his (Mohan's) rank if the lowest candidate is assigned rank 1?
(*a*) 44th (*b*) 45th
(*c*) 46th (*d*) Data inadequate

4. If Rahul finds that he is 12th from the right in a line of boys and 4th from the left, how many boys should be added to the line such that there are 28 boys in the line?
(*a*) 12 (*b*) 14
(*c*) 20 (*d*) 13

5. In a row of boys, Rajan is tenth from the right and Suraj is tenth from the left. When Rajan and Suraj interchange their positions, Suraj will be twenty-seventh from the left. Which of the following will be Rajan's position from the right?
(*a*) Tenth
(*b*) Twenty-sixth
(*c*) Twenty-ninth
(*d*) None of these

6. Mahesh and Suresh are ranked 11th and 12th respectively from the top in a class of 41 students. What will be their respective ranks from the bottom?
(*a*) 32nd and 33rd
(*b*) 29th and 30th
(*c*) 30th and 31st
(*d*) 31st and 30th

7. Uma ranked 8th from the top and 37th from bottom in a class. How many students are there in the class?
(*a*) 47 (*b*) 46
(*c*) 45 (*d*) None of these

8. In a queue, Sadiq is 14th from the front and Joseph is 17th from the end, while Jane is in between Sadiq and Joseph. If Sadiq be ahead of Joseph and there be 48 persons in the queue, how many persons are there between Sadiq and Jane?
(*a*) 5 (*b*) 6
(*c*) 7 (*d*) 8

9. Rohan ranked eleventh from the top and twenty-seventh from the bottom among the students who passed the annual examination in a class. If the number of students who failed in the examination was 12, how many students appeared for the examination?
(*a*) 48
(*b*) 49
(*c*) 50
(*d*) Cannot be determined

10. Some boys are sitting in a row. P is sitting fourteenth from the left and Q is seventh from the right. If there are four boys between P and Q, how many boys are there in the row?
(*a*) 19 (*b*) 21
(*c*) 25 (*d*) 23

EXPLANATORY ANSWERS

1. (*d*):

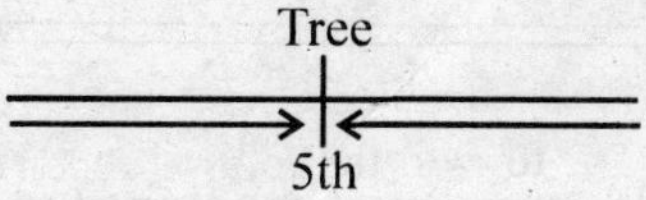

Total number of trees in the row are : $(5+5)-1=9$.

2. (*a*) :

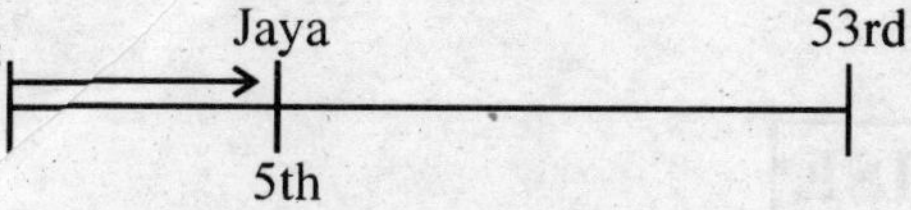

Jaya's rank from the bottom is : $(53-5)+1=49$th.

3. (*b*) :

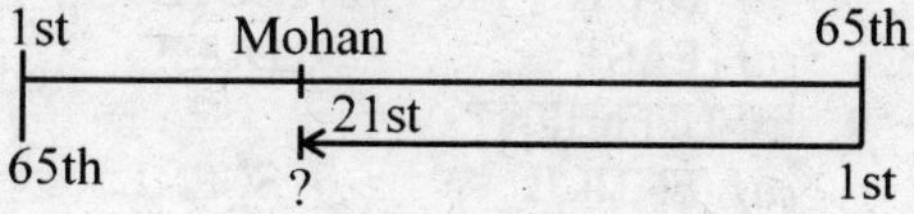

Note : Mohan's rank from the last or the question asked means the same.

Mohan's rank is $(65-21)+1=45$th.

4. (*d*) :

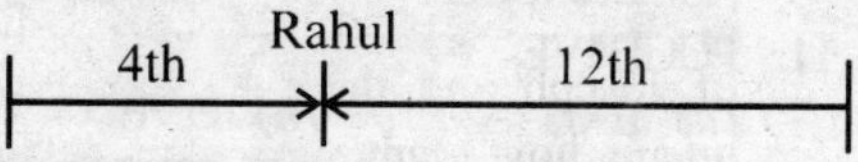

The number of boys in the line are : $(4+12)-1=15$

To make a line of 28 boys, $(28-15)$ *i.e.* 13 more boys are needed.

5. (*d*) :

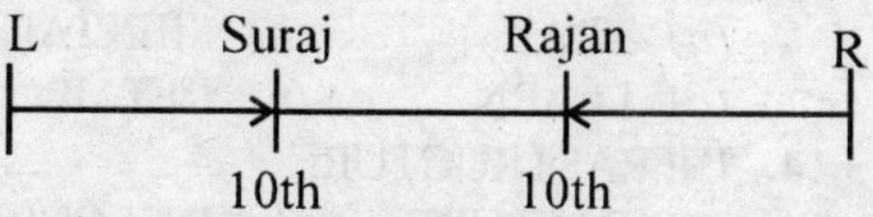

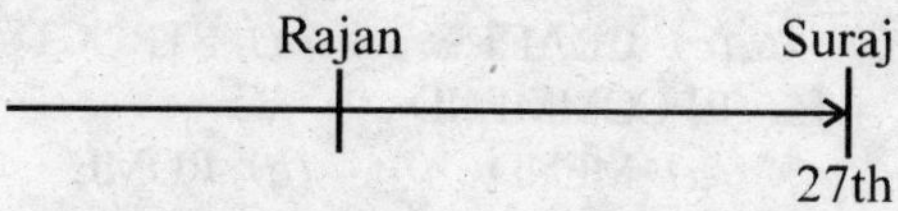

As the position of boys is equal from both ends, Rajan will also be 27th from the right after changing positions.

6. (*d*) :

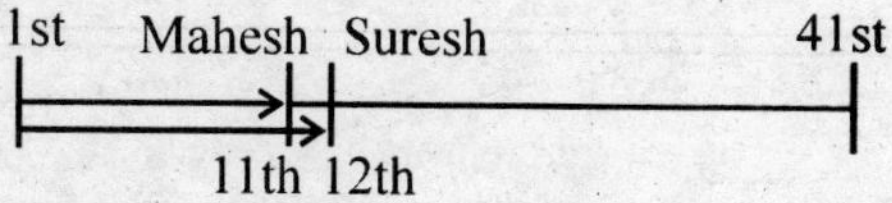

Mahesh's position from bottom is : $(41-11)+1=31$st

Suresh's position from bottom is : $(41-12)+1=30$th.

7. (*d*) :

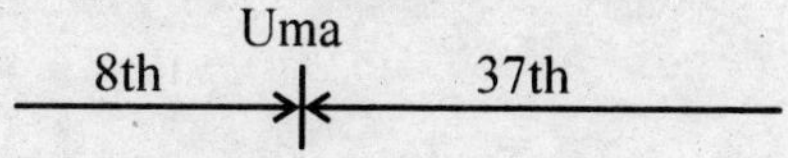

Total number of students in the class are : $(8+37)-1=44$.

8. (*d*) :

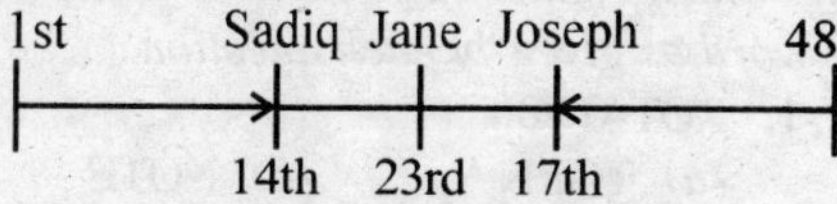

Sadiq's position from front : 14th

Joseph's position from last : 17th or $48-17+1=32$nd from front.

Middle postion between Sadiq & Joseph

$$=\frac{(32-14)}{2}+14=23\text{ rd.}$$

Hence, Jane position is 23rd from front

Person between Sadiq & Jane $=23-14-1=8$.

9. (*b*) :

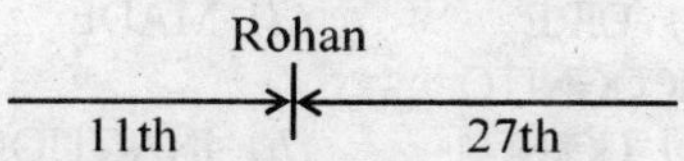

Number of students who passed the examination $(11+27)-1=37$

Those who failed = 12

Total number of students who appeared in the examination $=37+12=49$.

10. (*c*) :

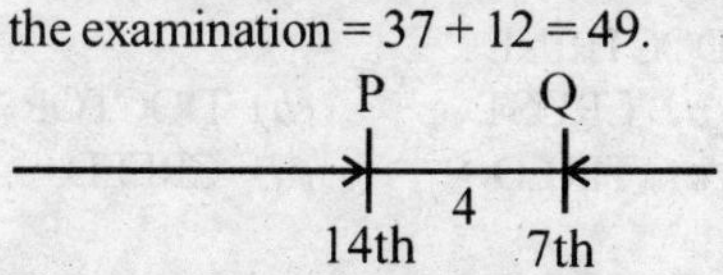

The number of boys in the row are : $(14+4+7)=25$.

15. PERMUTATIONS AND COMBINATIONS

In these type of questions, the only factor essential is alertness. In every question, a word is given. By using the letters of this given word the options are formed. The candidates are required to find from the given options the word *(i)* which cannot be formed by using the letters of the given word or *(ii)* which can be formed by using the letters of the given word.

EXERCISE

Directions : *Find out the one word among the options which cannot be formed by using the letters of the word as given in each question.*

1. ROTATION
   (a) TORN (b) NOTE
   (c) TART (d) RAIN
2. PHILOSOPHY
   (a) SOIL (b) SHIP
   (c) SOLO (d) SPIN
3. SLAVATION
   (a) SNORT (b) LATVIA
   (c) SALIVA (d) AVAIL
4. ACADEMY
   (a) DEMY (b) MACE
   (c) DIRE (d) MADE
5. INCOGNITO
   (a) GOING (b) INACTION
   (c) IGNITION (d) TONGO
6. JUDICIARY
   (a) INJURY (b) CADDY
   (c) DICY (d) ACRID
7. DOCTRINE
   (a) CRUST (b) DOCTOR
   (c) TIRED (d) CREED
8. EDUCATED
   (a) DATE (b) CUTE
   (c) EAST (d) DUCT
9. INSUFFICIENT
   (a) ENTICE (b) SCENT
   (c) SUFFICE (d) THENCE
10. DECEMBER
    (a) REDEEM (b) DECREE
    (c) BRACED (d) MEMBER
11. FUGITIVE
    (a) EXIT (b) FIVE
    (c) GIVE (d) GIFT
12. CATASTROPHE
    (a) TASTE (b) CHEAP
    (c) POUCH (d) STARE
13. TORRENTIAL
    (a) TRAIL (b) MENTAL
    (c) LEARN (d) RETAIL
14. INFRASTRUCTURE
    (a) RAPTURE (b) INSECURE
    (c) CRAFTS (d) STRUCTURE
15. RECOMMEND
    (a) MEND (b) ROME
    (c) CANE (d) OMEN

ANSWERS

1	2	3	4	5	6	7	8	9	10
(b)	(d)	(a)	(c)	(b)	(a)	(a)	(c)	(d)	(c)
11	**12**	**13**	**14**	**15**					
(a)	(c)	(b)	(a)	(c)					

16. SYMBOL SUBSTITUTION

Questions in these category are easy to attempt. Candidates must be quick in substituting symbols and calculations. The common pattern of questions asked are given below.

EXERCISE

1. If "+" means "–"; "–" means "×"; "×"means "÷" and "÷" means "+", then $15 \times 5 \div 10 + 5 - 3 = ?$

(a) 9.5 (b) 0
(c) –2 (d) 24

2. If "+" means "×"; "–" means "÷"; "÷"means "+" and "×" means "–", then what will be the value of $20 \div 40 - 4 \times 5 + 6 = ?$

(a) 60 (b) 1.67
(c) 150 (d) 0

3. If × stands for addition, < for subtraction, + stands for division, > for multiplication, – stands for equal to, ÷ for greater than, and = stands for less than, state which of the following is true?

(a) $5 \times 3 < 7 \div 8 + 4 \times 1$
(b) $3 \times 4 > 2 - 9 + 3 < 3$
(c) $5 > 2 + 2 = 10 < 4 \times 8$
(d) $3 \times 2 < 4 \div 16 > 2 + 4$

4. If → stands for subract, ← stands for add, •↑↑ stands for multiply, ↓↓ stands for divide, ↔ for greater than, ⟷ stands for equal to, then which of the following alternatives is true?

(a) 4 ← 6 ↑↑ 2 ⟷ 3 → 12 ← 12
(b) 10 ↓↓ 5 ↑↑ 5 ⟷ 9 → 3 ← 4
(c) 15 ↑↑ 2 → 5 ⟷ 12 ↓↓ 4 ← 3
(d) 13 ↓↓ 13 ← 1 ↔ 20 → 5 ↑↑ 2

5. If Δ denotes =; + denotes >, – denotes <, □ denotes ≠, × denotes > and ÷ denotes < then a + b – c denotes

(a) b Δ c □ a
(b) b □ a ÷ c
(c) a ÷ b × c
(d) b – a + c

6. If '✱' denotes '×', 'Δ' denotes '÷', '□' denotes '–', '●' denotes '+', 'α' denotes '=' and 'β' denotes ≠, then which of the following euations is correct?

(a) 2 □ 10 ✱ 4 Δ 5 α 5 ● 12 Δ 6
(b) 27 Δ 9 ● 6 β 3 ✱ 6 □ 9
(c) 4 Δ 2 ✱ 0 α 7 Δ 1 ✱ 0
(d) 5 ● 6 Δ 3 □ 2 α 8 Δ 4 ✱ 3

7. If ↓ stands for '÷', ↑ stands for '×', → stands for '+' and ← stands for '–', then 25 ↓ 5 → 3 ↑ 6 ← 8 = ?

(a) 9 (b) 12
(c) 16 (d) 15

8. If the + and × signs of the following equations are interchanged, which will be the correct equation?

(a) $7 \times 5 + 3 = 20$
(b) $4 + 9 \times 1 = 42$
(c) $6 \times 5 + 8 = 46$
(d) $2 + 11 \times 4 = 28$

9. If '+' stands for multiplication, '×' stands for addition, '÷' stands for subtraction and '–' stands for division, then what will be the result of the following equation?

$7 \times 4 \div 10 \times 2 + 5 = ?$

(a) 7 (b) 0
(c) 11 (d) 15

10. If 'A' means '÷', 'B' means '+', 'C' means '×' and 'D' means '–', then 12 C 4 A 24 D 10 B 1 = ?

(a) $11\frac{1}{3}$ (b) 23
(c) –7 (d) $16\frac{4}{5}$

EXPLANATORY ANSWERS

1. ***(c)*** **:** $15 \div 5 + 10 - 5 \times 3$

$3 + 10 - 15 = -2$

2. ***(d)*** **:** $20 + 40 \div 4 - 5 \times 6$

$20 + 10 - 30 = 0$

3. ***(c)*** **:** *(a)* $5 + 3 - 7 > 8 \div 4 + 1$

$1 > 3$

(b) $3 + 4 \times 2 = 9 \div 3 - 3$

$11 = 0$

(c) $5 \times 2 \div 2 < 10 - 4 + 8$

$5 < 14$

(d) $3 + 2 - 4 > 16 \times 2 \div 4$

$1 > 8$

4. ***(b)*** **:** *(a)* $4 + 6 \times 2 = 3 - 12 + 12$

$16 = 3$

(b) $10 \div 5 \times 5 = 9 - 3 + 4$

$10 = 10$

(c) $15 \times 2 - 5 = 12 \div 4 + 3$

$25 = 6$

(d) $13 \div 13 + 1 > 20 - 5 \times 2$

$2 > 10$

5. ***(d)*** **:** What is given is $a > b < c$

The equations are :

(a) $b = c \neq a$ which is wrong

(b) $b \neq a < c$ which is wrong

(c) $a < b > c$ which is wrong

(d) $b < a > c$ which is correct

Therefore, *(d)* is the answer.

6. ***(c)*** **:** The solved equations will be :

(a) $2 - 10 \times 4 \div 5 = 5 + 12 \div 6$

$2 - 8 = 5 + 2$

$-6 = 7$ which is wrong

(b) $27 \div 9 + 6 \neq 3 \times 6 - 9$

$3 + 6 \neq 18 - 9$

$9 \neq 9$ which is wrong

(c) $4 \div 2 \times 0 = 7 \div 1 \times 0$

$2 \times 0 = 7 \times 0$

$0 = 0$ which is correct

(d) $5 + 6 \div 3 - 2 = 8 \div 4 \times 3$

$5 = 6$ which is wrong

7. ***(d)*** **:** $25 \div 5 + 3 \times 6 - 8$

$5 + 18 - 8 = 15$

8. ***(c)*** **:** After interchanging the signs the equations are :

(a) $7 + 5 \times 3 = 22$ which is wrong

(b) $4 \times 9 + 1 = 37$ which is wrong

(c) $6 + 5 \times 8 = 46$ which is correct

(d) $2 \times 11 + 4 = 26$ which is wrong

9. ***(c)*** **:** $7 + 4 - 10 + 2 \times 5$

$7 + 4 - 10 + 10 = 11$

10. ***(c)*** **:** $12 \times 4 \div 24 - 10 + 1$

$2 - 10 + 1 = -7$

17. MISSING NUMBERS

Playing with numbers and mathematical skills are needed to attempt these type of tests. The candidates have to work out the right combination of arithmetical symbols to arrive at the answer options which will take the place of the interrogation sign in the given questions.

EXERCISE

Directions: *In each question given below which one number can be placed at the sign of interrogation?*

1. 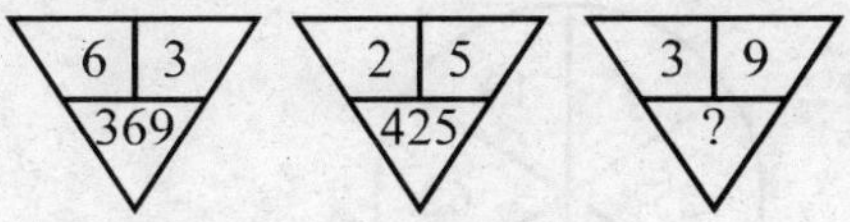

(*a*) 693 (*b*) 939
(*c*) 981 (*d*) 993

2. 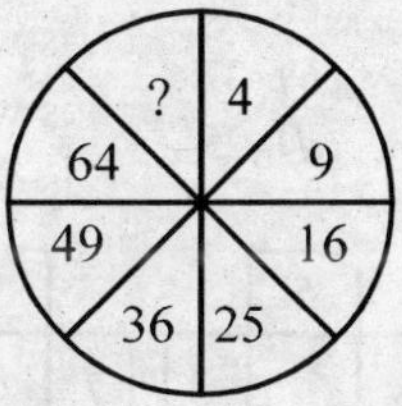

(*a*) 68 (*b*) 100
(*c*) 72 (*d*) 81

3. 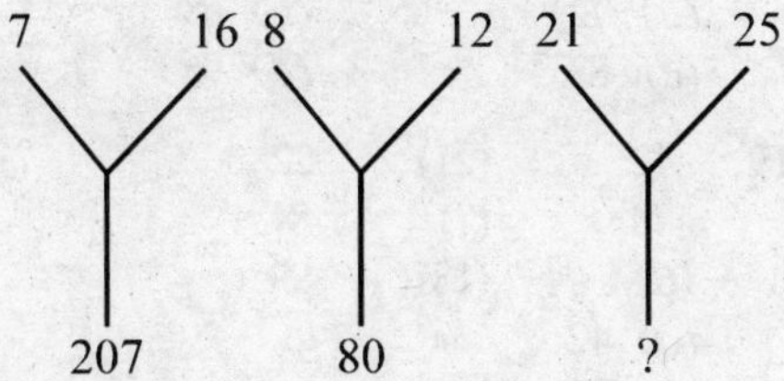

(*a*) 425 (*b*) 184
(*c*) 241 (*d*) 210

4. 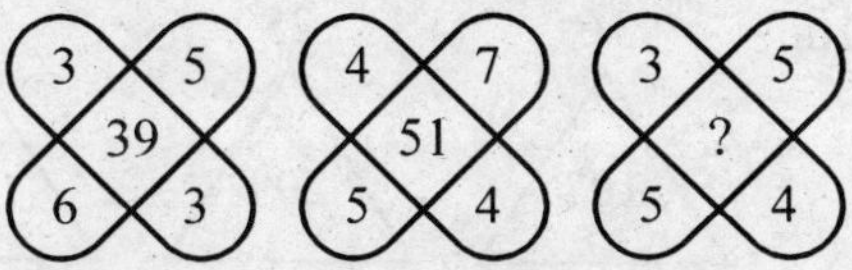

(*a*) 35 (*b*) 37
(*c*) 45 (*d*) 48

5. 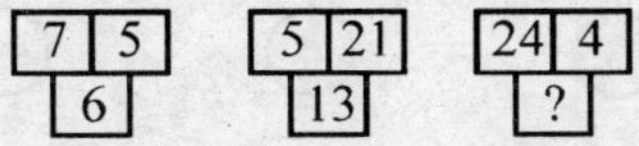

(*a*) 4 (*b*) 8
(*c*) 20 (*d*) 14

6.

14	9	4
12	7	2
10	5	0
16	11	?

(*a*) 9 (*b*) 6
(*c*) 3 (*d*) 7

7. 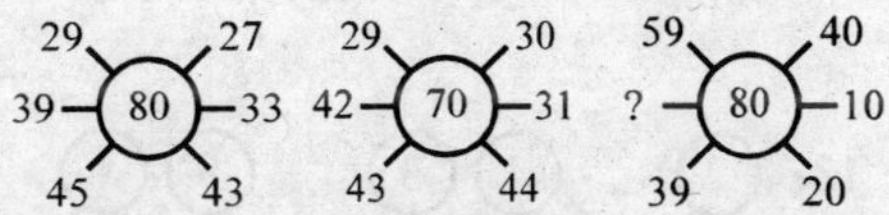

(*a*) 69 (*b*) 49
(*c*) 50 (*d*) 60

8. 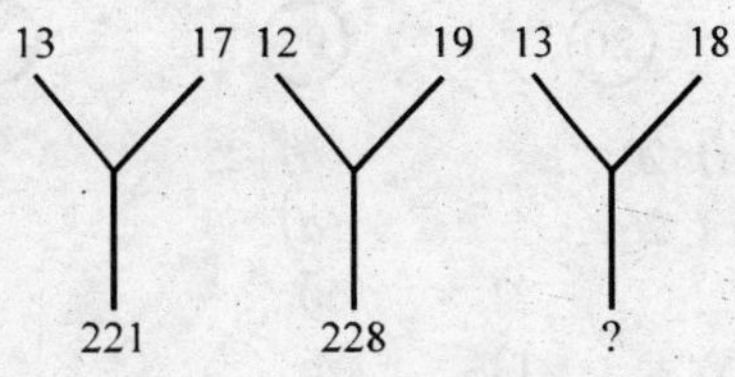

(*a*) 31 (*b*) 229
(*c*) 234 (*d*) 312

9. 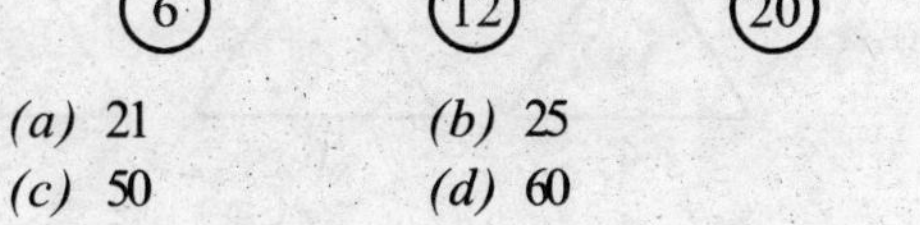

(*a*) 21 (*b*) 25
(*c*) 50 (*d*) 60

10. 51 (11) 61
64 (30) 32
35 (?) 43
(a) 25 *(b)* 27
(c) 32 *(d)* 37

11.

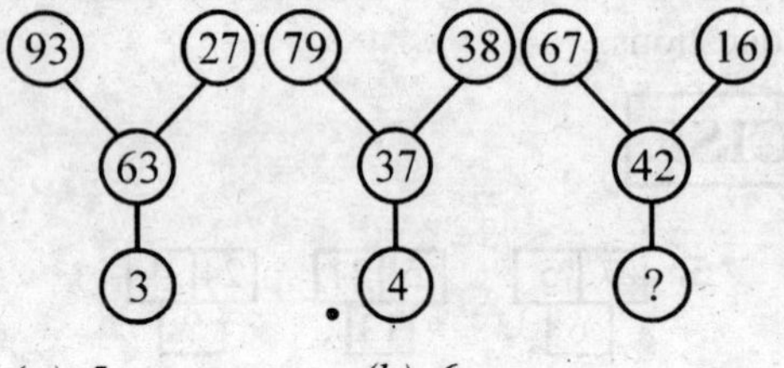

(a) 5 *(b)* 6
(c) 8 *(d)* 9

12.

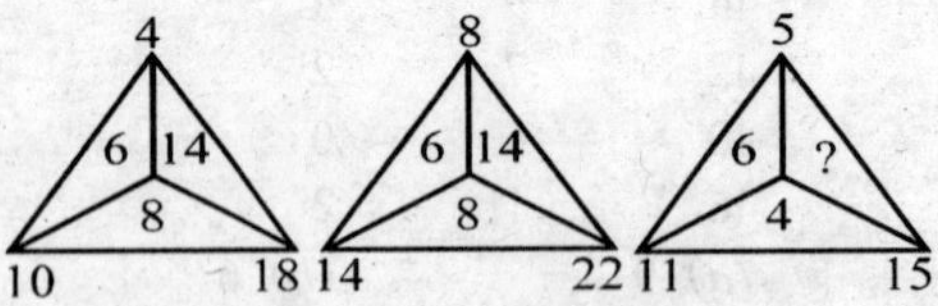

(a) 8 *(b)* 14
(c) 10 *(d)* 6

13.

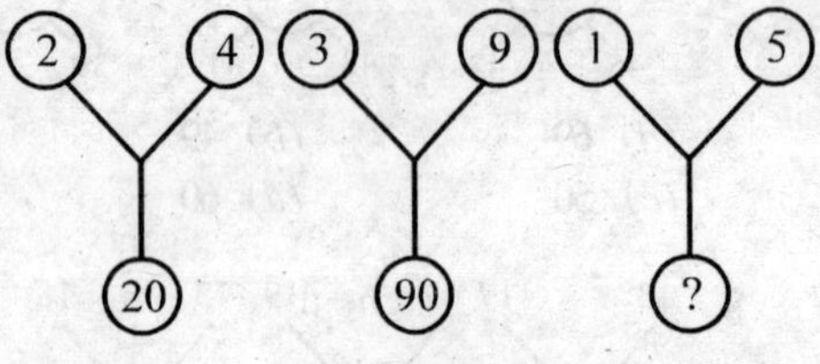

(a) 20 *(b)* 25
(c) 26 *(d)* 75

14. 27 22 50
13 12 26
9 2 ?
(a) 12 *(b)* 39
(c) 18 *(d)* 24

15.

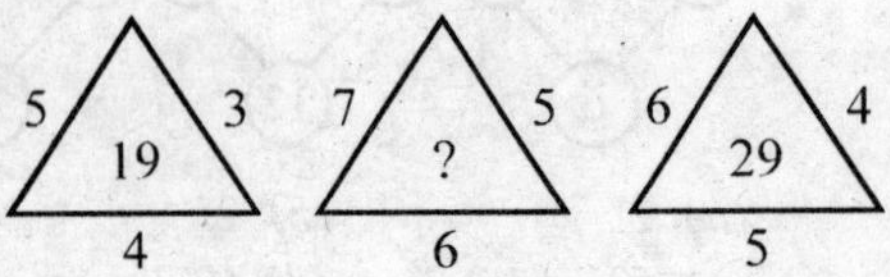

(a) 25 *(b)* 47
(c) 37 *(d)* 41

16.

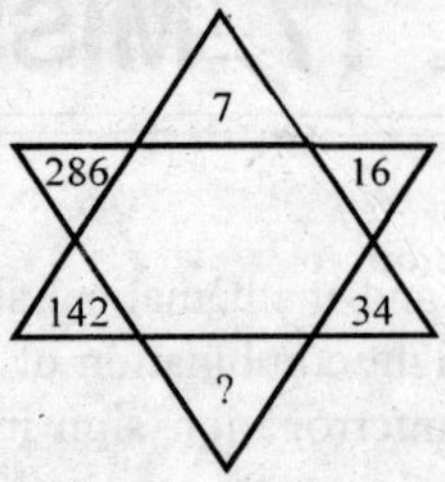

(a) 70
(b) 68
(c) 56
(d) 92

17.

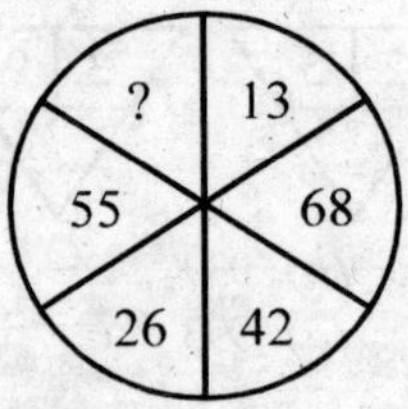

(a) 41 *(b)* 37
(c) 29 *(d)* 25

18.

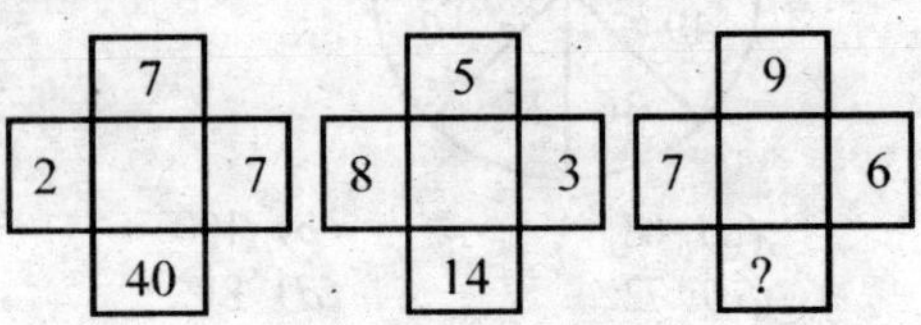

(a) 72 *(b)* 68
(c) 82 *(d)* 96

19. 42 (21) 22
78 (?) 84
162 (18) 99
(a) 12
(b) 13
(c) 60
(d) 72

20.

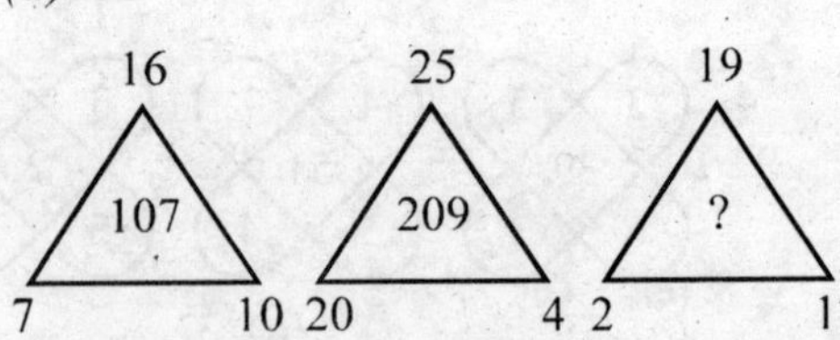

(a) 68 *(b)* 93
(c) 175 *(d)* 217

EXPLANATORY ANSWERS

1. (c) : The squares of two numbers on the top placed side by side gives the number inside the bottom triangle, *i.e.*,
6^2 and $3^2 = 369$
2^2 and $5^2 = 425$, similarly
3^2 and $9^2 = 981$.

2. (d) : Starting from number 4 the numbers are the squares of numbers in natural order *i.e.*, $2^2 = 4, 3^2 = 9, 4^2 = 16 \ldots\ldots 9^2 = 81$.

3. (b) : The number at the bottom is the difference of the squares of two numbers at the top, *i.e.*,
$16^2 - 7^2 = 256 - 49 = 207$
$12^2 - 8^2 = 144 - 64 = 80$, similarly
$25^2 - 21^2 = 625 - 441 = 184$.

4. (b) : The number in the centre is the sum of the products of diagonal numbers, *i.e.*,
$(3 \times 3) + (5 \times 6) = 39$
$(4 \times 4) + (7 \times 5) = 51$, similarly
$(3 \times 4) + (5 \times 5) = 37$.

5. (d) : Sum of two numbers on the top divided by 2 gives the third number, *i.e.*,
$(7 + 5) \div 2 = 6$
$(5 + 21) \div 2 = 13$, similarly
$(24 + 4) \div 2 = 14$.

6. (b) : The numbers in 2nd and 3rd columns are 5 less than the nunbers in 1st and 2nd columns respectively, *i.e.*,
$14 - 5 = 9$ and $9 - 5 = 4$
$12 - 5 = 7$ and $7 - 5 = 2, \ldots$ similarly
$16 - 5 = 11$ and $11 - 5 = 6$.

7. (a) : The sum of 3 numbers in each line in one figure is same, *i.e.*,
$29 + 80 + 43$ or $39 + 80 + 33$
or $45 + 80 + 27 = 152$
$29 + 70 + 44$ or $42 + 70 + 31$
or $43 + 70 + 30 = 143$,
similarly $59 + 80 + 20$ or $39 + 80 + 40 = 159$.
The missing number is :
$159 - (80 + 10) = 69$.

8. (c) : The number at the bottom is the product of two numbers at the top, *i.e.*,
$13 \times 17 = 221$
$12 \times 19 = 228$, similarly
$13 \times 18 = 234$.

9. (b) : Square of number at the bottom is equal to the product of two numbers at the top, *i.e.*,
$6^2 = 4 \times 9$, *i.e.*, 36
$12^2 = 9 \times 16$, *i.e.*, 144, similarly
$20^2 = 16 \times ?$, *i.e.*, 400. The missing number is $400 \div 16 = 25$.

10. (b) : The sum of the products of the digits of numbers in 1st and 3rd columns is the number in the 2nd column, *i.e.*,
$(5 \times 1) + (6 \times 1) = 11$
$(6 \times 4) + (3 \times 2) = 30$, similarly
$(3 \times 5) + (4 \times 3) = 27$.

11. (d) : The sum of numbers on right and centre subtracted from the number on the left gives the number at the bottom, *i.e.*,
$93 - (27 + 63) = 3$
$79 - (38 + 37) = 4$, similarly
$67 - (16 + 42) = 9$.

12. (c) : The number inside each triangle is the difference of the numbers at its base *i.e.*
$10 - 4 = 6, 18 - 4 = 14$ and $18 - 10 = 8$
$14 - 8 = 6, 22 - 8 = 14$ and $22 - 14 = 8$, similarly
$11 - 5 = 6, 15 - 5 = 10$ and $15 - 11 = 4$.

13. (c) : The sum of squares of two numbers at the top gives the third number below, *i.e.*,
$2^2 + 4^2 = 20$
$3^2 + 9^2 = 90$, similarly
$1^2 + 5^2 = 26$.

14. (a) : The sum of numbers in 1st and 2nd column plus 1 is the number in the 3rd column, *i.e.*,
$27 + 22 + 1 = 50$
$13 + 12 + 1 = 26$, similarly
$9 + 2 + 1 = 12$.

15. (d) : The product of numbers on either side of the triangle plus the number at the base is the number inside the triangle, *i.e.*,
$(5 \times 3) + 4 = 19$
$(6 \times 4) + 5 = 29$, similarly
$(7 \times 5) + 6 = 41$.

16. *(a)* : Clockwise starting from number 7, the next number is obtained by doubling the number and adding 2, *i.e.,*
$(7 \times 2) + 2 = 16$
$(16 \times 2) + 2 = 34 \ldots$, similarly
$(34 \times 2) + 2 = 70$
$(70 \times 2) + 2 = 142$
$(142 \times 2) + 2 = 286$.

17. *(c)* : The difference between the numbers in opposite sectors is 13, *i.e.,*
$26 - 13 = 13$
$68 - 55 = 13$, similarly
The missing number is $42 - 13 = 29$
($42 + 13 = 55$ is not given as option).

18. *(b)* : The number at the bottom is obtained by subtracting the sum of two numbers in the centre grid line from the square of the number at the top, *i.e.,*
$7^2 - (2 + 7) = 40$
$5^2 - (8 + 3) = 14$, similarly
$9^2 - (7 + 6) = 68$.

19. *(b)* : The number inside the brackets is obtained by multiplying the number on the left by 2 and then dividing the product by the sum of digits of number on the right, *i.e.,*
$(42 \times 2) \div (2 + 2) = 21$
$(162 \times 2) \div (9 + 9) = 18$, similarly
$(78 \times 2) \div (8 + 4) = 13$.

20. *(a)* : Subtracting the sum of squares of two numbers at the base from the square of number at the apex gives the number inside the triangle, *i.e.,*
$16^2 - (7^2 + 10^2) = 107$
$25^2 - (20^2 + 4^2) = 209$, similarly
$19^2 - (2^2 + 17^2) = 68$.

18. ALPHABET PROBLEMS

Alphabet problems are fun to attempt. They are based on alphabetical series in natural as well as reverse order.

Natural Order

A B C D E F G H I J K L M N O P Q R S T U V W X Y Z

Reverse Order

Z Y X W V U T S R Q P O N M L K J I H G F E D C B A

Note : The series starts from A on reaching Z and from Z on reaching A. Of these A E I O U are vowels and the rest are consonants.

EXERCISE

1. Which letter should be ninth letter to the left of ninth letter from the right if the first half of the alphabet is reversed?

(a) I *(b)* D
(c) F *(d)* E

2. Starting from the fifth letter from the left, if twelve letters are written in reverse order, then which letter will be the seventh to the left of the fourteenth letter from the right?

(a) N *(b)* H
(c) L *(d)* O

3. What letter will come in the centre of sixth letter from the right and thirteenth letter from the left?

(a) Q *(b)* R
(c) P *(d)* S

4. If in the word "DISTURBANCE", the first letter is interchanged with the last letter, the second letter is interchanged with the tenth letter and so on, which letter would come after the letter "T" in the newly formed word?

(a) I *(b)* U
(c) N *(d)* S

5. If it is possible to make a meaningful word with the third, the fifth, the seventh and the tenth letters of the word PROJECTION. If no such word can be made, give 'O' as the answer. If more than one such word can be made, give 'M' as the answer.

(a) T *(b)* N
(c) O *(d)* M

6. A meaningful word is made if we take the first, fourth, fifth, seventh, tenth, eleventh and the twelfth letters of the word "FELICITATIONS". Which of the following will be the fifth letter of that word from the right end of that word?

(a) T *(b)* C
(c) N *(d)* I

7. On rearranging the jumbled spelling of the word SKARTINS, a language is obtained. What is the fifth letter from the right of the rearranged word?

(a) N *(b)* K
(c) R *(d)* S

8. If the 1st, 3rd, 5th, 7th, 10th and 13th letters of the word "ENTERTAINMENT" are used to make a meaningful word, then what two letters will come in the centre?

(a) A M *(b)* T T
(c) RE *(d)* N A

9. On rearranging the jumbled spelling of the word GRUBY a sport is obtained. What is the letter in the centre?

(a) R *(b)* B
(c) G *(d)* U

10. If the letters 'ERVSECI' can be rearranged to form a meaningful word what will be the fifth letter from the right?

(a) R *(b)* V
(c) E *(d)* None of these

11. From the word HASTEN how many independent meaningful English words can be made without changing the order of the letters and using each letter only once?

(a) 1 *(b)* 2
(c) 3 *(d)* 4

EXPLANATORY ANSWERS

1. *(d)* : MLKJIGHFEDCBANOPQRSTUVWXYZ
9th 9th

2. *(d)* : ABCDPONMLKJIHGFEQRSTUVWXYZ
7th 14th

3. *(a)* :

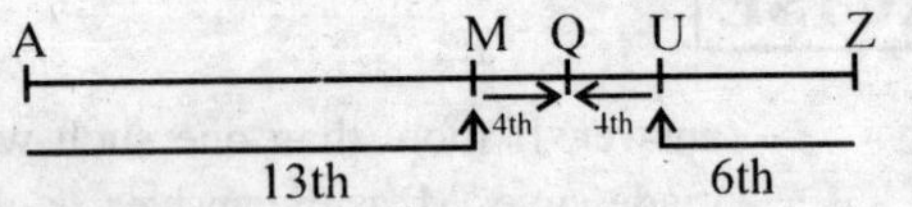

13th letter from left is 'M' and 6th letter from right is 'U'. The letter in the centre of 'M' and 'U' is 'Q'.

4. *(d)* : E C N A B R U T S I D

5. *(d)* : P R O J E C T I O N
The 3rd, 5th, 7th and 10th letters are OETN.
The words formed are TONE and NOTE.

6. *(b)* : F E L I C I T A T I O N S
The 1st, 4th, 5th, 7th, 10th, 11th and 12th lettes are FICTION.
The word is FICTION and 5th letter from right is 'C'.

7. *(d)* : The word is SANSKRIT and 5th letter from right is 'S'.

8. *(b)* : E N T E R T A I N M E N T
The 1st, 3rd, 5th 7th, 10th and 13th letters are ETRAMT.
The word formed is MATTER.

9. *(c)* : The sport is RUGBY. The letter in the centre is 'G'.

10. *(a)* : The word is SERVICE and fifth letter from right is 'R'.

11. *(b)* : The words formed are : HAS, TEN.

19. LOGICAL DIAGRAM

In these type of questions, a set of five different figures is given as options. Each figure represents a logical pattern of certain groups of related words wherein each word represents a class. One has to identify the most appropriate logical figure for the set of words given. Some of the relationships represented by these diagrams are given below. Understand the relationship patterns and then attempt the exercise following the explanation.

EXERCISE

Directions : *From the five logical Diagrams, select one which best illustrates the relationship among three given classes in the questions 1 to 10.*

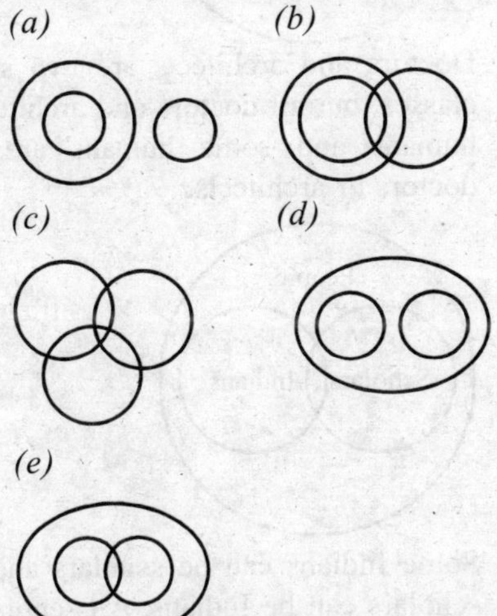

1. Birds, fruits, mangoes
2. Criminals, lawyers, bandits
3. Swimmers, bachelors, men
4. Smart, engineers, women
5. Vegetables, potatoes, brinjals
6. Grapes, sweet, fruit
7. Doctors, architects, humans
8. Scholars, people, Indians
9. Children, naughty, studious
10. Pens, pencils, stationery

Directions : *From the five logical diagrams select one which best illustrates the relationship among three given classes in questions 11 to 20.*

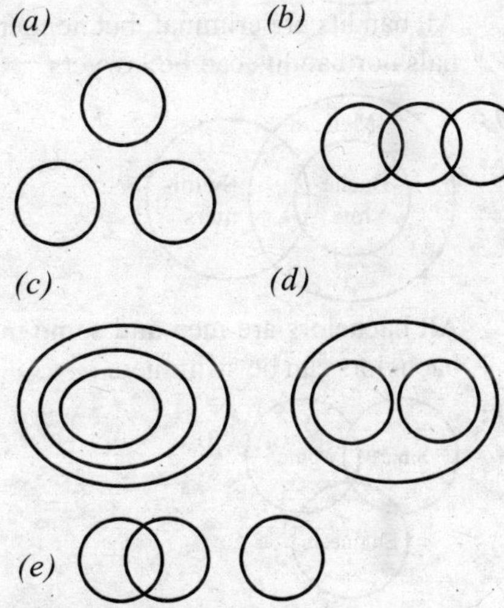

11. Ink, crayons, red
12. Canines, dogs, pups
13. Table, chair, stool
14. Ripe, mangoes, basket
15. Scholars, studious, illiterates
16. Cars, ships, means of conveyance
17. Age, number, thirteen
18. Country, state, continent
19. Father, parent, mother
20. Iron, metal, mercury

EXPLANATORY ANSWERS

1. ***(a)*** **:**

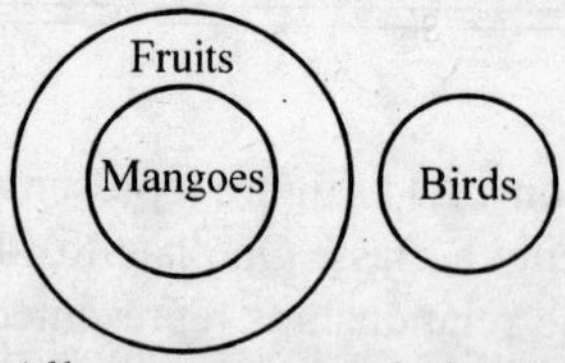

All mangoes are fruits, but neither fruits, nor mangoes can be birds.

2. ***(a)*** **:**

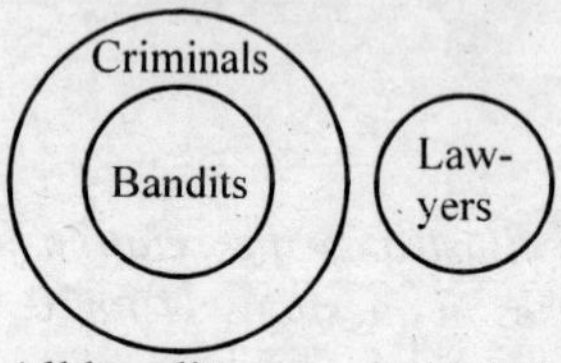

All bandits are criminal, but neither criminals nor bandits can be lawyers.

3. ***(b)*** **:**

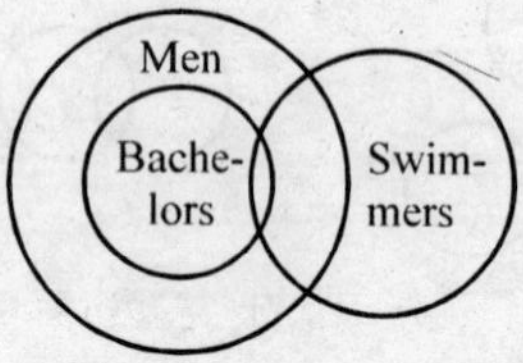

All bachelors are men and some men and bachelors can be swimmers.

4. ***(c)*** **:**

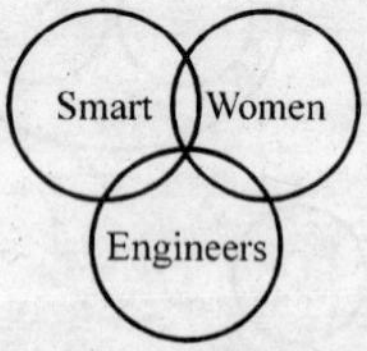

Some women can be smart and some women can be engineers and vice–versa. Some engineers can be women and some engineers can be smart and vice–versa.

5. ***(d)*** **:**

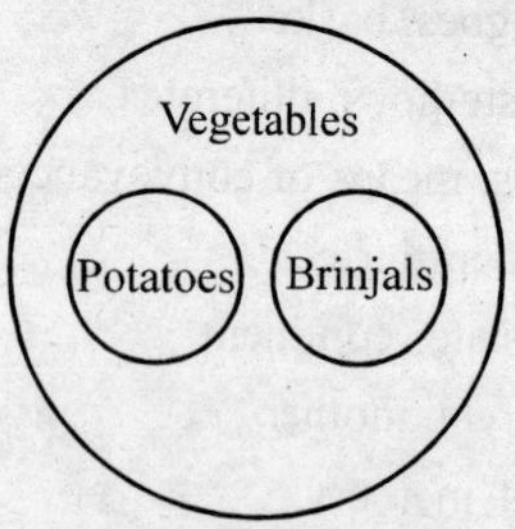

Potatoes and brinjals are vegetables but they have nothing in common. Some vegetables are potatoes and some are brinjals.

6. ***(b)*** **:**

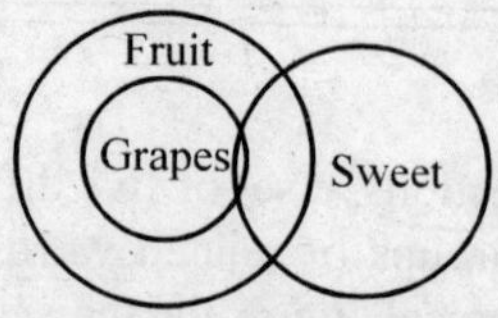

Some grapes are sweet and all grapes are fruit. But not all that is sweet is fruit.

7. ***(d)*** **:**

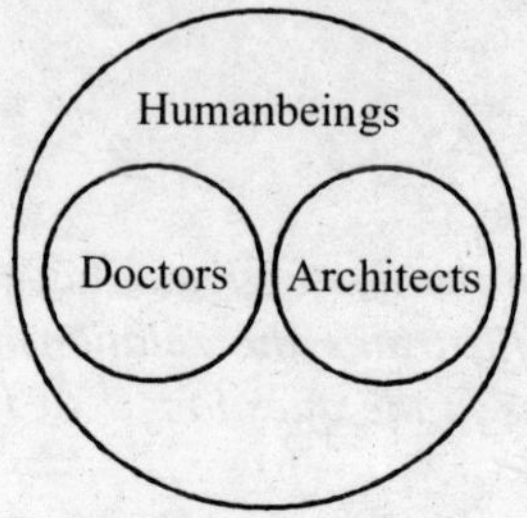

Doctors and architects are two separate classes, but all doctors and architects are humans and some humans are either doctors or architects.

8. ***(e)*** **:**

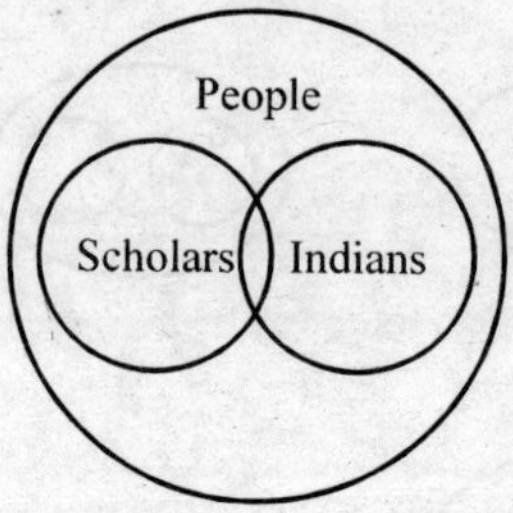

Some Indians can be scholars and some scholars can be Indians. All scholars and Indians are people.

9. ***(c)*** **:**

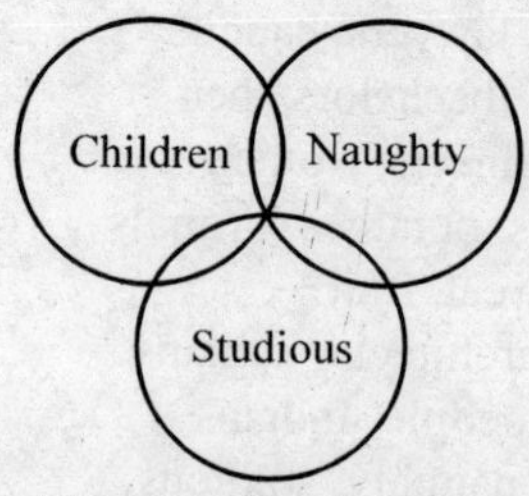

Some children can be naughty and some can be studious, some studious can be children and some naughty. Some naughty can be studious and some children.

10. *(d)* :

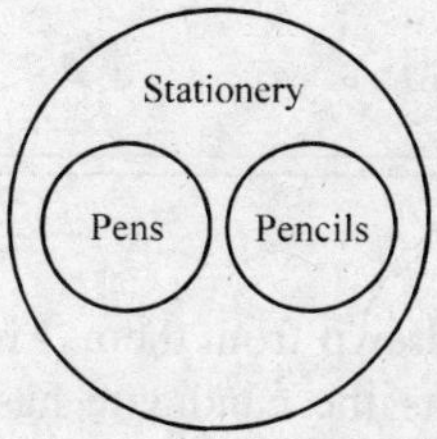

Pens and pencils both are items of stationery and some stationery is pens and pencils, but pens and pencils are two separate classes.

11. *(b)* :

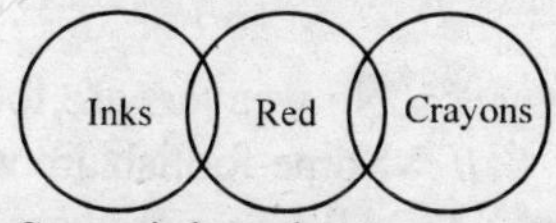

Some ink and some crayons can be red and some red units can be inks and crayons, but ink and crayon have nothing in common.

12. *(c)* :

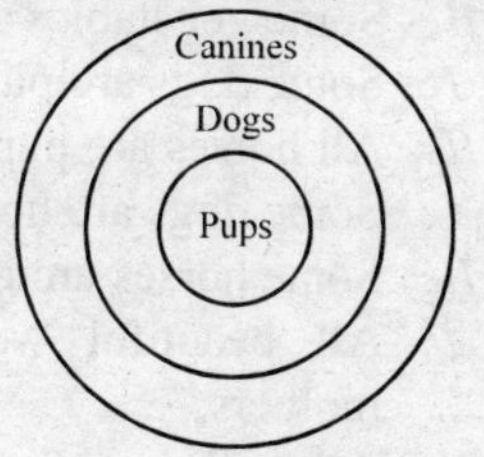

All pups are dogs and all dogs are canines. Some canines are dogs, of which some are pups.

13. *(a)* :

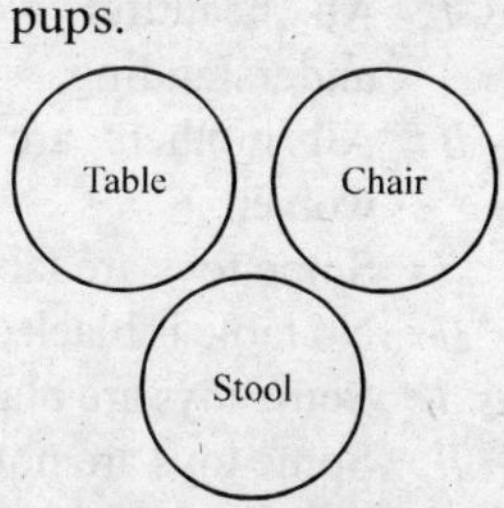

All three are different classes.

14. *(e)* :

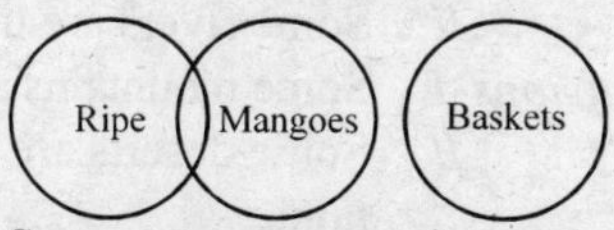

Some mangoes are ripe and some ripe units are mangoes, but neither ripe units nor mangoes can be baskets.

15. *(e)* :

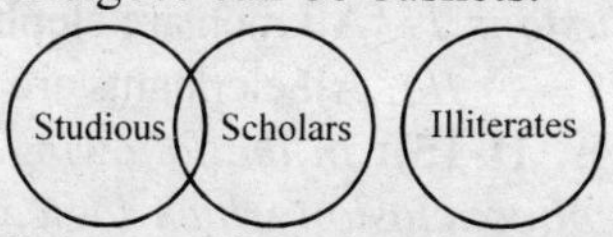

Some studious can be scholars and some scholars can be studious, but neither studious nor scholars can be illiterates.

16. *(d)* :

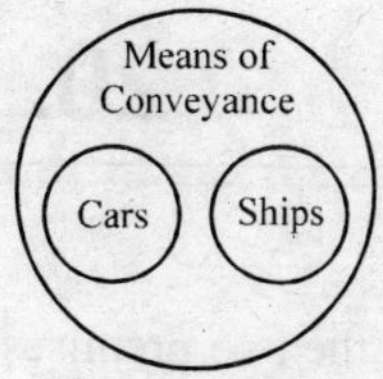

All cars and all ships are means of conveyance, but neither is contained in the other. Some means of conveyance are cars and some ships.

17. *(b)* :

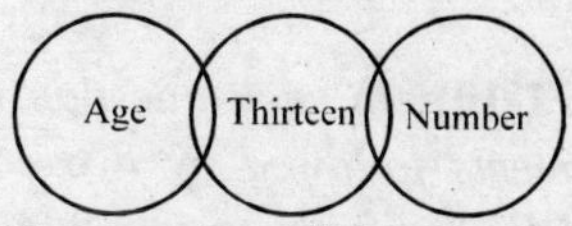

Some are aged thirteen and some numbers are thirteen. Some thirteen units are numbers and some ages. Age and number have nothing in common.

18. *(c)* :

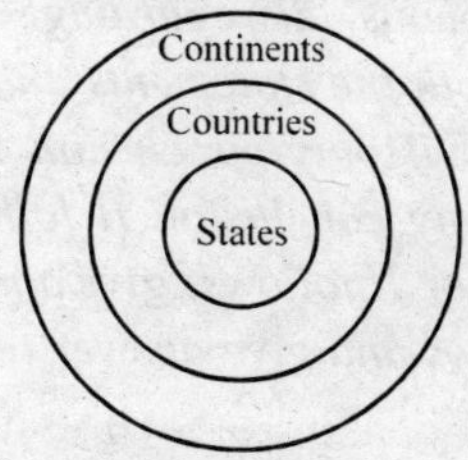

All continents contain countries within it and each country contains states within it.

19. *(d)* :

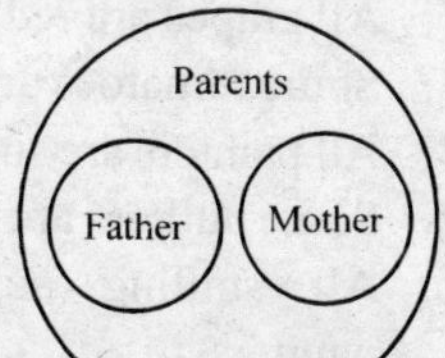

All fathers and mothers are parents, but they are two separate classes. Some of the parents are fathers and some are mothers.

20. *(d)* :

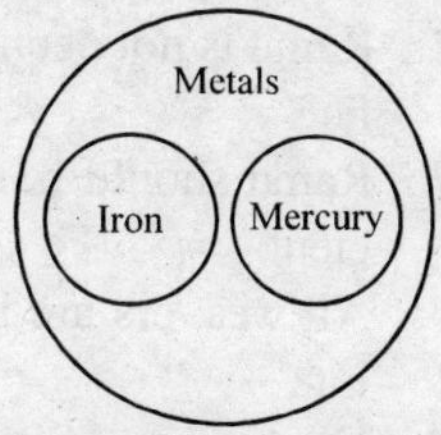

Iron and mercury are metals, but they have nothing in common. Some metals are iron and some mercury.

20. SYLLOGISM

In this reasoning pattern, the two premises are followed by two conclusions drawn from them. Five options *(a)*, *(b)*, *(c)*, *(d)* and *(e)* are given as answers. Based on the two statements the candidate has to select the right option as answer.

EXERCISE

Directions (Qs. 1-10): *In each question below are given two statements followed by two conclusions numbered I and II. You have to take the two given statements to be true even if they seem to be at variance from commonly known facts and then decide which of the given conclusions logically follows from the two given statements, disregarding commonly known facts. Read both the statements and—*

Give answer (a) if only conclusion I follows; give answer (b) if only conclusion II follows; give answer (c) if either I or II follows; give answer (d) if neither I nor II follows and give answer (e) if both I and II follows.

1. *Statements* *I*: All tomatoes are red.
II: All grapes are tomatoes.
Conclusions *I*: All grapes are red.
II: Some tomatoes are grapes.

2. *Statements* *I*: All painters are smiling.
II: Some authors are painters.
Conclusions *I*: All smiling authors are painters.
II: Some authors are smiling.

3. *Statements* *I*: All peons in this office are efficient.
II: Ramu is not efficient.
Conclusions *I*: Ramu is not peon in this office.
II: Ramu should be more efficient.

4. *Statements* *I*: All weavers are hard working.
II: No hard working men are foolish.
Conclusions *I*: No weavers are foolish.
II: Some foolish are weavers.

5. *Statements* *I*: All fishes are cars.
II: All cars are vegetables.
Conclusions *I*: Some vegetables are cars.
II: Some vegetables are fishes.

6. *Statements* *I*: Some dogs are pups.
II: All horses are pups.
Conclusions *I*: Some dogs are horses.
II: Some horses are dogs.

7. *Statements* *I*: All beautiful women are mothers.
II: All mothers are understanding.
Conclusions *I*: All beautiful women are understanding.
II: All mothers are beautiful women.

8. *Statements* *I*: Some toys are tables.
II: No table is black.
Conclusions *I*: Some toys are black.
II: Some toys are not black.

9. *Statements* *I*: All rivers are mountains.
II: Some rivers are deserts.
Conclusions *I*: Some mountains are deserts.
II: Some deserts are not mountains.

10. *Statements* *I*: All men are horses.
II: All horses are elephants.
Conclusions *I*: All men are elephants.
II: All elephants are men.

Directions (Qs. 11-15): *In the following questions, select the set of conclusion which logically follows from the given statements.*

11. *Statements* *I* : All foxes are plates.
II : All plates are trees.
Conclusions *I* : All foxes are trees.
II : All trees are foxes.
III : Some trees are foxes.
IV : Some trees are plates.
(a) All conclusions are correct.
(b) Only conclusions I, III, and IV follow.
(c) Only conclusions II, III, and IV follow.
(d) Only conclusions I and IV follow.
(e) None of the above.

12. *Statements* *I* : Some cubes are squares.
II : All squares are circles.
Conclusions *I* : All cubes are circles.
II : Some circles are cubes.
III : Some circles are squares.
IV : All squares are cubes.
(a) Only conclusion I follows.
(b) Only conclusion I, II and III follow.
(c) All conclusions are correct.
(d) Only conclusions II and III follow.
(e) None of the above.

13. *Statements* *I* : All cups are goats.
II : All goats are tins.
Conclusions *I* : All goats are cups.
II : All tins are goats.
III : No cups are tins.
IV : No tins are cups.
(a) Only conclusions III and IV follow.
(b) Only conclusios I and II follow.
(c) Only conclusions I, II and III follow.
(d) All conclusions are correct.
(e) None of the above.

14. *Statements* *I* : All bombs are bags.
II : Some bags are jets.
Conclusions *I* : All bombs are jets.
II : All jets are bombs.
III : Some jets are bombs.
IV : Some bombs are jets.
(a) Only conclusion III follows.
(b) Only conclusions I and II follow.
(c) All conclusions are correct.
(d) Only conclusions III and IV follow.
(e) None of these.

15. *Statements* *I* : Some thorns are jackets.
II : Some jackets are boats.
Conclusions *I* : No thorns are boats.
II : All jackets are boats.
III : Some boats are thorns.
IV : No jackets are thorns.
(a) Either conclusion I or IV follows.
(b) Either conclusion I or II follows.
(c) Either conclusion I or III follows.
(d) No conclusion is correct.
(e) All conclusions are correct.

EXPLANATORY ANSWERS

1. *(e)* : When all tomatoes are red and all grapes are tomatoes, then all grapes are also red. When all grapes are tomatoes, then some tomatoes must be grapes. Therefore, both conclusions I and II are correct.

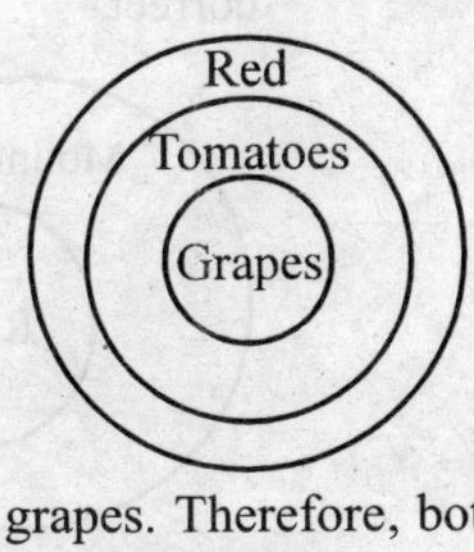

2. *(b)* : When all painters are smiling and some authors are painters, then some authors are smiling. Therefore, only conclusion II is correct.

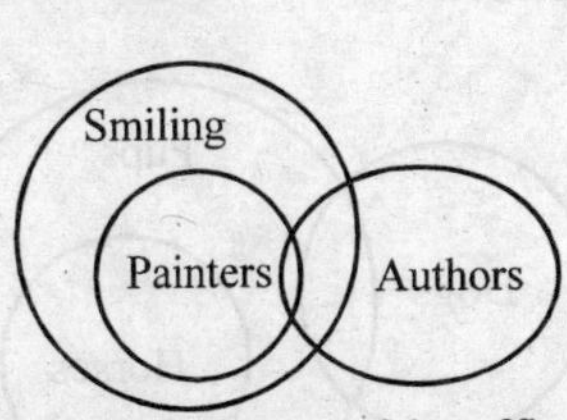

3. *(a)* : When all the peons of the office are efficient, then Ramu cannot be a peon in this office. Therefore, only conclusion I is correct.

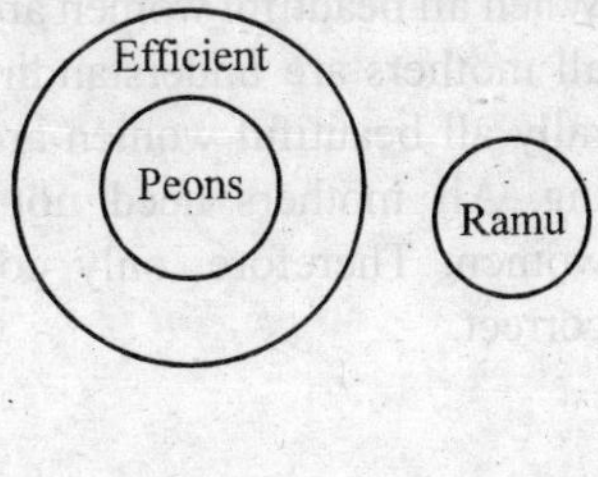

4. *(a)* : When all weavers are hardworking and no hardworking men are foolish, then no weavers are foolish. Therefore, only conclusion I is correct.

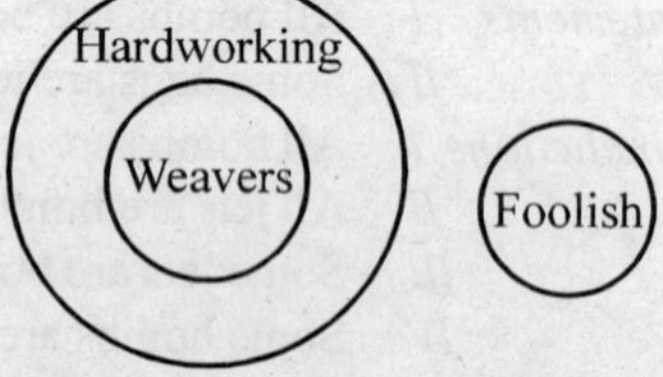

5. *(e)* : When all fishes are cars and all cars are vegetables, then all fishes will naturally be vegetables. This means that some vegetables are fishes. And when all cars are vegetables, then some vegetables will be cars naturally. Therefore, both the conclusions I and II are correct.

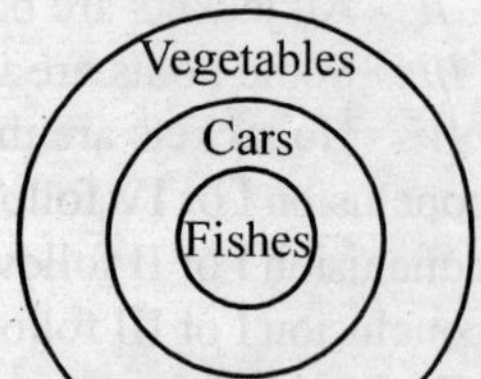

6. *(d)* : No relationship can be established between the two statements. Therefore, neither conclusion I nor conclusion II is correct.

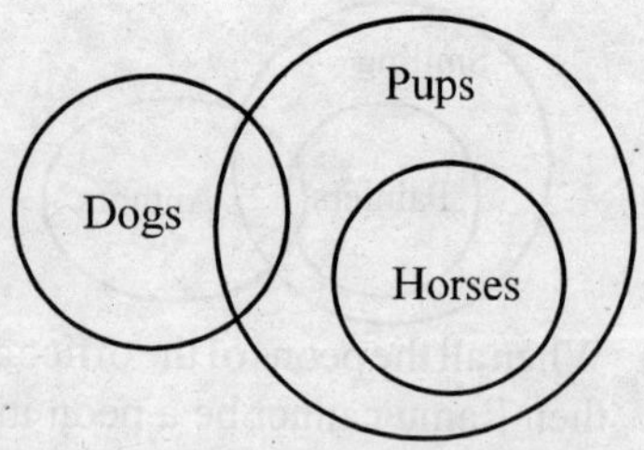

7. *(a)* : When all beautiful women are mothers and all mothers are understanding, then naturally all beautiful women are understanding. All mothers need not be beautiful women. Therefore, only conclusion I is correct.

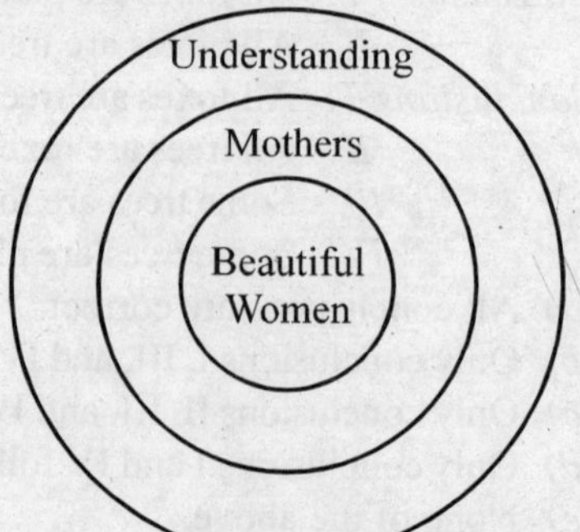

8. *(c)* : When some toys are tables and no table is black, then it is indicated that some toys can be black, as all toys are not tables. On the other hand, some toys may not be black. Therefore, there is a possibility that some toys may or may not be black. As such, either conclusion I or conclusion II can be correct.

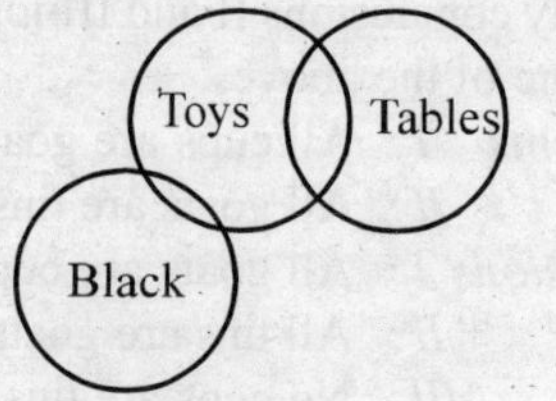

9. *(e)* : When all rivers are mountains and some rivers are deserts, then some deserts cannot be mountains and also, some mountains need not be deserts. Therefore, both conclusion I and conclusion II are correct.

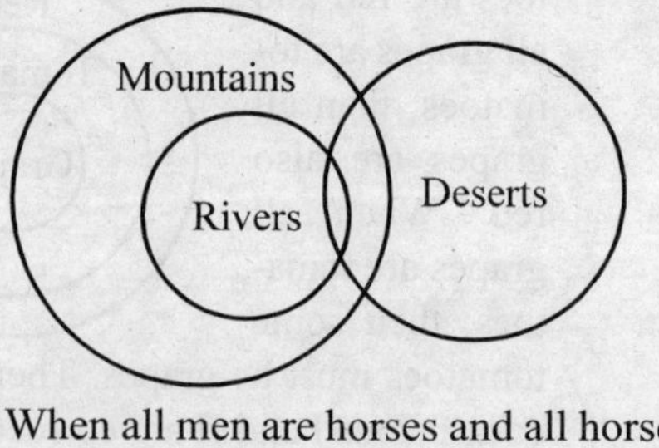

10. *(a)* : When all men are horses and all horses are elephants then, naturally all men are elephants, but all elephants need not be men. Therefore, only conclusion I is correct.

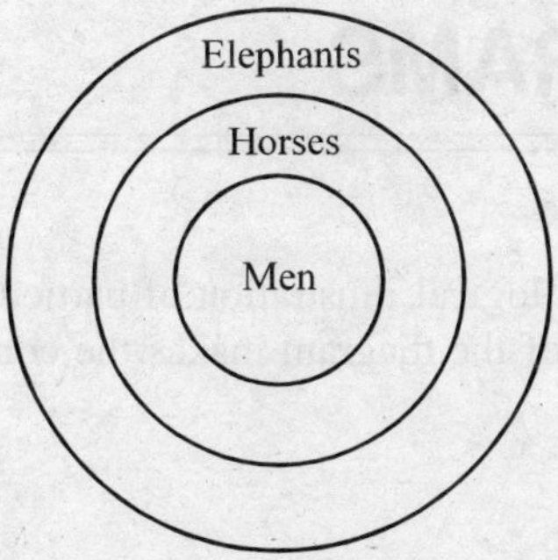

11. ***(b)*** **:**

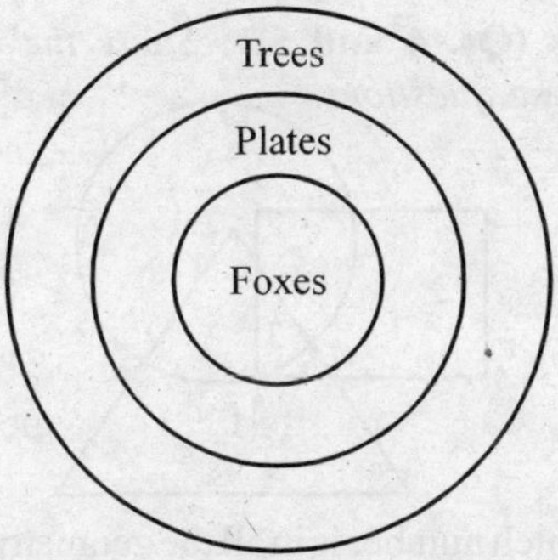

When all foxes are plates and all plates are trees, then naturally all foxes will be trees and some trees will then have to be foxes. And when all plates are trees then some trees will have to be plates. Therefore, only conclusions I, III and IV are correct.

12. ***(d)*** **:** When it is given that some cubes are squares and all squares are circles, then some cubes will naturally be circles, though all cubes cannot be circles. When some cubes are circles, then some circles will have to be cubes. And when all squares are circles, then some circles will have to be squares. As per given statement II, all squares are circles. Therefore all squares cannot be cubes. As such only conclusions II and III are correct.

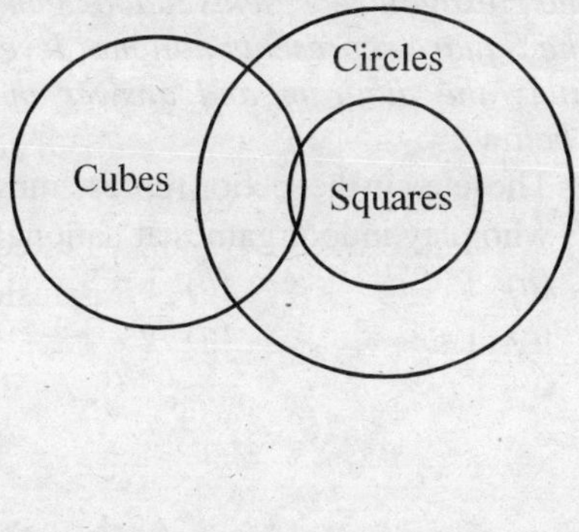

13. ***(e)*** **:** When all cups are goats, then only some goats can be cups. When all goats are tins, then only some tins can be goats. When all cups are goats and all goats are tins, then naturally all cups are tins and some tins must be cups. Therefore, all the conclusions are incorrect.

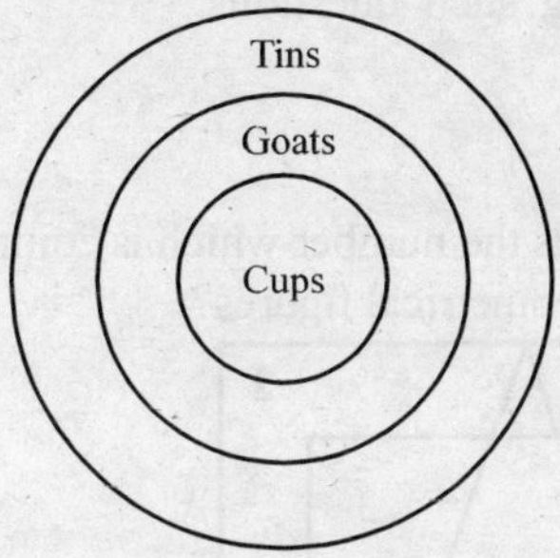

14. ***(e)*** **:** When all bombs are bags and some bags are jets then all bombs cannot be jets. 'Some bags' indicate that there is no chance of some bombs being jets, or some jets being bombs. Further all jets cannot be bombs. Therefore, all conclusions are incorrect.

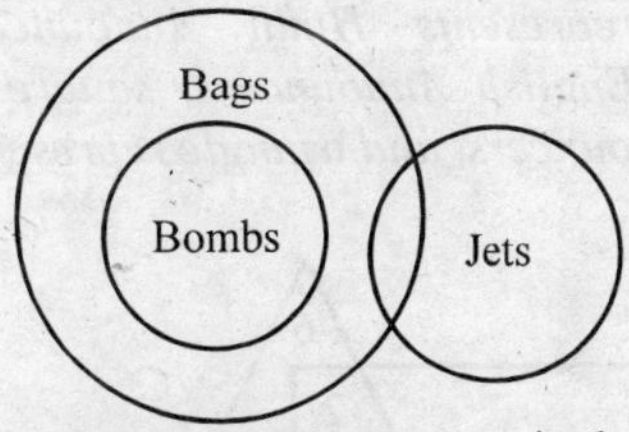

15. ***(d)*** **:** When some thorns are jackets and some jackets are boats, then some thorns may be boats but some boats cannot be thorns. As per Statement I, some thorns are jackets, some jackets need to be thorns. When Statement II conveys that some jackets are boats, then it is clear that all jackets cannot be boats. Therefore, no particular given conclusion can be drawn from the given statements.

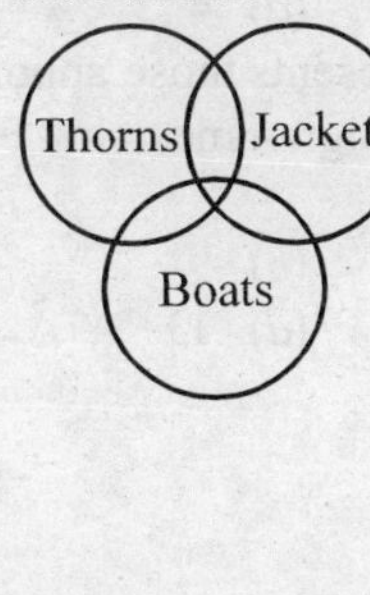

21. VENN DIAGRAMS

In these type of questions, diagrammatic representation presents a logical illustration of particular class or statements based on which the questions are asked. A clear view of the diagram makes the concepts clear for attempting such questions.

EXERCISE

1. What is the number which is common to only two geometrical figures?

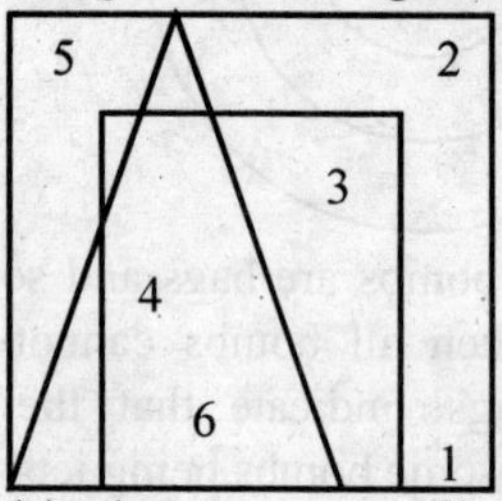

(*a*) 4 (*b*) 3
(*c*) 5 (*d*) 2

Directions (Qs. 2 and 3) : *In the following diagram, rectangle represents Hindi Announcers, circle represents English Announcers, square represents French Announcers, and triangle represents German Announcers.*

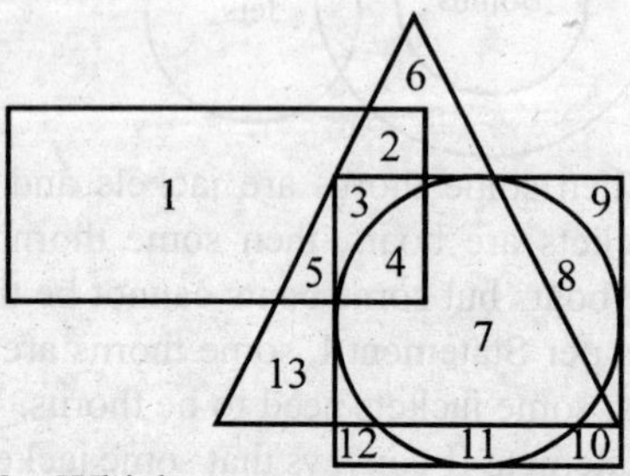

2. Which area represents those announcers who can present programmes in Hindi, French and German only?

(*a*) 1 (*b*) 2
(*c*) 3 (*d*) 4

3 Which area represents those announcers who can present programmes in French and English only?

(*a*) 7 (*b*) 9
(*c*) 11 (*d*) 13

Directions (Qs. 4 and 5) : *Study the diagram to answer these questions.*

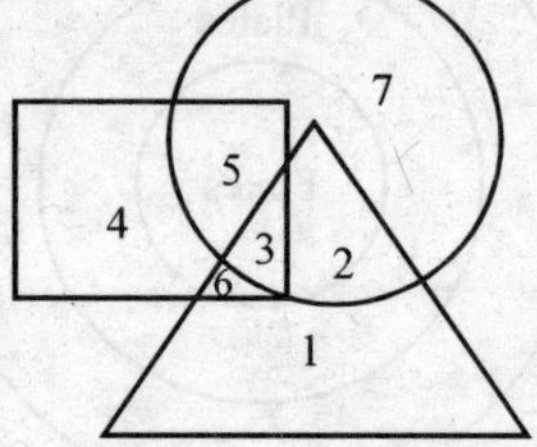

4. Which number is in all the geometrical figures?

(*a*) 5 (*b*) 6
(*c*) 2 (*d*) 3

5. Number 6 is in :

(*a*) Rectangle and triangle
(*b*) Circle and traingle
(*c*) Rectangle and circle
(*d*) Rectangle only

Directions (Qs. 6 to 9) : *In the following diagram*

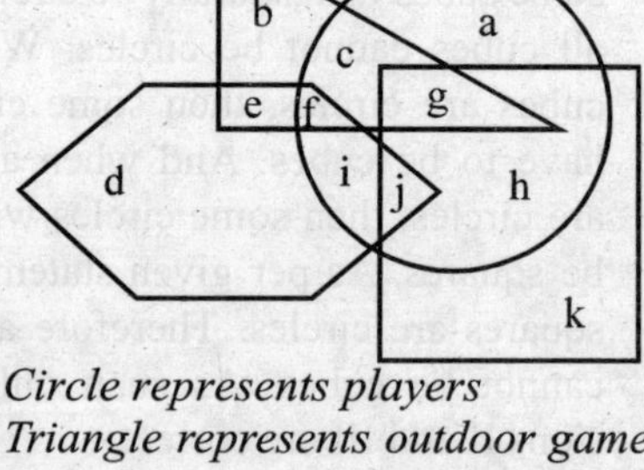

The Circle represents players
The Triangle represents outdoor games
The Hexagon represents indoor games and
The Square represents national level players
Study the diagram and answer the questions given below :

6. The letter in the section representing the players who play indoor games at national level is :

(*a*) f (*b*) i
(*c*) j (*d*) g

7. The letter representing the section of outdoor as well as indoor game players who do not play at the national level is :
(*a*) c (*b*) f
(*c*) e (*d*) i

8. The section representing national level players who do not play either outdoor or indoor games but still come under the category of players is :
(*a*) k (*b*) g
(*c*) c (*d*) h

9. Persons who play outdoor games but do not come under the category of players are represented in the section marked :
(*a*) b (*b*) c
(*c*) a (*d*) d

Direction (Qs. 10) : *Study the diagram given below.*

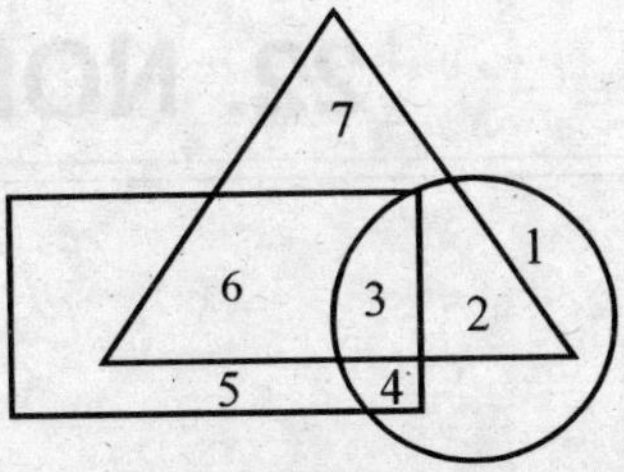

A college provides three different activities, students union represented by triangle, literary society represented by rectangle and social service league represented by circle.

10. Those who take part in both literary society and social service league but not in students union are represented by :
(*a*) 3 & 4 (*b*) 5 & 6
(*c*) 5 & 1 (*d*) 4

EXPLANATORY ANSWERS

1. *(b)* :

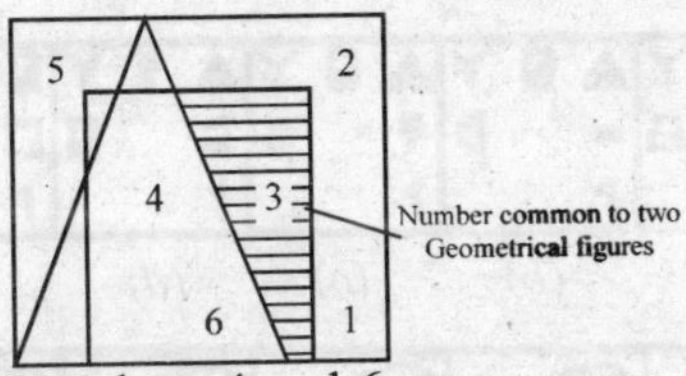

Note : Numbers 4 and 6 are common to all three geometrical figures.

2. *(c)*, 3. *(c)* :

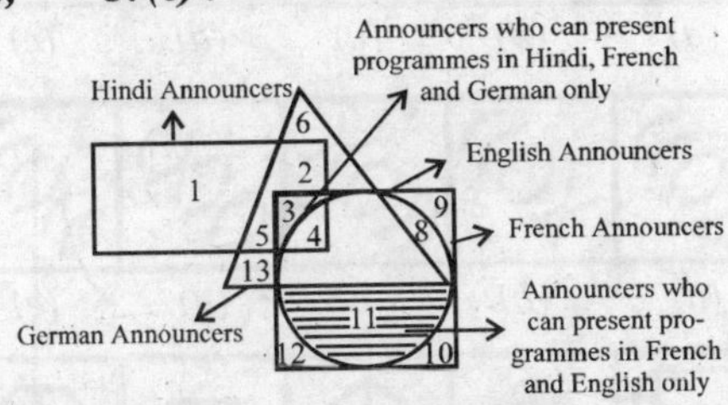

4. *(d)*, 5. *(a)* :

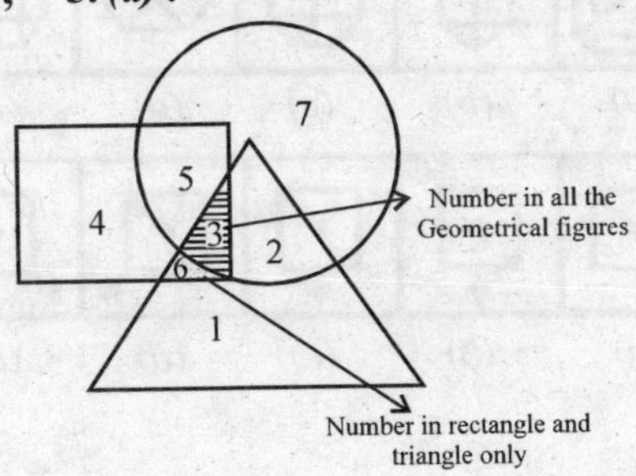

6. *(c)*, 7. *(b)*, 8. *(d)*, 9. *(a)* :

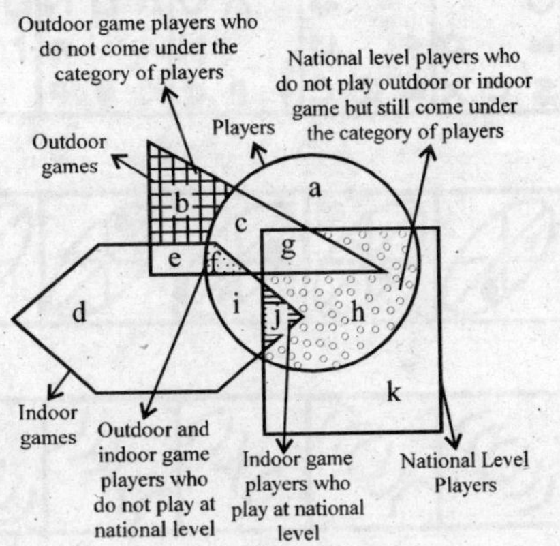

10. *(d)*

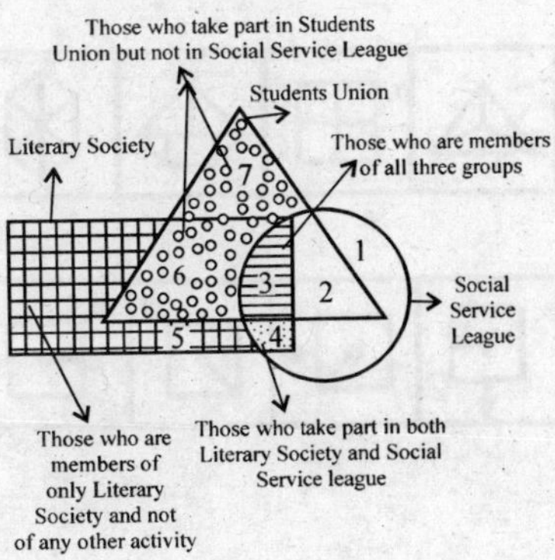

22. NON-VERBAL SERIES

EXERCISE

Directions (Q. 1–10) : *In each of the following questions which one of the five answer figures given below should come after the problem figures if the sequence are continued?*

Problem Figures | **Answer Figures**

1.  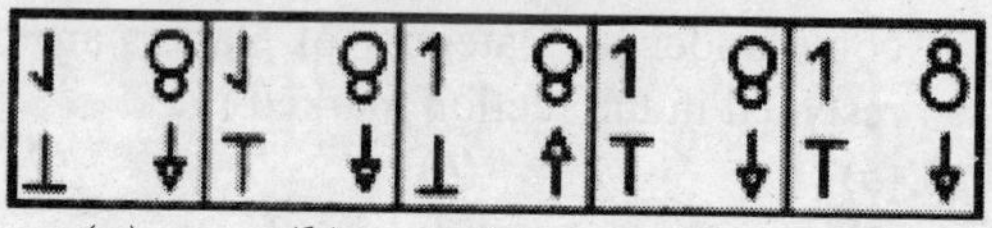

(a) (b) (c) (d) (e)

2. 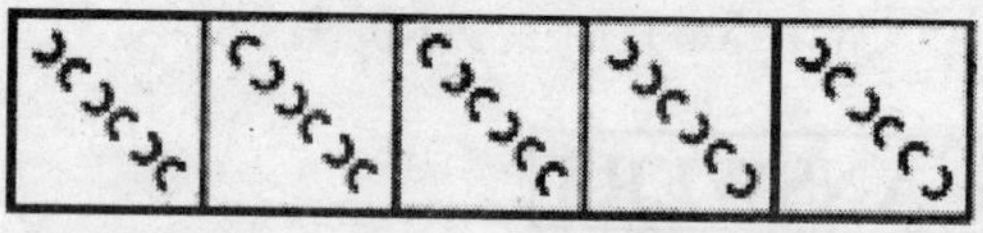 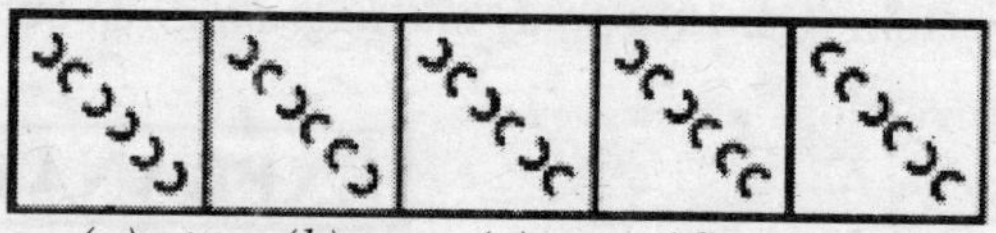

(a) (b) (c) (d) (e)

3. 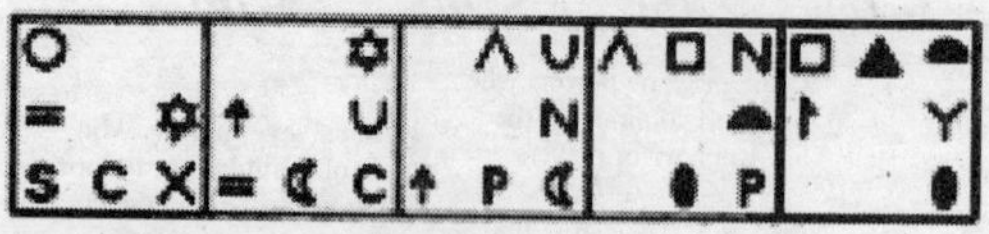 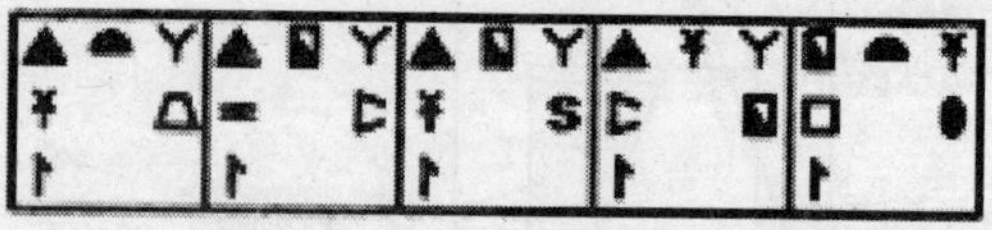

(a) (b) (c) (d) (e)

4.  

(a) (b) (c) (d) (e)

5.  

(a) (b) (c) (d) (e)

6.  

(a) (b) (c) (d) (e)

7.  

(a) (b) (c) (d) (e)

Problem Figures | **Answer Figures**

8.  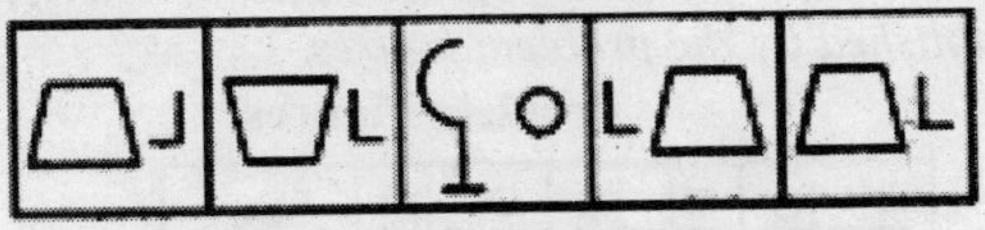

(a) (b) (c) (d) (e)

9. 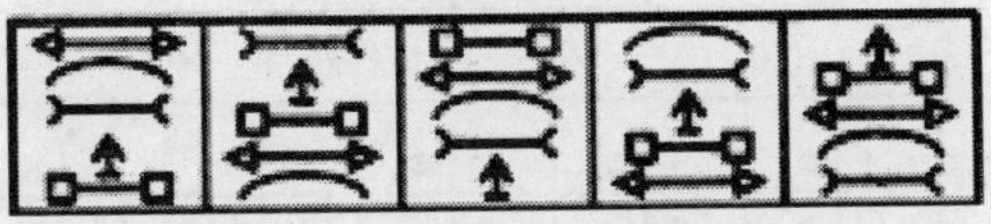 

(a) (b) (c) (d) (e)

10. 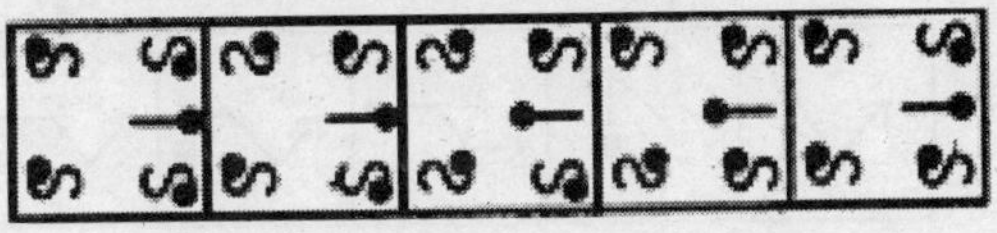 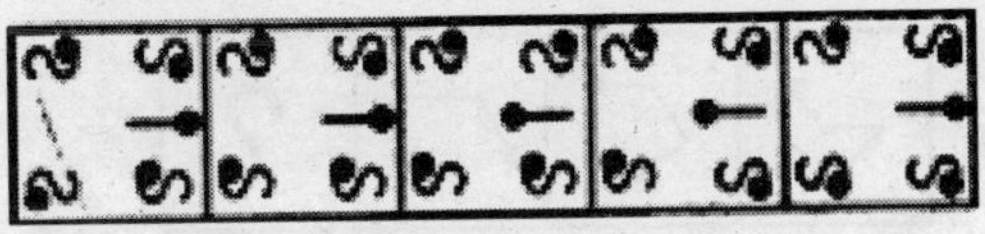

(a) (b) (c) (d) (e)

Directions (Q. 11-20) : *In each of these questions, a series begins with an unmarked figure on the extreme left in the row of figures. One and only one of the five lettered figures in the series does not fit into the series. The two unmarked figures, one on the extreme left and the other on the extreme right fit into the series. Take as many aspects into account as possible of the figures in the series and find out the one and only of the five marked figures which does not fit into the series. The letter of that figure is the answer.*

11. 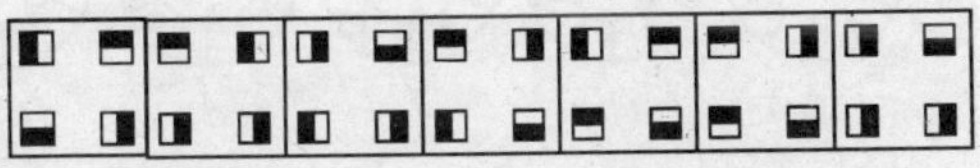

(a) (b) (c) (d) (e)

12. 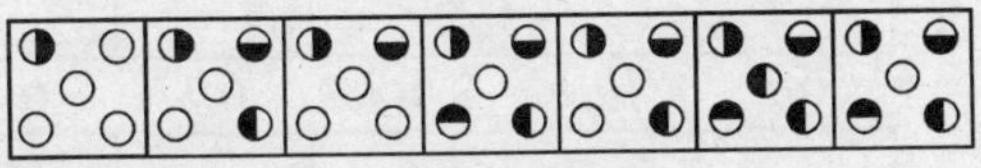

(a) (b) (c) (d) (e)

13. 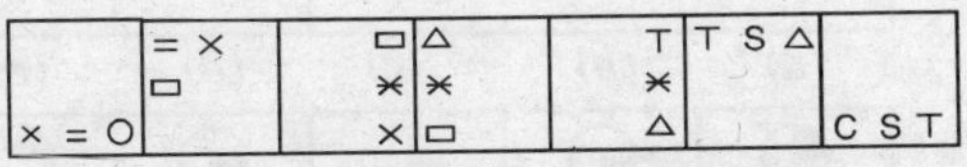

(a) (b) (c) (d) (e)

14. 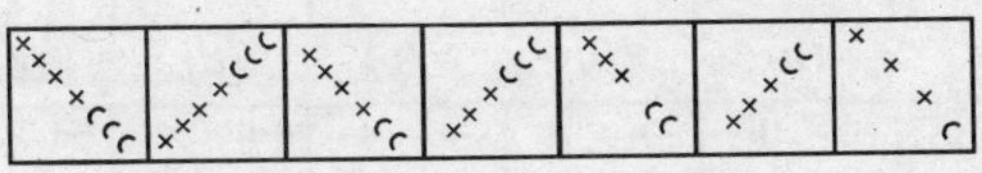

(a) (b) (c) (d) (e)

15. 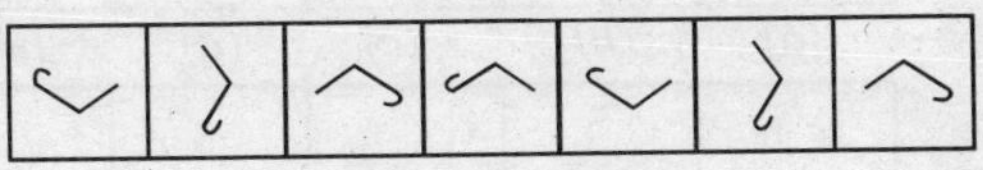

(a) (b) (c) (d) (e)

16. 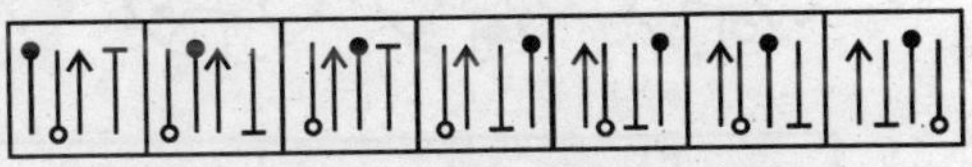

(a) (b) (c) (d) (e)

17. 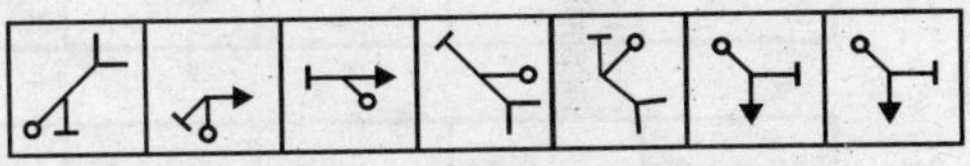

(a) (b) (c) (d) (e)

18. 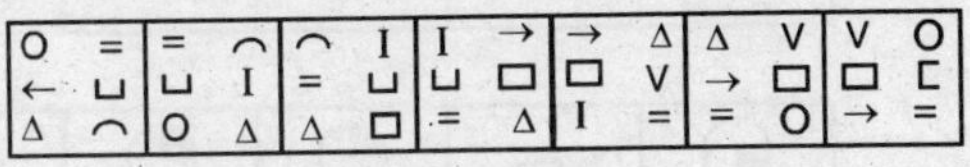

(a) (b) (c) (d) (e)

19. 

(a) (b) (c) (d) (e)

20. 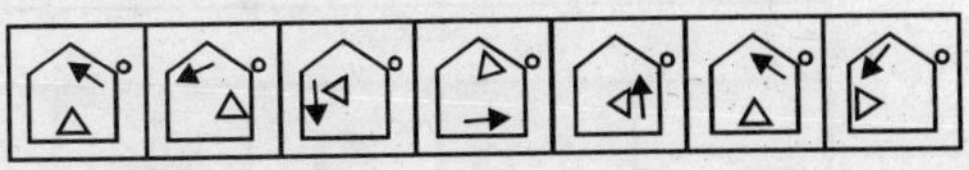

(a) (b) (c) (d) (e)

Directions (Q. 21–30) : *Each of the following questions consist of problem figures followed by answer figures. Select a figure from amongst the answer figures which will continue the same series or pattern as established by the problem figures.*

Problem Figures | **Answer Figures**

21. 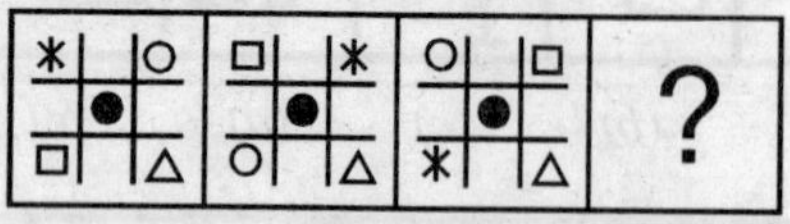 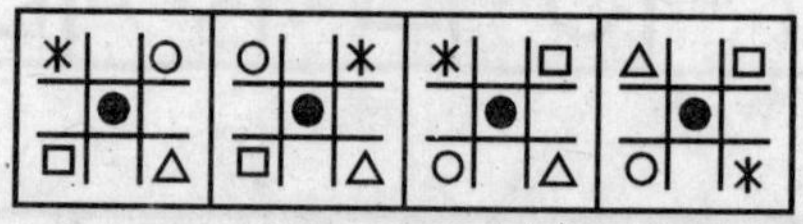

(a) (b) (c) (d)

22. 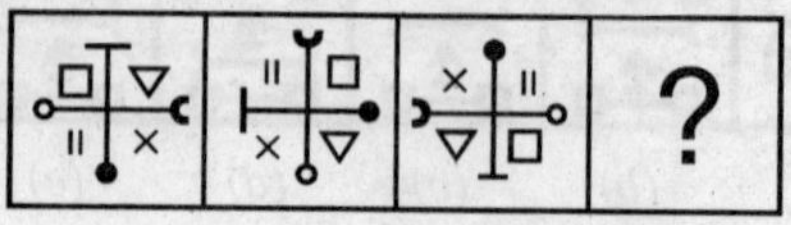 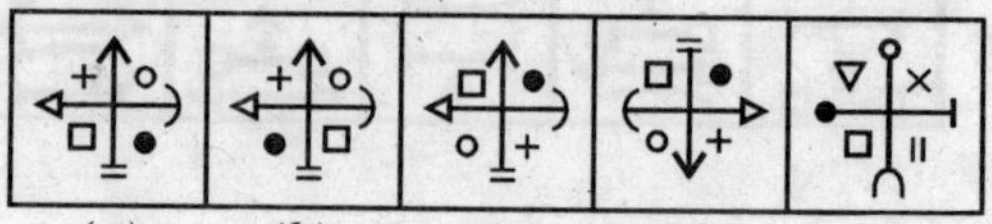

(a) (b) (c) (d) (e)

23. 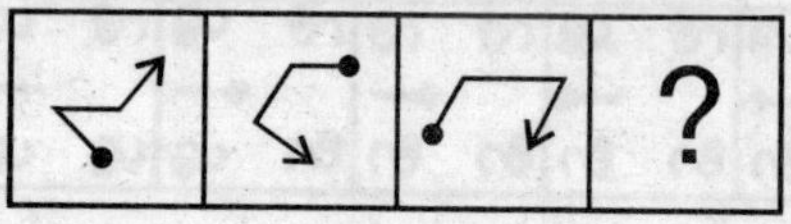 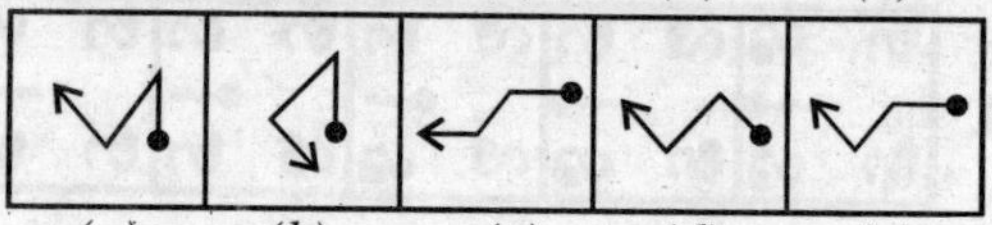

(a) (b) (c) (d) (e)

24. 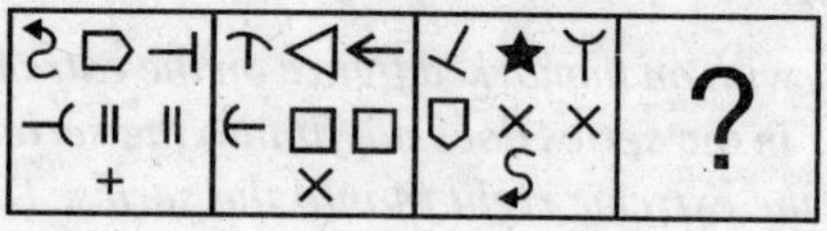 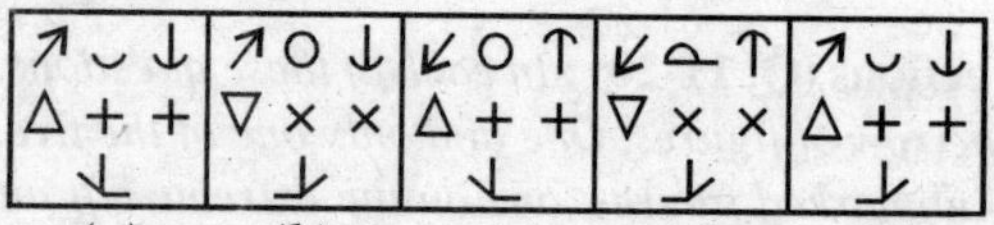

(a) (b) (c) (d) (e)

25. 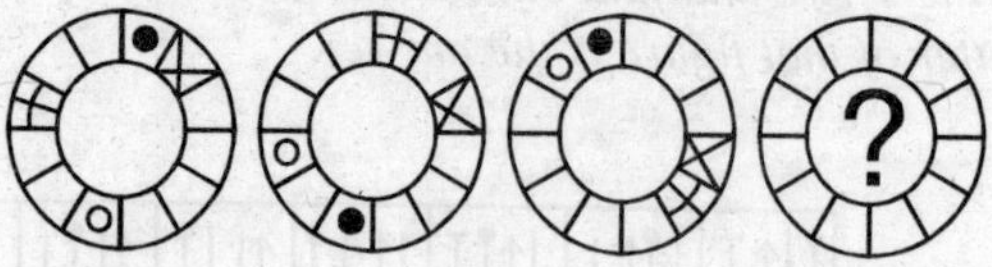 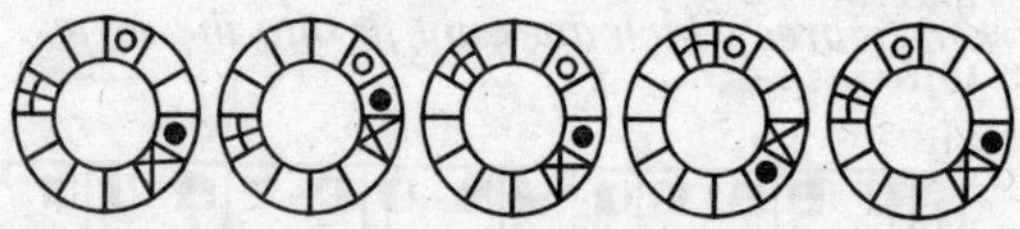

(a) (b) (c) (d) (e)

26.  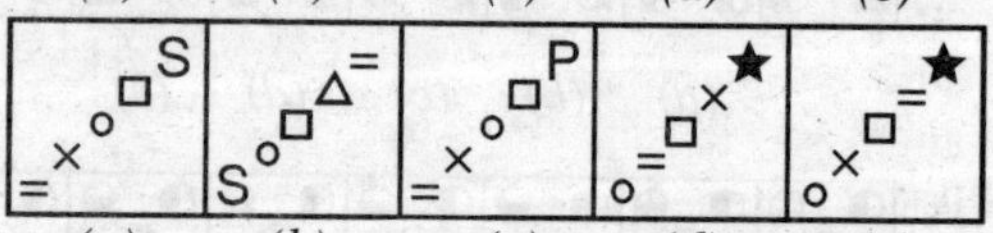

(a) (b) (c) (d) (e)

27. 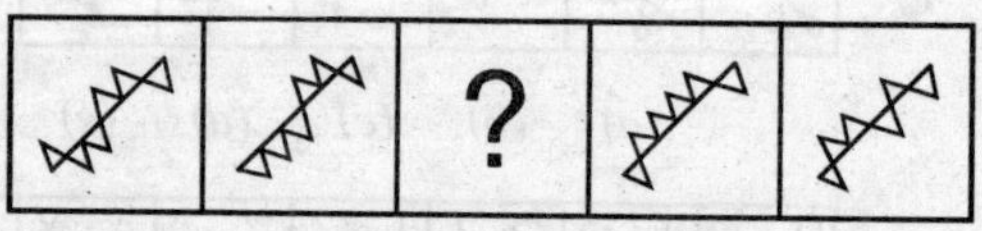 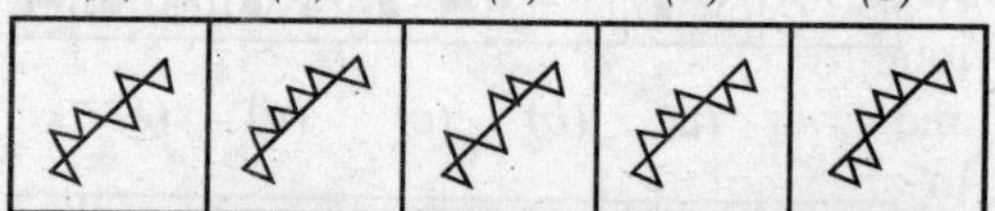

(a) (b) (c) (d) (e)

28. 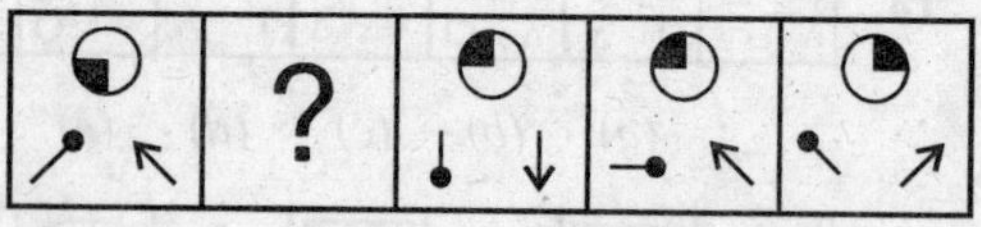 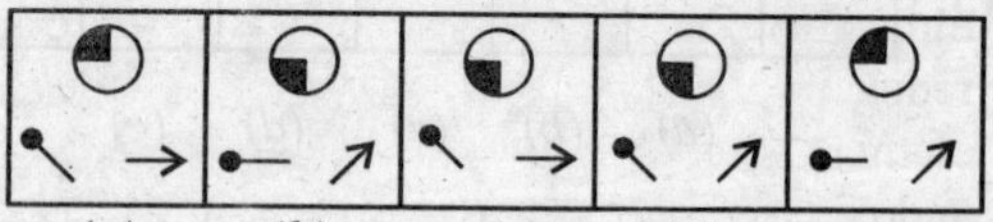

(a) (b) (c) (d) (e)

29. 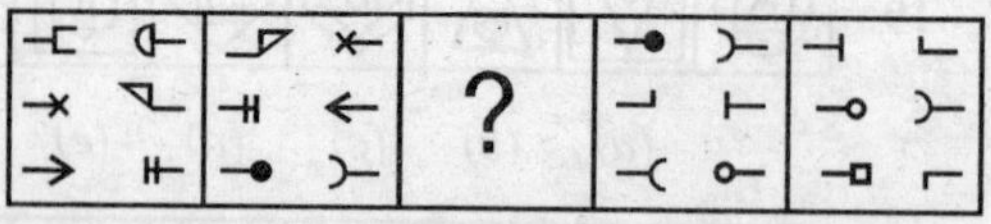 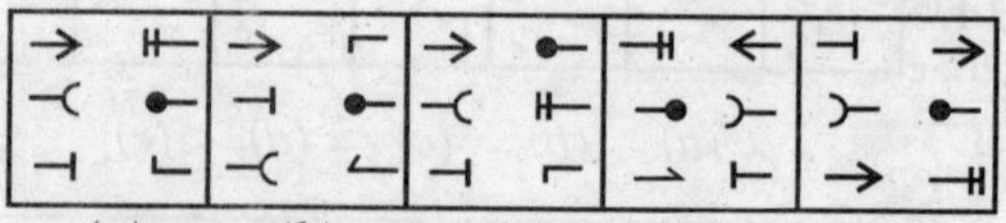

(a) (b) (c) (d) (e)

30.  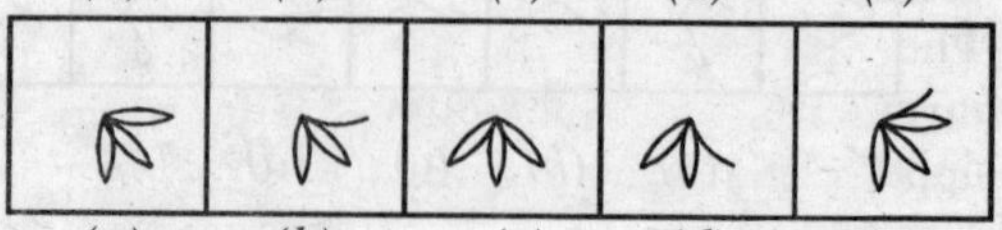

(a) (b) (c) (d) (e)

EXPLANATORY ANSWERS

1. *(d)* : In each step, all the elements move to the adjacent corner (of the square boundary) in a CW direction and the element that reaches the upper-left corner gets vertically inverted.

2. *(c)* : We can label the arcs as shown  . The arcs get inverted in the sequence (1 & 2), (3, 4 & 5), (6 & 1), (2, 3 & 4), (5 & 6), ...

3. *(d)* : All the elements move half-a-side of the square boundary in ACW direction in each step. Also, first, third and fifth elements are replaced by new elements in one step and second, fourth and sixth elements are replaced by new elements in the next step. The two steps are repeated alternately.

4. *(a)* : In each step, the dot moves one space CW and the arrow moves two spaces CW.

5. *(c)* : One arc and four arcs get inverted alternately.

6. *(e)* : The number of parts increases by one along with the number of sides in the figure.

7. *(c)* : The pin rotates 45°CW and 90°CW alternately and moves one space (each space is equal to half-a-side of the square) and two spaces CW alternately. The arrow rotates 90°ACW and 45°ACW alternately and moves two spaces and one space.

8. *(e)* : In one step, the two elements interchange positions and the smaller element gets enlarged while the larger element gets reduced in size. In the next step, the smaller element is replaced by a new small element and the larger element is replaced by a new large element.

9. *(c)* : In each step, the elements move in the order  .

10. *(b)* : The upper-left element gets laterally inverted in first, third, fifth. .... steps; the upper-right element gets rotated through 180° is first, fourth, seventh,.... steps; the lower-left element gets laterally inverted in second, fourth, sixth, ... steps; the lower-right element gets rotated through 180° in third, sixth,... steps and the pin at the middle-right position gets laterally inverted in every second step.

11. *(a)* : The shade in the top left square is moved one step clockwise till figure B and then reversed, the process is repeated. The shade in the top right square is moved one step anticlockwise till figure D and then reversed. The shade in the bottom left square is moved one step clockwise in alternate figures and the shade in bottom right square is moved one step clockwise after two figures. In figure 'A' the rule is isolated by the shade in the bottom left square.

12. *(e)* : In alternate figures a new circle is shaded clockwise. The pattern of the shade is also moved clockwise. In figure 'E' right half of the circle in the centre should have been shaded.

13. *(a)* : The three elements are placed either horizontally or vertically. In option 'A' neither of the placements can be applied.

14. *(c)* : The placement of elements is same in alternate figures. The number and type of elements is same in two subsequent figures. In this manner, figure 'C' should have four crosses and two C shapes.

15. *(c)* : The element is moved one step anticlockwise and the arc at one end is turned outside and inside alternately. In figure 'C' the element should be on the right side with the arc turned outside on the top side.

16. *(e)* : The left most element, line segment with the dot is moved one step towards right till figure C where it reaches the extreme right, position. This process is repeated from figure D where the element on the extreme left, line segment with a circle, is moved. In figure 'E' the placement of the elements does not follow the rule of the series.

17. ***(e)*** **:** The 'T' line is rotated 45° clockwise and the line with the circle 45° anticlockwise. The 'Y' shape and the arrow are repeated twice after two figures. In option E, the 'T' shape and the line with the circle are rotated by 90°.

18. ***(e)*** **:** First the elements in the four corners are moved one step anticlockwise, next the four elements from the top are moved one step anticlockwise and then the four elements from the bottom are moved one step anticlockwise. Of the remaining two elements, the one on the left is made new each time and then their places are interchanged. This process is repeated from figure D. In option 'E' open square should have been in place of circle to continue the series.

19. ***(a)*** **:** At each step the outermost figure is removed and a new figure is placed right in the centre of other two figures. In option 'A' the triangle is turned upside down, which violates the rule of the series.

20. ***(a)*** **:** The arrow is moved one step anticlockwise and the triangle one step clockwise. In figure 'A' the triangle should have been on the left side of the figure.

21. ***(a)*** **:** The places of star, circle and square are moved one step clockwise at each step.

22. ***(e)*** **:** The elements in the four quadrants are moved one step clockwise and the elements at the ends of the cross are moved one step anticlockwise in this series.

23. ***(a)*** **:** In alternate figures, the line with the dot is turned 90° clockwise and the arrow 180° clockwise.

24. ***(e)*** **:** In alternate figures, the element in the top left position is horizontally inverted and moved one and half steps anticlockwise, the top middle element is turned 90° clockwise and moved one step anticlockwise, the top right element is turned 135° clockwise and moved one step anticlockwise, the element at the bottom is replaced by a new element and moved to the top middle position, and the two identical elements are replaced by two new identical elements.

25. ***(a)*** **:** The cross and the circle move one and two steps clockwise respectively (at each step), the plus moves 3, 4 and 5 steps clockwise, and the dot 6, 5 and 4 steps clockwise.

26. ***(a)*** **:** At first step, the fifth or the bottom most element is moved to the second place from top, the second element moved to the fourth place, the fourth element is moved to the third place, the third element is moved to the first or the topmost place and the element on the top, which is made new, is moved to the last or the fifth place. At second step i.e., from second problem figure to third problem figure the above process is reversed. The bottom most element is the first and the top most element is the last or fifth. Hereafter, the process is repeated from the beginning. Option 'A' is the right answer.

27. ***(c)*** **:** Starting from the bottom, one triangle is moved to the opposite side at each step in upward order. Option 'C' fits into the question marked space.

28. ***(c)*** **:** The shade inside the circle is rotated clockwise in alternate figures; the line segment with a dot is rotated 135° clockwise in alternate figures and the arrow is rotated 135° anticlockwise in alternate figures. By this process answer figure 'C' completes the series.

29. ***(a)*** **:** At each step the elements are moved diagonally upward and then laterally inverted, and the top two elements are made new and placed at the bottom line. By this process, option figure 'A' completes the series.

30. ***(a)*** **:** The number of arcs making the petals of the flower are increased by one, one and half, two, two and half respectively at each step. Also, the flower is turned 45° anticlockwise. By this process, option 'A' is the right answer.

23. NON-VERBAL ANALOGY

EXERCISE

TYPE-I

Directions (Q. 1-15): *The second figure in the first unit of the Problem Figures bears a certain relationship to the first figure. Similarly, one of the figures in the Answer Figures bears the same relationship to the first figures in the second unit of the Problem Figures. Locate the figure which would fit the questions marks.*

Problem Figures | **Answer Figures**

1.

1 2 3 4

(a) (b) (c) (d) (e)

2.

1 2 3 4

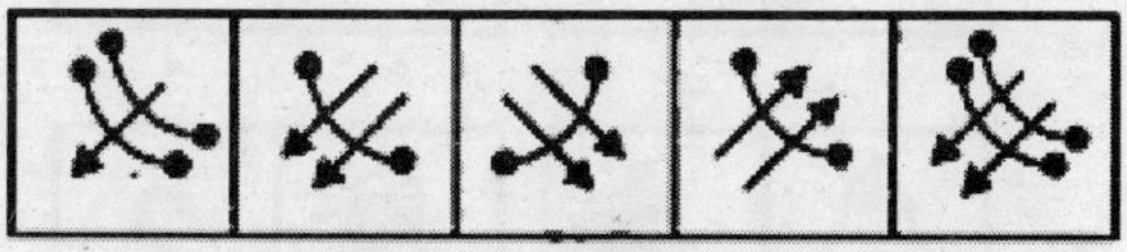

(a) (b) (c) (d) (e)

3.

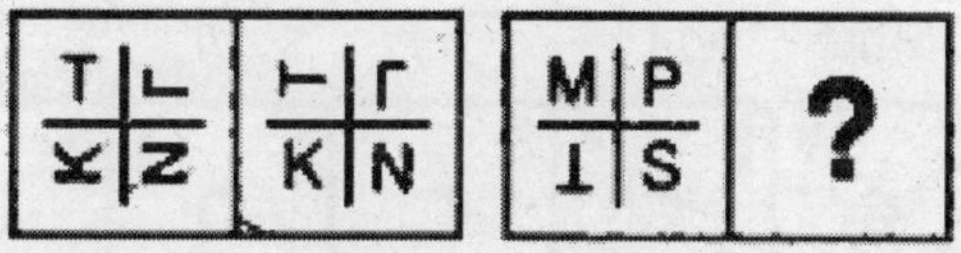

1 2 3 4

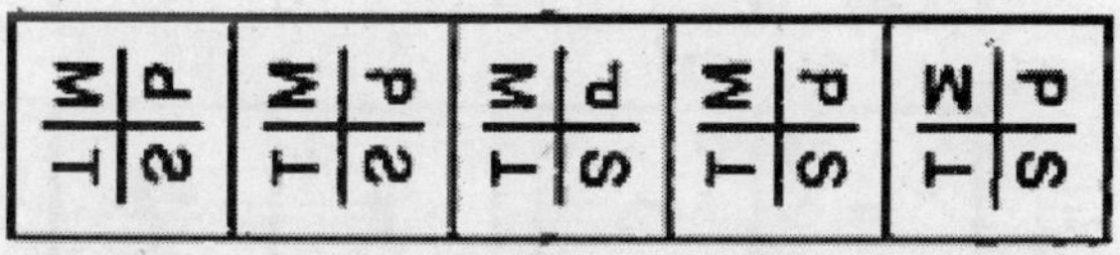

(a) (b) (c) (d) (e)

4.

1 2 3 4

(a) (b) (c) (d) (e)

5.

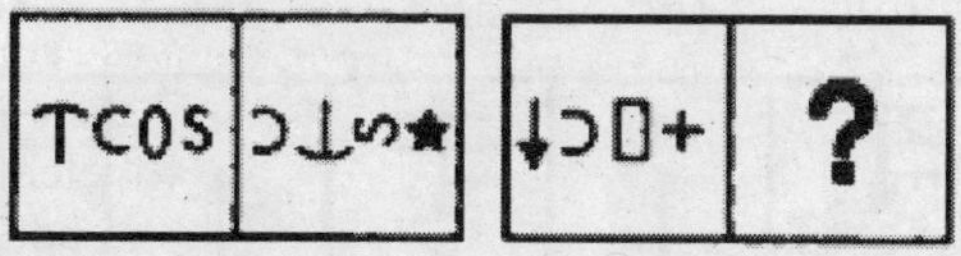

1 2 3 4

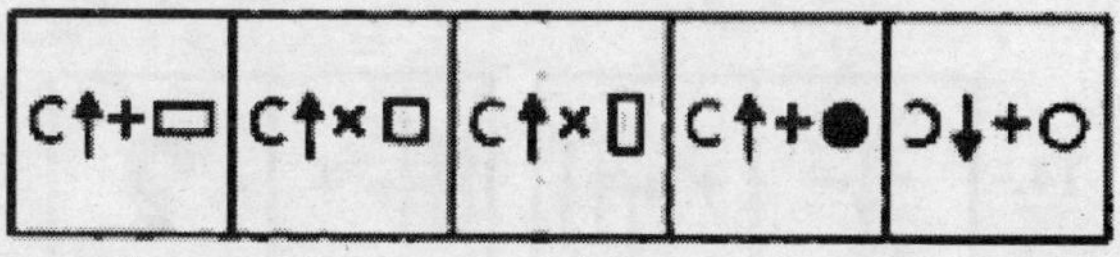

(a) (b) (c) (d) (e)

6.

1 2 3 4

(a) (b) (c) (d) (e)

Problem Figures | **Answer Figures**

7.

1 2 3 4 (a) (b) (c) (d) (e)

8.

1 2 3 4 (a) (b) (c) (d) (e)

9.
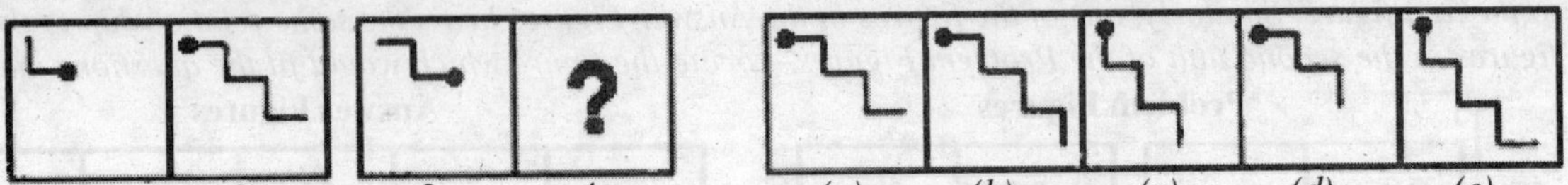
1 2 3 4 (a) (b) (c) (d) (e)

10.
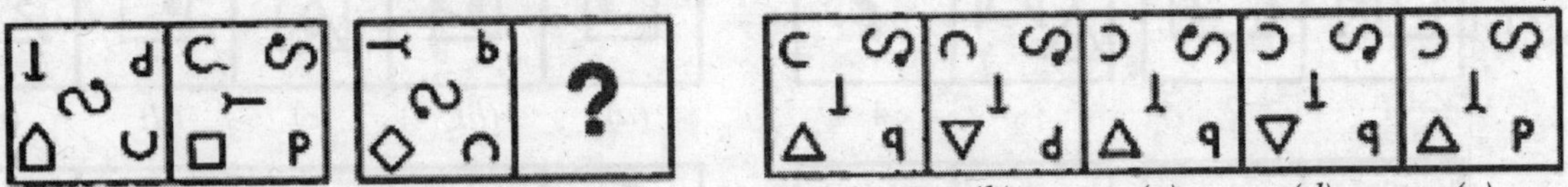
1 2 3 4 (a) (b) (c) (d) (e)

11.

1 2 3 4 (a) (b) (c) (d) (e)

12.
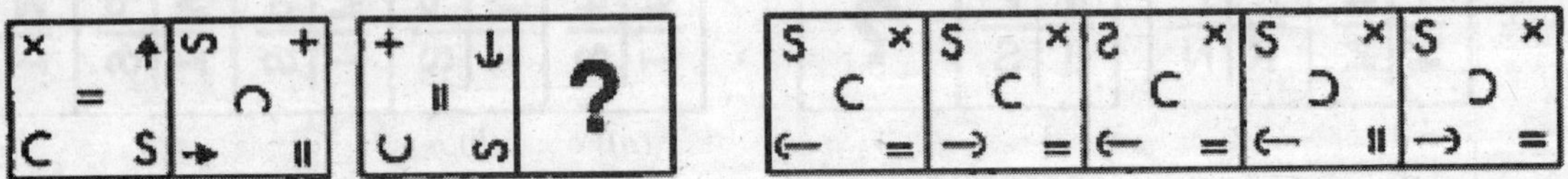
1 2 3 4 (a) (b) (c) (d) (e)

13.

1 2 3 4 (a) (b) (c) (d) (e)

14.
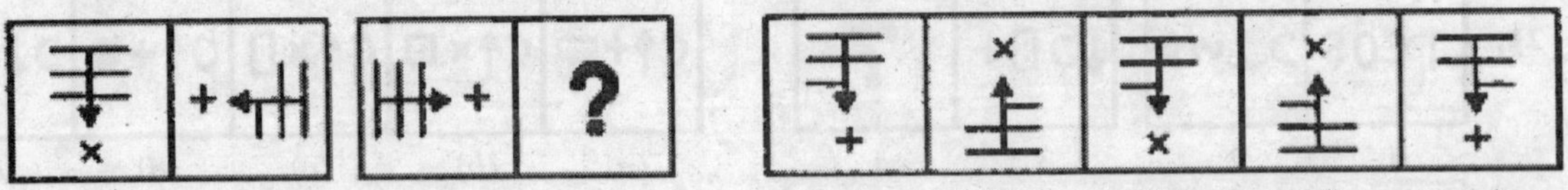
1 2 3 4 (a) (b) (c) (d) (e)

15.

1 2 3 4 (a) (b) (c) (d) (e)

TYPE-II

Directions (Q. 16–30): *In each of the following questions, a related pair of figures is followed by five numbered pairs of figures. Select the pair that has a relationship* **similar** *to that in the unnumbered pair.*

Problem Figure **Answer Figures**

16.

(a) (b) (c) (d) (e)

17.
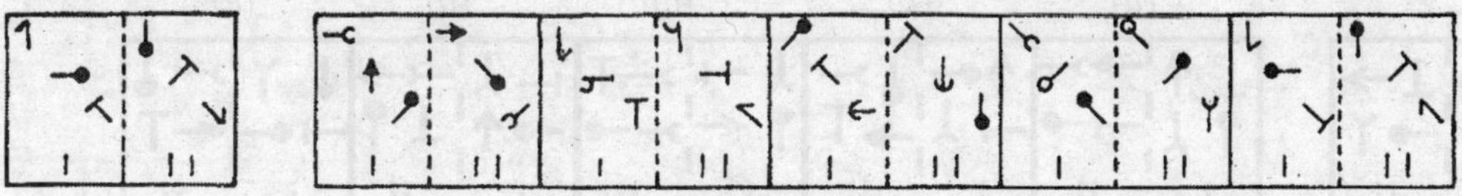
(a) (b) (c) (d) (e)

18.
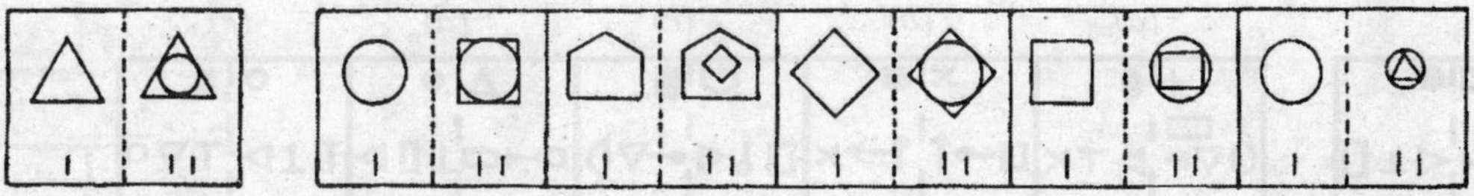
(a) (b) (c) (d) (e)

19.
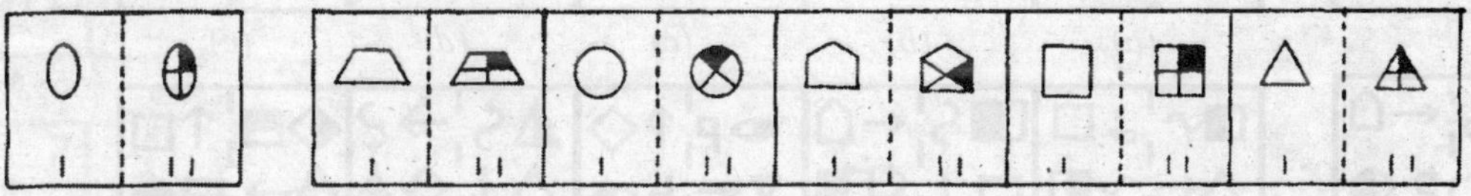
(a) (b) (c) (d) (e)

20.
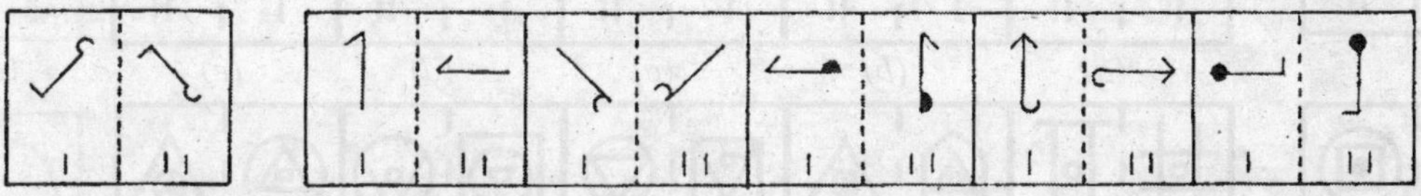
(a) (b) (c) (d) (e)

21.
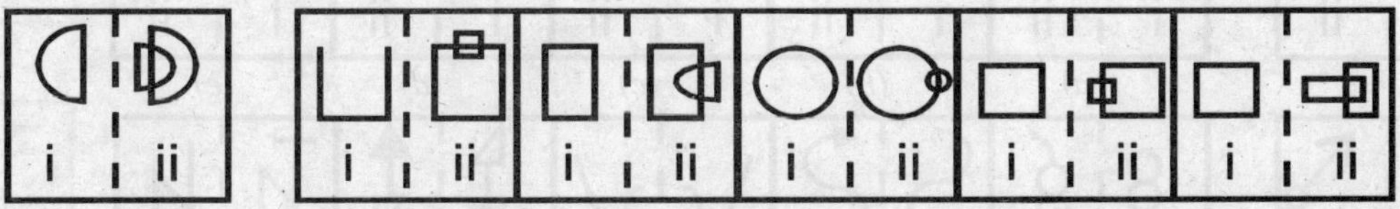
(a) (b) (c) (d) (e)

22.
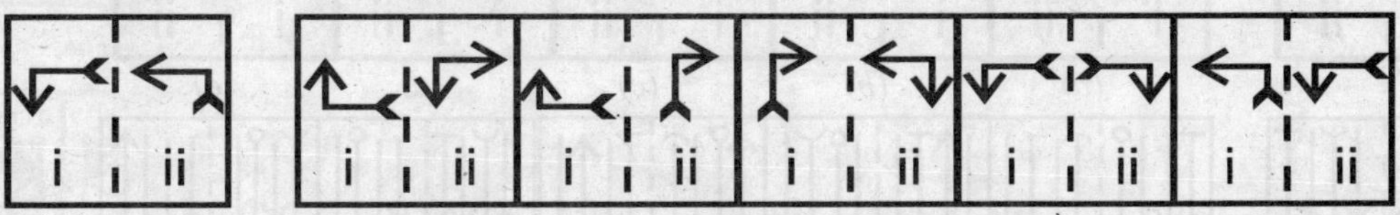
(a) (b) (c) (d) (e)

Problem Figure | **Answer Figures**

23. 

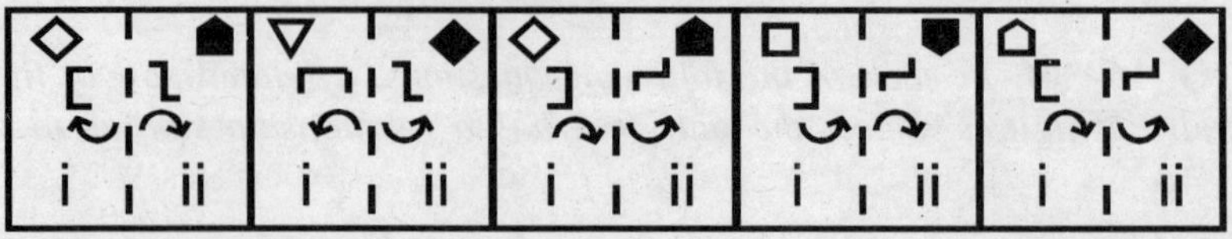

(a) (b) (c) (d) (e)

24. 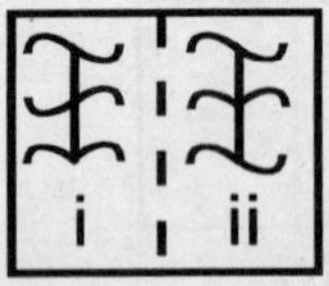

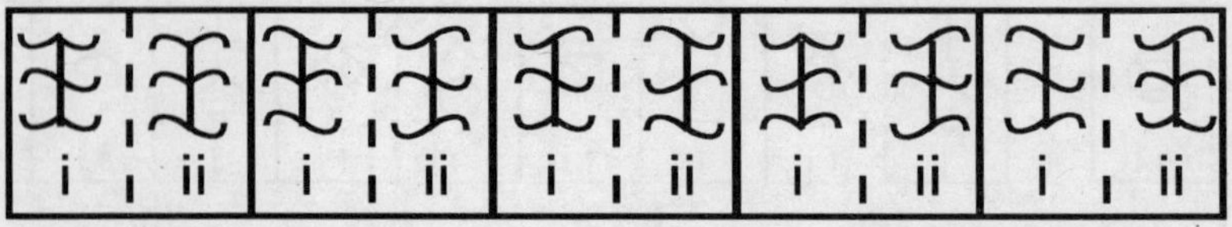

(a) (b) (c) (d) (e)

25. 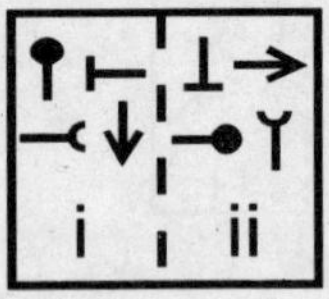

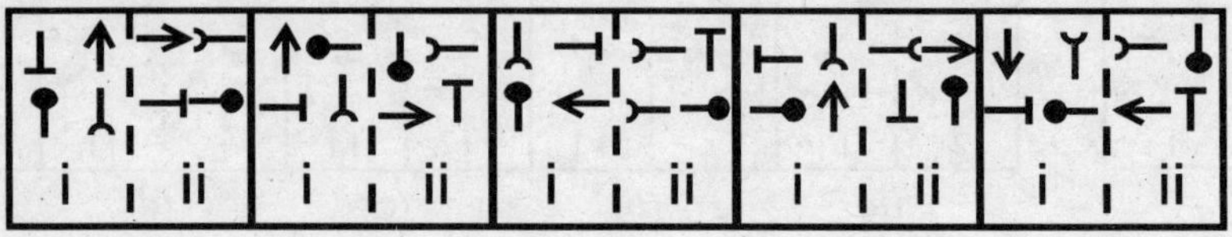

(a) (b) (c) (d) (e)

26. 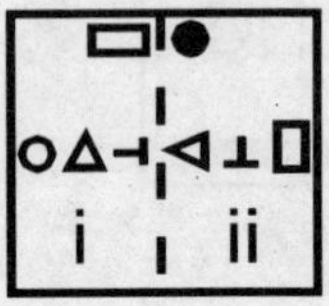

(a) (b) (c) (d) (e)

27. 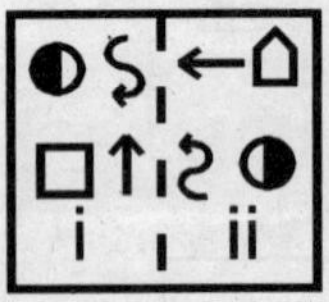

(a) (b) (c) (d) (e)

28. 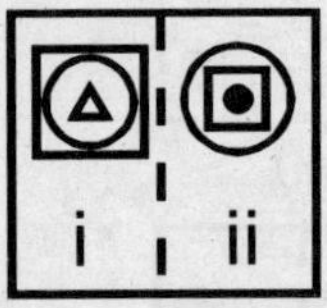

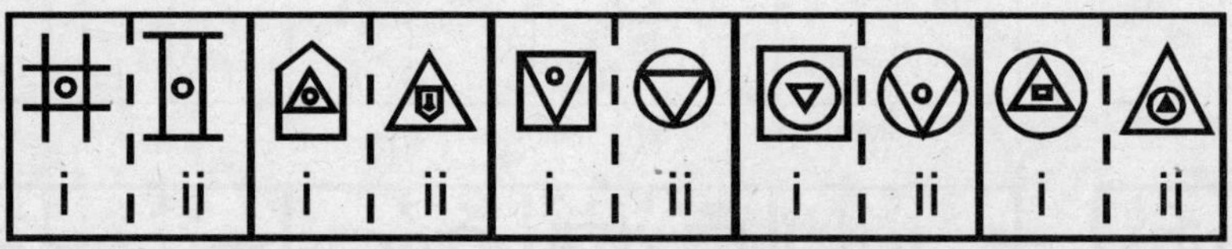

(a) (b) (c) (d) (e)

29. 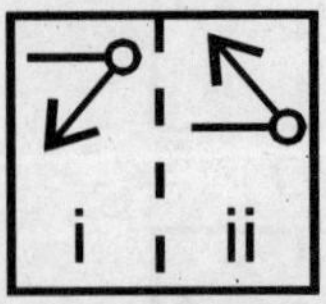

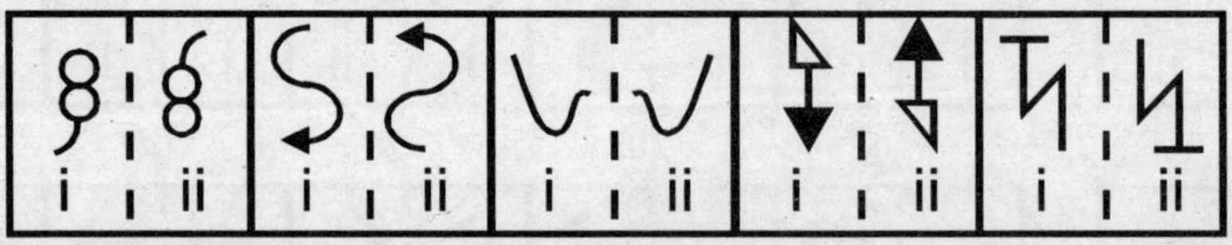

(a) (b) (c) (d) (e)

30. 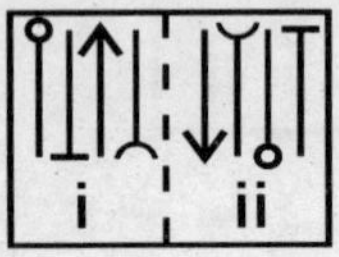

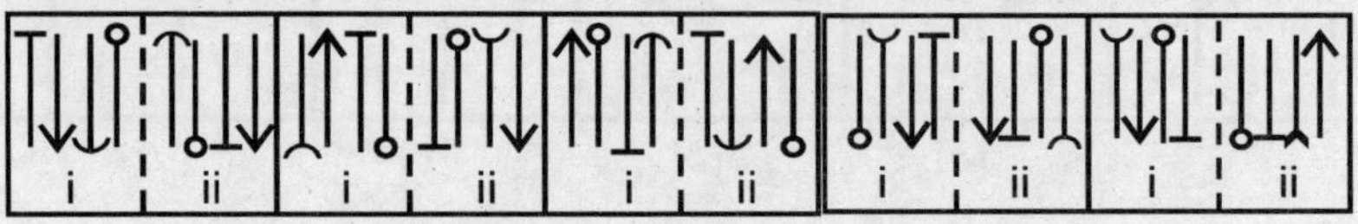

(a) (b) (c) (d) (e)

EXPLANATORY ANSWERS

1. *(b)* : The R.H.S. figure is fitted into the L.H.S. figure and the resulting figure is rotated 90° CW.

2. *(b)* : The figure rotates 45° ACW, the arrow changes to a curved line with dotted ends and the curved lines with dotted ends get converted to arrows.

3. *(d)* : The top left symbol rotates 90° ACW while all other symbols rotate 90° CW.

4. *(e)* : The black portion in top layer moves one step to the right; the black portions in the middle and the lower layers move one step to the left and the dot moves one step upwards.

5. *(d)* : The first and second symbols from the left interchange positions and the other two symbols also interchange positions. The symbol that reaches the first position from the left gets laterally inverted; the symbol that reaches the second position gets inverted, the third symbol rotates 90° CW and the fourth symbol gets replaced by a new one.

6. *(d)* : The single figure is replaced by a figure similar to the double figures and the double figures are replaced by figures similar to the single figure.

7. *(e)* : The figure rotates 135° ACW; a 'T' appears diagonally opposite to the black leaf and a 'Y' appears diagonally opposite to the white leaf.

8. *(c)* : The square rotates through 45°. The arrow moves 90° ACW and the pin moves 45° ACW.

9. *(b)* : The figure rotates through 180° and three lines forming a zig-zag, get attached to its lower end.

10. *(d)* : The symbols move in the order

The symbol that reaches the central position rotates 90° CW and its arc gets inverted; the 'P' shaped symbol rotates through 180°; the 'C' shaped symbol rotates 90° CW; the 'S' Shaped symbol gets laterally inverted and the fifth symbol gets replaced by a new one.

45°, the symbol that reaches the lower right corner rotates 90° ACW and a new symbol appears in middle-left position.

11. *(e)* : The upper and the lower parts of the figure get separated. Shading is removed from the upper part and the lower part is inverted. The two parts are then placed side by side.

12. *(a)* : The symbols move in the order

The symbol that reaches the top-left corner rotates 90° ACW; the symbol in the top-right corner rotates through 45°; the symbols in the lower-left corner and in the central positions rotates 90° CW and the symbol that reaches the lower-right corner rotates through 90°.

13. *(e)* : The figure gets laterally inverted. The dot on the larger arc, the pin and the small arc rotate 90° ACW. Also, the pin gets inverted.

14. *(c)* : The figure rotates 90° CW. One half of one of the lines on the arrow is lost. The figure in front of the arrowhead rotates through 45°.

15. *(d)* : The missing line segment in the first figure is replaced in second. Then moving ACW, the third line segment is removed along the two next consecutive sides of the square. Shaded portion in the first figure moves three steps ACW. Similarly, the third figure gives figure (D).

16. *(b)* : The uppermost design enters into innerside side of the lower design from Ist figure to the IInd figure.

17. *(a)* : In element I to II upper left design comes at lower right rotating 135° C.W. Middle design goes to upper left and rotates 90° CW. While lower right design goes to middle and it also rotates 90° C.W. The same changes occur in option A.

18. *(e)* : In element I to II and ellipse is put in the triangle. Similarly in option E a triangle is put in the ellipse.

19. *(d)* : From first figure to IInd figure, design is divided into four equal parts and right side of the upper portion becomes shaded.

20. *(e)* : From Ist figure to IInd figure, design is reversed after moving 90° anticlockwise direction.

21. *(d)* : The figure in the first part is laterally inverted and a similar but smaller design is placed on its left side in the second part.

22. *(e)* : The element in first part is moved by 90° and the places of short and long line segments are interchanged.

23. *(c)* : The number of sides making the top left figure is increased by one and a new figure is made, shaded and moved to the top right position. The element in the centre is turned 90° anticlockwise and the small line on the other side is turned by 180°. The element in the bottom right is turned upside down and moved to the bottom left position.

24. *(a)* : The direction of both arcs on the top, are on the middle right and arc on the bottom left in first part are turned to the other side in the second part.

25. *(b)* : From part one to part two, the element in the top left is turned 90° clockwise and the other three 90° anticlockwise, also the elements are moved one step anticlockwise.

26. *(b)* : From part one to part two, the top right element is turned by 90° and moved down, the lower right and middle elements are turned 90° clockwise and 90° anticlockwise respectively and moved to the left and the lower left element is shaded and moved up.

27. *(a)* : All the four elements exchange place diagonally and in doing so the top left element is laterally inverted, the top right element is horizontally inverted, the bottom right element is turned 90° anticlockwise and the number of lines making the element in bottom left is increased by one.

28. *(e)* : The innermost figure is removed and the new innermost figure also encloses the other two figures. The innermost and smallest figure is then shaded.

29. *(b)* : The design in the first part is horizontally inverted in the second.

30. *(b)* : All the elements in the first part are turned upside down and then 1st, 2nd, 3rd and 4th positioned elements become 3rd, 4th, 1st and 2nd elements in the second part.

24. ODD MAN OUT

In this type of reasoning a statement is followed by inferences drawn from it. From these inferences only one definitely follows which is the hidden proposition of the sentence and it is the right answer to the question.

EXERCISE

Directions (Q. 1–10) : *In each question below five figures are given. Four are similar in a certain way and so form a group. The question is— which one of the figures* ***does not*** *belong to that group?*

1. 

(a) (b) (c) (d) (e)

2. 

(a) (b) (c) (d) (e)

3. 

(a) (b) (c) (d) (e)

4. 

(a) (b) (c) (d) (e)

5. 

(a) (b) (c) (d) (e)

6. 

(a) (b) (c) (d) (e)

7. 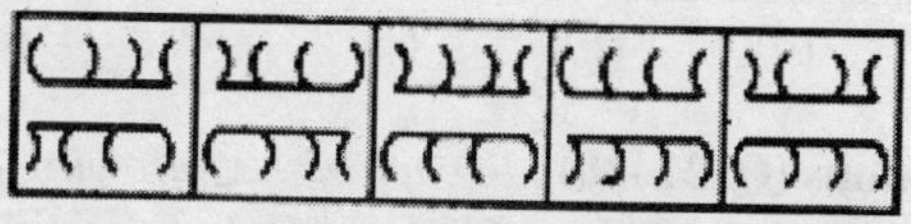

(a) (b) (c) (d) (e)

8. 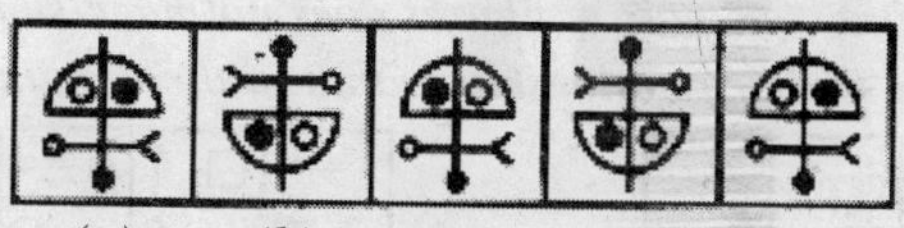

(a) (b) (c) (d) (e)

9. 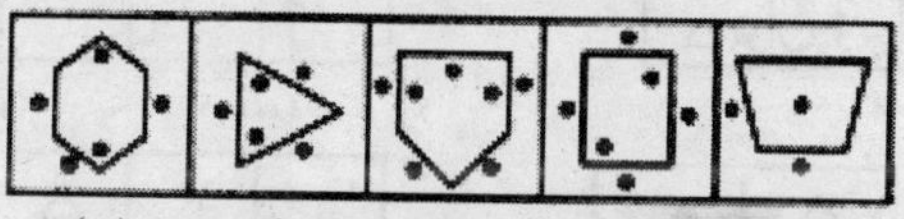

(a) (b) (c) (d) (e)

10. 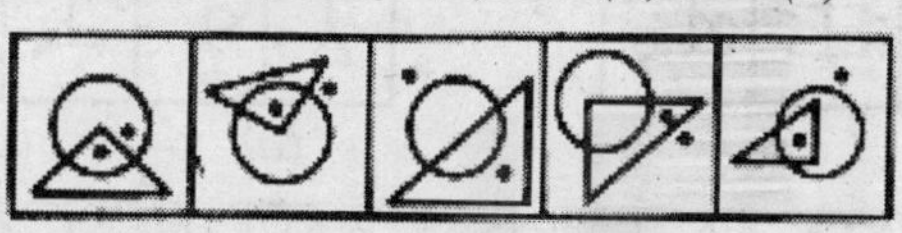

(a) (b) (c) (d) (e)

Directions (Q. 11–20) : *In each of the following questions, in four out of the five figures, element I is related to element II in the same particular way. Find out the figure in which the element I is* ***not*** *so related to element II.*

11. 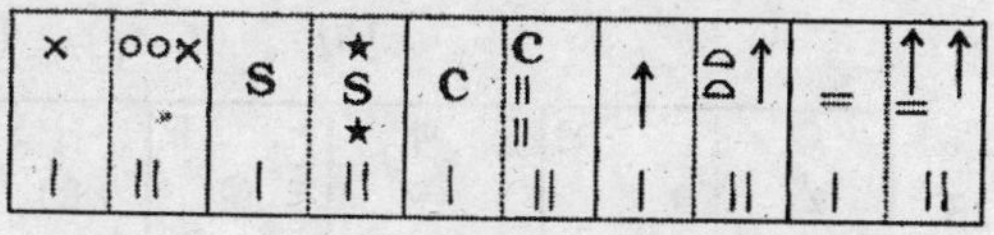

(a) (b) (c) (d) (e)

12. 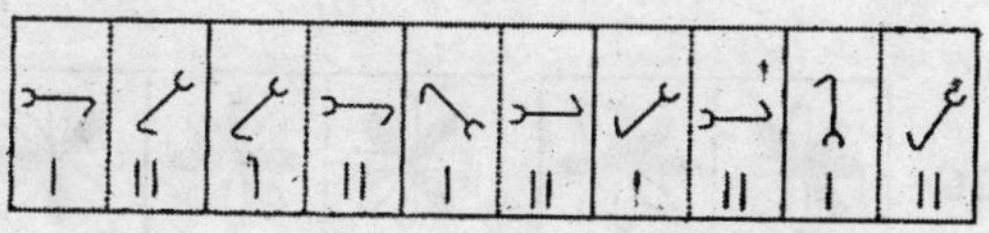

(a) (b) (c) (d) (e)

13. 
(a) (b) (c) (d) (e)

14. 
(a) (b) (c) (d) (e)

15. 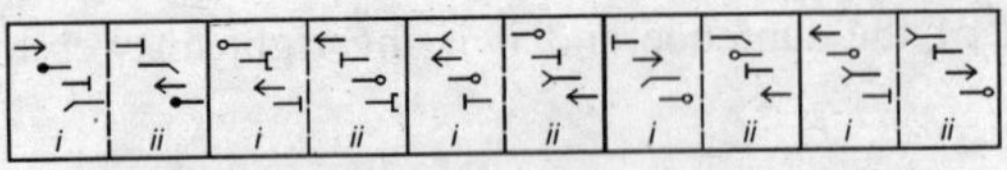
(a) (b) (c) (d) (e)

16. 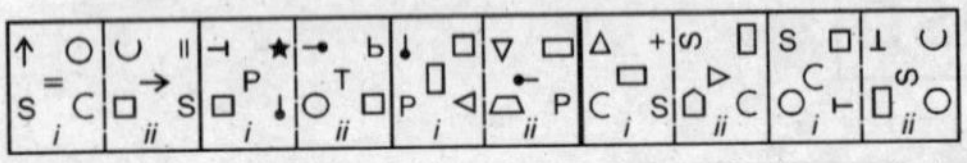
(a) (b) (c) (d) (e)

17. 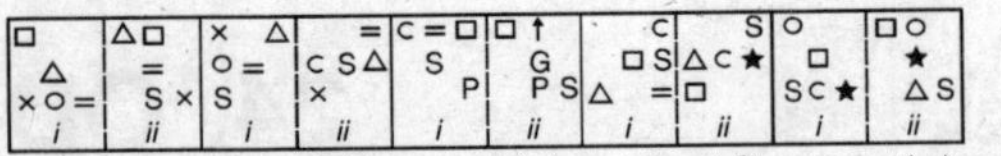
(a) (b) (c) (d) (e)

18. 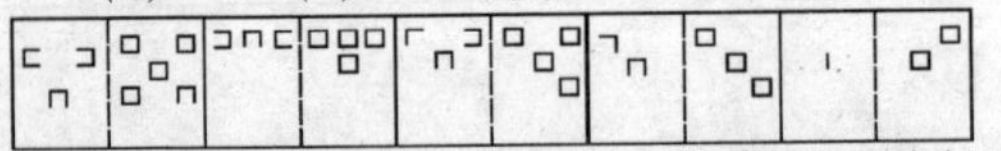
(a) (b) (c) (d) (e)

19. 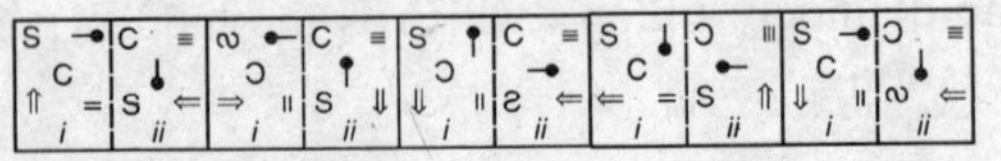
(a) (b) (c) (d) (e)

20. 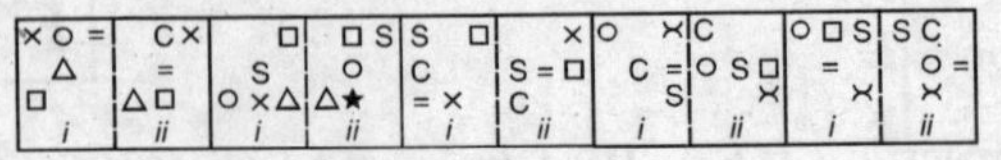
(a) (b) (c) (d) (e)

Directions (Q. 21–30) : *In each of the following questions, a related pair of figures (unnumbered) is followed by five numbered pairs of figures. Out of these five, four have relationship similar to that in the unnumbered pair. Only one pair of figures does not have similar relationship. Select that pair of figures which does not have a similar relationship to that in the unnumbered pair. Number of that pair is your answer.*

21. 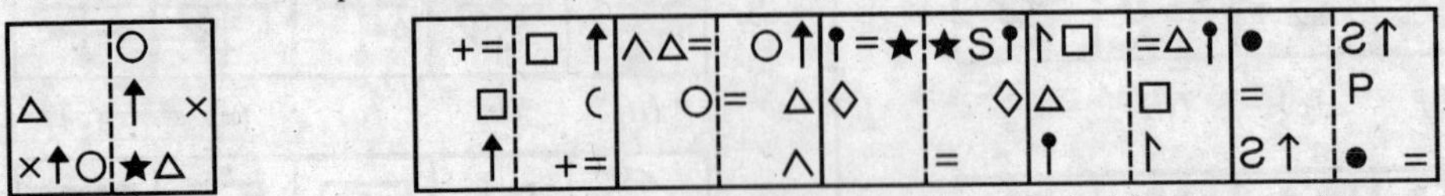
(a) (b) (c) (d) (e)

22. 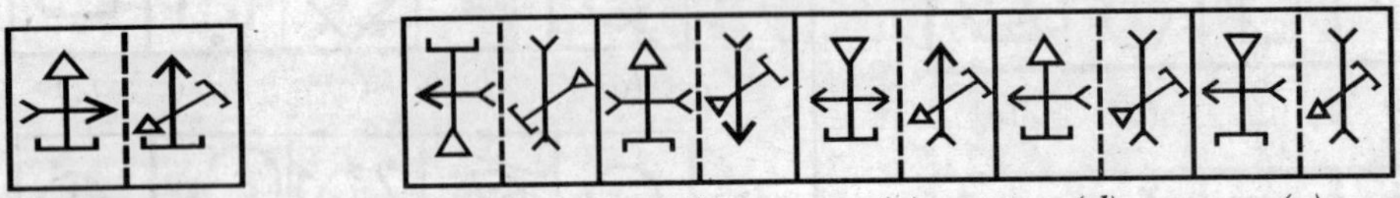
(a) (b) (c) (d) (e)

23. 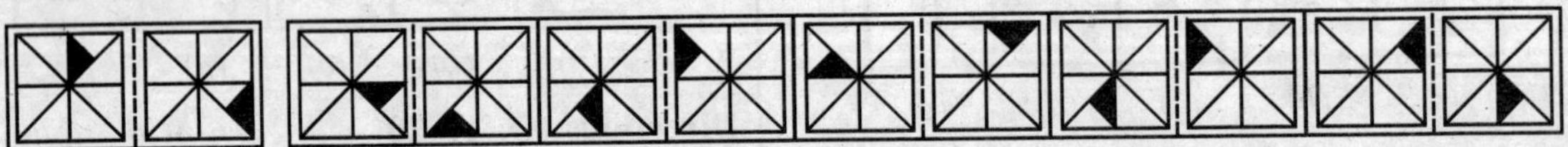
(a) (b) (c) (d) (e)

24. 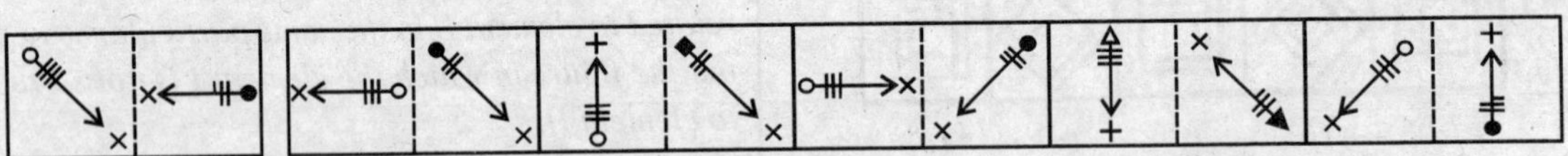
(a) (b) (c) (d) (e)

25. 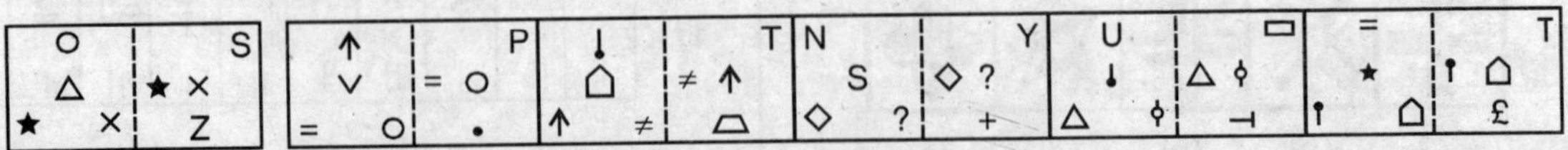
(a) (b) (c) (d) (e)

26. 
(a) (b) (c) (d) (e)

27. 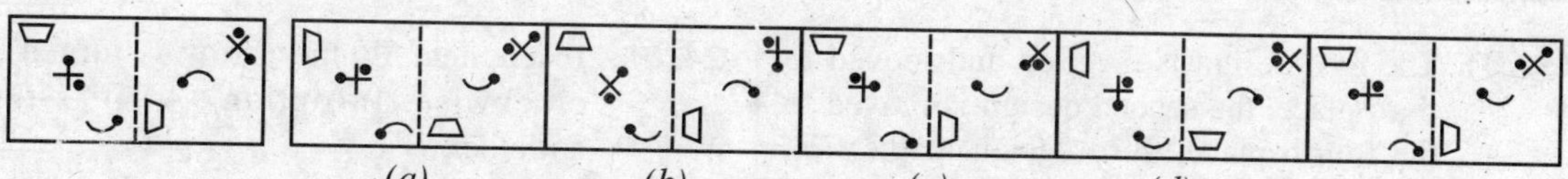

(a) (b) (c) (d) (e)

28. 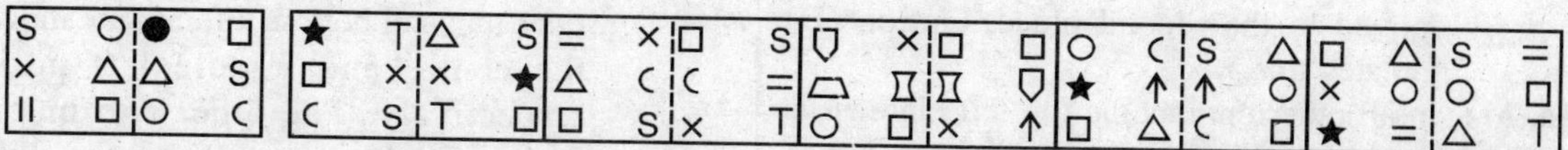

(a) (b) (c) (d) (e)

29. 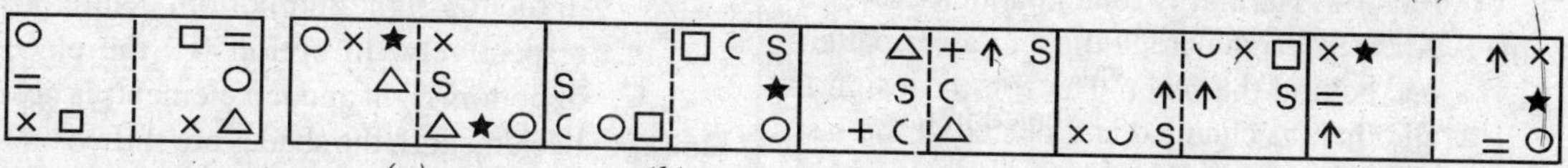

(a) (b) (c) (d) (e)

30. 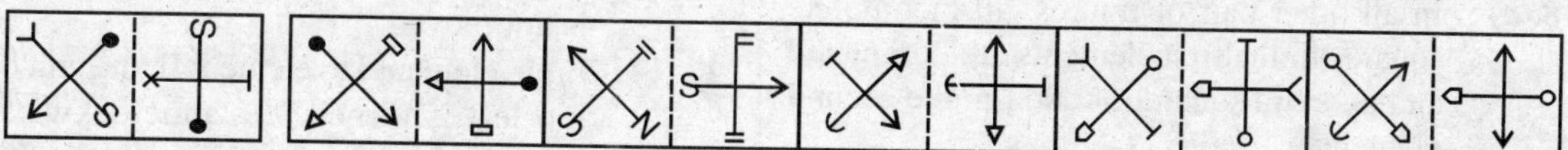

(a) (b) (c) (d) (e)

EXPLANATORY ANSWERS

1. *(d)* : In all other figures, the arrow and the + sign lie towards the black end of the main figure.

2.*(a)* : The pins, equal in number of sides in the main figure are attached to the midpoint of a side of the main figure in case of figures (B), (C), (D) and (E). In figure (A), these pins are attached to a vertex of the main figure.

3.*(c)* : In all other figures, the dot appears in the angle formed between the arrow and the pin.

4.*(a)* : All other figures can be rotated into each other. (In each figure except figure (A), the middle element is obtained by rotating the outer element through 90° CW and the inner element is obtained by rotating the middle element through 90° CW).

5.*(c)* : All other figures have at least one line of symmetry.

6.*(c)* : All other figures can be rotated into each other.

7.*(e)* : In each one of the other four figures, four arcs are curved towards the left and four other arcs are curved towards the right.

8.*(c)* : All other figures can be rotated into each other.

9.*(d)* : In all other figures, the number of dots outside the main figure is one more than the number of dots inside the main figure.

10.*(a)* : In all other figures, one of the dots lies outside the triangle as well as the circle.

11.*(e)* : Except in figure (B), in all other figures, from element I to II two new designs are added in one side of the main design.

12.*(c)* : In each figure from element I to II the main design rotates through 135° clockwise or anticlockwise. Except in figure (C), in all other figures, the smaller line segment moves to other side from element I to II.

13.*(a)* : In all other figures the element II can be obtained by the lateral inversion of the element I. In figure (A), the lower design has not been inverted.

14.*(b)* : In figure (B), the small segment is on the same side as that of the half shaded circle in both the elements.

15.(*d*) : The first design is inverted and moved to third place, the second design is moved to the fourth place, third design to the first place and fourth design is inverted and moved to the second place. Option (D) violates this.

16.(*b*) : In all other options the top-left element is moved to the centre with 90° clockwise rotation. Here, it is rotated anticlockwise.

17.(*d*) : All the designs are shifted in a set pattern one behind the other. The fourth design in all others is changed and placed in the last. Here, the fifth and last designs are changed.

18.(*a*) : In all other pair of figures, all incomplete squares in the first elements are completed and an extra square is added in the second element.

19.(*a*) : From element I to element II, the 'S' shape is turned 90° clockwise and moved down, the double arrow shape '⇒' is turned 90° clockwise and moved to the right, the two parallel lines one turned by 90°; one parallel line is added and all three lines are moved up, the line with a dot is turned 90° clockwise and moved to the centre and the 'C' shape in the centre is turned by 180° and moved to top left position. Here, the double arrow is turned anticlockwise.

20.(*c*) : Starting from one unit, all units are moved in a set pattern, the places of last two units moved are interchanged and the last unit is then made new. Here, no changes are made in the last two units.

21.(*d*) : From element I to element II clockwise the first unit is moved 2 steps forward, the second unit 1 step forward, the third unit 2½ steps forward and the fourth unit 3 steps forward. In option 'D' the third unit violates the rule.

22.(*e*) : From element I to element II, the horizontal bar is turned 135° anticlockwise and the unit at the lower end is turned by 180°. The vertical bar is turned 90° anticlockwise and the unit at the lower end is turned by 180°. In option 'E' one more unit at the top is turned by 180°.

23.(*e*) : In element II, the shade is moved two sections clockwise and shifted from the centre to the base. In option 'E' it is not so.

24.(*a*) : In element II, the arrow is turned 135° clockwise. In option 'A' it is turned anticlockwise.

25.(*b*) : From element I to element II, the bottom right unit and bottom left unit are moved to the centre and middle left position respectively. The other two units are removed and two new elements are placed in the top right and bottom centre position respectively. In option 'B' the placement of bottom right and left elements is not right.

26.(*c*) : In element II, the shades are shifted one petal clockwise. In option 'C' one of the shades is not moved.

27.(*b*) : From element I to element II, the unit on the top left is turned 90° anticlockwise and moved to the bottom right corner position, the unit in the centre is turned 135° anticlockwise and moved to the top right position, and the unit in the bottom right is turned by 180° and moved to the centre. In option 'B', the middle unit is turned 135° clockwise.

28.(*a*) : From element I to element II, a new unit is placed in the top left position, the top left unit is moved to the middle right position, the middle right unit is moved to the left position, the middle left unit is replaced by a new unit and placed in bottom right position, the bottom right unit is moved to the top right position, and the top right unit is moved diagonally to replace the bottom left unit. In option 'A', the middle left unit is not changed when moved to the bottom right position.

29.(*e*) : From element I to element II starting anticlockwise, the first and second units are moved 1½ steps clockwise respectively, the third unit ½ step anticlockwise, the fourth unit 2 steps clockwise, and a new unit is placed ahead of the first unit. Option 'E' violates the rules.

30.(*e*) : In element II, the cross is turned 135° clockwise and then the positions of left and top units on the cross are interchanged. In option 'E' it is not so.

ENGLISH LANGUAGE

1. Comprehension Passages

In the English language paper, questions on comprehension test are very important for the examinees appearing in the competitive examinations.

Comprehension means the act of comprehending or the capacity of the mind to understand. In the examination papers, questions on comprehension test are included to judge the ability of the examinees to understand the given passage.

Therefore, they should understand how to solve these questions. Practice of solving these questions will greatly help them in the examination.

Directions: *Read the following passages carefully and answer the questions given after each passage. Out of the four alternatives, choose the correct answer according to the context of the passage.*

PASSAGE-1

This is the age of the Machine, Machines are everywhere, in the fields, in the factory, at home, in the street, in the city, in the country, every where. To fly, it is not necessary to have wings; there are machines. The swim under the sea, it is not necessary to have gills; there are machines. To kill our fellowmen in over-whelming numbers, there are machines. Petrol machines alone provide ten times more power than all human beings in the world. In the busiest countries, each individual has six hundred human slaves in his machines.

What are the consequences of this abnormal power? Before the War, it looked as though it might be possible, for the first time in history to provide food and clothing and shelter for the teeming population of the world—every man, woman and child. This would have been the greatest triumphs of science. And yet, if you remember, we saw the world crammed, full of food and people hungry. Today, the larders are bare and millions, starving. That's the war, you would say. When the machines of peace once more begin to ....

1. According to the passage, which of the following is not necessary to fly?

A. Wings B. Arms
C. Feet D. Machines

2. Petrol machinery is used to provide:

A. ten times more power than human beings in the world
B. less power than human beings in the world
C. as much power as human beings in the world
D. none of the above is correct

3. What could be one of the greatest triumphs of science?

A. to provide food, clothing and shelter to everyone
B. none would get food, clothing and shelter
C. only rich people would get food, clothing and shelter
D. people would get only clothing

4. This is the age of the:

A. machine B. animal husbandry
C. agriculture D. wars

5. The machine age produces:

A. goods
B. food
C. goods but avoids the consequences
D. none of the above

Answers

1	2	3	4	5
A	A	A	A	C

PASSAGE-2

What are the good parts of our civilization? First and foremost there are order and safety. If today I have a quarrel with another man, I do not get beaten merely because I am physically weaker and he can knock me down. I go to law and the law will decide as fairly as it can between the two of us. Thus in disputes between man and man. Right has taken the place of might. Moreover, the law protects me from robbery and violence. Nobody may come and break into my house, steal my books or run off with my children. Of course, there are burglars, but they are very rare and the law punishes them whenever, it catches them.

It is difficult for us to realize how much this safety means. Without safety those higher activities of mankind which make up civilization could not go on. The inventor could not invent, the scientist find out or the artist make beautiful things. Hence, order and safety, although they are not themselves civilization, are things without which civilization could be impossible. They are as necessary to our civilization as the air we breathe is to us; and we have-grown so used to them that we do not notice them any more than we notice the air.

1. The first and foremost good parts of civilization are:
   A. order and insecurity
   B. only insecurity
   C. order and safety
   D. insecurity and lawlessness.
2. In disputes between man and man:
   A. right has taken the place of might
   B. might has taken the place of right
   C. might is right
   D. none of the above
3. According to the passage, the burglars are:
   A. many B. rare
   C. found nowhere D. not punished
4. An artist can create beautiful things only if:
   A. there is disorder
   B. there is no safety
   C. there is safety
   D. there is neither safety nor order
5. According to the writer, man does not notice order and safety as:
   A. he does not notice the air he breathes
   B. he does not notice the food he eats
   C. he does not notice the shelter he needs
   D. none of the above is correct

Answers

1	2	3	4	5
C	A	B	C	A

PASSAGE-3

The purpose of education is to make the student an expert in his subject. This must be clearly understood, and mere muddling through lessons and lectures and books and passing examination are relegated to secondary importance as means to the end—which is excellence in the field choosen.

But there are so many fields, and no man can become an expert in all the fields. It is necessary to decide which fields are the important ones that a man should know well.

It is clear that one's own work is the most important. This has been realised and modern civilization has accordingly provided vocational education. It is now possible to acquire high professional skill in the various fields, medicine, engineering production, commerce and so on—but with good and bad mixed together, and no standard for guidance.

1. The purpose of education is to make the student:
   A. an expert in all fields
   B. an expert in his subject
   C. only capable of earning
   D. confident only
2. What, according to the writer, is the end?
   A. excellence in the field choosen
   B. passing the examination
   C. earning more and more money
   D. cramming lectures and books
3. According to the passage, can a man become an expert in all fields?
   A. Yes B. Partially yes
   C. Sometimes D. No
4. According to the writer, which of the following is the most important work?
   A. someone else's work
   B. one's own work
   C. nobody's work
   D. everyone's work

5. The modern civilization has provided
   A. vocational education
   B. art of conversation
   C. adult education
   D. higher education

Answers

1	2	3	4	5
B	A	D	B	A

PASSAGE-4

English education, which was introduced in India in the earlier part of the nineteenth century, established her cultural contact with the West. Prior to this, India had for centuries remained in a state of isolation, although in very early times she had sent out cultural missions to the other Asiatic countries. India really began to borrow from the West and assimilate new ideas on an extensive scale only after the British had taken up the direction of her educational policy.

It is true that Western education at first exerted an unsettling: influence on young men and led to errors in life and conduct. They hated everything Indian, aped western manners and modes of life, and forgot their glorious past. There were scholars who ignored modern Indian languages, avoided classical Indian literature, and made a fetish of speaking and writing English.

1. When was English education introduced in India?
   A. in the twentieth century
   B. in the later part of the nineteenth century
   C. in the earlier part of the nineteenth century
   D. in the eighteenth century
2. When did India begin to borrow from the West?
   A. after the British had taken up the direction of her educational policy
   B. before the British had taken up the direction of her educational policy
   C. in the twentieth century
   D. none of the above is correct
3. What did India send out to other Asiatic countries?
   A. economic mission B. military forces
   C. cultural missions D. none of these
4. Western education exerted an unsettling influence on:
   A. old men B. young men
   C. old women D. children
5. Young men forgot their:
   A. glorious past B. present
   C. future D. originality

Answers

1	2	3	4	5
C	A	C	B	A

PASSAGE-5

Each nation has its own peculiar character which distinguishes it from others. But the peoples of the world have more points in which they are all like each other than points in which they are different. One type of person that is common in every country is the one who always tries to do as little as he possibly can and to get as much in return as he can. His opposite, the man who is in the habit of doing more than is strictly necessary and is ready to accept what is offered in return, is rare everywhere.

Both these types are usually unconscious of their character. The man who avoids effort is always talking about his 'rights'; he appears to think that society owes him a pleasant easy life. The man who is always doing more than his sheer talks of 'duties' feels that the individual is in debt to society, and not society to the individual. As a result of their view, neither of these men thinks that he behaves at all strangely.

1. What type of person is common in every nation?
   A. A person who wants to do little and get more
   B. A person who wants to do more and get little
   C. Each person is different
   D. There is no such type of person that is common in every country
2. A person doing more and getting little:
   A. is rare everywhere
   B. is found in our country
   C. is common in all countries
   D. is found nowhere

3. The man who talks about his 'rights':
   A. avoids meeting other people
   B. avoids hard work
   C. knows his duties well
   D. believes in hard work
4. The man who talks of 'duties':
   A. is always hard working
   B. avoids hard work
   C. does not know his duties well
   D. always thinks of his 'right' first
5. Which one of the following thinks that the individual is in debt to the society?
   A. a person who talks of his 'rights only'
   B. a person who is always doing more than his sheer talks of 'duties'
   C. every citizen of the country
   D. a person who talks of his 'duties' only

Answers

1	2	3	4	5
A	A	B	A	C

PASSAGE-6

The history of civilization shows how man always has to choose between making the right and wrong use of the discoveries of science. This has never been more true than in our own age. In a brief period amazing discoveries have been made and applied to practical purpose.

It would be ungrateful not to recognize how immense are the boons, which science has given to mankind. It has brought within the reach of multitudes benefits and advantages which only a short time ago were the privilege of the few. It has shown how malnutrition, hunger and disease can be overcome. It has not only lengthened life but it has deepened its quality. Fields of knowledge, experience and recration open in the past only a few, have been thrown open to millions. Through the work of science the ordinary man today has been given the opportunity of a longer and fuller life then was over possible to his grandparents.

1. Amazing discoveries of science have been made:
   A. in a brief period
   B. in a long period
   C. in our orefather's age
   D. in centuries
2. The boons of science are:
   A. few B. found nowhere
   C. immense D. very few
3. Which of the following can be overcome with the help of science?
   A. Malnutrition B. Disease
   C. Hunger D. All of these
4. Science provides a chance of:
   A. shorter and fuller life
   B. longer and fuller life
   C. longer and dull life
   D. none of these
5. What on the whole, has science done to mankind?
   A. It has reduced the quality of our life
   B. It has shortened our life
   C. It has deepened the quality of life
   D. It has done a great harm to mankind

Answers

1	2	3	4	5
A	C	D	B	C

PASSAGE-7

It is said that wars are fought for the sake of peace. Many a politician justifies wars as being the means of bringing about stability in the international relations. So far as the aim of those who are always busy in society is concerned, their motive is not always to achieve freedom from work. Their ultimate purpose is not to be idle. To be busy is a mode of life or habit. Those who are busy in society, say, businessmen, or people in authority, politicians or statesmen, officials or employees, are all part of the continuous machine which keeps the society going.

People are busy so that different activities of a society are carried out and the wherewithals which mankind badly needs are provided. No society, however, prosperous and endowed with bounties of nature, can afford to have the objective of being idle in the long run. No doubt, advanced countries ensured minimum facilities of living and amenities of work for their workmen; they even fix their working hours so that after their busy day's life they can have some leisure at their disposal for self development or peace of mind. Yet, with the passage of time a busy society has the tendency to become busier. Even with the best computers and automations at the disposal of the modern technocrats manpower continues to remain busy, as one phase of achievement leads automatically to the second phase of work. War may have the intention of peace but business is undending so long as a society has the objective of progress and does not become stationary or stagnant or decadent.

1. According to the passage, busy people:
- A. want freedom work
- B. want to be idle
- C. do not like rest
- D. are part of a machine which runs society

2. Why are people busy?
- A. to carry out different activities of society
- B. to provide needs of mankind
- C. both A and B
- D. none of the above

3. Author says that:
- A. no society can be idle
- B. developed countries can be idle
- C. underdeveloped countries can be idle
- D. all of the above

4. Computers and automations:
- A. have made man idle
- B. could not relieve man from busy life
- C. both of the above
- D. none of the above

5. With the passage of time man is becoming busier because
- A. he likes to be busy
- B. he is born to be busy
- C. to be busy is mode of life or habit
- D. all of the above

Answers

1	2	3	4	5
D	C	A	B	C

PASSAGE-8

Every genius that comes to the world, achieves greatness through the capacity of taking trouble. All great men of the world who have achieved impossible things in their life time have undergone hardships, sacrifices, trials and tribulations. There is no easy victory over failure. No hard achievement is smooth and easy. History of great men reminds us that with strong determination man can achieve any thing he may set his mind upon, however impossible it may seem apparently.

A man with determination and iron will can defeat all hurdles in the way of his mission. Even the most intelligent people suffer in life if they cannot cope with their circumstances and labour hard to achieve the goal of their life. A genius who is fired with real zeal and determination to achieve his ideal comes to possess the necessary capacity to bear the hardships, cross the hurdles and achieve the final victory. Genius and hard work go together to bring the desired results. The stage of greatness comes after many stages of frustration and disappointment. The weaker man gives way to those frustrations but the genius perseveres and holds on to their mission until they achieve the object of their life.

1. The writer feels that victory over failure:
- A. is not possible
- B. is not good
- C. is absolute
- D. is not easy

2. According to the passage genius implies:
- A. failing again and again
- B. capacity of taking trouble and hardship
- C. stages of frustration and disappointment
- D. escape from hardship

3. Which of the following is correct?
- A. Only dull people should work hard
- B. Intelligent people need not labour hard
- C. Even intelligent people have to cope with circumstances
- D. None of the above

4. It can be inferred that:
- A. genius and hard work go together
- B. genius and hard work are opposed to each other
- C. genius and hard work end in frustration
- D. all of the above

5. A man can defeat all hurdles by:
- A. coping with all situations
- B. strong determination and iron will
- C. becoming strong
- D. becoming tall

Answers

1	2	3	4	5
D	B	C	A	B

PASSAGE-9

Life is a struggle. "We live in deeds and not in years." If we rest, we rust. If we work we shine like jewels. Adventures are the essence of life but action also entails contemplation. Proper action needs the proper initiative. Napoleon took the wrong initiative and brought the downfall of France. Proper action is always taken by the wise persons. The wise persons always foreshadow the hardships for executing a policy. They become passive when they forecast that their efforts are at stake. All great leaders and diplomats take the steps keeping in view their reputation.

We should strike when the iron is hot. Some persons take the steps haphazardly with the result that they lose the opportunity and thus they are treated as fools. Angels are wise people and very particular about their action. It has been the aim of all philosophers to understand the world. After understanding, they move very gradually and not like fools who plunge into the situation without contemplation. Mr. Ayub Khan under Bhutto's influence plunged into war with India inflicting destruction to humanity. Our ex-prime Minister Lal Bahadur Shastri gauged the situation. He responded to the challenge of Pakistan and won the battle. Fools always meddle with the situation without bringing about any change but wise persons penetrate into the matter and take the appropriate action.

1. According to the writer:
- A. Napoleon acted wisely
- B. we may rust like iron
- C. we may shine like metals
- D. leaders and diplomats act keeping in view their reputation

2. Some people are treated as fools because
- A. they act haphazardly
- B. they strike when the iron is hot
- C. they act like philosophers
- D. all of the above

3. Mr. Ayub Khan was
- A. wise to decalre was against India
- B. foolish to disobey Bhutto
- C. not wise in declaring war against India
- D. none of the above

4. What is the aim of the philosopher?
- A. To act like angels
- B. To act like Ayub Khan
- C. To act like Bhutto
- D. To understand the world

5. The passage implies that
- A. one should act quickly
- B. understanding should precede action
- C. fools penetrate into the matter
- D. none of the above

Answers

1	2	3	4	5
D	A	C	D	B

PASSAGE-10

With human beings the world ever ensnared by the performance of mechanical tasks and the pursuit of equally mechanical distractions, the time is not distant when nothing but the most abominable entertainments will succeed in steering them. If it happens so, the present civilisation will emerge as a mere imitation of the Roman in which the Romans desired more gladiators, tightrope walking elephants and fantastically rare animals to be slaughtered. This is one danger which is likely to cut at the roots of the modern civilisation because it threatens the existence of mental activities.

I would prefer to be bored by an eight hour job in an office or writing streams of words of journalism rather than be amused by the monotony of modern pleasures. It is the lack of participation which is the most damaging aspect of modern pleasures. This organised distraction combines within itself the performance of movies, gramophones, radios and the press which go a long way in killing the residue of initiative or sense of participation. Even in the case of newspapers, no mental effort is required on the part of the readers as the contents are presented in such a cut and dried manner that one need not undergo the fatigue of a single thought.

Consequently for years together men continue scanning newspapers and magazines by merely moving their eyes.

If idealists failed to stem the rot, in future, pleasures will take on incredibly monostrous shape.

1. The writer feels that human activities and distractions are:
A. logical B. interesting
C. intellectual D. mechanical

2. According to the passage entertainments
A. relieve a man
B. are badly needed
C. threaten the existence of mental activities
D. are useless

3. The writer prefers
A. modern pleasures to office work
B. modern pleasures to journalism
C. neither journalism nor office work
D. journalism and office work to modern pleasures

4. Modern pleasures, according to the writer
A. are indispensable
B. are useless because they don't amuse men
C. cripple the sense of participation
D. do not make men take the initiative

5. Which of the following is correct?
A. The author says that reading newspapers is bad
B. Mental effort is not required in reading newspapers
C. We should imitate Romans
D. We should slaughter animals

Answers

1	2	3	4	5
D	C	D	C	B

PASSAGE-11

Courage is not only the basis of all virtue; it is its expression. Faith, hope, charity and all the rest don't become virtues until it takes courage to exercise them. There are roughly two types of courage. The first, an emotional state which urges a man to risk injury or death, is physical courage. The second, a more reasoning attitude which enables him to take coolly his career, happiness, his whole future, or his judgement of what he thinks either right or worthwhile, is moral courage.

I have known many men, who had marked physical courage, but lacked moral courage. Some of them were in high places, but they failed to be great in themselves because they lacked moral courage. On the other hand, I have seen men who undoubtedly possessed moral courage but were very cautious about taking physical risks. But I have never met a man with moral courage who couldn't, when it was really necessary, face a situation boldly.

1. All virtues become meaningful because of
A. faith B. charity
C. courage D. hope

2. Physical courage is an expression of
A. emotions B. deliberation
C. uncertainty D. defiance

3. People with physical courage often lack
A. mental balance
B. capacity for reasoning
C. emotional stability
D. will to fight

4. A man with moral courage can
A. defy his enemies
B. overcome all difficulties
C. face a situation boldly
D. be very pragmatic

5. A man of courage is
A. cunning B. intelligent
C. curious D. careful

Answers

1	2	3	4	5
C	A	B	C	D

2. Cloze Test

A cloze test is a procedure in which an examinee is asked to supply words that have been removed from a passage as a test of his ability to comprehend text. Practise it regularly to score well.

TEST 1

Today most Indian businessmen are very worried. To begin with, they are not used to competition. In the past, they sold whatever ..... (1) ..... produced at whatever prices thay chose. But ..... (2) ..... increasing competition, customers began to ..... (3) ..... and choose. Imports suddenly became ..... (4) ..... available and that too at cheaper ..... (5) .....

1. A. it B. he C. they D. we

2. A. with B. by C. after D. from

3. A. buy B. take C. pick D. want

4. A. hardly B. easily C. frequently D. conveniently

5. A. costs B. returns C. dividend D. prices

TEST 2

As a rule of thumb, a manned mission costs from fifty to a hundred times more than a comparable unamanned mission. Thus, for scientific exploration alone, ... (1) ..... missions, employing machine intelligence, are ..... (2) ..... However, there may well be ..... (3) ..... other than scientific for exploring ..... (4) ..... social, economic, political, cultural or ..... (5) .....

1. A. manned B. unmanned C. space D. lunar

2. A. liked B. wanted C. used D. preferred

3. A. reasons B. causes C. clues D. objects

4. A. moon B. sun C. space D. mission

5. A. casual B. historic C. historical D. histrionic

TEST 3

The principal advantage in having a clear-cut objective of business is that it does not derail; the enterprise does not stray ..... (1) ..... the direct route that it has set for ..... (2) ..... Enterprises with well-defined objectives can conveniently undertake ..... (3) ..... and follow long-range development policies. Recognition of objectives ..... (4) ..... the temptation to compromise long-range ..... (5) ..... for short-term gains and improves coordination in work and consistency in policy.

1. A. from B. on C. along D. towards

2. A. others B. industry C. itself D. government

3. A. production B. research C. audit D. appraisal

4. A. invites B. defers C. shifts D. removes

5. A. objectives B. losses C. interests D. profits

TEST 4

Let children learn to judge their own work. A child ..... (1) ..... to talk does not learn ..... (2) ..... being corrected all the time ..... (3) ..... corrected too much, he will ..... (4) ..... talking. He notices a thousand times a day the difference between the ..... (5) ..... he uses and the language those around him use.

1. A. endeavouring B. learning
C. experimenting D. experiencing
2. A. in B. on
C. by D. to
3. A. unless B. being
C. until D. if
4. A. stop B. halt
C. avoid D. shun
5. A. speech B. language
C. talk D. skill

6. A. told B. said
C. asked D. advised
7. A. explored B. exhorted
C. explained D. exported
8. A. wandered B. wondered
C. wondrous D. wounded
9. A. which B. what
C. whom D. whose
10. A. like B. lake
C. lick D. lack

TEST 5

His talk used to be full of wit and humours. He liked reading. He was a ..... **(1)** ..... reader and would pore over books ..... **(2)** ..... a wide range of interest as ..... **(3)** ..... he got them. He had ..... **(4)** ..... a standing order to two bookshops ..... **(5)** ..... city.

1. A. voracious B. fervent
C. anxious D. enthusiastic
2. A. covering B. barring
C. including D. containing
3. A. firmly B. quickly
C. soon D. urgently
4. A. offered B. proclaimed
C. intimated D. given
5. A. at B. in
C. within D. inside

TEST 6

An old scholar ..... **(1)** ..... that Truth was in the country. He ..... **(2)** ..... to find her, as he had devoted his life to studying her in all her ..... **(3)** ..... . He came upon the cottage in the ..... **(4)** ..... where Truth lived. He ..... **(5)** ..... on the door. Truth ..... **(6)** ..... what he wanted. The scholar ..... **(7)** ..... who she was. He added that he had ..... **(8)** ..... a thousand times ..... **(9)** ..... she really was ..... **(10)** .....

1. A. hard B. herd
C. heard D. hired
2. A. decide B. decides
C. decided D. decision
3. A. firms B. forms
C. farms D. ferns
4. A. maintain B. fountain
C. mountain D. plantain
5. A. locked B. shocked
C. knocked D. pocked

TEST 7

Each species has its special place or habitat. An ..... **(1)** ..... bird-watcher can look at ..... **(2)** ..... forest, meadow, lake, swamp or field and ..... **(3)** ..... almost exactly what birds he ..... **(4)** ..... find there ..... **(5)** ..... birds are found all over the world; others ..... **(6)** ..... themselves to certain areas. Still ..... **(7)** ..... migrate from one country to another in ..... **(8)** ..... in search of warmth and ..... **(9)** ..... and then return in spring, ... **(10)** ..... the season is more favourable.

1. A. expert B. experienced
C. advanced D. active
2. A. the B. some
C. a D. certain
3. A. predict B. suggest
C. prophesy D. calculate
4. A. should B. must
C. might D. will
5. A. more B. some
C. most D. all
6. A. keep B. entrust
C. confine D. involve
7. A. some B. others
C. few D. all
8. A. winter B. summer
C. spring D. autumn
9. A. seeds B. crops
C. fruit D. food
10. A. while B. until
C. after D. when

TEST 8

In the large shops ..... **(1)** ..... for Diwali are begun ..... **(2)** ..... or six weeks before ..... **(3)** ..... actual day. Shop owners ..... **(4)** ..... Diwali because lots of ..... **(5)**

..... are given, which means ..... **(6)** ..... goods are bought than ..... **(7)** ..... any other time of ..... **(8)** ..... year. The main shops ..... **(9)** ..... decorated many weeks before ..... **(10)** ..... to tempt people to buy things.

1.	A. preparations	B. shopping
	C. purchases	D. preparing
2.	A. two	B. five
	C. few	D. couple
3.	A. a	B. an
	C. the	D. which
4.	A. hate	B. anticipate
	C. recommend	D. like
5.	A. purchases	B. prizes
	C. presents	D. presentation
6.	A. many	B. more
	C. few	D. less
7.	A. at	B. in
	C. on	D. for
8.	A. any	B. a
	C. the	D. this
9.	A. were	B. are
	C. have been	D. will be
10.	A. occasion	B. festival
	C. festivities	D. Diwali

TEST 9

Many parents greet their children's teenage years with needless dread. While teens ..... **(1)** ..... assault us with heavy-metal music ..... **(2)** ..... outlandish clothes and spend all ..... **(3)** ..... time with friends, such behaviour ..... **(4)** ..... adds up to full-scale revolt. Teenage ..... **(5)** ..... according to psychologist Laurence Steinberg, has been ..... **(6)** ..... exaggerated. Sociologist Sanford Dornbusch agrees. "The ..... **(7)** ..... that teenagers inevitably rebel is a ..... **(8)** ..... that has the potential for great family ..... **(9)**," say Dornbusch. He believes the notion can ..... **(10)** ..... communication during this critical time for parents to influence youngsters.

1.	A. should	B. may
	C. must	D. can
2.	A. put	B. show
	C. dress	D. flaunt
3.	A. our	B. their
	C. his	D. her
4.	A. infrequently	B. sporadically
	C. scarcely	D. always
5.	A. revolution	B. mania
	C. subversion	D. rebellion
6.	A. greatly	B. hardly
	C. never	D. always
7.	A. surmise	B. idea
	C. complaint	D. accusation
8.	A. story	B. reality
	C. fact	D. myth
9.	A. ruin	B. harm
	C. defeat	D. downfall
10.	A. damage	B. destroy
	C. injure	D. suffocate

TEST 10

Well, it was done and the debt was paid. But I began to feel ..... **(1)** ..... sorry for myself that I could not ..... **(2)** ..... it. I made up my mind never to steal ..... **(3)** ..... I also made up my mind to tell ..... **(4)** ..... to my father. But I did not have the ..... **(5)** ..... to speak to him. It was not that ..... **(6)** ..... was afraid that my father would beat me. I ..... **(7)** ..... not remember any time when he beat ..... **(8)** ..... of us. I was afraid that my confession ..... **(9)** ..... cause him great pain. But I ..... **(10)** ..... felt that I had to take this risk. I would never be happy again unless I told everything to my father.

1.	A. so	B. as
	C. very	D. too
2.	A. accept	B. like
	C. bear	D. understand
3.	A. also	B. again
	C. still	D. ever
4.	A. anything	B. something
	C. nothing	D. everything
5.	A. bravery	B. courage
	C. fortitude	D. gallantry
6.	A. I	B. he
	C. she	D. me
7.	A. would	B. should
	C. do	D. did
8.	A. all	B. some
	C. any	D. none
9.	A. shall	B. can
	C. will	D. would
10.	A. soon	B. again
	C. once	D. since

TEST 11

It is difficult to find a person who would put in a good word for the kind of bureaucracy we have in India. Incidentally, things may now be seen as coming to a head. ..... **(1)** ..... the attainment of Independence, India ..... **(2)** from time to time several ..... **(3)** ..... power Committees or Commissions to ..... **(4)** ..... administration. In spite of all this, the impression ..... **(5)** ..... that the Indian variety of bureaucracy has been slow and slothful. Fact is that the ..... **(6)** ..... of bureaucracy happens to be ..... **(7)** ..... the same all over the world. Even in the U.S.A. Presidents have ..... **(8)** ..... a great deal of concern ..... **(9)** ..... the manner in which bureaucracy has been functioning at various levels. In spite of all this, not much change can be ..... **(10)** ..... in the near future. One may feel like hanging one's head the despair unless one believes in some super-human power that looks after our universe.

1. A. From B. With C. Till D. Since
2. A. arranged B. appointed C. framed D. selected
3. A. great B. super C. high D. multiple
4. A. perform B. reform C. revive D. transform
5. A. insists B. subsists C. consists D. persists
6. A. structure B. function C. growth D. behaviour
7. A. practically B. structurally C. precisely D. strictly
8. A. asserted B. declared C. voiced D. waged
9. A. on B. at C. with D. from
10. A. accepted B. expected C. affected D. admitted

ANSWERS

Test 1

1	2	3	4	5
C	A	C	B	D

Test 2

1	2	3	4	5
B	D	A	C	C

Test 3

1	2	3	4	5
A	C	A	D	A

Test 4

1	2	3	4	5
B	C	D	C	B

Test 5

1	2	3	4	5
A	A	C	D	B

Test 6

1	2	3	4	5
C	C	B	C	C
6	7	8	9	10
C	B	B	B	A

Test 7

1	2	3	4	5
A	C	D	B	B
6	7	8	9	10
C	A	A	D	D

Test 8

1	2	3	4	5
A	B	C	D	C
6	7	8	9	10
B	A	C	B	D

Test 9

1	2	3	4	5
B	D	B	D	D
6	7	8	9	10
B	B	B	A	D

Test 10

1	2	3	4	5
A	C	B	D	B
6	7	8	9	10
A	D	C	D	A

Test 11

1	2	3	4	5
D	B	C	B	D
6	7	8	9	10
B	A	C	B	B

3. Spot the Error

The most common errors in English are of spellings, grammar and usage of words. By regular practice, the errors can be easily spotted and minimised.

COMMON ERRORS WITH NOUNS AND NOUN-PHRASES

	Incorrect	Correct
1.	I have bought new *furnitures.*	I have bought new *furniture.*
2.	The wages of sin *are* death.	The wages of sin *is* death.
3.	She told these *news* to her mother.	She told her mother this *news.*
4.	He took *troubles* to do his work.	He took *trouble* (or pains) over his work.
5.	The *cattles* were grazing.	The *cattle* were grazing.
6.	He showered *many abuses* on me.	He showered *much abuse* on me.
7.	I spent the holidays with my *family members.*	I spent the holidays with my *family.*
8.	There is no *place* in this compartment.	There is no *room* in this compartment.
9.	Write this new *poetry* in your *copy.*	Write this new *poem* in your *note-book.*
10.	He took *insult* at this.	He took *offence* at this.
11.	Put your *sign* here.	Put your *signatures* here.
12.	She is my *cousin sister.*	She is my *cousin.*
13.	*Sunil's* my *neighbour's* house was burgled.	*Sunil* my *neighbour's* house was burgled.
14.	I lost a *ten-rupees* note.	I lost *a ten-rupee* note.
15.	Road closed for *repair.*	Road closed for *repairs.*
16.	His house is out of *repairs.*	His house is out of *repair.*
17.	What is the *reason* of an earthquake?	What is the *cause* of an earthquake?
18.	This building is made of *stones.*	This building is made of *stone.*
19.	I disapprove of *these kinds* of games.	I disapprove of *this kind* of games.
20.	Veena's and Sheela's father is ill.	Veena and Sheela's father is ill.
21.	His *son-in-laws* are doctors.	His *sons-in-law* are doctors.
22.	*Alms* is given to the *poor.*	*Alms* are given to the poor.
23.	He always keeps his words.	He always keeps his *word.*
24.	I carried the *luggages.*	I carried the *luggage.*
25.	*Two-third* of the work is left.	*Two-thirds* of the work is left.

COMMON ERRORS WITH PRONOUNS

	Incorrect	Correct
1.	Both did not go.	Neither went.
2.	We all did not go.	None of us went.
3.	Each of these boys play.	Each of these boys plays.
4.	Whoever does best he will get a prize.	Whoever does best will get a prize.
5.	One should not waste his time.	A man should not waste his time.
6.	I and she are sisters.	She and I are sisters.
7.	He is wiser than me.	He is wiser than I.
8.	Between you and I, Anil is not to be trusted.	Between you and me, Anil is not to be trusted.
9.	Nobody was there but I.	Nobody was there but me.
10.	Who is there ? It is me.	Who is there ? It is I.
11.	Only he and me can use this card.	Only he and I can use this card.
12.	Let you and I go now.	Let you and me go now.
13.	Everyone got one's pay.	Everyone got his pay.
14.	Everyone is frightened when they see a tiger.	Everyone is frightened when he sees a tiger.
15.	These two friends are fond of one another.	These two friends are fond of each other.
16.	I did not like him coming at that hour.	I did not like his coming at that hour.
17.	Who do you think I met?	Whom do you think I met?
18.	You should avail this opportunity.	You should avail yourself this opportunity.
19.	When you have read these books, please return the same to me.	When you have read the books, please return them to me.
20.	They that are humble need fear no fall.	Those that are humble need fear no fall.

COMMON ERRORS WITH ADJECTIVES

	Incorrect	Correct
1.	These all oranges are good.	All these oranges are good.
2.	He held the book in the both hands.	He held the book in both hands.
3.	Both men have not come.	Neither man has come.
4.	That man should do some or other work.	That man should do some work or other
5.	He is elder than I.	He is older than I.
6.	Shakespeare is greater than any other poets.	Shakespeare is greater than any other poet.
7.	He is a coward man.	He is a cowardly man.
8.	Many villagers cannot write his own name.	Many villagers cannot write their own name.
9.	Each of us loves our home.	Each of us loves his home.
10.	Much efforts bring their reward.	Much effort brings its reward.
11.	He found hundred rupees.	He found a hundred rupees.
12.	He had leave of four days.	He had four days leave.

Incorrect	Correct
13. This is a worth seeing sight.	This is a sight worth seeing.
14. He will spend his future life here.	He will spend the rest of his life here.
15. There is a best teacher in that class.	There is a very good teacher in that class.
16. Of the two plans this is the best.	Of the two plans this is the better.
17. He is becoming strong every day.	He is becoming stronger every day.
18. He is worst than I.	He is worse than I.
19. Jaipur is hot than Delhi.	Jaipur is hotter than Delhi.
20 In our library the number of books is less.	In our library the number of books is small.
21. From the three he is more clever.	He is the cleverest of the three.
22. India is the first peace-loving country in the world.	India is the foremost peace-loving country in the world.
23. Verbal instruction will not do.	Oral instruction will not do.
24. Her command over French is most excellent.	Her command over French is excellent.
25. He has not some money with him.	He has not any money with him.
26. I have visited Bombay many a times.	I have visited Bombay many a time.
27. Death is more preferable to dishonour.	Death is preferable to dishonour.
28. I gave him a few books I had.	I gave him the few books I had.
29. If he wants farther help send him to me.	If he wants further help, send him to me.
30. She is so cunning as a fox.	She is as cunning as a fox.

COMMON ERRORS WITH VERBS

Incorrect	Correct
1. He asked had we taken our luggage.	He asked if we had taken our luggage.
2. She asked what are you doing.	She asked what we were doing.
3. Rama asked to Anil why he is angry.	Rama asked Anil why he was angry.
4. He does not care for his money.	He does not take care of his money.
5. He does not care for his work.	He takes no care over his work.
6. No one cared for him after his mother died.	No one took care of him after his mother died.
7. He got angry before I said a word.	He got angry before I had said a word.
8. I met a man who was my tutor 20 years ago.	I met a man who had been my tutor twenty years ago.
9. I had been for walking yesterday.	I went for a walk yesterday.
10 If I shall do this I shall be wrong.	If I do this I shall be wrong.
11. I have left trekking.	I have given up trekking.
12. I came to know as to how he did this.	I learnt how he did this.
13. I came to know why he was sad.	I found out why he was sad.
14. He knows to swim.	He knows how to swim.
15. The criminal's head was cut.	The criminal's head was cut off.

Incorrect	Correct
16. I said to him to go.	I told him to go.
17. I told the teacher to excuse me.	I asked the teacher to excuse me.
18. He is troubling me.	He is giving me trouble.
19. I have got a hurt on my leg.	I have hurt my leg.
20. She gave a speech.	She made a speech.
21. He has given his examination.	He has sat for his examination.
22. He took out his shoes.	He took off his shoes.
23. I have ordered for a new car.	I have ordered a new car.
24. He would not hear me.	He would not listen to me.
25. I struck a blow on his face.	I struck him in the face.
26. He denied to come.	He refused to come.
27. He lived there for a day.	He stayed there for a day.
28. The book is not found.	The book is lost.
29. Shut the light.	Turn off the light.
30. I must revenge my brother.	I must avenge my brother.

COMMON ERRORS IN SUBJECT-VERB AGREEMENT

Incorrect	Correct
1. The owners of this factory *is* very rich.	The owners of this factory *are* very rich.
2. The pleasures of nature that one can experience at Shimla *is* beyond description.	The pleasures of nature that one can experience at Shimla *are* beyond description.
3. There *is* no street lights in our colony.	There *are* no street lights in our colony.
4. He and I *am* entrusted with the job.	He and I *are* entrusted with the job.
5. Rice and curry *are* his favourite dish.	Rice and curry *is* his favourite dish.
6. The honour and glory of our country *are* at stake.	The honour and glory of our country *is* at stake.
7. Time and tide *waits* for none.	Time and tide *wait* for none.
8. All the passengers with the driver *was* killed.	All the passengers, with the driver, *were* killed.
9. The teacher, with her students, *were* going out.	The teacher, with her students, *was* going out.
10. I as well as they *am* tired.	I as well as they *are* tired.
11. Not only the soldiers but their captain also *were* captured.	Not only the soldiers but their captain also *was* captured.
12. Neither you nor I *were* selected.	Neither you nor I *was* selected.
13. Either of these two applicants *are* fit for the job but neither want to accept it.	Either of these two applicants *is* fit for the job but neither wants to accept it.
14. One of these students are sure to stand first.	One of these students *is* sure to stand first.
15. Everyone of these workers want a raise.	Everyone of these workers wants a raise.
16. None of these letters has been answered so far.	None of these letters *have* been answered so far.

	Incorrect	Correct
17.	None of the girls were present at the party.	None of the girls *was* present at the party.
18.	Many a battle were fought on Indian soil.	Many a battle *was* fought on Indian soil.
19.	A lot of work remain to be done.	A lot of work *remains* to be done.
20.	The majority of these girls likes music.	The majority of these girls *like* music.
21.	The number of admissions are encouraging.	The number of admissions *is* encouraging.
22.	A large number of boys was present.	A large number of boys *were* present.
23.	A variety of books was on display.	A variety of books *were* on display.
24.	Variety are the spice of life.	Variety *is* the spice of life.
25.	If my estimates are correct. I will need another hundred rupees.	If my estimate is correct, I will need another hun dred rupees.
26.	Mathematics *are* my favourite subject.	Mathematics *is* my favourite subject.
27.	'Gulliver's Travels' *are* written by Swift.	'Gulliver's Travels' *is* written by Swift.
28.	Ten miles *are* a long distance to cover on foot.	Ten miles *is* a long distance to cover on foot.
29.	A new pair of shoes *are* to be purchased.	A new pair of shoes *is* to be purchased.
30.	The Committee *have* issued its report.	The Committee *has* issued its report.
31.	I, who am your friend, *has* always been on your side,	I, who am your friend, *have* always been on your side.
32.	I am the person who *have* always stood by you.	I am the person who *has* always stood by you.
33.	This is one of the best novels that *has* been published this year.	This is one of the best novels that *have* been published this year.
34.	Less than half the amount *have* been wasted.	Less than half the amount *has* been wasted.
35.	A lot of people *has* turned up for the show.	A lot of people *have* turned up for the show.
36.	Much of their honour *are* un-deserved.	Much of their honour *is* un-deserved.
37.	More than a decade *have* passed since this house was built.	More than a decade *has* passed since this house was built.
38.	Either she or he *are* mistaken.	Either she or he *is* mistaken.
39.	Plenty of information *are* available on the subject.	Plenty of information *is* available on the subject.
40.	Plenty of pamphlets *is* available on the subject.	Plenty of pamphlets *are* available on the subject.

COMMON ERRORS IN USE OF WILL, SHALL, WOULD, SHOULD, MAY, MIGHT, MUST

	Incorrect	Correct
1.	When I shall see him I shall tell him this.	When I *see* him, I shall tell him this.
2.	If I should do wrong, he would punish me.	If I *did* wrong, he would punish me.
3.	Until he will have confessed his fault, he will be kept in prison,	Until he *has* confessed his fault, he will be kept in prison.
4.	She will obey me.	She *shall* obey me.
5.	You would work hard.	You *should* work hard.
6.	You shall find him in the garden.	You *will* find him in the garden.

Incorrect	Correct
7. He must have died of exposure, but we cannot be certain.	He *might* have died of exposure, but we cannot be certain.
8. You might not show disrespect to your elders.	You *must* not show disrespect to your elders.
9. You may take exercise in order to maintain good health,	You *must* take exercise in order to maintain good health.
10. He must be a crook for all we know.	He *may* be a crook for all we know.

COMMON ERRORS IN THE USE OF ADVERBS

(Very, Much, Too, Enough, Quite, Hardly, Scarcely, Before, Ago, Since, Yet, Still, etc.)

Incorrect	Correct
1. He is very much angry.	He is *very* angry.
2. She was very good enough to help me.	She was *good enough* to help me.
3. She runs much fast.	She runs *very* fast.
4. She runs very faster than Seema.	She runs *much* faster than Seema.
5. It is bitter cold today.	It is *bitterly* cold today.
6. He is a much learned man.	He is a very learned man.
7 She is thinking very hardly.	She is thinking very hard.
8. To tell in brief the film was boring.	*In short* the film was boring.
9. He told the story in details.	He told the story *in detail.*
10. I did it anyhow.	I *managed to do* it somehow.
11. Aeroplanes reach Europe soon.	Aeroplanes reach Europe quickly.
12. Before long there were dinosaurs on the earth.	*Long ago,* there were dinosaurs on the earth.
13. This book is too interesting.	This book is *very* interesting.
14. He lives miserly.	He lives in *a miserly* way.
15. Just I had gone when she came.	I had just gone when she came.
16. He sings good.	He sings *well.*
17. He sings good than I.	He sings *better* than I.
18. Really speaking it is cold.	*As a matter of fact* it is cold.
19. He is enough tall to reach the ceiling.	He is *tall enough* to reach the ceiling.
20. He went directly to his college.	He went *direct* to his college.
21. He is presently at Delhi	He is at Delhi *at present.*
22. Last night she returned lately.	Last night she *returned late.*
23. He was even blamed by his friends.	He was *blamed even* by his friends.
24. I only employed him for a week.	I employed him for a week only.
25. I met him four months before.	I met him four *months ago.*

	Incorrect	Correct
26.	Anil seldom ever goes to school.	Anil *seldom goes* to school.
27.	I will wait here until you do not go.	I will wait here until *you go.*
28.	I never remember having met her before.	I *do not remember* having met her before.
29.	She has not been here too long to have many friends,	She has not *been here long* enough to have many friends.
30.	Hardly I have had any rest since one week.	Hardly have *I had* any rest for a week.
31.	Scarcely the water crossed the danger level, the warning signals were sounded.	Scarcely *had the* water *crossed the* danger level, when the warning signals were sounded.
32.	She is neat but fairly slow.	She is *neat* but rather slow.
33.	It is a rather good film.	It is a *fairly good* film.
34.	We yet have time to catch the bus.	We *still have* time to catch the bus.
35.	She has not still spent all her money.	She has *not yet* spent all her money.

COMMON ERRORS IN THE USE OF CONJUNCTIONS

	Incorrect	Correct
1.	As he is fat so he runs slowly.	As he is fat *he* runs slowly.
2.	If he is fat then he will run slowly.	If he is fat, he will run slowly.
3.	Though he is fat still he runs fast.	Though he is fat, *he runs* fast.
4.	*As* I pulled the trigger at the sametime he shook my arm.	As I pulled the trigger, he shook my arm.
5.	No sooner I had spoken than he left.	No sooner *had* I spoken than he left.
6.	Not only he will go, but also he will stay there.	Not only *will he* go, but he *will also* stay there.
7.	Neither he comes nor he writes.	Neither *does he* come nor *does he* write.
8.	Scarcely he entered the room than the telephone rang.	Scarcely *had* he entered the room *when the* telephone rang.
9.	Hardly she had left the house than it began to rain.	Hardly *had she* left the house *when* it began to rain.
10.	He is the fastest runner and he comes last.	He is the fastest runner *but* he comes last.
11.	She is as innocent as if she looks.	She is as innocent as she looks.
12.	Until he does not try he must be punished.	He must be punished unless he tries
13.	I want to know as to why you are late.	I want to know why you are late.
14.	I am fond of Chinese food as for example sweet and sour prawns.	I am fond of Chinese food, for example, sweet and sour prawns.
15.	He was angry therefore I ran away.	He was angry so I ran away.
16.	I was trying to work, at that time he was disturbing me.	While I was trying to work, he was disturbing me.
17.	Supposing if he is late, what will happen?	Supposing he is late (or if he is late) what will happen?
18.	He asked me that why I was late.	He asked me why I was late.

Incorrect	Correct
19. Let us catch a taxi lest we should not get late.	Let us catch a taxi lest we should get late.
20. She dresses herself like the teacher does.	She dresses herself as the teacher does.
21 Wait while I come.	Wait *until* (or *till)* I come.
22. Until, there is corruption in India, there can be little progress.	*As long* as there is corruption in India there can be little progress.
23. I have never told a lie nor cheated anybody.	I have never told a lie *nor have I* cheated anybody.
24. Both Mohan as well as Arun are responsible for this action.	Both Mohan *and* Arun are responsible for this action.
25. Hindus and Muslims both are to blame for the riots.	*Both Hindus* and Muslims are to blame for the riots.
26. I have bought paintings, books, records, and etc.	I have bought paintings, books *and records etc.*
27. He as well as you is a fool.	He as well as you *are* a fool.
28. He is so poor and he cannot save anything.	He is so *poor that* he cannot save anything.
29. Such a' book that you want is not available.	Such a book *as* you want is not available.
30. Such was her condition as everyone was moved to pity.	Such was her condition that everyone was moved to pity.

COMMON ERRORS IN THE USE OF PREPOSITIONS

Incorrect	Correct
1. I will not listen him.	I will not listen *to* him.
2. Copy this word by word.	Copy this word *for* word.
3. He enquired from her where she lived.	He enquired *of* her where she lived.
4. Sign here with ink.	Sign here *in* ink.
5. Has she come in train or by foot?	Has she come *by* train or *on* foot?
6. She said this at his face.	She said this *to* his face.
7. Open the book on page one	Open the book *at* page one.
8. I was invited for lunch.	I was *invited to* lunch.
9. I am ill since three months.	I have been *ill for* three months.
10. This paper is inferior than that.	This paper is inferior *to* that.
11. This resembles to that.	This *resembles* that.
12. My brother is superior than you in strength.	My brother is superior *to* you in strength.
13. He wrote me	He wrote *to* me.
14. I shall explain them this.	I shall explain this *to* them.
15. Send this letter on my address.	Send this letter *to* my address.
16. He suggested me this.	He suggested this *to* me.
17. He goes *on his* work.	He goes *to his* work.
18. He *reached to* Nagpur.	He *reached* Nagpur.
19. He told *to me* to go.	He told *me* to go.

	Incorrect	Correct
20	The term begins *from* July 1st.	The term begins *on* July 1st.
21.	There are many advantages *from* this.	The advantages *of* this are many.
22.	We waste much time *in* trifles.	We waste much time *on* (or *over*) trifles.
23.	He sat *on* a tree.	He sat *in* a tree.
24.	This is a comfortable house to *live*.	This is a comfortable house to *live in*.
25.	This is the road to *go*.	This is the road to *go by*.
26.	He married *with* an Indian lady.	He *married an Indian* lady.
27.	He accompanied *with* his friend.	He *accompanied his* friend.
28.	He went *for doing some* business.	He went away *on* business.
29.	He went for *riding*.	He went *for a ride*.
30.	I *pitied on* him.	I *pitied* him.
31.	When this was searched it was found.	When this was searched *for* it was found.
32.	I shall inform them *this*.	I shall inform them *of* this.
33.	*Due to illness* I cannot go to school.	*Owing* to illness I cannot go to school.
34.	He went *to the back side* of the house.	He went *behind* (or to the back of) the house.
35.	I must go; there is no *help*.	I must go; there is no help *for it*.
36.	I *met with your* friend there.	I *met your* friend there.
37.	The First World War was fought *during* 1914-1918.	The First World War was fought *between* 1914-1918.
38.	England grew prosperous *between* Queen Victoria's reign.	England grew prosperous *during* Queen Victoria's reign.
39.	He asked a holiday.	He asked *for* a holiday.
40.	I am obliged of you for this good turn.	I am obliged *to* you for this good turn.
41.	There is no harm to try.	There is no harm *in trying*.

MISCELLANEOUS ERRORS

(Including Ambiguities and Indianisms)

	Incorrect	Correct
1.	Many *homes* are lying vacant.	Many *houses* are lying vacant.
2.	It is cool in the *shadow* of the tree.	It is cool in the *shade* of the tree.
3.	She *keeps* good health.	She *enjoys* good health.
4.	My leg is *paining*.	*I am feeling pain* in my leg.
5.	*See* this word in the dictionary.	*Look up* this word in the dictionary.
6.	The train will arrive *just now*	The train will arrive *shortly*.
7.	They are *pulling* on well.	They are *getting* on well.
8.	The river has *over flown* its bank.	The river has *over flown* its banks.
9.	He was appointed *on* the post.	He was appointed *to* the post.
10.	Last but not *the least,* we have to discuss the problem of over population.	Last but not *least,* we have to discuss the problem of over population.

Incorrect	Correct
11. *Cities* after *cities* fell.	*City* after *city* fell.
12. What is the use Munir going there?	What is the use of Munir going there?
13. He *did many mischief.*	He *made much mischief.*
14. It is exact five *in* my watch.	It is exact five *by* my watch.
15. I will dine with them on *next Sunday.*	I will dine with them *Sunday next.*
16. Misfortunes when faced bravely and *manly* become less troublesome.	Misfortunes when faced bravely and *manfully* become less troublesome.
17. I am *laid down* with fever.	I am *laid up* with fever.
18. He is habituated to smoking.	He is *addicted* to smoking.
19. *According to my opinion* he is right.	*In my opinion* (or according *to me)* he is right.
20. Could you please *open* this knot?	Could you please *untie* this knot?

MULTIPLE CHOICE QUESTIONS

Directions: *In the following questions some of the sentences have errors and some are correct. Find out which part of a sentence has an error, the number of that part is your answer. If a sentence is free from errors, then your answer is D i.e., No error.*

1. (A) Either Ram or/(B) you is responsible/(C) for this action./(D) No error.

2. (A) The student flatly denied/(B) that he had copied/(C) in the examination hall./(D) No error.

3. (A) By the time you arrive tomorrow/(B) I have finished/(C) my work./(D) No error.

4. (A) The captain with the members of his team/(B) are returning/(C) after a fortnight./(D) No error.

5. (A) After returning from/(B) an all-India tour/(C) I had to describe about it./(D) No error.

6. (A) The teacher asked his students/(B) if they had gone through/(C) either of the three chapters included in the prescribed text./(D) No error.

7. (A) Do you know/(B) how old were you/(C) when you came here?/(D) No error.

8. (A) Beware of/(B) a fair-weather friend/(C) who is neither a friend in need nor a friend indeed./(D) No error.

9. (A) Copernicus proved/(B) that Earth/(C) moves round the Sun./(D) No error.

10. (A) The property/(B) was divided/(C) among the two brothers./(D) No error.

11. (A) I am quite certain/(B) that the lady is not only greedy/(C) but miserly./(D) No error.

12. (A) The brilliant success in the examination/(B) as well as his record in sports/(C) deserves high praise./(D) No error.

13. (A) I cannot find/(B) where has he gone/(C) though I have tried may best./(D) No error.

14. (A) If I was/(B) the Prime Minister of India/(C) I would work wonders/(D) No error.

15. (A) If it weren't/(B) for you,/(C) I wouldn't be alive today./(D) No error.

16. (A) He looked like a lion/(B) baulked from/(C) its prey./(D) No error.

17. (A) Widespread flooding/(B) is affecting/(C) large areas of the villages./(D) No error.

18. (A) If we really set to/(B) we can get the whole house/(C) cleaned in an afternoon./(D) No error.

19. (A) It's arrogant for you/(B) to assume you'll/(C)win every time./(D) No error.

20. (A) The two books are the same/(B) except for the fact that this/(C) has an answer in the back./(D) No error.

21. (A) Your husband doesn't/(B) believe that you are older/(C) than I./(D) No error.

22. (A) I could not/(B) answer to/(C) the question./(D) No error.

23. (A) Two years passed/(B) since/(C) my cousin died./(D) No error.

24. (A) I am learning English/(B) for ten years/(C) without much effect./(D) No error.

25. (A) Ramesh has agreed/(B) to marry with the girl/(C) of his parent's choice./ (D) No error.

26. (A) When he was arriving./(B) the party was/(C) in full swing./(D) No error.

27. (A) The most studious boy/(B) in the class/(C) was made as the captain./(D) No error.

28. (A) I am participating/(B) in the two-miles race/(C) tomorrow morning./(D) No error.

29. (A) When the boy committed a mistake/(B) the teacher made him to do/(C) the sum again./(D) No error.

30. (A) Whenever a person lost anything/(B) the poor folk around/(C) are suspected./(D) No error.

ANSWERS

1. **(B):** Replace 'is' by 'are'
2. **(D):** No error
3. **(B):** Replace 'have' by 'would have'
4. **(B):** Replace 'are' by 'its'
5. **(C):** Replace 'had to describe' by 'described'
6. **(C):** Replace 'either' by 'any'
7. **(D):** No error
8. **(D):** No error
9. **(B):** Omit 'that'
10. **(C):** Replace 'among' by 'between'
11. **(C):** Add 'also'
12. **(D):** No error
13. **(B):** Replace 'has he' by 'he has'
14. **(A):** Replace 'was' by 'were'
15. **(C):** Replace 'wouldn't be' by 'would not have been'
16. **(C):** Replace 'its' by 'his'
17. **(C):** Replace 'areas' by 'area'
18. **(A):** Replace 'set to' by 'set on'
19. **(A):** Replace 'for' by 'of'
20. **(C):** Replace 'in' by 'on'
21. **(C):** Replace 'I' by 'me'
22. **(B):** Omit 'to'
23. **(A):** Replace 'passed' by 'have passed'
24. **(A):** Replace 'am' by 'have been'
25. **(B):** Omit 'with'
26. **(A):** Replace 'was arriving' by 'arrived'
27. **(C):** Omit 'as'
28. **(B):** Replace 'in' by 'at'
29. **(B):** Omit 'to'
30. **(A):** Replace 'lost' by 'loses'

4. SENTENCE IMPROVEMENT

One may use the same words in many ways but the best way is only one that makes the perfect usage of the words and conveys the proper meaning of the expression. Try it yourself in this exercise.

MULTIPLE CHOICE QUESTIONS

Directions: *In these questions, a part of the sentence is* ***bold****. Below are given alternatives to the* ***bold*** *part at A, B and C which may improve the sentence. Choose the correct alternative to edit and improve the sentence. In case no improvement is needed, your answer is D.*

1. For most people who exercise **at the** morning, there is no getting around the question: Eat and run? Or run and eat later?
A. in the B. in
C. at the time of D. No Improvement

2. Are ad agencies even attempting to peer into the keyhole of this indulgence sanctum to garner consumer insights **ahead of** the curve?
A. above B. over
C. within D. No Improvement

3. Too many people rush into the world of credit and don't stop to think about how **their actions could affect their** credit score and ability to qualify for credit in the future.
A. their actions may affect their
B. their actions might affect their
C. their actions will affect their
D. No Improvement

4. According to the report, **number of deal with** vaccines were energized by concerns around avian flu, SARS, and biodefense products, while looming patent expirations led to more deals in generics.
A. number of deals in
B. number of deal in
C. number of deals with
D. No Improvement

5. This is how the Bombay High Court responded to the state government's purported **moral stand which** dance bars were causing grave harm to society.
A. moral stand in B. moral stand at
C. moral stand that D. No Improvement

6. If you have a high credit limit, use **at least a** third of it.
A. atleast a B. at last a
C. utmost a D. No Improvement

7. Fitness experts will say that **first eating provides** fuel for a proper workout.
A. eating in the beginning provides
B. first eat provides
C. eating first provides
D. No Improvement

8. One study that examined the claim directly in 2012 found that a group of people did **burned much calories from fat on days** when they exercised on an empty stomach than on days when they had a small breakfast first.
A. burn more calories from fat on days
B. burn more calorie from fat on days
C. burnt more calories from fat on days
D. No Improvement

9. Carefree children spent their afternoons **to run about barefoot**, their clothes dusty, and telltale twigs of the neighbour's mango tree in their hair.
A. running barefoot in the sun
B. run about barefoot in the sun
C. running about barefoot in the sun
D. No Improvement

10. A year ago, a 13-year-old girl attempted suicide because her mother **refuses to pay his** mobile bills.

A. refuses to pay her B. refused to pay her
C. refused to pay his D. No Improvement

11. Discreet salience **is extremely important** to create that 'irresistible-yet-unattainable' image for brands that want to take India seriously

A. was extremely important
B. is mainly important
C. was important extremely
D. No Improvement

12. This, over a designer outfit that he wanted for a friend's party and **that his sensitive** parents refused him.

A. which his sensitive
B. which his insensitive
C. that his insensitive
D. No Improvement

13. Goa was full of non-Goa property hunters **rushing about buying up the place** like tomorrow was an expired lease.

A. rushing in buying up the place
B. rushed about buying up the place
C. rushing about to buy up the place
D. No Improvement

14. Property hunting is a **tired and hungry** making business.

A. is a tiresome and hungry
B. is a tiring and hungry
C. is a tiring and waste
D. No Improvement

15. Cultural differences aside, **till luxury need speaks** in a manner that befits.

A. luxury still needs to speak
B. luxury still need to speak
C. luxury till need to speak
D. No Improvement

16. Indian food – the culinary avatar of the subcontinent's social history presented on a platter – **is without doubt the best food** in the world.

A. is undoubtly the greatest food
B. is without doubt greatest food
C. is best food without doubt
D. No Improvement

17. It must retain the language of poetry. **It needed to create** stories, and not statements.

A. It needed creating B. It needs creating
C. It needs to create D. No Improvement

18. In 2012, Asia-Pacific has become the first region **to reach aggregate profiting** in biotech.

A. to reach aggregated profi-tability
B. to reach aggregate profi-tability
C. to reach aggregate of profit
D. No Improvement

19. India is deviating to embrace the West. If Western luxury brands deviate a little, **albeit selectively**, they will find rich Indian arms open far and wide.

A. though selectively
B. however selectively
C. albeit selectedly
D. No Improvement

20. China and India continued to attract attention and deals, motivated by the desire to increase access to these **largest and growing** drug markets and by the need to lower the costs of drug development.

A. larger and growing B. large and growing
C. larger and grown D. No Improvement

21. Luxury brands are **still above of the** clover curve here, with their elite (small) audiences.

A. still ahead of the B. still in the
C. still far of the D. No Improvement

22. Agencies **hence needed to be** sure of returns before investing, say ad men.

A. hence needs to be B. so needs to be
C. hence need to be D. No Improvement

23. India is still a nascent market and that's the spirit everyone's **looking at it**.

A. looking for it B. looking in it
C. looking with it D. No Improvement

24. Questioning the state's move to allow women to serve liquor but not dance in bars **of the ground that** dancing aroused physical lust

A. on the grounds that
B. of the grounds that
C. over the grounds that
D. No Improvement

25. For England the positives from their crushing series lose come in the shape of James Anderson and Kevin Pietersen, **both of which** have made significant strides up the rankings

A. both of which B. both of whom
C. both of who D. No Improvement

26. International campaigns can work well for luxury here, **but context cannot be** ignored.

A. so context cannot be
B. but context cannot
C. but context couldn't
D. No Improvement

27. For one, the Indian luxury context, **while evolved rapidly**, still has its own meaning, and its own implications.

A. while evolved rapid
B. which evolving rapidly
C. while evolving rapidly
D. No Improvement

28. But too much of availability can compromise a luxury brand or **made it lose** its lustre.

A. make her lose B. make him lose
C. make it lose D. No Improvement

29. Still, it's under-the-upper **layers themselves who** are aspiring for slivers of luxury

A. layers themselves which
B. layer itself who
C. layers themself which
D. No Improvement

30. It is like saying Hindi movies, with skimpily dressed dancers, would **effect public** order

A. effect your B. affect public
C. affected public D. No Improvement

31. The court held that a few women being involved in prostitution was no **justice to deny other** bar girls the right to livelihood

A. justification to declare other
B. justification to deny other
C. justice to let other
D. No Improvement

32. All-rounder Irfan Pathan has also made some progress **over the** player rankings.

A. above the B. at the
C. up the D. No Improvement

33. Former PM on Sunday **joined hands** with suspended Lok Sabha members to float a new political outfit.

A. folded hands
B. walked hand in hand
C. shaked hands
D. No Improvement

34. Pakistan's former PMs will meet in London on Monday **to ask** a strategy to return home from exile.

A. to chalk out B. to negotiate
C. to create D. No Improvement

35. It's a family potboiler, medical thriller and political drama **all in one** – except that it's all too real and all too grim.

A. all 3 in one
B. all coupled into one
C. all rolled into one
D. No Improvement

ANSWERS

1	**2**	**3**	**4**	**5**	**6**	**7**	**8**	**9**	**10**
A	D	C	A	C	D	C	A	C	B
11	**12**	**13**	**14**	**15**	**16**	**17**	**18**	**19**	**20**
D	C	D	B	A	D	C	C	D	B
21	**22**	**23**	**24**	**25**	**26**	**27**	**28**	**29**	**30**
C	C	D	A	C	D	C	C	C	B
31	**32**	**33**	**34**	**35**					
B	C	C	A	C					

5. Reordering Words

The words form a sentence and convey their meaning only when they are arranged in a proper order. One must study and practise it regularly.

MULTIPLE CHOICE QUESTIONS

Directions: *In the following questions, some parts of the sentence have been jumbled up. You are required to rearrange these parts which are labelled P, Q, R and S to produce the correct sentence. Choose the option with proper sequence.*

1. We are doing
P : to the people
Q : to give relief
R : all we can
S : but more funds are needed
The correct sequence should be
A. P Q R S B. R Q P S
C. Q P R S D. S P Q R

2. The man
P : when he was
Q : in the office last evening
R : could not finish
S : all his work
The correct sequence should be
A. P Q R S B. Q R S P
C. R Q P S D. R S P Q

3. The people decided
P : they were going
Q : how much
R : to spend
S : on the construction of the school building
The correct sequence should be
A. Q P R S B. P Q R S
C. P R Q S D. S Q P R

4. The man said that
P : those workers
Q : would be given a raise
R : who did not go on
S : strike last month
The correct sequence should be
A. P Q R S B. P R S Q
C. Q P R S D. R S P Q

5. I think
P : the members
Q : are basically in agreement
R : of the group
S : on the following points.
The correct sequence should be
A. R Q P S B. S Q R P
C. P R Q S D. P Q S R

6. While it was true that
P : I had
Q : to invest in industry
R : some lands and houses
S : I did not have ready cash
The correct sequence should be
A. P Q R S B. P R S Q
C. S Q P R D. Q P R S

7. P : But your help
Q : to finish this work
R : it would not have been possible
S : in time
The correct sequence should be
A. P R Q S B. S P Q R
C. R P Q S D. P Q R S

8. The boy
P : in the competition
Q : who was wearing spectacles
R : won many prizes
S : held in our college

The correct sequence should be
A. P Q R S B. R P S Q
C. Q R P S D. Q P S R

9. About 200 years ago,
P : in the south of India
Q : an old king
R : ruled over a kingdom
S : called Rajavarman.
The correct sequence should be
A. Q S R P B. P Q R S
C. Q P S R D. Q S P R

10. P : his land
Q : a wooden plough
R : the Indian peasant still uses
S : to cultivate.
The correct sequence should be
A. R Q P S B. Q P S R
C. S R Q P D. R Q S P

11. He was a man,
P : even if he had to starve
Q : who would not beg
R : borrow or steal
S : from anyone.
The correct sequence should be
A. P Q R S B. P R Q S
C. Q R S P D. Q P R S

12. P : in the progress of
Q : universities play a crucial role
R : our civilization
S : in the present age.
The correct sequence should be
A. S Q P R B. Q R S P
C. Q R P S D. S Q R P

13. P : far out into the sea
Q : for the next two weeks there were further explosions
R : which hurled
S : ashes and debris.
The correct sequence should be
A. Q R P S B. R S P Q
C. Q R S P D. S R P Q

14. William Shakespeare,
P : in his lifetime
Q : the great English dramatist
R : wrote thirty-five plays
S : and several poems.
The correct sequence should be
A. P Q R S B. R S P Q
C. Q S R P D. Q R S P

15. Whenever I am,
P : with an old friend of mine
Q : in New Delhi
R : to have dinner
S : I always try.
The correct sequence should be
A. S Q P R B. Q S R P
C. R P S Q D. P R Q S

16. P : I don't know
Q : must have thought
R : what people sitting next to me
S : but I came away.
The correct sequence should be
A. R S Q P B. R Q S P
C. P Q R S D. P R Q S

17. P : in estimating the size of the earth
Q : but they were hampered by the lack of instruments of precision
R : ancient astronomers
S : used methods which were theoretically valid
The correct sequence should be
A. R P Q S B. P R Q S
C. R S Q P D. R P S Q

18. P : It is a pity that
Q : by offering a handsome dowry
R : a number of parents think that
S : they will be able to ensure the happiness of their daughters
The correct sequence should be
A. S Q R P B. P R S Q
C. P S R Q D. P R Q S

19. The common man
P : in nurturing
Q : a more active role
R : communal harmony
S : should play
The correct sequence should be
A. P R S Q B. S Q P R
C. S Q R P D. P R Q S

20. The doctor
P : able to find out
Q : what has caused

R : the food poisoning
S : has not been
The correct sequence should be
A. S P R Q B. P R Q S
C. P R S Q D. S P Q R

21. P : was suspended
Q : the officer being corrupt
R : before his dismissal
S : from service
The correct sequence should be
A. Q P S R B. Q P R S
C. R S Q P D. R S PQ

22. With an unsteady hand
P : on my desk
Q : from his pocket
R : he took an envelope
S : and threw it
The correct sequence should be
A. Q R P S B. Q R S P
C. R Q P S D. R Q S P

23. P : she gave her old coat
Q : to a beggar
R : the one with the brown fur on it
S : shivering with cold
The correct sequence should be
A. S Q R P B. S P R Q
C. P R Q S D. P S Q R

24. It is a privilege
P : to pay tax
Q : of every citizen
R : as well as the duty
S : as well as the duty who is well-placed
The correct sequence should be
A. R P S Q B. S P R Q
C. R Q S P D. S Q R P

25. It is not good
P : of the wicked persons
Q : to overthrow
R : to accept the help
S : the righteous persons
The correct sequence should be
A. R S Q P B. Q S R P
C. R P Q S D. Q P R S

26. Life is judged
P : and not by
Q : of work done
R : the longevity of years
S : by the quality
The correct sequence should be
A. Q S P R B. S Q R P
C. Q S R P D. S Q P R

27. P : When he learns that
Q : you have passed the examination
R : in the first division
S : your father will be delighted
The correct sequence should be
A. Q P S R B. S P Q R
C. Q R S P D. S R Q P

28. P : The journalist
Q : saw
R : countless number of the dead
S : driving across the field of battle
The correct sequence should be
A. P Q S R B. P Q R S
C. P S Q R D. S R Q P

29. P : Jane planned
Q : some stamps
R : to buy
S : this afternoon
The correct sequence should be
A. P R Q S B. P S Q R
C. Q R P S D. Q S P R

30. Her mother
P : when she was
Q : hardly four years old
R : began to teach Neha
S : English
The correct sequence should be
A. R S Q P B. S R P Q
C. R S P Q D. S R Q P

31. It was
P : in keeping with my mood
Q : a soft summer evening
R : as I walked sedately
S : in the direction of the new house
The proper sequence should be:
A. S R P Q B. Q R P S
C. Q P R S D. S Q P R

32. With her body
P : dragging her unwilling feet
Q : weak and infirm

R : doubled with age
S : she persisted in her mission
The proper sequence should be:
A. P Q R S B. Q P R S
C. R Q P S D. S R P Q

33. A.P.J. Abdul Kalam
P : is popularly know as
Q : from 2002 and 2007 and
R : was the 11th president of the country
S : 'Misile Man' of India
The proper sequence should be:
A. P Q R S B. Q P R S
C. S R P Q D. R Q P S

34. When he
P : did not know
Q : he was nervous and
R : heard the hue and cry at midnight
S : what to do
The proper sequence should be:
A. R Q P S B. Q S P R
C. S Q P R D. P Q R S

35. A French woman
P : committed suicide
Q : where she had put up
R : who had come to Calcutta
S : by jumping from the first floor balcony of the hotel
The proper sequence should be:
A. P R Q S B. Q S R P
C. R P S Q D. S R Q P

36. He has
P : while having a reverie
Q : found the book
R : at the bus-stop
S : he lost
The proper sequence should be:
A. Q R S P B. P R Q S
C. Q S R P D. P Q S R

37. Then the women
P : lamenting their evil desire
Q : that had brought
R : wept loudly
S : this sorrow upon them
The proper sequence should be:
A. R P Q S B. R Q P S
C. P Q S R D. P R Q S

38. It is easy to excuse
P : but it is hard
Q : in a boy of fourteen
R : the mischief of early childhood
S : to tolerate even unavoidable faults
The proper sequence should be:
A. R P Q S B. Q R S P
C. Q R P S D. R P S Q

39. I don't remember
P : I saw a man dying in front of a hospital
Q : but when I left Lucknow in 1984
R : hit apparently by a fast moving car
S : the exact date
The proper sequence should be:
A. S Q R P B. S Q P R
C. Q R P S D. S P R Q

40. Since the beginning of history
P : have managed to catch
Q : the Eskimos and Red Indians
R : by a very difficult method
S : a few specimens of this acquatic mammal
The proper sequence should be:
A. Q P R S B. S Q P R
C. S Q R P D. Q P S R

ANSWERS

1	2	3	4	5	6	7	8	9	10
B	D	A	B	C	C	A	C	A	D
11	**12**	**13**	**14**	**15**	**16**	**17**	**18**	**19**	**20**
C	A	C	D	B	D	C	B	B	D
21	**22**	**23**	**24**	**25**	**26**	**27**	**28**	**29**	**30**
B	D	C	C	B	D	B	C	A	C
31	**32**	**33**	**34**	**35**	**36**	**37**	**38**	**39**	**40**
C	C	D	A	C	C	A	D	B	D

6. Ordering of Sentences

A Paragraph is formed from sentences, it will convey its true meaning and purpose only when the sentences are arranged in a proper manner. Try and practise it in this exercise.

MULTIPLE CHOICE QUESTIONS

Directions: *A number of sentences are given below which when properly sequenced form a coherent paragraph. Each sentence is labelled as abcdef...... Choose the most logical order of sentences from among the given choices to construct a coherent paragraph:*

1. (a) The leopard was discovered in the servant quarters of a farmhouse.

(b) The injuries appeared to have been caused by the paws of the leopard, and were not teeth wounds.

(c) It took the wild life officials, Delhi Police and Delhi zoo vets eight hours to capture the leopard that had wandered into a factory in south Delhi.

(d) The leopard then jumped into the factory where the workers managed to lock it in a small generator room before calling in the police.

(e) Before its capture, the leopard attacked two women and a man in the farmhouse.

A. aebdc B. bdaec
C. eadbc D. adbec

2. (a) The project has already started on an experimental basis in the west district.

(b) A website is soon going to be launched where application forms can be downloaded and submitted.

(c) Standing in a queue at a government office to submit application form will be a thing of the past.

(d) A unique code will be alloted while submitting the form which will help in finding the status of the application.

A. abcd B. dabc
C. cbda D. badc

3. (a) Police suspect a carpenter working at John's house as he has not reported for work since the day the boy went missing.

(b) John did not return home in the afternoon.

(c) John's mother had herself put the boy on the vehicle in the morning.

(d) John smiled at him and was last seen walking up to him.

(e) His parents called the school and were told John had not been to school at all and had been marked absent.

(f) He was about to enter the school when someone called out his name.

A. cfdbea B. debfca
C. bfdaec D. abcdef

4. (a) A state champion from the past four years, Tushar began swimming at the age of six.

(b) But he has no plans of making swimming a career.

(c) Tushar's passion for swimming is unshakable.

(d) Something that began as a hobby rewarded him with all the fame he has achieved.

(e) His day begins at 4.30 am for a dip at Talkatora Stadium.

(f) He is determined to make a mark in the world of swimming.

A. dbaecf B. bcadef
C. edfbac D. cefadb

5. (a) However, the mayhem over the last few months is deeply shocking.

(b) Yet I do not agree with the prophets of doom who see nothing but disaster ahead.
(c) When I came back to my motherland India after a stay in Switzerland, I felt I was trading a hotbed of intense religious and political violence for peace and quiet.
(d) I think our nation is searching for an identity.
(e) And a new vision of the future will emerge from this.

A. abcde B. cabde
C. cebad D. bedca

6. (a) The universities in a democracy can no longer be content with the limited goal of scholarship.
(b) They are to respond to changed conditions and to new demands.
(c) Universities in the modern world are called upon to play a crucial role in the progress of our civilization.
(d) They have to devise new programmes and take into account the needs of society.
(e) They must not merely display their traditional resourcefulness but also must have the capacity for effective growth.

A. cbdae B. cbead
C. cadbe D. dbaec

7. (a) He decided to enter a new line by investing in some new equipments.
(b) Some of the old machines were to be sold to raise the money.
(c) Ram's business was not prospering.
(d) For this more money had to be found.
(e) He was still short of money and had to borrow some.

A. cadbe B. adebc
C. ebdac D. cbdae

8. (a) Parts of northern region were pounded by heavy rains today,
(b) Vehicular traffic came to a near halt.
(c) As mid and high altitude areas of Himachal Pradesh were in grip of severe cold wave with snow lashing the tribal areas and mid ranges receiving showers.
(d) As the sky remained heavily overcast with dark clouds reducing the visibility considerably.
(e) A large number of tourists were forced to buy heavy woollens and stay indoors due to inclement weather.

A. ecabd B. adecb
C. edabc D. acbde

9. (a) Clearly, age is not a deterrent in one's choice of learning.
(b) Perhaps, it was because of her childhood desire.
(c) When Rachna came to Delhi eight years back, she had not anticipated a career in the field of art.
(d) She has been successful in the various exhibitions that she has been part of in terms of business.
(e) She had got into expressing her thoughts with the help of a brush and colours only because her daughter refused to get initiated into it.
(f) She feels that her use of colour appeals to people.

A. aedcbf B. cdefba
C. cebadf D. acdebf

10. (a) The idea is that students should be able to find employment for themselves after the course.
(b) The Central Board of Secondary Education is planning a revamp of its vocational courses.
(c) For this it is necessary to tie up with the industry as well as mobilise schools for their support.
(d) While others will be made less academic and more in tune with the needs of the industry.
(e) A number of courses have been identified as 'deadwood' and will be done away with.

A. bedac B. abcde
C. acebd D. baced

11. (a) An integrated and combined approach was required to reveal the mystery of the brain – its structure, composition and function.
(b) Since the early 80's, scientists were clear that the brain would be the final frontier to conquer.
(c) The initiative was flagged off and came to be known as the Human Brain Project.

(d) But that wasn't easy because understanding the brain involved completely integrating information from the level of the gene to the level of behaviour.

(e) To fulfill this requirement a group of American scientists from various diciplines decided to work together.

A. acbed B. bdaec
C. abdec D. badec

12. (a) The rehabilitation record has been dismal.

(b) It has been two years years since the earthquake rudely rattled the people of Gujrat.

(c) And since then, life has been a constant struggle.

(d) The quake set Gujrat's clock back by 10 years.

(e) Things changed forever.

A. bedca B. bcade
C. dbace D. edcba

13. (a) In fact, success in exams depended on rote learning from old notes.

(b) when he was studying civil engineering in a college in Gujrat.

(c) He was detained for lack of attendance.

(d) Lectures were soporific, classes rarely worth attending and 80 per cent attendance compulsory.

(e) The college became a trap he hated.

(f) His is a plight many engineers across India would identify with.

(g) He found the going tough.

A. abcdgef B. bgdacef
C. fabcdge D. abcdefg

14. (a) In a country that has close to 600 recognised engineering colleges, there are only seven IITs.

(b) Barring a few exeptions, the academic atmosphere in these is moribund.

(c) The very best students usually get there.

(d) many waste themselves in frustration.

(e) Most of those who get into engineering are good students.

(f) but about 1.25 lakh others and up in the remaining colleges.

A. aecfbd B. abecdf
C. abcdef D. acfbed

15. (a) Whatever the job market, common wisdom says that IIT graduates will find jobs where others have failed.

(b) The IIT brand name is a ticket to success.

(c) When recruiters go headhunting, the IITs are still top of their list.

(d) Its possessor is understood to have an excellent academic record and the will to succeed.

(e) In the job market, that counts.

A. bdeac B. abcde
C. abdce D. dbace

16. (a) It will pave the way ....

(b) signalling a new beginning in strategic ties......

(c) for a tangible Indian economic presence in Iran and Central Asia.

(d) Iran has offered India valuable road linkages to central Asia ......

(e) aimed at promoting peace and economic cooperation in the region.

A. dbeac B. debca
C. acebd D. abced

17. (a) A good college is essential for a successful career and admissions are based on marks.

(b) The marks-based system followed by all the boards in the country recognises only a small percentage of students as successful.

(c) The marks one scores in the crucial board exams dictate the path his life takes.

(d) Anyone scoring below a certain percentage is automatically branded a 'failure'.

(d) So if you cannot make it into the best college, your career is over even before it has started.

A. abcde B. bcdea
C. bdcae D. abdec

18. (a) the pride of their batch.

(b) they're not too far off from taking charge of India's future.

(c) They were the toppers of their class

(d) they may have won accolades, made their schools and families proud, but

(e) Yesterday's toppers have their hands full.

(f) these confident go-getters have had their share of failure too.

A. eacfbd B. eadbfc
C. eadbcf D. cabedf

19. (a) Mistakes or errors should be treated as teacher.
(b) When you make mistake, you should neither feel ashamed nor desperate.
(c) Everybody makes mistakes.
(d) You should be bold enough to accept your mistakes before anybody.
(e) But the only sensible course is to study and analyse why you made that mistake.
(f) Only then you can learn not to make mistakes in future.
A. abfced B. acefbd
C. adbcfe D. cdfbea

20. (a) Our lessons in love and respect make us a tolerant people.
(b) I love Indian culture.
(c) I feel I have to repay my country whatever way I can.
(d) In no other country have I seen so much love and respect.
(e) I was born and brought up in this country and feel I owe everything to it.
A. bcade B. dcbea
C. acdeb D. ecbda

21. (a) To curb bio-terroriom is a difficult task.
(b) To check these attacks and lessen their impact, we need an impartial team of sincere, strong and dedicated men.
(c) The media can play a strong role in stopping this unnecessary spread of panic.
(d) Since Bio-terrorism is not visible or easily detectable, it can be used often.
(e) Men who honour the lives of their fellow countrymen before their own.
A. abcde B. dabce
C. adbec D. acbed

22. (a) He was dying.
(b) No one was ready to touch him as even shifting him from one place to another would lead to profuse bleeding.
(c) He was a five-day old infant, premature and bleeding profusely.
(d) Even if injected one small needle, blood would ooze out and continue to flow for an hour at a stretch.
(e) This small being had haematoma, a thick blood clot in his brain.
A. edbca B. cabde
C. eacdb D. cedba

23. (a) The day I don't treat a patient, I feel ......
(b) I have enough to eat, I crave for blessings now.
(c) But if a financially weak patient gives me only ₹ 50, I don't mind.
(d) Each month I do three to four operations free of cost.
(e) I have lost something in life.
(f) My consultation fee is ₹ 300.
A. fcdeab B. dfcbae
C. fcabde D. bdfcea

24. (a) When he was rushed to the nearby Primary Health Centre after his fall, the doctor referred him to a hospital.
(b) This worsened his injury.
(c) Had a little precaution been exercised after the accident, Tarun would have continued with his gymnastic classes.
(d) He was paralysed from waist downwards when he fell from the vaulting horse while doing gymnastics.
(e) However, the doctor forgot to tell Tarun's parents to take him on a stretcher as he had suffered spinal injuries.
(f) Tarun is wheelchair bound for two years.
A. fdeabc B. abcdef
C. fdcaeb D. fdbcae

25. (a) As the temperature rises, staying hydrated can become a greater challenge for people exercising both indoors and out.
(b) Several things can influence this process, including age, gender, physical conditioning. humidity and a lack of sufficient fluids.
(c) In hot weather, individuals can lose as much as two quarts of sweat per hour.
(d) As we age, we have a lower perceived level of thirst in response to fluid loss and early stages of dehydration.
(e) If not replenished, this can lead to dehydration, heat exhaustion and even heatstroke.
A. abcde B. dbcae
C. cbdea D. acebd

26. (a) Students become passive listeners in the class-room.
(b) Mostly lecturing method is preferred to cover the syllabus.
(c) I feel that there is a lacunae in the teaching techniques adopted by the lecturers in engineering colleges.
(d) Unless the teachers are exposed to different teaching techniques, they will not succeed in imparting knowledge.
(e) Lack of training in teaching can be ascribed to this sorry state of affairs.
A. dbeca B. cadbe
C. chaed D. dceab

27. (a) A product is something that is made in a factory, a brand is something that is bought by a consumer.
(b) The trick therefore, lies in the brand positioning.
(c) For a counsumer, the satisfaction of becoming associated with a name that is the 'best' and the 'leader' is far more important and at times makes him ignore the price factor.
(d) Brands come and go.
(e) Still there are those who manage to stay and develop an affinity with consumers.
A. aebcd B. debac
C. decab D. aecdb

28. (a) Many people fail simply because they make too many wrong decisions.
(b) Over a period of time you make a series of decisions, each seemingly of little consequence.
(c) So do people's lives.
(d) It has been said that history turns on small hinges.
(e) Yet the total of these decisions finally determines the outcome of your life.
(f) A successful life depends upon developing a higher percentage of wisdom than error.
A. acbedf B. adcbef
C. fedcba D. abcdef

29. (a) The younger you are when you discover this mighty power, the more likely you are to live successfully and happily.
(b) Everything you do has some effect upon others, as do their actions upon you.
(c) You are influenced by other people's acts and wishes, by law and custom, by your duties and your responsibilities.
(d) You live in a world filled with outside influences which impinge upon you.
(e) And yet you must find out how to live your own life.
A. abcde B. adebc
C. dcbea D. baedc

30. (a) She had wanted to go to Mars.
(b) Lots of young people talk about how they dream of this or that.
(c) Kalpana Chawla had wanted to make at least one more trip to space.
(d) She is one person who got to live out her dreams.
(e) She had also said that when it was time for her to die, she would like to die in space.
A. bcade B. bdeac
C. caebd D. cbead

ANSWERS

1	2	3	4	5	6	7	8	9	10
A	C	A	D	B	B	A	D	C	A
11	**12**	**13**	**14**	**15**	**16**	**17**	**18**	**19**	**20**
B	B	B	D	A	A	C	D	B	D
21	**22**	**23**	**24**	**25**	**26**	**27**	**28**	**29**	**30**
C	D	B	C	D	C	B	B	C	C

7. SENTENCE COMPLETION

A sentence conveys its meaning effectively only when it is completed in a proper way. Try and practise it in this exercise.

Directions: *In each question, an incomplete statement (Stem) followed by four fillers is given. Pick out the best one which can complete the incomplete stem correctly and meaningfully.*

1. He is so lazy that he .....
A. cannot depend on others for getting his work done.
B. cannot delay the schedule of completing the work.
C. can seldom complete his work on time.
D. dislike to postpone the work that he undertakes to do.

2. He always stammers in public meetings, but his today's speech .....
A. was fairly audible to everyone present in the hall.
B. was not received satisfactorily.
C. could not be understood properly.
D. was free from that defect.

3. In order to raise the company's profit, the employees .....
A. demanded two additional increments.
B. decided to go on paid holidays.
C. requested the management to implement new welfare schemes.
D. offered to work overtime without any compensation.

4. Although, he is reputed for making very candid statements, ...
A. his today's speech was not fairly audible.
B. his promises had always been realistic.
C. his speech was very interesting.
D. his today's statements were very ambiguous.

5. I felt somewhat more relaxed .....
A. but tense as compared to earlier.
B. and tense as compared to earlier.
C. as there was already no tension at all.
D. and tension-free as compared to earlier.

6. With great efforts his son succeeded in convincing him not to donate his entire wealth to an orphanage .....
A. and lead the life of a wealthy merchant.
B. but to a home for the forsaken children.
C. and make an orphan of himself.
D. as the orphange needed a lot of donations.

7. Even though it is a very large house, ...
A. there is a lot of space available in it for children.
B. there is hardly any space available for children.
C. there is no dearth of space for children.
D. the servants take a long time to clean it.

8. Practically, very little work could be completed in the last week as it was .....
A. full of working days.
B. a very hectic week.
C. full of holidays.
D. a very busy week.

9. He tames animals because he .....
A. is fond of them.
B. hates them.
C. is afraid of them
D. wants to set them free

10. He has no money now .....
A. although he was very poor once.
B. as he has given up all his wealth.
C. because he was very rich once.
D. because he has received huge donation.

11. The employer appeared to be in such an affable mood that Rohit .....
A. decided to ask for a raise in his salary.
B. was scared to talk to him about his leave.
C. felt very guilty for his inadvertent slip.
D. promised him that he would not commit mistake again.

12. Since people cannot learn through legitimate channels all that they are anxious to learn .....
A. they resort to ways and means without any ethical or moral considerations.
B. they join academics in order to quench their thirst for learning.
C. they adopt formal ways and means to achieve what they want to.
D. these social service organisations provide them the required input of knowledge.

13. It was an extremely pleasant surprise for the hutment-dweller when the Government officials told him that .....
A. he had to vacate hutment which he had been unauthorisedly occupying
B. he had been gifted with a furnished apartment in a multi-storeyed building.
C. he would be arrested for wrongfully encroaching on the pavement outside his dwelling.
D. they would not accede to his request.

14. Despite his best efforts to conceal his anger .....
A. we could detect that he was very happy.
B. he failed to give us an impression of his agony.
C. he succeeded in camouflaging his emotions.
D. people came to know that he was annoyed.

15. His appearance is unsmiling but .....
A. his heart is full of compassion for others.
B. he looks very serious on most occasions.
C. people are afraid of him.
D. he is uncompromising on matters of task performance.

16. The weather outside was extremely pleasant and hence we decided to .....
A. utilise our time in watching the television.
B. refrain from going out for a morning walk.
C. enjoy a morning ride in the open.
D. employ this rare opportunity for writing letters.

17. The officer who had neglected to file his income tax returns had to .....
A. return the files. B. pay a fine.
C. be rewarded. D. play mischief.

18. In order to help the company attain its goal of enhancing profit, all the employees .....
A. urged the management to grant paid leave.
B. appealed the management to implement new welfare schemes.
C. voluntarily offered to work overtime with lucrative compensation.
D. voluntarily offered to render additional services in lieu of nothing.

19. His behaviour is so unpredictable that he .....
A. never depends upon others for getting his work done.
B. is seldom trusted by others.
C. always finds it difficult to keep his word.
D. always insists on getting the work completed on time.

20. Since it is already midnight, we .....
A. had better leaving.
B. ought to have leave.
C. should take our leave.
D. might as well as leave.

21. It is not easy to remain tranquil when those around you .....
A. behave in a socially acceptable manner.
B. exhibit pleasant mannerism.
C. are losing their heads.
D. agree to whatever you say.

22. Although initial investigations pointed towards him, ...
A. the preceding events corroborated his involvement in the crime.
B. the additional information confirmed his guilt.
C. the subsequent events established that he was guilty.
D. the subsequent events proved that he was innocent.

23. Because he believes in democratic principles, he always .....
A. decides all the matters himself.
B. listens to others' views and enforces his own.
C. shown respect to others' opinions if they match his own.
D. reconciles with the majority's views and gives us his own.

24. Owing to the acute power shortage, the people of our locality have decided to .....
A. dispense with other non-conventional energy sources.
B. resort to abundant use of electricity for illumination.
C. off-switch the electrical appliance while not in use.
D. resort to use of electricity only when it is inevitable.

25. She never visits any zoo because she is a strong opponent of the idea of .....
A. setting the animals free into the forest.
B. feeding the animals while others are watching.
C. watching the animals in their natural abode.
D. holding the animals in captivity for our joy.

26. Unless you work harder you will fail, means .....
A. if you fail you will work harder.
B. you must at least plan well than you will not fail.
C. hardly you will fail if you do not desire so.
D. if you do not put more efforts, then you will fail.

27. Even if it rains I shall come, means .....
A. if I come it will not rain.
B. if it rains I shall not come.
C. I will certainly come whether it rains or not.
D. whenever there is rain I shall come.

28. Dinesh is as stupid as he is lazy means .....
A. Dinesh is stupid because he is lazy.
B. Dinesh is lazy because he is stupid.
C. Dinesh is either stupid or lazy.
D. Dinesh is equally stupid and lazy.

29. Mahesh needn't have purchased the bag, means .....
A. it was not necessary for Mahesh to purchase the bag but he has purchased it.
B. it was necessary for Mahesh to purchase the bag and he has not purchased it.
C. it was not necessary for Mahesh to purchase the bag and he has not purchased it.
D. it was necessary for Mahesh to purchase the bag but he has not purchased it.

30. The Manager would like you to help Dhiraj, means .....
A. the Manager would like you if you help Dhiraj.
B. the Manager desires you to help Dhiraj.
C. the Manager likes you because you help Dhiraj.
D. Dhiraj expects the Manager to tell you to help him.

ANSWERS

1	2	3	4	5	6	7	8	9	10
C	D	D	D	D	C	B	C	A	B
11	12	13	14	15	16	17	18	19	20
A	A	B	D	A	C	B	D	B	D
21	22	23	24	25	26	27	28	29	30
C	D	D	D	D	D	C	D	A	B

8. Nouns, Numbers & Pronouns

NOUN

A word which denotes a place, a thing, an animal or a person is said to be a noun.

1. Note the plurals of the following nouns:

Singular	Plural	Singular	Plural
copy	copies	cry	cries
baby	babies	duty	duties
body	bodies	country	countries
family	families	diary	diaries
fly	flies	fairy	fairies
city	cities	spy	spies
army	armies	storey	storeys
bay	bays	monkey	monkeys

2. The following nouns do not undergo any change in plural form, in general.

Singular	Plural	Singular	Plural
deer	deer	sheep	sheep
thousand	thousand	pair	pair
hundred	hundred	score	score
dozen	dozen	gross	gross

Note: We can write—
(*a*) thousands of men; (*b*) two pairs of shoes; (*c*) dozens of mangoes; (*d*) scores of people. etc. But—
(*a*) two thousand rupees; (*b*) three hundred men; (*c*) five dozen eggs, etc.

3. The following nouns are usually used in plural forms. They take a plural verb after them—

eatables	fetters	surroundings
riches	alms	spectacles
trousers	pants	scissors
premises	thanks	annals
congratulations	goods	shorts
tongs	pains	arms
breeches	(for troubles)	

4. The following are the nouns which are plural in appearance but are usually used in singular number. They are followed by a singular verb—

news	politics	physics
mathematics	economics	ethics
politics	classics	gallows
statistics	athletics	innings
mechanics	swnmons	mumps

5. Collective nouns often used as plurals—

public	police	cattle
audience	clergy	folk
people	poultry	nation
elite	gentry	glitterati

6. The nouns that are usually used in singular forms—

advice	hair	rice
fuel	alphabet	machinery
offspring	issue	furniture
mischief	stationery	luggage
bedding	information	abuse

7. Material nouns are always used in singular number—

gold	copper	milk
water	silk	wool

Note: They may be used in plural with a different meaning.

copper coins (coppers), chains or fetters (irons), cans made of tin (tins).

Formation of Feminine Gender from Masculine Gender

(*a*) By adding 'ess'/ 'trix'/ 'a' / 'sne' etc.
e.g., lion into lioness

(*b*) Placement of a word before or after noun
e.g., Servant into Maid-Servant; Milkman into Milkmaid

(*c*) A masculine noun containing vowel *e.g.,* Actor Avoid vowel and add 'ess' *i.e.,* Actress

(*d*) No specific note will be applied in some nouns (while changing into feminine gender) *e.g.,* Monk into Nun, Drone into Bee, Drake into Duck, Dog into Bitch.

THE PRONOUN

A pronoun is a word which is used in place of noun.

Kinds of Pronouns

(i) **Personal Pronoun:** I, we, my, mine, our, ours, you, he, she, they, him, her etc.

(ii) **Reflexive Pronoun:** Herself, himself, myself, yourself, themselves etc.

(iii) **Emphatic Pronoun:** I myself, we ourselves.

(iv) **Demonstrative Pronoun:** This, that, there, those etc.

(v) **Indefinite Pronoun:** Somebody, nobody, many, none, someone, few etc.

(vi) **Interrogative Pronoun:** What, who, whose, which, whom etc.

(vii) **Distributive Pronoun:** Neither, each, either, every, none, both etc.

(viii) **Relative Pronoun:** Who, which, whom etc.

MULTIPLE CHOICE QUESTIONS

Directions: *In the following questions choose the correct options to fill the blanks.*

1. The place was so dirty that ..... wished to run away from there.
A. everbody B. anybody
C. few D. some

2. ..... was there to help me.
A. Something B. Anything
C. Anybody D. Nobody

3. Is there .... to eat?
A. some B. something
C. any D. few

4. ..... of the students were making a great noise.
A. Anyone B. Somebody
C. Many D. Nobody

5. ..... of the students can solve this sum.
A. Someone B. Anybody
C. Somebody D. None

6. ...... of us should try our best to make India a heaven.
A. Any B. Somebody
C. Anybody D. All

7. ...... of us do not know the real meaning of our lives.
A. Any B. Something
C. Several D. Many

8. She presented me a ...... of flowers.
A. troup B. galaxy
C. bouquet D. cluster

9. There was a .... of eggs floating on the dirty water of the ditch.
A. clump B. shoal
C. clutch D. pile

10. A ...... of dancers was dancing on the stage.
A. troupe B. galaxy
C. herd D. clump

11. To save the drowning man, a ...... of sailors came out on the boats.
A. troop B. crew
C. band D. gang

12. A ...... (of stars) consists of millions of stars.
A. group B. herd
C. stack D. galaxy

13. Mr. Peter Cash was arranging a .... of bricks near his house.
A. group B. band
C. herd D. stack

14. A .... of geese was swimming in the water.
A. group B. gaggle
C. troupe D. bunch

15. There was a .... of mosquitoes hovering over the slum area.
A. swarm B. group
C. gang D. herd

16. Last night a .... of burglars broke into my house.

A. group B. cluster
C. clump D. gang

17. Devika lost her .... of keys.

A. bunch B. branch
C. band D. gang

18. I have some .... for you to do.

A. working B. worker
C. work D. works

19. They highly admire the .... of Kashmir.

A. scenery B. sceneries
C. scene D. scenes

20. I can easily read and write the English ....

A. alphabets B. alphabetic
C. alphabet D. alphabetical

21. I have met her many a ....

A. times B. timing
C. time D. timings

22. She has written many ....

A. poetry B. poetries
C. poem D. poems

23. One is supposed to do ....,.. .

A. our duty B. their duty
C. one's duty D. his duty

24. He is .... faithful partner.

A. Yours B. You
C. Your D. Your's

25. Ajay is more smart than ....

A. her B. hers
C. herself D. she

26. The ..... of the Minister's statement cannot be verified by people who have no access to official records.

A. veracity B. verbosity
C. ambiguity D. validity

27. Life is to death as pleasure is to ......

A. poverty B. suffering
C. anguish D. pain

28. 'Please' and 'Thank you' are the little courtesies by which we keep the ..... of life oiled and running smoothly.

A. path B. machine
C. garden D. river

29. Catching the earlier train will give us the ..... to do some shopping.

A. chance B. luck
C. possibility D. occasion

30. Leave a two-inch ..... on each page for the teacher's remarks.

A. border B. margin
C. blank D. gap

31. What is the ..... for an airletter?

A. fare B. value
C. postage D. stamp

32. The manner in which bombs exploded in five trains within a short span of time suggests that it is a part of a .....

A. game B. conspiracy
C. villainy D. sabotage

33. Some regions of our country still remain ..... to the average man.

A. inaccessible B. impossible
C. impermeable D. impenetrable

34. The old 'Nature Versus .....' debate regarding crime continues even today.

A. Man B. Universe
C. Culture D. Nurture

ANSWERS

1	2	3	4	5	6	7	8	9	10
A	D	B	C	D	D	D	C	C	A
11	12	13	14	15	16	17	18	19	20
B	D	D	B	A	D	A	C	A	C
21	22	23	24	25	26	27	28	29	30
C	D	C	C	D	A	D	B	A	B
31	32	33	34						
C	B	A	A						

9. Prepositions

A Preposition is a word which comes before a Pronoun or a Noun and expresses the relationship between Noun or Pronoun and some part of the remaining sentence.

(*a*) He is busy **with** his work.
(*b*) The boy jumped **into** the river.
(*c*) The birds are chirping *in* the trees.

In these sentences the words **with**, **into** and **in** show the relationship between the verbs **busy**, **jumped** and **chirping** with the nouns **work**, **river** and **trees** respectively.

Position of the Preposition

1. A Preposition usually precedes its object.
(*i*) He laughs **at** the poor.
(*ii*) He is angry **with** you.
(*iii*) She agrees **with** me.

2. In the case of Relative Pronouns it comes after the subject.
(*i*) This is the boy whom I was looking **for**.
(*ii*) That is the pen whose mention I was making **of**.

3. In the following cases, the Preposition comes after its object.
(*i*) Where is the boy you were complaining **against**?
(*ii*) What things are there you are looking **for**?
(*iii*) Who is there, you are waiting **for**?

Omission of the Preposition

In many cases when the sentences contain Nouns of Time or Place, the Prepositions **from**, **in** and **for** are often omitted.

(*i*) He walked many kilometres.
(*ii*) He came to see me last year.
(*iii*) As I could not find my puppy anywhere, I looked here and there.

Prepositions are small words that show the relationship between one word and another. Prepositions in the following sentences show the position of the paper in relation to the desk, the book, his hand and the door.

The paper is **on** the desk.
The paper is **under** the book.
The paper is **in** his hand.
The paper is **by** the door.

Common Prepositions

about	at	by
in	onto	toward
above	before	concerning
inside	out	under
across	behind	despite
into	over	until
after	below	down
like	since	up
against	beneath	during
near	through	upon
along	beside	except
of	throughout	with
amid	between	for
off	till	within
among	beyond	from
on	to	without

MULTIPLE CHOICE QUESTIONS

Directions: *Tick the correct Preposition for the blank in each of the following sentences.*

1. He applied ...... the manager.
A. for B. to
C. with D. by

2. Trust ...... God and do the right.
A. in B. for
C. to D. with

3. She is worthy ...... a prize.
A. with B. for
C. to D. of

4. Mr. Gomes has no taste ...... music.
A. of B. for
C. with D. to

5. You are hard ...... hearing.
A. at B. of
C. with D. for

6. He is sure ...... his success
A. for B. with
C. on D. of

7. Preeti was warned ...... the danger ahead.
A. for B. at
C. of D. about

8. I am thankful ...... you for a good advice.
A. for B. with
C. to D. from

9. Deepak would not surrender ...... the police.
A. with B. to
C. for D. on

10. The small plant in your lawn is very sensitive ...... touch.
A. on B. with
C. to D. for

11. Divya was sure to succeed ..... the examination.
A. for B. in
C. to D. with

12. Geeta was jealous ...... Ravina's beauty.
A. to B. with
C. for D. of

13. He was ignorant ..... what was happening there.
A. for B. of
C. to D. with

14. Your pen is inferior ...... mine.
A. than B. with
C. from D. to

15. Reenu is no match ...... Meenu.
A. to B. for
C. with D. upon

16. It is necessary ...... you to apply for this job.
A. on B. with
C. for D. to

17. Be loyal ...... your country.
A. for B. to
C. on D. with

18. Mukesh is junior ...... me.
A. than B. to
C. from D. of

19. Deepika was innocent ...... the crime.
A. of B. with
C. from D. to

20. I am desirous.... joining the Indian cricket team.
A. for B. of
C. to D. on

21. Pradeep is not eligible ...... the post.
A. to B. on
C. upon D. for

22. Does she believe ...... God?
A. to B. for
C. in D. over

23. Mr. Posh was charged..... the murder of his aunt.
A. for B. with
C. on D. to

24. Tagore is famous (or popular) ...... Indians.
A. for B. with
C. to D. towards

25. Kalidasa is famous ...... his drama the *Shakuntalam*.
A. for B. with
C. on D. about

26. He applied ...... the post of a teacher.
A. to B. on
C. for D. at

27. I differ ...... you in this matter.
A. from B. with
C. for D. above

28. My pen differs ...... yours.
A. with B. from
C. for D. upon

29. The air escaped out ...... the balloon.
A. from B. of
C. to D. under

30. I am confident ...... success.
A. of B. to
C. from D. about

31. He was deprived ...... his share and property.
A. of B. with
C. from D. about

32. He complains ...... headache.
A. about B. to
C. of D. in

33. My father deals ...... sugar.
A. with B. to
C. in D. about

34. His services were dispensed ......
A. for B. to
C. with D. of

35. Mohinder was born ...... a noble famly.
A. with B. about
C. towards D. in

36. He was born ...... poor parents.
A. of B. to
C. in D. on

37. A son was born ...... him.
A. to B. for
C. in D. upon

38. I was aware ...... the matter.
A. to B. of
C. in D. upon

39. He was absorbed ...... study.
A. in B. into
C. of D. under

40. The boy jumped ...... the river.
A. in B. under
C. below D. into

41. I agree ...... you.
A. upon B. to
C. with D. None of these

42. Wolves abound ...... this forest.
A. for B. in
C. with D. to

43. She did not agree ...... your proposal.
A. with B. in
C. to D. None of these

44. I was angry ...... his misconduct.
A. with B. to
C. at D. on

45. He is bent ...... mischief.
A. on B. of
C. to D. for

ANSWERS

1	2	3	4	5	6	7	8	9	10
B	A	D	B	B	D	C	C	B	D
11	**12**	**13**	**14**	**15**	**16**	**17**	**18**	**19**	**20**
B	D	B	D	B	C	B	B	A	B
21	**22**	**23**	**24**	**25**	**26**	**27**	**28**	**29**	**30**
D	C	B	B	A	C	B	B	A	A
31	**32**	**33**	**34**	**35**	**36**	**37**	**38**	**39**	**40**
A	C	C	C	D	A	A	B	A	D
41	**42**	**43**	**44**	**45**					
C	B	C	C	A					

10. Adjectives, Adverbs & Degree of Comparison

Some words tell more about another word they are called *modifiers*. There are two main kinds of modifiers: *adjectives* and *adverbs*.

Adjectives

An *adjective* modifies—tells more about—a noun or pronoun. It tells *what kind, how many,* or *which one*.

Example: *beautiful* music, *blue* sky, *large* room.

Adjectives are usually found right before a noun, right after a noun, or after a linking verb.

Note: Some adjectives, such as articles, numbers, and possessive adjectives, usually come before the noun.

Adverb

An *adverb* modifies—tells more about—a verb, adjective, or another adverb. It tells *how, when, where,* or *to what extent.*

Comparison and Adjectives

Adjectives and adverbs have three forms that show a greater or lesser degree of the characteristic of the basic word: the positive, the comparative, and the superlatives.

Use the comparative to compare two things:

1. Mary is the more lazy of the two.
2. I've tasted creamier cheese than this.
3. James is the shorter of the two boys.

Use the superlative to compare more than two things:

1. Mary is the laziest girl I know.
2. This is the creamiest cheese I've ever tasted.
3. James is the shortest boy in the class.

There are some words to which comparison does not apply, since they already indicate the highest degree of a quality.

Here are some examples:

Immediately	Superlative	First
Last	very	unique
Uniquely	universally	perfect
Perfectly	exact	complete
Correct	dead	deadly
Preferable	round	perpendicularly
Square	third	supreme
Totally	infinitely	immortal

Errors to Avoid in Comparison

Do not combine two superlatives:

Incorrect: That was the most bravest thing he ever did.

Correct: That was the bravest thing he ever did.

Incorrect: He grew up to be the most handsomest boy in the town.

Correct: He grew up to be the most handsome boy in the town.

Do not combine two comparatives:

Incorrect: Mary was more friendlier than Susan.

Correct: Mary was friendlier than Susan.

Incorrect: The puppy was more timider last week.

Correct: The puppy was more timid last week.

MULTIPLE CHOICE QUESTIONS

Directions: *In the following questions choose the correct option to fill the blank.*

1. The girl whom you met is the .... sister of Ravi.
A. eldest B. elder
C. older D. oldest

2. The historical place is ....
A. seeing worth B. worthy of seeing
C. worth seeing D. worthy seeing

3. These flowers smell ....
A. sweet B. sweetly
C. more sweetly D. most sweetly

4. .... aspirant can not pass the UPSC examination.
A. Each B. Every
C. All D. No

5. Harivansh Rai .... second Shakespeare.
A. is a B. is
C. is the D. is another

6. .... student in the class got prizes.
A. Each and every B. Every and each
C. Every D. Never

7. It is .... picture than the one we saw last Monday.
A. interesting B. much interesting
C. more interesting D. most interesting

8. She is clever ....
A. that her mother B. as her mother
C. so her mother D. than her mother

9. They will get ....
A. Red, green and black paper
B. Red, green black paper
C. Red and green and black paper
D. Either B or C

10. Health is .... wealth.
A. preferable to
B. more preferable than
C. more preferable to
D. most preferable then

11. .... water that was in the jug evaporated.
A. Little B. The little
C. Small D. A small

12. He has not sung .... songs.
A. much B. most
C. more D. many

13. Srishti has searched .... office.
A. whole the B. the whole
C. a whole D. some whole

14. K.R. Dhiraj was .... best and .... famous writer.
A. a, the most B. the, a most
C. the, more D. the, the most

15. Willam Shakespeare is famous as ....
A. a poet and a dramatist
B. a poet and dramatist
C. the poet and the dramatist
D. the poet and a dramatist

16. What does .... leader suggest?
A. other B. another
C. others D. anothers

17. He .... money
A. has few B. have few
C. has little D. have little

18. The .... boys are rewarded.
A. first two B. two first
C. firsts two D. two's first

19. He is .... brave.
A. strong B. stronger
C. more strong D. strong and

20. No sooner said ....
A. so done B. and done
C. than done D. but done

ANSWERS

1	2	3	4	5	6	7	8	9	10
A	C	A	B	C	C	C	D	A	A
11	**12**	**13**	**14**	**15**	**16**	**17**	**18**	**19**	**20**
B	D	B	D	B	A	C	A	D	C

11. Determiners & Articles

Determiners are actually Adjectives. They are always followed by nouns.

Determiners are of the following kinds:

(A) Demonstrative Determiners
this, that, these, those etc.

(B) Possessive Determiners
my, our, your, his, her, its, their etc.

(C) Quantitative Determiners
some, any, much, enough, sufficient, whole, a little, the little, little, all, both etc.

(D) Numerical Determiners
a few, some, few, the few, any, several, many, no, etc.
One, two, three .... (Cardinals)
First, second, third .... (Ordinals)

(E) Distributive Determiners
either, neither etc.

(F) Articles
Indefinite: a, an
Definite: the

MULTIPLE CHOICE QUESTIONS

Directions: *In the following questions choose the correct options to fill the blanks.*

1. Give me .... rice.
A. some B. few
C. a few D. any

2. .... sheep grazing on the slope of the hill had gone away.
A. Any B. The few
C. This D. Much

3. Have you got .... magazines to read?
A. all B. much
C. some D. little

4. I have ...... money that I want to spend on shares.
A. any B. much
C. less D. some

5. There is .... owl on the branch of the tree.
A. a B. the
C. an D. some

6. My brother is .... MBA.
A. a B. an
C. the D. any

7. Have you got .... cheese?
A. some B. many
C. a few D. few

8. No, I haven't got .... cheese.
A. many B. few
C. any D. some

9. There is only .... milk left in the bottle.
A. enough B. few
C. much D. a little

10. There is .... hope of his recovery.
A. any B. little
C. many D. few

11. .... dogs were barking at the strangers.
A. some B. any
C. much D. less

12. The girl bought her father .... juice.
A. few B. some
C. any D. many

13. You should take .... honey everyday.
A. any B. many
C. a little D. a few

14. .... boy was punished by the teacher.
A. Either B. All
C. Any D. Many

15. .... girl was asked to join the army.
A. None B. Neither
C. All D. Any

16. .... water in the jug has been drunk by Mohan.
A. The little B. The few
C. A few D. Few

17. I shall play .... piano at the party.
A. some B. any
C. the D. few

18. .... labourers were found dead in the mine.
A. Any B. Fewer
C. Many D. Less

19. Could I borrow .... umbrella?
A. our B. your
C. yours D. my

20. My brother is standing in the .... row.
A. any B. many
C. some D. first

21. Do you want .... tea?
A. any B. more
C. much D. few

22. He can fly .... aeroplane.
A. a B. an
C. some D. many

23. .... students were asked to bring their birth certificates.
A. Many B. Any
C. Much D. Less

24. .... gun needs oiling.
A. It B. This
C. These D. Those

25. .... shirts are mine.
A. These B. This
C. It D. That

26. .... child was allowed to enter the kitchen.
A. The B. All
C. Many D. A few

27. I have been waiting for you for .... hour.
A. a B. an
C. the D. a few

28. You must pay .... visit to your brothers.
A. the B. an
C. a few D. a

29. Why are you making .... noise?
A. your B. enough
C. a D. whole

30. He is .... honourable man.
A. a B. the
C. an D. much

31. .... cup is chipped.
A. These B. That
C. Those D. It

32. .... glasses belong to Mr. Jack.
A. This B. That
C. Those D. It

33. .... birds have colourful wings.
A. That B. These
C. This D. It

34. I want a car. I'll get ....one.
A. these B. this
C. those D. it

35. I need a camera. I'll get .... now.
A. it B. these
C. this D. those

ANSWERS

1	2	3	4	5	6	7	8	9	10
A	B	C	D	C	B	A	C	D	B
11	**12**	**13**	**14**	**15**	**16**	**17**	**18**	**19**	**20**
A	B	C	A	B	A	C	C	B	D
21	**22**	**23**	**24**	**25**	**26**	**27**	**28**	**29**	**30**
B	B	A	B	A	A	B	D	C	C
31	**32**	**33**	**34**	**35**					
B	C	B	B	A					

12. CONJUNCTIONS

A word which joins either two or more than two words/sentences is known as conjunction. e.g.,

Neither .... nor (in negative sense)
Either .... or (in affirmative sense)
Both .... and
Hardly .... when/before
No sooner .... than
Scarcely .... when/before
Though .... yet

Some illustrations based on above guidelines
Illustration:

(i) Yashwant is [neither] good [nor] bad.

(ii) It is [both] cheap [and] good.

(iii) [No sooner] did Ashok see the police [than] he ran away.

MULTIPLE CHOICE QUESTIONS

Directions: *In the following questions choose the correct options to fill the blanks.*

1. Neither he .... his friend is good.
A. or B. and
C. but D. nor

2. The officer asked the peon .... why he was late.
A. that B. if
C. but D. No word

3. Both Ajay .... Vijay are intelligent.
A. or B. nor
C. and D. No word

4. No sooner did the thief see the public .... he ran away.
A. then B. and
C. but D. than

5. Abhinav .... his brothers was going to Mumbai.
A. but B. yet
C. no word D. together

6. He behaves .... he were the captain of the team.
A. as if B. as
C. no word D. that

7. Either Rupali .... Sonali is going to attend the meeting.
A. and B. but
C. nor D. or

8. Neither Nirmal .... Ashwinee is going to listen the speech of the minister.
A. and B. but
C. nor D. or

9. Ravi .... Prakash are going to Kolkata.
A. or B. nor
C. but D. and

10. Rice .... curry is my usual breakfast.
A. and B. but
C. then D. than

11. Hardly had he left .... his brother came.
A. then B. than
C. when D. that

12. I would rather have a copy .... a book.
A. then B. than
C. when D. that

13. He is no other .... my friend.
A. then B. than
C. when D. but

14. He saw a snake ....he awoke.
A. then B. when
C. than D. No word

15. Ten years have passed .... my grandmother died.
A. since B. when
C. then D. than

16. She is .... good .... bad.
A. either, not B. neither, or
C. neither, nor D. neither, than

17. The cellphone is both cheap .... best.
A. than B. and
C. then D. or

18. No sooner did the thief see the police .... he ran away.
A. then B. than
C. so D. because

19. Srishti will go .... Sanju goes.
A. if B. than
C. then D. although

20. She is wise .... timid.
A. and B. yet
C. but D. however

21. Make hay .... the sun shines.
A. though B. while
C. after D. before

22. He is so weak .... he cannot walk.
A. but B. that
C. then D. so

23. Although he is rich, ... he is unhappy.
A. but B. yet
C. so D. still

24. Wait here .... I come back.
A. till B. until
C. before D. after

25. He is my friend .... I shall help him.
A. so B. hence
C. that is why D. therefore

26. He must go away .... he will be beaten.
A. otherwise B. and
C. or D. else

27. God loves good men .... good men love God.
A. and B. or
C. that D. those

28. He was late .... he was not punished.
A. but B. yet
C. still D. therefore

29. Walk slowly ...., you may fall.
A. and B. or
C. so D. otherwise

30. Work hard, ... you will fail.
A. and B. or
C. otherwise D. else

ANSWERS

1	2	3	4	5	6	7	8	9	10
D	D	C	D	D	A	D	C	D	A
11	**12**	**13**	**14**	**15**	**16**	**17**	**18**	**19**	**20**
C	B	B	B	A	C	B	B	A	C
21	**22**	**23**	**24**	**25**	**26**	**27**	**28**	**29**	**30**
B	B	B	A	B	C	A	C	D	D

13. TENSES & VERBS

1. Tense indicates a point in time or period of time in the past, present, or future tense.
2. The verb may consist of a single word, or a main verb and one or more auxiliary words. The key point is that tense is related to the form of verb. There are normally three forms of the verb, say, V_1, V_2, V_3 and for convenience a fourth form V_4 as verb+ing may be assumed.

A Comparative Chart Regarding Tenses and Verbs

Simple Present	**Simple Past**	**Simple Future**
V_1	V_2	shall/will + V_1
Present Continuous	**Past Continuous**	**Future Continuous**
is/am/are + V_4	was/were + V_4	shall/will + be + V_4
Present Perfect	**Past Perfect**	**Future Perfect**
has/have + V_3	had + V_3	shall/will + have + V_3
Present Perfect Cont.	**Past Perfect Cont.**	**Future Perfect Cont.**
has/have + been + V_4	had + been + V_4	shall/will + have been + V_4

SIMPLE PRESENT:

A. A present state of affairs. — A. My sister lives in Nagpur.
B. A general fact. — B. The sun rises in the east.
C. Habitual actions. — C. I listen to the radio in the mornings.
D. Future time-tables. — D. My flight leaves at 10:00.

PRESENT CONTINUOUS:

A. A specific action that is occurring. — A. Arvind is watching TV (right now).
B. A general activity that takes. — B. These days, I'm taking it easy.
C. Future arrangements. — C. I'm inviting Hari to the party on Friday.

SIMPLE PAST:

A. An action that began and ended at a particular time in the past. — A. The mail came early this Morning.
B. An action that occurred over a period of time but was completed in the past. — B. Dad worked in advertising in the past.
C. An activity that took place regularly in the past. — C. We jogged every morning before class.

PAST CONTINUOUS:

A. Interrupted Actions. — A. I was sewing when the telephone rang.

B. A continuous state over a period of time but was completed in the past.	B. She was looking very ill. I was meeting lots of people at that time.
C. Events planned in the past.	C. Neetu was leaving for Kolkata but had to make a last minute change
D. Expressing a future intent.	D. Jyoti is going to bring her sister tonight.
E. Predicting an event.	E. You are going to pass the test. Don't worry.

SIMPLE FUTURE:

A. Making a future decision.	A. I will call you after lunch.
B. Predicting a future event.	B. You will pass the test. Don't worry.
C. Indicating willingness to do something.	C. If I don't feel better soon, I will go to to the doctor.

FUTURE CONTINUOUS:

A. An action that will be going at a particular time in the future.	A. At noon tomorrow, I will be taking the children to their piano lessons.
B. Future actions which have already been decided.	B. I will be wearing my black dress to the dinner.

PRESENT PERFECT:

A. An action that happened at an unspecified time.	A. She has never climbed a mountain. I'm sorry. I have forgotten your Name.
B. An action that has recently occurred.	B. He's just gone to sleep.
C. An action that began in the past and continues up to the present (often used with "for" or "since").	C. Jack has lived in Chennai all his life. I have been here since Monday. He has known her for two weeks.
D. An action that happened repeatedly before now.	D. We have flown across the Pacific four times. I've failed my driver's test twice.

PRESENT PERFECT CONTINUOUS:

A. An action that began in the past and has just recently ended.	A. Have you been ringing the Bell?
B. An action that began in the past and continues in the present.	B. Lokesh has been studying for two hours.
C. An action repeated over a period of time in the past and continuing in present.	C. Suresh has been smoking since he was fifteen.

PAST PERFECT:

A. An action that occurred before another past action.	A. Tarun had left hours before we got there.
B. An action that was expected to occur in the past.	B. I had hoped to know about the job before now.

PAST PERFECT CONTINUOUS:

A. An action that occurred before another past action.	A. His eyes hurt because he had been Reading for eight hours.
B. An action that was expected to occur in the past.	B. I had been expecting a change in his attitude.

FUTURE PERFECT:

A. An action that will be completed before a particular time in the future.

A. By next July, my parents will have been married for fifty years.

FUTURE PERFECT CONTINUOUS:

A. Emphasizing the length of time that has occurred before a specific time in the future.

A. By May, my father will have been working at the same job for thirty years.

AGREEMENT OF THE VERB WITH THE SUBJECT

It is very important that the verb in a sentence should obey the subject, otherwise the sentence will be considered wrong.

I. When the Subject is a Singular Noun

A singular noun takes a singular verb.

(i) Mohit **makes** a noise in the class.

(ii) The child is **crying** for a cake.

II. When two singular nouns are joined with 'and'

When two singular nouns are joined with 'and' and they refer to two different persons, the plural verb should be used, *e.g.*,

(i) The novelist and the poet **were** honoured by the government.

(ii) The black and the white dogs **bark** at the strangers.

Note: Article 'the' is used with both the subjects. If article is used only once, the singular verb should be used.

(i) The painter and singer is going abroad.

(ii) The white and black dog has a bushy tail.

III. When the subjects together give a single idea, singular verb is used:

(i) Slow and steady wins the race.

(ii) Rice and curry is my favourite dish.

IV. A collective noun takes a singular verb when it acts as a whole, but it takes a plural verb when the individual, of which it is composed are considered separately.

(i) The committee was unanimous on imposing the new law.

(ii) The committee have given their separate opinions in the matter.

V. When the subjects are joined by neither . . . nor, either . . . or, and 'or', the verb should obey the last subject.

(i) Rakesh or his friends have been selected for the match.

(ii) His friends or Rakesh has been selected for the match.

(iii) Neither Rohit nor his brothers are going abroad.

(iv) Neither his brothers nor Rohit is going abroad.

(v) Either Sohan or his sisters were dancing at the function.

(vi) Either his sisters or Sohan was dancing at the function.

VI. Either, neither, either of, neither of, takes singular verb.

(i) Either boy was honest.

(ii) Neither girl was allowed to leave the premises.

(iii) Either of the boys was ready to help the old man.

(iv) Neither of the girls was asked to join the extra classes.

VII. Some nouns are always used as plurals so, they take plural verbs.

(i) Where are your glasses?

(ii) His pants are attractive.

(iii) Cattle are grazing in the field.

(iv) Whose scissors are these?

VIII. Some nouns are always used as singulars, so, they take singular verbs.

(i) What is the latest news?

(ii) The furniture in the house is of a poor quality.

(iii) Mumps is not a fatal disease.

(vi) Physics is a tough subject.

IX. Nouns formed by alongwith, as well as, together with, accompanied by, etc., take verb according to the first subject.

(i) I as well as you am to blame.
(ii) You as well as I are going to see a movie.
(iii) John accompanied by his parents is going to visit the Taj.
(iv) His parents accompanied by John are going to visit the Taj.
(v) His brothers together with Vivek are ready to whitewash the fence.

X. To indicate something hypothetical or not factually true, plural verb 'were' with *as if* is used.

(i) He talks as if he were a king.
(ii) She dresses herself as if she were a princess.

MULTIPLE CHOICE QUESTIONS

Directions: *Find the correct word(s) that correctly completes the sentence.*

1. A woman came in with a baby who, she said, ... a safety pin.
A. was just swallowing
B. swallowed
C. had just swallowed
D. just swallowed

2. The telephone ..... several times before I answered it.
A. was ringing B. has rung
C. had rung D. would ring

3. An employment advertisement should ..... the number of vacancies.
A. provide B. specify
C. contain D. declare

4. A crescendo of metallic thuds arose from the market, where the iron-smiths were ..... the pieces of metals.
A. flattening B. striking
C. hammering D. thrashing

5. Ambition is one of those ..... which are never satisfied.
A. ideas B. fancies
C. passions D. needs

6. The new education policy provides a useful ..... for the planners to remove illiteracy.
A. breakup B. breakthrough
C. breakaway D. break-in

7. The family gave father a gold watch on the ..... of his fiftieth birthday.
A. time B. event
C. occasion D. celebration

8. The passengers were afraid but the captain ..... them that there was no danger.
A. promised B. assured
C. advised D. counselled

9. It's very kind of you to ..... to speak at the meeting.
A. accept B. agree
C. comply D. concur

10. The miser gazed ..... at the pile of gold coins in front of him.
A. avidly B. admiringly
C. thoughtfully D. earnestly

11. The pilot had been warned about the storm before he .....
A. took away B. took up
C. took over D. took off

12. On account of the dearth of grass on the arid plains the cattle became .....
A. flippant B. jubilant
C. agitated D. emaciated

13. I saw a ..... of cows in the field.
A. group B. herd
C. swarm D. flock

14. He was sent to the prison for his .....
A. sin B. vice
C. crime D. guilt

15. ..... of old paintings is a job for the experts.
A. Resurrection B. Retrieval
C. Restoration D. Resumption

16. Once he has signed the agreement, he won't be able to .....
A. back up B. back in
C. back at D. back out

17. She ..... a brief appearance at the end of the party.
A. put on B. put in
C. put across D. put up

18. The battalion operating from the mountain was able to ..... three enemy divisions.
A. tie up B. tie down
C. tie on D. tie with

19. Do you know ..... ?
A. where she comes from
B. where does she come from
C. where from she comes
D. from where does she come

20. ..... works of reference are so valuable as the Encyclopaedia Britannica.
A. A few B. Few
C. The few D. Fewer

21. The paths of glory lead ..... to the grave.
A. straight B. but
C. in D. directly

22. Walking at three o'clock, I heard the ..... of thunder.
A. crackle B. rumble
C. ripple D. clank

23. The thief ..... all the money.
A. made up B. made off with
C. made do with D. made good

24. Either Surendra or his friends ..... asked to pay a visit to the university.
A. has been B. have been
C. has D. have

25. Where ..... your spectacles?
A. is B. are
C. were D. have

26. Measles ..... not a fatal disease.
A. is B. are
C. has D. have

27. He walks as if he ..... a prince.
A. was B. were
C. have been D. has been

28. The captain alongwith his team mates ..... reached the ground.
A. have B. has
C. is D. are

29. The jury ..... given its opinion.
A. has B. have
C. is D. are

30. Slow and steady ..... the race.
A. win B. wins
C. has wins D. have win

31. The poet and the novelist ..... invited by the PM.
A. is B. are
C. has D. have

32. Mathematics ..... a tough subject.
A. is B. are
C. has D. have

33. Either girl ..... in a sad mood.
A. was B. were
C. has D. have

34. You should not avoid ...... him.
A. for meeting B. in meeting
C. to meet D. meeting

35. Are you ...... you lessons?
A. busy for preparing
B. busy preparing
C. busy to prepare
D. busy of preparing

ANSWERS

1	2	3	4	5	6	7	8	9	10
C	C	B	C	C	B	C	B	B	A
11	**12**	**13**	**14**	**15**	**16**	**17**	**18**	**19**	**20**
D	D	B	C	C	D	B	B	A	B
21	**22**	**23**	**24**	**25**	**26**	**27**	**28**	**29**	**30**
B	B	B	B	B	A	B	B	A	B
31	**32**	**33**	**34**	**35**					
B	A	A	D	B					

14. Narration

The words spoken by a speaker are in Direct Speech.

The words spoken by somebody and expressed by someone else with some modification are known as Indirect Speech. *e.g.,*

(*a*) Rohit says to me, "You do not understand me." (Direct speech)

(*b*) Rohit tells me that I do not understand him. (Indirect speech)

MULTIPLE CHOICE QUESTIONS

Directions: *Each sentence in this assignment is followed by four options, only one is correct. Spot the correct answer.*

1. She said to me, "Keep quite and listen to my words".

A. She requested me to keep quite and listen to her words.

B. She ordered me to keep quite and listen to her words.

C. She entreated me to keep quite and listen to her words.

D. She told me to keep quite and listen to her words.

2. My brother said to me, "What are you doing here?"

A. My brother asked me that what I was doing there.

B. My brother asked me what I was doing there.

C. My brother asked me that what was I doing there.

D. My brother asked me what I was doing here.

3. Ravi said, "My father lived in this city two years ago."

A. Ravi said that his father had lived in that city two years before.

B. Ravi said that his father had lived in that city two years ago.

C. Ravi told that his father had lived in that city ago two years.

D. Ravi asked that his father had lived in that city before two years.

4. My brother said to me, "When I was young, I used to play cricket".

A. My brother told me that when I was young, I used to play cricket.

B. My brother told me that when I was young, I used to play cricket.

C. My brother told me that when he was young, I used to play cricket.

D. My brother told me that when he was young, he used to play cricket.

5. The student said, "Sir, I am not guilty".

A. The student said with respect that he was not guilty.

B. The student pleaded that he was not guilty.

C. The student pleaded with respect that he was not guilty.

D. The student said respectfully that he was not guilty.

6. She said, "I am an early-riser".

A. She regretted that she was an early-riser.

B. She said that she is an early-riser.

C. She said that she was an early-riser.

D. She regretted that she is an early-riser.

7. The police officer said to the criminal, "Speak as I tell you".

A. The police officer directed the criminal to speak as he told him.

B. The police officer told the criminal to speak as he told him.

C. The police officer advised the criminal to speak as he told him.

D. The police officer requested the criminal to speak as he told him.

8. The preacher said to me, "May God help you!"

A. The preacher prayed that God might help me.
B. The preacher prayed that God might help him.
C. The preacher requested that God might help me.
D. The preacher requested the God might help them.

9. She said to me, "Happy Diwali!"

A. She blessed me a happy Diwali.
B. She wished me a happy Diwali.
C. She prayed a happy Diwali.
D. She said to me a very happy Diwali.

10. He said, "Shall I open the gate?"

A. He asked that he should open the gate.
B. He asked if he should open the gate.
C. He ordered that he should open the gate.
D. He requested that he should open the gate.

11. I told Ravi, "Do have a cup of tea".

A. I ordered Ravi to have a cup of tea.
B. I advised Ravi to had a cup of tea.
C. I requested Ravi to have a cup of tea.
D. I said Ravi to have a cup of cold tea.

12. He told me, "Shall I go to the picture?"

A. He asked that he should go to the picture.
B. He asked me if he shall go to the picture.
C. He asked me if he should go to the picture.
D. He requested me to go to the picture.

13. The teacher says, "Two and two makes four".

A. The teacher says that two and two made four.
B. The teacher wishes that two and two makes four.
C. The teacher advises that two and two makes four.
D. The teacher says that two and two makes four.

14. Baby said, "I will go".

A. Baby said that she will go.
B. Baby said that she could go.
C. Baby say that she will go.
D. Baby said that she would go.

15. I said to my sister, "Please, give me more money".

A. I requested my sister to give me more money.
B. I ordered my sister to give me more money.
C. I advised my sister to gave me more money.
D. I requested my sister to give her more money.

16. He said, ''Bring a chair at once''.

A. He ordered to bring a chair at once.
B. He requested to bring a chair at once.
C. He told to bring a chair at once.
D. He says to bring a chair at once.

17. The teacher said, ''Don't make a noise''.

A. The teacher says to us not to make a noise.
B. The teacher asked us not to make a noise.
C. The teacher requested us not to make a noise.
D. The teacher asked us not to made a noise.

18. My father said, ''The earth is round''.

A. My father said that the earth was round.
B. My father says that the earth is round.
C. My father said that the earth is round
D. My father ordered that the earth is round.

19. We said, ''What a place it is!''

A. We said that it was a very fine place.
B. We said that is a very fine place.
C. We said that the place is fine.
D. We exclaimed with joy that the place was very fine.

20. She said, ''Shall I thread the needle?''

A. She asked if she should thread the needle
B. She asked if she shall thread the needle.
C. She requested if she should thread the needle.
D. She says that if she would thread the needle.

ANSWERS

1	2	3	4	5	6	7	8	9	10
B	B	A	D	C	C	A	A	B	B
11	**12**	**13**	**14**	**15**	**16**	**17**	**18**	**19**	**20**
C	C	D	D	A	A	B	C	D	A

15. ACTIVE & PASSIVE VOICE

An active sentence focuses on the person or thing doing the action. A passive sentence focuses on the person or thing affected by the action.

e.g., The tower was built. (Active voice)

Someone built the tower. (Passive voice)

Transformation of Voice

i.e., Active voice to Passive voice & vice versa.

- Voice and Tense are closely associated with each other.
- Tense plays an important role while transforming the voice.

MULTIPLE CHOICE QUESTIONS

Directions: *In these questions, the sentences have been given in Active/Passive voice. From the given options, choose the one which best expresses the given sentence in Passive/Active voice.*

1. Help the poor.
A. The poor should be helped.
B. The poor would be helped.
C. The poor must be helped.
D. The poor will be helped.

2. Bring a glass of water.
A. A glass of water will be brought.
B. A glass of water should be brought.
C. Let a glass of water be brought.
D. Let a glass of water will be brought.

3. He gave me a beautiful flower pot.
A. A beautiful flower pot was given to me by him.
B. A beautiful flower pot had given to me by him.
C. A beautiful flower pot had been giving by him.
D. I was giving him a beautiful flower pot.

4. Is he answering the question?
A. The question is answered by him.
B. The question is being answered by him.
C. Is the question being answered by him?
D. Is the question being answering by him?

5. Who gave you this letter?
A. This letter was given to you by whom?
B. This letter had given to you by whom?
C. Was this letter given to you?
D. By whom was this letter given to you?

6. The professor teaches students.
A. Students are being taught by the professor.
B. Students are taught by the professor.
C. The professor is being taught by students.
D. Students being taught by the professor.

7. M.S. Dhoni has created a world record.
A. A world record has been created by M.S. Dhoni.
B. A world record has created by M.S. Dhoni.
C. A world record is created by M.S. Dhoni.
D. A world record is being created by M.S. Dhoni.

8. Srishti sings a lovely song.
A. A lovely song had sung by Srishti.
B. A lovely song was sung by Srishti.
C. A lovely song is sung by Srishti.
D. A lovely song is sang by Srishti.

9. He was drawing a picture.
A. A picture was drawn by him.
B. A picture was being drawn by him.
C. A picture was drawing by him.
D. A picture was drew by him.

10. We made him leader.
A. He was made leader by us.

B. He was maded leader.
C. He made leader by us.
D. He was made leader.

11. There is no time to waste.
A. There is no time to be wasted.
B. No time to be wasted there.
C. No time to be wasted by there.
D. No time is to be wasted.

12. Take medicine in time.
A. In time medicine to be taken.
B. Medicine should be taken in time.
C. Medicine in time will be taken.
D. Medicine has to be in time taken.

13. He reads a novel.
A. A novel was read by him.
B. A novel has read by him.
C. A novel is being read by him.
D. A novel is read by him.

14. They had cleared the dues.
A. The dues had been cleared by them.
B. The dues had cleared by them.
C. The dues are being cleared.
D. The dues is cleared.

15. I invite you on the dinner.
A. On the dinner you have been invited.
B. On the dinner you are inviting.
C. You are inviting by me on the dinner.
D. You are invited by me on the dinner.

16. We chose him our leader.
A. He was chosen our leader.
B. He has been chosen our leader.
C. He had chosen our leader.
D. He have been chosen our leader.

17. Who made a maiden century?
A. By whose was a maiden century made?
B. By whom was a maiden century make?
C. By whom was a maiden century made?
D. By whom had a maiden century made?

18. I may help her in her project.
A. She might be helped by me in her project.
B. She may be helped by me in her project.
C. She might be helped in her project by me.
D. In her project, she may be help by me.

19. Take medicine in time.
A. Medicine should be taken in time.
B. Medicine will be taken in time.
C. Medicine will be took in time.
D. Medicine shall take in time.

20. I am solving the questions.
A. The questions are being solved by me.
B. The questions have been solved by me.
C. The questions are to be solved by me.
D. The question are solved by me.

21. May I take this pen?
A. May this pen will be taken by me?
B. May this pen shall be taken by me?
C. May this pen should be taken by me?
D. May this pen be taken by me?

22. Can we send it by air?
A. Can this be sent by air?
B. Can it be sent by air?
C. Can it go by air?
D. Can it be send by air?

23. Who wrote this book?
A. By whom was this book written?
B. By whom is this book written?
C. By whom was this book being written?
D. By whom is this book being written?

24. What did you buy?
A. What is bought by you?
B. What is being bought by you?
C. What was bought by you?
D. What was being bought by you?

25. Whom do you want?
A. Who is wanted by you?
B. Who is being wanted by you?
C. You are wanted by whom?
D. You are being wanted by whom?

ANSWERS

1	2	3	4	5	6	7	8	9	10
A	C	A	C	D	B	A	C	B	A
11	**12**	**13**	**14**	**15**	**16**	**17**	**18**	**19**	**20**
A	B	D	A	D	A	C	B	A	A
21	**22**	**23**	**24**	**25**					
D	B	A	C	A					

16. SYNONYMS, ANTONYMS & HOMONYMS

Synonym: A word or phrase that means the same as another word or phrase.
Antonym: A word or phrase that means the opposite of another word or phrase.
Homonyms: Two or more words having the same spelling or pronunciation but different meanings.

MULTIPLE CHOICE QUESTIONS

Directions: *In the following questions choose the word which best expresses the meaning of the given word.*

1. INDICT
   A. Condemn B. Reprimand
   C. Accuse D. Allege
2. SCINTILLATING
   A. Smouldering B. Gilittering
   C. Touching D. Warming
3. REFECTORY
   A. Restaurant B. Parlour
   C. Living Room D. Dining Room
4. DISTINCTION
   A. Diffusion B. Disagreement
   C. Different D. Degree
5. IMPROVEMENT
   A. Advancement B. Betterment
   C. Promotion D. Preference
6. ADVERSITY
   A. Failure B. Helplessness
   C. Misfortune D. Crisis
7. TURN UP
   A. Land up B. Show up
   C. Crop up D. Come up
8. DEIFY
   A. Flatter B. Challenge
   C. Worship D. Face
9. ERROR
   A. Misadventure B. Misgiving
   C. Ambiguity D. Blunder
10. SHALLOW
    A. Artificial B. Superficial
    C. Foolish D. Worthless
11. MASSACRE
    A. Murder B. Stab
    C. Assassinate D. Slaughter
12. COMBAT
    A. Conflict B. Quarrel
    C. Feud D. Fight
13. VORACIOUS
    A. Wild B. Hungry
    C. Angry D. Quick
14. IMPROMPTU
    A. Offhand B. Unimportant
    C. Unreal D. Effective
15. RABBLE
    A. Mob B. Noise
    C. Roar D. Rubbish
16. TEPID
    A. Hot B. Warm
    C. Cold D. Boiling
17. MAYHEM
    A. Jubilation B. Havoc
    C. Excitement D. Defeat
18. TIMID
    A. Fast B. Slow
    C. Medium D. Shy
19. CANTANKEROUS
    A. Quarrelsome B. Rash
    C. Disrepectful D. Noisy

20. PRECARIOUS
A. Cautious B. Critical
C. Perilous D. Brittle

Directions: *In the following questions choose the word which best expresses the opposite of the given word.*

21. DEAR
A. Priceless B. Free
C. Worthless D. Cheap

22. FLAGITIOUS
A. Innocent B. Vapid
C. Ignorant D. Frivolous

23. LIABILITY
A. Property B. Assets
C. Debt D. Treasure

24. VIRTUOUS
A. Wicked B. Corrupt
C. Vicious D. Scandalous

25. ENCOURAGE
A. Dampen B. Disapprove
C. Discourage D. Warn

26. MORTAL
A. Divine B. Immortal
C. Spiritual D. Eternal

27. LEND
A. Borrow B. Cheat
C. Pawn D. Hire

28. COMIC
A. Emotional B. Tragic
C. Fearful D. Painful

29. ADDITION
A. Division B. Enumeration
C. Subtraction D. Multiplication

30. MINOR
A. Big B. Major
C. Tall D. Heavy

31. REPEL
A. Attend B. Concentrate
C. Continue D. Attract

32. ARTIFICIAL
A. Red B. Natural
C. Truthful D. Solid

33. CAPACIOUS
A. Limited B. Caring
C. Foolish D. Changeable

34. PROVOCATION
A. Vocation B. Pacification
C. Peace D. Destruction

35. METICULOUS
A. Mutual B. Shaggy
C. Meretricious D. Slovenly

36. Choose the correct homonym for the word 'been'.
A. done B. being
C. bean D. covered

37. Choose the correct homonym for the word 'dose'?
A. doze B. does
C. douse D. dyes

38. Choose the correct homonym for the word 'would':
A. could B. weed
C. wood D. hold

39. Choose the correct homonym for the word 'load':
A. loud B. laud
C. lead D. lode

40. Choose the correct homonym for the word 'loan':
A. lawn B. lean
C. lone D. long

ANSWERS

1	2	3	4	5	6	7	8	9	10
C	B	D	C	B	C	B	C	D	B
11	**12**	**13**	**14**	**15**	**16**	**17**	**18**	**19**	**20**
D	D	B	A	A	B	B	D	A	B
21	**22**	**23**	**24**	**25**	**26**	**27**	**28**	**29**	**30**
D	A	B	C	C	B	A	B	C	B
31	**32**	**33**	**34**	**35**	**36**	**37**	**38**	**39**	**40**
D	B	A	B	D	C	A	C	D	C

17. ONE WORD SUBSTITUTION

There are many words in English language which can be perfectly used for a number of words. These words help in expressing ideas in a short and correct manner for the right occasion. Such words not only increase the vocabulary but also enable you to economise in the use of words to a great extent.

MULTIPLE CHOICE QUESTIONS

Directions: *In questions given below out of the four alternatives choose the one which can be substituted for the given words/sentence.*

1. Something that relates to everyone in the world
A. General B. Common
C. Usual D. Universal

2. An expression of mild disapproval
A. Warning B. Denigration
C. Impertinence D. Reproof

3. One who is not easily pleased by anything
A. Maiden B. Medieval
C. Precarious D. Fastidious

4. Murder of a king
A. Infanticide B. Matricide
C. Genocide D. Regicide

5. A remedy for all diseases
A. Stoic B. Marvel
C. Panacea D. Recompense

6. A dramatic performance
A. Mask B. Mosque
C. Masque D. Mascot

7. Study of birds
A. Orology B. Optology
C. Ophthalmology D. Ornithology

8. Ready to believe
A. Credulous B. Credible
C. Creditable D. Incredible

9. Incapable of being seen through
A. Ductile B. Opaque
C. Obsolete D. Potable

10. One who eats everything
A. Omnivorous B. Omniscient
C. Irresistible D. Insolvent

11. A place where bees are kept is called
A. An apiary B. A mole
C. A hive D. A sanctuary

12. One who cannot be corrected
A. Incurable B. Incorrigible
C. Hardened D. Invulnerable

13. One who is in charge of a museum
A. Curator B. Supervisor
C. Caretaker D. Warden

14. Continuing fight between parties, families, clans, etc.
A. Enmity B. Feud
C. Quarrel D. Skirmish

15. A voice loud enough to be heard
A. Audible B. Applaudable
C. Laudable D. Oral

16. A paper written by hand
A. Handicraft B. Manuscript
C. Handiwork D. Thesis

17. Habitually silent or talking little
A. Serville B. Unequivocal
C. Taciturn D. Synoptic

18. To slap with a flat object
A. Chop B. Hew
C. Gnaw D. Swat

19. A person who speaks many languages
A. Linguist B. Monolingual
C. Polyglot D. Bilingual

20. A light sailing-boat built specially for racing
A. Canoe B. Yacht
C. Frigate D. Dinghy

21. A fixed orbit in space in relation to earth
A. Geological B. Geo-synchronous
C. Geo-centric D. Geo-stationary

22. A style in which a writer makes a display of his knowledge
A. Pedantic B. Verbose
C. Pompous D. Ornate

23. A religious discourse
A. Preach B. Stanza
C. Sanctorum D. Sermon

24. A place that provides refuge
A. Asylum B. Sanatorium
C. Shelter D. Orphanage

25. Detailed plan of a journey
A. Travelogue B. Travelkit
C. Schedule D. Itinerary

26. A person who insists on something
A. Disciplinarian B. Stickler
C. Instantaneous D. Boaster

27. A drawing on transparent paper
A. Red print B. Blue print
C. Negative D. Transparency

28. One who believes that all things and events in life are predetermined is a
A. Fatalist B. Puritan
C. Egoist D. Tyrant

29. A school boy who cuts classes frequently is a
A. Defeatist B. Sycophant
C. Truant D. Martinet

30. The act of violating the sanctity of the church is
A. Blasphemy B. Heresy
C. Sacrilege D. Desecration

31. A place where monks live as a secluded community
A. Cathedral B. Diocese
C. Convent D. Monastery

32. One who is fond of fighting
A. Bellicose B. Aggressive
C. Belligerent D. Militant

33. Tending to move away from the centre or axis
A. Centrifugal B. Centripetal
C. Axiomatic D. Awry

34. A person of good understanding, knowledge and reasoning power
A. Expert B. Intellectual
C. Snob D. Literate

35. One absorbed in his own thoughts and feelings rather than in things outside
A. Scholar B. Recluse
C. Introvert D. Intellectual

36. One who does not marry, especially as a religious obligation
A. Bachelor B. Celibate
C. Virgin D. Recluse

37. A person who tries to deceive people by claiming to be able to do wonderful things.
A. Trickster B. Impostor
C. Magician D. Mountebank

38. To take secretly in small quantities
A. Robbery B. Pilferage
C. Theft D. Defalcation

39. Policemen riding on motorcycles as guards to a VIP.
A. Outriders B. Servants
C. Commandos D. Attendants

40. The part of a government which is concerned with making of rules.
A. Court B. Tribunal
C. Bar D. Legislature

ANSWERS

1	2	3	4	5	6	7	8	9	10
D	D	D	D	C	C	D	A	B	A
11	**12**	**13**	**14**	**15**	**16**	**17**	**18**	**19**	**20**
A	B	A	B	A	B	C	D	A	B
21	**22**	**23**	**24**	**25**	**26**	**27**	**28**	**29**	**30**
D	A	D	A	D	B	D	A	C	C
31	**32**	**33**	**34**	**35**	**36**	**37**	**38**	**39**	**40**
D	A	A	B	C	B	A	B	A	D

18. IDIOMS, PHRASES & PROVERBS

An idiom is a group of words established by usage as having a meaning different from the individual words.
A phrase is a small group of words standing together as an idiomatic expression.
A proverb is a short pithy saying in general use, stating a general truth or piece of advice.

MULTIPLE CHOICE QUESTIONS

Directions: *Some idioms/phrases are given below with their meanings. Choose their correct meanings.*

1. To beg the question
A. To refer to
B. To take for granted
C. To raise objections
D. To be discussed

2. To drive home
A. To find one's roots
B. To return to place of rest
C. Back to original position
D. To emphasise

3. To hit the right nail on the head
A. To do the right thing
B. To destroy one's reputation
C. To announce one's fixed views
D. To teach someone a lesson

4. To pick holes
A. To find some reason to quarrel
B. To destory something
C. To criticise someone
D. To cut some part of an item

5. To smell a rat
A. To see signs of plague epidemic
B. To get bad smell of a dead rat
C. To suspect foul dealings
D. To be in a bad mood

6. A black sheep
A. An unlucky person
B. A negro
C. An ugly person
D. A disgraced member

7. To catch a tarter
A. To trap wanted criminal with great difficulty
B. To catch a dangerous person
C. To meet with disaster
D. To deal with a person who is more than one's watch

8. To be above board
A. To have a good height
B. To be honest in any business deal
C. To have no debts
D. To try to be beautiful

9. To keep one's temper
A. To become angry
B. To be in good mood
C. To preserve one's energy
D. To be aloof from

10. To have an axe to grind
A. A private end to serve
B. To fail to arouse interest
C. To have no result
D. To work for both sides

11. To cry wolf
A. To listen eagerly
B. To give false alarm
C. To turn pale
D. To keep off starvation

12. A man of straw
A. A man of no substance
B. A very active person
C. A worthy fellow
D. An unreasonable person

13. To make clean breast of
A. To gain prominence
B. To praise oneself
C. To confess without reserve
D. To destroy before it blooms

14. To end in smoke
A. To make completely understand
B. To ruin oneself
C. To excite great applause
D. To produce no result

15. To leave someone in the lurch
A. To come to compromise with someone
B. Constant source of annoyance to someone
C. To put someone at ease
D. To desert someone in his difficulties

16. To play second fiddle
A. To be happy, cheerful and healthy
B. To reduce importance of one's senior
C. To support the role and view of another person
D. To do back seat driving

17. To set one's face against
A. To oppose with determination
B. To judge by appearance
C. To get out of difficulty
D. To look at one steadily

18. To put one's hand to the plough
A. To take up agricultural farming
B. To take a difficult task
C. To get entangled into unnecessary things
D. Take interest in technical work

19. To join issue with
A. To cooperate with others for a cause
B. To join any voluntary organisation for good purpose
C. To resolve dispute and restore peace
D. To enter into argument over any issue

20. To do oneself justice
A. To dispense justice on our own
B. To treat others with due respect
C. To defend one's point of view
D. To perform and be able

21. Once in a blue moon
A. Once in a while
B. Often
C. At a short interval
D. At a particular time

22. Necessity is the mother of invention
A. The mother of a girl named 'Necessity' made an invention.
B. She who can make some invention should be called 'mother'.
C. Your mother will feel happy if you make some invention.
D. A difficult problem compels people to think about its solution.

23. No pain, no gain
A. It is useless to suffer so much pain just for a little gain.
B. If you want to achieve something, you have to suffer to some extent.
C. Unless you have pain in your body, no doctor will care for you.
D. If you get injured in a competition, you will be allowed to get the prize.

24. Beauty is only skin deep
A. The real beauty of a person lies in his character and not in his outer appearance.
B. Only the quality of skin makes a person really beautiful.
C. If you want to be beautiful, give attention to your skin.
D. Rub cosmetics below the skin to get really beautiful.

25. Beggars cannot be choosers
A. Beggars are not allowed at all places.
B. Begging is prohibited by law.
C. It is not easy even to become a beggar.
D. Beggars have to accept (without choice) whatever is given to them.

ANSWERS

1	2	3	4	5	6	7	8	9	10
C	D	A	C	C	D	B	B	B	A
11	**12**	**13**	**14**	**15**	**16**	**17**	**18**	**19**	**20**
B	A	C	D	D	C	A	B	D	D
21	**22**	**23**	**24**	**25**					
A	D	B	A	D					

19. Modals & Auxiliaries

AUXILIARY VERBS

Modals are actually helping verbs. They help the finite verbs in framing sentences:

She **was** cooking food.

I **shall** guide you.

Kinds of Auxiliary Verbs

Auxiliary verbs are of two kinds:

A. Primary Auxiliaries (Modals)

B. Modal Auxiliaries (Auxiliary Modals)

A. Primary Modals

Primary modals work both as Helping Verbs and Finite Verbs.

Be = is, am, are, was, were, being, been

Have = has, have, had, having

Do = do, does, did, done, doing

(*a*) **Usage of be/have/do as Helping verbs:**

She **is** making a cane basket.

I **have** finished my homework.

She **does** know French.

(*b*) **Usage of be/have/do as Finite verbs:**

She **was** happy.

I **have** an expensive pen.

She **is doing** her homework.

B. Modal Auxiliaries

Shall, should, will, would, can, could, may, might, must, ought to, used to, have to, had to, dare, daren't, need needn't, mustn't are modal Auxiliaries.

Shall

'Shall' is used in the following ways:

(*a*) **With first Person Pronouns (I/we)**

I shall lend you my book.

We shall go to school together.

(*b*) **to express a suggestion**

Shall we go out for a walk?

Shall we meet the officer tomorrow?

Sometimes 'Shall' is used with Second and Third Person Pronouns as under:

(*a*) **to express a command**

You shall not tell a lie.

You shall not disturb us.

(*b*) **to express prohibition**

You shall not smoke here.

You shall not drink here.

(*c*) **to express a legal obligation**

You shall submit your sales tax return before the end of this month.

Should

'Should' is used in the following ways:

(*a*) **As Past Tense of 'shall'**

She said that she **should** settle in America.

(*b*) **to express duty and obligation**

You should do your duty honestly.

(*c*) **to express advice**

You should reach the station before time.

(*d*) **to express guess**

It should be 9 o'clock now.

(*e*) 'Should' is used with lest to express purpose.

Walk fast lest you should miss the train.

Will

'Will' is used in the following ways:

(*a*) **With Second and Third person Pronouns:**

You will dance at the party.

He will sing a song.

(*b*) **to express (Invitation/offer)**

Will you dine with me tonight?

(*c*) **to express an order**
Will you shut your big mouth?

(*d*) **to express probability**
He will come to see me tomorrow.

Sometimes 'Will' is used with 'I'

(*a*) **Determination**
I will win the first position.

(*b*) **A threat**
I will punish you.

(*c*) **A promise**
I will lend you Rs. 500/- tomorrow.

Would

'Would' is used in the following ways:

(*a*) **As Past Tense of 'will'**
He said that they would be attending the meeting the next day.

(*b*) **to express a desire or wish**
Would that I were a king!

(*c*) **to express a polite invitation**
Would you like some biscuits?

(*d*) **The usage of would in conditional sentences**
You would get good marks if you worked hard.
You would have won the race if you had run fast.

(*e*) **to express a piece of advice**
I would not meet him if I were you.

Can

'Can' is used in the following ways:

(*a*) **to express ability**
He can speak English fluently.

(*b*) **to grant permission**
You can go now.

(*c*) **to express impossibility**
Who can defeat his fate?

(*d*) **to make a request**
Can I use your motorbike?

Could

'Could' is used in the following ways:

(*a*) **As Past Tense of 'can'**
She said that she could see the sun rising.

(*b*) **to express past ability**
I could sing and dance when I was young.

(*c*) **to express a request**
Could I use your phone?

May

'May' is used in the following ways:

(*a*) **to express a request**
May I use your bicycle?

(*b*) **to seek and allow permission**
May I come in, sir?
Yes, you may.

(*c*) **to express possibility**
It may rain tonight.

(*d*) **In optative sentences**
May you live long!

Might

'Might' is used in the following ways:

(*a*) **As past tense of 'may'**
She said that her brother might come back home.

(*b*) **to express less possibility**
It might rain tonight.

(*c*) **to give and seek permission**
Might I come in, sir?
You might go home now.

Must

'Must' is used in the following ways:

(*a*) **to express duty**
You must serve your motherland.

(*b*) **to express obligation**
We must obey our elders.

(*c*) **to express advice**
You must take an umbrella before going to office.

(*d*) **to express probability**
'Must' expresses a stronger probability than may.
It must rain tonight.

Ought to

'Ought to' is used in the following ways:

(*a*) **to express obligation**
We ought to respect our teachers.

(*b*) **to express advice**
You ought to help the poor.

Used to

'Used to' is used in the following ways:

(*a*) **to express past habits**
He used to smoke.

(*b*) **to express past existence of something**
There used to be a five star hotel in this city.

Have to

'Have to' expresses compulsion in the present tense.

You have to sign the documents.

Had to

'Had to' expresses compulsion in the past time.

She had to join the office again.

Dare

'Dare' is used as a Modal only in Interrogative sentences.

How dare you touch my bag?

Dare not (Daren't)

'Dare not (Daren't)' is used in negative sentences.

She daren't complain against me.

Need

'Need' expresses an obligation/compulsion. It is used in Interrogative Sentences.

Need I say more?

Need not (Needn't)

'Need not (Needn't)' is used in negative sentences.

You needn't come here again.

Must not (Mustn't)

'Must not (Mustn't)' is the negative form of must.

You mustn't follow us.

MULTIPLE CHOICE QUESTIONS

Directions: *In the following questions choose the correct options to fill in the blanks:*

1. Work hard lest you .... fail.
A. should B. may
C. can D. must

2. .... I come in, madam?
A. Can B. May
C. Will D. Must

3. It ...... rain tonight.
A. shall B. will
C. may D. can

4. You ...... love your countrymen.
A. need to B. have to
C. had to D. ought to

5. .... you like some pastries?
A. Should B. Would
C. Could D. Will

6. ...... that I were an actor!
A. Would B. Should
C. Could D. Will

7. Had you made one more effort you ...... have won the race.
A. will B. may
C. would D. shall

8. I ...... solve any sum.
A. may B. am
C. must D. can

9. ...... I smoke here?
A. Can B. Will
C. Could D. Must

10. The passengers .... keep watch on their luggage.
A. has B. have
C. should D. had

11. You .... submit your file to the authorities within a week.
A. have B. had
C. should D. would

12. ...... I use your phone?
A. Have B. Could
C. Would D. Had

13. ..... you give me your pen?
A. May B. Can
C. Must D. Dare

14. There ...... be an hospital at this place.
A. have to B. may
C. used to D. might

15. He ...... read and write when he was young.
A. would B. could
C. should D. can

16. He said that he ..... sing a song at the party.
A. should B. would
C. can D. will

17. She asked if he ...... help her.
A. should B. can
C. must D. would

18. We .... respect our elders.
A. need to B. have to
C. ought to D. had to

19. Nothing .... be done under such circumstances.
A. can B. used to
C. must D. have to

20. She ..... not ask about it.
A. has B. have
C. had D. dare

21. You .... not bring the child here.
A. have B. had
C. need D. would

22. ..... you live long!
A. Will B. May
C. Shall D. Can

23. ..... God help you!
A. Can B. Will
C. May D. Shall

24. ..... that I were a leader!
A. Would B. Should
C. Could D. Will

25. It ...... be ten o'clock now.
A. could B. would
C. should D. will

26. He ..... have reached the station by now.
A. shall B. will
C. would D. should

27. Being a receptionist, she will ...... type a letter.
A. has to B. have to
C. need to D. must

28. The birds ...... fly high in the sky.
A. may B. should
C. can D. would

29. ...... I open the main gate?
A. Should B. Would
C. Could D. Must

30. If you played well, we ...... win the match.
A. would B. should
C. must D. need

31. If I were you I ... not attend the meeting.
A. can B. would
C. could D. should

32. She ...... smoke in those days.
A. used to B. could
C. would D. had to

33. You ...... take the child to an intelligent doctor.
A. shall B. will
C. ought to D. would

34. ..... I sit here for some time?
A. Can B. Shall
C. Will D. Must

35. I think you .... not mind my reciting the poem loudly.
A. should B. could
C. may D. would

ANSWERS

1	2	3	4	5	6	7	8	9	10
A	B	C	D	B	A	C	D	A	C
11	12	13	14	15	16	17	18	19	20
C	B	B	C	B	B	D	C	A	D
21	22	23	24	25	26	27	28	29	30
C	B	C	A	C	C	B	C	A	A
31	32	33	34	35					
B	A	C	A	D					

20. Non Finites

Read the following sentences:

1. She has decided to resign.
2. I see a thief running.
3. She insists on my sitting beside her.

In the above sentences, the underlined words are non-finites because they are not changed with the change of the subject, *e.g.*,

They have decided to resign.

She sees a thief running.

You insist on my sitting beside you.

Non-finites are of three kinds:

1. The Infinitives (to + v_1)
2. The Participles (v_1 + ing)
3. The Gerund (v_1 + ing)

1. THE INFINITIVE

To plus first form of the verb is called an Infinitive. It is often used as a Noun.

Uses of the Infinitive

(*a*) Subject of a sentence.
To laugh loudly is good for health.
To steal is bad.

(*b*) After a transitive verb.
He loves **to eat** sweets.
She likes **to play** tennis.

(*c*) After a preposition.
They are about **to leave.**

(*d*) As a complement after the verb 'be'.
Her ambition is **to be** a teacher.
His immediate aim is **to help** her.

(*e*) As an object.
He made me **weep.**
I saw him **go.**

(*f*) After an adjective.
Honey is sweet **to taste.**
He was ashamed **to talk** to his criminal friend.

(*g*) After a noun. (often in passive)
Here is a book **to be** read carefully.

Bare Infinitive

Some Infinitives are used without 'to' and are called Bare Infinitives.

You had better **go** home.
I saw him **go.**
I heard him **sing.**
He would rather **rest** than **play.**
I can **solve** this sum.
I watched him **steal** your purse.
I watched him **open** the safe.
Let him **come** in.
You had sooner **read** your book than **play.**

Note: Bare Infinitives are usually used after 'causal' (or 'causative') verbs and 'modals'.

2. THE PARTICIPLE

Participles serve the purpose of Adjectives.

I heard him **singing.**
I saw him **going.**

Kinds of Participles

Participles are of the following kinds:

I. Present Participle

I watched the boy **stealing** your purse.
I saw him **climbing** the hill.
She smelt something **burning.**
Don't let me catch you **smoking.**

II. Past Participle

I got the house **painted** last week.
I had my hair **cut.**
The rose has **faded.**

He had **written** five letters.

I want the office **built** in a month.

III. Perfect Participle

Having finished cooking, she started reading a novel.

Having dusted the room, the maid began to wash the dishes.

Having written a letter to her mother, she walked out of the room.

Joining of Sentences by using Participles

(I) By using Present Participles

1. Look at the boy. He is climbing the tree.
   Look at the boy climbing the tree.
2. He was dusting the room. He found a coin.
   While dusting the room, he found a coin.
3. The child opened the box. He found a toy.
   Opening the box, the child found a toy.

3. THE GERUND

A. (verb + ing) is usually used as a Gerund. Like a Noun, it is used as under.

(*a*) As a subject of the verb.
Killing birds is not good.
Smoking is injurious to health.

(*b*) As an object of the verb.
I like **singing.**
She loves **dancing.**

(*c*) As a complement of the verb 'be'.
What I hate the most is **drinking.**
What I love the most is **playing.**

(*d*) As an object of a preposition.
I am fond of **eating.**
She was punished for **telling** a lie.

B. In some cases, instead of Gerunds Infinitives can be used.

Subject + Verb	**Gerund or Infinitive**
I love	singing or to sing.
He hates	smoking or to smoke.
I like	dancing or to dance.
He prefers	reading novels/to read novels.
Your bike needs	oiling or to be oiled.

C. It + be + Adjective + Gerund (Phrase).

Subject + be	**Adjective/ Noun**	**Gerund (Phrase)**
It is	wrong	making so much noise.
It is	good	drinking juice in the evening.
It is	nice	walking in the moon light.

D. Subject + be + Adjective or Past Participle + Preposition + Gerund.

Subject + be	**Adjective/**	**Preposition Past Participle**	**Gerund (Phrase)**
He is	fond	of	swimming.
She was	annoyed	at	his talking so loudly.
He is	capable	of	solving all the sums.

MULTIPLE CHOICE QUESTIONS

Directions: *In the following questions choose the correct options to replace the words given in brackets.*

1. He came (run) to his aunt.
A. run B. running
C. to run D. in run

2. She dislikes (eat) meat.
A. eat to B. to eat
C. eating D. to eating

3. He likes (sing).
A. sing to B. singing
C. to sing D. to singing

4. We are ready (play) the match.
A. play to B. to playing
C. playing D. to play

5. (Smoke) is injurious to health.
A. Smoking B. To smoke
C. To smoking D. Smoke to

6. He loves (eat) raw vegetables.
A. eaten B. eating
C. to eating D. eat to

7. He seemed (have) finished his homework.
A. have to B. to have
C. having D. to having

8. It is not easy (achieve) this target.
A. achieve to B. achieving to
C. to achieve D. to achieving

9. It is always difficult (climb) a mountain.
A. climb to B. to climb
C. climbing to D. to climbing

10. She avoided (argue) with him.
A. argue to B. arguing
C. to arguing D. argues

11. I saw him (go).
A. to go B. to going
C. going D. gone

12. I heard him (sing).
A. to sing B. singing
C. to singing D. sung

13. She smelt something (burn).
A. burning B. to burn
C. to burning D. burn to

14. He claimed (be) the best player of hockey.
A. being to B. to be
C. been D. has been

15. We eat (live).
A. living B. to living
C. to live D. lively

16. He wanted (go) across the world.
A. go to B. to going
C. to go D. going to

17. I cannot bear (kill) birds.
A. killing B. to killing
C. to kill D. kill to

18. He wished (be) there inside the hotel.
A. being to B. to be
C. been D. been to

19. It is time (drink) some juice.
A. drinking B. to drinking
C. drink to D. to drink

20. He is too busy (take) care of his kids.
A. taking to B. to take
C. to taking D. take to

21. I forbore myself (slap) him on the face.
A. to slap B. slap to
C. slapping D. slapping to

22. She tried (open) the safe.
A. open to B. opening
C. to open D. to opening

23. It is no use (cry) over spilt milk.
A. cry to B. in crying
C. crying D. crying to

24. They enjoyed (fly) kites.
A. to fly B. fly to
C. flying D. flying to

25. It is your responsibility (keep) the accounts of every happening here.
A. keep to B. keeping to
C. to keep D. keeping

26. Please give me a pair of scissors (cut) cloth.
A. cut to B. cutting to
C. cutting D. to cut

27. She prefers (play) chess to sitting idly.
A. to playing B. playing
C. play to D. playing to

28. I prefer (talk) to the officer alone.
A. talk to B. talking to
C. to talk D. to talking

29. Would you mind your (bring) some cake for me?
A. to bring B. bring to
C. bringing to D. bringing

30. (Err) is human.
A. Err to B. Erring to
C. To erring D. To err

31. (Steal) is not good.
A. Stealing B. To steel
C. To stealing D. Stealing to

32. She heard the lion (roar).
A. to roar B. roaring
C. roar to D. to roaring

33. He is reported (be) dead.
A. be to B. to be
C. to being D. to been

34. You are ordered (bring) the file number 100.
A. bringing B. to bringing
C. bring to D. to bring

35. You are advised (take) part in sports.
A. taking to B. to taking
C. to take D. take to

36. He appeared (have) cast his vote in favour of us.
A. having B. to having
C. to have D. have to

37. His ambition is (become) a doctor.
A. becoming B. to becoming
C. to become D. become to

38. We are asked (be) there in the main hall.
A. being B. been
C. to be D. be to

39. Our immediate aim is (provide) financial help to the needy.
A. provide to B. providing to
C. to providing D. to provide

40. We read and write (become) civilized.
A. becoming B. becoming to
C. to become D. become to

41. You need (improve) your health.
A. improving B. improvinto to
C. to improve D. improve to

42. You are allowed (paint) this door.
A. painting B. painting to
C. to paint D. paint to

43. Remind me (post) this letter.
A. posting B. posting to
C. to post D. post to

44. The teacher forgot (bring) the roll call register.
A. bringing B. to bringing
C. bring to D. to bring

45. He was appointed (keep) a check on the accounts.
A. keep to B. keeping to
C. to keep D. keeping

46. Your activities are (be) noticed.
A. being B. been
C. to be D. be to

47. Stop (talk), please.
A. talk to B. talking
C. to talk D. to talking

48. He does not bother (listen to) anybody.
A. listen to B. to listen to
C. listening D. listening to

49. He is not accustomed to (have) soup before meal.
A. have to B. to have
C. having D. to having

50. She is glad (be) in the company of children.
A. being B. been
C. to be D. be to

ANSWERS

1	2	3	4	5	6	7	8	9	10
B	C	B	D	A	B	B.	C	B	B
11	**12**	**13**	**14**	**15**	**16**	**17**	**18**	**19**	**20**
C	B	A	B	C	C	A	B	D	B
21	**22**	**23**	**24**	**25**	**26**	**27**	**28**	**29**	**30**
C	C	C	C	C	D	B	C	D	D
31	**32**	**33**	**34**	**35**	**36**	**37**	**38**	**39**	**40**
A	B	B	D	C	C	C	C	D	C
41	**42**	**43**	**44**	**45**	**46**	**47**	**48**	**49**	**50**
C	C	C	D	C	A.	B	B	C	C

21. Commonly Confusing Words

There are many words in English which may look or sound similar but there is lot of difference in their meanings and usage. Learn more about such words in this exercise.

MULTIPLE CHOICE QUESTIONS

Directions: *In the following questions choose the correct word to fill the blank. Two words at A and B are provided for choice. If either of the words can be filled, mark C and if none of the word can be filled then mark D as your choice.*

1. She comes of a .... family.
   A. respectable   B. respectful
   C. Any one of these   D. None of these
2. It began to .... as I reached my office.
   A. reign   B. rain
   C. Any one of these   D. None of these
3. The teacher told the students to be ....
   A. quiet   B. quite
   C. Any one of these   D. None of these
4. The .... has gone to attend the meeting.
   A. principle   B. principal
   C. Any one of these   D. None of these
5. .... makes a man perfect.
   A. Practice   B. Practise
   C. Any one of these   D. None of these
6. Uttar Pradesh is the most .... state of India.
   A. popular   B. populous
   C. Any one of these   D. None of these
7. The bird had a .... of bread with beak.
   A. piece   B. peace
   C. Any one of these   D. None of these
8. As she read the letter, her face turned ....
   A. pail   B. pale
   C. Any one of these   D. None of these
9. Man is the maker of his own ....
   A. destination   B. destiny
   C. Any one of these   D. None of these
10. Try this medicine, it will prove ....
    A. effectual   B. effective
    C. Any one of these   D. None of these
11. Maninder has employed an .... boy for his office works.
    A. errand   B. errant
    C. Any one of these   D. None of these
12. The soldiers wanted to .... over their victory in the battle.
    A. exalt   B. exult
    C. Any one of these   D. None of these
13. When I asked him to accompany us, he .... illness.
    A. fained   B. feigned
    C. Any one of these   D. None of these
14. The books are lying on the .... piece.
    A. mantal   B. mantle
    C. Any one of these   D. None of these
15. Sohan lives a .... life.
    A. luxurious   B. luxuriant
    C. Any one of these   D. None of these
16. She is a lady of .... birth.
    A. lowly   B. low
    C. Any one of these   D. None of these
17. We should not be ....of other's wealth.
    A. jealous   B. zealous
    C. Any one of these   D. None of these
18. It is two days .... from Delhi to Kerala by train.
    A. journey   B. voyage
    C. Any one of these   D. None of these

19. My father makes a .... selection of books before buying.
A. judicial B. judicious
C. Any one of these D. None of these

20. Marconi had an .... mind.
A. ingenious B. ingenuous
C. Any one of these D. None of these

21. It is .... to spend more than what you earn.
A. impudent B. unprudent
C. Any one of these D. None of these

22. Orders for his arrest were issued by the .... court.
A. imperial B. imperious
C. Any one of these D. None of these

23. During the voyage she suffered from sea ....
A. sickness B. illness
C. Any one of these D. None of these

24. Akbar was a .... ruler.
A. human B. humane
C. Any one of these D. None of these

25. Gandhiji was a .... leader.
A. notorious B. famous
C. Any one of these D. None of these

26. The boys broke the window .... of the class room.
A. pain B. pane
C. Any one of these D. None of these

27. My new trousers are very ....
A. lose B. loose
C. Any one of these D. None of these

28. She has learnt her ....
A. lesson B. lessen
C. Any one of these D. None of these

29. Brutus is an .... man.
A. honorary B. honourable
C. Any one of these D. None of these

30. I have to replace the .... of my shoe.
A. heal B. heel
C. Any one of these D. None of these

31. Dara Singh .... from Punjab.
A. hales B. hails
C. Any one of these D. None of these

32. Constant worry .... his health.
A. affected B. effected
C. Any one of these D. None of these

33. John refused to .... his decision.
A. altar B. alter
C. Any one of these D. None of these

34. Vivek is a .... young man.
A. handsome B. beautiful
C. Any one of these D. None of these

35. He competed in the race .... footed.
A. bear B. bare
C. Any one of these D. None of these

36. She has given .... to a son.
A. birth B. berth
C. Any one of these D. None of these

37. Stalin was .... of poor parents.
A. borne B. born
C. Any one of these D. None of these

38. Please check your ....
A. brakes B. breaks
C. Any one of these D. None of these

39. The princess ordered for a new .... dress.
A. bridle B. bridal
C. Any one of these D. None of these

40. The .... of Plassey was fought in 1757.
A. War B. Battle
C. Any one of these D. None of these

ANSWERS

1	2	3	4	5	6	7	8	9	10
A	B	A	B	A	B	A	B	B	B
11	**12**	**13**	**14**	**15**	**16**	**17**	**18**	**19**	**20**
B	B	B	B	A	B	A	A	B	A
21	**22**	**23**	**24**	**25**	**26**	**27**	**28**	**29**	**30**
A	A	A	B	B	B	B	A	B	B
31	**32**	**33**	**34**	**35**	**36**	**37**	**38**	**39**	**40**
B	A	B	A	B	A	B	A	B	B

22. Spelling Errors

There are thousands of words in English language. It is difficult to remember the spellings and meanings of all at once. Try to learn as many as you can. Use a dictionary regularly.

MULTIPLE CHOICE QUESTIONS

Directions: *Find the correctly spelt words.*

1. A. Damage B. Dammage
C. Damaige D. Dammege

2. A. Efficiant B. Effecient
C. Efficient D. Eficient

3. A. Schedule B. Schdule
C. Schedale D. Schedeule

4. A. Occurad B. Occurred
C. Ocurred D. Occured

5. A. Grieff B. Grief
C. Grieef D. Grrief

6. A. Guarantee B. Garuntee
C. Guaruntee D. Gaurantee

7. A. Meddicine B. Medicine
C. Medicene D. Medicinne

8. A. Benefeted B. Benefitted
C. Benifited D. Benefited

9. A. Acommodation B. Acomodation
C. Accomodation D. Accommodation

10. A. Querrelsome B. Quarrelsame
C. Quarrelsome D. Querralsome

11. A. Sympathetic B. Smypathetic
C. Sympothetic D. Sympethetic

12. A. Prograssive B. Progressive
C. Progresive D. Prograsive

13. A. Uncivilized B. Uncevilized
C. Uncivillized D. Uncevelized

14. A. Extravagant B. Extreragent
C. Extreregant D. Extravegent

15. A. Missunderstood B. Miesunderstood
C. Misunderstood D. Misunderstod

16. A. Belligerent B. Beligirent
C. Belligarant D. Belligerrent

17. A. Astonished B. Astronished
C. Astoneshed D. Asstonished

18. A. Sincerely B. Sencerely
C. Sincerelly D. Sincerrely

19. A. Rigourous B. Rigerous
C. Rigorous D. Regerous

20. A. Satellite B. Sattellite
C. Satelite D. Sattelite

21. A. Pesanger B. Passenger
C. Pessenger D. Pasanger

22. A. Humurous B. Humorous
C. Humoreus D. Humorrous

23. A. Exeggerate B. Exaggerate
C. Exadgerate D. Exagerate

24. A. Fariegn B. Forein
C. Foriegn D. Foreign

25. A. Excesive B. Excessive
C. Exccessive D. Exccesive

26. A. Forcaust B. Forcast
C. Forecast D. Forecaste

27. A. Paralleled B. Paralelled
C. Parralleled D. Parallelled

28. A. Ocasion B. Occassion
C. Occasion D. Ocassion

29. A. Boquet B. Bouquet
C. Bouquete D. Bouquette

30. A. Chettering B. Chaterring
C. Chattering D. Chatering

31. A. Discourage B. Disscourage
C. Discourege D. Discaurage

32. A. Curageous B. Courageous
C. Courrageous D. Couregeous

33. A. Abandon B. Abanddon
C. Abendon D. Abbandon

34. A. Embarassment B. Emberrassement
C. Embarrassment D. Embbaresment

35. A. Eccintric B. Eccentrie
C. Eccentric D. Eccintrie

36. A. Occasional B. Occassional
C. Occesional D. Occessional

37. A. Querrel B. Querral
C. Quarrel D. Quarel

38. A. Contrebution B. Contribution
C. Contributtion D. Conterbution

39. A. Desgrace B. Disgrece
C. Disgrice D. Disgrace

40. A. Harassment B. Herassment
C. Harasment D. Harassmient

41. A. Imaginative B. Imeginative
C. Imagenative D. Imaginetive

42. A. Suficient B. Suficiant
C. Sufficient D. Sufficiant

43. A. Adequate B. Edequate
C. Adaquete D. Edaquete

44. A. Exparienced B. Experianced
C. Experienced D. Experrienced

45. A. Flatering B. Fletering
C. Flattering D. Fletaring

46. A. Cuttiveted B. Culltrivated
C. Cultivated D. Caltivated

47. A. Praiceworthy B. Peiseworthy
C. Praiseworthy D. Praisaworthy

48. A. Profesional B. Professionel
C. Professional D. Profissional

49. A. Ameteur B. Amateur
C. Amataur D. Amateor

50. A. Unfevourable B. Unfevaurable
C. Unfavourable D. Unfivourable

ANSWERS

1	2	3	4	5	6	7	8	9	10
A	C	A	B	B	A	B	D	D	C
11	**12**	**13**	**14**	**15**	**16**	**17**	**18**	**19**	**20**
A	B	A	A	C	A	A	A	C	A
21	**22**	**23**	**24**	**25**	**26**	**27**	**28**	**29**	**30**
B	B	B	D	B	C	A	C	B	C
31	**32**	**33**	**34**	**35**	**36**	**37**	**38**	**39**	**40**
A	B	A	C	C	A	C	B	D	A
41	**42**	**43**	**44**	**45**	**46**	**47**	**48**	**49**	**50**
A	C	A	C	C	C	C	C	B	C

23. PUNCTUATION

Punctuation marks help us to make grammatically correct sentences.

The following pairs of sentences will bring home to you the importance of punctuation marks:

(*a*) Jack, my neighbour, is going abroad.

(*b*) Jack, my neighbour is going abroad.

The sentence (*a*) means 'Jack' is my neighbour and he is going abroad. The sentence (*b*) means that I'm telling Jack that my neighbour is going abroad.

Learn and practise the correct usage of punctuation marks.

The following are some most commonly used punctuation marks:

(*i*)	Full Stop	(.)
(*ii*)	Note of Interrogation	(?)
(*iii*)	Note of Exclamation	(!)
(*iv*)	Comma	(,)
(*v*)	Inverted commas	(" ")
(*vi*)	Apostrophe	(')
(*vii*)	Capital Letters	(A)
(*viii*)	Colon	(:)
(*ix*)	Semicolon	(;)
(*x*)	Dash	(–)
(*xi*)	Oblique	(/)
(*xii*)	Parentheses	( )
(*xiii*)	Hyphen	(-)

MULTIPLE CHOICE QUESTIONS

Directions: *In the questions given below, which one alternative out of four has been applied with correct punctuation marks?*

1. When mankind passed through the grunt-and-groan stage and language had been invented everyone was happy

A. When mankind passed through the grunt-and-groan stage, and language had been invented, everyone was happy.

B. When, mankind passed through the grunt-and-groan stage, and language had been invented everyone was happy.

C. When mankind passed, through the grunt-and-groan stage and language had been invented everyone was happy.

D. When mankind, passed through the grunt-and-groan stage and language had been invented everyone was happy.

2. Communication has been established they said and now we can understand each other

A. Communication has been established, they said and now, we can understand each other.

B. ''Communication has been established,'' they said, ''and now we can understand each other.''

C. Communication has been established, they said, "and now we can understand, each other."

D. "Communication has been established" they said and now we can understand each other.

3. Then writing was developed so that words could be given some durability

A. Then, writing was developed so that words could be given some durability.

B. Then writing was developed, so that words could be given some durability.

C. Then writing was developed so that words could be given some durability.
D. Then writing was developed, so that words could be given, some durability.

4. How wonderful everyone exclaimed now we can read and write
A. How wonderful! everyone exclaimed, now we can read and write.
B. How wonderful everyone exclaimed! now we can read and write.
C. "How wonderful everyone exclaimed!" now we can read and write.
D. ''How wonderful!'' everyone exclaimed, ''Now we can read and write.''

5. But then they began to have difficulty understanding what was written down because everything seemed to run together
A. But then they began to have difficulty understanding what was written down, because everything seemed to run together.
B. But, then they began to have difficulty understanding, what was written down? because everything seemed to run together.
C. But then, they began to have difficulty understanding–what was written down? because everything seemed to run together.
D. But then they began to have difficulty, understanding what was written down because, everything seemed to run together.

6. How confusing they complained
A. "How confusing, they complained!"
B. "How confusing!" they complained.
C. "How confusing" they complained.
D. "How confusing?" they complained.

7. So they invented sentences phrases clauses and punctuation
A. So, they invented sentences phrases clauses and punctuation.
B. So they, invented sentences phrases clauses and punctuation.
C. So they invented sentences, phrases, clauses and punctuation.
D. So they invented, sentences, phrases, clauses and punctuation.

8. Now they stated gleefully we can set our thoughts down read them and understand just what is meant
A. Now, they stated gleefully, "we can set our thoughts down, read them and understand just what is meant.
B. Now, they stated, "gleefully we can set our thoughts down read them and understand just what is meant."
C. Now they stated gleefully, "we can set our thoughts down read them and understand," just what is meant.
D. ''Now,'' they stated gleefully, ''we can set our thoughts down, read them and understand just what is meant.''

9. Will you lend me ten rupees said sarla yes i will promila replied
A. "Will you lend me ten rupees?" said Sarla. "Yes, i will," promila replied.
B. "Will you lend me ten rupees," said Sarla. 'Yes, I will' Promila replied.
C. 'Will you lend me ten rupees?' said Sarla 'Yes, I will,' Promila replied.
D. "Will you lend me ten rupees?" said Sarla. "Yes, I will," Promila replied.

10. You are a thief policeman said the thief you asked for a bribe
A. "You are a thief!" policeman said, the thief, "You asked for a bribe."
B. "You are a thief policeman!" said the thief, You asked for a bribe.
C. "You are a thief policeman!" said, the thief, 'you asked for a bribe.'
D. "You are a thief, policeman!" said the thief, "You asked for a bribe."

ANSWERS

1	2	3	4	5	6	7	8	9	10
A	B	C	D	A	B	C	D	D	D

Computer Knowledge

COMPUTER KNOWLEDGE

INTRODUCTION

The term computer is derived from the Latin word compute, which means to calculate. A computer is an electronic machine, devised for performing calculations and controlling operations that can be expressed either in logical or numerical terms. In simple terms, a computer is an electronic device that performs diverse operations with the help of instructions to process the information in order to achieve the desired results. A Computer application extends to cover huge area including education, industries, government, medicine, scientific research etc.

A computer is one of the most influential forces available in modern times. Due to its memory, high speed and perfection, its application can be extended to almost infinite levels. Millions of complex calculations can be done in mere fraction of time. Difficult decisions can be made with accuracy for comparatively little cost. Computers are widely seen as instruments for future progress and as tools to achieve substantiality by way of improved access to information by means of video conferencing and e-mail. Indeed computers have left such on impression on modern civilization that we call this era as the information age.

CHARACTERISTICS OF COMPUTERS

The main characteristics of computers are:

(a) Speed　　*(b)* Storage
(c) Accuracy　　*(d)* Versatility
(e) Automation　　*(f)* Reliability

(a) **Speed :** Today's computers, according to their class, can perform from 4 MIPS (Millions of instructions per second) to 100 MIPS. What may take days for manual calculations may take only a few hours for computers to perform. Inside the computer the information signal travels at incredible electronic speed.

(b) **Storage:** This is expressed in terms of Kilobytes (or) Mega Bytes (MB) or Gega Bytes (GB) or Tera Bytes (TB). It is expressed as 'Main memory' or 'Primary storage' and through 'Auxiliary storage' or 'Secondary storage'. The Hard disks Floppy disk, Compact Disc (CD) and Magnetic Tape storage are examples of secondary storages.

(c) **Accuracy:** The accuracy of a Computer is consistently high. In fact, this quality of the computers make them indispensable in various fields such as Scientific Research, Space Research, Weather Predictions and many other areas where precision of a high order is required.

(d) **Versatility:** Computers are versatile in that they can perform almost any task, provided they are given the appropriate logical steps. For example, they are capable of performing wide ranging tasks such as construction of a payroll, inventory management in a factory, hotel billing, hospital management, banking applications and any imaginable task in every walk of life.

(e) **Automation:** The biggest advantage of computers is that it is automatic in its operation. Once a programming logic is initiated the computer performs repeated operations without human interventions until program completion.

(f) **Reliability:** The computers give very accurate results with predetermined values. They correct and modify the parameters automatically, giving suitable signals. They give formatted results with high degree of precisions.

HISTORY OF COMPUTERS

Abacus

Abacus was probably the earliest of counting devices. It consists of rectangular wooden frame with two compartments and beads sliding along the steel wires for counting. Multiplication and divisions are done using repeated additions and subtractions. Even today in which cross strings are fixed. Beads are inserted on to the strings. There are a number of rows of beads.

Pascal's calculator

A French mathematician, Blaise Pascal invented a machine based on gear wheels. He was the son of tax collector who had to do lot of calculations as part of his job. Blaise Pascal wanted to make his job easier by inventing a calculator. You might be familiar with gear wheels in use in your bicycle which meshes with a driving chain. He used similar gear wheels with ten teeth for each digit position. He fixed them together so that one wheel drives the other. When the wheel corresponding to units position rotated by ten teeth, it drove the wheel corresponding to the next higher position by one tooth. Thus one could make calculations. Pascal provided dials, which indicated numbers stored on each wheel. He also used suitable "dialing system" to operate the gear wheels. Other people also made a number of such calculators.

Babbage difference and Analytical Engines

Babbage, a British National and the son of a wealthy banker wanted to correct the errors in the logarithm tables being used during his time. In 1822, he made a machine which calculated the successive difference of expressions ($x^2 + ax + b$ is an example of an expression) and prepared table which helped him in his calculations. He wanted to make an accurate calculating machine called "Babbage's Analytical Engine". He conceived that his machine would use input devices, would have a processing part called "mill" where you can perform calculations, would also incorporate. Because of his contributions Charles Babbage is Known as the 'Father of Computing'.

Herman Hollerith's Machine

Dr. Herman Hollerith produced cards out of special paper pulp, designed punching machines to punch holes in the card to count census figures and invented sorting machines to read such punched card and collect data. He could complete the job within three years, achieving a speedup of about three times.

ABC Computer

In 1937, Dr. John Atanstoff with the help of his assistant Berry designed the Atanstoff Berry Computer (ABC). The machine laid the foundation for the development of electronic digital computer.

ENIAC- Electronic Numerical Integrator and Calculator

In 1947 John Mauchly and Eckart completed the first large scale Electronic Digital Computer, ENIAC. In this computer, each time a program was changed, the wiring had to be completely rearranged. It weighed 30 tons, contained 18,000 vacuum tubes and occupied a space of 30 50 feet.

UNIVAC-I – Universal Automatic Computers

In 1947, after ENIAC became operational Mauchly and Eckart formed their own Company- The Eckart-Mauchly Computer Corporation". Immediately after this they started the design of UNIVAC-I. This was purchased by US bureau of Census. UNIVAC was the first computer dedicated to business applications.

COMPUTER SYSTEM

A computer system is a combination of various components. It performs the system functions such as input, processing, output, storage and control. A computer system consists of the following components:

1. Hardware
2. Software

Hardware

The physical components of the computer, such as electrical, electronics and mechanical unit are known as the hardware of the computer. That is, the input units, output units and CPU are called hardware. Thus hardware is the equipment involved in the function of a computer. It consists of the components that can be physically handled.

Software

The computer performs operations like addition, subtraction, multiplication and division only when the user instructs it to do so. The user issues instructions and the CPU acts in accordance with the instructions. The sets of instructions, which control the sequence of operations, are known as programs, and collectively programs are called software. The software can be broadly classified into two types. They are: (a) System Software (b) Application Software.

Few terms related to software are :

Firmware

The computer programs permanently stored in ROM or PROM are called firmware. These programs are provided by hardware manufacturer along with the computers. Generally these are booting programs which help in the starting of a computer. Such programs cannot be erased or overwritten.

Bridge ware

The computer components and programs used to translate instructions and information written for one type of computer into a format that another type of computer can understand is called bridge ware. This is necessary because different computers are made by different manufacturers.

Freeware

This is freely available in market. Anybody can use this without any license.

GENERATIONS OF COMPTUERS

First Generation (1940-1956) : Vacuum Tubes

These computers used vacuum tubes for circuitry and magnetic drums for memory. A magnetic drum is a metal cylinder coated with magnetic iron-oxide material on which data and programs can be stored. Input was based on punched cards and paper tape, and output was displayed on printouts.

First generation computers relied on binary-coded language (language of 0s and 1s) to perform operations and were able to solve only one problem at a time. Each machine was fed with different binary codes and hence were difficult to program. This resulted in lack of versatility and speed. In addition, to run on different types of computers, instructions must be rewritten or recompiled.

Examples: ENIAC, EDVAC, and UNIVAC.

Characteristics of first generations computers:

- These computers were based on vacuum tube technology.
- These computers were very large, and required a lot of space for installation.
- Since thousands of vacuum tubes were used, they generated a large amount of heat. Therefore, air conditioning was essential.
- They were very expensive to operate and used a large amount of electricity.
- Since machine language was used, these computers were difficult to program and use.
- Each individual component had to be assembled manually. Hence, commercial appeal of these computers was poor.

Second Generation Computers (1956—1963) : Transistors

In the sixties, there was lot of development in semiconductor field - a field of materials. In 1946,Willam Shockley and a few of his colleagues invented transistors, which do not need any heating to liberate electrons in addition to being smaller in size, they saved power due to the absence of heating and hence the cooling needed. The smaller size resulted in smaller distances that the electrons have to travel to transmit information from one part of the computer to another. Hence calculations became faster. The reliability also increased.

Characteristics of second generation computers:

- These machines were based on transistor technology.
- Assemble language was used to program computers. Hence, programming became more time efficient and less cumbersome.
- Second generation computers still required air conditioning.

Third Generation Computers (1964-early 1970s): Integrated circuits

In second generation computers, one could recognize the circuit components such as transistors, resistors and capacitors distinctly. There were physically separate or "discreet". Slowly scientists started integrating these components together so that they are not separate. They were fused into the circuits. People called it large scale integrated circuits (LSI). Computers using such components were called third generation computers. Since components were packed together more densely, the size of computers became smaller. Progra-mmers also developed more sophisticated software. By 1970, engineers developed a device called microprocessor. Lot of circuits was packed into it. Intel 4004 was one such chip.

Characteristics of third generations computers:

- ❖ These computers were based on integrated circuit (IC) technology.
- ❖ Extensive use of high-level languages became possible.
- ❖ Commercial production became easier and cheaper.

Fourth Generation Computers (Early 1970s – till date) : Micro processors

More and more circuits were packed in a microprocessor. The components were integrated further and very large scale integration (VLSI) technology revolutionized computer field further. Intel Corporation made chips such as 8080 and 8086 to be followed by 80286, 80386, 80486 and now the Pentium processor. These chips perform calculations faster. They are not only used in computers, but also in measuring devices and even in house hold devices such as washing machines.

In course of time, the cost of these computers have come down so much that even individuals bought them so they came to be known as personal computers.

Characteristics of Fourth generation computers:

- Fourth generation computers are microprocessor-based systems.
- These computers are very small.
- These machines generate negligible amount of heat, hence they do not require air conditioning.
- GUI and pointing devices enable users to learn to use the computer quickly.
- Interconnection of computers leads to better communication and resource sharing.

Fifth Generation Computers (Present and beyond) : Artificial Intelligence

Up to fourth generation, the classification was based purely on hardware. Fifth generation computers are classified based on software also. VLSI technology is used in fifth generation computers. They have large main memories. The speed is also high. In addition to all this, Fifth generation computers run software called 'expert systems'.

VARIOUS TYPES OF COMPUTER SYSTEMS

Analog Computers

The analog computers operate by measuring instead of counting. The analog computer works on the supply of continuous electrical signals. The display is also continuous. Its output is in the form of graphs.

Analog Signal: An analog signal is a continuous variable electromagnetic wave. It can consume an infinite number of voltage or current values.

Characteristics of analog computer

The analog computer has the following important characteristics:

(a) It operates by measuring.
(b) It requires physical analog.
(c) It functions on continuously varying quantities.
(d) The output is usually represented in the form of graph.
(e) In analog, the calculations are first converted in equation and later converted into electrical signals.
(f) The accuracy of the output is poor.
(g) It has limited memory space.
(h) It is not versatile. i.e., it has limited application.
(i) The speed of analog computer is low.

Digital Computers

These computers work with quantities represented as digits. They operate on discrete quantities. In digital computer, both numeric and non-numeric information are represented as strings of digits. These computers use binary codes, 0's and 1's, to represent the information. The information is given to the computer in the form of discrete electrical signals.

Characteristics of Digital Computer

The digital computer has the following characteristics:

(a) The calculations are converted into binary numbers i.e., 1s and 0s.

(b) The output is represented in the form of discrete values.
(c) It is versatile in nature and is suitable for a number of applications
(d) In digital computers , the numbers, words and symbols can be used.
(e) Its processing speed is high.
(f) It is highly suitable for business application.

ANALOG Vs DIGITAL COMPUTER

S.No.	Analog Computer	Digital Computer
1.	It requires physical analog	It functions on discrete numbers
2.	The calculations are first converted to equations and later converted into electrical signals.	The calculations are converted into binary numbers (1s and 0s)
3.	Less accurate	More accurate
4.	Less speed	High speed
5.	Lacks flexibility	Highly flexible
6.	Cannot process alpha-numberic information	Can process alpha number information
7.	Limited application	More number of applications
8.	Not suitable for business applications	Highly suitable for business applications

Hybrid Computers

The computer which possess the features of both analog and digital computers are called hybrid computers. That is, the hybrid computers have the good qualities of both analog and digital computer.

Micro Computers

Because of its small size and the use of micro-processor, this computer is called micro computer. All the computers have three units namely input, output and central processing unit, (CPU). The entire CPU is contained in a single or a few microchips. When equipped with memory and input/output control circuitry, it is called micro computer. Its storage capacity is low when compared to mini and main frame computers. It is able to accept most of the high level languages. Large numbers of these can be packed tightly on to a single tiny piece of silicon. Silicon is a material found in sand. The microchip is made by building up a series of very thin layers of silicon and of the tiny components which are held in it.

Workstation

Workstation is a type of computer used for engineering applications (CAD/ CAM), desk top publishing, software development, and other types of applications that required a moderate amount of computing power and relatively high quality graphics capabilities. Workstations generally come with a large, high-resolution graphics screen, at least 64MB (Mega bytes) of RAM, built - in network support, and a graphical user interface. Most workstations also have a mass storage device such as a disk drive, but a special type of workstation, called a diskless workstation, comes without a disk drive. The most common operating systems for workstations are UNIX and Windows NT.

Mini Computers

The size of the mini-computer is in between the size of micro and main frame computers. It is more powerful than a micro computer. Mini computers are usually designed to serve multiple users.

Characteristics

1. It is a general purpose machine with a smaller CPU than a main frame
2. Its rate of acceptance and transfer of data is a maximum of 4 million bytes/seconds
3. It can support all high level languages
4. It can support many terminals i.e., more than 20 terminals

Super Computers

The super computers are very costly. Hence it is rarely used. Its capacity is abnormally high, it cannot be compared with any other computers in capacity, function, speed, accuracy, language etc., they have operations done in parallel, rather than sequential. They are employed for specialized applications that require immense amounts of mathematical calculations. The chief difference between a super computer and a main frame computer is that a super computer channels all its power into executing a few programs as fast as possible. But main frame uses its power to execute many programs concurrently. CRAY - 3, Cyber 205, and PARAM are some well known super computers.

Characteristics

(a) They use several processors working simultaneously.
(b) They process at a rapid speed.

(c) They have operations done in parallel, rather than sequentially. They are used in weather forecasting, supersonic aircrafts design and other works that require billions of calculations per second.
(d) They can be used for animated graphics-fluid dynamic calculations etc.,

Laptop

This is a small mobile computer, which usually weighs 2-18 pounds (1-6 kilograms), depending on size, materials, and other factors.

As personal computers, laptops are capable of the same tasks as a desktop computer. They contain components that are similar to their desktop counterparts and perform the same functions, but are miniaturized and optimized for mobile use and efficient power consumption.

BASIC PRINCIPLES OF OPERATION OF DIGITAL COMPUTER

A computer is basically a device used for processing of data, it performs the following three operations in sequence:

(a) Receives the data and instruction.
(b) Processes the data as per the instructions.
(c) Output the result i.e., information.

This cycle of operation of a computer is known as the input process - Output cycle.

The data are provided to the computer through the input devices. They are encoding such a way, which the computer can understand. The computer then processes the data with the help of instructions provided to it, then it produces a meaningful and desired output known as information.

The above functions are collectively known as the basic principles of operation of a digital computer. These can be expanded as follows:

(a) Accepting inputs
(b) Memory manipulation
(c) Arithmetic operations
(d) Decision making and
(e) Giving output

INPUT/OUTPUT DEVICES

INPUT DEVICES

An input device is any machine that feeds data into a computer. For example, a keyboard is an input device. Input devices other than the keyboard are sometimes called alternate devices. Trackballs and light pens are all alternate input devices.

Keyboard

Computer keyboards are similar to electric-typewriter keyboards but contain additional keys. The keys on computer keyboards are often classified as follows:

- **Alphanumeric Keys:** letters and numbers.
- **Punctuation Keys:** comma, period, semicolon, and so on.
- **Special Keys:** function keys, control keys, arrow keys, Caps Lock key, and so on.

The standard layout of letters, numbers, and punctuation is known as a QWERTY keyboard because the first five keys on the top row of letters spell QWERTY. Another keyboard design, which has letters positioned for speed typing, is the Dvorak keyboard.

There is no standard computer keyboard, although many manufacturers imitate the standards of PCs. There are actually three different PC standards: the original PC keyboard, with 84 keys; the AT keyboard, also with 84 keys; and the enhanced keyboard, with 101 keys. The three differ somewhat in placement of Function keys, the Control key, the Return key, and the Shift keys.

Mouse

Mouse is a device that controls the movement of the cursor or pointer on a display screen. Its name is derived from its shape, which looks a bit like a mouse, its connecting wire that one can imagine to be the mouse's tail, and the fact that one must make it scurry along a surface. As we move the mouse, the pointer on the display screen moves in the same direction. Mouse contains at least one button and sometimes as many as three, which have different functions depending on what program is running. Now-a-days, mouse is connected with computer through USB port.

Invented by Douglas Engelbart of Stanford Research Center in 1963.

Types of Mouse: There are three basic types of Mouse.

- **Mechanical:** It has a rubber or metal ball on its underside that can roll in all directions.

Mechanical sensors within the mouse detect the direction the ball is rolling and move the Screen pointer accordingly.

- **Optomechanical:** It is same as a mechanical mouse, but uses optical sensors to detect motion of the ball.
- **Optical:** It does a laser to detect the mouse's movement. One must move the mouse along a special mat with a grid so that the optical mechanism has a frame of reference. Optical mice have no mechanical moving parts. They respond more quickly and precisely than mechanical and optomechanical mice, but they are also more expensive.

Trackball

This is another pointing device. Essentially, a trackball is a mouse lying on its back. To move the pointer, we rotate the ball with our thumb, our fingers, or the palm of our hand. There are usually one to three buttons next to the ball, which we use just like mouse buttons.

Joystick

With a joystick, the pointer continues moving in the direction the joystick is pointing. Most joysticks include two buttons called triggers. It has a lever that moves in all directions and controls the movement of a pointer or some other display symbols. A joystick is similar to a mouse, except that with a mouse the cursor stops moving as soon as we stop moving the mouse. Joysticks are used mostly for computer games, but they are also used occasionally for CAD/CAM systems and other applications.

Scanners

Scanner is an input device that can read text or illustrations printed on paper and translate the information into a form that the computer can use. A scanner works by digitizing an image-dividing it into a grid of boxes and representing each box with either a zero or a one, depending on whether the box is filled in. The resulting matrix of bits, called a bit map, can then be stored in a file, displayed on a screen, and manipulated by programs.

Optical scanners do not distinguish text from illustrations; they represent all images as bit maps. Therefore, we cannot directly edit text that has been scanned. To edit text read by an optical scanner, we need an Optical Character Recognition (OCR) system to translate the image into ASCII characters.

Magnetic Ink Character Recognition [MICR]

This allows the computer to recognize characters printed using magnetic ink. MICR is a direct-entry method used in banks. This technology is used to automatically read those frustrating-looking numbers on the bottom of the cheque. A special-purpose machine known as a reader/sorter reads characters made of ink containing magnetized particles. A related technology is the magnetic strip, used on the back of credit cards and bank debit cards, that allows readers such as Automated Teller Machines (ATMs) to read account information and facilitate monetary transactions. Another example of magnetic strip technology is in ID cards, which can be used for a variety of functions from attendance monitoring to restricting access to specific locations.

Optical Character Recognition [OCR]

It refers to the branch of computer science that involves reading text from paper and translating the images into a form that the computer can manipulate. An OCR system enables to take a book or a magazine article and feed it directly into an electronic computer file.

All OCR systems include an optical scanner for reading text, and a sophisticated software for analyzing images. Most OCR systems use a combination of hardware (specialized circuit boards) and software to recognize characters, although some inexpensive systems do it entirely through software. Advanced OCR systems can read text in a large variety of fonts, but they still have difficulty with handwritten text.

The potential of OCR systems is enormous because they enable users to harness the power of computers to access printed documents. OCR is already being used widely in the legal profession, where searches that once required hours or days can now be accomplished in a few seconds.

Optical Mark Recognition [OMR]

OMR also called mark sensing, is a technology where an OMR device senses the presence or absence of a mark, such as a pencil mark. OMR is used in tests such as aptitude tests for different competition/ entrance examinations.

Bar Code Reader

Most of the persons are probably familiar with the bar code readers in supermarkets, bookshops, etc. Bar-code readers are photoelectric scanners that read the bar codes, or vertical zebra striped marks, printed on product containers. Supermarkets use a bar code system called the Universal Product Code (UPC).

The bar code identifies the product to the supermarket's computer, which has a description and the latest price of the product. The computer automatically tells the Point of Sales (POS) terminal what the price is.

Touch Screen

Touch screen is a type of display screen that has a touch sensitive transparent panel covering the screen. Instead of using a pointing device such as a mouse or light pen, we can use our finger to point directly to objects on the screen.

Light Pen

Light Pen is an input device that utilizes a light-sensitive detector to select objects on a display screen. A light Pen is similar to a mouse, except that with a light pen we can move the pointer and select objects on a display screen by directly pointing to the objects by light pen.

OUTPUT DEVICES

Output is anything that comes out of a computer. Output can be meaningful information or gibberish, and it can appear in a variety of forms - as binary numbers, as characters, as pictures, and as printed pages. Output devices include display screens, loudspeakers, printers, plotters, etc.

Monitor

Monitor is another term for the display screen. The term monitor, however, usually refers to the entire box, whereas display screen can mean just the screen. In addition, the term monitor often implies graphics capabilities.

Classification of Monitors: There are many ways to classify monitors.

(i) **Based on Color:** The most basic in terms of color capabilities.

(ii) **Based on Signals:** Another common way of classifying monitors is in terms of the type of signal they accept: analog or digital.

- **Digital Monitor:** A digital monitor accepts digital signals rather than analog signals. A digital monitor then translates the digital signals into analog signals that control the actual display.

  Although digital monitors are fast and produce clear images, they cannot display variable colors continuously.

- **Analog Monitor:** This is the traditional type of color display screen that has been used for years in televisions. In reality, all monitors based on CRT technology (that is, all monitors except flat-panel displays) are analog. Some monitors, however, are called digital monitors because they accept digital signals from the video adapter. EGA monitors, for example, must be digital because the EGA standard specifies digital signals. Digital monitors must nevertheless translate the signals into an analog form before displaying images.

Printer

Printer is a device that prints text or illustrations on paper and in many cases on transparencies and other media. There are many different types of printers. In terms of the technology utilized, printers fall into the following categories:

(i) **Daisy-wheel Printer:** Daisy-wheel printers are a type of printer that produces letter-quality type. A daisy-wheel printer works on the same principle as a ball-head typewriter. The daisy-wheel is a disk made of plastic or metal on which characters stand out in relief along the outer edge. To print a character, the printer rotates the disk until the desired letter is facing the paper.

(ii) **Dot-matrix Printer:** Dot-matrix printers create characters by striking pins against an ink ribbon. Each pin makes a dot, and combinations of dots form characters and illustrations.

These printers are inexpensive and relatively fast, but they do not produce high-quality output. Dot-matrix printers vary in two important characteristics:

- **Speed :** Measured in characters per second (cps), the speed can vary from about 50 to over 500 cps. Most dot-matrix printers offer different speeds depending on the quality of print desired.
- **Print quality :** Determined by the number of pins (the mechanisms that print the dots), it can vary from 9 to 24. The best dot-matrix printers (24 pins) can produce near letter-quality type, although we can still see a difference if we look closely.

(iii) Ink-jet Printer: Ink-iet printers work by spraying ionized ink at a sheet of paper. Magnetized plates in the ink's path direct the ink onto the paper in the desired shapes. Ink-jet printers are capable of producing high quality print approaching to that produced by laser printers. A typical ink-jet printer provides a resolution of 300 dots per inch, although some newer models offer higher resolutions.

(iv) Laser Printer: Laser printer utilizes a laser beam to produce an image on a drum. The light of the laser alters the electrical charge on the drum wherever it hits. The drum is then rolled through a reservoir of toner, which is picked up by the charged portions of the drum. Finally, the toner is transferred to the paper through a combination of heat and pressure. This is also the way copy machines work.

(v) WD & LED Printers: These are similar to a laser printer but uses liquid crystals or light-emitting diodes rather than a laser to produce an image on the drum.

(vi) Line Printer: Line printers are high-speed printers capable of printing an entire line at one time. A fast line printer can print as many as 3,000 lines per minute. The disadvantages of line printers are that they can print only one font, they cannot print graphics, the print quality is low, and they are very noisy.

Plotter

Plotter is a device that draws pictures on paper based on commands from a computer. Plotters differ from printers as they draw lines using a pen. As a result, they can produce continuous lines/ whereas printers can only simulate lines by printing a closely spaced series of dots. Multicolor plotters use different-colored pens to draw different colors. In general, plotters are considerably more expensive than printers. They are used in engineering applications where precision is mandatory.

Sound Cards & Speakers

Sound card is an expansion board that enables a computer to manipulate and output sounds. Sound cards enable the computer to output sound through speakers connected to the board, to record sound input from a microphone connected to the computer, and manipulate sound stored on a disk. Nearly all sound cards support MIDI, a standard for representing music electronically.

HARDWARE & SOFTWARE

A computer system consists of hardware, the physical unit (parts) of the computer that are capable of computing and manipulating information and software (set of instructions or programs) that carries out predefined tasks to complete a given job. The computer performs operations like addition, subtraction, multiplication and division only when the user instructs it to do so. The user issues instructions and the CPU acts in accordance with the instructions. The sets of instructions, which control the sequence of operations, are known as programs, and collectively programs are called software.

COMPONENTS OF HARDWARE

I. **Input unit:** This unit accepts instructions and data.

II. **Output unit:** This unit communicates the results to the user.

III. **Storage unit:** This unit stores temporary and final results.

IV. **Central Processing Unit (CPU):** This unit performs processing of instructions and data inside the computer.

The CPU has three components:

(a) The Control Unit

(b) The Arithmetic Logic Unit (ALU) and

(c) The Memory Unit.

(a) Control Unit: It controls the overall operation of the computer system. It is considered as the heart of the computer system. It controls all the other units, directs them to operate in a proper way and co-ordinates various operations performed.

It instructs the input device to transfer the data and instructions to the main memory and then to the arithmetic and logic unit (ALU). Then, it sends the processed result from ALU to the memory unit for storage and transfers it to the visual display unit or to the printer.

The control unit coordinates the various parts of the computer system - the arithmetic logic unit, the memory unit and the peripheral units. Besides, it controls the flow of data into, from and within the main storage as per the program instructions.

To perform its control operations effectively and quickly, the control unit has four basic components. They are

(i) Instruction Register
(ii) Decoder
(iii) Address Register and
(iv) Instruction Counter

The instruction register receives one by one the instructions to be executed in the required sequence. Then, the operation code of the instructions is transferred to decoder, which decodes the operation code. And it activates the appropriate circuits of the arithmetic and logic unit to perform the operation. The address register enables the data in the location specified in the instruction to be transferred to a specified accumulator for the arithmetic and logic unit.

(b) Arithmetic Logic Unit (ALU): This unit performs two kinds of operations, the arithmetic processing and logical processing. In arithmetic processing, it performs all mathematical operations such as addition, subtraction, multiplication and division. In logical processing, it performs the relational and logical operations such as comparing larger or smaller values, true or false statements, etc.

(c) Memory Unit: This unit holds the intermediate results during the course of calculations and provides the data as and when required. This internal storage is also called primary memory or main memory. This memory takes the data from an input device and stores it until the computer is ready to process it. It also stores processed data and intermediate results. When the processing is finished, it transfers the results to an output device.

SOFTWARE

Software is a generic term for organized collection of computer data and instructions. It is responsible for controlling, integrating, and managing the hardware components of a computer and to accomplish specific tasks. In other words, software tells the computer what to do and how to do it. For example, software instructs the hardware what to display on the user's screen, what kinds of input to take from the user, and what kinds of output to generate. Thus, software communicates with the hardware by organizing the control sequences, and the hardware carries out the instructions defined by the software.

A computer needs to be instructed to perform any task. These instructions are given in the form of computer programs, which are written in computer programming languages. A program controls the activity of the processor. The moment the hardware (processor, memory, etc.) acts as per the instructions of a program, the program is said to be in running or executing state.

A set of programs, which are specifically written to provide the user a precise functionality like solving a specific problem is termed as a software package. For example, word processing software package provides functionality to the computer so that it can be used to create text documents like letters and mailing lists. Similarly, an image processing software package assists a user in drawing and manipulating graphics.

DIFFERENCE BETWEEN HARDWARE & SOFTWARE

Hardware

1. It is the physical unit of the computer
2. Hardware understands only machine language, lower level language or binary
3. It works with binary code, the presence or absence of Pulses as 1's or 0's.

Software

1. It is a collection of programs to bring the hardware system into operation

2. It is written by a well versed programmer and generally in higher level language which is readable by human being.
3. It is represented by the Higher Level Languages such as BASIC, COBOL, Etc.,

COMPUTER MEMORY

There are two kinds of computer memory: primary and secondary. Primary memory is accessible directly by the processing unit. RAM is an example of primary memory. As soon as the computer is switched off the contents of the primary memory is lost. You can store and retrieve data much faster with primary memory compared to secondary memory. Secondary memory such as floppy disks, magnetic disk, etc., is located outside the computer. Primary memory is more expensive than secondary memory. Because of this the size of primary memory is less than that of secondary memory.

Computer memory is used to store two things: (i) instructions to execute a program and (ii) data. When the computer is doing any job, the data that have to be processed are stored in the primary memory. This data may come from an input device like keyboard or from a secondary storage device like a floppy disk. In computer's memory both programs and data are stored in the binary form.

PRIMARY MEMORY

The primary memory as you know in the computer is in the form of IC's (Integrated Circuits). These circuits are called Random Access Memory (RAM). A bit is an acronym for binary digit, which stands for one binary piece of information. This can be either 0 or 1. The Primary or internal storage section is made up of several small storage locations (ICs) called cells. Each of these cells can store a fixed number of bits called word length. Each cell has a unique number assigned to it called the address of the cell and it is used to identify the cells.

Capacity of Primary Memory

Each cell of memory contains one character or 1 byte of data. So the capacity is defined in terms of byte or words. Thus 64 kilobyte (KB) memory is capable of storing 64 × 1024 = 65,536 bytes. (1 kilobyte is 1024 bytes). A memory size ranges from few kilobytes in small systems to several thousand kilobytes in large mainframe and super computer.

Types of Primary Memory

Random Access Memory (RAM): The primary storage is referred to as random access memory (RAM) because it is possible to randomly select and use any location of the memory directly store and retrieve data. It takes same time to any address of the memory as the first address. It is also called read/write memory. The storage of data and instructions inside the primary storage is temporary. It disappears from RAM as soon as the power to the computer is switched off. The memories, which loose their content on failure of power supply, are known as volatile memories. So, now we can say that RAM is volatile memory.

Read Only Memory (ROM): There is another memory in computer, which is called Read Only Memory (ROM). Again it is the ICs inside the PC that form the ROM. The storage of program and data in the ROM is permanent. The ROM stores some standard processing programs supplied by the manufacturers to operate the personal computer. The ROM can only be read by the CPU but it cannot be changed. The basic input/output program is stored in the ROM that examines and initializes various equipment attached to the PC when the switch is made ON. The memories, which do not loose their content on failure of power supply, are known as non-volatile memories. ROM is non-volatile memory.

Programmable Read Only Memory (PROM): There is another type of primary memory in computer, which is called Programmable Read Only Memory (PROM). You know that it is not possible to modify or erase programs stored in ROM, but it is possible for you to store your program in PROM chip. Once the programmes are written it cannot be changed and remain intact even if power is switched off. Therefore programs or instructions written in PROM or ROM cannot be erased or changed.

Erasable Programmable Read Only Memory (EPROM): This stands for Erasable Programmable Read Only Memory, which over come the problem of PROM & ROM. EPROM chip can be programmed time and again by erasing the information stored earlier in it. Information stored in EPROM exposing the chip for some time ultraviolet light and it erases chip is reprogrammed using a special programming facility. When the EPROM is in use information can only be read.

Cache Memory

The speed of CPU is extremely high compared to the access time of main memory. Therefore the performance of CPU decreases due to the slow speed of main memory. To decrease the mismatch in operating speed, a small memory chip is attached between CPU and Main memory whose access time is very close to the processing speed of CPU. It is called CACHE memory. CACHE memories are accessed much faster than conventional RAM. It is used to store programs or data currently being executed or temporary data frequently used by the CPU.

Registers

The CPU processes data and instructions with high speed, there is also movement of data between various units of computer. It is necessary to transfer the processed data with high speed. So the computer uses a number of special memory units called registers. They are not part of the main memory but they store data or information temporarily and pass it on as directed by the control unit.

SECONDARY MEMORY

Therefore additional memory is required in all the computer systems. This memory is called auxiliary memory or secondary storage.

In this type of memory the cost per bit of storage is low. However, the operating speed is slower than that of the primary storage. Huge volume of data are stored here on permanent basis and transferred to the primary storage as and when required. Most widely used secondary storage devices are magnetic tapes and magnetic disk.

Magnetic Tape

Magnetic tapes are used for large computers like mainframe computers where large volume of data is stored for a longer time. In PC also you can use tapes in the form of cassettes. It can be 12.5 mm to 25 mm wide plastic film-type and 500 meter to 1200 meter long which is coated with magnetic material. It is similar to cassette tape recorder.

Magnetic Disk

Magnetic disks used in computer are made on the same principle. It rotates with very high speed inside the computer drive. Data is stored on both the surface of the disk. Magnetic disks are most popular for direct access storage device. Each disk consists of a number of invisible concentric circles called tracks. Information is recorded on tracks of a disk surface in the form of tiny magnetic spots.

Floppy Disk

It is similar to magnetic disk discussed. They are 5.25 inch or 3.5 inch in diameter. They come in single or double density and recorded on one or both surface of the diskette. The capacity of a 5.25-inch floppy is 1.2 mega bytes whereas for 3.5 inch floppy it is 1.44 mega bytes. It is cheaper than any other storage devices and is portable. The floppy is a low cost device particularly suitable for personal computer system.

Optical Disk

With every new application and software there is greater demand for memory capacity. It is the necessity to store large volume of data that has led to the development of optical disk storage medium. Optical disks can be divided into the following categories:

1. **Compact Disk/ Read Only Memory (CD-ROM):** CD-ROM disks are made of reflective metals. CD-ROM is written during the process of manufacturing by high power laser beam. Here the storage density is very high, storage cost is very low and access time is relatively fast. Each disk is approximately 4 1/2 inches in diameter and can hold over 600 MB of data. As the CD-ROM can be read only we cannot write or make changes into the data contained in it.
2. **Erasable Optical Disk:** These are optical disks where data can be written, erased and re-written. This also applies a laser beam to write and re-write the data. These disks may be used as alternatives to traditional disks. Erasable optical disks are based on a technology known as

magnetic optical (MO). To write a data bit on to the erasable optical disk the MO drive's laser beam heats a tiny, precisely defined point on the disk's surface and magnetises it.

CENTRAL PROCESSING UNIT [CPU]

The Central Processing Unit [CPU] is the brain of any computer system. In a computer system all major calculations and comparisons are made inside the CPU. The CPU is also responsible for activating and controlling the operations of other units of a computer system.

The control unit primary memory and the arithmetic logic unit of a computer system are jointly known as the Central Processing Unit. While the control unit takes care of the flow of data from input unit to storage unit and the flow of final results to the output unit, the arithmetic logic unit is the place where the actual execution of instructions taking place during the processing operation.

SOFTWARE

The computer being a machine cannot perform on its own. It needs to be instructed to perform even a simple task like adding two numbers. Computers work on a set of instructions called computer software (programs), which clearly specify the ways to carry out a task. Software can be categorized as system software and application software. System software is a generic term for referring to any computer program whose purpose is to help the user to run the computer system, whereas application software employes the capabilities of a computer directly to a task that the user wishes to perform.

CATEGORIES OF SOFTWARE

System Software

System software consists of several programs, which are directly responsible for controlling, integrating, and managing the individual hardware components of a computer system.

In simple terms, system software makes the computer functional. They provide basic functionality like file management, visual display, and keyboard input which are used by application software to accomplish these functions. Some examples of system software are:

1. OPERATING SYSTEM
2. DEVICE DRIVERS
3. LANGUAGE TRANSLATORS
4. SYSTEM UTILITIES

1. Operating System

It is the first layer of software loaded into computer memory when it starts up. As the first software layer, all other software that gets loaded after it depends on it for various common core services. These common core services include disk access, memory management, takes scheduling, and user interfacing. In addition, the operating system ensures that different programs executing at the same time do not interfere with each other. It provides a software platform on top of which other programs can run. In simple words, the operating system organizes and controls the hardware. Examples of operating systems are Windows XP, UNIX, and LINUX. The basic functions of an operating system are:

(*a*) Process Management: It handles the creation, deletion, suspension, resumption, and synchronization of process.

(*b*) Memory Management: It handles allocation and de-allocation of memory space as required by various programs.

(*c*) File Management: It is responsible for creation and deletion of files and directories. It also organizes, stores, retrieves, names, and protects all the files.

(*d*) Device Management: It manages all the devices of the computer system such as printers and modems. If any device fails, it detects the device failure and notifies the same to the user.

(*e*) Security Management: Protects system resources and information against destruction and unauthorized use.

(*f*) User interface: Provides the interface between the user and the hardware.

2. Device Drivers

Device drivers are system programs, which are responsible for proper functioning of devices. Every device, whether it is a printer, monitor, mouse or keyboard, has a driver program associated with it for its proper functioning.

4. System Utility

System utility programs perform day-to-day tasks related to the maintenance of the computer system. They are used to support, enhance, and secure existing programs and data in the computer system. They are generally small programs, having specific tasks to perform:

(a) ***File Management:*** These utilities make it easier to manage data files. Many programs are written to help users to find the files, create and organize directions, copy, move, and remove files.

(b) ***Backup:*** It may happen that sometime data files are corrupted, or accidentally deleted. In such a case, data backups become very useful. A backup system utility is essential for those organizations, which want to keep their data intact.

(c) ***Data Recovery:*** It is the process of retrieving deleted or inaccessible data from failed electronic storage media such as computer hard disk drives, removable media, optical devices, and tape cartridges.

(d) ***Virus Protection:*** Anti-virus programs are essential system utilities for a computer system functioning in a network. They provide the security to the system from viruses that can damage the computer system.

(e) ***Disk Management:*** Disk management program includes various system softwares like disk defragmenter, data compressor and disk formatting tools. De-fragmentation implies putting fragments of files in a sequential order onto the disk which reduces the time to access the file.

(f) ***Firewall:*** It is commonly used to protect information such as e-mail and data files within a physical building or organization. Essentially, a firewall is designed to protect a computer from unauthorized access, especially via network.

(g) ***Disk Cleanup:*** To keep a computer running smoothly, regular maintenance is vital. Therefore, one should use the disk cleanup utility, which easily determines which files on hard drive are no longer needed, then delete those files.

APPLICATION SOFTWARE

The most often seen software by a user is the application software. It is used to accomplish specific tasks rather than just managing a computer system. For a user, the computer system has no specific use without application software. Application software may consist of a single program, such as Microsoft's Note pad (for writing and editing simple text). It may also consist of a collection of programs, often called a software package, which work together to accomplish a task, such as database management software. Application software may also include a larger collection of related but independent programs and packages (a software suite), which have a common user interface or shared data format, such as Microsoft Office suite.

Applications softwares are dependent on system softwares. A system software (like operating system) acts as an interface between the user and the computer hardware, while application software performs specific tasks. Applications are pieces of software that perform tasks for the user besides helping the computer operate, which is the tasks of system software. Applications softwares are controlled by system software, which manages hardware devices and performs background tasks for them. The distinction between the two is important. Without system software, the computer will not run, and without application software, the computer, no matter how powerful, will not be helpful in meeting user requirements. Think of it this way applications apply the computer's thinking power to business tasks such as tracking the general ledger or billing your customers.

Application software ranges from games, calculators, and word processors (document creating programs), to programs that "paint" images on screen (image editors). Applications represent real world tasks. They can be easily divided by looking at exactly what function they serve. Some of the most commonly used application software is discussed below:

1. Word processor

A word processor is software used to compose, format, edit, and print electronic documents. Word processing is one of the earliest applications for office productivity and the personal computer. It involves not only typing, but also checking the spelling and grammar of the text and arranging it correctly on the page.

WORD KEYBOARD SHORTCUTS

Action	Key Stroke
Open a file	Ctrl + O
New file	Ctrl + N
Close a file	Ctrl + W
Save As	F12
Save	Ctrl+S or Shift+F12
Print Preview	Ctrl + F2
Print	Ctrl + P
Show/Hide paragraph symbols	Ctrl + *
Spelling and grammar	F7
Help	F1
Find	Ctrl + F
Replace	Ctrl + H
Go To	Ctrl + G
Select all - entire document	Ctrl + A
Select from cursor to beginning of line	Shift + Home
Select from cursor to end of line	Shift + End
Go to beginning of line	Home
Go to end of line	End
Go to beginning of document	Ctrl + Home
Go to end of document	Ctrl + End
Cut	Ctrl + X
Copy	Ctrl + C
Paste	Ctrl + V
Undo	Ctrl + Z
Redo	Ctrl + Y
Format painter	Ctrl + Shift + C
Left alignment	Ctrl + L
Center alignment	Ctrl + E
Right alignment	Ctrl + R
Justified	Ctrl + J

Action	Key Stroke
Delete previous word	Ctrl + Backspace
Apply bulleted list	Ctrl + Shift + L
Indent	Ctrl + M
Page break	Ctrl + Enter
Font face	Ctrl + Shift + F
Font size	Ctrl + Shift + P
Bold	Ctrl + B
Italics	Ctrl + I
Underline	Ctrl + U
Double underline	Ctrl + Shift + D
Word underline	Ctrl + Shift + A
Change case	Shift + F3
Subscript	Ctrl + =
Superscript	Ctrl + Shift + =
Make web hyperlink	Ctrl + K
Go to next cell	Tab
Go to previous cell	Shift + Tab
Go to beginning of column	Alt + PageUp
Highlight to beginning of column	Alt + Shift + PageUp
Go to end of column	Alt + PageDown
Highlight to end of column	Alt + Shift + PageDown
Go to beginning of row	Alt + Home
Highlight to beginning of row	Alt + Shift + Home
Go to end of row	Alt + End
Highlight to end of row	Alt + Shift + End
Column break	Ctrl + Shift + Enter
Copyright ©	Alt + Ctrl + C
Date field	Alt + Shift + D
Go to footnotes	Alt + Ctrl + F
Show/Hide ¶	Ctrl + Shift + 8
Theasaurus	Shift + F7

Note: *A plus sign indicates that the keys need to be pressed at the same time.*

2. Spreadsheets

One of the first commercial uses of computers was in processing payroll and other financial records, so the programs were designed to generate reports in the standard "spreadsheet" format bookkeepers and accountants used. A spreadsheet application is a rectangular grid, which allows text, numbers, and complex functions to be entered into a matrix of thousands of individual cells. The spreadsheet provides sheets containing cells each of which may contain text and / or numbers. Microsoft Excel and Lotus 1-2-3 are examples of spreadsheet applications.

3. Database management systems

Database management software is a collection of computer programs that allow storage, modification, and extraction of information from a database in an efficient manner. It supports the structuring of the database in a standard format and provides tools for data input, verification, storage, retrieval, query, and manipulation. FoxPro and Oracle are database management systems.

OPERATING SYSTEM

It is the first layer of software loaded into computer memory when it starts up. As the first software layer, all other software that gets loaded after it depends on it for various common core services. In simple words, the operating system organizes and controls the hardware. Examples of operating systems are Windows XP, UNIX, and Linux.

The operating system is a software program that acts as an interface between the user and the computer. It is used to control and manage the hardware components such as keyboard, monitor, printer, scanner etc.

FUNCTIONS OF AN OPERATING SYSTEM

(a) **Process Management:** It handles the creation, deletion, suspension, resumption, and synchronization of process.

(b) **Memory Management:** It handles allocation and de-allocation of memory space as required by various programs.

(c) **File Management:** It is responsible for creation and deletion of files and directories. It also organizes, stores, retrieves, names, and protects all the files.

(d) **Device Management:** It manages all the devices of the computer system such as printers and modems. If any device fails, it detects the device failure and notifies the same to the user.

(e) **Security Management:** Protects system resources and information against destruction and unauthorized use.

(f) **User interface:** Provides the interface between the user and the hardware.

TYPES OF OPERATING SYSTEM

These are the different types of operating system :

DOS (Disk Operating System)

MS-DOS was the widely used operating system before the introduction of the Windows operating system. The DOS is a set of computer programs. The main functions of DOS are to manage files, allocate system resources according to the requirement.

DOS Commands

We can type all DOS commands in either upper or lower case letters. There are two basic types of DOS commands:

- **Internal commands**

  These commands, like COPY, DEL, and TYPE, are stored in computers memory. Many DOS commands fall into this category.

- **External commands**

  This group of commands is stored on the disk. To use them, either insert the DOS floppy disk, or change to the directory on hard disk which contains DOS external commands. Examples of external commands include FORMAT, DISKCOPY, and CHKDSK.

  Some commands can take several forms. These separate forms are used by including various parameters with the command. Parameters, which will be discussed with each command, are indicated by a / mark. Here is an example of command with an attached parameter:

  C:\>DIR/W

  [DOS command DIR is attached with parameter W]

  All DOS commands must be activated by pressing the <Enter> key after typing the command.

WINDOWS OPERATING SYSTEM

Microsoft Windows is the most popular operating system around the world. Even those who are new to computers can use it with a little practice. With the help of Windows, we can operate the computer just by clicking the mouse buttons, Windows95, Windows98, Windows 2000 and Windows 7 are the various versions of Windows.

Windows is an operating system. It is the extension of the disk operating system.

THE UNIX OPERATING SYSTEM

Like DOS and windows, there's another operating system called UNIX.

PROGRAMMING LANGUAGES

Computers are machines. Unfortunately they cannot understand natural languages, such as Hindi, English, Tamil, etc. that human beings speak and understand. Therefore, to give instructions to computers, different languages have been developed. These languages are called computer languages. To get a particular work done by computers, programmers write instructions using these computer languages. Each computer language has its own vocabulary of a natural language that we speak. Each natural language has its rules and grammar. Similarly, each computer language too has its set of rules that are called as syntax. As computers are not intelligent, we have to use the exact syntax rules of the computer language whenever we write any computer program. Otherwise, the computer will not be able to understand our instructions.

Over the last few decades, several computer languages have developed. Different computer languages are suitable for different applications. For example, COBOL (Common business oriented Language) may be more suitable for business applications, whereas FORTRAN may be more suitable for scientific or engineering applications. We can classify all computer languages into three categories.

PROGRAMMING LANGUAGES

Computer languages are classified into three categories:

1. Low Level Language /Machine language
2. High level languages:

Low Level Language/Machine language

The form in which information is denoted or represented by a combination of "1" and "0"s is called machine language. Programs and data are ultimately represented in machine language in memory and other hardware of the computer.

To start with computer programmers used machine language for programming. It was tedious since each operation that the computer has to perform is denoted by a particular combination of"1"s and"0"s.Also each computer had its own machine language code. One has to remember all these codes to write a program.

High Level Languages

During 1960s computers started to gain popularity and it became necessary to develop languages that were more like natural languages such as English so that a common user could use the computer efficiently. Since assembly language required deep knowledge of computer architecture, it demanded programming as well as hardware skills to use computers. Due to computer's widespread usage, early 1960s saw the emergence of the third generations programming languages (3GL). Languages such as COBOL, FORTRAN, BASIC, and C are examples of 3GLs and are considered high-level languages.

High level languages are similar to English language. Programs written using these languages can be machine independent. A single high-level statement can substitute several instructions in machine or assembly language. Unlike assembly and machine programs, highlevel programs may be used with different types of computers with little or no modification, thus reducing the re-programming time.

Translating High-level Language to machine language:

Since computers understand only machine language, it is necessary to convert the highlevel language programs into machine language codes. This is achieved by using language translators or language processors, generally known as compilers, interpreters or other routines that accepts statements in one language and produces equivalent statements in another language.

Compiler

A compiler is a kind of translator that translates a program into another program, known as target language. Usually, the term compiler is used for language translator of high-level language into machine language. The compiler replaces single high-level statement with a series of machine language instruction.

Once the program has been compiled, the resulting machine code is saved in an executable file, which can be run on its own at any time. To be precise, once the executable is generated, there is no need for the actual source code file. Anyway, it is worthwhile to keep the source file(s) because if the source code is modified, it is necessary to recompile the program again to regenerate the executable file containing amendments.

Interpreter

Unlike compilers, an interpreter translates a statement in a program and executes the statement immediately, before translating the next source language statement. Similar to compilers, every interpreted language such as BASIC and LISP has its own interpreters.

Disadvantages of High-Level Languages:

The main disadvantages of this language are:

1. **Poor Control on Hardware:** High-level languages are developed to ease the pressure on programmers so that they do not have to know the intricacies of hardware. As a result, sometimes the applications written in high-level languages cannot completely harness the total power available at hardware level.
2. **Less Efficient:** The HLL applications are less efficient as far as computation time is concerned. This is because, unlike low-level languages, high-level languages must be created and sent through another processing program known as a compiler. This process of translation increases the execution time of an application. Programs written in high-level languages take more time to execute, and require more memory space. Hence, critical applications are generally written in low-level languages.

Type of High-Level Languages

Languages are often referred to as generations, the idea being that machine languages were the first generation and assembly languages were the second generation. High-level languages are sometimes used to refer all languages above the assembly level. Here we will subdivide high-level languages into three generation.

1. Procedural-oriented or third generation
2. Problem-oriented or fourth generation
3. Natural or fifth generation

Procedural-oriented Languages

High-level languages are often classified according to whether they solve general problems or specific problems. General-purpose programming languages are called procedural languages or third generation languages. They are languages such as Pascal, BASIC, COBOL, and FORTRAN, which are designed to express the logic, the procedure, of a problem. Because of their flexibility, procedural languages are able to solve a variety of problems. Procedural languages have many advantages over machine and assembly languages:

1. The program statements resemble English and hence are easier to work with.
2. Because of their English-like nature, less time is required to develop a program for a given problem.
3. Once coded, programs are easier to understand and modify.
4. The procedural languages are machine-independent.

However, procedure-oriented languages still have some disadvantages compared to machine and assembly languages:

1. Programs are executed more slowly.
2. The languages use computer resources less efficiently.

Problem-oriented Languages and Application Generators

Third-generation languages, such as BASIC or Pascal, require you to instruct the computer in step-by-step fashion. Fourth-generation languages, also known as problem-oriented languages, are high-level languages designed to solve specific problems or develop specific applications by enabling you to describe what you want rather than step-by-step procedures for getting there. Fourth-generation languages may be categorized into several kinds of application development tools:

1. Personal computer applications software
2. Query languages and report generators
3. Decision support systems and financial planning languages
4. Application generators

Natural Languages

Two popular natural languages are LISP and PROLOG. Natural languages have two characteristics:

1. They are designed to make the connections that humans have with computers more natural - more humanlike.
2. They are designed to allow the computer to become "smarter" - to actually simulate the learning process by remembering and improving upon earlier information.

STRUCTURED QUERY LANGUAGE(SQL) AND OTHER QUERY LANGUAGES

A query language is a set of commands to create, update and access data from a database allowing users to raise adhoc queries / questions interactively without the help of programmers. A structured query language (SQL) is a set of thirty (30) English like commands which has since become an adoptable standard. The structured query language syntax use some set of commands regardless of the database management system software like 'Select','From', 'Where'.

Some query languages have been designed in such a way that the command used is as close to Standard English text as possible. Query languages in a user-friendly way allow users to retrieve data from database without exposure to—

(i) file/record structure

(ii) processes that the system performs

(iii) Languages like Common Business Oriented Language (COBOL), Beginner's All-purpose Symbolic Instruction Code (BASIC) or such other standard programming languages. Data retrieving efficiency may be improved by gaining knowledge about query shortcuts, query strategies and the types of data used in the database. A training and development program for this purpose may prove useful for the end users.

LANGUAGE TRANSLATOR

A language translator is a system software which translates a computer program written by a user into a machine understandable form.The most elemental form of programming uses only the binary digits 0 and 1, which is directly understood by the electronic circuits. A program that have only binary digits is called a machine language program. It is difficult to write or understand machine language programs, as these consist of 0s and 1s.

ASSEMBLERS

Assemblers are used exclusively with assembly languages. They work similarly to compilers, translating an assembly language program into object code. Because assembly language programs are usually more machine efficient than those written in high-level languages, a two-step translation process may take place. First, the high-level language is translated to assembly language; then, using an assembler, it is converted to machine language.

DATA PROCESSING

DATA PROCESSING CONCEPTS

- **Data:** Data means any collection of raw hand figures facts. Data can be considered as the raw material of information. The data may be numerical such as payroll, employee Number, etc. or non-numerical like Student names, Product names, etc.
- **Data Processing:** As data is in its raw form it cannot solve any problem. The data needs some processing to make it useful. Data processing is the conversion of data into a more useful form. That is, transmission of data into meaningful information is called data processing.
- **Information:** The result obtained by data processing is called information. That is, the processed data is known as information. However, information produced in one data processing step may be used as data in the next data processing step.

DATA PROCESSING CYCLE

Data Processing is viewed as a system that accepts data as input, processes it into information as output. This can be explained with the help of the following diagram.

DATA TYPES

The data types may be as follows:

1. **Qualitative data**: It denotes the characteristics of things such as Average, Fair etc.

2. **Quantitative data:** It is expressed in terms of measurable quantities such as 10 KG, 40 degree Celsius etc.
3. **Numeric Types:** The data types may also be an integer (+, -) without any fractional part or real number which includes integers and fractions.
4. **Floating Point Representation:** These data types consist of 3 components namely: (1) Mantissa (2) Radix or Base and (3) Exponent. Besides the above, the data types include alphabetic data and alphanumeric data.

STEPS IN DATA PROCESSING

1. Identifying the Data
2. Input of Data
3. Manipulation of Data
4. Output of Information
5. Storage of Information.

The Data Processing System is used as a managerial aid in decision-making for solving business problems. It is also very useful in the areas of linear programming, PERT, CPM etc.

Today it appears that the computer is everywhere. Not only the business organization, the other institutions are also using data processing system for their regular use. We cannot think about a situation without a computer. Robotics and Artificial Intelligence are the two promising areas of applications.

DATA PROCESSING OPERATIONS

The data after some processing is transformed into information, which is organized and meaningful. It includes the following operations.

1. **Data Generation:** It involves the operation of collecting the original data. It implies that the raw data are collected and set out in the form of original document called a source document.
2. **Recording:** Here raw data is converted into an acceptable form. That is, the data is transcribed from the source documents on the cards or on some other specified forms and are made readable for the machines. This operation is performed throughout the IPO cycle. The punched cards and paper tapes, magnetic tapes, a magnetic disks, tape cassettes, floppy disks, magnetic drums, RAM cartridge, charged coupled devices, etc., are used as data recording media.
3. **Verification:** After the data have been recorded, their accuracy has to be checked. This can be done with the help of another machine called verifier or by re-reading.
4. **Classification:** Classification of information is the next important operation in which the data is separated into various categories.
5. **Sorting:** Sorting involves sequencing the data in a pre-determined order to facilitate processing. The order may be either alphabetic or numeric.
6. **Merging:** It is the operation of combining two or more ordered (sorted) sets of data to form another single ordered set.
7. **Calculating:** Here calculation of greater magnitude can be processed. Calculation involves solving equations and manipulation of the source data such as addition, subtraction, etc.
8. **Data Storage:** The results of processing one set of data are retained in storage for future use of reference. The basic requirement for utilizing the computer in all business applications is the ability to store and access data. The data is stored in a location called memory referred by its address. In large organizations, huge volume of data is to be stored and accessed. Hence, some auxiliary storage devices are also needed for the effective data processing.

The memory is measured by the following units:

(a) **BIT (Binary digit):** It is the smallest possible unit of information. It can be either 0 or 1.

(b) **NIBBLE:** Four bits form one nibble.

(c) **BYTE:** It is a unit of information consisting of fixed number of bits. It is a combination of 8 bits.

(d) **CHARACTER:** It is represented by one byte. It can be a letter, digit, punctuation mark or special characters.

(e) **WORD:** The combination of 2 bytes or 4 bytes or 8 bytes is a word.

The data measurement is as follows:

8 bits - 1 byte
1024 bytes - 1 Kilo Byte (KB)
1024 KB - 1 Mega Byte (MB)
1024 MB - 1 Giga Byte (GB)
1024 GB - 1 Tera Byte (TB)

(f) SECONDARY STORAGE (Backing/ Auxiliary Storage):

(a) Magnetic disk - it includes the following:
Hard disk – Rigid, Floppy disk - Flexible
(b) Magnetic tape
(c) Magnetic drum
(d) Mass storage Device - cartridge
(e) Optical Disks - CD ROM (Compact Disk - ROM)

9. **Data Retrieving:** Data retrieving is the process of searching or locating a data item from the storage. In EDP system, the data is retrieved from the storage device in sequential, indexed sequential or random access mode. The on-line data storage and retrieval is very useful for the proper functioning of a modern business establishment.

10. **Reporting:** Generally in business data processing, the processing operation comes to an end with the reporting of data. In this operation the results of the data processing are made available to others. The processed information may be reported in a number of ways depending on the use of results. The results may be printed out in the form of pay slips, bills, etc. or in the form of reports as ESI Reports, PF Reports or Sales Reports, etc.,

DATA PROCESSING SYSTEM

The methods of data processing are explained below:

1. **The single user system:** It is one-man show and is indicative of one of the earlier stages of computer development. Here only one person can work at a time. Hence, especially if the machine is meant for the use of many persons, much computer time is wasted waiting for one person to finish and debug his program on the machine.

2. **Batch Processing:** This is an old system but even today it is used for data processing in computing machines, in which the capacity of the CPU is limited. In this system, the data is collected for a predetermined period of time, after which it is accumulated in sequential manner.

In this system the source transaction documents are first collected before being sent to computer room. A batch of transactions is entered onto a computer media by data entry devices. The transactions are validated during data entry and verified with the source documents from the check lists. The validated and verified results on reports are returned to the user departments. In batch processing system the emphasis is on maximizing the computer resource utilization.

Examples of applications which can use batch processing are:

1. Payroll Processing: In payroll processing the data are collected for a stipulated period of time usually one month and processed at regular intervals after which payments are distributed to all the employees.
2. Telephone Billing: Here the subscriber does not get a bill for every call he makes. Instead, his calls are recorded at a centralized place and are processed on a predetermined period of time to prepare his bills.
3. Financial accessing
4. Budgeting and Budgeting control
5. Production planning and control
6. Project planning and control

MULTI-PROGRAMMING

In batch processing, programs are executed one by one. The memory and ALU of the machine are not being fully utilized. To get the maximum use of the machine, multiprogramming system is used. "Multi-programming enables to store and execute more than one program in the CPU at the same time". The multi-programming concept is event based. The purpose of multi-programming is to increase utilization of the computer system as whole.

Multi-programming is defined as execution of two or more program that all reside in primary storage. Since the CPU can execute only one instruction at a time, cannot simultaneously execute instructions from two or more program. However, it can execute instructions from one program then from second program then from first again, and so on. This type of processing is referred to as concurrent execution. Using concept of concurrent execution, multi-programming operate in the following way:

ON-LINE PROCESSING

Online processing refers to processing of individual transactions as they occur from their point of origin as opposed to accumulating them into batches. This is made possible by such direct access devices as Magnetic disk and Magnetic Drum and number of terminals connected to, and controlled by a central processor. In this way, various departments in a company can be connected to the process by cables. If operating companies are a number of miles away from the processor then they are linked by means of telegraph or telephone lines. This type of processing provides multi access to information files by terminal users and also enables them to update with transactions data.

It is a non-sequential process in which data is directly transmitted between input/ output device and a computer system via communication links. It is a method of processing where many users have direct access to the same system, and where the file is updated as soon as the transaction is completed.

Special Features

1. In this method data is not accumulated, instead it is entered and executed directly.
2. Quick Processing - By means of direct communication with the computer and continuous flow of input, the delay between transactions and their processing is avoided.
3. This method reduces the data entry errors, because the user who generates, the data is the one who keys it in.
4. This system validates data at various points and ensures that correct data is being entered.
5. Under this method the system performs the whole task in a conversational manner helping the data entry process.
6. In on line processing, one has the latest update immediately.

Online processing ensures that the records are in updated at any time whereas this is so with batch processing say once a week but the fact remains that online processing is usually more costly. Therefore in choosing one of the processing both updating of records and costs are to be considered.

REAL TIME PROCESSING

It is also called as interactive mode or Direct mode. This system makes the user to have direct contact with the computer through his terminal. It is an alternative approach to an on-line processing system. Here the data is processed, the instant it occurs. There is no delay between the time data is available, and the time it is processed.

The term real time refers to the technique of updating files transactions date immediately after the event to which it relates occurs. This is in distinction to batch processing which processes related data to batches of pre-defined periods of time. Real time systems are basically on-line systems with one specially in inquiry processing. The response of the system to the inquiry itself is used to control the activity. An on-line production data collection system that simply accepts input and utilities it for payroll and costing purposes cannot be termed real-time, but if, on the other hand, the system is designed to provide immediate information to monitor the production processes, it is a real time system.

Special Features

(a) Program is always under execution.

(b) It produces output to control, direct or affect the outcome of an ongoing activity or process.

(c) In this method, the control is exercised during the actual functioning.

(d) It is meant exclusively to perform one task.

(e) It is like an online system with; title constraints on response time availability.

(f) It is called a real time system because it has to give results based on dead lines which are imposed by the real world outside.

(g) The data which has to be produced by the systems has to be in such a less time, that they can influence the external events which are based on this data.

Thus the response of a real time system is one type of feedback control system. The response time would naturally differ from one activity to another. If the example, it is the launching of a space vehicle, the response time should be in split second whereas in business situation even a few minutes of response time may be alright. Online updating in real time usually leads to transaction as a by-product.

DISTRIBUTED PROCESSING

In computer science, a form of information processing in which work is performed by separate computers that are linked through a communications network. Distributed processing is usually categorized as either plain distributed processing or true distributed processing. Plain distributed processing shares the workload among computers that can communicate with one another. True distributed processing has separate computers perform different tasks in such a way that their combined work can contribute to a larger goal, such as the transfer of funds from one bank to another. This latter type of processing requires a highly structured environment that allows hardware and software to communicate, share resources, and exchange information freely. At the highest (and most visible) levels, such distributed processing can also require data transfer mechanisms that are relatively invisible to users but that enable different programs to use and share one another's data.

Distributed data processing system is a network of several computers in remote stations, each of which is linked to a single host computer. The larger, central computer maintains the firm's master data base and system log. Each remote system is a fully independent computer that maintains its own local data base in addition to communication with the master computer. These individual computers are tied together through a high speed communication network. This allows individual computers to communicate with one another in a variety of ways depending on the CIS requirements.

Many small computers (called nodes) are employed as data collection points in several departments. They are connected to a main computer system (called File Server) in a centralised department, which controls the entire database. The processing involved here is known as distributed processing.

The distributed data processing system exists because of the need for large interactive installations with a high degree of reliability and accuracy. Moreover, large number of mini computers can be connected in this system which results in cost reduction.

Features

(a) Decentralized computer system
(b) Interconnected by communication network
(c) More reliable
(d) Since more than one computer is used in the network, it is economical.

COMPUTER NETWORKS

BASIC OF COMPUTER NETWORKS

A **computer network**, often simply referred to as a **network**, is a collection of computers and devices connected by communications channels that facilitates communications among users and allows users to share resources with other users. Networks may be classified according to a wide variety of characteristics.

Computer networks can be used for several purposes:

- *Facilitating communications*: Using a network, people can communicate efficiently and easily via e-mail, instant messaging, chat rooms, telephony, video telephone calls, and video-conferencing.
- *Sharing hardware*: In a networked environment, each computer on a network can access and use hardware on the network. Suppose several personal computers on a network each require the use of a laser printer. If the personal computers and a laser printer are connected to a network, each user can then access the laser printer on the network, as they need it.
- *Sharing files, data, and information*: In a network environment, any authorized user can access data and information stored on other computers on the network. The capability of providing access to data and information on shared storage devices is an important feature of many networks.

Computer network has following basic concepts:

(*a*) Modes of Transmission
(b) Topology
(c) Categories of Network

Transmission Modes

It defines the direction of the data flow from sender to receiver.

Communication between two devices can be Simplex, Half Duplex and Full Duplex Mode.

(*i*) A simplex mode is a connection in which the data flows in only one direction, from the transmitter to the receiver. This type of connection is useful if the data do not need to flow in both directions (for example, from your computer to the printer or from the mouse to your computer...).

Simplex Connection

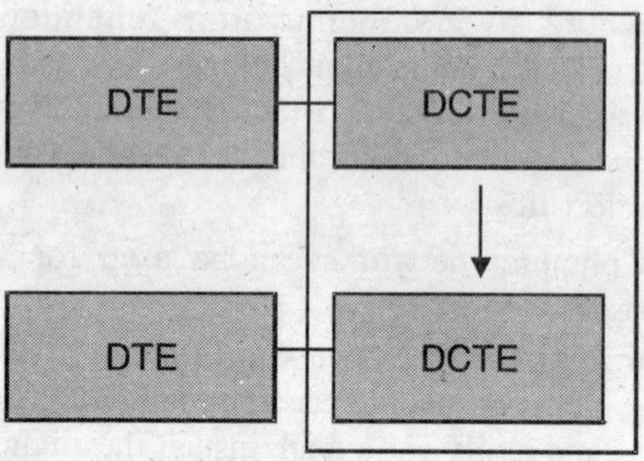

Simplex Mode

(*ii*) A half-duplex mode (sometimes called an alternating connection or semi-duplex) is a connection in which the data flows in one direction or the other, but not both at the same time. With this type of connection, each end of the connection transmits in turn. This type of connection makes it possible to have bidirectional communications using the full capacity of the line.

Half-duplex connection

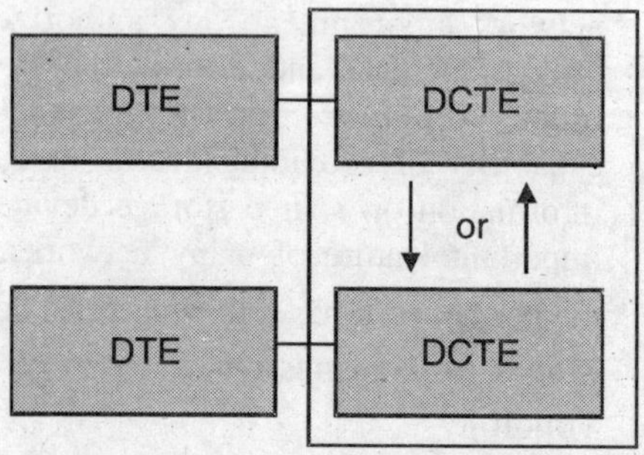

Half Duplex Mode

(*iii*) A full-duplex mode is a connection in which the data flow in both directions simultaneously. Each end of the line can thus transmit and receive at the same time, which means that the bandwidth is divided in two for each direction of data transmission if the same transmission medium is used for both directions of transmission.

Full-duplex connection

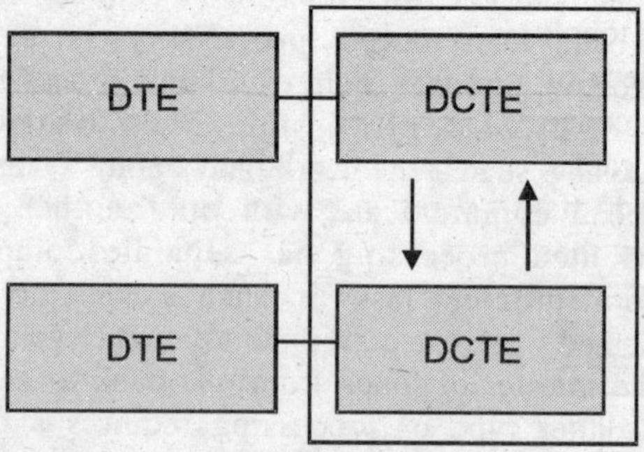

Full Duplex Mode

Topology

A computer network is made of computers which are linked to one another with communication lines (network cables, etc.) and hardware elements (network adapters, as well as other equipment for ensuring that data travels correctly). The physical arrangement - that is, the spatial configuration of the network - is called the **physical topology**.

The different kinds of topology are:

- Bus topology
- Star topology
- Ring topology
- Tree topology
- Mesh topology

Bus topology

Bus topology is the simplest way a network can be organized. In bus topology, all computers are linked to the same transmission line by using a cable, usually coaxial. The word "bus" refers to the physical line that joins all the machines on the network.

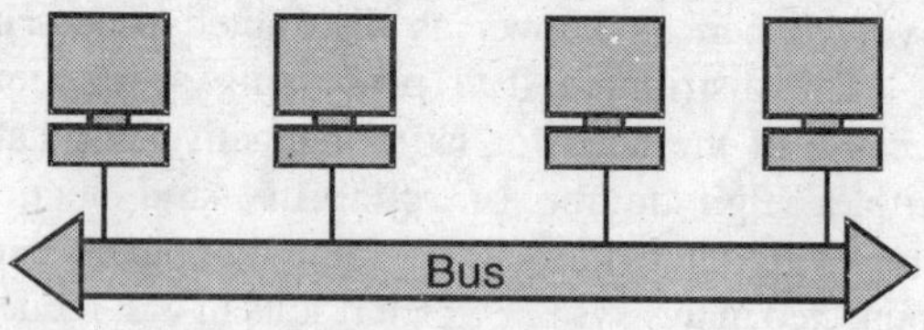

Bus Topology

The advantages of this topology are that it is easy to implement and functions easily; on the other hand, it is highly vulnerable, since if one of the connections is defective, the whole network is affected.

Star topology

In star topology, the network computers are linked to a piece of hardware called a hub. This is a box which contains a certain number of sockets into which cables coming out of the computers can be plugged. Its role is to ensure communications between those sockets.

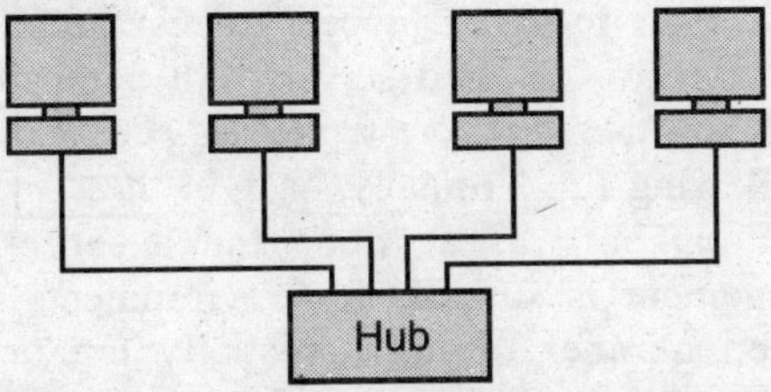

Star Topology

Unlike networks built with bus topology, networks which use star topology are much less vulnerable, as one of the connections can easily be removed by disconnecting it from the hub, without paralyzing the rest of the network. The critical point in this network is the hub, as without it, communication between the computers on the network is no longer possible.

However, a star topology network is bulkier than a bus network, as additional hardware is required (the hub).

Ring topology

In a ring-topology network, computers each take turns communicating, creating a loop of computers in which they each "have their turn to speak" one after another.

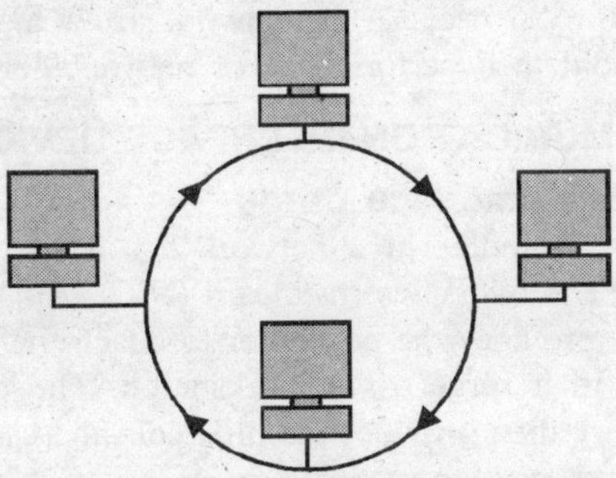

Ring Topology

In reality, ring topology networks are not linked together in loops. They are actually linked to a distributor (called a MAU, **Multi station Access Unit**) which manages communication between the computers linked to it, by giving each of them time to "speak."

Categories of Network

Network categories can be divided on the basis of its size, ownership, distance it covers and its physical architecture:

(i) LAN: LAN stands for Local Area Network. These networks evolved around the PC revolution. LANs enabled multiple users in a relatively small geographical area to exchange files and messages, as well as access shared resources such as file servers.

A local area network (LAN) is a network that connects computers and devices in a limited geographical area such as home, school, computer laboratory, office building, or closely positioned group of buildings. Each computer or device on the network is a node.

(ii) WAN: WAN stands for Wide Area Network. The interconnection of various LAN's through telephone network, which unites geographically distributed users, is achieved through WAN. In short when we log on to the internet, we become a part of a WAN.

Computers connected to a WAN are often connected through public networks, such as the telephone system (through a network service provider). Computers can also be connected through leased lines or satellites, also from a network service provider. The largest WAN in existence is the Internet.

(iii) MAN: MAN stands for Metropolitan Area Network. It is usually the interconnection between various LAN's in a particular geographical area like a metropolitan city like Bombay.

Internetworking evolved as a solution to three key problems: isolated LANs, duplication of resources, and a lack of network management. Isolated LANS made electronic communication between different offices or departments impossible. Duplication of resources meant that the same hardware and software had to be supplied to each office or department, as did a separate support staff. This lack of network management meant that no centralized method of managing and troubleshooting networks existed. A metropolitan-area network (MAN) is a data network designed for a town or city. A MAN can either be built as service provider or leased among multiple customers or a company can build its own private MAN. In terms of geographic breadth, MANs are larger than LANs, but smaller than WANs. MANs are usually characterized by high-speed connections using fiber-optic cable or other digital media and are often used by companies with several offices located within the same city. A corporation can extend the LAN services in each building across a metropolitan region by deploying a MAN to interconnect each corporate office.

(iv) Virtual private network: A virtual private network (VPN) is a computer network in which some of the links between nodes are carried by open connections or virtual circuits in some larger network (e.g., the Internet) instead of by physical wires. The data link layer protocols of the virtual network are said to be tunneled through the larger network when this is the case. One common application is secure communications through the public Internet, but a VPN need not have explicit security features, such as authentication or content encryption. VPNs, for example, can be used to separate the traffic of different user communities over an underlying network with strong security features.

A VPN may have best-effort performance, or may have a defined service level agreement (SLA) between the VPN customer and the VPN service provider. Generally, a VPN has a topology more complex than point-to-point.

NETWORK MODELS

Every computer networks supports two basic network models: **Client-Server and Peer-to- Peer.**

1. Client-Server: Client-Server networks consist of servers and clients. Servers are typically powerful computers running advanced network operating systems and user workstations (clients) which access data or run applications located on the servers.

While it is technically more complex and secure, the Client-Server network easier than ever to administer due to new centralized management software. It is also the most "scaleable" network configuration; additional capabilities can be added with relative case. The drawbacks to the Client-Server model are mostly financial. There is a large cost up front for specialized hardware and software. Also, if there are server problems, down time means that users lose access to mission-critical programs and data until the server can be restored.

2. Peer-to-peer: In peer-to-peer architecture, there are no dedicated servers. All computers are equal, and therefore, are termed as peer and shown in following fig. Normally, each of these machines functions both as a client and a server. This arrangement is suitable for environments with a limited number of users (usually ten or less). Moreover, the users are located in the same area and security is not an important issue while the network is envisaged to have a limited growth. At the same time, users need to freely access data and programs that reside on other computers across the network.

The basic advantage of this architecture is simplicity of design and maintenance. Since there is no server, all nodes on the network are fully employed and independent. Peer-to-peer networks are also known as workgroup. Computers participating in peer-to-peer network all are equal, so named as peer. No single computer holds the control of entire networks. Each system can install or upgrade their application/system software independently. A failure of a node on a peer-to-peer network means that the network can no longer access the applications or data on that node but other node can function properly. Lack of centralized control leads it is advisable to use less number of user system like 10 to 12 users. If the network size is higher than threshold then performance of network degraded.

COMMUNICATION INTERFACE DEVICES

Network Interface Cards

Every computer in a network has a special card called a network interface card (NIC). An NIC first of all, provides the connector to attach the network cable to a server or a workstation. The on-board circuitry then provides the protocols and commands required to support this type of network card. An NIC has additional memory for buffering incoming and outgoing data packets, thus improving the network throughput. A slot may also be available for remote boot PROM, permitting the board to be mounted in a diskless workstation. Network interface cards are available in 8-bit bus or in faster 16-bit bus standards. Characteristics of NICs include following:

- NIC construct, transmits, receives, and processes data to and from a host to network.
- Each NIC has a manufacturer provided 8 bytes permanent and unique MAC(media access control) address. This address is also known as physical address.
- The NIC requires drivers to operate.

Switches and Routers

Switches and Routers are hardware devices used to direct messages across a network. Switches create temporary point to point links between two nodes on a network and send all data along that link. Router computers are similar to bridges but have the added advantage of supplying the user with network management utilities. A switch is a kind of multi port connecting device which makes intelligent routing decisions on the basis of hardware (physical) addresses. It regenerates incoming signals and forwards it.

Router is a kind of connecting device which makes forwarding decisions of data packet on the basis of network addresses. Routers are the backbone of the Internet, as they can be used to interconnect different types of networks. Routers help administer the data flow by such means as redirecting data traffic to various peripheral devices or other computers. In an Internet work communication, routers not only pass on the data as necessary but also select appropriate routes in the event of possible network malfunctions or excessive use.

The primary purpose of a router is to examine the source and destination IP addresses of data packets it receives and to direct those packets out the appropriate port and over the best path available at the time. Routers accomplish this by using routing protocols and routing algorithms.

Hubs

A hub is a multi port connecting device that is used to interconnect LAN devices. Each node is connected to the hub by means of simple twisted pair wires. The hub then provides a connection over a higher speed link to other LANs, the company's WAN, or the Internet. A hub can be used to extend the physical length of a network. Hubs can be active and passive. In case of passive hub incoming signal is sent as it as output. Active hub can regenerate incoming signal. It supports homogeneous network only.

Bridges, Repeaters and Gateways

Bridges: The main task of a bridge computer is to receive and pass data from one LAN to another. In order to transmit this data successfully, the bridge magnifies the data transmission signal. This means that the bridge can act as a repeater as well as a link.

Repeaters: Repeaters are devices that solve the snag of signal degradation which results as data is transmitted along the various cables. What happens is that the repeater boosts or amplifies the signal before passing it through to the next section of cable.

Gateways: Gateways are also similar to bridges in that they relay data from network to network. They do not, as a rule, possess the management facilities of routers but like routers they can translate data from one protocol to another. Gateways are usually used to link LANs of different topologies, e.g., Ethernet and Token Ring, so enabling the exchange of data. The major point of distinction between gateways, bridge, and a router is that a gateway is a collection of hardware and software facilities that enables devices on one network to communicate with devices on another, dissimilar network. Bridges have the same general characteristics as gateways, but they connect networks that employ similar protocols and topologies. Routers are similar to bridges in that they connect two similar networks.

Modem

The coding/encoding device is called a modem. MODEM stands for Modulator/Demodulator. In the simplest form, it is an encoding as well as decoding device used in data transmission. It is a device that converts a digital computer signal into an analog telephone signal (i.e. it modulates the signal) and converts an analog telephone signal into a digital computer signal (i.e. it demodulates the signal) in a data communication system. Modems are used for handling data streams from a peripheral device to the CPU and vice versa through the common carrier network. Modems are required to telecommunicate computer data with ordinary telephone lines because computer data is in digital form but telephone lines are analogue. Modems are built with different ranges of transmission speeds.

Multiplexer

This device enables several devices to share one communication line. The multiplexer scans each device to collect and transmit data on a single line to the CPU. It also communicates transmission from the CPU to the appropriate terminal linked to the Multiplexer. The devices are polled and periodically asked whether there is any data to transmit. This function may be very complex and on some systems, there is a separate computer processor devoted to this activity and this is called a 'front-end-processor'.

Front-end Communication Processors

These are programmable devices which control the functions of communication system. They support the operations of a mainframe computer by performing functions, which it would otherwise be required to perform itself. These functions include code conversions, editing and verification of data, terminal recognition and control of transmission lines. The mainframe computer is then able to devote its time to data processing rather than data transmission.

COMMUNICATION CHANNEL (MEDIUM)

Communication media comprises different types of cables and wireless techniques that are used to connect network devices in a Local Area Network (LAN), Wireless Local Area Network (WLAN) or Wide Area Network (WAN). Choice of correct type of media is very important for the implementation of any network. Communication media is divided into two groups:

(i) **Guided Media :** Twisted Pair, Coaxial cable and Optical fiber.

(ii) **Unguided Media** : Wireless.

SERIAL VERSUS PARALLEL TRANSMISSION

The transmission mode refers to the number of elementary units of information (bits) that can be simultaneously translated by the communications channel. There are two modes of transmitting digital data. These methods are Parallel and Serial Transmissions.

- **Serial Transmission:**In serial transmission, the bits of each byte are sent along a single path one after another.
- **Parallel Transmission:** In parallel transmission, there are separate, parallel path corresponding to each bit of the byte so that all character bits are transmitted simultaneously.

Differences between Serial Transmission and Parallel Transmission

SERIAL TRANSMISSION

1. In this, the data bits are transmitted serially one after another.
2. Data is transmitted over a single wire.
3. It is a cheaper mode of transferring data.
4. Applicable for long distance data transmissions.
5. Relatively slower.

PARALLEL TRANSMISSION

1. In this, the data bits are transmitted simultaneously.
2. Data is transmitted over 8 different wires.
3. Relatively expensive.
4. Not practical for long distance communications as it uses parallel path, so cross talk may occur.
5. Relatively faster.

TRANSMISSION TECHNIQUES

Circuit Switching

A Circuit Switching network is one that establishes a fixed bandwidth circuit (or channel) between nodes and terminals before the users may communicate, as if the nodes were physically connected with an electrical circuit. In circuit-switching, this path is decided upon before the data transmission starts. The system decides on which route to follow, based on a resource-optimizing algorithm, and transmission goes according to the path. For the whole length of the communication session between the two communicating bodies, the route is dedicated and exclusive, and released only when the session terminates. Circuit switching is what most of us encounter on our home phones. We place a call and either get our destination party or encounter a busy signal, we can not transmit any message. A single circuit is used for the entire duration of the call.

Packet switching

It is a sophisticated means of maximizing transmission capacity of networks. Packet switching refers to protocols in which messages are broken up into small transmission units called packets, before they are sent. Each packet is transmitted individually across the net. The packets may even follow different routes to the destination, depends on the type of packet switching. Thus, each packet has header information which enables to route the packet to its destination. At the destination the packets are reassembled into the original message. Passwords and all types of data can be included within the packet and the transmission cost is by packet and not by message, routes or distance. Sophisticated error and flow control procedures are applied on each link by the network.

TRANSMISSION PROTOCOLS

Protocols are software that perform a variety of actions necessary for data transmission between computers. Stated more precisely, protocols are a set of rules for inter-computer communication that have been agreed upon and implemented by many vendors, users and standards bodies. Ideally, a protocols standard allows heterogeneous computers to talk to each other.

At the most basic level, protocols define the physical aspects of communication, such as how the system components will be interfaced and at what voltage levels will be transmitted.

At higher levels, protocols define the way that data will be transferred, such as the establishment and termination of sessions between computers and the synchronization of those transmissions. At still higher levels, protocols can standardize the way data itself is encoded and compressed for transmission.Thus we can say that, Network protocols which are essentially software, are sets of rules for-

- Communicating timings, sequencing, formatting, and error checking for data transmission.
- Providing standards for data communication

A transmission protocols is a set of conventions or rules that must be adhered to by both the communicating parties to ensure that the information being exchanged between the two parties is received and interpreted correctly.

TRANSMISSION CONTROL PROTOCOL/ INTERNET PROTOCOL

The protocols used on the Internet is called TCP/IP (Transmission Control Protocol/Internet Protocol). A TCP/IP protocol which has two parts.

(i) TCP deals with exchange of sequential data
(ii) IP handles packet forwarding and is used on the Internet.

BROAD BAND NETWORKS (ISDN)

Integrated Services Digital Network (ISDN) is a system of digital phone connections to allow simultaneous voice and data transmission across the world. Such voice and data are carried by bearer channels (B channels) having a bandwidth of 64 kilobits per second. A data channel can carry signals at 16kbps or 64kbps, depending on the nature of service provided.

There are two types of ISDN service . Basic Rate Interface (BRI) and Primary Rate Interface (PRI). BRI consists of two 64 kbps B channels and one 16kbps D channel for a total of 144kbps and is suitable for individual users. PRI consists of twenty three B channels and one 64kbps D channel for a total of 1536kbps and is suitable for users with higher capacity requirements. It is possible to support multiple primary PRI lines with one 64kbps D channel using Non Facility Associated Signaling (NFAS).

INTRUSION DETECTION SYSTEM (IDS)

ID stands for Intrusion Detection, which is the art of detecting inappropriate, incorrect, or anomalous activity. ID systems that operate on a host to detect malicious activity on that host are called host-based ID systems, and ID systems that operate on network data flows are called network-based ID systems. Sometimes, a distinction is made between misuse and intrusion detection. The term intrusion is used to describe attacks from the outside; whereas, misuse is used to describe an attack that originates from the internal network.

- The IDS is scalable so that the system grows with the organization, from smaller networks to enterprise installation.
- It provides automated network-based security assessment and policy compliance evaluation.

TECHNIQUES OF NETWORK SECURITY

Firewall is a device that forms a barrier between a secure and an open environment when the latter environment is usually considered hostile, for example the Internet. It acts as a system or combination of systems that enforces a boundary between more that one networks. Firewalls protect network from an un-trusted one. In that effect it has a routing ability.

INTERNET

Internet is a communication network which bridges all the small computer networks worldwide as a whole. Internet is based upon Internet technology, in particular World Wide Web (WWW), to build Information System within organization or enterprise to accomplish standardization and automation. Fundamentally, it means network computing environments which let the users share the information through the Internet and Web browsers. Ultimately, it allows a certain organization to build a Groupware within Web environment at low cost on top of existing network infrastructure. By doing this, closed organization network would be interconnected with existing worldwide Internet, which results in diverse information that strengthens competitive advantages of the organization. Basically, it runs on top TCP/IP and HTTP and filters out any illegal access through firewall.

If a corporate web connects two or more trading partners, it is often referred to as a business - to - business web, or an Intranet.

Note that internal webs - also known as intranets - are only logically "internal " to an organization. Physically they can span the globe, as long as access is limited to a defined community of interest.

INTERNET APPLICATIONS

The Internet has grown from a small project to today's biggest network of computers. Due to this colossal growth, the Internet has become the biggest domain of information. Now-a-days, an Internet user has access to a wide variety of services such as electronic mail, file transfer, vast information resources, interest group membership, interactive collaboration, multimedia displays, real-time broadcasting, shopping opportunities, and much more. Some of the important services provided by the Internet are briefed in the following few sections.

1. **World Wide Web: (WWW):** The World Wide Web (abbreviated as the web or WWW) is one of the most popular services available on Internet. Tim Berners Lee invented the World Wide Web (WWW) in 1989. It is a subset of the Internet and it presents text, images, animation, video, sound and other multimedia in a single interface. This greatly enhances the experience of the Internet surfer. Although the World Wide Web is often referred to as the Internet, they are actually two different concepts. The Internet is the decentralized global network of computers that transfer information and the bring that makes all this possible whereas the web is a collection of documents or websites, that users can access using the Internet and a web browser. The web is a part of the Internet and it refers to a system of Internet servers that supports hypertext using a specific Internet protocol called HTTP on a single interface (web browsers). In addition, almost every protocol type available on the Internet is accessible on the web. This includes e-mail, FTP, Telnet, and Usenet News. Since the WWW is a subset of the Internet, it stands to reason that the web could not exist without the Internet. However, the Internet would still be the Internet without the web.

   The operation of the web relies primarily on hypertext, as it is a means of information retrieval. Hypertext is a document containing words that connect to other documents. These words are called links, which the user can select. A single hypertext document can contain links to documents and resources throughout the Internet. With the ability of the web to work with multimedia and advanced programming languages, the World Wide Web is the fastest growing and the most interesting part of the Internet. With video conferencing and wireless applications, the Internet is ready to take us to the new realm of communication and information exchange.

2. **Electronic Mail (e-mail):** Electronic mail, or e-mail, is a fast, easy, and inexpensive way to communicate with other Internet users around the world. It is one of the basic and earliest services of the Internet and the most used application on the Internet too. E-mail overcomes most of the problems and delays of getting a physical document from one person to another. Rather, it has the dual advantage of not only being faster but cheaper to sue as well.
3. **File Transfer Protocol (FTP):** FTP or File transfer Protocol is a system of rules and a software program that enables a user to log on to another computer and transfer information between it and his/ her computer. It was the first service developed for the Internet so that government and educational institutions could easily exchange files. FTP allows the user to get access to the files stored in the directory of a remote computer that is connected to the Internet. Using FTP, one can upload and download files from the remote computer (known as FTP servers), if he/she has access permission on the remote machine.
4. **Telnet:** The word "telnet" is derived from telecommunications and network and is a protocol that allows a user to log on to a remote computer. Telnet is also known as remote login, which means connecting one machine to another in such a way that a person may interact with another machine as if it is being used locally.
5. **Internet Relay Chat (IRC):** IRC or Internet Relay Chat is a service on the Internet that allows people to communicate in real time and carry on conversations via the computer with one or more people. It provides the user with the facility to engage in simultaneous (synchronous) online "conversation" with other user from anywhere in the world.
6. **Chatting and Instant Messaging:** Chat programs allow users on the Internet to communicate with each other by typing in real time. They are sometimes included as a feature of a website, where users can log into chat rooms to exchange comments and information about the topics addressed on the site.
7. **Internet Telephony:** Internet telephone is the use of the Internet rather than the traditional telephone company infrastructure, to exchange spoken or other telephonic information. It consists of hardware and software that enable people to use the Internet as a transmission medium for telephone calls. There are many Internet telephony applications available. Some, such as Cool Talk and NetMeeting, come bundled with popular web browsers.
8. **Video Conferencing:** Video conferencing uses the same technology as IRC, but also provides sound and video pictures. It enables direct face-to-face communication across networks. A video conferencing system has to or more parties in different locations, which have the ability to communicate using a combination of video, audio, and data. A video conference can be person to person (referred to as "point-to-point") or can involve more than two people (referred to as "multipoint") and the video conferencing terminals are often referred to as "endpoints".
9. **Newsgroups (Usenet):** Newsgroups are international discussion groups that focus on a particular topic and helps in gathering information about that topic. The topics discussed here cover all the fields such as politics, computers, technology, and many more. The information or articles that make up the "news" are written by people interested in a specific topic. These articles are posted to the newsgroup so that others can read, reply, and comment on them.
10. **Mailing Lists (List server):** The Internet is home to a large community of individuals who carry out active discussions, organized around topic-oriented forums that are distributed via e-mail. This method of Internet communications is known as mailing list and it enables people with similar interests from all over the world to communicate and share information with each other.

INTRANET AND E-MAIL

An Intranet is a private network that uses the internet protocol and the public telecommunication system to securely share part of business information or operations with-suppliers, vendors, partners, customers, or other businesses.

Through e-mail, documents are prepared and sent electronically. The recipients need not be present at the other end to send the message. The message gets stored in the electronic mailbox of the addressee. The recipient can open the mailbox whenever he is free and can read or print the message.

INTRANET

An Intranet can be viewed a-part of a company's internal that is extended to users outside the company. It has also been described as a "state of mind" in which the internet is perceived as a way to do business with other companies as well as to sell products to customers. Intranet extends from one location to another across the internet by securing data flow, to another intranet to a business partner. In these way intranets of business partners, suppliers, creditors, distributors, customers, and the like are connected to Intranets by agreements.

An Intranet requires security and privacy. These require firewall server management, issuance and use of digital certificate or similar means of user authentication, encryption of messages, and the use of virtual private networks that tunnel through the public network.

Characteristics of Intranet

The following are the important characteristics of the Intranet.

(*a*) It is an extended internet-private business networks located outside of the corporate firewall.

(*b*) It can be referred to an intranet that is partially accessible to authorized outsiders.

(*c*) It is a network that uses the internet to link businesses with others that share the common goals.

Uses of Intranet

Companies can use an Intranet to:

(*a*) Exchange large volumes of data using Electronic Data Interchange.

(*b*) Share product catalogues exclusively with wholesalers or those in the Trade.

(*c*) Collaborate with other companies on joint development efforts.

(*d*) Jointly develop and use training programs with other companies.

(*e*) Provide or access services provided by one company to a group of other companies, such as an online banking application managed by one company on behalf of affiliated banks.

(*f*) Share news of common interest exclusively with partner companies.

(*g*) The manufacturing companies can coordinate the design manufacturing, scheduling and delivery across supply chain.

(*h*) With Intranet the technology firms can support for their customers and partners and makes it possible for remote access for employees.

(*i*) The financial services firms by using Intranet can reduce costs of proprietary networks.

(*j*) With Intranet the publishing companies can increase the speed of design and production cycles.

(*k*) Other benefits:

- Quicker turnaround time
- Improved communication
- Decreased paper flow
- Traceable correspondence
- Better service
- Lower overhead and expenses
- Improved employee morale
- Increased Margins
- Flexibility and scalability
- Reduced transitional barriers
- Versatility.

A brief list of examples of Intranet could include:

- Allowing suppliers access to relevant inventory levels
- Allowing clients to review their account records
- Allowing students to update address information in real time.

As with intranet, access is granted only where you establish that it is required. User access is controlled by the latest in security technologies, protecting sensitive material from intrusion.

WHAT IS THE RELATIONSHIP BETWEEN INTRANET, INTRANET AND E-COMMERCE?

The answer has three parts. First, Intranet, Intranet and e-commerce have in common the use of Internet (predominantly web) protocols to connect business users. Second, intranets are more localized and can therefore move data faster than more distributed Intranets. (Bandwidth limitations also apply to e-commerce.) Third, the amount of control that network managers can exert over users is different for the three technologies.

On an Internet, administrators can narrowly prescribe access and policy for a fixed group of users. For example, a company could specify Red Hat Linux as its standard desktop operating system, and Netscape Communicator 5 as its standard browser and mail client. The company could then write intranet workflow applications that leverage the uniform computing environment, over which it exercises strong control.

On a business-to business Intranet, system architects at each of the participating companies must collaborate to ensure a common interface and consistent semantics (data meanings). Since one company cannot reasonably enforce standards on its trading partners, Intranet application developers must taken into account a wider range of technologies than is the case for intranets. For example, one company participating in an Intranet might be using Microsoft Internet Explorer, another Netscape Navigator 4.5 and another Navigator Gold 3.x In order to collaborate via Intranet, the applications have to perform adequately on all represented platforms.

The same is true, even more, for e-commerce, in which the trading partners may be completely unknown to one another. This is the case when you walk into a supermarket: the common interest in communication is based on the need to transact business, and not necessarily on a long-term trust relationship. Thus, e-commerce applications often support a level of security and transactional integrity (for instance, non-repudiation of orders) not present in intranet or Intranet applications.

E-MAIL

E-mail is an electronic message sent from one computer to another. We can send or receive personal and business-related messages with attachments, such as pictures or formatted documents. We can even send songs and computer programs.

The e-mail communication is incredibly simple. A person with a PC and a modem to connect to the network can communicate with the other(s) so connected to the network. The message can be prepared and sent instantly. The other person finds the e-mail when he checks his mailbox and may reply to the message in the same way. The message sent is private and no other person can read it.

Each user of e-mail service has a user ID or password serving as e-mail address. First thing to do is to get online using modem and communication software. The system requires userid and password. Now the user can prepare his message in the form of a document using a word processor. The e-mail address of the recipient has to be typed in before the message is sent.

With e-mail each person connected to the system is allotted a mailbox and the software required for sending and receiving e-mail. The mailbox is simply a file into which the e-mail system stores electronic documents. The user can check his mailbox for messages over the network. The sender specifies his identify and that of the recipient. The sender then prepares the document or retrieves the stored document and sends it.

E-mail is a document communication facility. To ensure that the recipient also understands the emotions as well, a set of special symbols is used to convey some non-verbal signals. A few of such symbols are given below.

E-mail is the transmission of information electronically from terminal to terminal. The document is prepared in a word processor and is mailed electronically. The basic facilities in e-mail include message creation, message transfer and post delivery service. The e-mail service may be traditional mainframe based or minicomputer based or LAN based system with PCS to access from.

HOW E-MAIL WORKS?

The first thing to be done is to type the message and the e-mail address of the recipient. Once the 'send' button is clicked, this e-mail is sent through the telephone line after its conversion into analog signal by the modem. The e-mail message arrives at our service provider's server. If the server recognizes the e-mail address as valid, the mail will be sent either through the network of the service provider or through internet gateway to the service provider of the recipient.

To send e-mail, we need a connection to the internet and access to a mail server that forwards the mail. The standard protocol used for sending internet e-mail is called SMTP, short for Simple Mail Transfer Protocol. It works in conjunction with POP servers. POP stands for Post Office Protocol.

When we send an e-mail message, our computer routes it to an SMTP server. The server looks at the e-mail address (similar to the address on an envelope), then forwards it to the recipient's mail server. Once the message arrives at the destination mail server, It's stored until the addressee retrieves it. We can send e-mail anywhere in the world to anyone who has an e-mail address.

With the advent of MIME, which stands for Multipurpose Internet Mail Extension, and other types of encoding schemes, we can not only send messages electronically, but we can also send formatted documents, photos, sound files, and video files.

Infrastructure Requirement for E-Mail

- Personal Computer
- Telephone Connection
- Modem
- Mailing software viz., Outlook Express or Netscape communicator or Internet Explorer etc.

Advantages of E-mail

- Messages can be prepared and sent any time convenient for the sender.
- Message can be received at the convenience of the recipient.
- The transmission takes place instantly and the message gets stored in the mailbox of the recipient.
- The system can confirm delivery of message.
- Copies of message can be sent to multiple recipients.
- It reduces paper work.

Disadvantages

- Recipients must be having e-mail connectivity. They must have computer terminals, modem and telephone.
- They must be subscribing to the same e-mail service provider.
- Poor telecommunication affects the quality of message transmitted.
- Despite all the disadvantages e -mail is a cheap form of information transmission.

INDONET, NICNET, DARTMAIL and ICNET provide this service in India. A user can be a subscriber to such e-mail service providing agencies and use their facility.

ELECTRONIC COMMERCE

The growth of Internet into a global market place attracts more business firms to use this media for commerce. Business firms may use the Internet initially for communication. Websites are set up to provide information about its products and services. Business firms offer corporate information, product information, marketing related services etc,.

The Internet has integrated the fragment markets words over though in a modest way. But this interaction is growing rapidly. The most important advantage of the internet for business firms is that it allows reaching customers at very low costs.

Electronic commerce is the process of searching, choosing, buying and selling of product or service on the electronic network; it uses the computer and communication networks for promoting products, selling, delivery, collection and delivery service.

Electronic Commerce includes:

(a) Buying and selling on the internet

(b) Making payments electronically

(c) Business transaction in which there is no physical exchange or physical contact.

(d) It is transacting a business over am electronic network without physical contact.

These problems of authentication can be solved by using:

(a) Secure socket layer and hypertext transfer protocol

(b) Digital signatures

(c) Using public key cryptography

(d) Using digital certificates.

In E-commerce, the parties to a transaction interact electronically. They may be separated by long distances physically, yet the electronic network bring them together not only to complete a transaction but also to get after sales support, E-commerce is not just doing transaction over the Internet, it aims at few other things as well like:

- Web enabling an organization's business so that it can facilitate better customer interaction, handing customer enquiries receiving customer order and payments online.
- Improving customer service capabilities by allowing customers by providing Inert access to its databases containing customer interest information.
- Use the web to gather customer need information and thus to reducing cycle time by responding to customer needs quickly. It enables the firm in coming out with new available new product information to customers.
- Raising productivity of all activities in the organization by improving the flow of information in the organization.

FEATURES OF E-COMMERCE

E-Commerce has the following general features:

(a) It is a business strategy to cut down costs, while improving quality and increasing the speed of delivery of goods/services.

(b) It has ability to sell and purchase products/ services/information on computer networks.

(c) It is a solution for office automation and quick business transactions.

(d) It is a tool to improve intra business functioning like business re-engineering.

(e) It is tools to improve inter business communication through easy and accurate interaction and information interchange.

IMPORTANCE OF E-COMMERCE

E-Commerce becomes inevitable because of the following:

(a) **Low setup cost:** Any body can easily set up a website. In fact there are many organizations and training institutes who help customers in developing and launching websites. To market a product large retail showrooms are not required, just a web site showing the characteristics of the product including cost details are sufficient.

(b) **Global Free Market:** Nobody can dominate the global market as presence on the internet is easy not only for global giants, but even small organisations can participate actively at low costs and compete with stiff competition.

(c) **Global Access:** Since more than 200 countries are hooked onto the Internet, anybody who can afford a TV and a telephone can fully access the Internet and gain the information required.

(d) **Availability of Technology:** Since the same technology like web servers, browsers, engines, internet, etc., is used throughout the world therefore business can be easily conducted.

(e) **Multiple Opportunities:** By using E-Commerce multiple activities like selling, renting, purchasing etc. can be performed. In fact a whole variety of transactions can be provided all under one roof.

The benefits of electronic commerce are not just available to large corporations and government departments, and many small to medium businesses are discovering new cost -effective opportunities to use Internet-related technology to help their business operations locally and internationally.

E-COMMERCE ACTIVITIES

Business firms use the internet platform for communication and commerce. The e-commerce activities can be discussed as follows:

(a) **Direct marketing and selling:** Business firms set up websites for direct marketing and selling. Direct selling was one of the earliest forms of e-commerce. For example, Amazon.com, Barnes and noble and Dell computers engaged in direct selling. Gradually firm moved on to one or more complex operations on the web.

(b) **Value chain integration:** E-Commerce does not tolerate any kind of delay. Delay in inventory tracking and management can cripple the business. E-Commerce firm use EDI for exchanging transaction data among them so that transactions are automatically processed. Thus suppliers, customers and service providers will use open EDI for integrating their processing systems leading to mare efficient operations.

(c) **Corporate Purchasing:** Internet provides opportunities for business firms to reduce cost of purchasing. Suppliers keep their electronic catalogs updated. Comparative price information is also available. Ordering can be electronically done to reduce the laborious paper work in purchasing. Officers can approve purchase orders electronically. The firm can enforce policies; provide greater services to customers and suppliers.

(d) Financial and information services: A wide range of financial services are offered on the internet. They include:
- Online banking
- Online billing
- Online securities transactions
- Secure information distribution

(e) Mobile commerce: Mobile commerce is a part of e-commerce and differs from the latter on the use of mobile telecommunication communication network in place of telecommunication network. M-commerce includes only transactions with a monetary value and it excludes short message services. One condition essential for the success of mobile commerce is large user base of mobile phones. Adequate security for mobile transactions is another condition for its adoption in a big way.

MOBILE COMPUTING

Mobile Computing is a generic term describing your ability to use technology 'untethered'(wireless), that is not physically connected, or in remote or mobile (non static) environments. The term is evolved in modern usage such that it requires that the mobile computing activity be connected wirelessly to and through the internet or to and through a private network. This connection ties the mobile device to centrally located information and/or application software through the use of battery powered, portable, and wireless computing and communication devices. This includes devices like laptops with wireless LAN or wireless WAN technology, smart mobile phones, wearable computers and Personal Digital Assistants (PDAs) with Bluetooth or IRDA interfaces.

TYPES OF MOBILE COMPUTERS

Many types of **mobile computers** have been introduced since the 1990s, including the:

(a) Laptop computer
(b) Sub notebook
(c) Personal digital assistant (PDA)
(d) Portable data terminal (PDT)
(e) Mobile data terminal(MDT)
(f) Tablet personal computer
(g) Smart phone
(h) UMPC

Laptop Computer

As personal computers, laptops are capable of the same tasks as a desktop computer, although they are typically less powerful for the same price. They contain components that are similar to their desktop counterparts and perform the same functions, but are miniaturized and optimized for mobile use and efficient power consumption. Laptops usually have liquid crystal displays and most of them use different memory modules for their random access memory (RAM), for instance, SO-DIMM in lieu of the larger DIMMs. In addition to a built-in keyboard, they may utilize a touchpad (also known as a trackpad) or a pointing stick for input, though an external keyboard or mouse can usually be attached.

Sub Notebook

A sub notebook is a small and lightweight portable computer, with most of the features of a standard notebook computer but smaller. The term is often applied to systems that run full versions of desktop operating systems such as Windows or Linux. Sub notebooks are smaller than notebook computers but larger than handheld computers and ultra portables. They often have screens that are 10.4" (diagonal) or less, and weigh less than 1 kg; as opposed to full-size laptops with 12" or 15" screens and weighing 2 kg or more. The savings in size and weight are usually achieved partly by omitting ports or having removable media/optical drives; sub notebooks are often paired with docking stations to compensate. Sub notebooks are a niche IT product and rarely sell in large numbers.

Personal Digital Assistants (PDAs)

Personal digital assistants (PDAs) are handheld computers, but have become much more versatile over the years. PDAs are also known as pocket computers or palmtop computers. PDAs have many uses: calculation, use as a clock and calendar, accessing the Internet, sending and receiving E-mails, video recording, typewriting and word processing, use as an address book, making and writing on spreadsheets, scanning bar codes, use as a radio or stereo, playing computer games, recording survey responses, and Global Positioning System (GPS). Newer PDAs also have both color screens and audio capabilities, enabling them to be used as mobile phones (smart phones), web browsers, or portable media players. Many PDAs can access the Internet, intranets or Intranets via Wi-Fi, or Wireless Wide-Area Networks (WWANs). Many PDAs employ touch screen technology.

Mobile Data Terminal (MDT)

A mobile data terminal (MDT) is a computerized device used in police cars, taxicabs, courier vehicles, service trucks, commercial trucking fleets, military logistics, fishing fleets, warehouse inventory control, and emergency vehicles to communicate with a central dispatch office.

Mobile data terminals feature a screen on which to view information and a keyboard or keypad for entering information, and may be connected to various peripheral devices. Standard peripherals include two-way radios and taximeters, both of which predate computer assisted dispatching. MDTs may be simple display and keypad units, intended to be connected to a separate black-box or AVL computer. On the other end of the spectrum, MDTs may contain full, PC-equivalent hardware. The function and programmability of the devices is similarly broad.

Tablet PC

A Tablet PC is a notebook- or slate-shaped mobile computer. Its touch screen or digitizing tablet technology allows the user to operate the computer with a stylus or digital pen, or a fingertip, instead of a keyboard or mouse.

The form factor offers a more mobile way to interact with a computer. Tablet PCs are often used where normal notebooks are impractical or unwieldy, or do not provide the needed functionality.

Smart Phone

A smart phone is a full-featured mobile phone with personal computer like functionality. Most smart phones are cell phones that support full featured e-mail capabilities with the functionality of a complete personal organizer. An important feature of most smart phones is that applications for enhanced data processing and connectivity can be installed on the device, in contrast to regular phones which support sandboxed applications. These applications may be developed by the manufacturer of the device, by the operator or by any other third-party software developer. "Smart" functionality includes any additional interface including a miniature QWERTY keyboard, a touch screen, or even just secure access to company mail, such as is provided by a BlackBerry.

Ultra Mobile PC

The Ultra-Mobile PC (abbreviated UMPC), previously known by its codename Project Origami, is a specification for a small form factor tablet PC. It was developed as a joint development exercised by Microsoft, Intel, and Samsung, among others. Current UMPCs feature the Windows XP Tablet PC Edition 2005, Windows Vista Home Premium Edition, or Linux operating system and low-voltage Intel Pentium or VIA C7-Mprocessors in the 1 GHz range.

OFFICE AUTOMATION SYSTEMS AND TRANSACTION PROCESSING SYSTEMS

The introduction of mini computer in to office in the late sixties has since then changed very significantly the way the work is done in office. Office automation is an assorted mix of technologies with the basic objective of improving the efficiency of office work. Office automation systems include the application of computer-based office- oriented technologies such as word-processing, desktop publishing, electronic mail, teletext and teleconferencing.

Business transactions are certain events that occur routinely in a business firm such as purchase and issue of raw materials. The nature and volume of transactions depend on type and size of business. These transactions are to be recorded to measure efficiency of operations and resource use. The transaction processing system (TPS) is the most important and rich source of data for a business firm.

OFFICE AUTOMATION SYSTEMS

The important areas in office automation are:

Word processing: Word processing permits typing in documents, manipulation of such documents and their storage and retrieval.

Desktop publishing: This uses computer hardware and software to produce documents of professional print quality. The use can combine test, artwork, photos and a variety of fonts to produce the document.

Electronic mail: E-mail is the fastest growing communication mode. Computer network facilitate communication between computers. The electronic transfer of messages between computers is quick, convenient and economic.

Facsimile (FAX): The FAX machine sends and receives text and images. The text and images are converted into digital form and at the receiving end it is converted into text and image form.

Voice Mail: Voice mail sends digitized speech over phone to a mailbox and the message is digitally stored at the receiving end, which can be accessed using telephone.

Teleconferencing: It is the use of telecommunication technology to see people face to face without their physical proximity to each other. The participants gather in specially equipped rooms capable of simultaneous audio and video transmission.

Image storage and retrieval systems: These systems convert paper documents into electronic files and images for easy storage and retrieval.

Electronic fund transfer: It is a facility to transfer funds between accounts of customers with banks. At the point of sale counter customers presents his card and keys in a code and if the card and code tally the bill amount id transferred to the account of the retailer and the customer's account is updated.

Multimedia systems: The multimedia systems store, retrieve and process different types of data such as text, graphics, audio, video and animation. They facilitate information storage, retrieval and presentation in a variety of impressive ways.

TRANSACTION PROCESSING SYSTEMS

The transaction processing system (TPS) was the earliest form of computerized management information system. Originally, business transactions were processed manually. This was partly replaced by machine-assisted data processing systems. Gradually, electronic data processing was introduced to record business transactions. TPS is today an integral part of computer-based information systems. It is very difficult to imagine an organization without a functional TPS. For example, if an airline reservation system breaks down for a day or two, it will cripple the company and the flights will be in disarray causing untold miseries to customers.

In a business firm, there are two types of flows in and out of the firm. The first is a physical flow. It is the flow of inputs through various processes within the firm and the output of products and services out of the firm. The second is information flow. Information system tracks the physical flow. The physical flow of input and output is measured and recorded. These records are the sources of data for information corresponding to the physical flow.

The operations management takes care of the physical flow of resources and the transaction processing system takes care of the information flow. The transaction processing system processes all transactions and records them. This results in generation of transaction data which are structured and stored in databases. Apart from recording routine transactions, TPS also updates master files and databases.

TRANSACTION PROCESSING CYCLE

Transaction processing is a basic activity in organizations. It is a routine and repetitive activity that triggers a few other activities like updating database and generation of documents forming a cycle. The transaction processing cycle consists of six steps such as:

(a) Data entry
(b) Input data validation
(c) Transaction processing and validation of results
(d) File and database maintenance
(e) Document and report generation, and
(f) Inquiry processing

The transactions are measured in some convenient unit for recording such as money unit for expenses, hours in case of labour etc. Data pertaining to the transaction must be entered into the system. The source of this data usually is a document such as sales order from customers, invoice from suppliers etc., these are called source documents and they provide the basic data for TPS. The data is entered using either the traditional data entry methods or the direct data entry methods. In the former method the source documents like purchase order are prepared and usually accumulated into batches. The direct entry method uses automated systems for data capturing and recording. Point of sale terminals, optical scanners and MICR devices are used in capturing data and transferring data to computers in real time for transactions processing.

Input data validation is the next step in TPS. It checks the accuracy and reliability of data by comparing it with range data or standards etc. It involves error detection and error correction. Checking for errors include checking the data for appropriate format, missing data and inconsistent data. If the data value falls outside the normal range it is invalid. For example, if a firm's orders for materials in kilograms ranging from 100 to 1000 kilograms and if that range is accepted as normal data range for purchase orders, then this range is coded into the program for validation checking. That whenever a purchase order is prepared, as soon as quantity is entered in the appropriate column the system check whether the quantity entered is between 100 and 1000. Otherwise it will give an error message as "Check the Quantity Entered, it is out of range" or some other error message as is coded.

Processing of transaction data is the next step. This involves some computation, checking and comparing etc. For instance, if it is a credit sale transaction, then the total value of the transaction has to be computed, the system should check whether the value is within the credit limit sanctioned to the customer, it should check the availability of stock, delivery data possible etc.

Once the transaction is processed, certain output needs to be generated. The output may be some documents like sales invoices, pay slips etc. or screen displays or the output data may used to update related databases. Files and databases have to be updated with each transaction or each batch of transactions. In case of applications that are not time critical, the transactions may be processed in batch mode. Certain systems like airline reservation require updating with every transaction for giving status information in real time. Direct data entry devices have to be used to capture transaction data and update related files and databases to provide current information to users.

Inquiry processing is another activity of transaction processing system which involves providing information on current status like inventory levels, customer credit limit, dues from a particular customer, inbound supply, etc. The inquiry response is pre-planned and the on-screen display or output is formatted for the convenience of the requester.

A business transaction with a customer involves a good or service that a customer want and the business provides for a price. The TPS supports the delivery process.

To complete a transaction with an external entity like customer, supplier etc. a series of activities is involved such as checking of account, current inventory balance, delivery time and price.

For instance, the transaction at a bank counter involves checking of account balance, withdrawal of money or deposit of money. In the case of some transactions, an activity serves as a trigger and a series of activities follow it. For example, a sales order from a customer is followed by a number of activities; some of these are queries like:

- Checking whether the customer is an existing or a new customer,
- Checking customer's credit limit to know whether the transaction is within the permitted credit limit or not,
- Checking inventory balance to know whether the order can be fulfilled within the time the customer needs it,
- Checking production schedule to know how much will be added to finished stock at the end of a production period,
- Checking of back orders to know how much stock will be left to meet this sale order.
- Once this querying is over and if adequate stock is available for meeting the order, the sales order is approved and the transaction is processed. This involves
- Debiting customer account with the value of goods
- Crediting sales file with the value of goods
- Updating inventory file with the quantity of stock sold

- Generating a packing list for the Dispatch department to assemble the order
- Generating documents like sales invoice bill of exchange etc.
- Packing the goods and handing them to the delivery staff, and
- Delivering the goods.

TPS actually tracks the physical workflows. Each operation of the workflow is recorded. At each of these points in the sales order processing, the information about the state of the order is recorded.

TRANSACTION DOCUMENTS

Processing of transactions results in certain documents. These documents may be classified into any of the following types:

Informational Documents: These documents just inform that something has taken place or is taking place. For example, a sale confirms that the order has been received from the customer and has been verified.

Action Oriented Documents: These documents need to be acted upon. For example, a purchase order initiates a purchase. Similarly a production order instructs the production department to start production of the products mentioned in the production order.

Investigational Documents: These are generated on an exceptional basis. For example, whenever operations are not conforming to the range of deviations permitted, the variations are tracked and analyzed. A report is generated to enable the control point to take corrective action.

TRANSACTION PROCESSING MODES

Transactions may be processed individually or in batches. Similarly, the processing may be done at local offices or at the head quarters of companies. The type of processing depends on a set of factors like the volume of data, complexity of data processing operations, processing time constraints, computational demands and the degree of decentralization of authority. Thus, the processing modes are as follows:

- Batch Processing
- On-line Processing
- On-line, Real Time Processing
- Distributed processing
- Online Transaction Processing Systems

Glossary

Accumulator: A Storage area in memory used to develop totals of units or of aiounts being computed.

ActiveX: A Microsoft programming architecture that allows programs to interact with other programs over a network, such as the Internet. The controls created with ActiveX enable developers to add extra capabilities to Web sites, such as animation.

Address: A name, numeral, or other reference that designates a particular location in storage or some other data source or designation.

Note: Numerous types of addresses are employed in computer programming; for example; direct address, symbolic address.

ADSL: Asymmetric Digital Subscriber Line, a modem arrangement, connected to ends of a telephone line, that allows for high-speed transmissions of data — useful for interactive video and data communications. See also DSL, xDSL.

ALGOL (Algorithmic Language): A standard procedure oriented language for expressing computational algorithms developed as a result of international cooperation. ALGOL is designed to serve as a means for communicating computational procedures among humans, as well as to facilitate the preparation of such procedures for execution on any computer for which a suitable ALGOL compiler exists.

Note: The basic elements of ALGOL are arithmetic expressions containing numbers, variables and functions. These are combined to form self-containing units called assignment statements. Declarations are non-computational instructions which inform the compiler of characteristics such as the dimensions of an array or the class of a variable. A sequence of declarations followed by a sequence of statements, all enclosed within "begin" and "end" instruction, constitutes an ALGOL program block. ALGOL is very popular in Europe.

Alignment: Process of organising and fixing the position and order of words and lines in a document.

Analog Transmission: There are two ways that 'Information' can travel along a telecommunications network: either as an analog or a digital signal. Analog signals are like the spoken word - the signal is continuous and carried by a changing wavelength (pitch) and amplitude (loudness). A digital signal, on the other hand, is like the binary information which is stored in a computer. The signal consists of discrete on-off (1 and 0) bits. Although analog and digital information cannot be changed in form, the electronic signal the network uses to transmit it can. Analog information can be transmitted directly or encoded into digital bits; digital information can be transmitted directly or modulated into analog form. The choice between transmission systems depends upon the relative volumes of analog and digital information, the relative costs of codes (analog to digital coders-decoders) and modems (digital to analog modulators - demodulators) and the relative efficiencies of digital and analog transmission.

Applet: A small application program, made with the object-oriented programming language Java, which can be sent along the Web to a user. Applets can perform animations, calculations and other tasks without sending the user back to a server.

Application Program: A computer program used to perform a specific task, such as word processing, spreadsheet creation, or database management.

ASCII: Acronym for American Standard Code for Information Interchange. A standard set of characters used to enable compatibility between different computer devices.

Assemble: To prepare a machine language from a program written in symbolic coding by substituting absolute operation codes for symbolic operation codes and absolute or re-locatable addresses for symbolic addresses. For example, the symbolic instruction ADD TAX might be assembled into the machine instruction 24 1365, where 24 is the operation code of addition and 1365 is the address of the storage location labeled TAX. Contrast with compile.

Assembler: A computer program that assembles programs written in symbolic coding to produce machine language programs.

Note: Assemblers are an important part of the basic software for most computers and can greatly reduce the human effort required to prepare programs.

Asynchronous Communication: Transmission system in which the speed of operation is not related to any frequency in the system to which it is connected. In the transmission system each character is preceded by a start signal and succeeded by a stop signal. This means that 'asynch', as it is usually referred to, is rather slow.

Attachment: Content included in an e-mail, either as extra text or as a file.

Auxiliary Storage: Storage that supplements a computer's primary internal storage.

Note: In general, that auxiliary storage has a much larger capacity but a longer access time than the primary storage. Synonymous with mass storage. Same as secondary storage.

Backbone: The main pathway of a high-speed network.

Backup: Pertaining to equipment or procedures that are available for use in the event of failure or overloading of the normally used equipment or procedures.

Note: The provision of adequate backup facilities is an important factor in the design of all data processing systems and is especially vital in the design of real-time systems, where a system failure may bring the entire operation of a business to virtual standstill.

Bandwidth: How much data one can send through a connection. Usually measured in bits-per-second. A full page of English text is about 16,000 bits. A fast modem can move about 15,000 bits in one second. Full-motion, full-screen video would require roughly 10,000,000 bits per second, depending on compression.

BASIC (Beginner's All-purpose Symbolic Instruction Code): A programming language developed in the mid - 1960's as an easy-to learn, easy-to-use language to teach students how to program. The language contains a limited set of powerful commands designed especially for use in a time sharing environment.

Batch file: It is like a mini program, a series of commands that are given to the personal computer to execute in sequence.

Batch processing: A technique in which items to be processed are collected into groups (batched) to permit convenient and efficient processing. **Note:** Most business applications are of the batch processing type; the records of all transactions affecting a particular master file are accumulated covering a period of time, (e.g., one day); then they are arranged in sequence and processed against the master file.

Baud: In common usage, the baud rate of a modem is how many bits it can send or receive per second. Technically, baud is the number of times per second that the carrier signal shifts value. For example, a 1200 bit-per-second modem actually runs at 300 baud, but it moves 4 bits per baud ($4 \times 300 = 1200$ bits per second).

BBS: Bulletin Board System, a computer that creates a forum for sharing and exchanging messages and/or files. Most BBS's operate independent of the Internet, and must be reached with a modem or Telnet. But many BBS's have Web sites, as do service providers.

BCD (Binary Coded Decimal) : Pertaining to a method of representing each of the decimal digits zero through 9 by a distinct group of binary digits. For example, in the "8-4-2-1" BCD notation, which is used in numerous digital computers, the decimal number39 is represented as 0011 1001 (whereas in pure binary notation it would be represented as 100111).

Binary: Pertaining to the number system with a radix of 2, or to a characteristic or property involving choice or condition in which there are two possibilities. For example, the binary numeral 1101 means: $(1 \times 2^3) + (1 \times 2^2) + (0 \times 2^1) + (1 \times 2^\circ)$ which is equivalent to decimal 13.

Note: The binary number system is widely used in digital computers because most computer components, e.g., vacuum tubes, transistors, and integrated chips) are essentially binary in that they have two stable states.

BIOS (Basic Input Output System): Commands of function when a computer is switched on.

Bit: A binary digit; a digit (0 or 1) in the representation of a number in binary notation.

Booster Keys: Keys that do not perform actions by themselves but can be used with other keys to issue commands. The booster keys are Ctrl, Alt, and Shift.

Boot: To start a computer and load the operating system into RAM.

Bps - (Bits-per-Second): A measurement of how data is moved from one place to another. A 28.8 modem can move 28,800 bits per second.

Browser: A Client program (software) that is used to look at various kinds of Internet resources. Mosaic, Netscape Navigator and Internet Explorer are some of the commonly used browsers.

Buffer Memory: This is the internal memory of a microcomputer or word processor. Data is stored in this memory until transferred to its permanent store on a disk system. Buffer memories also hold the software used by the system.

Buffer: A storage device used to compensate for differences in the rates of flow of data or in the times of occurrence of events when transmitting data from one device to another. For example, a buffer holding the characters to print one line is associated with most line printers to compensate for the difference between the high speed at which the computer transmits data to the printer and the relatively low speed of the printing operation itself.

Bug: A mistake in the design of a program or a computer system, or an equipment fault.

BUS: Internal communication path in a computer.

Byte: A byte is eight bits.

Cell: The smallest unit of a spreadsheet filled with information.

Central Processor: The unit of a computer system that includes the circuits which controls the interpretation and execution of instructions. Synonymous with CPU (Central Processing Units) and main frame.

Chat: A chat, in general means talking to other people, by typing, who are using the Internet the same time as you. Most of this communication is done at a specific site. Chats can be ongoing or scheduled, group or one-to-one. Chats may also use sound and video where applicable.

Chip: An integrated electronic circuit consisting of miniature transistors and other circuit elements contained on a silicon wafer.

CIS development: The section of computer installation responsible for the analysis, design, and development of new systems and programs.

Client: A software program that is used to contact and obtain data from a Server software program on another computer, often across a great distance. Each Client program is designed to work with one or more specific kinds of Server programs and each Server requires a specific kind of Client. A Wed Browser is a specific kind of Client.

Clipart: These are pre-prepared graphic images that one can incorporate into a document with a word processor or a desktop publishing program.

COBOL (Common Business Oriented Language): A procedure-oriented language developed to facilitate the preparation and inter-change of programs which form business data processing functions.

Note: Designed in 1959 by a committee representing the U.S. Government and several computer manufacturers, COBOL has evolved through several versions (e.g., COBOL-60, COBOL-61, COBOL 61-Extended, COBOL-65). Every COBOL source program has four divisions, whose names and functions are as follows: (1) Identification Division, which identifies the source program and the output of a compilation, (2) Environment Division, which specifies those aspects of a data processing problem that are dependent upon the physical characteristics of a particular computer, (3) Data Division, which describes the data that the object program is to accept as input, manipulate, create, or produce as output, and (4) Procedure Division, which specifies the procedures to be performed by the object program, by means of English-like statements such as: "Subtract tax from gross pay giving net pay".

Cold Boot: To start a computer and load the operating system into RAM.

Collage: A single picture formed by pasting parts of different pictures or objects.

Command Name: The component of a command that specifies what action DOS is to perform.

Command: An instruction for DOS to perform a specific action.

Compile: To prepare a machine language program (or a program expressed in symbolic coding) from a program written in another programming language (usually a procedure oriented language such as BASIC, COBOL or FORTRAN). The compilation process usually involves examining and making use of the overall structure of the program and/or generating more than one object program instruction for each source program statement. Contrast with assemble.

Compiler: A computer program that compiles. Compilers are an important part of the basic software for most computers permitting the use of procedure-oriented languages which can greatly reduce the human effort required to prepare computer programs.

Computer information system (CIS): A coordinated collection of hardware, software, people, data, and support resources to perform an integrated series of functions that can include input, processing, output, and storage.

Computer-aided instruction (CAI): Interactive use of a computer to deliver educational contents to individuals and to adjust presentations according to learner responses.

Console: A portion of a computer that is used for communication between operators or maintenance engineers and the computer, usually by means of displays and manual control.

Cookie: A type of text file given to a browser by a server, used to record specific information about a user's preferences.

Corel DRAW: An application software for vector drawing.

CR - Carnage Return: This is the most important key on a computer or word processor keyboard. It is used to activate most of the functions on the system. It is usually identified by a reverse L-symbol with an arrow on the end of the horizontal bar.

Current Directory: The directory that DOS is currently using.

Current Drive: The disk drive that DOS is currently using.

Cursor: A symbol on the screen that marks the location where characters will appear as they are typed from the keyboard. The cursor usually displays as a blinking vertical line in a word processor or as a blinking underscore.

Data Base Administrator (DBA): The person in charge of defining and managing the content of a data base.

Data Base Management System (DBMS) : Software to manage and control data resources.

Data Bus: The internal pathway in a computer on which data moves.

Data dictionary: A document listing and defining all items or processes represented in data flow diagrams or used within a system.

DDR (Double Data Rate): A mechanism used to produce computer memory.

Debug: To trace and eliminate mistakes in a program or faults in equipment. The process is often assisted by a diagnostic routine.

Decompression: Process of enlarging a compressed file in a computer to its original size. (Also called unzipping.)

Default: An assumed value or option the computer uses when none is specified. Synonymous with regular, normal, or primary (as in a printer). Or as in normal or standard settings in an application or software program. Default in computers has NOTHING to do with finances.

Density: The data storage capacity of a disk.

Desk checking: A manual checking process in which representative data items, used for detecting errors in program logic, are traced through the program before the latter is checked on the computer.

Dialog Box: A small window that opens up on the computer screen to the user request or put in information relating to a task (such as printing) or give the information to the user, such as when there is an error.

Digitize: The process of converting lines, drawings and pictures to digital form by scanning the drawings and pictures with a device that converts sensed highlights into numbers or horizontal and vertical coordinates.

Direct access device: A hardware unit that can read and write records from or to a file without processing all preceding records.

Direct data entry: Entry of data directly into the computer through machine-readable source documents or through use of on-line terminals. Direct entry is a by-product of source business transactions, without requiring manual transcription from original paper documents.

Directory: An area on a disk where you store a group of related files under an identifying name. Also a list of files contained on a disk.

Disk Drive: A mechanism that reads and writes data on a disk.

Disk Operating System (DOS): The name used for various operating systems. The primary function of a disk operating system is to control the flow of data to and from the CPU and peripherals.

Disk: A circular platter with a magnetic coating on both sides. The most common medium for storing computer data.

Diskette: A removable computer storage medium made of plastic and covered with a magnetic coating. Usually 3_" in size (5_" floppy diskettes are obsolete). See also *Disk* and *Hard Disk*.

Domain Name: The location or address of an entity on the Internet. They must contain a top level domain name (such as .com, .org or .net) and a second-level domain name, such as DigitalMadurai. Second level domain names for the root (top level) .edu, .com, .org, .gov and .net domains in North America must be registered with Internic.

Domain Name: The unique name that identifies an Internet site. Domain Names always have 2 or more parts, separated by dots. The part on the left is the most specific, and the part on the right is the most general. A given machine may have more than one Domain Name but a given Domain Name points to only one machine. For example, the domain names : matisse.net, mail.matisse.net, workshop.matisse.net, can all refer to the same machine, but each domain name can refer to no more than one machine.

Double-Density: The diskette type that holds 720 Kb of data in 3_" diskettes (360 Kb of data in obsolete 5_" diskettes).

Down time: Time at which the computer is not available for processing.

dpi - Dots Per Inch: The unit of resolution indicating the number of dots printed per inch of a raster picture.

Drag: To move something around the computer with the help of the mouse. This involves holding down one of the mouse buttons while user moves it.

DTP (Desk Top Publishing) : The process of making publication and taking printouts using specially designed computer software's.

Dump: (1) To copy the contents of a set of storage locations, usually from an internal storage device (such as disk storage) to an external storage medium (such as magnetic tape or floppy disk), and usually for diagnostic or rerun purposes. (2) The data that results from the process defined in (1).

EBCDIC (Extended Binary Coded Decimal Interchange Code): An 8-bit code that represents an extension of a 6-bit "BCD" code that was widely used in computers of the first and second generations. EBCDIC can represent upto 256 distinct characters and is the principal code used in many of the current computers.

E-mail - (Electronic Mail): Messages, usually text, sent from one person to another via computer. E-mail can also be sent automatically to a large number of addresses (Mailing List).

Ethernet: A very common method of networking computers in a LAN. Ethernet will handle about 10,000,000 bits-per-second and can be used with almost any kind of computer.

External Commands: Commands stored in program files on a disk, which can only be executed when the program file is present in the current directory or in a directory, specified in a path statement.

Eye of Gnome: The GNU/Linux software to view pictures.

Facsimile Transmission System: Often abbreviated to 'Fax', this system is employed to relay alphanumeric and graphic data to other Fax machines at distant sites along a telephone or other telecommunications link. A fax device produces a facsimile copy of the original in the same manner as an office copier, except that the original is received electronically.

FAQ: Frequently Asked Question, a common format Web site authors use to answer questions.

File maintenance: The updating of a file to reflect the effects of period changes by adding, altering data; e.g., the addition of new programs to program library on magnetic disk.

File processing: The periodic updating of master files to reflect the effect of current data, often transaction data contained in detail files; e.g., a weekly payroll run updating the payroll master file.

File: A collection of related records, usually (but not necessarily) arranged in sequence according to key contained on each record.

Note: A record, in turn, is a collection of related items; an item is an arbitrary quantity of data that is treated as a unit. In payroll processing, an employee's pay rate forms an item; a group of items relating to one employee form a record, and the complete set of employee records forms a file.

Filter: Either a program that sorts data or a pattern that is used to determine which type of data is accepted. Often used with e-mail to separate messages.

Firewall: A system that protects a private network and its resources from unauthorized access.

Fixed length record: A record that always contains the same number of characters. The restriction to a fixed length may be deliberate, in order to simplify and speed processing or it may be dictated by the characteristics of the equipment used. Contrast with variable-length record.

Fixed word length: Pertaining to a machine word or operand that always has the same number of bits or characters. Contrast with variable word length. Most scientific computers are of the fixed word length type for maximum computational speeds, while many business oriented computers have variable word length to permit efficient handling of items and records of varying sizes. Some computers types have both fixed and variable words.

Floppy Disk: A removable computer storage medium made of plastic and covered with a magnetic coating. Usually 3_" in size (5_" floppy diskettes are obsolete).

Font: A character set in a particular style and size of type, including all alphanumeric characters, punctuation marks and special symbols.

Format: (Dual meaning) (a) To prepare a disk (or Drive) for data storage by creating sectors and cleaning (erasing) any and all files. (b) The layout or appearance of a document in terms of fonts, margins, etc. A special formula will have a certain format (sometimes also referred to as syntax), or appearance.

FORTRAN (Formula Translation): A procedure oriented language designed to facilitate the preparation of computer programs that performs mathematical computations. It was designed by IBM in the 1950's to use symbols and expression similar to those of algebra, FORTRAN was not originally intended to be a common language. However, it has evolved through several basic versions (*e.g.* FORTRAN II, FORTRAN IV) plus numerous dialects, has become largely machine-independent and has been approved as a USA standard programming language in two versions (FORTRAN and basic FORTRAN). FORTRAN is widely used procedure-oriented language in the United States and is being effectively employed in certain business as well as scientific applications. The essential elements of the FORTRAN is the assignment statement; *e.g.* Z = X + Y causes the current value of the variables X and Y to be added together and their sum to replace the previous value of the variable Z.

Fourth Generation Languages: These are infact sophisticated software packages that permit users to query data bases and extract the information needed to solve problems and prepare reports. With these languages, very complex operations are accomplished by just pressing a few keystrokes. Some examples of fourth generation languages are dBASE, FRED and PC/FOCUS.

FTP - (File Transfer Protocol): A very common method of moving files between two Internet sites. FTP is a special way to login to another Internet site for the purposes of retrieving and/ or sending files. There are many Internet sites that have established publicly accessible repositories of material that can be obtained using FTP.

Function Keys : Keys from F1 to F12 of a keyboard, which has specific function in application programms (Eg. For Help press F1)

GUI (Graphical User Interface): A computer mode of interaction using graphics.

Hard Disk: A large built-in storage capacity medium for computer data.

Hardware: Any of the mechanical or electrical components of a computer such as the CPU, memory chips, disk drives, keyboard, and monitor.

Header label: A machine-readable record at the beginning of the file containing data identifying the file and data used in control.

Hollerith code: A widely used code for representing alphanumeric data on punched cards, named after Herman Hollerith, the originator of punched card tabulating. Each card column holds one character, and each decimal digit, letter, and special character is represented by one, two or three holes punched into designated row positions of the column.

Host: Any computer on a network that is a repository for services available to other computers on the network. It is quite common to have one host machine providing several services, such as WWW and USENET.

HTML - (Hyper Text Markup Language): The coding language used to create Hypertext documents for use on the World Wide Web. HTML looks a lot like old fashioned typesetting code, where you surround a block of text with codes that indicate how it should appear. Additionally, in HTML one can specify that a block of text, or a word, is linked to another file on the Internet. HTML files are meant to be viewed using a World Wide Web client Program, such as Netscape Navigator, Internet Explorer or Mosaic.

HTML Editors: Software for easy HTML page creation.

HTTP: Hypertext Transfer Protocol, the definitive manner in which messages are formatted, transmitted and received on the World Wide Web.

Hyper text: A text format with facilities like Link, Bold, Italics etc. like an HTML life.

Hyperlink: A pointer or reference to another document. Usually underlined text or a picture, it accesses another document when clicked on.

Hyperlink: A technique to open another page from a web page.

IDE Port: Port on motherboard to which Hard Disk, CD Drive, Floppy Drive etc. are connected.

IDP (Integrated Data Processing): Data processing by a system that coordinates a number of previously unconnected processes in order to improve overall efficiency by reducing or eliminating redundant data entry or processing operations. An example of IDP is a system in which data describing orders, production, and purchases is entered into a single processing scheme that combines the functions of scheduling, invoicing, inventory control, etc.

Input Device: A mechanism, such as a keyboard or a mouse, used to give instructions to a computer for processing.

Input: Any data entered into a computer for processing.

Integrated Circuit (IC): A device incorporating circuitry and semiconductor components within a single unit, usually a miniature chip. Circuit elements and components are created as part of the same manufacturing procedures.

Interface Card: Special utility cards like Sound card, Network card etc. connected to the mother board.

Interface Slot: Slot in mother board to connect interface cards.

Interlocked Gap: The distance on a magnetic tape between the end of one block and the beginning of the next. Within this distance, the tape can be stopped and brought up to the normal speed again. Since the tape speed is not constant when stopping, no reading or writing is permitted in the gap. Synonymous with inter-record gap and record gap, though the use of these two terms is not recommended because of the important distinction between blocks and records.

Internal Commands: Commands that are loaded into RAM with DOS when a computer is booted and which can be executed whenever the system prompt is displayed.

Internet - (Upper case I): The vast collection of inter-connected networks that all use the TCP/IP protocols and that evolved from the ARPANET of the late 60's and early 70's. The Internet now connects more than 70,000 independent networks into a vast global internet.

Interpreter: Language translator that converts source code to machine code and executes it immediately, statement by statement.

Intranet: A private network inside a company or organization that uses the same kind of software that one would find on the public Internet, but that is only for internal use. As the Internet has become more popular, many of the tools used on the Internet are being used in private networks. For example, many companies have web servers that are available only to employees. Note that an Intranet may not actually be an internet — it may simply be a network.

IP: Internet Protocol, specifies and addresses the packets that the messages transmitted on the Internet are composed of. It usually works with another protocol called TCP, or Transfer Control Protocol, which establishes a connection between a destination and a source.

IRC: Internet Relay Chat, a client/server-software chat system that allows people anywhere on the Internet to join in live discussions.

ISP - (Internet Service Provider): An institution that provides access to the Internet in some form, usually for money. For example, in India, VSNL (Videsh Sanchar Nigam Limited) is the Internet Service Provider.

ISP: Internet Service Provider, an outfit or company which offers access to the Internet, usually for a fee.

Java: Java is a network-oriented programming language invented by Sun Microsystems that is specifically designed for writing programs that can be safely downloaded to one's computer through the Internet and immediately run without fear of viruses or other harm to one's computer or files. Using small Java programs (called "Applets"), Web pages can include functions such as animations, calculations, and other fancy tricks. One can expect to see a huge variety of features added to the Web using Java, since a Java program can be written to do almost anything a regular computer program can do, and then include that Java program in a Web page.

Joystick: A vertical lever, usually in a ball socket, which can be tilted in any direction and is used to move a cursor around the screen or display unit of a computer.

JPEG: A format to save and keep picture files.

Kb or K or Kilobyte: 1,024 bytes or characters.

Label: A name attached to or written alongside the entity it identifies e.g. a key that is attached to the item or record it identifies, or a name written alongside a statement on a coding sheet.

LAN: Local Area Network, a computer network for a relatively small geographic area. Each workstation or personal computer within the LAN has access to the devices shared by the LAN server or processor.

Layer Box: Dialogue box showing details of layers in a picture file.

Layer: A technique applied to prepare picture files.

Layout: Total design and positions of letters and graphics in a page.

Link: A pointer or reference to another document. Usually underlined text or a picture, it accesses another document when clicked on. (See also Hyperlink.)

Live Cam: A video camera attached to a computer. Its latest image is downloadable off the World Wide Web. Also called a Netcam.

Lock Up: When a computer does not accept input from the keyboard or any other input device, and the cursor does not move. A computer that locks up may have to be restarted again.

Login: Noun or a verb. ***Noun :*** The account name used to gain access to a computer system. Not a secret (contrast with Password). ***Verb:*** The act of entering into a computer system.

LOL: Laugh Out Loud, an e-mail or chat abbreviation.

Machine language: A language that is used directly by a computer. Thus, a "Machine language program" is a set of instructions which a computer can directly recognize and execute and which will cause it to perform a particular process. In Machine-oriented language there is a general (though not necessarily strict) one-to one correspondence between the statements of source program and the instructions of the object program (which will normally be a machine language program ready for executing on a particular computer). The input to an assembler is usually expressed in a machine-oriented language. Contrast with procedure-oriented language.

Maintenance (file): Process of changing a master file through the addition of new records, the deletion of old records and changing the contents of existing records.

Mark sensing: A technique for detecting pencil marks entered by hand in prescribed places on some preprinted documents. The marked data may be converted into light patterns and transmitted directly to a computer.

Master file: A file containing relatively permanent information which is used as source of reference and is generally updated periodically. Contrast with detail file.

Maximise Button: A button by which a software/ window under use can be maximised.

Media player: A software in Windows to watch movies.

Memory Slot: Part of a motherboard to connect memory cards.

Menu: Table that shows the available directions of a software.

Merge: To form a single sequenced file by combining two or more similarly sequenced files. Merging may be performed manually, by a collator, or by a computer system for which a "merge routine" is available. Repeated merging, splitting and remerging of strings of records can be used to arrange the records in sequence; this process, called a "merging sort," is frequently used as the basis for sorting operations on computer systems.

Message Switching System: A facility which uses computer techniques to transmit and receive, and store and retrieve textual information. It is a means of communicating in a fast, cost-effective and reliable way, using modern technology. These systems allow immediate access to any person or office using the facilities and all massages are transmitted and received instantly whether addressee is in the next office or the other side of the world.

MICR (Magnetic Ink Character Recognition): The automatic reading by machine of graphic characters printed with magnetic ink.

Module: In programming, a solution document representing a processing function that will be carried out by a computer.

Monitor: The visual display unit of a computer system.

Motherboard: The main circuit board of a microcomputer.

Mouse: A small, hand-held mechanism that controls the movement of the cursor or a pointer on a computer screen.

Move Tool: Tool to change the position of a picture.

MP3: MPEG-1 Audio Layer-3, a technology that compresses sound files from much larger files into very small files roughly one-twelfth the size, while retaining sound quality. Usually download-and-play files rather than streaming audio, MP3 players are available for download at several MP3 sites.

MPEG: The Moving Pictures Experts Group, a consortium which develops standards for digital audio and video compression. To play an MPEG file a computer must have certain amounts of speed, hard disk space and memory, as well as an MPEG viewer or other software.

MS Backup: A utility program used to back up a large number of files.

MS-DOS Operating System or Microsoft Disk Operating System: The operating system used by most of the major personal computer systems, especially the IBM Personal Computer 'look-likes'. IBM personal computers used a variation known as PC-DOS.

Multiprocessing: The simultaneous execution of two or more sequences of instructions in a single computer system. Frequently refers to simultaneous execution accomplished by the use of a system with more than one central processor.

Multi-programming: A technique for handling two or more independent programs simultaneously by overlapping or interleaving their execution. The overlapping or interleaving of the execution of the various programs is usually controlled by an operating system which attempts to optimize the performance of the computer system in accordance with the priority requirements of the various jobs.

Nautilus: File manager in Linux.

Netscape: A WWW Browser and the name of a company. The Netscape browser was originally based on the Mosaic program developed at the National Center for Supercomputing Applications (NCSA). Netscape has grown in features rapidly and is widely recognized as the best and most popular web browser. Netscape Corporation also produces web server software. Netscape provided major improvements in speed and interface over other browsers.

Node: Any single computer connected to a network.

OCR (Optical Character Recognition): The automatic reading by machine of graphic characters through the use of light-sensitive devices.

Operating System: An organized collection of routines and procedures for operating a computer. These routines and procedures will normally perform some or all of the following functions - (1) Scheduling, loading, initiating and supervising the execution of programs; (2) allocating storage, input/output units and other facilities of the computer system; (3) initiating and controlling input/output operations; (4) handling errors and restarts; (5) coordinating communication between the human operator and the computer system; (6) maintaining a log of system operations, and (7) controlling operation in a multi-programming, multi-processing or time-sharing mode. Among the facilities frequently included within an operating system are an executive routine, a scheduler, an IOCS, utility routines, and monitor routines.

Output Device: A mechanism, such as a printer or a monitor, used to retrieve and view data after it has been processed by a computer.

Output: Data that is generated from a computer after processing.

Overflow: In an arithmetic operation, the generation of a quantity beyond the capacity of the register or storage location which is to receive the result.

Overlay: To transfer segment of program from auxiliary storage into internal storage for execution, so that two or more segments occupy the same storage locations at different times. This technique makes it possible to execute programs which are too large to fit into the computer internal storage at one time, it is also important in multi-programming and time-sharing operations.

Parallel Interface: Generally used to link a printer into a computer or word processor. This interface allows the printer to accept transmission of data which is sent in parallel bit sequences. (See also Serial Interface.)

Parallel Port: The port used to connect associated devices like a printer to a computer, which help speedy transfer of data.

Parity Bit: A bit (binary digit) appended to an array of bits to make the sum of all the 1-bits in the array either always even ("even parity") or always odd ("odd parity").

Parity Checks: A check that tests whether the number of 1-bits in an array is either even ("even parity check") or odd ("odd parity check").

Peripheral equipment: The input/output units and secondary storage units of a computer system. **Note:** The central processor and its associated storage and control units are the only units of a computer system which are not considered peripheral equipment.

Peripherals: Additional components which enhance computer performance.

Port: Device by which different component in and out of a system unit can be connected.

PPP - (Point to Point Protocol): Most well known as a protocol that allows a computer to use a regular telephone line and a modem to make TCP/IP connections and thus be really and truly on the Internet.

Printer: A device for generating computer output on paper.

Problem-oriented language: A language whose design is oriented toward the specification of a particular class of problems, such as numerical control of machine tools. Sometimes used as a general term to describe both procedure and problem-oriented languages.

Procedure-oriented language: A language designed to permit convenient specification, in terms of procedural or algorithmic steps, of data processing or computational processes. Examples include ALGOL, COBOL and FORTRAN. Contrast with problem-oriented language and machine-oriented language.

Program: A set of instructions that a computer follows to perform a task.

Programmable read-only memory (PROM): Computer memory chips that can be programmed permanently, by burning the circuits in patterns, to carry out predefined process.

Programming language/1: (PL/1) A general-purpose, high level language that is designed to combine business and scientific processing features and that can be easily learned by novice programmers, yet contains advanced features for experienced programmers.

Protocol Translator: A peripheral device which converts the communications protocol of one system into the protocols of another system so that the two systems are compatible enabling data to be transferred between them.

PSET: Command in BASIC to show a point on the screen.

QuickTime: A multimedia plug-in program from Apple. It can play sound, animation, text and video in a single file.

RAM: Randon Access Memory, the part of the computer which keeps operating system and applications' data. RAM is very fast to access, but it only stays as long as the computer is running.

Random Access Memory (RAM): Temporary memory that holds application programs and data which you create and manipulate.

Random access: Pertaining to a storage device whose access time is not significantly affected by the location of the data to be accessed, thus, any item of data which is stored online can be accessed within a relatively short time (usually in part of a second). Same as direct access. Contrast with serial access.

Read-Only Memory (ROM): Permanent memory that hold the programs which are responsible for the initial phases of starting a computer.

Reboot: To restart a computer by turning it off and then on again by pressing Ctrl, Alt, Del, or by pressing a reset button.

Redundancy check: A check based on the transfer of more bits or characters than the minimum number required to express the massage itself, the added bits or characters having been inserted systematically for checking purposes. The most common type of redundancy check is parity check.

Residue check: A check of numeric data or arithmetic operation in which each number A, is divided by the modulo, N, and the remainder, B, accompanies A as a check digits. For example, in modulo 4 checks, B will be either 0, 1, 2 or 3; if the remainder formed when A is divided by 4 does not equal B, an error is indicated. Synonymous with modulo N check.

Resolution: It indicates the degree of details—that can be perceived. The higher the resolution, the finer the detail.

Router: A special purpose computer (or software package) that handles the connection between 2 or more networks. Routers spend all their time looking at the destination addresses of the packets passing through them and deciding which route to send them on.

Run manual: A manual documenting the processing system, program logic, controls, program changes, and operating instructions associated with a computer run.

Run: A performance of a specific process by a computer on a given set of data i.e., the execution of one routine or of several routines which are linked to form one operating unit, during which little or no human intervention is required.

Scanner: Device used to copy pictures from papers or photographs to computer.

Scroll: To move a graphics image or the text on the monitor up, down, right, or left, in a smooth, usually continuous and reversible action.

Search Engine: A program, or a system of programs, which uses keywords to find Web pages containing matching words, returning the results to the user.

Secondary storage: Storage that supplements a computer's primary internal storage. Synonymous with auxiliary storage.

Security program: Systems program that controls access to data in files and permits only authorized use of terminals and other equipments. Control is usually through various levels of pass words assigned on the basis of need to know.

Server: A computer, or a software package, that provides a specific kind of service to client software running on other computers. The term can refer to a particular piece of software, such as a WWW server, or to the machine on which the software is running e.g., Our mail server is down today, that's why e-mail isn't getting out. A single server machine could have several different server software packages running on it, thus providing many different servers to clients on the network.

Shareware: Shareware is software that is initially free to download, with the agreement that the user may have to pay for it later.

SMPS (Switched Mode Power Supply) : The part of a system unit which distributes power supply to all segments of a computer.

Software: 1. A collection of programs and routines associated with a computer (including assemblers, compilers, utility routines, and operating systems) which facilitates the programming and operation of the computer. Contrast with hardware.

2. Any set of instructions or data a computer may use. The programs that tell a computer what to do and how to do it.

Sound Card: An electronic circuit card which can convert the data from computer on sound waves to pan it to speakers.

Source Program: A program written in a source language (e.g., written in COBOL, C, FORTRAN, or symbolic coding for input to a compiler or assembler).

Spam: Internet slang for unsolicited, and often commercial, e-mail or newsgroup postings.

Spider: A program that automatically culls Web pages. Spiders are often used in search engines.

Spooling: Computer processing technique under which input and output files originating on and destined for slow-speed devices are written to high-speed storage devices prior to and following processing. Thus, processing can take place at high speeds while input and output can be handled separately at relatively slow speeds.

Spreadsheet An electronic grid of rows and columns used to enter, organize and analyze a collection of numbers or data.

SQL - (Structured Query Language): A specialized programming language for sending queries to databases.

Status line: An area - a strip -at the bottom of the screen that tells the user about the operations of a program he/she is working in. For instance, a status line could tell that the file is now being saved, or that it is being printed.

Storage allocation: The assignment of specific programs, program segments, and or block of data to specific portions of a computer's storage.

Streaming: Continuously playing audio (streaming audio) or video (streaming video). Users don't need to wait for large files to download before listening or viewing. Instead, the media plays as it arrives.

Subdirectory or Subfolder: A directory that is contained within or is subordinate to another directory.

Surf: Internet term for exploring **the** Internet without a pre-set agenda. See also Browse.

System development life cycle (SDLC): Activities required to develop, implement and install a new or revised system. Standard activity phases include investigation, analysis and general design, detailed design and implementation, installation, and review.

T-1, T-3: Bell introduced the T-carrier system, the first successful system to support digital transmission, in the 1960s. The original rate, T-1 (1.544 Mbps) is a higher-speed line commonly used by ISPs (Internet Service Providers). T-3 (44.736 Mbps) is an even higher speed line.

Tab: (1) Facility to move the curser at prefixed small distance between words, to prepare small tables. (2) The space given between two words using the tab key. (3) Mechanism in dialogue boxes like paragraph in word processors to organize more than one information in the same box.

Task Bar: The bottom portion of a window where the start button, time button etc. are usually placed.

TCP/IP - (Transmission Control Protocol/Internet Protocol): This is the suite of protocols that defines the Internet. Originally designed for the UNIX operating system, TCP/IP software is now available for every major kind of computer operating system. To be truly on the Internet, your computer must have TCP/IP software.

Template: A previously made model slide.

Toggle: A switch or control code that turns an event on or off by repeated action or use; to turn something on or off by repeating the same action.

Track: That part of a data storage medium that is influenced by (or influences) one head; e.g., the ring-shaped portion of the surface of a disk, or one of several divisions (most commonly seven or nine) running parallel to the edges of a magnetic tape.

Translator: A device or computer program that performs translation from one language or code to another - e.g., an assembler or compiler.

UNIX Operating System: Computer operating system developed by the Bell Telephone Laboratories in the USA. Currently considered to be the system of the future with many manufacturers adopting UNIX for their new ranges of equipments. Office automation software is, on the whole, not very well represented in the UNIX area. There are some world processing packages, such as Q-One from Quadratronic, an offering from Interplex within an integrated package, Crystalwriter from Syntactics and UNIX-option Multimate which will be available shortly.

UNIX: An operating system developed in the early '70s. It was the first operating system written with the C language, and was the first open or standard operating system. UNIX is popular with workstations, but not personal computers.

Unpack: To separate short units of data that have previously been packed i.e., to reverse a packing operation.

Update: To incorporate into a master file the changes required to reflect recent transactions or other events.

URL - (Uniform Resource Locator): The standard way to give the address of any resource on the Internet that is part of the World Wide Web (WWW). A URL looks like this : http://www.icai.org/seminars.htnnl or telnet://well.sf.ca.in or newsmew.newusers.questions etc. The most common way to use a URL is to enter into a WWW browser program, such as Netscape, or Lynx.

USB Port (Universal Serial Bus Port): A way by which external equipments can be attached to a computer.

Utility routine: A standard routine used to assist in the operation of a computer by performing some frequently required processes such as sorting, merging, report program generation, data transcription, file maintenance, etc. Utility routines are important components of the software supplied by the manufacturers of most computers.

Vector File: A file stored with vector graphics or pictures.

Vector Image: Picture file madeup of geometric shapes like circuts, rectangles, ovals etc.

Very large scale integration (VLSI): Design and production techniques to place thousands of electronic components within small integrated circuit chips to reduce their sizes and costs.

Webmaster: Individual who creates and or manages a Web site. May also be the individual who manages the technical aspects of a Web site.

Wildcard Characters: Special characters that can be used in most DOS commands as substitutes for other characters. The asterisk (*) and the question mark (?) symbols are wildcard characters.

Word Length: The number of bits or characters in a word.

WWW: World Wide Web, all the resources on the Internet that use HTTP, or hypertext transfer protocol, e.g. Web pages.

Zip Drive: Durable disk drive that uses 100 MB disks. Popular for backing up hard drives, or transporting large files.

Zip File: File made up of several other files compressed into one.

Zoom: The command to see a thing on the screen as enlarged or as reduced.

Computer Abbreviations

ACC	Accumulator
ACK	Acknowledge character
A/D	Analog to Digital
ADCCP	Advanced Data Communication Control Procedure
ADP	Automatic Data Processing
ALGOL	ALGOrithmic Language
ALU	Arithmetic Logic Unit
AM	Amplitude Modulation or Accounting Machine or Access Mechanism
ANSI	American National Standards Institute
APDOS	Apple DOS Operating System
AP	Attached Processor
APL	A Programming Language
ASCII	American Standard Code for Information Interchange
ASR	Automatic Send and Receive
ATM	Automatic Teller Machine
AU	Arithmetic Unit
BASIC	Beginner's All-purpose Symbolic Instruction Code
BCD	Binary Coded Decimal
BCS	British Computer Society
BDOS	Basic Disk Operating System
BIT	Binary digit
BIOS	Basic Input/Output System
BMC	Bubble Memory Control
Bps	Bits per second
BPI	Bytes per Inch
BROM	Bipolar Read Only Memory
BSAM	Basic Sequential Access Method
BSC	Binary Synchronous Communications
CAD	Computer Aided (Assisted) Design
CAD/CAM	Computer-Aided Design/Computer-Aided Manufacturing
CAFS	Contents Addressable File Store
CAI	Computer Aided (Assisted) Instruction
CAL	Computer Aided (Assisted) Learning
CAM	Computer Aided (Assisted) Manufacturing or Content Addressed Memory
CASE	Computer Aided Software Engineering
CAT	1. Computer Aided (Assisted) Training
	2. Computer Aided (Axial) Topography
CCD	Charge Coupled Device
CGA	Colour Graphics Adapter
CDAC	Centre for Development of Advanced Computing
CDROM	Computer Disk Read Only Memory
CICS	Computer Information Control System
CIM	Computer Input Microfilm
CLIP	Computer Language Information Processing
CMI	Computer Managed Instruction
CMOS	Complementary Metal Oxide Semiconductor
CML	Computer Managed Learning
CNC	Computer Numerical Control
COBOL	Common Business Oriented Language
CODASYL	Conference on Data System Languages
COM	Computer Output (Originated) Microfilm

COMAL	Common Algorithmic language
CORAL	Class Oriented Ring Associated Language
Cps	Characters per second
CPM	Control Program for Microprocessor
CPU	Central Processing Unit
CROM	Control Read Only Memory
CRT	Cathode Ray Tube
CSI	Computer Society of India
DS/HD	Double Sided, high density
DS/DD	Double Sided, double density
DAD	Direct Access Devices
DASD	Direct Access Storage Device
DBMS	Data Base Management System
DBTG	Data Base Task Group (of CODASYL)
DCE	Data Communications Equipment
DDL	Data Description (or Definition) Language
DDP	Distributed Data Processing
DOS	Disk (based) Operating System
DP	Data Processing
DPI	Dots per inch
DTP	Desktop Publishing
DPM	Data Processing Manager
DPS	Data Processing System
DRO	Destructive Read Out
DSS	Decision Support System
EBCDIC	Extended Binary Coded Decimal Interchange Code
ECMA	European Computer Manufacturers Association
ECOM	Electronic computer oriented mail
EDI	Electronic Data Interchange
EDS	Exchangeable Disk Store
EEPROM	Electrically Erasable Programmed Read Only Memory
EDP	Electronic Data Processing (equivalent to DP)
EFTS	Electronic Funds Transfer System
ENIAC	Electronic Numerical Integrator and Calculator
EPROM	Erasable Programmable Read Only Memory
FGCS	Fifth Generation Computer System
FEP	Front-End Processor
FORTRAN	Formula Translation
GB	Giga Bytes
GIGO	Garbage In/Garbage Out
GUI	Graphical User Interface
HIPO	Hierarchical Input/Process/Output
HLL	High Level Language
Hz	Hertz
IBG	Inter Block Gap
IC	Integrated Circuit
IDP	Integrated Data Processing
IFIP	International Federation for Information Processing
IMPLE	Initial Micro Program Load
I/O	Input/Output
IOCS	Input/Output Control System
IPS	Instructions per second
ISAM	Index(ed) Sequential Access method
ISDN	Integrated Services Digital Network
ISO	International Standards Organisation
ISR	Information Storage Retrieval
JCL	Job Control Language
K	Kilo-1000 in decimal; 1024 (210) in binary system
KBS	Kilo-Bytes per second
LAN	Local Area Network
LAP	Link Access Protocol
LCD	Liquid Crystal Display
LED	Light Emitting Diode
LISP	LIST Processing
LSI	Large Scale Integration

MB	Mega bytes.1 million in decimal; 1,048, 576 (220) in binary system
MAR	Memory Address Register
MCI	Magnetic Character Inscriber
MDR	Memory Data Register
MICR	Magnetic Ink Character Recognition
MIPS	Millions of instructions per second
MIS	Management Information System (or Services)
MPU	Micro-Processor Unit
MSI	Medium Scale Integration
MVS	Multiple Virtual Storage
NCC	National Computing Centre
NS	Nano Second
OCR	Optical Character Recognition (Reading)
OMR	Optical Mark Recognition (Reading)
OOF	Office of the Future
OOP	Object Oriented Programming
OS	Operating Systems
OPS	Operating per second
OSI	Open systems Interconnection
PBX	Private Branch Exchange
PCB	Printed Circuit Board
PC	Personal Computer
POS	Point-of Sale
PIN	Personal Identification Number
PL/1	Programming Language/1
PMOS	P-Channel Metal Oxide Semiconductor
PROLOG	Programming in Logic
PROM	Programmable Read Only Memory
PSE	Packet Switched System

PSTN	Public Switched Telephone network
QBE	Query By Example
RAM	Random Access Memory
RCS	Realtime Communication System
RJE	Remote Job Entry
ROM	Read Only Memory
RPG	Report Program Generator
RTL	Real Time language
RDBMS	Relational Data Base Management Systems
SOP	Standard Operating Procedure
SNOBL	String Oriented Symbolic Languages
SNA	Systems Network Architecture
SQL	Structured Query Language
SSI	Small Scale Integration
TDM	Time Division Multiplexing
TPI	Tracks Per inch
TRS	Tandy Radio Shack
T/S	Time Sharing
TSS	Time Sharing System
TTY	Tele Typewriter
UG	User Group
UNIVAC	Universal automatic computer
VDU	Visual Display Unit
VAN	Value Added Network
VLDB	Very Large Data Base
VGA	Video Graphics Adapter
VLSI	Very Large Scale Integration
WAN	Wide Area Network
WORM	Write Once, Read Memory
WP	Word Processing

Multiple Choice Questions

1. The word size of a microprocessor refers to—
   (*a*) The amount of information that can be stored in a byte
   (*b*) The amount of information that can be stored in a cycle
   (*c*) The number of machine operations performed in a second
   (*d*) The maximum length of an English word that can be input to a computer

2. Bar codes store information using—
   (*a*) Punch holes
   (*b*) Thick and thin lines
   (*c*) Magnetized spots
   (*d*) Bits

3. Below are examples of real security and privacy risks EXCEPT—
   (*a*) hackers (*b*) identity theft
   (*c*) spam (*d*) viruses

4. Which is an electronic device that can store temporarily a single bit of data.
   (*a*) Accumulator (*b*) Buffer
   (*c*) Memory (*d*) Latch

5. The first generation computers were characterised by—
   (*a*) Micro processor chips
   (*b*) Thermionic valves
   (*c*) Transistors
   (*d*) Integrated circuits

6. The ability to recover and read deleted or damaged files from a criminal computer is an example of a law enforcement specialty known as—
   (*a*) robotics
   (*b*) computer forensics
   (*c*) simulation
   (*d*) animation

7. A modern digital computer has—
   (*a*) Extremely high speed
   (*b*) Large memory
   (*c*) Almost unlimited army
   (*d*) All of these

8. What is the full form of COBOL?
   (*a*) Common Business Objective Language
   (*b*) Command Byte Oriented Language
   (*c*) Common Business Oriented Language
   (*d*) Character Business Oriented Language

9. Find the invalid combination.
   (*a*) Dot Matrix Printer - Impact Printer
   (*b*) Laser Printer - Non Impact Printer
   (*c*) Daisy Wheel printer - Non Impact Printer
   (*d*) Inkjet Printer - Non Impact Printer

10. In which generation of computers transistors were used?
    (*a*) First generation computers
    (*b*) Second generation computers
    (*c*) Third generation computers
    (*d*) Fourth generation computers

11. Which computer system is mainly used in Weather forecasting and Disaster control?
    (*a*) Super computer
    (*b*) Mainframe computer
    (*c*) Micro computer
    (*d*) Personal computer

12. A factor which would strongly influence a business person to adopt a computer is its—
    (*a*) Accuracy (*b*) Reliability
    (*c*) Speed (*d*) All of these

13. The output quality of a printer is determined by—
    (*a*) Dot per sq. inch
    (*b*) Dot per inch
    (*c*) Dots printed per unit time
    (*d*) All of above

14. The first microprocessor built by the Intel Corporation was called—
(*a*) 8008 (*b*) 8080
(*c*) 4004 (*d*) 8800

15. When was the first minicomputer built?
(*a*) 1965 (*b*) 1962
(*c*) 1971 (*d*) 1966

16. The first digital computer built with IC chips was known as—
(*a*) IBM 7090 (*b*) Apple-1
(*c*) IBM System/360 (*d*) VAX-780

17. What is the name of the British gentleman who was the first to put forward in 1952 the idea for the integrated circuit?
(*a*) Jack S. Kilby
(*b*) G.W. Dummer
(*c*) William Shockley
(*d*) John Bardeen

18. The magnetic tape consists of a plastic type with a surface coating of magnetic material. When was it invented?
(*a*) 1968 (*b*) 1964
(*c*) 1956 (*d*) 1946

19. In the third generation of computers—
(*a*) Distributed data processing first became popular
(*b*) An operating system was first developed
(*c*) High-level procedural languages were first used
(*d*) On-line, realtime systems first became popular

20. In analog computer—
(*a*) Input is first converted to digital form
(*b*) Output is displayed in digital form
(*c*) Input is never converted to digital form
(*d*) All of above

21. Which of the following devices can be used to directly input 'Text books'?
(*a*) OCR (*b*) OMR
(*c*) MICR (*d*) None of these

22. Ascending order of a data hierarchy is—
(*a*) Bit-byte-record field-file-database
(*b*) Bit-byte-field-record-file-database
(*c*) Byte-bit record file-database
(*d*) None of the above

23. Personal computers are also called—
(*a*) Desktop computers
(*b*) Portable computers
(*c*) Advanced computers
(*d*) Palmtop computers

24. ENIAC stands for—
(*a*) Electronic Number Instruction and Code
(*b*) Electronic Number Integrated and Calculator
(*c*) Electronic Number Instruction Access Calculator
(*d*) None of these

25. An IP address contains four sets of numbers ranging from—
(*a*) 1 to 100 (*b*) 1 to 1000
(*c*) 0 to 255 (*d*) 1 to 500

26. In 3rd generation computers, the instructions are executed—
(*a*) Both sequentially and parallel
(*b*) Parallel only
(*c*) Sequentially only
(*d*) All of above

27. EPROM consists of—
(*a*) bipolar transistors (*b*) easily erasable
(*c*) MOSFETs (*d*) Diodes

28. Which of the following is used only for data entry and storage, and never for processing?
(*a*) Mouse (*b*) Dumb terminal
(*c*) Microcomputer (*d*) None of these

29. Different components on the motherboard of a PC processor unit are linked together by sets of parallel electrical conducting lines. What are these lines called?
(*a*) Conductors (*b*) Buses
(*c*) Connectors (*d*) None of these

30. Where have the program and data to be located before the ALU and control unit of a computer can operate on it?
(*a*) Internal memory
(*b*) Secondary memory
(*c*) Microprocessor
(*d*) Magnetic types

31. Which chips are erasable by ultra-violet rays after removing them from the main circuit?
(*a*) EPROM chips (*b*) EEPROM chips
(*c*) PROM chips (*d*) All of these

32. A memory bus is mainly used for communication between—
(*a*) processor and memory
(*b*) processor and I/O devices
(*c*) I/O devices and memory
(*d*) input device and output device

33. A name or number used to identify a storage location is called—
(*a*) A byte (*b*) A record
(*c*) An address (*d*) All of these

34. Which of the following is not a primary storage devcie?
(*a*) Magnetic type (*b*) Magnetic disk
(*c*) Optical disk (*d*) None of these

35. Which of the following is the user programmed semiconductor memory?
(*a*) SRAM (*b*) DRAM
(*c*) EPROM (*d*) All of the above

36. CD-ROM is a—
(*a*) Semiconductor memory
(*b*) Memory register
(*c*) Magnetic memory
(*d*) None of these

37. A characteristic of the ASCII code is—
(*a*) its use of the zone code 1010, 1011 and 1100
(*b*) its limitation to a maximum of 96 character configurations
(*c*) its independence from the Hollerith code
(*d*) All the above

38. A temporary storage area, attached to the CPU, for I/O operations is a—
(*a*) Chip (*b*) Buffer
(*c*) Register (*d*) Core

39. In magnetic disks, data is organized on the platter in a concentric sets of rings called—
(*a*) Sector (*b*) Track
(*c*) Head (*d*) Block

40. Who designed the first electronics computer - ENIAC?
(*a*) Van-Neumann
(*b*) Joseph M. Jacquard
(*c*) J. Presper Eckert and John W Mauchly
(*d*) Richard Davis

41. A code used for standardizing the storage and transfer of information amongst various computing devices is called—
(*a*) CRT (*b*) CPU
(*c*) ASCII (*d*) Dvorak

42. What is the name of the logic circuit which can add two binary digits?
(*a*) Full adder (*b*) Half adder
(*c*) Buffer (*d*) Register

43. Who invented the high level language C?
(*a*) Dennis M. Ritchie (*b*) Donald Kunth
(*c*) Niklaus Writh (*d*) Seymour Papert

44. Two new types of semiconductor memories are—
(*a*) Magnetic disks
(*b*) Charge-coupled devices
(*c*) Magnetic bubble memory
(*d*) Both (b) and (c)

45. Magnetic tape is used for—
(*a*) Historical storage (*b*) Computer input
(*c*) Both (a) and (b) (*d*) Neither (a) nor (b)

46. A byte is comprised of—
(*a*) one bit (*b*) four bits
(*c*) eight bits (*d*) sixteen bits

47. The CPU chip used in a computer is partially made up of—
(*a*) copper (*b*) iron
(*c*) gold and silver (*d*) silica

48. The silicon chips used for data processing are called—
(*a*) RAM chips (*b*) ROM chips
(*c*) micro processor (*d*) PROM chips

49. The hardware in which data may be stored for a computer system is called—
(*a*) Registers (*b*) Bus
(*c*) Control unit (*d*) Memory

50. A half byte is known is—
(*a*) Data (*b*) Bit
(*c*) Half byte (*d*) Nibble

51. The most common binary code in use today is the 8 bit ASCII code. What do the letters ASCII stand for?
(*a*) American Standard Code for International Interchange

(*b*) American Standard Code for Information Interchange
(*c*) American Standard Code for Intelligence Interchange
(*d*) American Scientific Code for Information Interchange

52. Personnel who design, program, operate and maintain computer equipment known as—
(*a*) Console-operator
(*b*) Programmer
(*c*) System Analyst
(*d*) Peopleware

53. Which of the following is an example of nonvolatile memory?
(*a*) ROM (*b*) VLSI
(*c*) LSI (*d*) RAM

54. Which is used for manufacturing chips?
(*a*) Bus (*b*) Control unit
(*c*) Semiconductors (*d*) (a) and (b) only

55. The computer code for the interchange of information between terminals is—
(*a*) ASCII (*b*) BCD
(*c*) EBCDIC (*d*) All of these

56. What is the name of the storage device which is used to compensate for the difference in rates of flow of data from once device to another?
(*a*) Cache (*b*) Concentrator
(*c*) Buffer (*d*) I/O device

57. Which is the most popular medium for direct-access secondary storage of a computer?
(*a*) Magnetic tape (*b*) Magnetic disk
(*c*) RAM (*d*) ROM

58. When did arch rivals IBM and Apple Computers Inc. join hands?
(*a*) 1978 (*b*) 1991
(*c*) 1984 (*d*) 1990

59. An error in software or hardware is known as bug. What is the alternative computer jargon for it?
(*a*) Leech (*b*) Squid
(*c*) Glitch (*d*) Slug

60. A type of semiconductor memory that usually has small capacity but very fast access is—
(*a*) PROM (*b*) RAM
(*c*) scratchpad (*d*) ROM

61. A single primary storage location in the processor unit—
(*a*) can hold several different data items at the same time
(*b*) can hold data items but not program instructions
(*c*) is identified by a built-in and unique number called an address
(*d*) is identified by a number that varies with the contents in the location

62. A storage device where the access time is dependent upon the location of the data is—
(*a*) Random access
(*b*) Serial access
(*c*) Sequential access
(*d*) Transaction access

63. Memory that holds microprograms is—
(*a*) core memory (*b*) ROM
(*c*) RAM (*d*) control memory

64. Octal numbers are used—
(*a*) In computer hardware
(*b*) When binary numbers are too long
(*c*) Internal to the computer
(*d*) In preference to 'hex' number

65. Binary numbers need more places for counting because—
(*a*) They are always big numbers
(*b*) Any no. of 0's can be added in front of them
(*c*) Binary base is small
(*d*) 0's and 1's have to be properly spaced apart

66. Any tape of storage that is used for holding information between steps in its processing is—
(*a*) CPU
(*b*) Primary storage
(*c*) Intermediate storage
(*d*) Internal storage

67. PROM is a type of computer memory. What does PROM stands for?
(*a*) Powered Read Only Memory
(*b*) Programmable Read Only Memory
(*c*) Permanent Read Only Memory
(*d*) Powered Read & Write Only Memory

68. Which one of the following is not a correct definition?
(*a*) SRAM → Static Random Access Memory
(*b*) PROM → Programmable Read Only Memory
(*c*) DRAM → Dynamic Random Access Memory
(*d*) SAM → Static Access Memory

69. Which of the following are the type of the secondary storage?
(*a*) Floppy Disk & Hard Disk
(*b*) Floppy Disk & ROM
(*c*) Hard Disk & RAM
(*d*) None of the above

70. Who defined the binary number system?
(*a*) Pascal (*b*) A.D. Leibniz
(*c*) Newton (*d*) Aristotle

71. Find the valid statements—
(*a*) A floppy has more capacity than a hard disk
(*b*) Hard disk is a primary memory device
(*c*) RAM stands for Read Access Memory
(*d*) ROM is a permanent memory

72. A set of programs that handle firm's data base responsibilities is called a—
(*a*) Data Base Management System (DBMS)
(*b*) Data Base Processing System (DBPS)
(*c*) Data Management System (DMS)
(*d*) All of the above

73. A computer will function only if it:
(*a*) Has a control unit
(*b*) Is given input data
(*c*) Has a program in its memory
(*d*) Has software package

74. The comparison of data inside the arithmetic logic unit is referred to as a—
(*a*) Instruction
(*b*) Data operation
(*c*) Conditional question
(*d*) Logical operation

75. Which of the following statement is false?
(*a*) Generally, computers don't make mistake
(*b*) Computers eliminate jobs
(*c*) Computers can think
(*d*) Maths is necessary to understand computers

76. Surgeons can perform delicate operations by manipulating devices through computers instead of manually. This technology is known as—
(*a*) Computer forensics (*b*) Simulation
(*c*) Forecasting (*d*) Robotics

77. A programme written in machine language is called—
(*a*) Assembler (*b*) Object
(*c*) Computer (*d*) Machine

78. Data transfer using telephone system is—
(*a*) Time division multiplexing
(*b*) Space division multiplexing
(*c*) Frequency division multiplexing
(*d*) All of the above

79. Software instructions intended to satisfy a user's specific processing needs are called_________.
(*a*) Systems software
(*b*) A microcomputer
(*c*) Documentation
(*d*) Application software

80. Which of the following is responsible for coordinating various operations using timing signals?
(*a*) Arithmetic-logic unit (*b*) Control unit
(*c*) Memory unit (*d*) Input/Output unit

81. A single but structure is primarily found in—
(*a*) Main frames
(*b*) Super computers
(*c*) High performance machines
(*d*) Mini and micro-computers

82. The study of molecules and structures whose size ranges from 1 to 100 nanometers.
(*a*) Nanoscience
(*b*) Artificial intelligence
(*c*) Microelectrodes
(*d*) Computer forensics

83. What is the term which represents the used of links between information of all softs whether text, graphics, video or audio-based?
(*a*) Hypertext (*b*) Hypermedia
(*c*) HyperCard (*d*) Wild Card

84. The two basic types of record-access methods are—
(*a*) Sequential and random
(*b*) Sequential and indexed

(*c*) Direct and immediate
(*d*) On-line and realtime

85. Modern Computer are very reliable but they are not
(*a*) Fast (*b*) Powerful
(*c*) Infallible (*d*) Economical

86. The language that the computer can understand and execute is called—
(*a*) machine language
(*b*) application software
(*c*) system program
(*d*) all of the above

87. Where was the India's first computer installed and when?
(*a*) Institute of Social Science, Agra, 1955
(*b*) Indian Institute of Statistics, Delhi, 1957
(*c*) Indian Statistical Institute, Calcutta, 1955
(*d*) Indian Institute of Science, Bangalore, 1971

88. The first electronic digital computer contained?
(*a*) Electronic valves
(*b*) Vacuum tubes
(*c*) Transistors
(*d*) Semiconductor memory

89. The first computer made available for commercial use was—
(*a*) Mark-I (*b*) ENIAC
(*c*) EDSAC (*d*) UNIVAC

90. The third generation of computer covers the period—
(*a*) 1971-1982 (*b*) 1982-1984
(*c*) 1959-1964 (*d*) 1964-1977

91. What was the computer conceived by Babbage?
(*a*) Analytical Engine
(*b*) Arithmetic Machine
(*c*) Donald Knuth
(*d*) All of the above

92. The process of starting or restarting a computer system by loading instruction from a secondary storage device into the computer memory is called—
(*a*) Duping (*b*) Booting
(*c*) Padding (*d*) All of the above

93. Who invented the microprocessor?
(*a*) Marcian E. Huff
(*b*) Herman H. Goldstein
(*c*) Joseph Jacquard
(*d*) All of the above

94. In which year were chips used inside the computer for the first time?
(*a*) 1964 (*b*) 1975
(*c*) 1977 (*d*) 1981

95. Computers on an internet are identified by—
(*a*) E-mail address (*b*) Street address
(*c*) IP address (*d*) All the these

96. Which one of the following is different from other members?
(*a*) Google (*b*) Windows
(*c*) Linux (*d*) Mac

97. The proper definition of a modern digital computer is—
(*a*) an electronic automated machine that can solve problems involving words and numbers
(*b*) a more sophisticated and modified electronic pocket calculator
(*c*) any machine that can perform mathematical operations
(*d*) a machine that words on binary code

98. Personal computers have number of chips mounted on a main circuit board. What is the common name for such boards?
(*a*) Motherboard (*b*) Father board
(*c*) Breadboard (*d*) Daughter board

99. In analog computer:
(*a*) input is first converted to digital form
(*b*) input is never converted to digital form
(*c*) output is displayed in digital form
(*d*) all of the above

100. Data processing computer built to conventional architecture is known as—
(*a*) Super computer (*b*) Mainframe
(*c*) Micro computer (*d*) Mini computer

101. Operatinng System concept started in _______
(*a*) First generation computer
(*b*) Second generation computer
(*c*) Third generation computer
(*d*) Fourth generation computer

102. A German mathematician who invented a calculator, for addition, subtraction, multiplication and division, His name was—
(*a*) Napier (*b*) Pascal
(*c*) Leibniz (*d*) Hollerith

103. Who invented analytical machine?
(*a*) Charles Babbage (*b*) Hollerith
(*c*) Pascal (*d*) Napier

104. Modern computers are very reliable but they are not—
(*a*) Fast (*b*) Powerful
(*c*) Infallible (*d*) Cheap

105. A complete microcomputer system consists of—
(*a*) Microprocessor
(*b*) Memory
(*c*) Peripheral equipment
(*d*) All of the above

106. Modem is a/an—
(*a*) input device (*b*) output device
(*c*) both (a) and (b) (*d*) storage device

107. Computer peripherals do not include—
(*a*) UPS (*b*) Speaker
(*c*) Microphone (*d*) Microwave

108. This device helps us to change our voice into electronic signals, is called—
(*a*) Speakers (*b*) Mouse
(*c*) Microphone (*d*) Motherboard

109. Which one of the following is Essential Peripheral?
(*a*) Printer (*b*) Keyboard
(*c*) Mouse (*d*) All of the above

110. Which is not a 'Computer Peripherals—
(*a*) Scanner (*b*) Speaker
(*c*) CPU (*d*) Printer

111. ________ is an input device used for computer.
(*a*) Scanner (*b*) Joystick
(*c*) Light pen (*d*) All of these

112. In most IBM PCs, the CPU, the device drives, memory expansion slots and active components are mounted on a single board. What is the name of this board?
(*a*) Breadboard (*b*) Daughter board
(*c*) Grandmother board (*d*) Motherboard

113. The output that is printed on paper is called—
(*a*) Hard copy (*b*) Soft copy
(*c*) Both (a) and (b) (*d*) All of the above

114. In which kind of printers, a light beam is used to print?
(*a*) Dot-matrix printers (*b*) Line printers
(*c*) Inkjet printers (*d*) Laser printers

115. ________ printers are used for very good quality printout.
(*a*) Dot-matrix (*b*) Line
(*c*) Inkjet (*d*) Laser

116. Mouse, Keyboard, Monitor and Printer etc are examples of—
(*a*) Software (*b*) Memory
(*c*) Peripherals (*d*) CPU

117. A computer program that translates program instructions into machine language is called a/an
(*a*) Interpreter (*b*) Loader
(*c*) Compiler (*d*) Simulator

118. Which is not an input device?
(*a*) CRT (Cathode Ray Tube)
(*b*) Optical scanners
(*c*) Voice recognition devices
(*d*) COM (Computer Micro film)

119. Which is considered a direct entry input device?
(*a*) Optical scanner (*b*) Mouse
(*c*) Light pen (*d*) All of above

120. What of the following terms is related to a monitor?
(*a*) Screen
(*b*) Monochrome monitor
(*c*) RGB monitor
(*d*) Video display

121. The computer device primarily used to provide hardcopy is the—
(*a*) CRT (*b*) line printer
(*c*) computer console (*d*) card reader

122. Which of the following is a non-impact printer?
(*a*) Daisy wheel printer (*b*) Drum printer
(*c*) Laser printer (*d*) All of the above

123. The input unit of a computer ________
(*a*) feeds data to the CPU or Memory
(*b*) retrieves data from CPU
(*c*) directs all other units
(*d*) All of the above

124. Direct entry data devices include—
(*a*) telephone, communications and bar codes
(*b*) keyboards, cartridges and bar code reader
(*c*) machine communication, key boards and data collection devices

(*d*) analog computers, digital computers and time clocks

125. A disadvantage of the laser printer is—
(*a*) It is quieter than an impact printer
(*b*) It is very slow
(*c*) The output is of a lower quality
(*d*) None of these

126. Which of the following is used only for data entry and storage, and never for processing?
(*a*) Mouse
(*b*) Dumb terminal
(*c*) Microcomputer
(*d*) Dedicated data entry system

127. A small or intelligent device is so called because it contains within it a
(*a*) Program (*b*) Sensor
(*c*) Computer (*d*) Microcomputer

128. Compact discs, hold how many minutes of data?
(*a*) 56 mins (*b*) 60 mins
(*c*) 60 mins (*d*) 74 mins

129. Which of the folloiwng is a device that changes data from coded form to clear form—
(*a*) Keyboard (*b*) Decoder
(*c*) Mnemonics (*d*) Bar code

130. An input device that reads printed text employing optical character pattern matching is known as—
(*a*) Scanner (*b*) Magnetic disk
(*c*) Mouse (*d*) Magnetic tape

131. A hand-held device which reads marks or characters on paper by detecting photo-sensitivity is known as—
(*a*) light pen (*b*) optical wand
(*c*) plotter (*d*) all of the above

132. A stand-alone system which produces one page of printed output at a time is—
(*a*) Page printer (*b*) Line printer
(*c*) Laser printer (*d*) Dot matrix printer

133. A mouse is used as—
(*a*) a way to entertain children
(*b*) a pointing device
(*c*) an easy way to input information in your computer
(*d*) both (b) and (c)

134. Which device can produce the final product of machine processing into a form usable by human?
(*a*) Storage (*b*) Input device
(*c*) Output device (*d*) Control

135. A peripheral device in which the storage medium used in magnetic tape is—
(*a*) Keyboard (*b*) VDU
(*c*) Punched card (*d*) Tape deck

136. The devices attached to the computer and controlled by computers control unit are known as—
(*a*) Peripheral devices (*b*) Program
(*c*) Software (*d*) Utility

137. A peripheral device—
(*a*) tears easily on the dotted line
(*b*) is another name for an add-on component of a computer system
(*c*) sits on the sidelines and never gets involved
(*d*) none of these

138. Which of the following statements is not true?
(*a*) A notebook computer weighs less and actually look like a notebook
(*b*) A palmtop computer weighs at most a few pounds and can fit into a pocket
(*c*) A palmtop computer is also called a picocomputer
(*d*) None of these

139. Which of the following options correctly expresses the meaning of the term 'PCs'?
(*a*) Independent computers for all working staff
(*b*) Personal Computers widely available to individual workers with which they can access information from larger systems and increase their personal productivity
(*c*) Packed computer system formed by joining together of various computer terminals
(*d*) Computers manufactured by the Pentium Company

140. What do you understand by the term 'downsizing'?
(*a*) The recession in the jobs in software companies
(*b*) The reduction in the memory of a computer
(*c*) Offloading the applications from a central mainframe computer to a smaller system
(*d*) Restricting the number of programs run by a PC

141. Which supercomputer is developed by the Indian Scientists?
(*a*) Param (*b*) Super 301
(*c*) Compaq Presario (*d*) CRAY YMP

142. One Gigabyte is Approximately equal is—
(*a*) 1000,000 bytes
(*b*) 1000,000,000 bytes
(*c*) 1000,000,0000,000 bytes
(*d*) None of these

143. Check the odd term out—
(*a*) Internet (*b*) Linux
(*c*) Unix (*d*) Windows

144. The errors that can be pointed out by the compiler are—
(*a*) Syntax error (*b*) Symantic error
(*c*) Logical error (*d*) Internal error

145. What is the control unit's function in the CPU—
(*a*) To transfer data to primary storage
(*b*) To store program instructions
(*c*) To perform logic functions
(*d*) To decode program instructions

146. 'DTP' stands for ?
(*a*) Digital Transmission Protocol
(*b*) DeskTop Publishing
(*c*) Data Type Programming
(*d*) Document Type Processing

147. When we opens an Internet site we see www. What is the full form of www?
(*a*) world wide word
(*b*) world wide web
(*c*) word widing works
(*d*) words wide spiderman web

148. Which of the following commands is given to reboot the computer?
(*a*) Ctrl + Alt + Del
(*b*) Ctrl + Alt + Tab
(*c*) Ctrl + Shift + Del
(*d*) Ctrl + Shift + Del

149. The background of any Word document—
(*a*) is always white colour
(*b*) is the colour you present under the Options menu
(*c*) is always the same for the entire document
(*d*) can have any colour you choose

150. The blinking symbol on the computer screen is called the—
(*a*) mouse (*b*) logo
(*c*) hand (*d*) cursor

151. Which function calculates the largest value in a set of numbers in Excel?
(*a*) Average (*b*) Count
(*c*) Minimum (*d*) Maximum

152. To move to the bottom of a document, press—
(*a*) Auto Summarize (*b*) Home key
(*c*) Ctrl key + End key (*d*) End key

153. The Word function that corrects text as you type is referred to as—
(*a*) Auto Summarize (*b*) Auto Insert
(*c*) Auto Correct (*d*) Track Changes

154. To find and load a file that has been saved—
(*a*) select the Close command
(*b*) select the New command
(*c*) select the Save command
(*d*) select the Open command

155. What displays the content of the active cell is Excel?
(*a*) Name box (*b*) Row Headings
(*c*) Formula bar (*d*) Taskpane

156. In Word you can force a page break—
(*a*) by positioning your cursor at the appropriate place and pressing the F1 key
(*b*) by positioning your cursor at the appropriate place and pressing Ctrl + Enter
(*c*) by using the Insert/Section Break
(*d*) by chaning the font size your document

157. Which of the following refers to a small, single-site network?
(*a*) LAN (*b*) DSL
(*c*) RAM (*d*) USB

158. By default, your documents print in-mode.—
(*a*) Landscape (*b*) Portrait
(*c*) Page Setup (*d*) Print View

159. How do you prevent e-mailed word documents from always opening in the Reading Layout?
(*a*) From the Tools Menu > Options > General Tab > uncheck the 'Allow starting in Reading Layout'
(*b*) From the View Menu > Reading Layout > General Tab > uncheck the 'Allow starting in Reading Layout'

(c) From the Format Menu > Autoformat > Edit Tab > uncheck the 'Use with e-mailed attachments'.
(d) All the above

160. Which of these is a quick way to copy formatting from a selected cell to two other cells on the same worksheet?
(a) Use CTRL to select all three cells, then click the Paste Button image button on the Standard toolbar.
(b) Copy the selected cell, then select the other two cells, click Style on the Format menu, then click Modify
(c) Click Format Painter Button image on the Formatting toolbar twice, then click in each cell you want to copy the formatting to
(d) Use Alt to select all three cells, then click the Paste Button image button on the Standard toolbar

161. Select the odd one out—
(a) Interpreter (b) Operating System
(c) Compiler (d) Assembler

162. Which of the following places the common data elements in order from smallest to largest?
(a) Character, file, record, field, database
(b) Character, record, field, file, database
(c) Character, field, record, file, database
(d) Bit, byte, character, record, field, file, database

163. The Assistant is—
(a) an application that allows you to take notes and save them in a file
(b) an animated character that provides help and suggestions
(c) a button on the standard Toolbar that executes the Print command
(d) a collection of frequently mis-spelled words in a dictionary file

164. Suppose you have coloumns of data span more than one printed page. How can you automatically print the column headings on each page?
(a) Click Page Setup on the File menu, click the Sheet tab, and enter the row that contains these column headings under Print titles
(b) Click Page Setup on the File menu, click the Page tab, click the Options button, then enter your choices
(c) Click Page Preview on the File menu, click the Sheet tab, and enter the row that contains these column headings under Print titles
(d) Click Page Setup on the File menu, click the Sheet tab, and make a selection under the Print heading

165. Which of the following describes a relational database?
(a) It provides a relationship between integers
(b) It consists of separate tables or related data
(c) It retrieves data related to its queries
(d) It provides a relationship between floats

166. What do you press to enter the current date in a cell?
(a) CTRL + ; (semicolon)
(b) CTRL + SHIFT + : (colon)
(c) CTRL + F10
(d) CTRL + F11

167. What happens when you press Ctrl + V key?
(a) A Capital V letter is typed into your document at the cursor point
(b) The selected item is pasted from the Clipboard
(c) The selected item is pasted from the Clipboard
(d) The selected drawing objects are distributed vertically on the page

168. CRM means—
(a) Customer Relationship Management
(b) Customer Retention Manager
(c) Customers' Relatives Meet
(d) Channel Route Market

169. The term PC means—
(a) Private Computer
(b) Personal Computer
(c) Professional Computer
(d) Personal Calculator

170. Silicon Valley of India is located in—
(a) Dehradun
(b) Bangalore
(c) Hyderabad
(d) Srinagar

171. Collection of two or more computers that are located within a limited distance of each other and that are connected to each other directly or indirectly?
(*a*) Innernet
(*b*) Intranet
(*c*) Local Area Network
(*d*) Wide Area Network

172. Part of a database that holds only one type of information?
(*a*) Report (*b*) Record
(*c*) File (*d*) Field

173. Which of the following is true?
(*a*) Plotters are not available for microcomputer systems
(*b*) Micro-computer are not programmed like conventional computers
(*c*) Mini-computers are task-oriented
(*d*) The contents of ROM are easily changed

174. ROM is composed of—
(*a*) Magnetic cores
(*b*) Micro-processors
(*c*) Photoelectric cells
(*d*) Floppy disks

175. The computer code for interchange of information between terminals is—
(*a*) ASCII (*b*) BCD
(*c*) BCDIC (*d*) Hollerith

176. A temporary storage area, attached to the CPU, for I/O operations, is a—
(*a*) Channel (*b*) Buffer
(*c*) Register (*d*) Core

177. Which one of the following is a file?
(*a*) Floppy disk (*b*) Magnetic drum
(*c*) Magnetic tape (*d*) None of these

178. An I/O device which provides photographic outputs for printing galleys, is the—
(*a*) Camera printer
(*b*) Automatic typesetter
(*c*) Radix printer
(*d*) All of these

179. A term used interchangeably with diskette is—
(*a*) Disk cartridge
(*b*) Disk pack
(*c*) Floppy disk
(*d*) Packette disk

180. A peripheral device used in a word processing system is—
(*a*) Floppy disk
(*b*) Magnetic card reader
(*c*) CRT
(*d*) All of these

181. MS-DOS is the name of a/an—
(*a*) Application software (*b*) Hardware
(*c*) System software (*d*) None of these

182. The daily processing of corrections to customer accounts best exemplifies the processing mode of—
(*a*) batch processing
(*b*) real-time processing
(*c*) time-sharing
(*d*) off-line processing

183. Which of the following terms could be used to describe the concurrent processing of computer programs via CRTs, on one computer system?
(*a*) Time sharing
(*b*) On-line processing
(*c*) Interactive processing
(*d*) All of these

184. The retrieval of information from the computer is defined as
(*a*) Collection of data
(*b*) data retrieval operations
(*c*) output
(*d*) data output collection

185. An advantage of a distributed word processing network is
(*a*) increased number of reports handled
(*b*) less delay in inter-office communications
(*c*) greater corporate control over outputs
(*d*) All of these

186. Which one of the following is not a computer language?
(*a*) BASIC (*b*) COBOL
(*c*) LOTUS (*d*) FORTRAN

187. Which of the following packages is used for composition in printing press?
(*a*) Lotus (*b*) dBase
(*c*) Page Maker (*d*) Word Perfect

188. Which one of the following is not a programming language of a computer?
(*a*) BASIC (*b*) FORTRAN
(*c*) LASER (*d*) PASCAL

189. The window which shows icons for things like the mouse, sound, and display is...?
(*a*) My Computer (*b*) Explorer
(*c*) Control Panel (*d*) Taskbar

190. The brain of a computer is
(*a*) CPU (*b*) CD
(*c*) Floppy disc (*d*) Megabyte

191. On the Task bar the time is shown in the
(*a*) Notification area or Tray
(*b*) Start menu
(*c*) Scrollbar
(*d*) Desktop

192. Charles Babbage invented
(*a*) ENIAC
(*b*) Difference engine
(*c*) Electronic computer
(*d*) Punched card

193. Which one of the following is a stored program machine?
(*a*) Micro-processor (*b*) Calculator
(*c*) Analog-computer (*d*) Micro-computer

194. Computers can be classified in which of the following hierarchical orders?
(*a*) PC, Large, Super Micro, Super Computer
(*b*) Super Micro, PC, Large, Super Computer
(*c*) PC, Super Micro, Large, Super Computer
(*d*) Large, Super Micro, Super Computer, PC

195. The computer device primarily used to provide hard copy is the
(*a*) CRT (*b*) Line Printer
(*c*) Computer Console (*d*) Card Reader

196. Consider the following statements about Internet facility:
(*a*) It serves as the largest one-line information system.
(*b*) It provides the most dependable and latest mode for sending E-mail.
(*c*) Recurring expenditure on communication E-mail is very high.
(*d*) It is often misused and has triggered cyber-crimes.

197. Which of the following circuit is used as a 'Memory device' in computers?
(*a*) Rectifier (*b*) Flip-Flop
(*c*) Comparator (*d*) Attenuator

198. Personnel who design, program, operate and maintain computer equipment refers to
(*a*) Console-operator (*b*) Programmer
(*c*) Peopleware (*d*) System Analyst

199. For reproducing sound, a CD (Compact Disc) audio player uses a—
(*a*) quartz crystal
(*b*) titanium needle
(*c*) laser beam
(*d*) barium titanium ceramic

200. When a CD (Compact Disc used in audio and Video system) is seen in sunlight, rainbow like colours are seen. This can be explained on the basis of phenomenon of
(*a*) reflection of diffraction
(*b*) reflection and transmission
(*c*) diffraction and transmission
(*d*) refraction, diffraction and transmission

201. Pickup wrong definition
(*a*) Offline-is a system peripheral equipment not controlled by CPU
(*b*) Online - is a system in which peripheral equipment is in direct contact with CPU
(*c*) PL/I is the acronym Peripheral Listing/ Index.
(*d*) Program or routine is a set sequence of instructions given to computer for problem solving

202. The most important advantage of a video disk is
(*a*) Compactness
(*b*) Potential capacity
(*c*) Durability
(*d*) Cost effectiveness

203. WAN means—
(*a*) Wide Area Network
(*b*) Wine Area Network
(*c*) Woll Area Network
(*d*) Wide Allen Network

204. Which of the following is the universal gate?
(*a*) NAND-Gate (*b*) OR-Gate
(*c*) AND-Gate (*d*) NOT-Gate

205. The translator program that converts source code in high level language into machine code line by line is called—
(*a*) Assembler (*b*) Compiler
(*c*) Loader (*d*) Interpreter

206. Which of the following is not an image file?
(*a*) JPEG (*b*) GIF
(*c*) TMP (*d*) BMP

207. Before a disk drive can access any sector record, a computer program has to provide the record's disk address. What information does this address specify?
(*a*) Track number (*b*) Sector number
(*c*) Surface number (*d*) All of above

208. What is the capacity of a standard PC floppy?
(*a*) 2MB (*b*) 1.44KB
(*c*) 1.44MB (*d*) 120 MB

209. What is downloading?
(*a*) Sending a file on the Internet
(*b*) Retrieving a file on the Internet
(*c*) Moving a file from a floppy
(*d*) Scanning a picture

210. What is a cookie?
(*a*) Cooking software
(*b*) Web site
(*c*) Internet information file
(*d*) Hacker file

211. What is degauss?
(*a*) Attachment for CPU
(*b*) Creating magnetic media
(*c*) Erasing magnetic media
(*d*) Medical software

212. A Computer Virus cannot be contracted by
(*a*) Floppy diskette
(*b*) E-mail
(*c*) Scanner
(*d*) Internet Downloads

213. Hardware devices that are not part of the main computer system and are often added later to the system.
(*a*) Clip art (*b*) Highlight
(*c*) Execute (*d*) Peripheral

214. A Cathode Ray Tube (CRT) is found is what?
(*a*) CPU (*b*) Printer
(*c*) Monitor (*d*) Scanner

215. What does the term IRQ stand for?
(*a*) Input Request Que
(*b*) Interrupt Request Que
(*c*) Interrupt Request
(*d*) Input Request

216. The Intel Pentium bug/flaw was an issue with the:
(*a*) Cache
(*b*) FPU
(*c*) Socket
(*d*) There was no bug/flaw

217. What does the term MIME stand for?
(*a*) Mail Internet Mail Exchange
(*b*) Mail Interleave Method Exchange
(*c*) Multipurpose Internet Mail Extensions
(*d*) Multipurpose Interleave Mail Exchange

218. Which of the following is not a network protocol?
(*a*) HTTP (*b*) RIP
(*c*) PIM (*d*) PSI

219. The main computer that stores the files that can be sent to computers that are networked together is ___
(*a*) File server (*b*) Clip art
(*c*) Mother board (*d*) Peripheral

220. Which of the following is an example of Binary?
(*a*) 123 (*b*) 111 1011
(*c*) 7B (*d*) All of the above

221. Which of the following will not help your computer's security?
(*a*) Firewall
(*b*) VLAN
(*c*) Good Password
(*d*) Updated software

222. What is IRC?
(*a*) Internet Relay Channel
(*b*) Internet Respond Channel
(*c*) Internet Relay Chat
(*d*) Internet Response Cache

223. Which of the following is not a mouse technology?
(*a*) Mechanical
(*b*) Optical
(*c*) Motorized
(*d*) Optical-Mechanical

224. Which of the following is not a programming language?
(*a*) Lisp (*b*) See
(*c*) Java (*d*) Perl

225. Which of the following is not related to e-mail?
(*a*) BCC (*b*) SPAM
(*c*) Pen (*d*) Pine

226. Which of the following is part of a hard disk drive?
(*a*) Mother Board (*b*) Platter
(*c*) Laser (*d*) Riser Board

227. Which of the following is not a network device?
(*a*) Core (*b*) Switch
(*c*) Hub (*d*) Router

228. Which of the following is not a Unix or Linux variant?
(*a*) SunOS (*b*) RedHat
(*c*) DOS (*d*) Debian

229. Which of the following is a PC video file extension?
(*a*) .MVE (*b*) .MP3
(*c*) .AVI (*d*) .VDO

230. Which of the following is not an operating system?
(*a*) MP3 (*b*) AIF
(*c*) WAV (*d*) COM

231. Which of the following is not an operating system?
(*a*) SuSE (*b*) Unix
(*c*) OSD (*d*) DOS

232. Which of the following is a broadband Internet connection?
(*a*) 28.8k (*b*) 56k
(*c*) Cable (*d*) Modem

233. Which of the following is not an Internet browser?
(*a*) Internet Explorer (*b*) AOL
(*c*) Netscape (*d*) Opera

234. Which of the following is not a network command?
(*a*) Ping (*b*) Winipcfg
(*c*) Netcfg (*d*) Tracert

235. Microsoft Windows XP is an upcoming operating system, what is XP short for?
(*a*) Whistler
(*b*) eXtra Powerful
(*c*) eXPerienced
(*d*) It is not an acronym

236. Unix is short for what?
(*a*) UNIt eXchange
(*b*) UNIform eXchange
(*c*) UNIt X
(*d*) It is not an acronym

237. How many bits are in a megabit?
(*a*) 1000000 or 10^6 (*b*) 1024
(*c*) 256 (*d*) 8

238. Which of the following file systems or file allocation tables did Windows 95 not provide?
(*a*) NTFS (*b*) ext3
(*c*) HPFS (*d*) All of the above

239. Which of the following is not related to a computer hard disk drive?
(*a*) Platter (*b*) Pwrite
(*c*) Access Arm (*d*) MFM

240. To select text by shading as you drag the mouse arrow over the text is known as—
(*a*) Clip art (*b*) To highlight
(*c*) To fetch (*d*) To decode

241. Which of the following is not a search engine?
(*a*) Google (*b*) Zeal
(*c*) Amazon (*d*) Hotbot

242. CPU is also known as—
(*a*) Execute (*b*) Microprocessor
(*c*) Micro chip (*d*) Decode

243. Which Linux command sets a file's permission?
(*a*) attrib (*b*) Chmod
(*c*) properties (*d*) rights

244. Which of the following is not a keyboard layout?
(*a*) QWERTY (*b*) Maltron
(*c*) Sholes (*d*) Dvorak

245. Which of the following is the directory commonly used to store a website?
(*a*) /home (*b*) /public
(*c*) /home_html (*d*) /public_html

246. Which of these are not computer?
(*a*) Aptiva (*b*) Macintosh
(*c*) Acorn (*d*) Paseo

247. Which of the below does not have the ability to allow a user to communicate with another computer?
(*a*) Network Card (*b*) Serial Port
(*c*) VGA Port (*d*) Modem

248. Which of the below is not a type of live communication?
(*a*) Chat (*b*) E-mail
(*c*) Instant Messaging (*d*) IRC

249. Which of the below is an input device?
(*a*) Monitor (*b*) Printer
(*c*) Scanner (*d*) Speakers

250. Which characteristic of computer distinguishes it from electronic calculators?
(*a*) Accuracy
(*b*) Storage Capacity
(*c*) Versatility
(*d*) Automatic

251. Which of the below is not a type of DVD drive?
(*a*) DVD-RD (*b*) DVD-RW
(*c*) DVD+RW (*d*) DVD-RAM

252. Name of the computer terminal which gives paper printout?
(*a*) Hard copy terminal (*b*) Display screen
(*c*) Soft copy terminal (*d*) Plotter

253. Which of the below is related to memory?
(*a*) PS (*b*) DSP
(*c*) Flops (*d*) Cache

254. Which of the following is not related to computer video?
(*a*) Direct X (*b*) AC-3
(*c*) GeForce (*d*) OpenGL

255. Which of the following is not related to chat?
(*a*) IRC (*b*) IM
(*c*) Op (*d*) AutoPlay

256. Which of the following is not considered a super user?
(*a*) Admin (*b*) Agent
(*c*) Op (*d*) Root

257. Which of the below commands displays the time on most Linux and Unix computers?
(*a*) time (*b*) date
(*c*) timex (*d*) now

258. What is 10100110?
(*a*) 4 (*b*) 19
(*c*) 151 (*d*) 166

259. Which of the below is not a codec?
(*a*) DivX (*b*) EVid
(*c*) FLAC (*d*) XviD

260. A device that uses words or messages recorded on a magnetic medium to produce audio response is
(*a*) Magnetic tape
(*b*) Voice response unit
(*c*) Voice recognition unit
(*d*) Voice band

261. What does LOL stand for?
(*a*) Log Off Laptop
(*b*) Laughing Out Loud
(*c*) Lack Of Laughter
(*d*) Lag On Laptop

262. What command comments out a line in a batch file?
(*a*) # (*b*) ;
(*c*) Hide (*d*) Rem

263. Which of the below is not a PC game?
(*a*) Dune (*b*) Oregon trail
(*c*) Tropico (*d*) Ultimate defense

264. Which of the below is not a network connectors?
(*a*) DVI (*b*) RJ-45
(*c*) BNC (*d*) DB-15

265. What is the .tbz file extension?
(*a*) Compressed text file
(*b*) Text file
(*c*) Audio file
(*d*) Compressed tar file

266. Which of the below HTML tags is correct for inserting an image?
(*a*) <a img=""> (*b*) <img src="">
(*c*) <image source=""> (*d*) <image="">

267. What of the following will happen when data is entered into a memory location?
(*a*) It will add to the content of the location
(*b*) It will change the address of the memory location
(*c*) It will overlap the previous content
(*d*) It will not be fruitful if there is already some data at the location

268. Which of the below people is credited for developing the World Wide Web?
(*a*) Alan Kay
(*b*) Tim Berners-Lee
(*c*) Jack Kilby
(*d*) Robert Noyce

269. Which of the below is not a type of printer?
(*a*) Bubble Jet printer
(*b*) LED printer
(*c*) Thermal printer
(*d*) Microwave printer

270. Which year was Microsoft Windows XP released?
(*a*) 2000 (*b*) 2001
(*c*) 2002 (*d*) 2003

271. What is another name for a motherboard?
(*a*) CPU (*b*) Fatherboard
(*c*) Main system (*d*) System board

272. Which of the below is not a type of game?
(*a*) FPS (*b*) RTS
(*c*) RPG (*d*) ETS

273. Which of the below is a type of memory that cannot have information written to it?
(*a*) DRAM (*b*) RAM
(*c*) ROM (*d*) SRAM

274. Which of the below is not a type of network?
(*a*) MAN (*b*) HAN
(*c*) LPN (*d*) VPN

275. Which of the below is not a text editor?
(*a*) Vim (*b*) Perl
(*c*) Pico (*d*) Vi

276. Which of the following is not a social network site?
(*a*) Amazon (*b*) MySpace
(*c*) Orkut (*d*) Twitter

277. What command clears the screen in MS-DOS and the Windows command line?
(*a*) cd (*b*) clear
(*c*) cls (*d*) echo

278. What MS-DOS command can display hidden files?
(*a*) attrib (*b*) cd
(*c*) ls (*d*) more

279. A storage area used to store data to adjust for the difference in speed at which the different units can handle data is
(*a*) Memory (*b*) Accumulator
(*c*) Address (*d*) Buffer

280. Which of the following is not an antivirus company?
(*a*) AVG (*b*) Panda
(*c*) Xymantec (*d*) Xargon

281. Who created the first mouse?
(*a*) Bill Gates
(*b*) Douglas Englebart
(*c*) John Mauchly
(*d*) Robert Noyce

282. Which of the below is not a type of computer memory?
(*a*) DIMM (*b*) MIMM
(*c*) RIMM (*d*) SIMM

283. Which of the below is the GUI commonly user with Linux?
(*a*) LUI (*b*) GNU
(*c*) GPL (*d*) GNOME

284. Which of the below examples of a programming code contains an example of a regular expression?
(*a*) $expression = 1;
(*b*) my@expression;
(*c*) $total = $exp + $exp2;
(*d*) $total =~s/[0-9]+^*//g;

285. What is the name of the below image? A type of protection that requires users to enter the letters seen in the image when filling out information on the Internet and is an easy method of identifying humans from computer.

(*a*) Captcha (*b*) Decepcha
(*c*) Gotcha (*d*) GenImage

286. Which part of the computer does an EIDE cable connect to?
(*a*) Floppy drive (*b*) Hard disk drive
(*c*) Sound card (*d*) Video card

287. What is Apache?
(*a*) browser (*b*) computer
(*c*) operating system (*d*) web server

288. Which of the below is not related to the Internet and web development?
(*a*) DOS (*b*) HTML
(*c*) Java (*d*) PHP

289. Which of the below options is not an iPod Apple as released?
(*a*) iPod Mini (*b*) iPod Nano
(*c*) iPod Shuffle (*d*) iPod Vision

290. Which of the below power line issues can cause problems with your computer?
(*a*) Line sag (*b*) Line surge
(*c*) Line noise (*d*) All of the above

291. Where are the device drivers settings for Microsoft Windows stored?
(*a*) BIOS (*b*) CMOS
(*c*) EEPROM (*d*) Registry

292. Which of the below options is a type of connector used with a CD-ROM or other disc drive?
(*a*) DB-15 (*b*) Molex
(*c*) PS/2 (*d*) RJ-11

293. What is the name of the section of Microsoft Windows shown in the below picture?

(*a*) Quick Launch (*b*) Notification area
(*c*) Taskbar (*d*) Time

294. Who was one of the original founders for the Intel corporation?
(*a*) Bill Gates (*b*) Jerry Yang
(*c*) Gordon E-Moore (*d*) Sergey Brin

295. Where of the below versions of Windows was the first to be released after Windows 98?
(*a*) Windows 99 (*b*) Windows 2000
(*c*) Windows ME (*d*) Windows XP

296. Where is the BIOS stored?
(*a*) On the hard drive
(*b*) On a diskette
(*c*) On a USB drive
(*d*) On a flash memory chip

297. What is BIOS short for?
(*a*) Not short for anything
(*b*) Basic Input/Output System
(*c*) Binary Input/Output System
(*d*) Bus Input/Output System

298. Which below IP address would be used for a local network?
(*a*) 74.125.127.100 (*b*) 69.72.169.241
(*c*) 192.168.1.100 (*d*) 209.131.36.100

299. Which of the below media type hold the most information?
(*a*) Blue-ray (*b*) CD
(*c*) DVD (*d*) Floppy diskette

300. Which of the below utilities allow you to view a drives partition information?
(*a*) Chkdsk
(*b*) Disk Management
(*c*) Device Manager
(*d*) Scandisk

301. What is XML short for?
(*a*) eXtensive Markup Language
(*b*) eXtensive Markup List
(*c*) eXtension Markup List
(*d*) eXtensible Markup Language

302. What is the name of the port in the below picture?

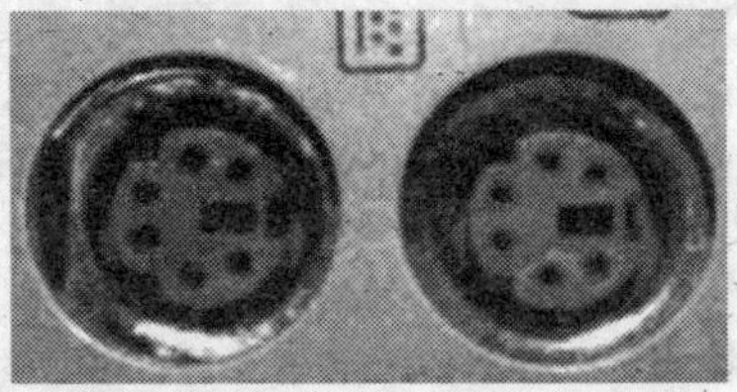

(*a*) AT (*b*) Mouse
(*c*) PS/2 (*d*) USB

303. The task of performing arithmetic and logical operations is called:
(*a*) ALU (*b*) Editing
(*c*) Storage (*d*) Output

304. The process of producing results from the data for getting useful information is called:
(*a*) Output (*b*) Input
(*c*) Processing (*d*) Storage

305. Speed of Dot Matrix Printer is measured in
(*a*) SPS (*b*) UPS
(*c*) CPS (*d*) LPS

306. _______ are used to produce high quality drawings and images, such as construction plans for buildings or blueprints for mechanical objects.
(*a*) Monitor (*b*) Plotter
(*c*) Printer (*d*) Mouse

307. The software (set of programs) that reads a program written in high level language and translates it into an equivalent program in machine language is called as—
(*a*) Assembler (*b*) Compiler
(*c*) Translator (*d*) All of these

308. The software (set of programs) that reads a program written in assembly language and translates it into an equivalent program in machine language is called as
(*a*) Compiler
(*b*) Assembler
(*c*) Plotter
(*d*) All of these

309. Deleted files or folders are stored in the—
(*a*) Recycle bin (*b*) My Document
(*c*) Not Stored (*d*) All of these

310. Whenever a program is run or a window is opened, an icon representing the program appears on the—
(*a*) Taskbar (*b*) My Document
(*c*) Control Panel (*d*) All of these

311. For viewing files—
(*a*) Double left click of the mouse on that file
(*b*) Single left click of the mouse on that role
(*c*) Right click of the mouse on that file
(*d*) All of these

312. Which of the following can be used to open a file?
(*a*) Ctrl + O (*b*) Ctrl + N
(*c*) Ctrl + A (*d*) All of these

313. Which of the following can be used to create a new file?
(*a*) Ctrl + N (*b*) Ctrl + P
(*c*) Ctrl + M (*d*) All of these

314. Which of the following can be used to close a file?
(*a*) Ctrl + W (*b*) Ctrl + O
(*c*) Ctrl + N (*d*) All of these

315. Which is the shortcut key using keyboard to save a new file?
(*a*) F12 (*b*) F2
(*c*) F7 (*d*) F4

316. Which of the following can be used to save the existing file?
(*a*) Ctrl + S (*b*) Ctrl + O
(*c*) Ctrl + D (*d*) All of these

317. Which of the following can be used for Print Preview?
(*a*) Ctrl + F2 (*b*) Ctrl + F3
(*c*) Ctrl + F4 (*d*) All of them

318. Which of the following can be used to check spelling and grammar?
(*a*) F7 (*b*) F8
(*c*) Ctrl + F9 (*d*) All of these

319. Which of the following can be used for 'Help'?
(*a*) F1 (*b*) F8
(*c*) F9 (*d*) F12

320. Which of the following can be used for 'Go to beginning of line'?
(*a*) HOME (*b*) END
(*c*) SHIFT (*d*) All of these

321. Which of the following can be used for 'Go to end of line'?
(*a*) HOME (*b*) END
(*c*) CTRL (*d*) SHIFT

322. Which of the following can be used for 'Go to beginning of document'?
(*a*) CTRL + End (*b*) CTRL + Home
(*c*) CTRL + C (*d*) All of these

323. Which of the following can be used for 'Go to end of document'?
(*a*) CTRL + End (*b*) CTRL + C
(*c*) CTRL + W (*d*) All of them

324. Which of the following can be used to 'Cut' a selected text?
(*a*) CTRL + X (*b*) CTRL + Y
(*c*) CTRL + Z (*d*) All of these

325. Which of the following can be used to 'Copy' a selected text?
(*a*) CTRL + C (*b*) CTRL + X
(*c*) CTRL + Y (*d*) All of these

326. Which of the following can be used to 'Page break'?
(*a*) CTRL + ENTER
(*b*) CTRL + SHIFT
(*c*) CTRL + Z
(*d*) All of these

327. Which of the following can be used to add page numbers to a document?
(*a*) Selected Insert from main tab bar → Page Numbers
(*b*) Select Review from main tab bar → Page Numbers
(*c*) Select Tools → Page Numbers
(*d*) All of these

328. Which of the following is not an example of hardware?
(*a*) WORD (*b*) Printer
(*c*) Monitor (*d*) Mouse

329. Which of the following is not a storage medium?
(*a*) hard disk (*b*) flash drive
(*c*) DVD (*d*) monitor

330. To see the document before the printout is taken, use—
(*a*) Insert Table (*b*) Paste
(*c*) Format Painter (*d*) Print Preview

331. To save a document for the first time, ... option is used.
(*a*) Save as (*b*) Save first
(*c*) Save on (*d*) Copy

332. What is a device that can change images into codes for the computer?
(*a*) mouse (*b*) printer
(*c*) joystick (*d*) scanner

333. To specify margins in word, the user has to select page setup option from the ______ menu.
(*a*) Edit (*b*) Table
(*c*) Auto correct (*d*) File

334. The computer specially designed that perform complex calculations extremely rapidly.
(*a*) Servers (*b*) Laptops
(*c*) Mainframes (*d*) Supercomputers

335. Which part of the computer can display the user's work?
(*a*) Mouse (*b*) Keyboard
(*c*) Disk Drive (*d*) Monitor

336. When a computer prints a report, this output is called ________
(*a*) Program (*b*) Soft copy
(*c*) Hard copy (*d*) Execution

337. Print command is found inside the ______ menu.
(*a*) View (*b*) Edit
(*c*) Tools (*d*) File

338. Function of ALU is—
(*a*) To control the execution of instruction
(*b*) To perform arithmetic and logical operation on data
(*c*) To store the result in main memory
(*d*) All the above

339. A file can be created using _____ command.
(*a*) Save (*b*) Open
(*c*) New (*d*) Edit

340. Backup is—
(*a*) Deleting all data from disk drive
(*b*) Moving all data from original location to another storage media
(*c*) Protecting data by copying it from source location to another location
(*d*) Accessing data from a tape drive

341. The default alignment of text inside a column is—
(*a*) Left (*b*) Right
(*c*) Center (*d*) Justify

342. A _____ is secret word or string of characters that is used for authentication to gain access to a resource.
(*a*) Token (*b*) Keyword
(*c*) Passward (*d*) Identifier

343. What is the name of list that stores the URLs of Web pages and links visited in past few days?
(*a*) Link list (*b*) Page list
(*c*) History list (*d*) All of them

344. The operating system is a type of—
(*a*) System software
(*b*) Application software
(*c*) Language processor
(*d*) All of these

345. Word wrap means—
(*a*) Inserting spaces between words
(*b*) Aligning text with the right margin
(*c*) Moving text automatically to the next line
(*d*) All of these

346. Which one of the following is not available in format menu of Notpad Window?
(*a*) Word wrap (*b*) Font
(*c*) Paragraph (*d*) All of these

347. Which one of the following is dangerous for computers?
(*a*) Worms (*b*) Virus
(*c*) Both (*a*) and (*b*) (*d*) All of these

348. If the monitor has more resolution then:
(*a*) Colour will not be good
(*b*) Picture quality is good

(c) Text will not be good
(d) All of these

349. For graphics printing we use
(a) Dot Matrix Printer (b) Scanner
(c) Plotter (d) All of these

350. Which is impact printer:
(a) Laser Printer
(b) Thermal Printer
(c) Ink Jet Printer
(d) Dot Matrix Printer

351. Internet is—
(a) A local computer network
(b) A world wide network of computers
(c) An interconnected network of computers
(d) A world wide interconnected network of computers which use a common protocol to communicate with one another

352. A hub is a—
(a) Router (b) Bridge
(c) Repeater (d) All of these

353. Most appropriate definition of a computer network is—
(a) System allows making requests for information from central computer
(b) An organised way of storing information about a set of similar things
(c) System that receives data and messages enabling two or more computers to communicate
(d) All of these

354. A communication network which supports audio and video data transfer is known as
(a) Data Network
(b) Image Network
(c) Multimedia Network
(d) Voice Network

355. What is a NIC?
(a) Netware Intranet Controller
(b) No Internet Connection
(c) Network Interference Control
(d) Network Interface Card

356. What is a MAC?
(a) A computer made by Apple
(b) Memory Address Corruption
(c) Mediocre Apple Computer
(d) Media Access Control

357. What do we call a collection of two or more computers that are located within a limited distance of each other and that are connected to each other directly or indirectly?
(a) Innernet
(b) Intranet
(c) Local Area Network
(d) Wide Area Network

358. ____________ is the science revolving around the use of nanostructures to build devices on an extremely small scale.
(a) Micro-technology
(b) Computer forensics
(c) Artificial intelligence
(d) Nanotechnology

359. MAN coverage is limited to
(a) Peer-to-Peer
(b) City
(c) Country
(d) Client Server

360. A virus that neither replicates or copies itself, but does compromises the security of the computer is?
(a) Joke Program (b) Worm
(c) Trojan Horse (d) Hoax

361. A computer which CPU speed more than 100 million instruction per second and with the word length of around 64 bits is known as
(a) Super computer
(b) Desktop computer
(c) Micro computer
(d) Macro computer

362. Which one of the following is NOT a network topology?
(a) Star (b) Bus
(c) Linear (d) Ring

363. Cursor is a—
(a) Pixel
(b) Thin blinking line
(c) Pointing device
(d) All of these

364. The ________ on the keyboard enables you to enter numbers quickly.
(a) Alphabetic keys (b) Numeric keys
(c) Control keys (d) Function keys

365. The arrow keys can be used to _______
(*a*) delete text
(*b*) more the cursor in the text that has already been entered
(*c*) Save the document
(*d*) more the cursor while deleting text

366. The scanner scans _______
(*a*) Pictures
(*b*) Texts
(*c*) Pictures & Texts
(*d*) Neither Picture nor Texts

367. HTML is basically used to design
(*a*) web-page
(*b*) website
(*c*) graphics
(*d*) Tables and Frames

368. You click at B to make the text—
(*a*) OCR
(*b*) Optical scanners
(*c*) Voice recognition device
(*d*) Fiber Optics

369. The term 'Pentium' is related to what?
(*a*) Mouse
(*b*) Hard Disk
(*c*) Microprocessor
(*d*) DVD

370. Which of the following is not a database?
(*a*) Oracle (*b*) AJAX
(*c*) MySQL (*d*) SQL Server

371. What is CGI?
(*a*) Computed Gateway Interface
(*b*) Compliant Gateway Interface
(*c*) Case Gateway Interface
(*d*) Common Gateway Interface

372. Which of the following is not a Web Server?
(*a*) Apache (*b*) IIS
(*c*) Jigsaw (*d*) Zoab

373. How many layers are described in networking?
(*a*) 5 (*b*) 6
(*c*) 7 (*d*) 8

374. Which of there is a correct format of IP address?
(*a*) 192.168.1.1
(*b*) 192.168.111.1111
(*c*) 192.168.900.1
(*d*) 192.900.168.1

375. Which of the following is the first web-based e-mail service?
(*a*) Gmail
(*b*) Yahoo Mail
(*c*) Hotmail
(*d*) Rediff Mail

376. The central processing unit (CPU) consists of
(*a*) Control unit, primary storage, and secondary storage
(*b*) Input, output and processing
(*c*) Control unit, processing and primary storage
(*d*) Control unit, arithmetic-logic unit and primary storage

377. Memory Management is a feature of—
(*a*) Processor
(*b*) Operating System
(*c*) MS word
(*d*) Animation

378. A computer programmer
(*a*) Dies all the thinking for a computer
(*b*) Can enter input data quickly
(*c*) Can operate all types of computer equipment
(*d*) Can draw only flowchart

379. Which of the following performs modulation and demodulation?
(*a*) Satellite (*b*) Switch
(*c*) Optical Fibre (*d*) Modem

380. The way of manipulating data into information is called—
(*a*) Storing (*b*) Processing
(*c*) Deletion (*d*) Organising

381. In computer, 'TMP' extension refers usually to what kind of file?
(*a*) Temporary file (*b*) Image file
(*c*) Video file (*d*) Text file

382. Java is a—
(*a*) Compiler
(*b*) Operating system
(*c*) Input Device
(*d*) Programming Language

383. In computers, a collection of raw data is known as what?
(*a*) Information (*b*) Output
(*c*) Data (*d*) Query

384. From among the following pick out the item that does not belong to computer:
(*a*) Mouse (*b*) OCR
(*c*) MICR (*d*) Plotter

385. Which software application is used for accessing sites or information on a network (as the World Wide Web)?
(*a*) Operating System (*b*) Web Browser
(*c*) Microsoft Word (*d*) Microsoft Excel

386. Who is known as the father of the Java programming language?
(*a*) Bill Board (*b*) James Gosling
(*c*) Jame Smith (*d*) Sabeer Bhatia

387. What does BCC means in E-mail?
(*a*) Black Carbon Copy
(*b*) Blind Carbon Copy
(*c*) Business Computer Center
(*d*) Business Computer Card

388. WAV file format is associated with what type of files?
(*a*) Video (*b*) Sound
(*c*) Image (*d*) Word Document

389. What is JVM?
(*a*) Jumber Verbose Machines
(*b*) A part of IIS
(*c*) Java Virtual Machine
(*d*) Net Framework

390. Which of these is a correct format of E-mail address?
(*a*) contact.website.into
(*b*) contact website.info
(*c*) contact@website.info
(*d*) contact@website@into

391. A program that can copy itself and infect a computer without the permission or knowledge of the owner is called what?
(*a*) Floppy (*b*) Virus
(*c*) Java (*d*) Monitor

392. 'DB' computer abbreviation usually means?
(*a*) Database (*b*) Double Byte
(*c*) Data Block (*d*) Driver Boot

393. On the Task bar the time is shown in the ______
(*a*) Start menu
(*b*) Scroll bar
(*c*) Desktop
(*d*) Notification area or Tray

394. Information to be communicated via a data communications system is the ______
(*a*) Medium (*b*) Protocol
(*c*) Message (*d*) Transmission

395. Hardware devices that are not part of the main computer system and are often added later to the system—
(*a*) Peripheral (*b*) Clip art
(*c*) Highlight (*d*) Execute

396. To select text by shading as you drag the mouse arrow over the text is known as—
(*a*) Clip art (*b*) To highlight
(*c*) To fetch (*d*) To decode

397. Computers on an internet are identified by—
(*a*) E-mail address
(*b*) Street address
(*c*) IP address
(*d*) All of these

398. When does a computer add and compare its data?
(*a*) CPU (*b*) Memory
(*c*) Hard disk (*d*) Floppy disk

399. Which one of the following is different from other members?
(*a*) Google (*b*) Windows
(*c*) Linux (*d*) Mac

400. Which is the largest unit of storage among the following?
(*a*) Terabyte (*b*) Megabyte
(*c*) Kilobyte (*d*) Gigabyte

401. Which one of the following is not a network device?
(*a*) Router (*b*) Switch
(*c*) Hub (*d*) CPU

402. HTML is basically used to design—
(*a*) Web-page (*b*) Web-site
(*c*) Graphics (*d*) Tables and Frames

403. An E-mail address is composed of—
(*a*) two parts (*b*) three parts
(*c*) four parts (*d*) five parts

404. A key board has at least—
(*a*) 91 keys (*b*) 101 keys
(*c*) 111 keys (*d*) 121 keys

405. The 'brain' of a computer which keeps peripherals under its control is called
(*a*) Common Power Unit
(*b*) Common Processing Unit
(*c*) Central Power Unit
(*d*) Central Processing Unit

406. OCR stands for—
(*a*) Optical Character Recognition
(*b*) Optical CPU Recognition
(*c*) Optimal Character Rendering
(*d*) Other Character Restoration

407. Transfer of data from one application to another line is known as—
(*a*) Dynamic Disk Exchange
(*b*) Dodgy Data Exchange
(*c*) Dogmetic Data Exchange
(*d*) Dynamic Data Exchange

408. 'Dpi' stands for—
(*a*) Dots per inch
(*b*) Digits per unit
(*c*) Dots pixel inch
(*d*) Diagrams per inch

409. Which part of the Central Processing Unit (CPU) performs calculation and markes decisions:
(*a*) Arithematic Logic Unit
(*b*) Alternating Logic Unit
(*c*) Alternate Local Unit
(*d*) American Logic Unit

410. Information and Communication Technology includes—
(*a*) Online learning
(*b*) Learning through the use of EDUSAT
(*c*) Web Based Learning
(*d*) All of these

411. If a new device is attached to a computer, such as a printer or scanner, its ________ must be installed before the device can be used.
(*a*) Buffer
(*b*) Driver
(*c*) Pager
(*d*) Server

412. The software that allows users to surf the Internet is called a/an—
(*a*) Search engine
(*b*) Internet Service Provider (ISP)
(*c*) Multimedia application
(*d*) Browser

413. A tuple is a—
(*a*) Column of a table
(*b*) Two dimensional table
(*c*) Row of a table
(*d*) Key of a table

414. The method of file organization in which data records in a file are arranged in a specified order according to a key field is known as the—
(*a*) Direct access method
(*b*) Queuing method
(*c*) Predetermined method
(*d*) Sequential access method

415. In Excel, ________ contains one or more worksheets.
(*a*) Template (*b*) Workbook
(*c*) Active cell (*d*) Label

416. Which of the following is a popular programming language for developing multimedia web pages, websites, and web-based application?
(*a*) COBOL (*b*) JAVA
(*c*) BASIC (*d*) Assembler

417. Compiling creates a(n)—
(*a*) program specification
(*b*) algorithm
(*c*) executable program
(*d*) subroutine

418. A CD-RW disk—
(*a*) has a faster access than an internal disk
(*b*) is a form of optical disk, so it can only be written once
(*c*) holds less data than a floppy disk
(*d*) can be erased and rewritten

419. The first page of a Web site is called the—
(*a*) Homepage
(*b*) Index
(*c*) Java Script
(*d*) Book mark

420. A word in a web page that, when clicked, opens another document—
(*a*) Anchor
(*b*) URL
(*c*) Hyperlink
(*d*) Reference

ANSWERS

1	2	3	4	5	6	7	8	9	10
(*b*)	(*b*)	(*c*)	(*d*)	(*b*)	(*d*)	(*d*)	(*c*)	(*c*)	(*b*)
11	**12**	**13**	**14**	**15**	**16**	**17**	**18**	**19**	**20**
(*a*)	(*d*)	(*b*)	(*c*)	(*a*)	(*c*)	(*b*)	(*d*)	(*d*)	(*c*)
21	**22**	**23**	**24**	**25**	**26**	**27**	**28**	**29**	**30**
(*a*)	(*b*)	(*a*)	(*b*)	(*c*)	(*d*)	(*c*)	(*b*)	(*b*)	(*a*)
31	**32**	**33**	**34**	**35**	**36**	**37**	**38**	**39**	**40**
(*a*)	(*a*)	(*c*)	(*d*)	(*c*)	(*d*)	(*c*)	(*b*)	(*b*)	(*c*)
41	**42**	**43**	**44**	**45**	**46**	**47**	**48**	**49**	**50**
(*c*)	(*b*)	(*c*)	(*d*)	(*c*)	(*c*)	(*d*)	(*c*)	(*d*)	(*d*)
51	**52**	**53**	**54**	**55**	**56**	**57**	**58**	**59**	**60**
(*b*)	(*c*)	(*a*)	(*c*)	(*a*)	(*c*)	(*b*)	(*d*)	(*c*)	(*c*)
61	**62**	**63**	**64**	**65**	**66**	**67**	**68**	**69**	**70**
(*c*)	(*b*)	(*c*)	(*c*)	(*c*)	(*c*)	(*b*)	(*d*)	(*a*)	(*b*)
71	**72**	**73**	**74**	**75**	**76**	**77**	**78**	**79**	**80**
(*d*)	(*d*)	(*c*)	(*d*)	(*c*)	(*d*)	(*b*)	(*b*)	(*d*)	(*b*)
81	**82**	**83**	**84**	**85**	**86**	**87**	**88**	**89**	**90**
(*d*)	(*c*)	(*b*)	(*a*)	(*c*)	(*a*)	(*c*)	(*a*)	(*a*)	(*d*)
91	**92**	**93**	**94**	**95**	**96**	**97**	**98**	**99**	**100**
(*a*)	(*c*)	(*a*)	(*b*)	(*c*)	(*b*)	(*a*)	(*a*)	(*b*)	(*b*)
101	**102**	**103**	**104**	**105**	**106**	**107**	**108**	**109**	**110**
(*c*)	(*c*)	(*a*)	(*c*)	(*d*)	(*c*)	(*a*)	(*d*)	(*d*)	(*c*)
111	**112**	**113**	**114**	**115**	**116**	**117**	**118**	**119**	**120**
(*d*)	(*c*)	(*a*)	(*d*)	(*d*)	(*c*)	(*a*)	(*d*)	(*d*)	(*d*)
121	**122**	**123**	**124**	**125**	**126**	**127**	**128**	**129**	**130**
(*b*)	(*c*)	(*a*)	(*b*)	(*d*)	(*b*)	(*d*)	(*a*)	(*b*)	(*a*)
131	**132**	**133**	**134**	**135**	**136**	**137**	**138**	**139**	**140**
(*b*)	(*a*)	(*d*)	(*c*)	(*d*)	(*a*)	(*b*)	(*d*)	(*b*)	(*c*)
141	**142**	**143**	**144**	**145**	**146**	**147**	**148**	**149**	**150**
(*a*)	(*b*)	(*a*)	(*a*)	(*c*)	(*b*)	(*b*)	(*a*)	(*b*)	(*d*)
151	**152**	**153**	**154**	**155**	**156**	**157**	**158**	**159**	**160**
(*d*)	(*c*)	(*c*)	(*d*)	(*c*)	(*b*)	(*a*)	(*b*)	(*a*)	(*c*)
161	**162**	**163**	**164**	**165**	**166**	**167**	**168**	**169**	**170**
(*b*)	(*c*)	(*b*)	(*a*)	(*b*)	(*a*)	(*b*)	(*a*)	(*b*)	(*b*)
171	**172**	**173**	**174**	**175**	**176**	**177**	**178**	**179**	**180**
(*c*)	(*c*)	(*c*)	(*b*)	(*a*)	(*b*)	(*d*)	(*d*)	(*c*)	(*d*)
181	**182**	**183**	**184**	**185**	**186**	**187**	**188**	**189**	**190**
(*c*)	(*a*)	(*d*)	(*c*)	(*b*)	(*c*)	(*c*)	(*c*)	(*c*)	(*a*)
191	**192**	**193**	**194**	**195**	**196**	**197**	**198**	**199**	**200**
(*b*)	(*b*)	(*d*)	(*c*)	(*b*)	(*a*)	(*b*)	(*b*)	(*c*)	(*d*)
201	**202**	**203**	**204**	**205**	**206**	**207**	**208**	**209**	**210**
(*c*)	(*b*)	(*a*)	(*a*)	(*d*)	(*c*)	(*c*)	(*c*)	(*b*)	(*c*)
211	**212**	**213**	**214**	**215**	**216**	**217**	**218**	**219**	**220**
(*c*)	(*c*)	(*c*)	(*c*)	(*c*)	(*b*)	(*c*)	(*d*)	(*b*)	(*b*)

221	222	223	224	225	226	227	228	229	230
(b)	(c)	(c)	(b)	(c)	(b)	(a)	(c)	(c)	(d)
231	232	233	234	235	236	237	238	239	240
(c)	(c)	(b)	(c)	(c)	(d)	(a)	(e)	(b)	(d)
241	242	243	244	245	246	247	248	249	250
(c)	(d)	(b)	(c)	(d)	(b)	(c)	(b)	(c)	(a)
251	252	253	254	255	256	257	258	259	260
(a)	(c)	(d)	(b)	(d)	(b)	(b)	(d)	(b)	(a)
261	262	263	264	265	266	267	268	269	270
(b)	(d)	(d)	(a)	(d)	(b)	(b)	(b)	(d)	(b)
271	272	273	274	275	276	277	278	279	280
(d)	(d)	(c)	(c)	(b)	(a)	(c)	(a)	(d)	(d)
281	282	283	284	285	286	287	288	289	290
(b)	(b)	(d)	(d)	(a)	(b)	(d)	(a)	(d)	(d)
291	292	293	294	295	296	297	298	299	300
(d)	(b)	(b)	(c)	(b)	(d)	(b)	(c)	(a)	(b)
301	302	303	304	305	306	307	308	309	310
(d)	(c)	(a)	(a)	(c)	(b)	(b)	(b)	(a)	(a)
311	312	313	314	315	316	317	318	319	320
(a)	(a)	(a)	(a)	(a)	(a)	(a)	(a)	(a)	(a)
321	322	323	324	325	326	327	328	329	330
(b)	(b)	(a)	(a)	(a)	(a)	(a)	(a)	(d)	(d)
331	332	333	334	335	336	337	338	339	340
(a)	(d)	(d)	(c)	(d)	(c)	(d)	(b)	(c)	(c)
341	342	343	344	345	346	347	348	349	350
(a)	(c)	(a)	(a)	(c)	(c)	(c)	(b)	(c)	(d)
351	352	353	354	355	356	357	358	359	360
(d)	(c)	(c)	(c)	(d)	(d)	(c)	(b)	(b)	(b)
361	362	363	364	365	366	367	368	369	370
(b)	(c)	(b)	(b)	(b)	(c)	(a)	(d)	(c)	(b)
371	372	373	374	375	376	377	378	379	380
(d)	(d)	(c)	(d)	(c)	(d)	(b)	(c)	(d)	(b)
381	382	383	384	385	386	387	388	389	390
(a)	(d)	(d)	(d)	(b)	(b)	(b)	(b)	(c)	(c)
391	392	393	394	395	396	397	398	399	400
(b)	(a)	(d)	(b)	(a)	(b)	(c)	(a)	(b)	(a)
401	402	403	404	405	406	407	408	409	410
(d)	(a)	(a)	(b)	(a)	(a)	(d)	(a)	(a)	(d)
411	412	413	414	415	416	417	418	419	420
(b)	(a)	(c)	(d)	(b)	(b)	(c)	(d)	(a)	(c)

GENERAL AWARENESS

1. OUR INDIA

INDIA : AT A GLANCE

Population (2011)	:	1,21,08,54,977
Capital	:	New Delhi
Area	:	32,87,263 sq km
Geographic Location	:	Between 8º4' and 37º6' north latitudes
	:	Between 68º7' and 97º25' east longitudes
Coastline Length	:	7,516.6 km including the coastline of Lakshadweep, Andaman & Nicobar Islands.
Major Languages	:	22
National Anthem	:	Jana Gana Mana
National Currency	:	Rupee (₹)
National Animal	:	Tiger
National Aquatic Animal	:	Dolphin
National Bird	:	Peacock
National River	:	Ganga
Characteristics of Indian	:	Socialist, Secular, Democratic, Republic
Legislature	:	Bicameral Legislature at the Centre
	:	Uni/Bicameral Legislatures in States
Executive	:	President, Vice-President and Council of Ministers at the Centre
		Governor and Council of Ministers in States
Judiciary	:	Independent from Executive with Supreme Court at the apex of the hierarchy
Total Road Length	:	66.7 lakh kilometres (March 2024)

India: States & Union Territories

States/Union Territories	*Capital*	*Area in (Sq. Km.)*	*Language*
Andhra Pradesh	Amaravati	1,60,229	Telugu
Arunachal Pradesh	Itanagar	83,743	Nyishi, Dafla, Miji, Wancho etc.
Assam	Dispur	78,438	Assamese
Bihar	Patna	94,163	Hindi, Maithili
Chhattisgarh	Raipur	136,034	Hindi
Goa	Panji	3,702	Marathi and Konkani
Gujarat	Gandhinagar	1,96,024	Gujarati
Haryana	Chandigarh	44,212	Hindi
Himachal Pradesh	Shimla	55,673	Hindi and Pahari
Jharkhand	Ranchi	79,714	Hindi, Santhali
Karnataka	Bengaluru	1,91,791	Kannada
Kerala	Thiruvananthapuram	38,863	Malayalam
Madhya Pradesh	Bhopal	308,000	Hindi
Maharashtra	Mumbai	307,713	Marathi
Manipur	Imphal	22,327	Manipuri
Meghalaya	Shillong	22,429	Khasi, Garo and English
Mizoram	Aizawl	21,081	Mizo and English
Nagaland	Kohima	16,579	Sema, English
Odisha	Bhubaneswar	155,707	Odiya
Punjab	Chandigarh	50,362	Punjabi
Rajasthan	Jaipur	3,42,239	Hindi and Rajasthani
Sikkim	Gangtok	7,096	Bhutia, Nepali, Lepcha and Limbu
Tamil Nadu	Chennai	1,30,058	Tamil
Telangana	Hyderabad	1,14,840	Telugu, Urdu
Tripura	Agartala	10,491	Bengali, Kakborak, Manipuri
Uttar Pradesh	Lucknow	2,40,928	Hindi and Urdu
Uttarakhand	Dehradun	53,484	Hindi
West Bengal	Kolkata	88,752	Bengali
Jammu & Kashmir	Srinagar (Summer) Jammu (Winter)	2,22,236*	Kashmiri, Urdu, Dogri
Andaman & Nicobar Island	Sri Vijaya Puram	8,249	Bengali, Hindi, Nicobarese, Tamil, Telugu, and Malayalam
Chandigarh	Chandigarh	114	Hindi, Punjabi
Dadara and Nagar Haveli and Daman and Diu	Daman	603	Gujarati and Hindi
Delhi	Delhi	1483	Hindi, Punjabi and Urdu
Lakshadweep	Kavaratti	32	Malayalam
Puducherry	Puducherry	492	Tamil, Telugu, Malayalam, English and French
Ladakh	Leh	—	Ladakhi

* Including areas of Ladakh and illegally occupied by China and Pakistan.

POPULATION

Second Largest Nation : In terms of the size of population, India is the second largest country in the world, next only to China. China tops the list with 1341.0 million people. India's population constitutes nearly 17.5 per cent of the total world population while her geographical area is only 2.42 per cent of the world area. With such a huge population to support on so small an area, the country finds herself in great difficulty in making any significant dent on its poverty and economic backwardness. India's national income, which is barely 2 per cent of the total global income, clearly shows the tremendous strain of population on her economy.

2011 Census Highlights

Population of India–Total Indian population is 17.5% of total world population	:	1,21,08,54,977 (Male: 62,32,70,258; Female: 58,75,84,719)
Decadal Growth (2001-2011)	:	17.7 per cent (Males: 17.1 per cent; Females: 18.3 per cent)
Hightest Decadal Growth (State-wise)	:	Meghalaya (27.9 per cent)
Lowest Decadal Growth (State-wise)	:	Nagaland (–0.6 per cent)
Most populous State	:	Uttar Pradesh (16.51 per cent of National Population)
Density of population	:	382 persons per sq. km.
Most densly populated State	:	Bihar : 1106 per sq. km
Sex Ratio	:	943 females per 1000 males
Total Literacy Rate	:	73% (Males – 80.9%), (Females – 64.6%)
Highest Literacy (State-wise)	:	Kerala (94%)
Lowest Literacy (State-wise)	:	Bihar (61.8)

OTHER DETAILS

(a) Population of India

1951	36,10,88,090	1961	43,92,34,771
1971	54,81,59,652	1981	68,33,29,097
1991	84,64,21,039	2001	102,87,37,436
2011	1,21,08,54,977		

(b) Density of Population (Persons per square kilometre)

1951	113	1961	138
1971	177	1981	216
1991	267	2001	324
2011	382		

(c) Annual Compound Rate of Growth

1941-1951	1.25 per cent	1951-1961	1.96 per cent
1961-1971	2.22 per cent	1971-1981	2.20 per cent
1981-1991	2.14 per cent	1991-2001	1.95 per cent
2001-2011	1.64 per cent		

2011 CENSUS OF INDIA : POPULATION DISTRIBUTION, POPULATION DENSITY AND LITERACY RATE

S. No.	State/ Union Territories*	Population 2011			Population Density (per sq. km.)	Literacy Rate 2011		
		Persons	Males	Females	2011	Persons	Males	Females
	INDIA	**1,21,08,54,977**	**62,32,70,258**	**58,75,34,719**	**382**	**73.0**	**80.9**	**64.6**
1.	Jammu and Kashmir	1,25,41,302	66,40,662	59,00,640	124	67.2	76.8	56.4
2.	Himachal Pradesh	68,64,602	34,81,873	33,82,729	123	82.8	89.5	75.9
3.	Punjab	2,77,43,338	1,46,39,465	1,31,03,873	551	75.8	80.4	70.7
4.	Chandigarh	10,55,450	5,80,663	4,74,787	9,258	86.0	90.0	81.2
5.	Uttarakhand	1,00,86,292	51,37,773	49,48,519	189	78.8	87.4	70.0
6.	Haryana	2,53,51,462	1,34,94,734	1,18,56,728	573	75.6	84.1	65.9
7.	Delhi	1,67,87,941	89,87,326	78,00,615	11,320	86.2	90.9	80.8
8.	Rajasthan	6,85,48,437	3,55,50,997	3,29,97,440	200	66.1	79.2	52.1
9.	Uttar Pradesh	19,98,12,341	10,44,80,510	9,53,31,831	829	67.7	77.3	57.2
10.	Bihar	10,40,99,452	5,42,78,157	4,98,21,295	1,106	61.8	71.2	51.5
11.	Sikkim	6,10,577	3,23,070	2,87,507	86	81.4	86.6	75.6
12.	Arunachal Pradesh	13,83,727	7,13,912	6,69,815	17	65.4	72.6	57.7
13.	Nagaland	19,78,502	10,24,649	9,53,853	119	79.6	82.8	76.1
14.	Manipur	28,55,794	14,38,586	14,17,208	115	79.2	86.1	72.4
15.	Mizoram	10,97,206	5,55,339	5,41,867	52	91.3	93.3	89.3
16.	Tripura	36,73,917	18,74,376	17,99,541	350	87.2	91.5	82.7
17.	Meghalya	29,66,889	14,91,832	14,75,057	132	74.4	76.0	72.9
18.	Assam	3,12,05,576	1,59,39,443	1,52,66,133	398	72.2	77.8	66.3
19.	West Bengal	9,12,76,115	4,68,09,027	4,44,67,088	1,028	76.3	81.7	70.5
20.	Jharkhand	3,29,88,134	1,69,30,315	1,60,57,819	414	66.4	76.8	55.4
21.	Odisha	4,19,74,218	2,12,12,136	2,07,62,082	270	72.9	81.6	64.0
22.	Chhattisgarh	2,55,45,198	1,28,32,895	1,27,12,303	189	70.3	80.3	60.2
23.	Madhya Pradesh	7,26,26,809	3,76,12,306	3,50,14,503	236	69.3	78.7	59.2
24.	Gujarat	6,04,39,692	3,14,91,260	2,89,48,432	308	78.0	85.8	69.7
25.	Daman and Diu	2,43,247	1,50,301	92,946	2,191	87.1	91.5	79.5
26.	Dadra & Nagar Haweli	3,43,709	1,93,760	1,49,949	700	76.2	85.2	64.3
27.	Maharashtra	11,23,74,333	5,82,43,056	5,41,31,277	365	82.3	88.4	75.9
28.	Andhra Pradesh	4,93,86,799	2,47,38,068	2,46,48,731	308	67.4	74.8	60.0
29.	Karnataka	6,10,95,297	3,09,66,657	3,01,28,640	319	75.4	82.5	68.1
30.	Goa	14,58,545	7,39,140	7,19,405	394	88.7	92.6	84.7
31.	Lakshadweep	64,473	33,123	31,350	2,149	91.8	95.6	87.9
32.	Kerala	3,34,06,061	1,60,27,412	1,73,78,649	860	94.0	96.1	92.1
33.	Tamil Nadu	7,21,47,030	3,61,37,975	3,60,09,055	555	80.1	86.8	73.4
34.	Puducherry	12,47,953	6,12,511	6,35,442	2,547	85.8	91.3	80.7
35.	Andaman & Nicobar Island	3,80,581	2,02,871	1,77,710	46	86.6	90.3	82.4
36.	Telangana	3,51,93,978	17,704,078	17,489,900	308	66.5	75.0	57.9

2. NATIONAL SYMBOLS

State Emblem: The State Emblem of India is an adaptation from the Sarnath Lion Capital of Ashoka. It was adopted by the Government of India on January 26, 1950. In the adapted form, only three lions are visible, the fourth being hidden from the view. The wheel (Dharma Chakra) appears in relief in the centre of the abacus with a bull on the right and a horse on the left. The bell-shaped lotus has been omitted. The words ''Satyameva Jayate'' meaning ''Truth alone triumphs'' are inscribed below the Emblem in Devanagari script.

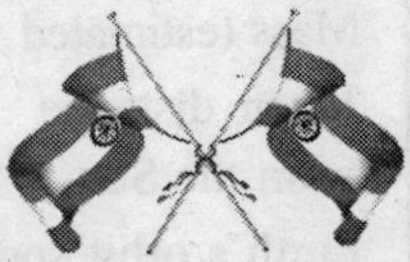

National Flag: The National Flag of India is a horizontal tricolour of deep saffron (Kesari), white and dark green in equal proportion. In the centre of the white band there is a wheel in navy blue colour. It has 24 spokes. The ratio of the length and the breadth of the flag is 3 : 2. Its design was adopted by the Constituent Assembly of India on July 22, 1947.

National Anthem: Rabindranath Tagore's song 'Jana-gana-mana' was adopted by the Constituent Assembly as the National Anthem of India on January 24, 1950.

Jana-gan-mana-adhinayaka jaya he,
Bharata-bhagya-vidhata
Punjab-Sindh-Gujarat-Maratha-Dravida-
Utkala-Banga
Vindhya-Himachala-Yamuna-Ganga Uchhala-
jaladhi-taranga.
Tava subha name jage, Tava subha asisa mange,
Gahe tava jaya gatha,
Jana-gana-mangala-dayak, jaya he Bharata
bhagya vidhata,

Jaya he, jaya he, jaya he, Jaya jaya jaya,
jaya he.

National Song: Bankim Chandra Chatterji's 'Vande Mataram' which was a source of inspiration to the people in their struggle for freedom, has been adopted as National Song. It has an equal status with the National Anthem.

Vande Mataram

Sujalam, suphalam, malayaja-shitalam,

Shasya shyamalam, Mataram

Shubhrajyotsna,pulkita yaminim,

Phulla kusumita drumadalashobhinim,

Subhasinim sumadhura—bhashinim,

Sukhadam, Varadam, Mataram.

National Bird and Animal of India: Peacock and Tiger; **National Aquatic Animal:** Dolphin; **National Flower:** Lotus; **National Calendar:** It was adopted on March 22, 1957. It has 365 days in the year and the first month of the year is Chaitra.

Months of the National Calendar

(1) Chaitra, (2) Vaishakha, (3) Jaishtha, (4) Ashadha, (5) Shravan, (6) Bhadra, (7) Ashvina, (8) Kartika, (9) Marga-Shirsha, (10) Pausha, (11) Magha, (12) Phalguna.

* * * * *

3. THE UNIVERSE

The Solar System: Some Facts

Number of Planets: 8—Mercury, Venus, Earth, Mars, Jupiter, Saturn, Uranus and Neptune.

Largest most

Massive planet	Jupiter
Brightest planet	Venus
Brightest star	Sirius
Fastest orbiting planet	Mercury
Longest (Synodic) day	Mercury
Planet with largest moon	Jupiter
Greatest average density	Jupiter
Tallest mountain	Mars
Strongest magnetic fields	Jupiter
Most circular orbit	Venus
Shortest (synodic) day	Jupiter
Hottest planet	Venus
No moons	Mercury, Venus
Planet with moon with most eccentric orbit	Neptune
Lowest average density	Saturn
Greatest amount of liquid on the surface	Earth

The Earth: Facts and Data

Composition of the Earth: Aluminium (0.4%), Sulphur (2.7%), Silicon (13%), Oxygen (28%), Calcium (1.2%), Nickel (2.7%), Magnesium (17%), Iron (35%)

Surface area	:	510100500 sq km
Land Surface (29.1%)	:	148950800 sq km
Ocean Surface (70.9%)	:	361149700 sq km
Type of water	:	97% salt, 3% fresh
Total area of water	:	382672000 sq km
Equatorial diameter	:	12753 km
Equatorial Circumference	:	40066 km
Polar Circumference	:	39992 km
Polar diameter	:	12710 km
Equatorial radius	:	6376 km
Polar radius	:	6335 km
Mass (estimated weight)	:	594×10^{19} metric tons
Mean distance from the Sun	:	149407000 km
Earth's orbit speed (around sun)	:	107320 kmph
Period of Revolution (round the sun)	:	365 days 5 hrs 48 min. 45.51 seconds
Time of Rotation (on its axis)	:	23 hrs 56 min. 4.09 seconds
Inclination of the axis (to the plane of the eclipitc)	:	23°27'

Solar Statistics

Distance from the Earth	:	149.8 million km
Absolute Visual Magnitude	:	4.75
Diameter Core	:	13,84,000 km
Temperature	:	15000000 K
Photosphere Temperature	:	5770 K

Rotation as seen from the Earth (at the equator)	:	25.38 days
Rotation as seen from the Earth (near the poles)	:	33 days
Chemical Composition	:	Hydrogen 71% Helium 26.5% Other elements 2.5%
Age	:	About 4.5 billion years
Expected lifetime of a normal star	:	About 10 billion years

Oceans of the World

Pacific	16,62,41,000 sq km
Atlantic	8,65,57,000 sq km
Indian	7,34,27,000 sq km
Arctic	94,85,000 sq km

Longest Rivers

Name	*Country/ Continent*	*Length in Kilometres*
Nile	Africa	6650
Amazon	S. America	6437
Mississippi-Missouri	USA	6020
Yangtze-Kiang	China	5494
Ob-Irtysh	Russia	5410
Lena	Russia	4400
Hwang Ho	China	4344
Niger	Africa	4180
St. Lawrence	Canada (USA)	4023
Murray-Darling	Australia	3780
Volga	Russia	3690
Indus	Asia	2900
Danube	Europe	2850
Orinoco	S. America	2575

Major Riverside Cities

City	*River*	*Country*
Alexandria	Nile	Egypt
Amsterdam	Amsel	Netherland
Ankara	Kizil	Turkey
Baghdad	Tigris	Iraq
Bangkok	Menam	Thailand
Belgrade	Danube	Yugoslavia
Berlin	Spree	Germany
Budapest	Danube	Hungary
Cairo	Nile	Egypt
Chittagong	Karnaphuli	Bangladesh
Karachi	Indus	Pakistan
Khartoum	Blue & White Nile	Sudan
Lahore	Ravi	Pakistan
Lisbon	Tagus	Portugal
Liverpool	Mersey	England
London	Thames	England
Moscow New	Moskva	Russia
Orleans	Mississipi	USA
New York	Hudson	USA
Paris	Seine	France
Yangon	Irawadi	Myanmar
Rome	Tiber	Italy

Major Gulfs of the World

Names	*Areas (Sq. Km.)*
Gulf of Mexico	15,44,000
Gulf of Hudson	12,33,000
Arabian Gulf	2,38,000
Gulf of St. Lawrence	2,37,000
Gulf of California	1,62,000
English Channel	89,900

Major Mountain Ranges of the World

Range	*Location*	*Length (km)*
Andes	South America	7,200
Himalayas-Karakoram-Hindukush	South Central Asia	5,000
Rockies	North America	4,800

Range	Location	Length (km)
Great Dividing Range	East Australia	3,600
Atlas	North West Africa	1,930
Western Ghats	Western India	1,610
Caucasus	Europe	1,200
Alaska	USA	1,130
Alps	Europe	1,050

Largest Deserts of the World

Subtropical

Sahara, North Africa	94,00,000 sq. km.
Kalahari, Southern Africa	9,00,000 sq. km.
Thar, India/Pakistan	2,00,000 sq. km.
Great Sandy, Australia	4,00,000 sq. km.

Cool Coastal

Atacama, Chile S.A.	1,40,000 sq. km

Cool Winter

Gobi, China	13,00,000 sq. km.
Colorado, Western USA (also called the painted desert)	3,37,000 sq. km.

Atmosphere

Composition of Gases in Atmosphere

Nitrogen	78.03%
Oxygen	20.99%
Argon	0.93%
Carbon dioxide	0.03%
Hydrogen	0.01%
Neon	0.0018%
Helium	0.0005%
Crypton	0.0001%
Xenon	0.000,005%
Ozone	0.000,0001%

World Important Local Winds

Chinoon: A warm day wind frequently experienced on the eastern side of the Rocky Mountains.

Fohn: A warm dry wind descending a mountain, as on the north side of the Alps.

Haboob: A sand storm or a dust storm in north and north-east Sudan near Khartoum.

Bagrrio: It is the tropical cyclone of the Philippine Island.

Loo: A hot wind which blows in summer season in Indian sub-continent.

Papasago: A cold northerly wind sometimes felt on the Mexico plateau.

Bora: It is the name given to the cold dry wind experienced particularly in winter along the eastern coast of the Atlantic Ocean and in northern Italy.

Black Toller: A hot dust wind which blows in the vast plain of North America.

Principal Mountain Peaks of the World

Mountains	Height in Metres	Range	Date of First Ascent
1. Mount Everest	8,848	Himalayas	May 29, 1953
2. K-2 (Godwin Austen)	8,611	Karakoram	July 31, 1954
3. Kanchenjunga	8,597	Himalayas	May 25, 1955
4. Lhotse	8,511	Himalayas	May 18, 1956
5. Makalu I	8,481	Himalayas	May 15, 1955
6. Dhaulagiri I	8,167	Himalayas	May 13, 1960
7. Mansalu I	8,156	Himalayas	May 9, 1956
8. Chollyo	8,153	Himalayas	Oct. 19, 1954
9. Nanga Parbat	8,124	Himalayas	July 3, 1953
10. Annapurna I	8,091	Himalayas	June 3, 1950

Mountains	Height in Metres	Range	Date of First Ascent
11. Gasherbrum I	8,068	Karakoram	July 5, 1958
12. Broad Peak I	8,047	Karakoram	June 9, 1957
13. Gasherbrum II	8,034	Karakoram	July 7, 1956
14. Shisha Pangma (Gosainthan)	8,014	Himalayas	May 2, 1964
15. Gasherbrum III	7,952	Karakoram	Aug. 11, 1975

Types of World Agriculture

Viticulture: The cultivation of the vine for production of grapes and wine.
Pisciculture: The breeding, rearing and transplantation of fish by artificial means.
Sericulture: The raising of silk worms for the production of raw silk.
Horticulture: To grow flower front, vegetables on small plots.
Apiculture: Bee keeping on a commercial scale for the sale of honey.
Floriculture: The cultivation of flowers or flowering plants.
Mariculture: Sea farming, or the cultivation of marine plants and animals for commercial purposes.
Olericulture: The cultivation of vegetables and kitchen herbs.

Famous Straits of the World

Strait	Between	Country
Malacca Strait	Andaman Sea and South China Sea	Indonesia
Palk Strait	Mannar and Bay of Bengal	India-Sri Lanka
Magellan Strait	Pacific and South Atlantic Ocean	Chile
Dover Strait	English Channel and North Sea	England-France
Berring Strait	Berring Sea and Chukasi Sea	Alaska-Russia
Sugaroo Strait	Japan Sea and Pacific Ocean	Japan
Sunda Strait	Java and Indian Ocean	Indonesia
Gibralter Strait	Mediterranean Sea and Atlantic Ocean	Spain
Harmuj Strait	Persia and Bay of Oman	Oman-Iran
Hudson Strait	Bay of Hudson and Atlantic Ocean	Canada

World's Famous Official Documents

White Paper: India; **Orange Book:** Netherlands; **Yellow Book:** France; **Green Book:** Italy and Iran; **White Book:** Portugal, China and Germany; **Grey Book:** Japan and Belgium.

Famous Newspapers of the World

Newspaper	Place of Publishing	Language
Daily News	New York (America)	English
Guardian	London (Britain)	English
Pravada	Moscow (Russia)	Russian
Al-Ahram	Cairo (Egypt)	Arabic
Merdeca	Jakarta (Indonesia)	Indonesian
Times	London (Britain)	English
People's Daily	Beijing (China)	Chinese
New Statesman	Britain	English
Daily Mirror	Britain	English
Hindu,		

Newspaper	Place of Publishing	Language
Hindustan Times, Times of India, Tribune, Statesman, Indian Express, Economic Times	India	English
Hindustan, Nav Bharat Times, Rashtriya Sahara, Dainik Jagaran, Punjab Kesari	India	Hindi

Important Boundary Lines

Boundary Line	Countries
Hindenberg Line	Germany-Poland
Maginot Line	France and Germany
Mannerhein Line	Russia-Finland
Mc Mahon Line	India and China
Order Niesse Line	Germany-Poland
Radcliff Line	India-Pakistan
Seigfrid Line	Germany-France
Durand Line	Pakistan and Afghanistan
17th Parallel	The line which defined the boundary between North Vietnam and South Vietnam before the two were united.
38th Parallel	North Korea and South Korea
49th Parallel	U.S.A. and Canada

10 Largest Countries

In Area

Rank	Country	Area (sq. km)
1.	Russia	1,70,75,000
2.	Canada	99,76,186
3.	China	95,96,960
4.	United States	93,72,614
5.	Brazil	85,11,965
6.	Australia	76,82,300
7.	India	32,87,263
8.	Argentina	27,76,654
9.	Kazakhstan	27,17,300
10.	Algeria	23,81,741

In Population (million)

Rank	Country	Population (2021)
1.	China	1,398
2.	India	1,339
3.	USA	335
4.	Indonesia	275
5.	Pakistan	238
6.	Nigeria	219
7.	Brazil	213
8.	Bangladesh	164
9.	Russia	142
10.	Japan	125

10 Smallest Countries

In Area

Rank	Country	Area (sq. km)
1.	Vatican City	0.44
2.	Monaco	1.95
3.	Nauru	21.00
4.	Tuvalu	26.00
5.	San Marino	62.00
6.	Liechtenstein	160.00
7.	Marshall Islands	181.00
8.	St. Kitts-Nevis	269.00
9.	Maldives	298.00
10.	Malta	316.00

In Population

Rank	Country	Population (2021)
1.	Vatican City	1,000
2.	Nauru	9,770
3.	Tuvalu	11,448
4.	Palau	21,613
5.	Monaco	31,223
6.	San Marino	34,467
7.	Liechtenstein	39,425
8.	St. Kitts-Nevis	54,149
9.	Dominica	74,584
10.	Marshall Islands	78,831

Signals/Signs and Meaning

Signal/Sign	Meaning
Red Triangle	Family Planning
Red Cross	Medical Help
Red Light	Danger, 'Stop' for the movement of vehicles
Green Light	Go
Olive Branch	Peace
White Pigeon or Dove	Peace
Black Strip on Arm	(i) Opposition (ii) Sorrow
Black Flag	Opposition
Red Flag	(i) Danger (ii) Revolution
White Flag	Treaty or Surrender
Yellow Flag	Vehicles with patients of contagious diseases
Two Bones across with a Skull	Danger of electricity
Half mast flown Flag	National mourning
Lotus	Sign of civilization and culture
Wheel (Chakra)	Sign of Progress
A blind folded woman with scale in hand	Sign of Justice
Reversed flown	National calamity flag

National Emblems of Important Countries

Country	National Emblem
America	Golden Rod
Australia	Kangaroo
Ireland	Shamrock
Italy	White Lily
Israel	Candelabrum
Iran	Rose
Canada	White Lily
Great Britain	Rose
Chile	Candor and Huemul
Germany	Corn Flower
Japan	Chrysanthemum
Zimbabwe	Zimbabwe Bird
Denmark	Beach
Turkey	Crescent and Star
The Netherlands	Lion
New Zealand	Kiwi, Fern Southern Cross
Norway	Lion
Nepal	Kukri
Pakistan	Crescent
Poland	Eagle
France	Lily
Belgium	Lion
Bangladesh	Water Lily
Mongolia	The Soyombo
Russia	Double headed eagle
Lebanon	Cedar Tree
Sudan	Secretary Bird
Syria	Eagle
India	Lioned Capital

Region wise Population

Region	Population (2021)	World Share (in percentage)
Asia	4,584,249,616	59.1%
Africa	1,375,397,882	17.4%
Europe	747,142,309	9.8%
Latin America and the Caribbean	651,321,069	8.4%
Northern America	373,076,833	4.8%
Oceania	41,663,096	0.5%

International Date Line

It roughly corresponds to 180°E or W meridian of longitude which falls on the opposite side of the Greenwich meridian and the date changes by one day (i.e. 24 hours), as this line is crossed. On crossing this line from east to west a day is added, and a day is subtracted on crossing it from west to east.

* * * * *

4. UNITED NATIONS ORGANISATION

- **Origin:** UN Charter was signed by 50 members on June 26, 1945. It officially came into existence on October 24, 1945.
- **UN Charter:** The Charter is the Constitution of the UNO and contains its aims and objectives and rules and regulations for its functioning.
- **Aims and Objectives:** They are security, welfare and human rights.
- **Headquarters:** New York.
- **Flag:** The flag is light blue in colour, and emblazoned in white, in its centre is the UN symbol—a polar map of world embraced by twin olive branches open at the top.
- **Official Languages:** The official languages of the UN are: English, French, Chinese, Russian, Arabic and Spanish. However, working languages are English & French only.
- **Main Organs of the UNO:** There are six main organs:
  1. **General Assembly:** It consists of representative of all members of the UN. Each member country has only one vote. It meets once a year and passes UN Budget.
  2. **Security Council:** It is the Executive body of the UN and is mainly responsible for maintaining international peace and security. It has 15 members, 5 of which (USA, UK, France, Russia and China) are permanent members. The 10 non-permanent members are elected by General Assembly for two-year term and are not eligible for immediate re-election.
  3. **Economic and Social Council:** It has 54 members elected by General Assembly.
  4. **Trusteeship Council:** It looks after interest of the people in areas not yet independent and leads them towards self-government.
  5. **International Court of Justice:** It has 15 judges, no two of whom may be nationals of the same state. They are elected by General Assembly and Security Council for a term of 9 years. The Court elects its President and Vice-President for a 3-year term.
  6. **Secretariat:** It is the Secretariat of the UN and is headed by the Secretary General.

Years Observed by United Nations Organisation

1967: International Tourism Year
1968: Human Rights Year
1970: International Education Year
1972: International Book Year
1973: Copernicus Year
1974: World Population Year
1975: International Women's Year
1979: International Year of the Child
1981: International Year of Disabled
1983: World Communication Year
1985: International Youth Year
1986: International Year of Peace
1987: International Year of Shelter for the Homeless
1990: International Literacy Year
1992: International Space Year
1993: International Year for World's Indigenous People
1994: International Year of Family

1995: International Year of Tolerance
1996: International Year for Eradication of Poverty
1998: Human Rights Year
1999: Year of Older Persons
2000: Year of the Culture of Peace
2001: International Year of Volunteer
2002: International Year of Eco-tourism
2003: International Year of Fresh Water
2004: International Rice Year
2005: International Year of Sports and Physical Education
2006: International Year of Deserts & Desertification
2008: International Year of Potato
2009: International Year of Astronomy
2010: International Year of Bio-diversity
2011: International Year of Forest
2012: International Year of Cooperatives
2013: International Year of Water Cooperation
2014: International Year of Family Farming
2015: International Year of Soil
2016: International Year of Pulses
2017: International Year of Sustainable Tourism for Development
2019: International Year of Indigenous Languages
2020: International Year of Plant Health
2021: International Year of Peace and Trust
2022: International Year of Artisanal Fisheries and Aquaculture
2023: International Year of Millets
2024: International Year of Camelids
2025: International Year of Glaciers Preservation; International Year of Quantum Science and Technology; International Year of Cooperatives; International Year of Peace and Trust.

- **Present Membership:** At present 193 countries are members of the UNO. South Sudan is the latest entrant to this world organisation.

Famous International Organisations, Headquarters and Year of Establishment

International Organisations	*Headquarters*	*Year of Establishment*
United Nations Organisations (U.N.O.)	New York	1945
International Monetary Fund (I.M.F.)	Washington	1945
World Health Organisation (W.H.O.)	Geneva	1948
Food & Agricultural Organisation (FAO)	Rome	1945
International Labour Organisation (ILO)	Geneva	1919
UNESCO	Paris	1946
International Court of Justice	The Hague	1945
Universal Postal Union (UPU)	Berne	1874
International Civil Aviation Organisation (ICAO)	Montreal	1947
UNIDO	Vienna	1966
International Atomic Energy Agency (IAEA)	Vienna	1957
International Finance Corporation (IFC)	Washington	1956
United Nations Development Programme (UNDP)	New York	1965
UNICEF	New York	1946
International Maritime Organisation (IMO)	London	1948
World Meteorological Organisation (WMO)	Geneva	1950
International Telecommunication Union (ITU)	Geneva	1865

International Organisations	Headquarters	Year of Establishment
Arab League	Cairo	1945
Commonwealth of Nations	London	1931
World Trade Organisation (WTO)	Geneva	1995
International Development Association (IDA)	Washington D.C.	1960
International Bank for Reconstruction and Development (IBRD)	Washington D.C.	1944
World Intellectual Property Organisation (WIPO)	Geneva	1967
Organisation of Islamic Conference (OIC)	Jeddah (Saudi Arabia)	1969
Red Cross	Geneva	1863
Interpol	Lyons	1923
Asian Development Bank (ADB)	Manila	1966
North Atlantic Treaty Organisation (NATO)	Brussels	1949
Association of South East Asian Nations (ASEAN)	Jakarta	1967
South Asian Association for Regional Cooperation (SAARC)	Kathmandu	1985
Asia-Pacific Economic Cooperation (APEC)	Singapore	1989
Organisation for Economic Cooperation and Development (OECD)	Paris	1961
Organisation of Petroleum Exporting Countries (OPEC)	Vienna	1960
Commonwealth of Independent States (CIS)	Minsk, Belarus	1991
International Olympic Committee (IOC)	Switzerland	1894
European Union (EU)	Brussels	Changed form of EEC Established in 1958
Amnesty International (AI)	London	1961
Shanghai Cooperation Organisation (SCO)	Beijing	2001

* * * * *

5. INDIAN CONSTITUTION & POLITY

INDIAN CONSTITUTION

India, as a sovereign state, has its own Constitution. The Indian Constitution has undergone a lengthy process over the years before its formal compositions. In fact, a number of legal developments contributed a lot in this direction. These developments, now acknowledged as the process of the constitutional development, are quite significant and these developments paved the way for the creation of an ideal constitution by a Constituent Assembly following a rigorous exercise.

CONSTITUENT ASSEMBLY

In accordance with the recommendation of the Cabinet Mission, which consisted of Lord Pethick-Lawrence, Sir Stafford Cripps and A.V. Alexander and which visited India in March 1946, the Constituent Assembly of India was elected by the Provincial Assemblies in July 1946. It had 389 members in all, including 93 representatives of Indian Princely States.

The important Committees of the Constituent Assembly were:

(*a*) **Union Powers Committee:** It had 9 members. Shri Jawaharlal Nehru was its Chairman;

(*b*) **Committee on Fundamental Rights and Minorities:** It had 54 members. Sardar Vallabhbhai Patel was its Chairman;

(*c*) **Steering Committee:** It had 3 members. Dr. K.M. Munshi (Chairman); Shri Gopalswamy Ayyangar and Shri Bishwanath Das;

(*d*) **Provincial Constitution Committee:** 25 members. Sardar Patel as Chairman;

(*e*) **Committee on Union Constitution:** 15 members. Pandit Nehru as Chairman.

The first session of the Assembly was held in New Delhi on December 9, 1946. It was attended by 207 members. Sachchidanand Sinha, as the oldest member of the Constituent Assembly, was elected provisional chairman of the session. However on December 11, 1946, Dr. Rajendra Prasad was elected as the Permanent Chairman of the Constituent Assembly.

THE LONG JOURNEY

- Demand for a Constituent Assembly composed of the people of India officially asserted by the Congress for the first time in 1935.
- Cripps' proposals of 1942 accepted this demand.
- The election for Indian Constituent Assembly held in 1946 according to the Cabinet Mission plan.
- First meeting of the Constituent Assembly for undivided India held on December 9, 1946.
- On 26 July, 1947, separate Constituent Assembly for Pakistan created.
- The sovereign Constituent Assembly for the Dominion of India (*i.e.,* excluding Pakistan) met for the first time on 14 August, 1947.
- Members of the Constituent Assembly indirectly elected.
- The electoral college consisted of members of the Provincial Legislative Assemblies (Lower Houses only).

- Each Province and each Indian State or group of States allotted seats in the Constituent Assembly proportional to their respective population (roughly in the ratio of one to a million).
- In all, provinces to elect 292 members and Indian states 93.
- Principle of Communal Electorate valid for election to the Constituent Assembly (Muslims, Sikhs, General).
- Method of election—proportional representation with single transferable vote.
- As the result of partition, membership of the CA reduced to 299.
- Constitution of India declared passed on 26th November, 1949.
- On 26th November, 1949, 284 members appended their signature to the Constitution.
- Drafting Committee of the Constituent Assembly chaired by Dr. Ambedkar.
- The Constitution underwent three readings before finalisation.
- Provisions relating to citizenship, elections, provisional parliament, temporary and transitional provisions came into effect on November 26, 1949.
- The Date of Commencement of Indian Constitution fixed for 26th January 1950.

Indian Constitution is a comprehensive document and it is the lengthiest written Constitution in the World.

The Preamble of the Constitution: "We the people of India, having solemnly resolved to Constitute India into a Sovereign, Socialist, Secular Democratic Republic and to secure to all its citizen."

Justice: Social, economic and political.

Liberty: Of thought, expression, belief, faith and worship.

Equality: Of status and of opportunity, and to promote among them all.

Fraternity: Assuring the dignity of the individual and the unity and integrity of the nation. In our Constituent Assembly, this twenty-sixth day of November, 1949, do hereby adopt, enact and give to ourselves this constitution."

SCHEDULES TO THE CONSTITUTION

The Constitution of India originally contained only eight schedules. Presently there are 12 schedules in the constitution.

First Schedule: It consists the list of the States and Union territories. ***Second Schedule:*** This Schedule is related to salary and allowances of the President, Governors, Speaker, Supreme Court and High Court Judges etc. ***Third Schedule:*** Contains forms of oath and affirmation. ***Fourth Schedule:*** Contains allocation of seats to each State and Union territory in the Council of States. ***Fifth Schedule:*** Provides for administration and control of scheduled areas and scheduled tribes. ***Sixth Schedule:*** Provides for administration of Tribal Areas in Assam, Meghalaya and Mizoram. ***Seventh Schedule:*** Distribution of powers and functions between the centre and state governments under three lists. ***Eighth Schedule:*** The languages recognised by Parliament. ***Ninth Schedule:*** It contains laws passed by the Union or States which cannot be taken to courts. ***Tenth Schedule:*** Provisions as to disqualification on the ground of political defection. ***Eleventh Schedule:*** Provisions regarding powers, authority etc. of Panchayati Raj institutions. ***Twelfth Schedule:*** Provisions regarding powers, authority etc. of Municipalities etc.

Foreign Sources of Indian Constitution

Foreign Sources	*Subject*
Britain	Parliamentary system, collective responsibilities of Cabinet
America	Fundamental right, Citizenship, Independent Judiciary, Judicial review
Canada	Division of powers
Ireland	Directive principles
Germany	Emergency provisions
Russia	Fundamental duties
Australia	Concurrent list

THE SUPREME COURT

The Supreme Court of India consists of the Chief Justice and other Judges whose number is prescribed by the Parliament from time to time. In 1950 there was a Chief Justice and there were 7 Judges. But the number of Judges continued increasing as per the need. The Supreme Court, at present, consists of the Chief Justice and 33 Judges.

The Chief Justice and other Judges of the Supreme Court are appointed by the President of India. For appointing the Chief Justice of India, the other Judges of the Supreme or High Courts may be consulted. Usually, the senior-most Judge in the Supreme Court is appointed as the Chief Justice. For the appointment of other Judges of the Supreme Court, the Chief Justice has to be consulted. Usually, the Chief Justice himself consults a collegium of the four senior-most Judges, and all of them need to agree for any candidate to be recommended for the appointment of a judge.

A person can be appointed as a Judge of the Supreme Court only if he/she:

I. is a citizen of India;

II. must have been at least a Judge of a High Court or of two or more such Courts in succession for at least five years; or

III. must have been an advocate of a High Court or of two or more such Courts in succession for at least ten years; or

IV. is, in the opinion of the President, a distinguished jurist.

Judges of the Supreme Court hold office till they attain the age of 65 years. But they may be removed from office by an order of the President, passed after an address by each House of Parliament supported by a special majority on the ground of proved misbehaviour or incapacity.

The Jurisdiction and Powers of the Supreme Court

The Supreme Court of India is a powerful judiciary. The Constitution of India has defined its jurisdiction and powers in detail, it has Original. Appellate and Advisory Jurisdictions Besides these jurisdictions, it has a few other important functions.

(*i*) **Original Jurisdiction:** The Supreme Court alone has the authority to hear directly certain cases. These are:

(*a*) Disputes between the Union government and one or more State governments,

(*b*) Disputes between two or more States,

(*c*) Disputes between the Government of India and one or more States on the one side and one or more States on the other side.

(*ii*) **Appellate Jurisdiction:** The power of a superior or higher court to hear and decide appeals against the judgment of the lower court is called appellate jurisdiction. The Supreme Court is a court of appeal for constitutional, civil and criminal cases. It can hear appeals against the judgments of the High Courts. It also has the power to review its own judgment. It may in its own discretion grant special lease to appeal against any judgment or order delivered or passed by any court or tribunal within the territory of India.

Moreover, an Appeal may come to the Supreme Court in any criminal case, if the High Court certifies that the case is fit for appeal to the Supreme Court. The special appellate power has become a handy weapon in the hands of the Court to review the decisions pertaining to elections and Labour and Industrial Tribunals.

(*iii*) **Advisory Jurisdiction:** The Supreme Court has a special advisory jurisdiction in matters which may specifically be referred to it by the President of India. If at any time, it appears to the President that a question of law or fact has arisen or is likely to arise, which is of such public importance that it is urgent to obtain the opinion of the Supreme Court on it, he/she may refer it to the Supreme Court. The Supreme Court may, after such hearing as it thinks fit, report to the President its opinion thereon. The report or the opinion of the Supreme Court is of course, not binding on the President. Similarly, there is no compulsion for the Court to give its advice.

(*iv*) **Judicial Review:** The Supreme Court of India has the power to examine the validity of laws or executive orders. The Supreme Court has the powers to interpret the Constitution, and through this it has assumed the power of judicial review.

(*v*) **Guardian of the Constitution:** As the interpreter of the Constitution, the Supreme Court has the power to protect and defend the Constitution. If the Court finds that any law or executive order is against the Constitution, the same can be declared unconstitutional or invalid. Similarly the Supreme Court also acts as the custodian and protector of Fundamental Rights.

PARLIAMENT

Parliament is the national legislature of the Indian Union. It consists of two Houses known as the Council of States or the Rajya Sabha and the House of People or Lok Sabha. The President is an integal part of Parliament.

Rajya Sabha

The Rajya Sabha is the Upper House of the Parliament and it is constituted of representatives from the States or the Constituent units of the Indian Union. It is a permanent body, one third of its members retiring after every two years. Its maximum strength is 250. Out of these, twelve members are nominated by the President from well-known personalities in the realm of Science, Art, Literature and Social Service. Rest of 238 representatives of the States and Union Territories are elected. Rajya Sabha at present consists of 245 members.

Lok Sabha

The Lok Sabha whose life is five years, is the Lower House of Parliament and comprises of members directly elected by the people. The House of the people (Lok Sabha) at present consists of 543 members directly elected from the states and Union Territories. Two members were nominated from the Anglo-Indian Community by the President, but by the 104th amendment of the constitution this provision have been abolished. The House of the People shall continue for five years (unless sooner dissolved) from the date of its meeting and no longer and the expiry of the said period of 5 years shall operate as dissolution of the House.

Parliamentary Committees

There are several Parliamentary Committees to assist the Parliament in its deliberations. These are appointed or elected by the respective Houses of Lok Sabha and Rajya Sabha on a motion made or are nominated by their presiding officers, i.e., the Speaker of Lok Sabha and the Chairman of Rajya Sabha respectively. Broadly, Parliamentary Committees are of two kinds–standing committees and ad-hoc committees. Among the Standing Committees, three are financial Committees:

(*i*) Public Account Committee;

(*ii*) Estimate Committee;

(*iii*) Public undertaking Committee.

Ad-hoc Committees are appointed as the need arises and cease to exist when the work is over.

Speaker of Lok Sabha

Speaker is elected by the Lok Sabha from among its members. The Speaker will have the final power to maintain order within the House of the People and to interpret its rules of procedure. Speaker decides whether a bill is a money bill or a non-money bill.

Table of Precedence

1. President
2. Vice-President
3. Prime Minister
4. Governors of States within their respective states
5. Former Presidents

5A. Deputy Prime Minister

6. Chief Justice of India, Speaker of Lok Sabha
7. Cabinet Ministers of the Union, Chief Ministers of States within their respective States, Deputy Chairman NITI Aayog

   Leaders of opposition in Rajya Sabha and Lok Sabha

7A. Holders of the Bharat Ratna Decoration

8. Ambassadors Extraordinary and Plenipotentiary and High Commissioners of Commonwealth Countries accredited to India
Chief Ministers of States outside their respective States
9. Judges of the Supreme Court
10. Deputy Chairman Rajya Sabha, Deputy Chief Minister of States
Deputy Speaker Lok Sabha, Members of the NITI Aayog, Minister of State of the Union and Other Minister in the Ministry of Defence.

PRESIDENT

The President is the Constitutional head of the Republic of India. He is more or less the titular head of the executive. Really speaking, he is the constitutional head but not the real executive. The real power is vested in the hands of the Council of Ministers.

Qualifications

(*i*) Indian citizen,
(*ii*) age not less than 35 years,
(*iii*) should have qualification for election to Lok Sabha,
(*iv*) should not hold any office of profit,
(*v*) should not be a Member of Parliament or State Legislature.

Powers

The Constitution has vested the President with the following powers:

(*i*) **Executive powers:** executive authority is exercised in his name. He is the supreme commander of armed forces and declares war and makes peace. He appoints all important executive officials, like Prime Minister, Governors etc.;

(*ii*) **Legislative Powers:** The President is a part of the Parliament; he summons and prorogues both the Houses jointly and separately; he nominates 12 members in Rajya Sabha. His assent to the bills is essential; money bills are introduced with his recommendation;

(*iii*) **Financial Powers:** He acts as a custodian of Contingency Fund; appoints Finance Commission;

(*iv*) **Judicial powers:** He appoints Chief Justice and other judges of the Supreme Court—he can seek the advice of the Chief Justice on any matter of public importance; he can grant pardon and reprieve, commute or suspend sentence; he is not answerable before any court;

(*v*) **Diplomatic powers:** He enjoys the right to represent India in international sphere; he has power to receive and send envoys, conclude international treaties etc.;

(*vi*) **Emergency Powers:** He enjoys extensive powers, dealing with three types of emergencies:

(*a*) emergency due to war or external aggression or internal rebellion;
(*b*) emergency due to the failure of constitutional machinery in the state; and
(*c*) emergency due to financial instability.

During emergencies, the President assumes extraordinary powers. The position of the President has been finally determined by 42nd Amendment. It has made it obligatory on the part of the President to act on the advice of the Council of Ministers.

Term and Emolument

The President holds the office for a period of five years. He is eligible for re-election. He draws a fix salary per month with various allowances. He is also entitled to rent free official residence called Rashtrapati Bhawan.

VICE-PRESIDENT

The Vice-President is elected by the elected members of the both Houses of the Parliament. A candidate for the office of Vice-President should be:

(*i*) above 35 years of age;
(*ii*) citizen of India;

(*iii*) eligible for election as a member of Rajya Sabha;

(*iv*) should not hold any office of profit;

(*v*) should not be a member of parliament; and

(*vi*) should not be of unsound mind.

Vice-President holds office for 5 years and can be removed from office earlier through a resolution passed by a two-third majority of Rajya Sabha agreed to by the Lok Sabha.

The Presiding Officer

Vice-President is the ex-officio chairman of Rajya Sabha and presides over the sessions of the Upper House. He performs all the duties of the President when the office of the President falls vacant due to the death, resignation or absence of the President. He draws a fix salary per month in his capacity of being the Chairman of the Rajya Sabha.

COUNCIL OF MINISTERS AND PRIME MINISTER

The Constitution of India provides for a parliamentary system of government under which the President is only a constitutional ruler and the real power is exercised by the Council of Ministers, headed by the Prime Minister. The members of the Council of Ministers hold office during the pleasure of the President but actually they stay in office as long as they enjoy the confidence of the majority in the Lok Sabha. As per the Constitution, the Council of Ministers is only an advisory body to assist the President but in reality, it enjoys extensive powers. Constitutionally, the executive authority has been vested in the President but in reality, these powers are exercised by the Prime Minister and the Council of Ministers.

PRIME MINISTER

The Prime Minister is the leader of the majority party in the Parliament and the President cannot exercise his discretion in the appointment of the Prime Minister. He stays in office till the majority of the members of Lok Sabha has confidence in him. He occupies an important position in relation to the Council of Ministers. He recommends the names of the persons to be included in the Council of Ministers. He allocates portfolios among them and can ask any minister to tender resignation. He can drop a minister while reshuffling the ministry. He coordinates the administration of various departments. He is the chief link between the President and the Council. He is the leader of the majority party and so, he has a great influence on the Parliament and the party. The Prime Minister enjoys such extensive powers as have been described as the virtual ruler of the country.

FUNDAMENTAL RIGHTS

Following fundamental rights are enjoyed by every Indian citizen, irrespective of caste, colour, creed and sex:

1. **Right to Equality:** No special privileges, no distinction on grounds of religion, caste, creed and sex.
2. **Right to Freedom:** The right to freedom of expression and speech, the right to choose one's own profession, the right to reside in any part of the Indian Union.
3. **Right to Freedom to Religion:** Except when it is in the interest of public order, morality, health or other conditions, everybody has the right to profess, practice and propagate his religion freely.
4. **Cultural and Educational Rights:** The Constitution provides that every community can run its own institutions to preserve its own culture and language.
5. **Right against Exploitation:** Traffic in human beings and forced labour and the employment of children under 14 years in factories or mines, are punishable offences.
6. **Rights to Constitutional Remedies:** When a citizen finds that any of his fundamental rights has been encroached upon, he can move the Supreme Court, which has been empowered to safeguard the fundamental rights of a citizen (Article 32).

Jurisdiction and Seat of High Courts

Name	Year	Territorial Jurisdiction	Seat
Allahabad	1866	Uttar Pradesh	Prayagraj (Bench at Lucknow)
Andhra Pradesh	2019	Andhra Pradesh	Amaravati
Bombay	1862	Maharashtra, Goa, Dadar and Nagar Haveli and Daman and Diu	Mumbai (Benches at Nagpur, Panaji and Sambhaji Nagar)
Calcutta	1862	West Bengal and Andaman & Nicobar Islands	Kolkata (Circuit Benches has at Shri Vijaya Puram and Jalpaiguri)
Chhattisgarh	2000	Chhattisgarh	Bilaspur
Delhi	1966	Delhi	Delhi
Gauhati	1948	Assam, Nagaland, Mizoram and Arunachal Pradesh	Guwahati (Benches at Kohima, Aizawl and Itanagar)
Gujarat	1960	Gujarat	Ahmedabad
Himachal Pradesh	1971	Himachal Pradesh	Shimla
Jammu & Kashmir and Ladakh	1928	Jammu & Kashmir, Ladakh	Srinagar and Jammu
Jharkhand	2000	Jharkhand	Ranchi
Karnataka	1884	Karnataka	Bengaluru (Circuit Benches at Dharwar and Gulbarga)
Kerala	1958	Kerala & Lakshadweep Islands	Kochi
Madhya Pradesh	1956	Madhya Pradesh	Jabalpur (Benches at Gwalior and Indore)
Madras	1862	Tamil Nadu & Puducherry	Chennai (Bench at Madurai)
Orissa	1948	Odisha	Cuttack
Patna	1916	Bihar	Patna
Punjab and Haryana	1966	Punjab, Haryana and Chandigarh	Chandigarh
Rajasthan	1949	Rajasthan	Jodhpur (Bench at Jaipur)
Sikkim	1975	Sikkim	Gangtok
Uttarakhand	2000	Uttarakhand	Nainital
Tripura	2013	Tripura	Agartala
Meghalaya	2013	Meghalaya	Shillong
Manipur	2013	Manipur	Imphal
Telangana	2019	Telangana	Hyderabad

FUNDAMENTAL DUTIES

The fundamental duties for the Indian citizens have been incorporated in the Constitution through the Constitution (42nd) Amendment Act, 1976. These duties are:

(*i*) to abide by the Constitution and respect its ideals and institutions, the National Flag and the National Anthem;

(*ii*) to cherish and follow the noble deeds which inspired our national struggle for freedom;

(*iii*) to uphold and protect the sovereignty, unity and integrity of India;

(*iv*) to defend the country and render national service when called upon to do so;

(*v*) to promote harmony and the spirit of common brotherhood amongst all the people transcending religious, regional or sectional diversities and to renounce practices derogatory to the dignity of women;

(*vi*) to value and preserve the rich heritage of our composite culture;

(*vii*) to protect and improve natural environment including forests, lakes, rivers and wildlife, and to have compassion for living creatures;

(*viii*) to develop the scientific temper, humanism and the spirit of inquiry and reform;

(*ix*) to safeguard public property and to abjure violence;

(*x*) to strive towards excellence in all spheres of individual and collective activity so that the nation constantly rises to higher levels of endeavour and achievement.

(*xi*) who is parent or guardian to provide opportunities for education to his child or, as the case may be, ward between age of six and fourteen years.

DIRECTIVE PRINCIPLES OF STATE POLICY

The Directive Principles of State Policy are contained in Article 36 to 51 in Part IV of the constitutions. Directive principles are not enforceable through courts. Main aim of Directive principles is to provide social and economic base of a genuine democracy.

Some Important Directive Principles:

- Provisions for adequate means of livelihood for all citizens (Art. 39).
- Right to work (Art. 41).
- Right to human condition of work and maternity relief (Art. 42).
- Right to a living wage and condition of work ensuring decent standard of life of worker (Art. 43).
- Common Civil Code (Art. 44).
- Prohibit consumption of liquor (Art. 47).
- Prevent slaughter of useful cattle (Art. 48).
- Organise Panchayati Raj (Art. 40).
- Separate the judiciary from the executive (Art. 50).
- Protect and maintain places of historic monuments (Art. 49).
- International peace (Art. 51).

Voting Age: The voting age in the election to the Lok Sabha and State Legislative Assemblies has been reduced from 21 to 18 years by the Constitution (61st) Amendment Act, 1989.

GOVERNOR

The Governor is appointed by the President and holds office during the pleasure of the President. Apart from the power to appoint the council of ministers, if the governor finds that the government of state cannot be carried on in accordance with the provisions of the constitution (Art. 356), he may send his report to the President who may assume to himself the functions of the government of the state. (This is popularly known as 'President's Rule').

THE ATTORNEY GENERAL OF INDIA

The Attorney General of India is the first law officer of the Government of India. Though he is not a member of cabinet he has the right to speak in the

House of Parliament, but he has no right to vote. The Attorney General of India shall be appointed by the President and shall hold office during his pleasure.

His duty shall be to give advice on such legal matter from time to time as may be referred to him by the President.

COMPTROLLER & AUDITOR GENERAL OF INDIA (CAG)

The Comptroller and Auditor General of India is guardian of the public purse and it is his duty to see that not a *paisa* is spent out of consolidated fund of India or of a state without the authority of the appropriate legislature. He is appointed by President of India.

Status

- Appointed by the President.
- A person with long administrative experience & knowledge of accounts is appointed.
- Holds office for 6 yrs or till 65 yrs of age.
- The President can remove him only on the recommendation of the 2 houses of Parliament (as in case of judge of Supreme Court).

UNION PUBLIC SERVICE COMMISSION (U.P.S.C.)

The UPSC has one chairman and nine members. The members as well as the chairman are appointed by the President. Roughly, one half of the members of UPSC should be persons who have held important offices under the central or the state government for at least 10 years. They retire after 6 years. The chairman or a member of the UPSC can be removed from the office by the President but after referring the case to the supreme Court, which, after holding enquiry, recommends for the same. The functions of the UPSC are:

(*i*) to conduct examination for appointment to the services of the Union;

(*ii*) to advise the government on the methods of recruitment; and

(*iii*) to advise the government on disciplinary method affecting a person who is serving under the government of India.

INTER-STATE COUNCILS

Article 263 provides for inter-state councils. The power of the President to set up Inter-State Councils not only for advising upon disputes but also for investigating and discussing subjects in which some or all of the states, or the Union and one or more of the states have common interest.

STAFF SELECTION COMMISSION

The Union Government has constituted the Staff Selection Commission for recruitment to non-technical Group C and some of Group B posts in the central departments and in subordinate offices. The administrative Reforms Commission had recommended the setting up of such a Commission.

* * * * *

6. PLANNING IN INDIA

The need for planning was felt in India even before independence. A National Planning Committee was set up by the Indian National Congress as early as 1938. The Planning Commission was set up in 1950. It is an advisory body engaged in the task of meaningful national planning. The main objectives of India's Economic Planning are as follows : (*i*) securing an increase in National Income; (*ii*) achieving a planned rate of investment within a given period to bring the actual investment as a proportion of national income to a higher level; (*iii*) reducing inequality in the distribution of income and wealth; (*iv*) providing additional employment; (*v*) adopting measures to increase agricultural production, manufacturing capacity for producers and a favourable balance of payments.

Five Year Plans in India

Plans	Period	Investment (₹ Crore)	Objectives
First Plan	April 1, 1951–March 31, 1956	1,960	Priority to agriculture, electricity and irrigation.
Second Plan	April 1, 1956–March 31, 1961	4,672	Development of basic and heavy industries.
Third Plan	April 1, 1961–March 31, 1966	8,577	Long term development of India's economy.
Annual Plan	April 1, 1966–March 31, 1967	2,137	
Annual Plan	April 1, 1967–March 31, 1968	2,205	
Annual Plan	April 1, 1968–March 31, 1969	2,283	
Fourth Plan	April 1, 1969–March 31, 1974	15,779	Enlarge the income of rural population and supply of goods of mass consumption.
Fifth Plan	April 1, 1974–March 31, 1979	39,426	Attain increased self reliance and employment avenues.
Annual Plan	April 1, 1979–March 31, 1980	12,176	
Sixth Plan	April 1, 1980–March 31, 1985	1,09,292	Removal of unemployment
Seventh Plan	April 1, 1985–March 31, 1990	2,18,730	Food work and productivity were the basic priorities.
Eighth Plan	April, 1992–March 31, 1997	4,95,670	Raising employment
Ninth Plan	April 1, 1997–March 31, 2002	9,41,041	Agriculture and rural development
Tenth Plan	April 1, 2002–March 31, 2007	14,91,610	Growth rate 7.8 percent per annum.
Eleventh Plan	April 1, 2007–March 31, 2012	36,44,718	Literacy, Employment, Rural development & Transport development.
Twelfth Plan	April 1, 2012–March 31, 2017	43,30,000	Long term development of India's economy.

INDIA'S AMBITIOUS 15-YEAR VISION PLAN

Niti Aayog has come forward with a draft 15-year vision plan to catapult the country's economy to more than three times as compared to the present day. The new plan is set to replace the centralised five-year plans the country has been following for decades.

The new plan is accompanied by shorter sub-plans—a seven-year strategy for 2017-24, and a three-year 'Action Agenda' from 2017-18 to 2019-20. No less than 300 specific action points covering a wide range of sectors have been drawn up as part of the 15 year vision.

The salient features of 15-year vision plan are:

- India aims to more than triple the size of its economy in 15 years with gross domestic product (GDP) expected to rise to ₹ 469 lakh crores from ₹ 137 lakh crore in 2015-16. Per capita GDP is expected to rise by three times to ₹ 3,14,667 in 2015-2016.
- NITI Aayog plans to work closely with staes to boost infrastructure and services, including regions that require special attention. The gov-ernment made a big push for Goods and Services Tax (GST), urging the state governments to speed up the legislation of state GST bills.
- India's urban population is expected to increase by 22 crores by 2031. The plan is likely to lay emphasis on urban development, taking a note from China's elaborate long-term development agenda.
- The plan envisages a central body for overseeing the implemention of sustainable development goals. Specific goals will cover clean water, removing hunger, climate efforts, responsible consumption, clean energy, quality educaiton, reduced inequality and gender equality, among others.
- The NITI Aayog will work as a "collaborative federal body whose strength is in its ideas, rather than in administrative or financial control."

NITI AAYOG

The National Institution for Transforming India, also called NITI Aayog, was formed via a resolution of the Union Cabinet on January 1, 2015. NITI Aayog is the premier policy 'Think Tank' of the Government of India, providing both directional and policy inputs. While designing strategic and long term policies and programmes for the Government of India, NITI Aayog also provides relevant technical advice to the Centre and States. At the core of NITI Aayog's creation are two hubs - *Team India Hub* and the *Knowledge and Innovation Hub*. The Team India Hub leads the engagement of states with the Central government, while the Knowledge and Innovation Hub builds NITI's think-tank capabilities. These hubs reflect the two key tasks of the Aayog.

FINANCE COMMISSION

Article 280 of the Constitution provides for the appointment of a finance commission every five year. President appoints chairman and members of this commission. Finance commission are to recommend to President the basis for the distribution of the net proceeds of taxes between the centre and the states and the principles which should govern the grants-in-aid to be given to the states out of the consolidated funds of India.

NATIONAL DEVELOPMENT COUNCIL

The National Development Council, set-up in 1952, consists of representatives of the Central Government as well as the State governments. It is the supreme body insofar as planning is concerned and it determines policies, issues guidelines, reviews working of the plan and finally approves the plan. The Council consists of the Prime Minister (Chairman), all Union Cabinet Ministers, Chief Ministers of all States and Union Territories and the Vice Chairman and members of the NITI Aayog. For matters relating to Plans and planning, the Union Minister of Planning is responsible to the Parliament.

RESERVE BANK OF INDIA

It is the Central Bank of the country. The Reserve Bank of India was established in 1935 with a capital of ₹ 5 crore. This capital of ₹ 5 crore was divided into 5 lakh equity shares of ₹ 100 each. In the beginning the ownership of almost all the share capital was with the non-government shareholders. In order to prevent the centralisation of the equity shares in the hands of a few people, **the Reserve Bank of India was nationalised on January 1, 1949.**

Establishment Years of Major Financial Institutions of India

Institution	Year
• Imperial Bank of India	1921
• Reserve Bank of India (Nationalisation of RBI took place on January 1, 1949)	April 1, 1935
• Industrial Finance Corporation of India	1948
• State Bank of India	July 1, 1955
• Unit Trust of India	Feb. 1, 1964
• Bifurcation of UTI (UTI-I & UTI-II)	Feb. 2003
• IDBI	July 1964
• NABARD	July 12, 1982
• IRBI (Now it has been renamed a IIBIL since March 6, 1997)	March 20, 1985
• SIDBI	1990
• EXIM Bank	January 1, 1982
• National Housing Bank	July 1988
• Life Insurance Corporation (LIC)	September 1956
• General Insurance Corporation (GIC)	November 1972
• Regional Rural Banks	Oct. 2, 1975
• Technology Development & Information Co. of India Ltd.	1989
• Infrastructure Leasing & Financial Services Ltd.	1988
• Housing Development Finance Corporation Ltd. (HDFC)	1977

*****

7. GENERAL SCIENCE

INVENTIONS AND DISCOVERIES

Important Inventions

Name of Invention	*Inventor*	*Nationality*	*Year*
Aeroplane	Orville & Wilbur Wright	U.S.A.	1903
Ball-Point Pen	John J. Loud	U.S.A.	1888
Barometer	Evangelista Torricelli	Italy	1644
Bicycle	Kirkpatrick Macmillan	Britain	1839-40
Bifocal Lens	Benjamin Franklin	U.S.A.	1780
Car (Petrol)	Karl Benz	Germany	1888
Celluloid	Alexander Parkes	Britain	1861
Cinema	Nicolas & Jean Lumiere	France	1895
Clock (mechanical)	I-Hsing & Liang Ling-Tsan	China	725
Diesel Engine	Rudolf Diesel	Germany	1895
Dynamo	Hypolite Pixii	France	1832
Electric Lamp	Thomas Alva Edison	U.S.A.	1879
Electric Motor (DC)	Zenobe Gramme	Belgium	1873
Electric Motor (AC)	Nikola Tesla	U.S.A.	1888
Electro-magnet	William Sturgeon	Britain	1824
Electronic Computer	Dr. Alan M. Turing	Britain	1943
Film (moving outlines)	Louis Prince	France	1885
Film (musical sound)	Dr. Le de Forest	U.S.A.	1923
Fountain Pen	Lewis E. Waterman	U.S.A.	1884
Gramophone	Thomas Alva Edison	U.S.A.	1878
Helicopter	Etienne Oehmichen	France	1924
Jet Engine	Sir Frank Whittle	Britain	1937
Laser	Charles H. Townes	U.S.A.	1960
Lift (Mechanical)	Elisha G. Otis	U.S.A.	1852
Locomotive	Richard Trevithick	Britain	1804
Machine Gun	James Puckle	Britain	1718
Microphone	Alexander Graham Bell	U.S.A.	1876
Microscope	Z. Janssen	Netherlands	1590
Motor Cycle	G. Daimler	Germany	1885
Photography (on film)	John Carbutt	U.S.A.	1888
Printing Press	Johann Gutenberg	Germany	c.1455
Razor (safety)	King C. Gillette	U.S.A.	1895
Refrigerator	James Harrison & Alexander Catlin	U.S.A.	1850

Name of Invention	Inventor	Nationality	Year
Safety Pin	Walter Hunt	U.S.A.	1849
Sewing machine	Barthelemy Thimmonnier	France	1829
Ship (steam)	J.C. Perier	France	1775
Ship (turbine)	Hon. Sir C. Parsons	Britain	1894
Skyscraper	W. Le Baron Jenny	U.S.A.	1882
Slide Rule	William Oughtred	Britain	1621
Steam Engine (condenser)	James Watt	Britain	1765
Steel Production	Henry Bessemer	Britain	1855
Steel (stainless)	Harry Brearley	Britain	1913
Submarine	David Bushnell	U.S.A.	1776
Tank	Sir Ernest Swinton	Britain	1914
Telegraph	M. Lammond	France	1787
Telegraph Code	Samuel F.B. Morse	U.S.A.	1837
Telephone (perfected)	Alexander Graham Bell	U.S.A.	1876
Television (mechanical)	John Logie Baird	Britain	1926
Television (electronic)	P.T. Farnsworth	U.S.A.	1927
Thermometer	Galileo Galilei	Italy	1593
Transformer	Michael Faraday	Britain	1831
Transistor	Bardeen, Shockley & Brattain	U.S.A.	1948
Washing Machine (elec.)	Hurley Machine Co.	U.S.A.	1907
Zip-Fastener	W.L. Judson	U.S.A.	1891

Important Discoveries

Discovery	Discoverer	Nationality	Year
Aluminium	Hans Christian Oerstedt	Denmark	1827
Atomic number	Henry Moseley	England	1913
Atomic structure of matter	John Dalton	England	1803
Chlorine	C.W. Scheele	Sweden	1774
Electromagnetic induction	Michael Faraday	England	1831
Electromagnetic waves	Heinrich Hertz	Germany	1886
Electromagnetism	Hans Christian Oersted	Denmark	1920
Electron	Sir Joseph Thomson	England	1897
General theory of relativity	Albert Einstein	Switzerland	1915
Hydrogen	Henry Cavendish	England	1766
Law of electric conduction	Georg Ohm	Germany	1827
Law of electromagnetism	Andre Ampere	France	1826
Law of falling bodies	Galileo	Italy	1590
Laws of gravitation & motion	Isaac Newton	England	1687
Laws of planetary motion	Johannes Kepler	Germany	1609-19
Magnesium	Sir Humphry Davy	England	1808
Neptune (Planet)	Johann Galle	Germany	1846
Neutron	James Chadwick	England	1932
Nickel	Axel Cronstedt	Sweden	1751
Nitrogen	Daniel Rutherford	England	1772

Discovery	Discoverer	Nationality	Year
Oxygen	Joseph Priestly C.W. Scheele	England Sweden	1772
Ozone	Christian Schonbein	Germany	1839
Pluto (Planet)	Clyde Tombaugh	U.S.A	1930
Plutonium	G.T. Seaborg	U.S.A	1940
Proton	Ernest Rutherford	England	1919
Quantum Theory	Max Planck	Germany	1900
Radioactivity	Antoine Bacquerel	France	1896
Radium	Pierre & Marie Curie	France	1898
Silicon	Jons Berzelius	Sweden	1824
Special theory of relativity	Albert Einstein	Switzerland	1905
Sun as centre of solar system	Copernicus	Poland	1543
Uranium	Martin Klaproth	Germany	1789
Uranus (Planet)	William Herschel	England	1781
X-rays	Wilhelm Roentgen	Germany	1895

Geographical Explorations/Discoveries

Place	Explorer/Discoverer	Nationality	Year
America	Christopher Columbus	Italy	1492
Hawaii Islands (Sandwich Islands)	Captain James Cook	England	1778
Newfoundland	John Cabot	England	1497
New Zealand	Abel Janszoon Tasman	Holland	1642
North Pole	Robert Peary	USA	1909
Sea Route to India (via Cape of Good Hope)	Vasco da Gama	Portugal	1498
South Pole	Roald Amundsen	Norway	1911

Scientific Instruments

Name of Instrument	Used for
Altimeter	measuring altitude
Ammeter	measuring strength of an electric current
Anemometer	measuring the velocity of wind
Audiometer	measuring level of hearing
Barometer	measuring atmospheric pressure
Callipers	measuring the internal and external diameters of tubes
Calorimeter	measuring quantity of heat
Compass	finding out direction
Dynamo	converting mechanical energy into electrical energy
Eudiometer	measuring volume changes during chemical reactions between gases
Galvanometer	detecting and determining the strength of small electric currents
Hydrometer	measuring specific gravity of a liquid
Hygrometer	measuring the humidity in the atmosphere
Lactometer	measuring the purity of milk
Manometer	measuring the gaseous pressure
Micrometer	measuring minute distances, angles, etc.

Name of Instrument	Used for
Microscope	seeing magnified view of very small objects
Periscope	with the help of this instrument an observer in a submarine can see what is going on the surface of the sea
Photometer	measuring intensity of light from distant stars
Pyrometer	measuring high temperatures
Radar	detecting and finding the presence and location of moving objects like aircraft, missile, etc.
Radiometer	measuring the emission of radiant energy
Rain Gauge	measuring the amount of rainfall
Seismograph	measuring and recording the intensity and origin of earthquake shocks
Sextant	measuring altitude and angular distances between two objects or heavenly bodies
Spectrometer	measuring the refractive indices
Spherometer	measuring the curvature of spherical objects/surface
Sphygmomanometer	measuring blood pressure
Stethoscope	ascertaining the condition of heart and lungs by listening to their function
Stroboscope	viewing objects that are moving rapidly with a periodic motion as if they were at rest
Tachometer	measuring the rate of revolution or angular speed of a revolving shaft
Telescope	viewing magnified images of distant objects
Theodolite	measuring the horizontal and vertical angles
Thermocouple	measuring the temperature inside furnaces and jet engines
Thermometer	measuring human body temperature
Thermostat	regulating constant temperature
Ultrasonoscope	measuring utrasonic sounds
Viscometer	measuring the viscosity of a fluid
Voltmeter	measuring potential difference between two points.

Diseases and the Parts of Body they Affect

Disease	Part of body affected
AIDS	Immune system of body
Arthritis	Inflammation of joints
Asthma	Lungs
Cataract	Eyes
Conjunctivitis	Eyes
Diabetes	Pancreas
Diphtheria	Throat
Glaucoma	Eyes
Eczema	Skin
Goitre	Front of the neck (due to enlargement of thyroid gland)
Gout	Joints of bone

Disease	Part of body affected
Jaundice	Liver
Meningitis	Brain or spinal cord
Pleurisy	Pleura (inflammation of)
Polio	motor neurons
Pneumonia	Lungs
Pyorrhoea	Sockets of teeth
Tuberculosis	Lungs
Typhoid	Intestine
Malaria	Spleen
Leukaemia	Blood
Rickets	Bones

8. SPACE RESEARCH

First in Space

First creator of rules regarding space research	—	Isaac Newton
First artificial satellite launched in space	—	Sputnik-1 (1957)
First living being sent in space	—	Louika (a dog)
Firstever manned spacecraft	—	Vostok-I
First man in space	—	Yuri Gagarin, U.S.S.R. (1961)
First woman in space	—	Valentina Tereshkova, U.S.S.R. (June 1963)
First man who moved in space out of the spacecraft	—	Alexi Livonov, U.S.S.R. (June 1965)
First person to land on moon	—	Neil Armstrong, America (21st July, 1969)
First fourwheeled carriage without human being on moon	—	Leunokhev-I, U.S.S.R. (1970)
First space lab in orbit	—	Skylab (America, 1973)
First space shuttle	—	Columbia (America, 1981)
First Indian (man) in space	—	Squadron leader—Rakesh Sharma (13th April, 1984)
First Indian (Woman) in space	—	Kalpana Chawla (19th Nov., 1997)
First American woman in space	—	Sailyride (1983)
First spacecraft on Mars	—	Pathfinder (6 July, 1997)
First woman who lead spacecraft	—	Allin Collis (America)
First spacecraft without man	—	Shenzoo, China (20th Nov. 1999)

Indian Space Programme : At a Glance

Satellite	*Date*	*Type*	*Launch Vehicle*	*Result*
Aryabhatta	19-04-75	Scientific	Cosmos	successful
Bhaskara I	07-06-79	Geosurvey	Cosmos	successful
Rohini	10-08-79	Geosurvey	S.L.V.3	unsuccessful
Rohini D-1	18-07-80	Geosurvey	S.L.V.3	successful
Rohini	31-05-81	Scientific	S.L.V.3	successful
Apple	19-06-81	Communication	Ariane	successful
Bhaskara II	20-11-81	Geosurvey	Cosonos	successful
INSAT-1A	10-04-82	Multipurpose	Delta	unsuccessful
Rohini	17-04-83	Scientific	S.L.V.3	successful
INSAT-1B	30-08-83	Multipurpose	Space Shuttle	successful
SROSS I	24-03-87	Technical	ASLV-D1	unsuccessful
IRS-1A	17-03-88	Remote sensing	Vostok	successful
INSAT-1D	12-06-90	Multipurpose	Delta	successful

Satellite	Date	Type	Launch Vehicle	Result
IRS-1B	29-08-91	Remote sensing	Vostok	successful
IRS-ID	29-09-97	Remote sensing	PSLV	successful
INSAT-3C	24-01-2002	Communication	Ariane-4	successful
CARTOSAT-2	10-01-2007	Communication	PSLV-C7	successful
INSAT-4CR	02-09-2007	Communication	GSLV-F04	successful
CARTOSAT-2A	28-04-2008	Communication	PSLV-C9	successful
Chandrayaan-I	22-10-2008	Maping and Scientific	PSLV-C11	successful
Oceansat-2	24-09-2009	Remote Sensing	PSLV-C14	successful
CARTOSAT-2B	12-07-2010	Communication	PSLV-C15	successful
Megha-Tropiques	12-10-2011	Maping and Scientific	PSLV-C18	successful
Spot-6	09-09-2012	Remote Sensing	PSLV-C21	successful
SARAL	25-02-2013	Scientific	PSLV-C20	successful
GSAT-7	30-08-2013	Defence	Ariane-5	successful
MOM	5-11-2013	Mapping	PSLV-C25	successful
GSAT-14	05-01-2014	Communication	GSLV-D5	successful
IRNSS-1B	04-04-2014	Mapping and Scientific	PSLV-C24	successful
Spot-7	30-06-2014	Remote Sensing	PSLV-C23	successful
GSAT-16	07-12-2014	Communication	Ariane-5	successful
IRNSS-1D	28-03-2015	Mapping and Scientific	PSLV-C27	successful
GSAT-6	27-08-2015	Communication	GSLV-D6	successful
Astrosat	28-09-2015	Mapping and Scientific	PSLV-C30	successful
GSAT-15	11-11-2015	Communication	Ariane-5	successful
TELEOS-1 & others	16-12-2015	Mapping and Scientific	PSLV-C29	successful
IRNSS-1E	20-01-2016	Mapping and Scientific	PSLV-C31	successful
IRNSS-1F	10-03-2016	Mapping and Scientific	PSLV-C32	successful
IRNSS-1G	28-04-2016	Mapping and Scientific	PSLV-C33	successful
CARTOSAT-2 & others	22-06-2016	Mapping and Scientific	PSLV-C34	successful
INSAT-3DR	08-09-2016	Meteorology	GSLV-F05	successful
SCATSAT-1 & others	26-09-2016	Multipurpose	PSLV-C35	successful
CARTOSAT-2 & 103	15-02-2017	Multipurpose	PSLV-C37	successful
GSAT-9	06-05-2017	Communications	GSLVMK-II	successful
GSAT-19	05-06-2017	Communications	GSLVMK-III-DI	successful
CARTOSAT-2E	23-06-2017	Earth Sciences	PSLV-C38	successful
GSAT-17	29-06-2017	Communications	Ariane-5 ECA	successful
GSAT-7A	19-12-2018	Military Satellite	GSLV-MKII-F11	successful
KalamSAT-V2	23-01-2019	Student Satellite	PSLV-C44	successful
Chandrayaan-2	22-07-2019	Lunar Exploration	GSLV-MKIII MO1	—
Cartosat-3	27-11-2019	Earth Imaging Satellite	PSLV-C47	successful
GSAT-30	17-01-2020	Communication	Ariane-5	successful
E0S-01	07-11-2020	Earth Observation	PSLV-C49	successful
Amezonia & 19 others	28-02-2021	Communication	PSLV-C51	successful
E0S-04	14-02-2022	Radar Imaging	PSLV-C52	successful
TelEOS-02 and LUMILITE-4	22-04-2023	Multipurpose	PSLV-C55	successful
Chandrayaan-3	14-07-2023	Lunar Exploration	LVM3M4	successful
Aditya-L1	02-09-2023	Solar Energy Observation	PSLV-C57	successful
XPoSAT	01-01-2024	Earth Observation	PSLV-C58	successful
INSAT-3DS	17-02-2024	Meteorological	GSLV-F14	successful
EOS-08	16-08-2024	Earth Observation	SSLV-D3	successful
Proba-3	05-12-2024	Earth Observation	PSLV-C59	successful
NVS-02	29-01-2025	Navigation	GSLV-F15	successful

* * * * *

9. INDIAN HISTORY

Famous Sites of Indus Valley Civilization

Name of Site	Year of Excavation	River/ Sea coast	Discoverer
Harappa (Montgomery–Pakistan)	1921	Ravi River	Dayaram Sahney
Mohanjodaro (Larkana–Pakistan)	1922	Indus River	Rakhal Das Banerjee
Chanhudaro (Sindh–Pakistan)	1931	Indus River	N.G. Mazumdar
Alamgir pur (Meerut – U.P.)	1952-55	Hindan River	Yagyadatta Sharma
Ropar (Punjab)	1953	Sutlej River	Yagyadatta Sharma
Rangpur (Kathiabar–Gujarat)	1953	Bhabar River	Madho Swaroop Vatsa, Rang Nath Rao
Kotdigi (Sindh–Pakistan)	1953	Indus River	Fazal Ahmed Khan
Lothal (Ahmedabad–Gujarat)	1954	Bhogwa River	Rang Nath Rao
Kalibanga (Ganganagar–Rajasthan)	1961	Ghaggar	Brajwasi Lal
Surkotara (Kutch–Gujarat)	1967	Ghaggar River	Ravindra Singh Vishta
Banawali (Hissar–Haryana)	1973	Ghaggar River	Ravindra Singh Vishta
Balakote	1979	Arabian Sea	George F. Dales
Dhaulavira (Gujarat)	1963-68	—	J.P. Joshi
	1990-91	—	Dr. R.S. Vishta

Wellknown Quotations

"Swarajya is My Birthright"	— Bal Gangadhar Tilak
"Give me blood, I shall give you freedom"	— Netajee Subhash Chandra Bose
"Inqalab Zindabad"	— Bhagat Singh
Saare Jahan Se Achcha, Hindustan Hamara"	— Dr. Mohammed Iqbal
"Dilli Chalo"	— Subhash Chandra Bose
"Sarfaroshi ki tamanna, Ab Hamare Dil Mein Hai."	— Ram Prasad Bismil
"I am socialist by nature".	— Jawahar Lal Nehru
"Go to Vedas"	— Swami Dayanand
"Aaram Haram Hai"	— Jawahar Lal Nehru
"Jai Jawan, Jai Kisan"	— Lal Bahadur Shastri
"Jai Jawan, Jai Kisan, Jai Vigyan"	— Atal Bihari Vajpayee
"Speak less, work more"	— Sanjay Gandhi
"Vijayee Vishwa Tiranga Pyara"	— Shyam Lal Gupta

"Quit India"	— Mahatma Gandhi
"Hindi, Hindu, Hindustan"	— Bhartendu Harishchandra
"Purna Swarajya"	— Jawahar Lal Nehru
"Every lathi blow inflicted on my body will prove a nail in British coffin"	— Lala Lajpat Rai
"Jai Hind"	— Subhash Chandra Bose
"Do or die"	— Mahatma Gandhi
"Who lives if India dies"	— Jawahar Lal Nehru
"Vande Mataram"	— Bankim Chandra Chatterjee
"Jana Gana Mana Adhinayaka Jai Hai"	—Rabindranath Tagore
"Hate sin, not the sinner."	— Mahatma Gandhi
"Service of the people is the service of God"	— Swami Vivekananda
"Truth and non-violence are my God."	— Mahatma Gandhi

Battles and Wars in India

War	Year	Result
Battle of Kalinga	(261 B.C.)	Ashoka defeated the king of Kalinga
Second battle of Tarain	(1192 A.D.)	Muhammad Gori defeated Prithviraj Chauhan
First battle of Panipat	(1526 A.D.)	Babar defeated Ibrahim Lodi
Battle of Khanwa	(1527 A.D.)	Babar defeated Rana Sanga
Battle of Chausa	(1539 A.D.)	Shershah Suri defeated Humayun and became ruler of Delhi
Second Battle of Panipat	(1556 A.D.)	Akbar defeated Hemu
Battle of Talikota	(1565 A.D.)	Allied forces of Bijapur, Bidar, Golkunda and Ahamadnagar defeated the King of Vijay Nagar
Battle of Haldighati	(1576 A.D.)	Some historian say that this battle was indecisive but some say that Rana Pratap was defeated by Akbar.
Battle of Palasey	(1757 A.D.)	British forces defeated Nawab of Bengal Sirajudoulla
Battle of Wandiwash	(1760 A.D.)	British forces defeated the French
Third battle of Panipat	(1761 A.D.)	Maratha were defeated by Ahmad Shah Abadali
Battle of Buxar	(1764 A.D.)	British forces defeated the combined forces of Mir Quasim, Shah Alam Mughal empire and Awadh's Nawab
Third Anglo-Maratha War	(1792 A.D.)	Maratha were conclusively defeated
Fourth Anglo-Mysore War	(1799 A.D.)	Tipu Sultan died fighting the British forces
Second Anglo-Sikh War	(1848 A.D.)	British forces annexed Punjab from Sikh rulers
Indo-China War	(1962 A.D.)	China attacked India unilaterally and annexed some area
Indo-Pak War	(1965 A.D.)	Pakistan attacked India but had to suffer severe setbacks
Indo-Pak War	(1971 A.D.)	Pak declared war against India.

* * * * *

10. WORLD GEOGRAPHY

Earth: The earth constitutes land, water and air. Land is made up of rocks and soil. It is distributed in continents and islands. The water found in oceans, seas, lakes, etc. occupies about 2/3 of the earth's surface. The earth is surrounded by a cover of air, called atmosphere, which extends up to several hundred kilometres above its surface.

Shape: In ancient times people believed that the earth was flat in shape. Greek philosopher Pythagoras (6th century BC) was the first person to declare that the earth was round. After careful measurement, the scientists have found that the earth is slightly oblate (flattened at poles) and not exactly round.

Motions: The earth has two motions: *(i) Rotation:* Earth makes a complete round on its axis once each 24 hours (more exactly 23 hours, 56 minutes and 4.09 seconds). It causes days and night on the earth. *(ii) Revolution:* The earth makes a complete round of the Sun in one year. This revolution of earth produces alternate seasons.

Some Facts: **(1)** Equal Day and Night — March 21 and September 23. **(2)** Longest Day — June 21. **(3)** Shortest Day — December 22. **(4)** The sunlight takes eight minutes in travelling from the Sun to the Earth. **(5)** Average speed of the earth in orbit ---- 66,600 miles (107,220 km) per hour. **(6)** Earth's equatorial diameter is about 7926 miles (12,756 km). **(7)** Water (oceans, seas, lakes and rivers) occupies nearly 75 per cent of the surface of the earth. **(8)** Earth's average distance from the Moon — 2,38,857 miles (3,84,400 km). **(9)** Earth's average distance from the Sun — 93 million miles (149.4 million km).

Greenwich Time: It is the local time of the Greenwich observatory in London on 0° meridian. Greenwich time is international standard time.

International Date Line: Half way round the earth from the Greenwich is International Date Line on 180° longitude. It runs down mid-Pacific. It is one day earlier on the east of this line than it is on the west of the line. When it is Monday east of the line, it is Tuesday west of the line.

Zones: On the basis of temperature and distribution of solar heat on the surface of the earth, the earth has been divided into five zones: (1) Torrid Zone, (2) North Temperate Zone, (3) South Temperate Zone, (4) Arctic Zone, and (5) Antarctic Zone.

Continents: Large land masses forming large geographical divisions are called continents. There are seven continents: (1) Asia (29.5%), (2) Africa (20%), (3) Europe (6.5%), (4) North America (16.3%), (5) South America (11.8%), (6) Australia (5.2%), and (7) Antarctica (9.6%).

Highest Mountain Peaks: (1) Everest (Asia-8848 metres), (2) Aconcagua (South America-6960 metres), (3) Mckinley (North America-6194 metres), (4) Kilimanjaro (Africa-5895 metres), (5) Elbrus (Europe-5642 metres), (6) Vinson Massif (Antarctica-5140 metres), (7) Kosciusko (Australia-2228 metres).

Largest Oceans: (1) Pacific Ocean (The largest, covers almost 1/3 of the earth's total area, and the deepest about 6.8 miles at Mariana Trench in western Pacific); (2) Atlantic Ocean, and (3) Indian Ocean. Other seas and gulfs are — the Mediterranean Sea, South China Sea, Bering Sea, Caribbean Sea, East China Sea, Sea of Japan, North Sea, Baltic Sea, Hudson Bay and Gulf of Mexico.

Longest Rivers: (1) Nile (6650 km-Africa), (2) Amazon (6570 km-South America), (3) Mississippi-Missouri (5970 km-North America), (4) Yangtze Kiang (5470 km-Asia), (5) Ob Irtysh (5150 km-Europe), (6) Congo (4666 km-Africa).

Highest Waterfalls: (1) Angel (807 m-Venezuela), (2) Mongefossen (774 m-Norway), (3) Kukenaam (610 m-Venezuela), (4) Ribbon (491 m-USA), (5) King George VI (487 m-Guyana), (6) Upper Yosemite (435 m-USA).

Great Deserts: (1) Sahara (94 lakh sq km-North Africa), (2) Libyan (11.65 lakh sq km-North Africa), (3) Australian (16 lakh sq km-Australia), (4) Gobi (13 lakh sq km-Mongolia), (5) Great Victoria (6,47,000 sq km-Australia), (6) Syrian (5,20,000 sq km Arabia), (7) Arabian (23,30,000 sq km Arabia).

Largest Islands: (1) Greenland (21,75,600 sq km) (2) New Guinea (7,77,000 sq km), (3) Borneo (7,25,545 sq km), (4) Malagasy (5,90,000 sq km), (5) Baffin Island (4,76,070 sq km).

Major Producers of Crops, Minerals and Industrial goods

Coal	China, USA, India, Australia, Indonesia, Russia
Cocoa	Cote d'Ivaire, Ghana, Indonesia, Nigeria
Coffee	Brazil, Vietnam, Columbia, Indonesia
Copper	Chile, Peru, China, USA
Cotton	China, India, USA, Pakistan, Brazil
Gold	China, Australia, Russia, USA, Canada
Grapes	China, Italy, USA, France, Spain
Iron ore	Australia, Brazil, China, India
Jute	India, Bangladesh, China
Manganese	South Africa, China, Australia
Petroleum	Russia, Saudi Arabia, USA, Iraq
Rice	China, India, Indonesia, Bangladesh
Rubber	Thailand, Indonesia, Malaysia, Vietnam, India
Silk	China, India, Uzbekistan, Thailand
Silver	Mexico, Peru, China, Chili
Steel	China, Japan, India, USA
Tea	China, India, Kenya, Sri Lanka
Wheat	China, India, USA, France, Russia
Diamond	Russia, Australia, Congo, Botswana
Tobacco	China, Brazil, India, USA, Indonesia

The Highest, Biggest and Longest in the World

Airport	*Largest*	King Fahd International Airport, Dammon (Saudi Arabia)
Animal	*Tallest*	Giraffe (Average height 6.09 m)
	Largest & Heaviest	Blue Whale (190 tonnes)
	Longest recorded	Boot lace Worm (55 m)
	Fastest	Cheetah (Approximately 100 km/hr)
Bay	*With max. shore line*	Hudson Bay (Canada: 12268 km)
	With maximum area	Bay of Bengal (India: 217 million hc)
Building	*Tallest*	Burj Khalifa in Dubai (818 meter)
Canal	*Big ship (longest)*	Suez Canal (160 km) Busiest Kiel Canal (North Sea)
Church	*Largest*	Basilica of St. Peter (Vatican City Rome–Area 23000 sq. m.
Continent	*biggest*	Asia (31,845,872 km^2)
	Smallest	Australia Mainland (Area 76,17,930 km^2)

Country,	*Largest in Population*	China (over 139.7 crore)
	Largest in Area	Russia (17,098,242 sq. km)
	With largest electorate	India (over 90 crores)
	Smallest independent	State of Vatican City (0.44 km^2)
Delta	*Largest*	Sundarban's Ganga-Brahmaputra delta (1,05,000 sq. km)
Epic	*Longest*	Mahabharata
Film	*Most Oscars*	Ben Hur (11 Oscars—1959); Titanic (11 Oscars—1998); The Lord of Rings : The Return of the King (11 Oscars—2003).
Island	*Biggest*	Greenland (2,175,600 sq km)
Lake	*Largest*	Caspian Sea (Azerbaijan, Russia, Iran border: 37.18 lakh km^2)
	Deepest	Baikal (Siberia)
	Largest (fresh water)	Superior Lake (USA—Canada border: 82,350 km^2)
Mountain	*Highest peak*	Mt. Everest (8848 m; Nepal)
	Highest range	Himalayas, Asia (upto 4200 m)
	Greatest mountain range	Himalaya-Karakoram (96 out of 109 peaks over 7315 m are here)
Ocean	*Largest and Deepest*	The Pacific (Area: 166,240,000 km^2; Depth: 10,924 m)
Planet	*Biggest*	Jupiter (equatorial diameter 142984 km)
	Brightest, hottest and nearest to Earth	Venus
	Nearest to Sun	Mercury
Plateau	*Highest*	Tibetan Plateau (Central Asia: 4900 m)
Platform	*Longest (rail)*	Shri Siddharoodha Swamiji Railway Station, Hubballi, Karnataka (India)
Religion	*Oldest*	Hinduism
Religion	*Largest*	Christianity
Rivers	*Longest*	(i) Nile (6650 km) (ii) Amazon (6437 km)
Star	*Brightest*	Sirius A (also called Dog Star)
Swimming course	*Longest recognised*	English Channel
Tunnel	*Longest (railway)*	Gotthard Base Rail Tunnel (Switzerland; 57.1 km)
	Largest (road)	Laerdal, Norway (24.51 km)
Wall	*Longest*	Great Wall of China (main length 3460 km; branches length 2860 km)
Waterfall	*Highest*	Salto-Angel (in Venezuela on a branch of river Carrao, 807 m.)

Capital & Currencies

Country	Capital	Currency
✶ Afghanistan	Kabul	Afghani
✶ Albania	Tirana	Lek
✶ Algeria	Algiers	Dinar
✶ Angola	Luanda	New Kwanza
✶ Argentina	Buenos Aires	Peso
✶ Armenia	Yeravan	Dram
✶ Australia	Canberra	Dollar
✶ Austria	Vienna	Euro
✶ Azerbaijan	Baku	Manat
✶ Bahrain	Manama	Dinar
✶ Bangladesh	Dhaka	Taka
✶ Barbados	Bridgetown	Dollar
✶ Belarus	Minsk	Ruble
✶ Belgium	Brussels	Euro
✶ Benin	Porto Novo	Franc
✶ Bhutan	Thimphu	Ngultrum[1]
✶ Bolivia	La paz	Dollar
✶ Botswana	Gaborone	Pula
✶ Brazil	Brasilia	Real
✶ Bosnia Herzegovina	Sarajevo	Dinar
✶ Bulgaria	Sofia	Lev
✶ Cambodia	Phnom-Penh	Riel
✶ Canada	Ottawa	Dollar
✶ Chile	Santiago	Peso
✶ China	Beijing	Yuan
✶ Colombia	Bogota	Peso
✶ Congo	Brazzaville	Franc
✶ Croatia	Zagreb	Kuna
✶ Cuba	Havana	Peso
✶ Cyprus	Nicosia	Euro
✶ Czech Republic	Prague	Koruna
✶ Denmark	Copenhagen	Krone
✶ Ecuador	Quito	Sucre
✶ Egypt	Cairo	Pound
✶ Estonia	Tallinn	Euro
✶ Ethiopia	Addis Ababa	Birr
✶ Fiji	Suva	Dollar
✶ Finland	Helsinki	Euro
✶ France	Paris	Euro
✶ Georgia	Tbilisi	Lari
✶ Germany	Berlin	Euro
✶ Ghana	Accra	Cedi
✶ Greece	Athens	Euro
✶ Guatemala	Guatemala City	Quetzal

Country	Capital	Currency
✶ Guyana	George Town	Dollar
✶ Hungary	Budapest	Forint
✶ Iceland	Reykjavik	Krona
✶ India	New Delhi	Rupee
✶ Indonesia	Jakarta	Rupiah
✶ Iran	Teheran	Rial
✶ Iraq	Baghdad	Dinar
✶ Ireland	Dublin	Euro
✶ Israel	Jerusalem	Shekel
✶ Italy	Rome	Euro
✶ Jamaica	Kingston	Dollar
✶ Japan	Tokyo	Yen
✶ Jordan	Amman	Dinar
✶ Kazakhstan	Akmola	Tenge
✶ Kenya	Nairobi	Shilling
✶ Korea (S)	Seoul	Won
✶ Korea (N)	Pyongyang	Won
✶ Kyrgyzstan	Bishkek	Som
✶ Kuwait	Kuwait City	Dinar
✶ Laos	Vientiane	Kip
✶ Latvia	Riga	Euro
✶ Lebanon	Beirut	Pound
✶ Liberia	Monrovia	Dollar
✶ Libya	Tripoli	Dinar
✶ Lithuania	Vilnius	Litas
✶ Luxembourg	Luxembourg	Euro
✶ Macedonia	Skopje	Dinar
✶ Malawi	Lilongwe	Kwacha
✶ Malaysia	Kuala Lumpur	Ringgit
✶ Maldives	Male	Rufiyaa
✶ Mali	Bamako	Franc
✶ Mauritius	Port Louis	Rupee
✶ Mexico	Mexico City	Peso
✶ Moldavia	Chisinau	Leu
✶ Mongolia	Ulan Bator	Tugrik
✶ Morocco	Rabat	Dirham
✶ Mozambique	Maputo	Metical
✶ Myanmar	Nay Pyi Taw	Kyat
✶ Namibia	Winohoek	Dollar
✶ Nepal	Kathmandu	Rupee
✶ Netherlands	Amsterdam	Euro
✶ New Zealand	Wellington	Dollar
✶ Nigeria	Abuja	Naira
✶ Norway	Oslo	Krone
✶ Oman	Muscat	Rial
✶ Pakistan	Islamabad	Rupee

Country	Capital	Currency
✶ Panama	Panama City	Balboa
✶ Peru	Lima	New Sole
✶ Philippines	Manila	Peso
✶ Poland	Warsaw	Zloty
✶ Portugal	Lisbon	Euro
✶ Qatar	Doha	Riyal
✶ Romania	Bucharest	Leu
✶ Russia	Moscow	Ruble
✶ Saudi Arabia	Riyadh	Rial
✶ Senegal	Dakar	Franc
✶ Slovakia	Bratislava	Euro
✶ Spain	Madrid	Euro
✶ Sri Lanka	Colombo	Rupee
✶ Sudan	Khartoum	Dinar
✶ Suriname	Paramaribo	Guilder
✶ Sweden	Stockholm	Krona
✶ Switzerland	Berne	Swiss Francs
✶ Syria	Damascus	Pound
✶ South Africa	Capetown (Legislative) Pretoria *(Administrative)*	Rand
✶ Tadzhikistan	Dushanbe	Ruble
✶ Taiwan	Taipei	Dollar
✶ Tanzania	Dodoma	Shilling
✶ Thailand	Bangkok	Baht
✶ Tunisia	Tunis	Dinar
✶ Turkiye	Ankara	Lira
✶ Turkmania	Ashikabad	Manat
✶ Uganda	Kampala	Shilling
✶ Ukraine	Kiev	Hyrvnia
✶ United Arab Emirates	Abu Dhabi	Dirham
✶ U.K.	London	Pound Sterling
✶ U.S.A.	Washington	Dollar
✶ Uruguay	Montevideo	Peso
✶ Uzbekistan	Tashkent	Som
✶ Venezuela	Caracas	Bolivar
✶ Vietnam	Hanoi	Dong
✶ Yemen	Sana'a	Rial
✶ Zimbabwe	Harare	Dollar
✶ Congo (Democratic Republic)	Kinshasa	Franc
✶ Zambia	Lusaka	Kwacha

First in the World

First Chinese visitor to India	Fahien
First foreign invader of India	Alexander, the Great (Greek)
First person to climb Mt. Everest	Tenzing Norgay (India) and Edmund Hillary (New Zealand) (1953)
First atom bomb dropped at	Hiroshima (Japan)
First man in the space	Yuri Gagarin (former USSR)
First woman in the space	Valentina Tereshkova (former USSR)
First person to walk in the space	Alexei Leonov (former USSR)
First person to land on the moon	Neil Armstrong (USA)
First and the only woman to have climbed Mt. Everest twice	Santosh Yadav (Indian; May 12, 1992; May 10, 1993)
First person on Mt. Everest without oxygen	Phu Dorjee (Indian; May 9, 1984)
First person to climb Mt. Everest twice	Nawang Gombu
First President of the USA	George Washington
First woman Prime Minister	Sirimavo Bandaranaike (Sri Lanka)
First person to swim across English Channel	Mathew Webb
First woman to swim across English Channel	Gertrude Caroline Ederle
First woman to climb Mt. Everest	Junko Tabei (Japan)
First woman to climb Mt. Everest alone and without oxygen supplies	Alison Hargreaves (Briton: May 13, 1995)

First Aeroplane to fly around the world without refuelling	Voyager (Dec. 1986)
First test-tube Baby	Louise Brown (UK; 1978)
First all-talking Film	Jaz Singer (1927)
First Secretary-General of the UN	Trygve Lie (Norway: 1946-53)
First woman President of the UN General Assembly	Vijayalakshmi Pandit (India: 1953)
First woman to reach North Pole	Ann Bancroft (1986)
First person to reach North Pole	Robert Peary
First person to reach South Pole	Amundsen (1911)
First woman to command Spacecraft in space	Ellin Collins

Popular Names

Popular Name	*Real Name*
Badshah Khan	Abdul Ghaffar Khan
Bapu, Father of Nation	M.K. Gandhi
Bard of Avon	William Shakespeare
Chachaji *or* Panditji	Jawaharlal Nehru
Desert Fox	Gen. Rommel (Germany)
Desh Bandhu	C.R. Das
Father of English Poetry	Geoffrey Chaucer
Fuhrer	Adolf Hitler
Grand Old Man of India	Dadabhai Naoroji
Grand Old Man of Britain	W.E. Gladstone
Gurudev	Rabindra Nath Tagore
Guruji	M.S. Golwalkar
Grand Commoner	Pitt, the younger
Iron Man of India	Sardar Patel
Lady with the Lamp	Florence Nightingale
Lal, Bal, Pal	Lala Lajpat Rai, Bal Gangadhar Tilak, Bipin Chandra Pal
Li-Kwan	Pearl Buck
Little Corporal *or* Man of Destiny	Napoleon Bonaparte
Lokmanya	Bal Gangadhar Tilak
Lok Nayak	Jayaprakash Narain
Mahamana	Pt. Madan Mohan Malaviya
Maid of Orleans	Joan of Arc
Maiden Queen	Queen Elizabeth I
Man of Blood and Iron	Prince Bismark
Netaji	Subhash Chandra Bose
Nightingale of India	Sarojini Naidu
Priyadarshini	Indira Gandhi
Punjab Kesari	Lala Lajpat Rai
Wizard of the North	Walter Scott

Geographical Surnames

Geographical Surname	*Real Name*
Bengal's Sorrow	Damodar River
Blue Mountains	Nilgiri Hills
China's Sorrow	Hwang-Ho
City of Palaces	Kolkata
City of Skyscrapers *or* Empire City	New York
City of Dreaming Spires	Oxford
Cockpit of Europe	Belgium
Dark Continent	Africa
Emerald Isle	Ireland
Eternal City	Rome
Forbidden City	Lhasa (Tibet)
Gateway of India	Mumbai
Gate of Tears	Strait of Bab-el-mandab
Gift of the Nile	Egypt
Granite City	Aberdeen (Scotland)
Hermit Kingdom	Korea
Holy Land	Jerusalem (Israel)
Island of Pearls	Bahrain (Persian Gulf)
Island of Cloves	Zanzibar
Key to the Mediterranean	Gibraltar
Land of Five Rivers	Punjab
Land of Golden Pagoda	Myanmar (Burma)
Land of Kangaroo	Australia
Land of Maple Leaf/Lillies	Canada
Land of Midnight Sun	Norway
Land of Morning Calm	Korea
Land of the Rising Sun	Japan
Land of Thousand Lakes	Finland
Land of Thunderbolt	Bhutan
Land of the White Elephants	Thailand
Manchester of the Orient	Osaka (Japan)
Pearl of the Antilles *or* Sugar Bowl of the World	Cuba
Pink City	Jaipur
Playground of Europe	Switzerland
Queen of the Adriatic	Venice (Italy)
Roof of the World	Pamirs
Sick Man of Europe	Turkey
Venice of the North	Stockholm (Sweden)
Windy City	Chicago
Whiteman's Grave	Guinea Coast of Africa
World's Loneliest Island	Tristan de Cunha

Countries'/Cities' Names—Old and New

Old Name	New Name
Abyssinia	Ethiopia
Basutoland	Lesotho
Bechuanaland	Botswana
British Honduras	Belize
Burma	Myanmar
Ceylon	Sri Lanka
Zaire	Congo
Constantinople	Istanbul
Dahomey	Benin
Dutch East Indies	Indonesia
East Pakistan	Bangladesh
Formosa	Taiwan
Gold Coast	Ghana
Leningrad	St. Petersburg
Leopoldville	Kinshasa
Mesopotamia	Iraq
North Rhodesia	Zambia
Nyasaland	Malawi
Peking	Beijing
Persia	Iran
Rangoon	Yangon
Salisbury	Harare
Siam	Thailand
South West Africa	Namibia
Southern Rhodesia	Zimbabwe
Turkey	Turkiye

IMPORTANT RESIDENCES

• **Buckingham Palace (London):** King/Queen of Britain • **10, Downing Street (London):** Prime Minister, Britain • **Elysee Palace (Paris):** President, France • **Rashtrapati Bhawan (New Delhi):** President, India • **White House (Washington):** President, USA • **Vatican (Rome):** Pope

Important towns situated on the River Banks

Town	River
Agra	Yamuna
Ahmedabad	Sabarmati
Prayagraj	Confluence of the Ganga and the Yamuna
Ayodhya	Saryu
Baghdad	Tigris
Berlin	Spree
Cairo	Nile
Kolkata	Hooghly
Cuttack	Mahanadi
Delhi	Yamuna
Dibrugarh	Brahmaputra
Dublin	Liffey
Hardwar	Ganga
Hyderabad	Musi
Jabalpur	Narbada
Kanpur	Ganga
Karachi	Indus
Lahore	Ravi
Leh	Indus
London	Thames
Lucknow	Gomati
Nasik	Godavari
New York	Hudson
Paris	Seine
Patna	Ganga
Rome	Tiber
Srinagar	Jhelum
Surat	Tapti
Sydney	Murray-Darling
Varanasi	Ganga
Vienna	Danube
Washington	Potamac
Yangon	Irawadi

Books and Authors

FOREIGN

Book	Author
Aesop's Fables	Aesop
Adventure of Robinson Crusoe	Daniel Defoe
Adventures of Sherlok Holmes	Arthur Conan Doyle
Alice in Wonderland	Lewis Carrol
Apple Cart	G.B. Shaw
Arabian Nights	Sir Richard Burton
As You Like It	William Shakespeare
A Tale of Two Cities	Charles Dickens
A Tale of Two Gardens	Octavio Paz
A Thousand Suns	Dominique Lapierre
August Coup	Mikhail S. Gorbachev
Ben Hur	Lewis Wallace
Candida	G.B. Shaw
Das Kapital	Karl Marx
David Copperfield	Charles Dickens
Divine Comedy	A. Dante
Doctor's Dilemma	G.B. Shaw
Famished Road	Ben Okri
Freedom From Fear	Aung San Suu Kyi
Gulistan Bostan	Sheikh Saadi
Gulliver's Travels	Jonathan Swift
Hamlet	William Shakespeare
Iliad	Homer
Inferno	A. Dante
In Memoriam	Lord Tennyson
Ivanhoe	Walter Scott
Julius Caesar	William Shakespeare
Lady Chatterley's Lover	D.H. Lawrence
Lajja	Taslima Nasreen
Les Miserable	Victor Hugo
Leviathan	Thomas Hobbes
Lolita	V. Nobokov
Lycidas	John Milton
Mein Kampf	Adolf Hitler
Merchant of Venice	William Shakespeare
Midnight's Children	Salman Rushdie

Book	Author
Moor's Last Sigh	Salman Rushdie
Mother	Maxim Gorky
Mother India	Katherine Mayo
Nana	Emile Zola
Ninteen Eighty Four	George Orwell
Odyssey	Homer
Origin of Species	Charles Darwin
Othello	William Shakespeare
Paradise Lost	John Milton
Paradise Regained	John Milton
Path to Power	Margaret Thatcher
Pickwick Papers	Charles Dickens
Pride and Prejudice	Jane Austen
Razor's Edge	Somerset Maugham
Republic	Plato
Romeo and Juliet	William Shakespeare
Round the World in Eighty Days	Jules Verne
Rubaiyat-i-Omar Khayyam	Edward Fitzgerald (Translator)
Shape of Things to Come	H.G. Wells
The Satanic Verses	Salman Rushdie
The Social Contract	Rousseau
The Tempest	William Shakespeare
Time Machine	H.G. Wells
Tom Sawyer	Mark Twain
Treasure Island	R.L. Stevenson
Twelfth Night	William Shakespeare
Uncle Tom's Cabin	H.B. Stowe
Unto This Last	John Ruskin
Utopia	Thomas More
Universe Around Us	James Jeans
Vicar of Wakefield	Oliver Goldsmith
War and Peace	Leo Tolstoy
Wealth of Nations	Adam Smith
Wonder That was India	A.L. Basham
Wuthering Heights	Emily Bronte

INDIAN

Book	Author
Abhigyan Shakuntalam	Kalidas
Ain-i-Akbari	Abul Fazal

Book	Author
Anand Math	Bankim Chandra Chatterjee

Book	Author
Arthashastra	Kautilya
A Suitable Boy	Vikram Seth
Bhagwat Gita	Ved Vyas
Chidambara	Sumitranandan Pant
Devdas	Sarat Chandra Chatterjee
Diwan-i-Ghalib	Mirza Ghalib
Discovery of India	Jawaharlal Nehru
Essays on Gita	Aurobindo Ghosh
Eternal India	Indira Gandhi
Faces of Everest	Major H.P.S. Ahluwalia
Ganadevata	Tarashankar Bandopadhyaya
Geet Govind	Jaya Dev
Geetanjali	R.N. Tagore
Glimpses of World History	Jawaharlal Nehru
Godaan	Prem Chand
Gul-e-Nagma	Firaq Gorakhpuri
Gunahon ka Devta	Dharmveer Bharti
Harsh Charita	Bana Bhatta
Hindu View of Life	S. Radhakrishnan
Idols	Sunil Gavaskar
India Divided	Dr. Rajendra Prasad
The Judgement	Kuldip Nayyar
Juhi ki Kali	Surya Kant Tripathi 'Nirala'
Justice of Peace ke Aansu	Janardan Prasad Singh
Chand ka Munh Terha Hai	Muktibodh
Kapalkundala	Bankim Chandra Chatterjee
Kadambari	Bana Bhatta
Kagaz Te Kanwas	Amrita Pritam
Kamayani	Jai Shankar Prasad
Kitni Nawon	S.H. Vatsyayan
Kumar Sambhav	Kalidas
Mahabharata	Ved Vyas

Book	Author
Malgudi Days	R.K. Narayan
Manvini Bhavai	Pannalal Patel
Mati Matal	Gopi Nath Mohanty
Meghdoot	Kalidas
Meri Ekyavan Kavitain	Atal Bihari Vajpayee
Meri Sansadiya Yatra	Atal Bihari Vajpayee
Mritunjaya	B.K. Bhattacharya
Mudrarakshasa	Vishakhadatta
My Experiments with Truth	M.K. Gandhi
My Own Boswell	M. Hidayatullah
My Presidential Years	R. Venkataraman
Nisheeth	Uma Shankar Joshi
'No, Sir'	P.G. Mavlankar
One Day Wonders	Sunil Gavaskar
Panchtantra	Vishnu Sharma
Passage to England	Nirad C. Chaudhuri
Prison Diary	Jaya Prakash Narayan
Raghuvansha	Kalidas
Rajtarangini	Kalhana
Ramayana	Balmiki
Ramcharit Manas	Tulsidas
Rukh Te Rishi	Harbhajan Singh
Satyarth Prakash	Swami Dayanand
Sur Sagar	Surdas
The Guide	R.K. Narayan
The Insider	P.V. Narasimharao
The Post Office — *Dak Ghar*	Rabindra Nath Tagore
The God of Small Things	Arundhati Roy
Urvashi	Ram Dhari Singh 'Dinkar'
Yama	Mahadevi Verma
My Country : My Life (Autobiography)	L.K. Advani
The Test of My Life	Yuvraj Singh
Twenty Years in a Decade	Shah Rukh Khan

IMPORTANT BOOKS WRITTEN IN JAIL

Book	Author
My Experiments with Truth	Mahatma Gandhi
Glimpses of World History Discovery of India	Jawaharlal Nehru
Gita Rahasya	Lokmanya Bal Gangadhar Tilak
Pilgrim's Progress	John Bunyan
Bible (in German language)	Martin Luther
Les Miserables	Victor Hugo
Long Walk to Freedom	Nelson Mandela

11. FIRST IN INDIA

First in India

Nobel Prize for Literature (1913)	Rabindra Nath Tagore
Nobel Prize for Physics (1929)	C.V. Raman
Nobel Prize for Peace (1979)	Mother Teresa
Nobel Prize for Economics (1998)	Amartya Sen
Special Oscar award winner (1992)	Satyajit Ray
First and the last Indian Governor-General of free India	C. Rajagopalachari
Woman Governor of the State	Smt. Sarojini Naidu
Indian Commander-in-Chief	General K.M. Cariappa
Woman Chief Minister of a State	Smt. Sucheta Kripalani
Woman President of United Nations General Assembly (1954)	Smt. Vijaylakshmi Pandit
President of International Court of Justice	Dr. Nagendra Singh
Woman to swim across the English Channel	Ms. Aarti Saha
Miss Universe	Miss Sushmita Sen
Miss World	Reita Faria
Indian to swim across the English Channel	Mihir Sen
Field Marshal	S.H.F.J. Manekshaw
Indian recipient of Victoria Cross	Khudadad Khan
Indian to conquer Mt. Everest	Sherpa Tenzing, May 29, 1953
Indian male cosmonaut (1984)	Rakesh Sharma
Indian female cosmonaut	Kalpana Chawla (19 Nov., 1997)
Woman to climb Mt. Everest	Miss Bachendri Pal, May 23, 1984
Woman to get Olympic Medal	Karnam Malleswari
Indian to address the UN General Assembly in Hindi	Atal Bihari Vajpayee
Newspaper	Bengal Gazette, Jan 27, 1780
Postage Stamp issued	In 1852
Telegraph line laid	In 1851, Kolkata; Diamond Harbour
Railways run	April 16, 1853; Bombay-Thana
Electric Train run	1925: Bombay-Kurla
Atomic Power Station	Tarapore (Maharashtra)
Passenger-cum-cargo ship made in India	Harshavardhan
Satellite	Aryabhatta (1975)
Rocket	Rohini (1967)
Atomic Reactor	Apsara (1956)
Climb Everest without oxygen	Phu Dorjee (1987)
First film (movie)	Raja Harishchandra (1913)
First film (talkie)	Alam Ara (1931)
Metro Railway	Kolkata Metro Railway

Test-tube baby, scientifically documented	Born on August 6, 1986 at K.E.M. Hospital, Mumbai
TV Centre	At Delhi
Indian to get an Oscar	Bhanu Athaiya
Woman pilot in IAF	Ms Harita Kaur Deol
Cellular Phone	Kolkata, August 1, 1995
Women president of Indian National Congress	Smt. Annie Besant
President of Indian National Congress	W.C. Banerjee (1885)
Indian who passed in I.C.S. Examination	Satendra Nath Tagore
Woman chief justice of High Court	Lila Saith (Himachal Pradesh)
Woman Foreign Secretary	Chokila Iyyar

First Important Officials of India

The Governor-General of free India	Lord Mountbatten
President	Dr. Rajendra Prasad
President (Female)	Pratibha Patil
Vice-President	Dr. S. Radhakrishnan
Prime Minister	Jawahar Lal Nehru
Prime Minister (Female)	Indira Gandhi
Deputy Prime Minister	Sardar Vallabhbhai Patel
Chief Justice	Harilal J. Kania
First Female Judge in Supreme Court	Smt. Meera Sahib Fatima Bibi
Speaker, Lok Sabha	Ganesh Vasudeo Mawlankar
Woman Speaker of Lok Sabha	Meira Kumar
Chief Election Commissioner	Sukumar Sen
Chief of Defence Staff (CDS)	General Bipin Rawat
Female Minister	Raj Kumari Amrit Kaur (Health Minister)
Female Governor	Sarojini Naidu (U.P.)
Female Chief Minister	Sucheta Kripalani (U.P. 1963)
Finance Commissioner	K.C. Niyogi
Leader of Opposition in Lok Sabha (Recognised)	Y.V. Chavan (Congress)
Leader of Opposition in Rajya Sabha (Recognised)	Kamalapati Tripathi (Congress)

Highest, Biggest, Largest & Longest in India

Award for Gallantry, highest	Param Vir Chakra
Award, highest civilian	Bharat Ratna
Bank, with largest number of branches	State Bank of India
Road Bridge, Longest	Bhupen Hazarika Setu, Across Lohit River (9.15 km)
Cattle fair, largest	Sonepur (Bihar)
Cellular Phone, First	Kolkata, August 1, 1995
City, Most Populous	Mumbai
Corridor, Longest	Rameshwaram Temple corridor (4,000 ft.)
Desert, Largest	Thar (Rajasthan)
Dam, Longest	Hirakud Dam (Odisha)

Delta, Largest	Sunderban's Delta
Dome, Largest	Gol Gumbaj (Bijapur)
Dam, Highest	Tihri Dam 261 m. (855 ft.)
Gateway, Highest	Buland Darwaja at Fatehpur Sikri (176 ft.)
Lake, Largest (Fresh water)	Wular Lake (Kashmir)
Literacy, Highest	Kerala (94%)
Museum, Largest	Indian Museum (Kolkata)
Mosque, Biggest	Jama Masjid (Delhi)
Peak, Highest	K-2 (Pak-Occupied Kashmir)
Platform, Longest	Shree Siddharoodha Swamiji Railway Station Hubballi, Karnataka (1507 m. long)
Railway Bridge, Longest	Vembanad Bridge, Kerala (4.6 km)
River, Longest	The Ganges (2525 Km)
Rainfall, Highest (annual mean)	Mowsynram near Cherrapunji (1178 cm)
Road, Longest	NH-44 (3,745 km)
Road-Rail Longest Bridge	Bogibeel bridge, Assam (4.94 km)
State, (Largest population)	Uttar Pradesh
State, Largest (in area)	Rajasthan
State, with maximum forest cover	Madhya Pradesh
State, with maximum density of population	Bihar
Tunnel, Longest (Road)	Dr. Shyama Prasad Mukherjee Tunnel (9.28 kms, J & K)
Tunnel, Longest (Railway)	T-50 Tunnel, Khari-Sumber section (12.77 kms) Jammu & Kashmir.
Minar, Highest	Qutub Minar (Delhi, 72.5 m.)
Waterfall, Highest	Kunchikal Waterfall (Karnataka: 455 m.)
Zoo, Largest	Arignar Anna Zoological Park, Chennai, Tamil Nadu

Table of Precedence

1. President
2. Vice-President
3. Prime Minister
4. Governors of States within their respective states
5. Former Presidents

5A. Deputy Prime Minister

6. Chief Justice of India, Speaker of Lok Sabha
7. Cabinet Ministers of the Union, Chief Ministers of States within their respective States, Deputy Chairman NITI Aayog, Former Prime Ministers. Leaders of opposition in Rajya Sabha and Lok Sabha

7A. Holders of the Bharat Ratna Decoration

8. Ambassadors Extraordinary and Plenipotentiary and High Commissioners of Commonwealth Countries accredited to India, Chief Ministers of States outside their respective States, Governors of States outside their respective states.
9. Judges of the Supreme Court

9A. Chairperson Union Public Service Commission, Chief Election Commissioner, Comptroller & Auditor-General of India.

10. Deputy Chairman Rajya Sabha, Deputy Chief Minister of States, Deputy Speaker Lok Sabha, Members of the NITI Aayog, Minister of State of the Union and Other Minister in the Ministry of Defence.

* * * * *

12. CULTURAL ACTIVITIES

AKADEMIES

There are three akademies for promotion of creative art.

1. **Lalit Kala Akademi, New Delhi:** Established in 1954, the Lalit Kala Akademi strives for the popularisation of Indian art within the country and in various countries of the world through exhibitions, publications, workshops and camps. Every three year it organises the Triennale India, an international exhibition. It publishes research papers on Indian arts. Besides organising seminars, it honours eminent artists. The Akademi has set up regional centres called Rashtriya Lalit Kala Kendras at Lucknow, Kolkata, Chennai and Bhubaneswar and a small office at Mumbai.
2. **Sangeet Natak Akademi, New Delhi:** The Sangeet Natak Akademi, set-up in 1953, aims at the promotion and development of dance, drama and music. It holds seminars and festivals, presents awards to the eminent artists and extends financial assistance to traditional teachers and scholarships to students. It also operates a scheme of exchange of troupes.
3. **Sahitya Akademi, New Delhi:** The Sahitya Akademi, established in 1954, has the main functions of development of Indian letters, setting up high literary standards, translation of literary works of one Indian language into other Indian languages, publication of books on history of literature and criticism, bibliographies and reference books. The Akademy has regional offices at Mumbai, Kolkata, Bengaluru and Chennai.
4. **National School of Drama:** It is one of the top theatre training institutes in the world and only one of its kind in India. It was set up in 1959 under Sangeet Natak Akademi but was later made autonomous organisation in 1975.

SCULPTURE

Archaeological Survey of India, set up in 1861, is responsible for preservation and maintenance of sculptures and historical monuments and manages a number of archaeological museums.

National Archives of India, established in 1891, it is the official custodian of all non-current records of permanent value of the Government of India and its predecessor bodies.

MUSEUMS

They are repositories of the cultural heritage and conserve and preserve historical technical and other materials against decay and transmit them to posterity as records of history.

MUSIC

Main Schools of Classical Music: There are two main schools of classical music, namely, the Hindustani and the Carnatic. The Hindustani school of classical music is in vogue in north-western India, eastern India and northern parts of the South India.

Musical Instruments: They are: Tabla, Mridangam, Pakhawaj, Chandai, Dholak, Veena, Sitar, Sarod, Gootuvadhyam, Sarangi, Flute, Nadaswaram, Shehnai, Shringi and Turahi.

DANCE

India has a very rich tradition of tribal, folk and classical dances.

Classical Dance

Dance	State	Famous Artists
Bharat Natyam	Tamil Nadu	Yamini Krishnamurthy, Rukmini Devi Arundale, Swapna Sundari, Sonal Mansingh, Vaijanti Mala, Mrinalini Sarabhai, Chandralekha, Indrani, Ram Gopal, Bal Saraswati
Kathakali	Kerala	Gopinath, K.K. Nayar, Kunju-Kurup, T.K. Chandu
Kuchipudi	Andhra Pradesh	Sapna Sundari, Raja Reddy, Shobha Nayar, Radha Reddy, Vedantam Satyanarayan, Vimpanti Chinna Satyam.
Kathak	North India	Birju Maharaj, Gopi Krishna,, Shambhu Maharaj, Sitara Devi, Vishnu Sharma, Durga Lal, Shobhana Narayan
Odissi	Odisha	Kelucharan Mahapatra, Indrani Rehman, Madhavi Mudgal, Protima Bedi, Samyukta Panigrahi, Sonal Mansingh, Debudas
Manipuri	Manipur	Uday Shankar, Bipin Singh, Suryamukhi, Darohra Jhaveri

Famous Folk-Dance

State/(UT)	Folk Dance
Andhra Pradesh	Dandari, Banjara
Assam	Bihu, Keli Gopal, Sataria
Bihar	Chhau, Magahi, Durga dance
W. Bengal	Kirtan, Kalatri, Asweabadh, Brita, Kalidance
Chhattisgarh	Saila, Karama, Bhagoria
Gujarat	Garba, Rasalila, Tippani, Dandia,
Haryana	Damyal, Lahoor
Himachal Pradesh	Dussehra dance, Hikat, Notio
Jammu & Kashmir	Dumhal
Jharkhand	Jhau, Ghumakudia, Jadur, Sarhul, Soharai, Karama, Vaima, Loojhari, Jat-Jatin, Vidayat
Karnataka	Yakshagan, Dolu Kunitha
Kerala	Mohini Attam, Padayuni
Madhya Pradesh	Lota Nritya, Jawara
Maharashtra	Tamasha, Dahi Handi, Gof, Deepak Dindi
Manipur	Dhol Cholam
Meghalaya	Nongakarem
Nagaland	Bamboo dance
Odisha	Chhau, Maya Shabari, Dalachai
Punjab	Gidda, Bhangra, Panihari
Rajasthan	Thumar, Kathaputali, Tera Tali
Tamil Nadu	Terukalathu, Kabalatam, Kargam, Pulivesham
Tripura	Hazagiri
Uttar Pradesh	Rasalila, Nautanki, Thali, Dhurang, Jhumela, Huraka, Bol.
Uttarakhand	Kajari, Karan
Goa	Dhode Modini

Musical Instruments and Artists

Musical Instrument	*Artists*	*Musical Instrument*	*Artists*
Flute	Hari Prasad Chaurasia, Panna Lal Ghosh, T.R. Mahalingam, N. Ramani, Vijaya Raghava Rao	Sitar	Pandit Ravishankar, Vilayat Khan
		Santur	Shiv Kumar Sharma
		Rudraveena	Zia Mohiuddin Dagar
Tabla	Allah Rakha, Gudai Maharaj, Latif Khan, Zakir Hussain	Pakhawaj	Govind Rao, Anokhe Lal, Kanthi Maharaj
		Mridanga	Palghat R. Raghu, U.S. Burman
Violin	Lalgudi Jayaraman, L. Subramaniam, M.S. Gopal Krishnan, S. Subrahmaniam, V.G. Jog, N. Rajan	Harmonium	Purushottam Walawakar, M. Dhaulpuri
		Guitar	Pt. Vishnu Mohan Bhatt, Brij Bhushan Kalra
Shehnai	Bismilla Khan, Imrat Khan Ali Akbar	Ghatam	T.H. Vinayakaram
Sarod	Khan, Amjad Ali Khan, Alauddin Khan, Saren Rani, Brij Narayan	Janjira	V. Nagarajan
		Symphony	Jubin Mehta

Major Wild Life Sanctuary in India

India is rich in flora and fauna. However, due to increasing population and industrial and commercial activities, there has been acute pressure on forests. The Government has taken several steps to check the sharp fall in the number of these species. Among the measures are declaration of certain habitats as national parks and sanctuaries. 106 national parks and 573 sanctuaries have been established till **March** 2025, important ones being given below:

Assam: Kaziranga National Park (know for one-horn Rhinoceroses); Manas Sanctuary.
Jharkhand: Hazaribagh National Park; Betla Tiger Reserve Palamau.
Gujarat: Valvadar National Park, Bhavnagar; Marine National Park, Gir Forests.
Himachal Pradesh: Rohla National Park; Motichur Sanctuary.
Jammu & Kashmir: Dachigam Sanctuary.
Karnataka: Bandipur National Park; Bannargheta National Park, Bangalore; Nagorhole National Park, Coorg; Ranganthitto Bird Sanctuary.
Kerala: Eravikulam Rajmallay National Park, Idduki; Periyar Game Sanctuary.
Madhya Pradesh: Kanha National Park; Bandhavgarh National Park, Shahdol; Shivpuri National Park.
Maharashtra: Taloba National Park, Chandrapur; Panch National Park, Nagpur; Borivali National Park, Mumbai; Nawagaon National Park, Bandara; Melghat National Park.
Manipur: Keibul Lamjao National Park.
Odisha: Simlipal, Tiger Sanctuary.
Rajasthan: Sariska Sanctuary; Ghana Bird Sanctuary, Ranthambhor Sanctuary.
Sikkim: Khangchandzenda National Park, Gangtok.
Tamil Nadu: Vedanthangal Bird Sanctuary; Guindy National Park, Chennai; Mudumalai Sanctuary; Kalakad-Munden Thurai Reserve.
Uttar Pradesh: Chandraprabha Sanctuary; Dudhwa National Park, Lakhimpur.
West Bengal: Jaldapara Sanctuary; Sunderbans.
Uttarakhand: Corbett National Park; Nainital.

* * * * *

13. AWARDS

NATIONAL AWARDS

- **Bharat Ratna:** This is India's highest civilian award. It is given for exceptional work on art, literature, science and recognition of public service of the highest order. Government servants are not eligible for it.
- **Padma Vibhushan:** The **Padma Vibhushan** is the second-highest civilian award of the Republic of India, preceded by Bharat Ratna and followed by Padma Bhushan. Instituted on 2 January 1954, the award is given for "exceptional and distinguished service", without distinction of race, occupation, position, or sex. The award criteria include "service in any field including service rendered by Government servants" including doctors and scientists, but excludes those working with the public sector undertakings.

  During 1 May and 15 September of every year, the recommendations for the award are submitted to the Padma Awards Committee, constituted by the Prime Minister of India. The recommendations are received from all the state and the union territory governments, the Ministries of the Government of India, the Bharat Ratna and previous Padma Vibhushan award recipients, the Institutes of Excellence, the Ministers, the Chief Ministers and the Governors of State, and the Members of Parliament including private individuals. The committee later submits their recommendations to the Prime Minister and the President of India for the further approval. The award recipients are announced on Republic Day.
- **Padma Bhushan:** The **Padma Bhushan** is the third-highest civilian award in the Republic of India, after the Bharat Ratna and the Padma Vibhushan, but coming before the Padma Shri. It is announced on the occasion of Republic Day of India every year. It is conferred by the President of India at a function held at Rashtrapati Bhavan sometime around March or April. The award was established on 2 January 1954 by the president of India. It is awarded to recognize distinguished service of a high order to the nation, in any field.
- **Padma Shri: Padma Shri** (also Padmashree) is the fourth highest civilian award in the Republic of India, after the Bharat Ratna, the Padma Vibhushan and the Padma Bhushan. Awarded by the Government of India, it is announced every year on India's Republic Day.

  Padma Awards were instituted in 1954 to be awarded to citizens of India in recognition of their distinguished contribution in various spheres of activity including the Arts, Education, Industry, Literature, Science, Sports, Medicine, Social Service and Public Affairs. It has also been awarded to some distinguished individuals who were not citizens of India but did contribute in various ways to India.

  The selection criteria have been criticized in some quarters with the claim that many highly deserving artists have been left out in order to favor certain individuals.

  On its obverse, the words "Padma", meaning lotus in Sanskrit, and "Shri", a Sanskrit-derived honorific equivalent to 'Mr.' or 'Ms.', appear in Devanagari above and below a lotus flower. The geometrical pattern on either side is in burnished bronze. All embossing is in white gold.

GALLANTRY AWARDS

- ★ **Param Vir Chakra:** The highest award for bravery or some daring and pre-eminent act of valour or self-sacrifice in the presence of the enemy, whether on land, at sea or in the air.
- ★ **Mahavir Chakra:** It is the second highest decoration and is awarded for acts of conspicuous gallantry in the presence of the enemy, whether on land, at sea or in the air.
- ★ **Vir Chakra:** It is the third in order of awards given for acts of gallantry in the presence of enemy, whether on land, at sea or in the air.
- ★ **Ashok Chakra:** This medal is awarded for the most conspicuous bravery or some daring or pre-eminent act of valour or self-sacrifice on land, at sea or in the air but not in the presence of enemy.
- ★ **Vishishta Sewa Medal:** It is awarded to personnel of all the three Services in class I, II and III in recognition of distinguished service of the "most exceptional" and "exceptional" and a "high" order respectively. Prefixes *Parma* and *Ati* are added before first two categories of medals respectively.
- ★ **Jeewan Raksha Padak:** Awarded for meritorious acts or a series of acts of a human nature displayed in saving life from drowning, fire and rescue operations in mines etc.

National Sports Awards

- ★ **Major Dhyan Chand Khel Ratna Award:** The scheme was launched in the year 1991-92 with the objective of honouring sportspersons to enhance their general status and to give them greater dignity and place of honour in society. Under this scheme, an amount of ₹ 25 lakh is given as award for the most spectacular and outstanding performance by a sportsperson over a period of four years immediately preceding the year in which award is to be given.
- ★ **Dronacharya Award:** Dronacharya Award is an award presented by ministry of youth Affairs and Sports, Government of India for excellence in sports coaching. The Dronacharya (Lifetime) awardees gets ₹ 15 lakh and Dronacharya (Regular) awardees gets ₹ 10 lakh a bronze statuette of Dronacharya and scroll of honour. The award was instituted in 1985.
- ★ **Arjuna Award:** The Arjuna Awards are given by the ministry of youth Affairs and sports, government of India to recognize outstanding achievement in National sports. Instituted in 1961 the award carries a cash prize of 15,00,000 a bronze statue of Arjuna and a scroll.
- ★ **Arjuna Award (Lifetime):** Arjuna Award (Lifetime) is India's highest award for lifetime achievement in sports and games, given by the ministry of youth Affairs and sports, government of India. The award is initiated in 2002. The award carries a cash prize of ₹ 10,00,000 a plaque and a scroll of honour.
- ★ **Maulana Abul Kalam Azad Trophy:** This trophy was instituted in 1956-57. The top overall performing university in the inter-university tournaments is given the Maulana Abul Kalam Azad (MAKA) Trophy, which is a rolling trophy. A small replica of the MAKA Trophy is also awarded for retention by the university. In addition, the university also gets a cash prize of ₹ 15 lakh. The second and third best universities also receive cash awards amounting to ₹ 5 lakh and ₹ 3 lakh respectively.

Other Awards

- ★ **Jnanpith Award:** Awarded to outstanding authors of creative literature in any of the Indian languages recognised by the Constitution of India. It was sponsored by the Bharatiya Jnanpith a culturo-literary society founded in 1944 by Shanti Prasad Jain, an eminent industrialist.
- ★ **Sahitya Akademi Award:** It is awarded for outstanding literary works and comprises a cash prize of ₹ 1,00,000 in each of the 22 languages mentioned in the Eighth schedule of the Constitution and Rajasthani and English that it supports and a copper plaque.

★ **Saraswati Samman:** The award is given by K.K. Birla Foundation to an outstanding author for his literary work in any Indian language mentioned in the Eighth Schedule of the Constitution and published during the last 10 years.

★ **Dada Saheb Phalke Award:** The prestigious Dada Saheb Phalke Award is given to the persons for outstanding contribution to the growth and development of Indian cinema. First presented in 1969, the award was introduced by the government of India to commemorate Dadasaheb Phalke's contribution to Indian Cinema. Phalke, who is popularly known as and often regarded as a the Father of Indian Cinema was an Indian film-maker who directed India's first-length feature film, Raja Harishchandra. The first recipient of the award was actress Devika Rani, who was honoured at the 17th National film Awards.

★ **Indira Gandhi Award:** The award has been instituted for promoting national integration and understanding amongst the religious groups, communities and ethnic groups of India.

★ **Gujar Mal Modi Award:** The award carries ₹ 2.01 lakh as cash prize, apart from a silver shield and a scroll and is given to the best scientist of the year who makes an outstanding contribution to research resulting in new innovative technology.

★ **Vachaspati Puraskar:** K.K. Birla Foundation's prestigious Vachaspati Puraskar carries a cash award of ₹ 1,50,000 for outstanding Sanskrit works published during the last ten years.

★ **Bhartendu Harishchandra Awards:** The Bhartendu Harishchandra Awards were instituted in 1983, by the Ministry of Information and Broadcasting for original Hindi writing on any subject in mass communications like journalism, publication, advertising, broadcasting films, etc.

★ **Kabir Samman:** The award is conferred annually on a person of literature of very high order on the basis of his or her superb creativity and consistent commitment to the most recent and latest trends of literary creation in any of the Indian languages. The award carries ₹ 3 lakh and a letter of citation.

INTERNATIONAL AWARDS

★ **Nobel Prizes:** The most prestigious award in the world is supported by the Nobel Foundation of US. This award was set up in 1900 under the will to Alfred Bernhard Nobel (1833-96). Alfred Nobel was an unmarried, Swedish scientist and chemical engineer who discovered Nitroglycerin ($C_3H_5N_3O_9$) and its use in the manufacture of dynamite in 1966. The interest accrued on the fortune left by him is divided annually among the persons who have made outstanding contribution in science, literature, peace and economics. Swedes found out about the prizes only after his death in 1896. When they read his will in which he had donated the annual income from his fortune to support the awards. In his will he ordered that 'the most worthy shall receive the prize, whether he is Scandinavian or not. This led to his criticism as being unpatriotic for not reserving the prizes only for Swedes.

Nobel Foundation's Prize Awarding Bodies

(*i*) The Royal Swedish Academy of Sciences, awards the Nobel prize in Physics and Chemistry.

(*ii*) The Nobel Assembly of Karolinska Chirugical Institute. Sweden, awards the Nobel Prize in Medicine and Physiology.

(*iii*) The Swedish Academy awards the Prize in Literature.

(*iv*) The Committee of the Norwegian Parliament awards the Prize for Peace.

(*v*) The Bank of Sweden awards the Nobel Prize in Economics.

★ **Ramon Magsaysay Award:** The Raman Magsaysay Award, named after a Philippines President, who died in an air crash in 1957, is given annually to Asian nationals or institutions who have made worthy contributions to public service, community leadership, journalism, literature and the creative arts and international understanding. It carries a gold medal, a certificate and US$ 50,000. It is awarded on August 31, every year.

- **Pulitzer Prize:** Instituted in 1970 and named after the US publisher Joseph Pulitzer (1847-1911). It is conferred annually in the United States for accomplishment in journalism, literature and music under the management to the Pulitzer Prize Board at Columbia University.
- **Man Booker Prize:** Instituted in 1968, it is the highest literary award set up by the Booker Company and the British Publishers Association along the lines of the Pultizer Prize, of USA, worth £ 20,000 (1992). The Booker Prize has only been shared in 1974 and 1992. Since 2002, it has been known as the **'Man Booker Prize'**, reflecting the sponsorship by an investment company, the Man Group plc. The winner receives £ 50,000 and both the winner and the shorlisted authors are guaranteed a world wide readership plus a dramatic increase in book sales.
- **Oscar Awards:** The annual Oscar presentation has been held since 1929. After three-quarters of a century of recognizing excellence in cinema achievement, the annual presentation of the Oscars has become the Academy of Motion Picture Arts and Sciences' most famous activity.
- **Kalinga Award:** The award given for popularisation of science is an international award conferred annually by the United Nations Educational, Scientific and Cultural Organisation (UNESCO) to a person with a distinguished career of service in the interpretation of science and research to the public. The award was instituted in 1952 at the initiative of Mr Biju Patnaik the founder of the Kalinga Foundation Trust in Odisha.
- **Grammy Award:** The Grammy Foundation was established in 1989 to cultivate an awareness, appreciation and advancement of the contribution of recorded music American culture from the and technical legends of the past to the still unimagined musical breakthroughs of the future generations of the music professionals. The Grammy Foundation works in partnership with its founder, the Recording Academy, to bring national attention to important issues such as the value and impact of music and arts education and the urgency of preserving our rich cultural legacy.

Highest Honours of Some Countries

Country	*Highest Honour*	*Country*	*Highest Honour*
India	Bharat Ratna	Britain	Member of British Empire, Victoria Cross
Pakistan	Nishan-e-Pakistan		
Kuwait	Mubarak-Al-kabir Medal	Japan	Order of Moulovenice Sun
Saudi Arabia	Shah Abdul Aziz Medal	Denmark	Order of Diana Brog
Argentina	The Order of Sona Martin	France	Legend of Honour
Nicaragua	Augusto-Caesar Sandino Order	America	Presidential Medal of Freedom
Vietnam	The order of the Golden Star	Germany	Pore Lee Merit Iron Cross
Hungary	The Order of Banner	The Netherlands	Netherlands Lion

* * * * *

14. COMPUTER

The computer is the system of that electronic device through which various informations are processed on the basis of a definite set of instructions called program and mathematical (numerical) and non-mathematical both types of informations are processed. The first mechanical computer was composed or fabricated by Blaise Pascal in 1642 and it is called Pascalene. But in 1833, Charles Babbage first time conceived an automatic calculator or computer. Charles Babbage is called the father of modern computer. Herman made an electronic tabulating machine based on punch cards which operates automatically. In 1937, first mechanical computer mark-I was fabricated by Howard Akeen. The most outstanding contribution in the development of modern computer goes to John Wan Newmaan who brought the 2nd revolution in the area of computer in 1951. He discovered EDVAC (Electronic Discrete Variable Automatic Computer) and utilised the stored program and the binary number system in the computer.

Functions of Computer

1. Collection and composition (input) of datas;
2. Storage of datas.
3. Processing of datas.
4. Retrieval or output of the proccessed informations and datas.

Units of Computer

1. Input unit.
2. Central processing unit–CPU.
3. External Memory unit.
4. Output unit.

The CPU of the computer is called brain of the computer and sometimes CPU is also called Micro Processor of the computer. The data is entered through the input unit in the computer and through the central processing unit with the help of External Memory Unit datas are arranged and processed. Ultimately by the output unit these datas or informations are issued or released.

Parts of Computer

- **Monitor :** The monitor of the computer is like a television in which the picture appears in the form of doted points on the screen and these are called pixcels.
- **Hard Disc and Floppy Disc :** The Hard Disc is the permanent disc in the computers while the Floppy Disc is the disc utilised when datas or informations are to be transferred from one computer to another.
- **Mouse :** The mouse of the computer is like the remote control of TV through which computer is directly regulated or controlled without utilising the key-board.
- **Printer :** The printer is a device which prints any documents or processed informations of the computer.

Some high level languages

1. **FORTRAN :** This language was developed for solving the mathematical formulae very quickly and conveniently.
2. **COBOL :** This language was developed for the commerical purposes. For the processing of this language a group of sentences is selected called paragraph and all paragraphs composed are called a section, while all sections composed are called a division.
3. **BASIC :** In basic a definite part of the prescribed instruction is only inserted in the computer.

4. **ALGOL :** This was basically fabricated and designed for the complex algebraic calculations.
5. **PASCAL :** It is an amplified and modified form of ALGOL.
6. **COMAL :** This computer language is used for the students of secondary level.
7. **LOGO :** This language is used for children and kids for drawing Graphic line diagrams.
8. **PROLOG :** This language is developed in 1973 in France and this language is used for Artificial Intelligence which is capable and equivalent to the logical program.
9. **FORTH :** This language was invented by Charles Mure which is frequently used in all types of the works in the computer.

Computer Virus

The computer virus is an electronic code which is used to abolish or erradicate the inclusive informations or programs of the computer. Some important computer viruses are Micheleanjalo, Dork Avangor, kilo, filip, Macmug, Scores, Casecade, Jeruslem, Date crime, Coloumbs crime, Internet virus, Pachcom, Pach EXE, COM-EXE, Marizuana, C-brain, bloody, Chenge Mungu and Desi etc.

Computer Networking

There are two types of networkings which are usually occur—Local Area Networking (LAN) and Wide Area Networking (WAN). By LAN all the computers of the same buildings are connected like the computers of university premises, computers of offices etc. By WAN all the comptuers of a large area are connected like the computers of all the offices of a city or town etc. In India a very large computer network namely INDONET has been installing through which all the main towns and cities has to be interlinked.

Computer Terminology

- **Bit :** The bit is a unit of measurement of the electronic data. One bit is either 0 or 1 but not both. On composing 8 bits, 1 byte is formed.
- **Bug :** The Bug is the error in the computer program or system and its eradication is called Debug.
- **Byte :** Total eight bits compose a byte. Thus 8 bits = 1 byte.
- **CD-ROM :** A CD like of music CD in which data can be stored substantially called CD-ROM. In a CD with comparison to floppy extremely more datas can be stored but one problem in it is that one time recorded data can not be deleted or modified.
- **Chip :** It is a thin slice on which by a special mechanism a circuit is designed which is normally made from Silicon.
- **Memory System :** The place where computer data and program are temporarily kept is called Memory system. Usually memory is implied from RAM.
- **Modem :** The device which converts digital signals into analogue signals and vice-versa is called Modem.
- **RAM :** It is Random Access Memory (a place) where datas to be processed are kept temporarily and it is unstable memory.
- **ROM :** It is Read Only Memory and it is stable or Non-valatile memory which doesn't ended after power off.
- **Scanner :** It is a device through which graphic image is transformed to digital image and the scanners are of usually two types one desktop and another hand operating.

Programing

Computers perform phenomenal feats of calculation, but they do not do so in a complicated way. They actually carry out very simple operations, such as addition and subtraction. They achieve their fantastic computing power by carrying out these operations at incredible speed.

The programme, or set of instructions for operating the computer, is therefore written as a sequence of very simple steps. (See box below) Several computer languages have been developed for different applications, including BASIC, COBOL, FORTRAN and PASCAL. Writing programmes is very skilled and time-consuming work. But for most typical computer applications ready-written programmes are available, called "packages".

* * * * *

15. SPORTS

Important Cups & Trophies

International

• *American Cup*	: Yacht Racing	• *Walker Cup*	: Golf
• *Ashes*	: Cricket	• *Westchester Cup*	: Polo
• *Benson and Hedges*	: Cricket	• *Wightman Cup*	: Lawn Tennis
• *Canada Cup*	: Golf	• *World Cup*	: Cricket
• *Colombo Cup*	: Football	• *World Cup*	: Hockey
• *Corbitton Cup*	: Table Tennis (Women)	• *Reliance Cup*	: Cricket
• *Davis Cup*	: Lawn Tennis	• *Rothman's Trophy*	: Cricket
• *Derby*	: Horse Race	• *William's Cup*	: Basketball
• *Grand National*	: Horse Streple Chase Race	• *European Champions Cup*	: Football
• *Jules Rimet Trophy*	: World Soccer Cup	• *Eisenhower Cup*	: Golf
• *King's Cup*	: Air Races	• *Essande Champions Cup*	: Hockey
• *Merdeka Cup*	: Football	• *Rene Frank Trophy*	: Hockey
• *Ryder Cup*	: Golf	• *Grand Prix*	: Table Tennis
• *Swaythling Cup*	: Table Tennis (Men)	• *Edgbaston Cup*	: Lawn Tennis
• *Thomas Cup*	: Badminton	• *Grand Prix*	: Lawn Tennis
• *Uber Cup*	: Badminton (Women)	• *World Cup*	: Weightlifting
• *U. Thant Cup*	: Tennis		

National

• *Agarwal Cup*	: Badminton	• *C.K. Naidu Trophy*	: Cricket
• *Agha Khan Cup*	: Hockey	• *Chakola Gold Trophy*	: Football
• *All India Women's Guru Nanak Championship*	: Hockey	• *Divan Cup*	: Badminton
• *Bandodkar Trophy*	: Football	• *Deodhar Trophy*	: Cricket
• *Bangalore Blues Challenge Cup*	: Basketball	• *Duleep Trophy*	: Cricket
• *Barna-Bellack Cup*	: Table Tennis	• *D.C.M. Cup*	: Football
• *Beighton Cup*	: Hockey	• *Durand Cup*	: Football
• *Bombay Gold Cup*	: Hockey	• *Dhyan Chand Trophy*	: Hockey
• *Burdwan Trophy*	: Weightlifting	• *Dr. B.C. Roy Trophy*	: Football (Junior)
• *Charminar Trophy*	: Atheletics	• *Ezra Cup*	: Polo
• *Chadha Cup*	: Badminton	• *F.A. Cup*	: Football
		• *G.D. Birla Trophy*	: Cricket
		• *Ghulam Ahmed Trophy*	: Cricket
		• *Gurmeet Trophy*	: Hockey

- *Guru Nanak Cup* : Hockey
- *Gyanvati Devi Trophy* : Hockey
- *Holkar Trophy* : Bridge
- *Irani Trophy* : Cricket
- *I.F.A. Shield* : Football
- *Indira Gold Cup* : Hockey
- *Jawaharlal Challenge* : Air Racing
- *Jaswant Singh Trophy* : Best Services Sportsman
- *Kuppuswamy Naidu Trophy* : Hockey
- *Lady Rattan Tata Trophy* : Hockey
- *MCC Trophy* : Hockey
- *Moinuddaula Gold Cup* : Cricket
- *Murugappa Gold Cup* : Hockey
- *Modi Gold Cup* : Hockey
- *Narang Cup* : Badminton
- *Nehru Trophy* : Hockey
- *Nixan Gold Cup* : Football
- *Obaidullah Gold Cup* : Hockey
- *Prithi Singh Cup* : Polo
- *Rani Jhansi Trophy* : Cricket
- *Ranji Trophy* : Cricket
- *Rangaswami Cup* : Hockey
- *Ranjit Singh Gold Cup* : Hockey
- *Rajendra Prasad Cup* : Tennis
- *Ramanujan Trophy* : Table Tennis
- *Rene Frank Trophy* : Hockey
- *Radha Mohan Cup* : Polo
- *Raghbir Singh Memorial* : Football
- *Rohinton Baria Trophy* : Cricket
- *Rovers Cup* : Football
- *Sanjay Gold Cup* : Football
- *Santosh Trophy* : Football
- *Sir Ashutosh Mukherjee* : Football
- *Subroto Cup* : Football
- *Scindia Gold Cup* : Hockey
- *Sahni Trophy* : Hockey
- *Sheesh Mahal Trophy* : Cricket
- *Todd Memorial Trophy* : Football
- *Tommy Eman Gold Cup* : Hockey
- *Vittal Trophy* : Football
- *Vizzy Trophy* : Cricket
- *Vijay Merchant Trophy* : Cricket
- *Wellington Trophy* : Rowing
- *Wills Trophy* : Cricket

Sports Measurements

- *Badminton Courts:* 44 ft. by 20 ft. (doubles) 44 ft. by 17 ft. (singles)
- *Boxing Ring:* 12 ft. by 28 ft. Sq.
- *Cricket Pitch:* 22 yards (distance)
- *Derby Course:* 1½ miles. (2.4 km)
- *Football Field:*
  (a) Length : 100 – 120 yards.
  [Breadth: 50 – 56 yards.
  (b) Rugby : 100 yards by 75 yards
- *Hockey Ground:* 100 yards by 55 to 60 yards
- *Lawn Tennis Court:* 78 ft. by 36 ft. (double), 78 ft. by 28 ft. (single)
- *Marathon Race:* 26 miles, 385 yards
- *Polo Ground:* 300 yards by 200 yards (if boarded)
- *Golf:* Hole 4½ inches in diameter.

Sports Terms

- **Badminton:** Mixed doubles; Deuce; Drop; Smash; Let; Foot work; Setting.
- **Base Ball:** Pitcher; Put out, Strike; Home; Bunt.
- **Billiards:** Cue; Jigger; Pot; Break; In Baulk; In Off; Cannons.
- **Boxing:** Upper cut; Round; Punch; Bout; Knock down; Hitting below the belt; Ring.
- **Bridge:** Finesse; Dummy; Revoke; Grand Slam; Little Slam; No Trump; Rubber.
- **Chess:** Bishop, Gambit; Checkmate; Stalemate.
- **Cricket:** L.B.W. *(leg before wicket)*; Creases, Popping-creases; Stumped; Bye; Leg-Bye; Googly; Hattrick; Maiden over; Drive; Bowling; Duck; Follow-on; No ball; Leg Break; Silly point; Cover point; Hit-wicket; Late-cut; Slip; Off-spinner; In-swing.

- **Football:** Off Side; Block; Drop-kick; Penalty-kick (or *goal kick*); Corner-kick; Free-kick; Dribble; Thrown-in; Foul.
- **Golf:** Boggy; Foursome; Stymic; Tee; Put; Hole; Niblic; Caddie; Links; The green; Bunker.
- **Hockey:** Carried; Short Corner; Bully; Sticks; Off side; Roll in; Striking Circle; Under-cutting; Dribble.
- **Horse racing:** Jockey; Punter.
- **Polo:** Bunker; Chukker; Mallet.
- **Tennis:** Back hand drive; Volley; Smash; Half-volley; Deuce; Service; Let; Grand Slam.

Name of Playing Compound of Different Games

Name of Compound	*Related Sports*	*Name of Compound*	*Related Sports*
Court	Lawn Tennis, Badminton, Netball, Hand ball, Volleyball, Squash, Kho-Kho, Kabaddi	Pool	Swimming
		Alley	Bowling
		Mat	Judo, Karate II
Diamond	Baseball	Arena	Horse Riding
		Vellodrum	Cycling
Ring	Boxing, Skating, Wrestling, Circus, Riding display	Field	Polo, Football, Hockey
		Track	Athletics
Course	Golf	Pitch	Cricket, Rugby
Board	Table Tennis	Rink	Ice Hockey

National Sports and Games of Some Countries

Australia	Cricket	Spain	Bull Fighting
Canada	Ice Hockey	USA	Baseball
England	Cricket and Rugby Football	China	Table Tennis
Japan	Ju-Jitsu	Malaysia	Badminton
Russia	Chess	Pakistan	Hockey
Scotland	Rugby Football		

Number of Players in Some Games/Sports

Sports	*No. of Players*	*Sports*	*No. of Players*
Badminton	1 or 2	Lacrosse	12
Baseball	9	Netball	7
Basketball	5	Polo Rugby	4
Billiards (Snooker)	1	Football (Rugby)	15
Boxing	1	Table Tennis	1 or 2
Bridge	2		
Chess	1		
Cricket	11	Lawn Tennis	1 or 2
Croquest	13 or 15		
Football (Soccer)	11	Volleyball	6
Hockey	11	Water Polo	7

OLYMPIC GAMES

First of all these games were held by the Greeks in 776 B.C. on Mount Olympus in honour of the Greek God Zeus. In this way, the history of Olympic Games is about twenty eight hundred years old. These games continued to be held every four years until 394 A.D. When these games were stopped by a royal order of the emperor of Rome. The modern Olympic Games which started in Athens in 1896, are the result of the devotion and dedication of a French educator Baron Pierre de Coubertin and the first Olympic meet in the modern series was held in 1896 in Athens, the Capital of Greece. Since then, they are being held every four years except for breaks during world wars. The Olympic flag is white in colour with five coloured rings, each ring symbolic of a continent. Summer as well as winter Olympics are held in the same year.

ASIAN GAMES

After the Second World War, most of the Asian Countries gained independence. On the lines of Olympic Games, Asian Games were planned every four years. India hosted the first Asian Games in 1951.

COMMONWEALTH GAMES

The Commonwealth Games are held every four years, in the year in which Asian Games are held. All the Commonwealth Countries (former colonies of Britain) can take part in it. The first Commonwealth Games were held in 1930 at Hamilton (Canada).

CRICKET WORLD CUP

The first Cricket World Cup was organised in England in 1975. A separate women's Cricket World Cup has been held every 4 years since 1973. Australia is the winner of 2023 Cricket World Cup.

HOCKEY WORLD CUP

The first Hockey World Cup was organised in Barcelona (Spain) in 1971. Women's Hockey World Cup has been held since 1974.

FOOTBALL WORLD CUP

The Football World Cup is organised by FIFA (Federation of International Football Association). The World Cup is called 'Jules Rimet Cup' named after the name of FIFA President Jules Rimet. The first Football World Cup was organised in Uruguay in 1930.

Personalities Associated with Sports

- **Athletics:** Carl Lewis, Linford Christy, Ben Johnson, Calvin Smith, Edwin Moses, Sergei Bubka, Sebestian Coe, Florence Griffith Joyner, Rosa Mota, Harold Schmidt, Milkha Singh, P.T. Usha, Shiny Abraham, Vandana Rao, Jesse Owens, Jyotirmoy Sikdar.
- **Boxing:** Cassius Clay (Mohammad Ali), Joe Frazier, Mike Tyson, Larry Holmes, Frank Bruno, Henry Cooper, Archie Moore, Evander Holyfield, George Foreman.
- **Badminton:** Prakash Padukone, Syed Modi, Dinesh Khanna, Jamie Paulson, Nandu Natekar, Liem Swie King, Saina Nehwal, P.V. Sindhu.
- **Billiards:** Wilson Jones, Geet Sethi, Michael Ferreira, Pankaj Advani.
- **Chess:** Boris Spausky, Gary Kasparov, Anatoly Karpov, Victor Korchonoi, Vishwanathan Anand, Konern Humpy, Parveen Thipsay, Rohini Khadilkar.
- **Cricket:** Sunil Gavaskar, Bishen Singh Bedi, Kapil Dev, Mohd. Azharuddin, Sachin Tendulkar, G.R. Vishwanath, Lala Amarnath, Ajit Wadekar, B.S. Chandrashekhar, E.A.S. Prasanna, S. Venkatraghvan, Don Bradman, Richard Hadlee, Gary Sobers, Ian Botham, Vivian Richards, Clive Llyod, Dilip Sardesai, Charles Griffith, Imran Khan, Mushtaq Mohammad, Geoff Boycott, Tony Greg, Wasim Akram, Richie Benaud, Michael Holding, Greg Chappell, Javed Miandad, Vijay Manjrekar, M.A.K. Pataudi, S.M.H. Kirmani, Frank Worrell, Bill Lawry, Clive Rice, Mark Taylor, Joel Garner, Arjuna Ranatunga, Arvinda De'Silva, Saurav Ganguly,

Virat Kohli, M.S. Dhoni, Ajit Agarkar, Jacques Kallis, John Traicos, Brian Mcmillan, W.R. Hammond, Sanath Jaisurya.

- **Hockey:** Dhyan Chand, Ashok Kumar, Ajit Singh, Pargat Singh, Pritpal Singh, Zafar Iqbal, Shankar Laxman, Mervyn Fernandes, Mohammad Shahid, R. Charlesworth, Balbir Singh, Terry Walsh, Kishan Lal, Udlam Singh, Dhanraj Pillai.
- **Football:** Pele, Diego Maradona, Franz Beckenbour, Socrates, Raud Gullit, Garry Linekar, Emilo Butraguino, Coreca, P.C. Bannerji, Arunlal Ghosh, Chuni Goswami, Inder Singh, Davor Suker, Ronaldo, Rivaldo, Deschamps.
- **Tennis (Lawn):** Bjorn Borg, Jimmy Connors, John Mcenroe, Ivan Lendl, Pete Sampras, Billie Jean Kings, Chris Evert Lloyd, Martina Navratilova, Steffi Graf, Stefan Edberg, Andre Agassi, Michael Chang, Ramesh Krishnan, Boris Becker, Leander Paes, Ramanathan Krishnan, Zeeshan Ali, Vijay Amritraj, Anand Amritraj, Jaideep Mukherjee, Rod Laver, Roy Emerson, Naresh Kumar, Premjit Lall, John Newcombe, Martina Hingis, Arantxa Sanchez Vicario, Mary Pierce, Jana Novotna,Rozer Federer.
- **Golf:** Greg Norman, Jack Nikalus, Sandy Lyle, Seve Bellestros, Nick Faldo, Nick Price, Sher Ali, Jeeve Milkha Singh, S. Choudhary, R.K. Pitamber, Vikramjit Singh.
- **Gymnastics:** Nadia Comaneci, L. Latynina, V. Kaslavska, E. Szebo, W. Kim. Y. Ma, Y. Shrusunova, Daniela Silivas, A. Braglia, V. Chukarin, N. Andrianov, Sergi Kharkhov.
- **Swimming:** Arti Gupta, Arun Kumar Shaw, Baidyanath, Dawn Frazer, Mihir Sen, Aarti Saha, Mark Spitz.
- **Wrestling:** Dara Singh, Bhim Sen, Mukhtiar Singh, Sudesh Kumar, Chandagi Ram.

Stadia in Various Cities of India

- **Delhi:** Ambedkar Stadium, Arun Jaitley Stadium, Jawaharlal Nehru Stadium, Indira Gandhi Indoor Stadium, Shivaji Stadium, National Stadium.
- **Mumbai:** Brabourne Stadium, Wankhede Stadium.
- **Kolkata:** Eden Gardens, Salt Lake Stadium, Ranjit Stadium, Subhas Sarovar.
- **Chennai:** Nehru Stadium, Chidambaram Stadium, Chepauk.
- **Cuttack:** Barabati Stadium.
- **Kanpur:** Green Park.
- **Jamshedpur:** Keenan Stadium.
- **Nagpur:** Vidarbha CA Ground
- **Jaipur:** Swai Mansingh Stadium
- **Gwalior:** Roop Singh Stadium
- **Pune:** Nehru Stadium
- **Vadodara:** Moti Bagh Stadium
- **Patna:** Moin-ul-Haq Stadium
- **Hyderabad:** Lal Bahadur Stadium
- **Patiala:** Yaduvindra Stadium.
- **Bengaluru:** Chinnaswami Stadium.
- **Siliguri:** Kanchenjunga Stadium.
- **Faridabad:** Mayur Stadium.
- **Vishakhapatnam:** Indira Priyadarshini Stadium.

* * * * *

MULTIPLE CHOICE QUESTIONS

GENERAL AWARENESS

1. The part of the Sun, which is visible during eclipses only, is known as
A. photosphere
B. chromosphere
C. corona
D. all the parts are visible with naked eye

2. Sphygmomanometer is used for
A. measuring the brain pulse of a patient
B. measuring the systolic and diastolic blood pressures of man
C. measuring the amount of blood in a human body
D. measuring the haemoglobin count in a human body

3. The most abundant gas in air is
A. nitrogen B. hydrogen
C. oxygen D. ozone

4. The most commonly found acid in nature is
A. hydrochloric acid B. sulphuric acid
C. lactic acid D. acetic acid

5. This bomb is used to destroy living beings but would not damage the buildings and other property
A. napalm bomb B. neutron bomb
C. hydrogen bomb D. None of the above

6. Electrical energy is measured in terms of units which are also termed as
A. KW B. KWH
C. WH D. KVAR

7. In cold countries, the radiator water of cars is mixed with glycerol. This is done to
A. increase the specific heat of water
B. reduce the freezing point of water
C. improve the engine efficiency
D. glycerol is not added in radiator water

8. If the Richter scale shows a value of 7.2, then the seismograph indicates
A. an earthquake of low intensity
B. an earthquake of very high intensity
C. an earthquake of moderate intensity
D. either A or C

9. The theory of origin of species is based primarily on
A. the process of biological evolution
B. the process of natural selection
C. the evolution of life from the oceans
D. the evolution of man from apes

10. Common coal used in our households is
A. Anthracite B. Bituminous coal
C. Lignite D. All of the above

11. Some recent findings on moon, which point out towards the possibility of settlement of man on moon, include
A. nil atmospheric gases
B. ice reserves on the poles
C. micro-organisms
D. None of the above

12. Viagra is a medicine for
A. treatment of AIDS
B. treatment of female fertility
C. treatment of male impotency
D. treatment of Lukaemia

13. Rickets is a disease which is caused by the deficiency of
A. Vitamin A B. Riboflavin
C. Vitamin C D. Vitamin D

14. When a ship enters waters of the sea from a river, then its level
A. rises as the sea water is saline and hence bouyancy force is more
B. decreases as ocean is a large mass of water
C. remains the same as water is the same for the river and the sea
D. None of the above

15. The major constituent of pearl is
A. calcium carbonate
B. calcium oxide and ammonium chloride
C. organic mass
D. calcium carbonate and silica

16. A healthy person needs ..... calories per day.
A. 2200 B. 2400
C. 2500 D. 1800

17. The value of one (marine) Naut is
A. 1951 metre per hour
B. 1852 metre per hour
C. 2305 metre per hour
D. 1860 metre per hour

18. Acid and base combine to form
A. salt and nitrogen
B. nitrogen and oxygen
C. salt and water
D. acid and alkali

19. Cellulose could be obtained from
A. wood and cotton B. silk and cotton
C. paper and silk D. wood and silk

20. ELISA test is done for the detection of
A. cancer B. AIDS
C. diabetes D. None of the above

21. Triple Antigen, prevents
A. small pox, malaria, whooping cough
B. tetanus, diphtheria, small pox
C. whooping cough, tetanus, polio
D. diphtheria, tetanus, whooping cough

22. A freely falling body
A. would fall towards the surface of the earth
B. would have no weight
C. would have one half of its original weight
D. None of the above

23. If the motor neurons of the spinal cord of a child are damaged, then he would develop the following disease.
A. Rickets B. Polio
C. Diphtheria D. Jaundice

24. Which one of the following is not a part of the balanced diet?
A. Vitamins B. Carbohydrate
C. Proteins D. Alcohol

25. Which statement is not correct in connection with human physiology?
A. The length of the small intestine is 7 metres and its diameter is 2.5 cm.
B. There are 639 muscles in a human body
C. An infant breathes 45 times per minute whereas a six year old child breathes 25 times per minute
D. The weight of the adult human brain is nearly 700 gms

26. The bottles of beer are not kept in the deep freezer because
A. beer is an alcohol which could burst under conditions of low temperature
B. alcohol could damage the deep freezer due to its corrosive action if the bottles break accidently
C. water content in beer gets converted into ice which expends (after change of state from water to ice) and this could lead to bursting of beer bottles
D. the low temperature could degrade the beer and hence, it may not good remain for consumption

27. Rocket works on the basis of
A. principle of conservation of momentum
B. principle of relativity
C. principle of conservation of mass
D. principle of conservation of energy

28. Which one of the following groups is more closely related from the viewpoint of taxonomy?
A. silverfish, starfish, cuttlefish
B. earthworm, seahorsc, hookworm
C. housefly, dragonfly, butterfly
D. None of the above

29. Red blood corpuscles are produced in
A. liver B. spleen
C. bone marrow D. kidneys

30. The disease for which the first oral drug has been developed for treatment.
A. Cancer B. Pneumonid
C. Small pox D. Plauge

31. E-comm is a short form of
A. Engineering Commercial
B. Electronic Commercial
C. Electronic Commerce
D. None of the above

32. High AC voltages are used for transmitting electric power because
A. at high voltages, current is low and hence, losses are low

B. the transmission of power is quicker
C. the high voltages a consumé lesser materials for transmission
D. None of the above

33. There is a hole in the boat through which, water is seeping into the boat. Just before the boat capsizes
A. water level would decrease
B. water level would increase
C. water level would remain the same
D. None of the above

34. During which month, the rate of rotation of the earth on its axis is the fastest?
A. December
B. May
C. the rate of rotation is fixed
D. It is fastest when the earth is closest to the Sun.

35. The time taken by the Sun rays to reach the earth is
A. 9 minutes B. 10 minutes
C. 7 minutes D. 8 minutes

36. The outer planets are
A. Moon, Earth, Mercury, Venus
B. Jupiter, Saturn, Uranus, Earth, Mars
C. Jupiter, Uranus, Saturn, Neptune
D. None of the above

37. According to the astrophysicists
A. the universe is mobile and expanding
B. the universe is heading for a collision with another universe
C. the universe is stationary
D. the doomsday of universe is near due to the formation of many new black holes

38. Which is popular as the White City?
A. New York B. Belgrade
C. Bangalore D. Bab-el-mandab

39. The national currency of Haiti is
A. Rupiah B. Gourde
C. Quetzal D. Dong

40. Which one is not a news agency of India?
A. UNI
B. PTI
C. Hindustan Samachar
D. Reuters

41. The abundant element of the earth's atmosphere is:
A. Oxygen B. nitrogen
C. hydrogen D. CO_2

42. The first talking movie of India was ..... and the first silent movie of India was .....
A. Aan, Aawara
B. Raja Harish Chandra, Alamara
C. Alamara, Raja Harish Chandra
D. Purana Mandir, Raja Harish Chandra

43. Hair becomes grey because
A. rays of the Sun force it to become grey
B. the quantity of melanin is reduced in human body with growing age
C. there is a lack of vitamins in the body due to growing age
D. None of the above

44. Salaries of Supreme Court judges are drawn from:
A. Law Ministry Grants
B. Consolidated Fund of India
C. Home Ministry Grants
D. Parliamentary Grants

45. The term "Paper-gold" is associated with
A. deficit budgeting
B. loans from the World Bank
C. Special Drawing Rights (SDRs) from the IMF
D. None of the above

46. TRAI refers to
A. Terresteral Remote Sensing Authority of India
B. Telecommunication Research Authority of India
C. Transport Regulatory Authority of India
D. Telecom Regulatory Authority of India

47. NSDL is an organisation in India which
A. provides security to depositors
B. accepts deposits from recognised bodies
C. provides data security for on-line computer systems
D. None of the above

48. The enzyme pepsin converts
A. proteins into peptones
B. fats to amino acids
C. carbohydrates to sugars
D. proteins to amino acids

49. Who among the following is not a winner of the PVC?
A. Bana Singh

B. Nirmal Jeet Singh Sekhon
C. Somnath Sharma
D. Shanti Swaroop Rana

50. Which one of the following pairs is not correct?
A. Narmada – Betul district
B. Krishna – near Mahabaleshwar
C. Chambal – near Mhow
D. Godavari – Nashik district

51. The Japanese art of flower arrangement is known as
A. Bonsai B. Ongami
C. Ikebota D. None of the above

52. The meaning of the Latin word *Vive Rex* is
A. Long live the king!
B. Let the Nation Live
C. A middle course
D. Nothing wrong here

53. The permanent station of India in Antarctica is known as
A. *Vikalp*
B. Antarctica India Station
C. *Maitri*
D. *Dakshin Yamunotri*

54. A man dies due to electrocution because
A. electric current passes through his body to earth which leads to sudden contraction and expansion of muscles (including heart muscles) and this, alongwith development of heat in the body, leads to heart failure.
B. there is no resistance offered by the body
C. the body allows the current to flow through the blood which cannot circulate any longer
D. None of the above

55. "Blue Dwarfs" are
A. members of the Russian circus
B. warriors of Mongolia
C. young stars of the universe
D. naval officers in the high seas

56. What is a fly leaf?
A. thin paper sheet for making packaging material
B. a blank page at the beginning or end of a book
C. a marker in a book
D. a sheet of paper next to the main title of the book

57. Who is associated with the theory of inheritance of acquired characters?
A. Spencer B. Mandeleev
C. Lamarck D. All of the above

58. Ligaments and tendons in the body are made up of
A. skeletal tissue B. muscular tissue
C. connective tissue D. epithelial tissue

59. A cell membrane is
A. completely permeable
B. impermeable
C. semi-permeable
D. None of the above

60. The tenure of the non-permanent members of the UN Security Council is
A. one year
B. three years
C. two years
D. there is no fixed tenure

61. Why proper earthing is necessary?
A. It reduces the consumption of electricity
B. It allows the current to flow through the earth wire and into the earth, thus protecting the person
C. It allows the appliance to operate efficiently
D. None of the above

62. Which one of the following items has not been included in the minimum needs programme?
A. unemployment allowance
B. rural water supply
C. rural electrification
D. adult education

63. This is not the principle organ of digestion and absorption in the human body.
A. small intestine B. stomach
C. large intestine D. Both A and B

64. Which are the two stars which appear as morning stars in the Eastern sky and evening stars in the Western sky?
A. Jupiter and Mars
B. Mars and Venus
C. Saturn and Mercury
D. Mercury and Venus

65. Which planet rotates on its axis from East to West?
A. Mercury B. Jupiter
C. Earth D. Venus

66. The chemical compound present in the stone of human kidney is
A. calcium phosphate B. calcium carbonate
C. silica D. calcium oxalate

67. Which one of the following diseases would be caused by bacterial infection?
A. tetanus B. rabies
C. cancer D. malaria

68. India On-line Limited is
A. an advertising agency
B. a reservation office
C. an information service
D. an internet services provider

69. CTBT is related to
A. economic sanctions imposed by the USA on India
B. the codename of Pokharan-II blasts
C. the nuclear test ban treaty which India is being forced to adhere to
D. codename of Pakistani nuclear arsenal

70. The disagreement between Lok Sabha and Rajya Sabha is solved by:
A. setting up Joint Select Committee
B. dissolving Lok Sabha
C. setting up adjudication committee
D. calling a joint session

71. The national anthem was written by ..... and was translated into English by .....
A. Bankim Chandra Chatterji, Aurobindo Ghosh
B. Rabindra Nath Tagore, Aurobindo Ghosh
C. Bankim Chandra Chatterji, Rabindra Nath Tagore
D. the national anthem was originally written in English and was translated later

72. The tear in human body is a solution of :
A. Sodium hydroxide and sodium chloride
B. Calcium bicarbonate and sodium chloride
C. Magnesium bicarbonate and sodium hydroxide
D. Sodium bicarbonate and Magnesium chloride

73. The drug seroxat is
A. a new medicine for treating the lepers.
B. a new medicine developed by British scientists and is used for the treatment of shyness and social phobia
C. is anti-AIDS therapy developed by France
D. is an antacid developed in India under guidance of WHO

74. What is "Bermuda Triangle" sometimes referred to as the "Grakeyard of ships", located?
A. in the South Pacific ocean
B. in the North Atlantic ocean
C. in the Indian ocean
D. in the Arctic ocean

75. The theory propounded by Nobel laurate Professor Amartya Sen–is commonly known as
A. The Famine Economics
B. The Theory of Economic Divide
C. The Amartya Sen Shift
D. The Amartya Sen Divide

76. Which is known as the Electronics City of India?
A. Tumkoor B. Secunderabad
C. Bhopal D. None of the above

77. The main objective behind the creation of concept of *Navratnas* in the public sector was
A. to increase the control of the PSUs over economy
B. to boost local manufacturing and exports in the core sectors
C. to improve the functional autonomy
D. to improve their image and efficiency by giving them high status

78. The North American seaport on the Pacific side is
A. Baltimore B. Boston
C. New York D. Seattle

79. The old name of Harare was
A. Sam B. Rhodesia
C. Salisbury D. Batavia

80. The famous Prince of Wales Museum is located in
A. Mumbai B. Kolkata
C. Vadodara D. Bangalore

81. Who invented Atom Bomb (Uranium Fission)?
A. A W Haffmann B. Otto Hahn
C. A Einstein D. None of the above

82. The first ever woman to go into space was
A. Kalpana Chawla
B. Valentina Tereshkova
C. Mary Pierce
D. None of the above

83. The highest mountain peak in India is
A. K-2 B. Everest
C. Kanchanjunga D. Makalu-I

84. The "Garden City" of England is
A. Portsmouth B. Manchester
C. Kent D. Warwickshire

85. *Habeas Corpus* is
A. an order of the International Court of Justice
B. a type of writ issued by a High Court or Supreme Court against illegal detention of a person.
C. the petition of a lawyer in the Supreme Court on behalf of his client for bail against the orders of any other court in India
D. None of the above

86. If impeachment motion is passed by the American Senate against the US President, he would have to
A. leave office and all his assets created by him during Presidency
B. leave office, lose his pensions, security cover and all those benefits that are accorded to a retired US President
C. jailed for five years and will not get any benefits.
D. retire honourably with all his benefits, compensations, assets and pensions remaining intact

87. Who appoints the non-permanent members of the UN Security Council?
A. the permanent members
B. the General Assembly
C. the International Court of Justice
D. None of the above

88. The Preamble of the Constitution was amended by:
A. 1st amendment B. 26th amendment
C. 42nd amendment D. 44th amendment

89. The only President to be elected twice is:
A. S. Radhakrishnan B. V.V. Giri
C. Rajendra Prasad D. N.S. Reddy

90. The official airline of Australia is
A. SIA B. Lufthansa
C. Modiluft D. None of the above

91. Which one of the following types of coal contains a higher percentage of carbon than the rest?
A. Bituminous Coal B. Lignite
C. Anthracite D. Peat

92. Ten Commandments were revealed by God to:
A. Abraham B. Moses
C. Jesus D. Peter

93. Kalinga in older days, is now known as:
A. Odisha B. Kohima
C. Karnataka D. Maharashtra

94. Bihu festival is celebrated in:
A. Gujarat B. Assam
C. Bihar D. West Bengal

95. Milk is an example of
A. gel B. emulsion
C. suspension D. mixture

96. The President can dissolve the Lok Sabha before expiry of its term, on the advice of:
A. Prime Minister
B. Speaker
C. Vice-President
D. Election Commissioner

97. In a landmark judgement, the Allahabad High Court ruled that
A. Capital Sentence is not to be imposed upon the rapists
B. pension is the fundamental right of the government employees
C. the Supreme Court should not be bothered for cases of financial compensation
D. None of the above

98. Tughlaq dynasty occupied Delhi throne after decline of:
A. Suri dynasty B. Slave dynasty
C. Lodhi dynasty D. Khilji dynasty

99. Governors of states are:
A. appointed by Chief Ministers
B. appointed by the President
C. elected by members of Legislative Assembly
D. elected by people

100. The partition of Bengal was carried out by:
A. Lord Curzon B. Lord Minto
C. Lord Canning D. Lord Ripon

101. The Air Force Day falls on
A. October 10 B. October 9
C. September 5 D. October 8

102. MAD stands for
A. Most Active Disease
B. Mica Aluminium Duo
C. Mutually Assured Death
D. Mutually Assured Destruction

103. "Disguised Unemployment" means
A. more persons employed for a job that only a few could accomplish
B. people without any technical jobs
C. woman without jobs in rural areas
D. employment of children in factories

104. In India, an active volcano is situated at
A. Lakshadweep
B. Chhotanagpur Plateau
C. Andaman and Nicobar
D. Malawa Plateau

105. The first country to establish trade relationships with India was
A. England B. France
C. Holland D. Portugal

106. Which has the highest share of electrical power generation in India?
A. thermal power
B. nuclear power
C. hydro-power
D. naphtha-based and gas-based power

107. The great ocean liner, known to be the best and luxurious during her times, sank in the year
A. 1902 B. 1912
C. 1908 D. 1889

108. Who among the following is known as the Indian Napoleon?
A. Chandra Gupta Maurya
B. Bindusar
C. Samudra Gupta
D. Harshvardhana

109. Time gap between two sessions of Parliament cannot exceed:
A. 3 months B. 6 months
C. 1 year D. no fixed gap

110. In which state, Panchayati Raj was introduced for the first time?
A. Bihar B. Punjab
C. Rajasthan D. Andhra Pradesh

111. Which one is not a national duty?
A. Respect the Constitution
B. Respect the President
C. Defend the country
D. Protect natural environment

112. Treaty of Seringapatam was signed between:
A. Tipu Sultan and Nawab of Hyderabad
B. Tipu Sultan and English
C. Tipu Sultan & Rani of Jhansi
D. Tipu Sultan and French

113. NHRC stands for
A. National Hydro Research Committee
B. National Handicapped Rahabilitation Council
C. National Human Rights Commission
D. None of the above

114. "Water water everywhere but not a drop to drink" who stated these lines in a poem?
A. John Milton
B. Samuel Taylor Coleridge
C. Lord Byron
D. P.B. Shelley

115. Rabindranath Tagore gave up his knighthood after:
A. Jallianwala Bagh Tragedy
B. Introduction of separate electorates
C. Bengal faminine
D. Bengal Partition

116. Which country is known as the land of golden wool?
A. India B. Turkey
C. Australia D. Myanmar

117. BIFR stands for
A. Bilateral and International Foreign Regulation
B. Board of Industrial Financial Resurrection

C. Board of Industrial and Financial Reconstruction
D. None of the above

118. Pinaca is a
A. drug for curing AIDS
B. multi-barrel rocket system
C. fighter aircraft developed by HAL
D. codename of the nuclear test operation carried out on May 11, 1998

119. Vice-President is ex-officio:
A. Member of Rajya Sabha
B. Chairman of Rajya Sabha
C. Member of Lok Sabha
D. Speaker of Lok Sabha

120. Vitamin C is not available in this food in sufficiently large quantities.
A. lemon B. tomato
C. cod liver oil D. fresh fruits

121. This book was not written in a jail
A. *Glimpses of World History* – J L Nehru
B. *The Bible* (German) – Martin Luther
C. *Les Miserables* – Victor Hugo
D. *Yama* – Mahadevi Verma

122. Who among the following can be removed from office through impeachment by Parliament?
A. Speaker of Lok Sabha
B. Prime Minister
C. President of India
D. Vice-President of India

123. The following is not the function of the liver.
A. to store excesssive sugar in the form of glycogen
B. the produce an antidote for neutralising poison
C. to manufacture red blood corpuscles
D. to purify the blood through bile

124. A fascist is a person whose views are extremely
A. left-winged B. rational
C. right-winged D. liberal

125. The famous mathematician and a professor of Astronomy designed this building in London
A. Westminister Abbey
B. St Paul's Cathedral
C. Stock Exchange
D. Tower of London

126. Which one of the following sounds cannot be heard by a human ear?
A. 30,000 vibrations per second
B. 10,000 vibrations per second
C. 1,000 vibrations per second
D. 300 vibrations per second

127. A weather balloon may not be inflated completely on the ground because
A. it cannot withstand the atmospheric pressure if inflated fully
B. if the balloon is inflated fully on ground, fuel consumption would be higher
C. the air inside the balloon expands as it rises and hence, the balloon could get burst
D. None of the above

128. Which one of the following vitamins is stored in the liver?
A. Vitamin C
B. Vitamin B_{12}
C. Vitamin A
D. Vitamin K and Vitamin A

129. All of the following are plant products except
A. silk B. cork
C. hemp D. linen

130. Which one of the following organs in the human body is known as "Adam's Apple"?
A. thyroid B. liver
C. thymus D. adrenal

131. Insecticides or medicines could be harmful
A. to the insects and weeds as they kill them instantaneously upon consumption
B. to the habitat as the environment could become polluted due to excessive usage of chemicals in our crop management processes
C. to the human beings and animals who consume the food adulterated by the insecticides and weedicides
D. to the transporters and movers of the crops who could inhale noxious fumes of insecticides and weedicides

132. Name the assassin of John Lennon
A. Art Buchwald
B. Lee Oswald
C. Mark David Chapman
D. None of the above

133. Which one of the following is not a sprinter?
A. Marion Jones
B. Florence Griffith Joyner
C. Ben Johnson
D. Susie O' Neill

134. Which of the following is called the "Gateway to the Pacific"?
A. Suez Canal B. Bering Sea
C. Panama Canal D. Gulf of Alaska

135. Which one of the following statements is true regarding the treaty on banning the land-mines?
A. the USA does not want to sign the CTBT
B. the treaty was kept open for signatures in Ottawa in December, 1997.
C. India has already signed it
D. A and B are true

136. Similipal Tiger reserve is situated in:
A. Madhya Pradesh B. Uttarakhand
C. Maharashtra D. Odisha

137. The famous Gandhian, who was also known as the "Frontier Gandhi," is
A. Liaqat Ali Khan
B. Yusuf Khan
C. Khan Abdul Ghaffar Khan
D. Abdul Wali Khan

138. Which one of the following is an alloy?
A. copper B. lanthanum
C. bronze D. uranium

139. World Environment Day is celebrated on
A. June 4 B. June 5
C. June 7 D. March 5

140. This country is the largest producer of cotton in the world.
A. India B. China
C. Egypt D. the USA

141. The quorum required to the Rajya Sabha is:
A. 100 B. 35
C. 25 D. 30

142. The temples of Khajuraho were built by
A. Chalukyas B. Pallavas
C. Rashtrakutas D. Chandelas

143. National Remote Sensing Agency (NRSA) is located at:
A. Hyderabad
B. Bengaluru
C. Thiruvananthapuram
D. Gadanki, near Tirupati

144. The clones for .... and .... have been developed.
A. man, cow B. crow, sheep
C. rat, cat D. sheep, rat

145. AWWA stands for
A. All Women Welfare Association
B. Army Wives Welfare Association
C. Airport Weather and Welfare Authority
D. None of the above

146. The popular book *The Gift of Time* by Jonathan Schell, deals with
A. the lewid affair of Bill Clinton and Monica Lewinsky
B. the elimination of nuclear weapons from the world
C. Indo-US relationships
D. the deteriorating environment in industrial America

147. How can a person move on a hard icy surface?
A. he should use roller skates
B. he should hop, sneeze, jump and step in the direction which is opposite to the direction of his required movement
C. he should hop, sneeze, jump and step in the direction in which the movement is required
D. he should skid on his knees and hands

148. The first conference of Non-Aligned Movement was held at:
A. The Hague
B. Moscow
C. Great Britain
D. Belgrade

149. Who is regarded as the founder of the scientific socialism?
A. Rousseau B. Karl Marx
C. Engles D. Lenin

150. Pyroclastics are
A. non-toxic gases
B. lava flows
C. fragments of hot rock and spattering lava
D. pollutant chemicals from a leather factory

151. Which one of the following is not a sedimentary rock?

A. slate B. limestone
C. clay D. sandstone

152. Oketa is

A. used to define human-induced climatic changes
B. used to describe increasing drought periods of high magnitudes
C. a unit to describe the prevailing cloudiness
D. None of the above

153. The following state produces the maximum quantities (85 percent) of raw silk in India

A. Kerala B. Jammu & Kashmir
C. Karnataka D. Tamil Nadu

154. Salal Hydro Electric Project is situated on the river

A. Beas B. Jhelum
C. Chenab D. Sutlej

155. Which is the largest island sea in the world?

A. Caribbean Sea B. Mediterranean Sea
C. Red Sea D. Beaufort Sea

156. What is the name of the bell used at the Lloyds in London?

A. The Great Bell B. The Charmer
C. The Tower Bell D. Lutine

157. What are "The Hagiographs?"

A. These are the poems written by Lord Byron
B. These are the holy writings of Jewish scriptures
C. These are the geographical lines representing same rainfall levels
D. None of the above

158. Which one of the following forms would provide the lowest protection?

A. Patent B. Trademark
C. Copyright D. Logo

159. The twenty-fifth State of India is

A. Goa B. Nagaland
C. Mizoram D. Delhi

160. What does the 17th Parallel line separate?

A. South and North America
B. North and South Korea
C. South and North Yemen
D. South and North Vietnam

161. Operation Flood-II, the prestigious milk products revolution of India, was initiated on

A. October 1, 1979 B. October 2, 1979
C. January 26, 1979 D. October 2, 1978

162. After World War I, the peace treaty was signed in:

A. Geneva B. Versailles
C. Paris D. Venice

163. Potassium chloride is given to the patient for

A. curing his bleeding gums
B. reducing his cholestrol level
C. reducing his blood pressure
D. alleviating his arthiritis pain

164. What is notation?

A. It is another word for "Mutually Assured Destruction"
B. It is the Latin deformation of the phrase "to swim"
C. It is a term used to denote the growth of illeterate masses
D. None of the above

165. The hideout of Adolf Hitler in the mountains was

A. Stuttgart B. Heidelberg
C. Berchtesgaden D. Both A and C

166. Who stated, "Where wealth accumulates decay?"

A. J M Keynes B. Adam Smith
C. Frederic Engels D. Oliver Goldsmith

167. Who was the national leader who wrote History of India on the walls of the Andaman Cellular Jail?

A. Ambedkar B. Vir Savarkar
C. Nandlal Bose D. Jyotiba Phule

168. The USA does not possess the following space shuttle

A. Columbia B. Atlantis
C. Challenger D. Discovery

169. The term "White Elephant" is used to denote

A. very bright and white item
B. very costly and expensive item
C. an item or a head that is very costly to maintain
D. an item or a head that is a part of the national economic budget of a country

170. Kolar Gold Mines are in this state.

A. Karnataka B. Bihar
C. Odisha D. Madhya Pradesh

171. Which of the following is a plant hormone?
A. Oestrogen B. Cytokinin
C. Thyroxin D. Insulin

172. Which one of the following is not an alkali?
A. sodium hydroxide
B. calcium carbonate
C. magnesium hydroxide
D. sodium sulphate

173. Polar ice is melting due to greenhouse effect. This would lead to
A. more melting of the polar glaciers and hence, subsequent submerging of land areas of earth
B. increasing temperatures on polar caps
C. reduction in temperature of ocean waters and rise in temperature of the Arctic circle waters as well as those of the Antartic circle waters
D. no impact

174. *India 2020* is a book written by
A. Trilok Gurtu
B. Khushwant Singh
C. P Chidambaram
D. A P J Abdul Kalaam

175. The Panama Canal connects:
A. The Pacific and Atlantic Oceans
B. The Pacific and Arctic Oceans
C. The Atlantic and Arctic Oceans
D. The Atlantic and Indian Oceans

176. The following are single cell structures
A. Paramaecium B. Amoebia
C. Both A and B D. None of A or B

177. 'The Last Supper' was painted by:
A. Picasso B. Francis Bacon
C. Michaelangelo D. Raphael

178. The plants, which can resist high temperatures, are known as
A. thermophilic B. thermophobic
C. thermoduric D. Both A and B

179. Which one of the following vaccines is used for controlling tuberculosis among the cattle?
A. Cell Culture Vaccine
B. Goat Tissue Adapted Vaccine
C. Adjuvant Vaccine
D. BCG Vaccine

180. Which one of the following chemicals is carcinogenic if inhaled?
A. carbon dioxide
B. suspended particulate matter
C. lead oxide
D. sulphur dioxide

181. What is a "Tenurial System?"
A. It is a system that identifies the ownership of land and the relationship of the land owner with the actual cultivator
B. It identities the land size and the *modus-operandi* of its usage
C. It identifies the ownership of the land
D. None of the above

182. Pulses are deficient in
A. methionine B. lysine
C. leusine D. iso-leusine

183. Which types of roses are grown in India for industrial applications?
A. R Centripetala and Bushra Rose
B. R Damascena Var Bifera
C. Rosa Damascena
D. A, B and C

184. Why sprinkler irrigation is preferred over other methods of irrigation?
A. It is a cheap method and does not require canal-digging and canal maintenance
B. It uses water effectively and water resolves are optimally utilised
C. It does not require well-digging measures which are costly
D. It supplies water only to those fields where the same is required

185. The size of clay particles is
A. greater than 0.2 mm
B. 0.02 mm – 0.2 mm
C. 0.002 mm – 0.02 mm
D. less than 0.002 mm

186. Which one of the following plants is of great medicinal value?
A. Ranwolfia Serpentiana
B. Thea Sinesis
C. Coffea Robusta
D. Ficus Religiosa

187. Biological control agents of soil borne plant pathogens act by
A. rapidly repleting nutrients and thereby, causing starvation and death of the pathogen

B. secreting toxic metabolitics
C. direct parastism or predation on the pathogens
D. All of the above

188. Nearly 80 percent of sugarcane in India is planted during
A. July – December B. May – August
C. June – August D. December – April

189. Soluble salt content of soil is determined by measuring its
A. pH Value
B. organic matter content
C. Sulphur content
D. electrical conductivity

190. Operation Flood is related to ..... whereas development of fisheries is related to .....
A. white revolution, black revolution
B. white revolution, blue revolution
C. green revolution, blue revolution
D. blue revolution, green revolution

191. An upper air wind system with very high velocities in certain parts of the atmosphere is called
A. Cyclone B. Anticyclone
C. Jet stream D. Tsunami

192. "Mixed Farming" refers to
A. farming by traditional and modern methods
B. agriculture and dairy farming clubbed together
C. farming without synthetic fertilisers but with traditional manure
D. farming with synthetic fertilisers and with traditional manure

193. The main constituent of *Gobar Gas* is
A. butane B. carbon monoxide
C. methane D. octane

194. Speed of sound waves is maximum in
A. solids B. liquids
C. gases D. vacuum

195. When a body gets positively charged, it actually
A. gains electrons
B. loses electrons
C. becomes a donor of ions
D. becomes a receptor of ions

196. Which type of nerves carries impulses from the sense organs in response to the stimulus?
A. sensory B. motor
C. secretory D. None of the above

197. Which gas does not pollute air (for human and animal consumption)?
A. carbon monoxide B. nitrogen dioxide
C. sulphur dioxide D. carbon dioxide

198. The human brain sends and receives signals as
A. electrical impulses B. chemical impulses
C. motor movements D. either A or B

199. "Foot and Mouth" disease attacks
A. cattle B. pigs and cattle
C. sheep and pigs D. cattle, sheep and pigs

200. While returning to earth, the spacecraft has a total communication blackout. The reason is
A. during the re-entry period, the density of the plasma generated by the intense functional heat is so high that the operational frequencies used for communication become much lesser than the plasma cut-off frequency, thus resulting in a total blackout
B. the electromagnetic waves present in the space above the earth temporarily over-power the communication system of the aircraft, thus completely crippling its operation and transmission
C. the force of gravity counters the radiowaves emitted by the aircraft
D. None of the above

ANSWERS

1	2	3	4	5	6	7	8	9	10
C	B	A	D	B	B	B	B	B	A
11	**12**	**13**	**14**	**15**	**16**	**17**	**18**	**19**	**20**
B	C	D	A	A	C	B	C	A	B

21	22	23	24	25	26	27	28	29	30
D	B	B	D	D	C	A	C	C	C
31	**32**	**33**	**34**	**35**	**36**	**37**	**38**	**39**	**40**
C	A	A	C	D	C	A	B	B	D
41	**42**	**43**	**44**	**45**	**46**	**47**	**48**	**49**	**50**
B	C	B	B	C	D	A	A	D	A
51	**52**	**53**	**54**	**55**	**56**	**57**	**58**	**59**	**60**
D	A	C	A	C	B	C	A	C	C
61	**62**	**63**	**64**	**65**	**66**	**67**	**68**	**69**	**70**
B	A	C	B	D	D	A	C	C	D
71	**72**	**73**	**74**	**75**	**76**	**77**	**78**	**79**	**80**
B	B	B	B	C	D	C	D	C	A
81	**82**	**83**	**84**	**85**	**86**	**87**	**88**	**89**	**90**
B	B	A	C	B	B	B	C	C	D
91	**92**	**93**	**94**	**95**	**96**	**97**	**98**	**99**	**100**
C	B	A	B	B	A	B	D	B	A
101	**102**	**103**	**104**	**105**	**106**	**107**	**108**	**109**	**110**
D	D	A	C	D	A	B	C	B	C
111	**112**	**113**	**114**	**115**	**116**	**117**	**118**	**119**	**120**
B	B	C	B	A	C	C	B	B	C
121	**122**	**123**	**124**	**125**	**126**	**127**	**128**	**129**	**130**
D	C	D	C	B	A	C	C	A	A
131	**132**	**133**	**134**	**135**	**136**	**137**	**138**	**139**	**140**
C	C	D	C	D	D	C	C	B	B
141	**142**	**143**	**144**	**145**	**146**	**147**	**148**	**149**	**150**
C	D	A	D	B	B	B	D	B	C
151	**152**	**153**	**154**	**155**	**156**	**157**	**158**	**159**	**160**
A	C	C	C	B	D	B	A	A	D
161	**162**	**163**	**164**	**165**	**166**	**167**	**168**	**169**	**170**
B	B	C	B	C	D	B	C	C	A
171	**172**	**173**	**174**	**175**	**176**	**177**	**178**	**179**	**180**
B	D	A	D	A	C	C	C	D	C
181	**182**	**183**	**184**	**185**	**186**	**187**	**188**	**189**	**190**
A	A	D	B	D	A	D	D	D	B
191	**192**	**193**	**194**	**195**	**196**	**197**	**198**	**199**	**200**
C	B	C	A	B	A	D	B	D	A

SPORTS

1. The first winning stroke in Lawn Tennis gives the player:
A. 2 points B. 1 point
C. 10 points D. 15 points

2. Which of the following game is played for stipulated period of 70 minutes?
A. Hockey B. Football
C. Rugby D. Basketball

3. 'Merdeka cup' is associated with:
A. Golf
B. Football
C. Squash
D. Hockey

4. Arjuna Award has been instituted for outstanding contribution in the field of
A. Social Service

B. Games and Sports
C. Literature
D. Art and Music

5. Murugappa Gold Cup is associated with:
A. Football B. Polo
C. Hockey D. Bridge

6. Jimmy Connors and Geoff Boycott are related with following games respectively:
A. Tennis, Football B. Tennis, Cricket
C. Chess, Cricket D. Football, Hockey

7. The winner of the Golden Boot Award at the World Cup Soccer tournament organised in Yokohama was .... and he scored ...... goals.
A. Zinedine Zidane, four
B. Davor Suker, six
C. Ronaldo, eight
D. None of the above

8. Number of players in a team of Water polo is:
A. 7 B. 5
C. 9 D. 11

9. The term 'Steeple Chase' is associated with which of the following games
A. Polo B. Tennis
C. Horse Racing D. Cricket

10. Who is known as Father of India's "White Revolution" and "Operation Flood"?
A. Dr. Verghese Kurien
B. J.B. Kripalani
C. Baba Amte
D. Har Gobind Khorana

11. The first Olympic games were revived by ..... in 1896 at Athens
A. Lord Welsley
B. Queen Elizabeth-I
C. Baron Piere de Cubertin
D. None of the above

12. The national game of the USA is
A. swimming B. baseball
C. athletics D. None of the above

13. Jules Rimmet Cup is associated with
A. hockey B. archery
C. football D. table tennis

14. The approximate weight of a cricket ball is
A. 5.25 Oz B. 6.30 Oz
C. 7.20 Oz D. 8.25 Oz

15. The number of players on each side in a basketball match is
A. 10 B. 6
C. 5 D. 8

16. The first woman in the history of US open Championship to have played 100 matches, is:
A. Martina Navaratilova
B. Chris Evert
C. Steffi Graf
D. Helena Sukova

17. Swaythling Cup is associated with
A. World Table Tennis Tournament (men)
B. World Table Tennis Tournament (university)
C. World Table Tennis tournament (women)
D. World Hockey Tournament (university)

18. Which one of the following is not a cricket - playing nation?
A. West Indies B. Zimbabwe
C. Kenya D. Columbia

19. The first recipient of Major Dhyan Chand Khel Ratna Award (1991-92) was:
A. Geet Sethi B. N Kunjurani Devi
C. V Anand D. P K Garg

20. The first Olympic Games were held at Olympia (Greece) in the year:
A. 300 BC B. 776 BC
C. 500 BC D. 394 AD

21. Which of the following is the National Game of Spain?
A. Bull fighting B. Baseball
C. Rugby D. Golf

22. 'Ashes' is the name of a series between ..... and ..... and it relates to .....
A. Pakistan, Australia, Hockey
B. India, England, Cricket
C. England, Australia, Cricket
D. New Zealand, Australia, Cricket

23. The term "Butterfly Stroke" is associated with
A. Kabaddi B. Wrestling
C. Polo D. Swimming

24. Neeraj Chopra is associated with which sports?
A. Javelin Throw B. Tennis
C. Hockey D. Football

25. 'Gambit' is a term normally associated with
A. Bridge B. Chess
C. Billiards D. Polo

26. 'Bunker' and 'Chukker' are the two terms associated with
A. Polo B. Rowing
C. Bungey Jumping D. Ice Hockey

27. A Lawn Tennis court measures
A. 78 feet by 28 feet
B. 79 feet by 29 feet
C. 76 feet by 26 feet
D. 70 feet by 24 feet

28. Who scored the fastest timing (in case of an under-13 swimmer) for crossing the English Channel?
A. Arati Saha
B. Uday Shenoy
C. Rihen Mehta
D. Rupali Ramdas Ropal

29. Which one of the following has been entrusted with the responsibility of training coaches in various disciplines of sports?
A. Tata Football Academy
B. Ministry of Human Resource Development
C. Netaji Subhash Institute of Sports
D. Lakshmibai National College of Physical Education

30. The term 'Tee' is associated with which of the following sports?
A. Table Tennis
B. Polo
C. Golf
D. Judo

31. 'Deodhar Trophy' is associated with which of the following games?
A. Hockey B. Cricket
C. Football D. Basketball

32. Who was the first deaf & dumb swimmer in the world to swim 30 km Gibralter strait?
A. Des Renford
B. Mihir Sen
C. Arti Pradhan
D. Taranath Shenoy

33. The height of the net in the centre of the tennis court is
A. 3 feet, 5 inches B. 3 feet, 2 inches
C. 2 feet, 8 inches D. 2 feet, 6 inches

34. 'Canon' is a sports term associated with the following game.
A. Billiards B. Volleyball
C. Shot-Put D. Table Tennis

35. The Himalayan Mountaineering Institute is located in
A. Leh B. Darjeeling
C. Kohima D. Dispur

36. The diameter of a golf hole is
A. 4.36 inches B. 4.50 inches
C. 5.63 inches D. 4.75 inches

37. The total distance of a Marathon Race is ..... miles and ..... yards.
A. 29, 388 B. 26, 380
C. 26, 385 D. 25, 372

38. The first woman, who won six gold medals in a single Olympics tournament, was
A. Evelyn Ashford
B. Florence Griffth Joyner
C. Kristin Otto
D. Susi Susanti

39. In which year on account of a decree issued by Roman Emperor the Olympic Games were ceased to be played?
A. 350 AD B. 394 AD
C. 300 BC D. 384 AD

40. Putney (UK) is a place most frequently associated with
A. swimming B. horse racing
C. boat rowing D. polo

41. Rafael Nadal is associated with which sports?
A. Tennis B. Badminton
C. Cricket D. None of the above

42. The term 'Finesse' is normally associated with this game.
A. Chess B. Bridge
C. Snooker D. Rowing

43. The following trophy is not associated with cricket.
A. Ranji Trophy
B. Rohintan Baria Trophy
C. Singer-Akai-Nidahas Trophy
D. Lady Rattan Tata Trophy

44. Tonya Harding is a controversial athlete and has been associated with the following game.
A. Rowing B. Table Tennis
C. Figure Skating D. Boxing

45. When and where the first Asian Games were held?

A. 1955, Seoul B. 1951, New Delhi

C. 1954, Manila D. 1970, Bangkok

46. Who among the following won Gold medal in Tokyo Olympics 2020?

A. Pradeep Verma

B. Mangal Singh

C. Neeraj Chopra

D. P.V. Sindhu

47. What is the measurement of a Golf Hole?

A. 3½ inch in diameter

B. 4½ inch in diameter

C. 7½ centimeter in diameter

D. 10 inch in diameter

48. The term 'Diamond' is associated with the game of:

A. Baseball B. Bridge

C. Basketball D. Billiards

49. K Sasikaran is well known as a

A. table tennis player B. swimmer

C. chess player D. football player

50. Who won men's single at the Australian Open 2025?

A. Jannik Sinner

B. Roger Federer

C. Stanislas Wawrinka

D. Alexander Zverev

ANSWERS

1	**2**	**3**	**4**	**5**	**6**	**7**	**8**	**9**	**10**
D	A	B	B	C	B	C	A	C	A
11	**12**	**13**	**14**	**15**	**16**	**17**	**18**	**19**	**20**
C	B	C	A	C	B	A	D	C	B
21	**22**	**23**	**24**	**25**	**26**	**27**	**28**	**29**	**30**
A	C	D	A	B	A	A	D	C	C
31	**32**	**33**	**34**	**35**	**36**	**37**	**38**	**39**	**40**
B	D	B	A	B	B	C	C	B	C
41	**42**	**43**	**44**	**45**	**46**	**47**	**48**	**49**	**50**
A	B	D	C	B	C	B	A	C	A

HONOURS AND AWARDS

1. In which of the following years 'Nobel Prizes' were instituted?

A. 1910 B. 1905

C. 1901 D. 1911

2. The writer who refused the Nobel Prize for Literature was:

A. Winston Churchill

B. Prem Chand

C. Jean Paul Sartre

D. None of the above

3. Which country awards the Noble Prize?

A. USA B. India

C. Russia D. Sweden

4. In which of the following years Arjuna Awards were instituted

A. 1951 B. 1971

C. 1961 D. 1965

5. National Awards for Popularising Science was instituted in the year

A. 1981 B. 1985

C. 1987 D. 1988

6. The Government of which state has instituted the 'Tansen Samman'?

A. Madhya Pradesh B. Uttar Pradesh

C. Gujarat D. Maharashtra

7. The Lifetime Achievement Award, instituted by DRDO, has been awarded to an eminent nuclear scientist. His name is

A. Dr A P J Abdul Kalam

B. Mr B D Nagchowdhary

C. Mr George Fernandes

D. Mr Mulayam Singh Yadav

8. Who returned the award of 'Sir' given by the British government in protest against the "Jallianwala Bagh Massacre" on April 13, 1919?
A. Prem Chand
B. Thomas Roe
C. Rabindra Nath Tagore
D. Dada Bhai Nauroji

9. Nobel Prize is not awarded in the following disciplines
A. Chemistry and Physics
B. Literature and Peace
C. Economics and Medicine
D. Geography and Space Research

10. In which year Nehru Award for International Understanding instituted
A. 1965 B. 1969
C. 1974 D. 1964

11. Which of the following Indians was awarded Legion D award, the highest civilian awards of France
A. Jawahar Lal Nehru B. Satyajit Ray
C. Mother Teresa D. Shahrukh Khan

12. 'Pulitzer' prizes are awarded to Americans for excellence in
A. Films B. Journalism
C. Medicine D. Social Work

13. C.V. Raman received Nobel Prize in the year
A. 1934 B. 1931
C. 1932 D. 1930

14. Saraswati Samman is awarded by
A. Government of India
B. Sahitya Academy
C. K.K. Birla Foundation
D. Lalit Kala Akademi

15. On which day every year National Awards for Teachers are announced?
A. August 15 B. September 5
C. November 19 D. November 14

16. The National Award given to the distinguished sportsmen/women in India is known as
A. Dronacharya Award
B. Param Vir Chakra
C. Arjun Award
D. Nehru Award

17. The prestigious Ramon Magsaysay Award was instituted in the memory of Mr Ramon Magsaysay who was
A. the Secretary – General of UN
B. the Commander of NATO in Europe
C. the President of the Philippines
D. the President of Cambodia

18. The Kalinga Prize is awarded by UNESCO but it was founded by an Indian. His name is
A. Biju Patnaik B. Sharad Pawar
C. C V Raman D. Piloo Modi

19. Who was the first Indian to receive the World Food Prize?
A. Dr. Verghese Kurien
B. Dr. Amrita Patel
C. Dr. M.S. Swaminathan
D. None of these

20. Jesse Owens Global award is given in the field of:
A. Literature B. Sports
C. Science D. Journalism

21. Nobel Alfred Bernhard after whom Nobel Prizes are given was:
A. Engineer B. Doctor
C. Chemist D. Pilot

22. Grammy Awards are given in the field of
A. painting B. architecture
C. music D. rock dance

23. The highest civilian award of India is
A. *Padma Vibhushan* B. *Padma Shri*
C. *Bharat Ratna* D. *Param Vir Chakra*

24. The highest military award of India is
A. Shaurya Chakra
B. Param Vishisht Sewa Medal
C. Param Vir Chakra
D. Kirti Chakra

25. The first ever B R Ambedkar National Award was given to
A. Baba Amte
B. T Shiv Shankar Pillai
C. International Red Cross
D. National Institute for Social Work and Social Sciences

26. 'Victory Medal' is awarded in:
A. UK B. USA
C. Russia D. France

27. Which one of the following is not a Shram Award

A. Shram Bhushan B. Shram Dev
C. Shram Devi D. Shram Vir

28. Dr Shanti Swaroop Bhatnagar Awards are given in any field of science by

A. Indian Council of Applied Economic Research
B. Defence Research and Development Organisation
C. National Institute for Social Work and Social Sciences
D. Tata Institute of Fundamental Research

29. Who is the winner of the Miss World-2025 contest?

A. Nadia Ferreira
B. Opal Suchata Chuangsri
C. Lalela Mswane
D. Toni-Ann Singh

30. First Miss World Competition was established by 'Miss World Incorporation' in the year

A. 1941 B. 1950
C. 1951 D. 1957

31. The size of an Olympic medal is ..... mm and thickness is ..... mm.

A. 50, 2.5 B. 60, 3.0
C. 60.5, 3.5 D. 55.2, 2.5

32. "Dhanwantari Award" is given in the field of

A. swimming B. Bharata Natyam
C. cinema D. medicine

33. Nobel Prizes are not given for which of the following fields?

A. Physics B. Chemistry
C. Music D. Peace

34. Which is the second Highest Civilian award in India?

A. Padam Vibushan B. Padam Shri
C. Bharat Ratna D. Ashok Chakra

35. Abel Prize is associated with:

A. Mathematics B. Film
C. Music D. Writing

36. The second highest gallantry award in India is:

A. Padam Bhushan B. Vir Chakra
C. Mahavir Chakra D. Ashok Chakra

37. 'Mubarak-Al-Kabir' medal is the highest honour of

A. Kuwait B. Iran
C. Afghanistan D. Iraq

38. Bharatendu Harish Chandra awards are given annually for:

A. best local self administration
B. showing kindness and generosity of unusual kind
C. promoting original writing in Hindi
D. None of the above

39. Who won the Man Booker Prize 2024 for 'Orbital'?

A. Samantha Harvey
B. Subhash Khot
C. Maryam Mirzakhani
D. Arthur Avila

40. Who has been selected for the prestigious Jnanpith award for the year 2024?

A. Alok Puranik
B. Vinod Kumar Shukla
C. Mrinal Pandey
D. Vishwanath Tiwari

41. Name the women sportsperson, who became the first Indian women to hold an honorary rank of Lieutenant Colonel in the countrys's defence forces.

A. Krishna Punia B. Saina Nehwal
C. Sania Mirza D. MC Mary Kom

42. Oscar award is related to

A. books
B. politics
C. European Community
D. films

43. Miss Universe award 2024 has been won by whom?

A. Victoria Kjaer Theilvig
B. Manya Singh
C. Olivia Yace
D. Shree Saini

44. Out of the Gallantry awards — PVSM, AVSM and VSM — the most exceptional medal is

A. PVSM
B. AVSM
C. VSM
D. All have equal recognition status

45. *Jeewan Raksha Padak* is awarded for
A. bravery in the battle front
B. fine display of vocal music skills
C. saving the life of human beings
D. None of the above

46. Who is not eligible for Bharat Ratna?
A. A government official
B. A sportsperson
C. A film actress
D. A Prime Minister

47. Jamnalal Bajaj award is given in the field of
I. Social Work
II. Fine Arts
III. Application of Science and Technology
IV. Literature
A. I and II B. I, II and III
C. II and IV D. I and III

48. In which year Indira Gandhi Peace Prize was instituted?
A. 1985 B. 1984
C. 1986 D. 1987

49. Borlaug Award was instituted for recognising outstanding contribution in the field of:
A. Ecology B. Medicine
C. Agriculture D. Journalism

50. Except Dr. Nelson Mandela, who is the other non-Indian so far honoured with Bharat Ratna
A. Dr. Julius Nyerere
B. Helen Hint
C. Hideki Yuka
D. Khan Abdul Ghaffar Khan

ANSWERS

1	2	3	4	5	6	7	8	9	10
C	C	D	C	C	A	B	C	D	D
11	**12**	**13**	**14**	**15**	**16**	**17**	**18**	**19**	**20**
B	B	D	C	B	C	C	A	C	B
21	**22**	**23**	**24**	**25**	**26**	**27**	**28**	**29**	**30**
C	C	C	C	D	B	B	C	B	C
31	**32**	**33**	**34**	**35**	**36**	**37**	**38**	**39**	**40**
B	D	C	A	A	C	A	C	A	B
41	**42**	**43**	**44**	**45**	**46**	**47**	**48**	**49**	**50**
D	D	A	A	C	A	D	C	C	D

BOOKS AND AUTHORS

1. The book "*The Insider*" is written by
A. Madhav Rao Scindia
B. Nana Patekar
C. Shobha De
D. P V Narasimha Rao

2. *India Wins Freedom* was written by
A. Dadabhai Nauroji
B. Ashfaqulla Khan
C. Sarojini Naidu
D. Maulana Abul Kalam Azad

3. *A Tale of Two Cities* is, in fact, the story of two famous cities. Those cities are
A. Paris and New York
B. London and New York
C. London and Paris
D. Stockholm and New York

4. *Ben Hur* was penned by
A. Lewis Wallace
B. Lord Byron
C. William Shakespeare
D. None of the above

5. *Panchatantra* was written by
A. R K Narayan B. R K Laxman
C. Vishnu Sharma D. None of the above

6. Arundhati Roy has been awarded the prestigious

A. Booker's Prize – 1997
B. Jnanpeeth Award – 1997
C. Sahitya Akademi Award – 1998
D. None of the above

7. Who wrote *Odyssey?*
A. George Orwell B. Homer
C. Dom Moraes D. None of the above

8. Which one of the following was not written by Shakespeare?
A. *As You Like It*
B. *Mcbeth*
C. *Hamlet*
D. *A Farewell to Arms*

9. Lewis Carol wrote a masterpiece. What is its name?
A. *Don Quixote*
B. *Alice in Wonderland*
C. *Adventures of Robinson Crusoe*
D. *Great Expectations*

10. The *Tamil Ramayana* is the work of
A. Tulsidas B. Jayangondar
C. Kambar D. Veda Vyas

11. In *Shrimad Bhagwat Geeta,* Lord Krishna teaches his disciple Arjuna to
A. rise to the occasion and fight with his near and dear ones
B. withdraw from the battlefield
C. do his duty and not to expect anything in return
D. attack the enemy in a planned and meticulous approach

12. Who wrote *Origin of Species?*
A. Charles Darwin
B. Alexander Flaming
C. G.B. Shaw
D. D.H. Lawrence

13. The poet and the well-known friend of Prithvi Raj Chauhan, who wrote *Prithvi Raj Raso,* was
A. Harisena B. Vishnu Datt
C. Chand Bardai D. None of the above

14. The first book was printed in India in the year 1561. Its name was
A. *The spiritual Compendium of the Christian Life*
B. *Aain-e-Akbari*
C. *Babur Nama*
D. *Ram Charit Manas*

15. The famous book *Runs and Ruins* was written by
A. Sir Donald Bradman
B. Sunil Gavaskar
C. Kapil Dev
D. Richard Hadlee

16. Adam Smith wrote the following famous book
A. The Wreck
B. Dr Zhivago
C. The Wealth of Nations
D. Tarzan of the Apes

17. H G Wells is known as a
A. poet
B. science-fiction writer
C. thriller-fiction writer
D. essay writer and critic

18. Tukaram wrote his devotional songs in this language
A. Urdu B. Gujarati
C. Hindi D. Marathi

19. Our ancient scholars and writers used this language for their social, religious and political books and works
A. Tamil
B. Sanskrit
C. Urdu
D. Hindi *(Devanagari)*

20. *Gora* is the hero of a book written by Rabindra Nath Tagore. What is the name of the book?
A. *Geetanjali* B. *Patanjali*
C. *Gora* D. *Twelfth Night*

21. Shylock is
A. the villain *in A Pound of Flesh* by William Shakespeare
B. an old Jew who is a famous hero of the Israeli nation
C. the hero of *Miranda,* written by William Shakespeare
D. the comic character of *Alice In the Wonderland* by Lewis Caroll

22. The following was a famous Hindi author and story-writer

A. Shobha De B. Aruna Asaf Ali
C. Mahadevi Verma D. Amrita Pritam

23. *Mudrarakshasa* was composed by
A. Vishakhadatta B. Bhavabhuti
C. Sivananda D. Jayadeva

24. *Razor's Edge* was written by
A. Toni Morrison
B. Saul Bellow
C. W Somerset Maugham
D. None of the above

25. *Sakharam Binder* is a famous play written by
A. Anil Barve B. Vijay Tendulkar
C. V S Naipaul D. Tasleema Nasreen

26. The major work of Sir Isaac Newton is
A. *Principia*
B. *Heritage*
C. *Human knowledge*
D. *I Dare*

27. The hero of *The Jungle Book,* written by Rudyard Kipling, is
A. the lion
B. Mowghuli
C. the father of Mowghuli
D. there is no hero

28. Who stated, "Peace hath her victories, no less renowned than war?"
A. Alfred Lord Tennyson
B. William Shakespeare
C. John Milton
D. None of the above

29. Macawber is a character who was created by
A. Thomas Hardy B. P G Wodehouse
C. Charles Dickens D. J W Von Goethe

30. *Pride and Prejudice* was written by
A. Anton Chekhov B. Maxim Gorky
C. Jane Austen D. Anthony West

31. *In the Afternoon Time* is the English translation of the autobiography of the famous poet, Harivansh Rai Bachchan. The autobiography was translated into English by
A. Vikram Seth B. Dr Rupert Snell
C. William Faulkner D. P D Tandon

32. Who is the author of the book *The Celestine Vision?*
A. Paul Hockins B. Salman Rushdie
C. Joseph Conrad D. James Redfield

33. The author of the famous book *Blue Mountain Revisited* is
A. Charles Kingsley
B. Virginia Woolf
C. Arthur Koestler
D. Peter Topkins

34. Homer was the great poet of the following language
A. Italian B. Greek
C. Arabic D. French

35. Hard Choices is a famous book written by :
A. Hillary Clinton
B. Barack Obama
C. Narendra Modi
D. Imran Khan

36. *Godaan* was written by Munshi Prem Chand and it depicts
A. the methodology for taking adequate care of the cows
B. exploitation of simple rural folk by the rich landlords of rural India
C. the mutiny of 1857 in which, Indians refused to bite the *Kartoos* made with cow beef
D. None of the above

37. Manu wrote a book during ancient times in which, he divided the Aryan society into four distinct classes. What was the name of the book?
A. *Arthashastra*
B. *Manusmriti*
C. *Moti Mahal*
D. *My Truth*

38. R. Venkataraman wrote *My Presidential Years.* What was the main theme of the book?
A. It described the aristocratic procedures being followed in the *Rashtrapati Bhawan* during his tenure as President
B. It described the power equations and ploys in the centre and in the states during his term
C. It described how he felt caged while he was President due to a load of procedures and formalities
D. It explained the machinations of the political party which was in power during his tenure as President

39. The hero of the play cried in the end, "Et Tu, Brute!" and died. Which is the play and who is the author?
A. The Wealth of Nations — Adam Smith
B. Mein Kempf — Adolf Hitler
C. Julius Caesar — William Shakespeare
D. None of the above

40. Don Veto Corleone was the undisputed king of the underworld in this novel. This masterpiece was also converted into a film in which Al Pacino played the role of the Don. What is the name of the novel and that of the author?
A. *A Farewell to Arms* — E Hemingway
B. *The Godfather* — Mario Puzo
C. *From Here to Eternity* — James Jones
D. *Dialogue with Death* — Arthur Koestler

41. *Gypsy Camp Vanishes Into the Blue* was a famous blockbuster movie made by the erstwhile USSR. The original story was written by a famous author. His name is
A. Leo Tolstoy
B. Anton Chekhov
C. Maxim Gorky
D. Leon Uris

42. The total number of *Puranas* written during the Vedic age is
A. 22 B. 9
C. 18 D. 25

43. Who wrote Monsoon Memories?
A. Jo Nesbo
B. Ratna
C. Renita D'Silva
D. Amartya Sen

44. 'Waiting for a Visa' is the autobiography of which of the following persons:
A. Indira Gandhi
B. Mahatma Gandhi
C. Jawaharlal Nehru
D. B.R. Ambedkar

45. According to *The Ramayana,* who received the last teaching lessons from the knowledgeable Ravana while he was on his death-bed?
A. Rama
B. Sugreeva
C. Laxmana
D. Both A and C

46. He was a German but he saved many a Jew from the cruel hands of the Nazis. A movie was made on this theme which won the coveted Oscar Prize. The book and the author are
A. *Operation Shylock* — Philip Roth
B. *Schindler's List* — Thomas Keneally
C. *The Rescue* — Joseph Conrad
D. *The Slave* — Isaac Bashevis Singer

47. He was the favourite assistant of Sherlock Holmes, the famous character created by Arthur Conan Doyle. His name is
A. Zhivago B. Watson
C. Hawkins D. Hector

48. He was a former member of British Parliament. He has written many hit fiction novels. One of his novels is
A. Shall We Tell the President?
B. The Rape of the Lock
C. Snow Country
D. Small Land

49. He wrote *Sharmili, Gaylord* and *Kati Patang*. His novels were written in Hindi and some of them have been converted into films also. His name is
A. Gita Mehta
B. B N Mullick
C. Nirad C Chaudhary
D. Gulshan Nanda

50. 'The Lives of Others' is written by..........
A. Neel Mukherjee
B. Charu Singh
C. R.D. Pradhan
D. Shivani Lohia

ANSWERS

1	2	3	4	5	6	7	8	9	10
D	D	C	A	C	A	B	D	B	C

11	12	13	14	15	16	17	18	19	20
C	A	C	A	B	C	B	D	B	C
21	22	23	24	25	26	27	28	29	30
A	C	A	C	B	A	B	C	C	C
31	32	33	34	35	36	37	38	39	40
B	D	D	B	A	B	B	C	C	B
41	42	43	44	45	46	47	48	49	50
C	C	C	D	C	B	B	A	D	A

ECONOMY, BUSINESS AND COMMERCE

1. Who is the Chairman of Island Development Authority?
A. President
B. Prime Minister
C. Finance Minister
D. Minister of Environment

2. World Economic Situation and Prospects Report is associated with:
A. IMF B. World Bank
C. United Nations D. WTO

3. The economies of the Oriental countries depend upon the growth or decline of
A. the American economy
B. the Japanese economy
C. the Korean economy
D. the Thai economy

4. The difference between the monetary policy and the fiscal policy is
A. fiscal policy tries to control aggregate demand through budgetary means whereas monetary policy controls the same through the quantity of money and the rate of interest
B. monetary policy is related to the money supply whereas the fiscal policy is related to the rate of interest
C. monetary policy is automatic whereas the fiscal policy is discretionary
D. both the policies are similar and have similar objectives

5. Which one of the following is a *Navratna* Company?
A. Delhi Vidyut Board
B. National Textiles Corporation
C. Mahanagar Telephone Nigam Ltd
D. Electronics Corporation of India Ltd

6. Which country holds the dubious distinction of becoming the biggest user of anti-dumping duty (ADD) since the Uruguay Round?
A. China B. Japan
C. US D. India

7. Find the odd city with the viewpoint of Indian Railways
A. Chittaranjan B. Chennai
C. Kapurthala D. Trombay

8. Which company released the slogan "Redefining the value of Rupee?"
A. Toshiba B. Samsung
C. Akai D. Panasonic

9. 'Shishu', 'Tarun' and 'Kishore' named enterprises are associated with:
A. SBI
B. IDBI
C. MUDRA Bank
D. NABARD

10. The major field of research of the Nobel laureate, Amartya Sen, is
A. mixed economy
B. welfare economics
C. the Amartya Sen Shift
D. capitalistic economy

11. GST has been implemented in:
A. 2014 B. 2015
C. 2016 D. 2017

12. Which one of the following is not a chief characteristic of FEMA?
A. Current account transactions are permitted unless there are RBI restrictions
B. Capital accounts transactions are permitted unless there are RBI transactions

C. Treatment for violations is harsh and is deemed to be a congnisable and non-bailable offence

D. Enforcement Directorate can arrest the accused in case of violations

13. The current market trends are

A. recession oriented
B. inflation oriented
C. recession oriented with inflation
D. boom oriented

14. Which of the following is not helpful in controlling money supply?

A. CRR
B. Bank Rate
C. Free Market Policy
D. Change in margin requirement

15. This company does not deal in consumer durables?

A. Samsung B. Akai
C. Godrej D. Nestle

16. Find the odd one out.

A. Lintas B. HTA
C. Contract D. LML

17. E-com does not require?

A. Internet connectivity
B. Technological inputs
C. Negotiations through E-mail
D. Knowledge about entertainment groups

18. Which one of the following is not an infrastructure related project?

A. Narmada Valley Project
B. North-South and East-West Corridors
C. Software exports
D. Railway modernisation

19. When the stock markets crash, then

A. stocks sell at lower prices than anticipated
B. scrips sell at higher prices than anticipated
C. the sellers are not very keen to sell in anticipation of sudden rise in values of stocks
D. None of the above

20. What is 'Dumping?'

A. It is the term given by the economists to excavation and digging activities of the MNCs that deal in earth moving equipment
B. It is the sale of the products and services by foreign nations and firms at very low prices so that they could find firm markets in India
C. It is the excessive supply of fast moving consumer goods by a developed country to an under-developed country
D. It is a series of measures taken by Government of India to facilitate international trade

21. Varishtha Pension Bima Yojna has been launched by

A. National Insurance Co.
B. LIC of India
C. Oriental Insurance Co.
D. United India Insurance Co.

22. Which company is the manufacturer of the product brand name 'Spectra?'

A. Telco B. Kinetic
C. LML D. None of the above

23. Who wrote the General Theory of Employment, Interest and Money?

A. Kaldor B. Marx
C. Keynes D. Marshall

24. Which one of the following is not an electronics products manufacturer?

A. Samsung B. Matsushita
C. Motorola D. Ford

25. World Economic Situation and Prospects Report is associated with—

A. IMF
B. World Bank
C. United Nations
D. WTO

26. What is the base year of newly introduced Consumer Price Index (CPI)?

A. 2000 B. 2004
C. 2012 D. 2011

27. The spirit of JIT is to

A. produce that much which could be sold and acquire that much of material inputs that could justify the sales
B. produce less but buy still lesser
C. collect orders from the markets and then produce
D. keep your inventory levels just equal to the market demand for the products

28. 'New Silk Route' is a rail route which links China with the European country—
A. France B. Germany
C. Italy D. Japan

29. Who among the following was first among the European nations to trade with India?
A. Britain B. Spain
C. Portugal D. France

30. GTX Extra is a brand name associated with
A. MRF B. HP
C. IOL D. Castrol

31. In India, the first bank of limited liability managed Indians and founded in 1881 was
A. Hindustan Commercial Bank
B. Oudh Commercial Bank
C. Punjab and Sind Bank
D. Bank of India

32. In the new millennium, the industries related to.....would be facing maximum growth rates?
A. manufacturing
B. FMCGs
C. information technology
D. consumer non-durables

33. Which one of the following items is not exported from India?
A. gold ornaments B. leather items
C. software products D. nuclear weapons

34. The stock value index of the registered companies of a stock exchange is known as
A. Nikkei B. Dow-Jones
C. Sensex D. None of the above

35. India has her only OTCEI in
A. Kolkata B. Indore
C. Mumbai D. New Delhi

36. Estimates of National Income in India are prepared by
A. Ministry of Finance
B. NITI Aayog
C. Reserve Bank of India
D. Central Statistical Organisation

37. If the Rupee becomes stronger vis-a-vis the US Dollar, then
A. exports would rise
B. imports would remain stagnant
C. exports would decline
D. None of the above

38. Which of the following is a subsidiary of RBI?
A. SIDBI
B. NABARD
C. National Housing Bank
D. All of the above

39. Which one of the following is not a core operation of L & T group?
A. Electricals
B. Construction Machinery
C. Shipping
D. Cement

40. The famous breakfast cereal Kellogg was started as .... during its early days of inception.
A. medicine
B. diet for patients in a nursing home
C. breakfast food for some top businessmen of the USA
D. diet enriching ingredient for the school-going children in Europe

41. Who observed, "as the population increases, the economic means of supporting that population do not grow in the same proportion?"
A. Goldsmith B. Malthus
C. Frederic Engels D. Adam Smith

42. The eminent Nobel Laureate–Amartya Sen is known for his research in
A. welfare economics
B. draughts and famines
C. poverty elimination
D. free market system of economy

43. Index 'Residex' is associated with:
A. Share Prices
B. Mutual Fund Prices
C. Land Prices
D. Price Inflation Index

44. The new industrial policy of India was announced in
A. 1996 B. 1991
C. 1997 D. 1998

45. If supply of onions is reduced, then
A. the demand would rise and the prices of the existing stocks would jump up
B. the demand would rise but prices would remain unaffected

C. the demand would fall as the users would avoid taking onions because of the fear of a sharp price rise

D. None of the above

46. How could the government break the vicious cycle of poverty among the poor masses?

A. By providing them with money

B. By providing them with opportunities of employment and entreprenenrship

C. By educating them about family planning

D. By getting loans for them from global financial agencies

47. WTO is dedicated to

A. liberal trade terms between the member nations

B. removal of all the trade protection procedures by all the member nations

C. agreements on patents of agricultural commodities like rice etc.

D. None of the above

48. Under which clause of Income Tax Act, taxpayer gets tax rebate on the premium paid for health insurance?

A. 80A B. 80C

C. 80D D. 80G

49. The basic objective of SIDBI is to

A. give more loans for infrastructure development to the corporate sector

B. grant loans to agricultural farmers for export of their commodities

C. solve the financial problems of small scale industries

D. assist IDBI and ICICI in the process of national industrial development

50. The major function of the Food Corporation of India is:

A. to control the demand side of foodgrains

B. to distribute high yielding variety seeds

C. to check the fluctuation in foodgrain price by controlling supply

D. to extend credit to farmers

ANSWERS

1	2	3	4	5	6	7	8	9	10
B	B	B	A	C	D	D	C	C	B
11	**12**	**13**	**14**	**15**	**16**	**17**	**18**	**19**	**20**
D	D	C	C	D	D	D	C	A	B
21	**22**	**23**	**24**	**25**	**26**	**27**	**28**	**29**	**30**
B	D	C	D	B	C	A	B	C	D
31	**32**	**33**	**34**	**35**	**36**	**37**	**38**	**39**	**40**
B	C	D	C	C	D	C	C	C	B
41	**42**	**43**	**44**	**45**	**46**	**47**	**48**	**49**	**50**
B	A	C	B	A	B	A	C	C	C

BANKING AND FINANCE

1. Which one of the following services is not provided by the mobile banking service?

A. Checking of balance of an account

B. Requesting for an accounts statement

C. Enquiring details of the fixed deposit

D. Asking for share prices of all the stocks at the BSE

2. Scheduled bank is that bank which is:

A. Nationalised

B. Not-nationalised

C. Based at foreign country

D. Included in the Second Schedule of R.B.I.

3. Grameen Bank and Micro Credit are asociated with:

A. Manmohan Singh B. Bill Gates

C. Md. Yunus D. Aung San Su Ki

4. ICICI Bank, prior to commencing its operations as a bank was a/an:

A. Market research group

B. Industrial finance corporation

C. Small-time player in consumer durables
D. Conduct for RRBs

5. If there is a capital flight from India:
A. Exchange rate of rupee will fall
B. Share prices will rise
C. Interest rate will fall
D. Exchange rate of rupee will rise

6. The headquarters of standard Chartered Bank are located at:
A. New York B. Hawai
C. London D. New Delhi

7. The term 'Orange Economy' is referred to:
A. Orange Farming
B. Creative Economy
C. Food Processing Industry
D. Silk Industry

8. India's first floating ATM has been launched in Kerala by
A. Canara Bank
B. Corporation Bank
C. HDFC Bank
D. State Bank of India

9. Which are the three international credit card companies?
A. Amex, Citibank, Master
B. Master, Amex, HSBC
C. Amex, Master, Visa
D. Visa, Citibank, Standard Chartered

10. Name the first bank in India to start using PKI (Public Key Infrastructure) based digital signatures for electronic fund transfer.
A. Bank of Punjab
B. Punjab National Bank
C. Canara Bank
D. Bank of Baroda

11. Federal Reserves is the Central Bank of...
A. Britain B. U.S.A.
C. Japan D. Canada

12. Capital market means
A. Mutual funds B. Money market
C. Direct taxes D. Securities market

13. The World Bank has given a go-ahead to India on the Baglihar Hydro-electric Project being build on the river:
A. Jhelum B. Sutlej
C. Chenab D. Beas

14. Which state has maximum branches of public sector commercial banks?
A. U.P. B. Maharashtra
C. Karnataka D. Gujarat

15. The "Adhoc Treasury Bill System" of meeting budget deficit in India was replaced by 'Ways and Means Advances System' which has come into force on:
A. March 31, 1997 B. April 1, 1996
C. April 1, 1997 D. None of these

16. Plastic money relates to:
A. Plastic currency B. Paper currency
C. ATM cards D. Credit cards

17. What is the minimum period for which banks may accept term deposits, according to RBI guidelines?
A. 15 days B. 30 days
C. 46 days D. 91 days

18. In the context of stock market, the abbreviation IPO stands for
A. Immediate Payment Order
B. Internal Policy Obligation
C. External Policy Obligation
D. Initial Public Offering

19. The Reserve Bank of India (RBI) keeps on modifying various rates/ratios to keep the flow of liquidity in the market in a balanced situation. Which of the following rates/ratios/indexes is not directly controlled by the RBI?
A. Cash Reserve Ratio (CRR)
B. Bank Rate
C. Repo Rate
D. Wholesale Price Index (WPI)

20. Which bank launched the first international credit card in India?
A. Hong Kong Bank B. Citibank
C. SBI D. Deutsche Bank

21. What is near money?
A. Money that is banked in nearby banks
B. Assets that are easily convertible into cash
C. Money held in local currency
D. Money that can be recalled easily

22. What is fiat money?
A. Money not backed by gold or any other valuable goods
B. Money issued by a government fiat
C. Money used to buy worthless assets
D. Assets that are easily convertible into cash

23. Which bank introduced the first Automatic Teller Machine (ATM) in India?
A. State Bank of India
B. Citibank
C. Bank of America
D. Hong Kong Bank

24. Bank of Rajasthan, belongs to which business family of India?
A. Hindujas B. Singhanias
C. Bangurs D. Modis

25. Which company launched the first electronic cash card in India?
A. Kotak Mahindra B. SBI
C. Bank of Baroda D. Escorts Finance

26. Where is the foreign exchange of India deposited?
A. Reserve Bank of India
B. State Bank of India
C. Both (A) and (B)
D. Union Finance Ministry

27. The apex institution in the field of industrial development banking in India is:
A. IFCI B. ICICI
C. LIC D. IDBI

28. Banking Sector will fall under which of the following sectors?
A. Agricultural Sector B. Service Sector
C. Manufacturing Sector D. Industrial Sector

29. Which of the following types of borrowings from the IMF has the softest servicing conditions?
A. Second Tranch Loan B. SAF
C. ESAF D. Oil facility

30. If the cash-reserve ratio is lowered by the Central Bank, what will be its effect on credit creation?
A. It will decrease credit creation
B. It will not decrease credit creation
C. It will increase credit creation
D. It will not change credit creation

31. "Conditionality" of an I.M.F. loan to a member country stands for:
A. Schedule of disbursement of loan instalments
B. Interest and repayment terms of the loan
C. The policy steps which the borrower country must take
D. An assessment of the credit-worthiness of the borrower

32. Credit is a:
A. Stock concept B. Flow concept
C. A stock-flow concept D. None of these

33. The IBRD aims at:
A. Promoting international monetary co-operation
B. Helping in reconstruction and development of economics
C. Helping children all over the world
D. Promoting the peaceful uses of atomic energy

34. People's Bank of India was founded in the year:
A. 1910 B. 1911
C. 1901 D. 1920

35. The RBI was established in the year:
A. 1935 B. 1936
C. 1940 D. 1945

36. Blank cheque is:
A. Without date
B. A cheque which has been signed and dated but in which the amount payable has not been filled in
C. Without signatures
D. None of the above

37. The United Commercial Bank was started by the Birlas in the year:
A. 1948 B. 1943
C. 1949 D. 1950

38. Financial Investment is:
A. Any investment
B. Investment which cannot be traded
C. Any investment which can be traded, such as shares, certificates of deposit, etc
D. None of the above

39. A Joint Account is:
A. A firm account
B. A bank account owned jointly by two or more people
C. A shop account
D. None of the above

40. The Foreign Investments Board was set up in the year:
A. 1960 B. 1968
C. 1969 D. 1970

41. The SBI floated its first Mutual Fund in the year:
A. 1987 B. 1988
C. 1989 D. 1990

42. Loan Shark is:
A. A person who lends money at a very high interest rate
B. Lending money at lower rates
C. Lending money without interest
D. None of the above

43. The IDBI started its operations in year:
A. 1964 B. 1965
C. 1966 D. 1967

44. Banking Companies Act was passed in the year:
A. 1947 B. 1948
C. 1949 D. 1950

45. Bearer Cheque is a cheque that is payable to:
A. A person whosoever present it to the banker
B. Only to the account person
C. Only to the account holder
D. None of the above

46. The Imperial Bank was converted to State Bank of India in the year:
A. 1950 B. 1955
C. 1956 D. 1957

47. The Unit Trust of India was launched in the year:
A. 1964 B. 1965
C. 1966 D. 1967

48. Treasury Bills are:
A. Taxes
B. Marketable financial bills of the central government
C. Acts
D. None of the above

49. CACS (Capital Adequacy, Asset Quality, Compliance and Systems) is a rating model used by RBI. This system is used by RBI to rate:
A. State run banks outside India
B. Foreign banks operating in India
C. Private banks in India
D. Co-operative banks

50. Name of the first Indian financial institution to be listed on the New York Stock Exchange (NYSE).
A. IFCI B. UTI
C. ICICI D. IDBI

ANSWERS

1	2	3	4	5	6	7	8	9	10
D	D	C	B	A	C	B	D	C	A
11	**12**	**13**	**14**	**15**	**16**	**17**	**18**	**19**	**20**
B	D	C	A	C	D	B	D	D	A
21	**22**	**23**	**24**	**25**	**26**	**27**	**28**	**29**	**30**
B	A	D	C	D	A	D	B	C	C
31	**32**	**33**	**34**	**35**	**36**	**37**	**38**	**39**	**40**
C	C	B	C	A	B	B	C	B	B
41	**42**	**43**	**44**	**45**	**46**	**47**	**48**	**49**	**50**
A	A	A	B	A	B	A	B	B	C

* * * * *